THE RHETORIC OF
BLAIR,
CAMPBELL,
AND
WHATELY

THE RHETORIC OF BLAIR, CAMPBELL, AND WHATELY

James L. Golden
and
Edward P. J. Corbett
Ohio State University

HOLT, RINEHART AND WINSTON, INC.
New York · Chicago · San Francisco · Atlanta · Dallas
Toronto · Montreal · London

*Gratefully dedicated to
our wives and children*

PREFACE

This text reprints what experts on British rhetoric generally regard as the most signicant portions of Hugh Blair's *Lectures on Rhetoric and Belles Lettres* (1783), George Campbell's *The Philosophy of Rhetoric* (1776), and Richard Whately's *Elements of Rhetoric* (1828). Until a few years ago it was still possible to pick up secondhand copies of these once widely circulated and often reprinted texts, but lately students have had to rely on the scarce supply of copies in their college libraries. In order to make these texts more accessible, the Southern Illinois University Press in 1963 and 1965 published handsome facsimile editions of the Blair, Campbell, and Whately texts, with excellent Introductions by Harold F. Harding, Lloyd F. Bitzer, and Douglas Ehninger. Students who want to read the complete text of these rhetorics can consult these reprints. This text is designed for those who want the convenience of having substantial excerpts from these rhetorics in a single volume.

The selections from Blair's *Lectures on Rhetoric and Belles Lettres* are reprinted here from the one-volume Philadelphia edition, which betv·een 1784 and 1853 went through at least thirty-seven printings; Campbell is reprinted from the single-volume 1850 London edition; and Whately is reprinted from the seventh edition of 1846, which incorporated all the expansions and revisions Whately made after the original edition in 1828. We have taken the liberty of abbreviating or omitting entirely some of the long, inconsequential footnotes and of replacing some of the Latin quotations with English translations.

The bibliographies in this text are intended to serve two purposes: (1) to guide interested students to further reading in primary and secondary works, and (2) to acknowledge in a general way our heavy indebtedness, in the writing of our Introduction and headnotes, to scores of books and articles.

With rhetoric presently commanding a renewed interest in departments of Speech and English, we hope that this text will help to acquaint modern

students with those three British rhetoricians who preserved the best of
the "old rhetoric" and pointed the way to the development of a "new
rhetoric."

J. L. G.
E. P. J. C.

Columbus, Ohio
June 1968

Preface to the 1980 Reprinting

The recent increase in the number of undergraduate and graduate
courses in rhetoric being offered at American colleges and universities has
created a renewed demand for reprints of classic primary texts of rhetoric.
That demand has prompted the reprinting of this collection of substantial
portions of the rhetorics of Hugh Blair, George Campbell, and Richard
Whately. Although these three rhetoricians came at the end of the long
tradition that began in fifth-century Athens, their oft-reprinted texts kept
the tradition alive, if not flourishing, during the nineteenth century and
had a profound effect on the development of the "new" rhetoric in the
twentieth century.

We have provided addenda to the bibliographies in order to record
some of the more important books and articles that have appeared during
the twelve years that have elapsed since this collection first appeared in
1968. Unquestionably, the most important new book on rhetoric for the
period covered by this anthology is Wilbur Samuel Howell's *Eighteenth-
Century British Logic and Rhetoric* (Princeton, N.J.: Princeton University
Press, 1971). In 1980, the G. K. Hall Company will publish the comprehensive annotated bibliography of primary and secondary rhetorical works,
from the time of Aristotle through the nineteenth century, which Winifred
Horner of the University of Missouri—Columbia and four other scholars
have compiled. The section on the eighteenth century, which Winifred
Horner herself prepared, carries almost fifty entries on primary works and
about 120 entries on secondary works.

J.L.G.
E.P.J.C.

Columbus, Ohio
January 1980

CONTENTS

꙳꙳꙳꙳꙳꙳꙳꙳꙳꙳

THE PHILOSOPHY OF RHETORIC

Book I. The Nature and Foundations of Eloquence

Book II. The Foundations and Essential Properties of Elocution

ELEMENTS OF RHETORIC

Part I. Of the Invention, Arrangement, and Introduction of Propositions and Arguments

THE RHETORIC OF
BLAIR,
CAMPBELL,
AND
WHATELY

INTRODUCTION

Hugh Blair, George Campbell, and Richard Whately constituted the great triumvirate of British rhetoricians who came at the end of a long tradition of rhetoric which had its beginning in fifth-century Greece. But these men did not so much terminate a tradition as initiate the period of modern or new rhetoric. Space does not permit a survey here of the 2000-year history of rhetoric, a history which includes dozens of the most illustrious names associated with Western culture. Students interested in pursuing that history can turn to the surveys listed in the bibliography at the end of this introduction. Here, however, we can put Blair, Campbell, and Whately into context by reviewing the main rhetorical doctrines and movements from the beginning in ancient Greece to the incipient decline of traditional rhetoric in early eighteenth-century England.

Although Aristotle, in a now lost history of rhetoric, named Empedocles of Agrigentum as the first teacher of rhetoric, Corax and his pupil Tisias are commonly accepted as having produced the first handbooks of rhetoric in Sicily during the first quarter of the fifth century B.C. Rhetoric began and for a long time remained exclusively the organon of oral, persuasive discourse of the courtroom. With the expulsion of a long line of tyrants, the citizens of Sicily rushed to court to plead their own cases for the recovery of their confiscated property, and in preparation for this special pleading before a jury of their peers they turned eagerly to anyone who could train them for this encounter. Gorgias of Leontini introduced rhetoric to Athens in 427, when he was sent on an embassy to that intellectually vibrant city. The Athenians were enthralled by Gorgias' eloquence, and soon numerous schools, taught by "rhetors" or "sophists," sprang up.

Not all Athenians, however, were impressed by this new art of persuasive oratory. The most prestigious opponent of the art was Plato, who echoed and reaffirmed the objections of his teacher, Socrates. As we learn from the *Gorgias* and the *Phaedrus*, Plato regarded rhetoric as a meretricious art, if indeed it was an art at all. For him, rhetoric was a mere "knack," a form of flattery, appealing to men's passions and emotions rather than reason; moreover, it based arguments on appearances and opinions rather than on

1

reality and truth. Interestingly enough, Plato's strictures on rhetoric are the same objections that men of all ages have leveled against this seductive art. In the *Phaedrus,* however, Plato did admit that there could be such a thing as a "true rhetoric," but it would come about only if rhetoricians were to probe for the *truth* in all matters, attempt to formulate essential definitions of particulars, and study man's psychological dispositions so that they could adapt and arrange their arguments to suit the temper of an audience.

Aristotle responded to that challenge. His *Rhetoric,* composed over the period from 342 to 330 B.C., represents his efforts to compose a philosophical, scientific rhetoric, an eminently realistic rhetoric which took man as he was, not as Plato wished him to be. Since Aristotle's *Rhetoric* is the fountainhead of the system of rhetoric commonly labeled "classical," we can use his treatise as the basis of an exposition of the key doctrines and terminology of classical rhetoric. The reader should understand, however, that not all of the classical system is found in Aristotle's *Rhetoric* in a fully developed form. It was Quintilian's *Institutio Oratoria,* written in the first century A.D., that presented the fullest exposition of classical rhetoric, and it was Aristotle's contemporary, Isocrates, who, with his commitment to humanistic, moral, one-world ideals, proved to be the most popular and influential teacher of rhetoric in his era.

One of the key terms in the *Rhetoric* and a term which represents one of Aristotle's chief contributions to the development of "an art of rhetoric" was *probability.* Aristotle astutely recognized that many matters connected with human affairs were not susceptible to the kind of absolute, infallible proof that could be managed in logic or in a scientific demonstration. It is not always possible, for instance, to establish with absolute certainty that a man has committed the crime of which he is accused or that the passage of a proposed tax bill will inevitably produce the benefits its exponents claim for it. In such situations, the lawyer or the statesman can produce only a high degree of probability; he must, in other words, *persuade* his audience that his claims are "true" or "beneficial." That notion of probability is implicit in Aristotle's definition of rhetoric as "the faculty of discovering the available means of persuasion in any given case."

What are the means of rhetorical proof, the means of winning assent to the probable truth of a proposition? Aristotle designated three modes of rhetorical proof: (1) *logos*—the appeal to the reason of the audience; (2) *pathos*—the appeal to the emotions of the audience; (3) *ethos*—the appeal that is exerted by the character and personality, by the "image," of the speaker or writer. In appealing to reason, we argue either inductively or deductively—"There is no other way," Aristotle says. The rhetorical equivalent of a full induction in logic is the *example,* a single instance of an analogous event or situation; the rhetorical equivalent of the syllogism in logic is the *enthymeme,* whose essential difference from the syllogism is not so much that one of the premises is left unstated as that the deductive argument is based on premises that are only probably or usually true rather than universally and infallibly true. The *topics* represented a system for probing any subject matter to discover something to say on that subject. Lines of argument, for instance, might be worked off from a *definition* of terms (what is the nature of the thing?) ; or from *comparison* (what is it like? what is it unlike? how does it differ in degree from something else?) ; or from *relationship* (what is the cause of this effect? what are the effects of this cause? if this antecedent condition exists, what consequences follow?) ; or from *authority* (for these arguments one must go outside the subject matter for such supporting evidence as testimony, statistics, maxims, documents, laws, and so on).

These were the so-called common topics, sources of arguments on virtually any subject. There were special topics, too, which Aristotle designated in relation to the three kinds of persuasive discourse: (1) the *deliberative* or *political*—the kind of discourse in which we seek to induce an audience to adopt a particular point of view or a particular course of action, usually in matters concerning public affairs; (2) the *judicial* or *forensic*—in particular the persuasive discourse of the courtroom but in general any discourse which seeks to accuse or exonerate someone of crime, malfeasance, or misconduct; (3) the *epideictic* or *ceremonial*—discourse intent on praising or blaming some person or institution or event (for example, a funeral oration, a Fourth of July speech, "The Gettysburg Address"). In deliberative discourse, where we are seeking to win acceptance for a thesis or a course of action, we come down hard on the special topics of the *good* (something worthy of pursuit for its own sake) or the *advantageous* (something useful or benficial) ; in judicial discourse, where we are seeking to indict or defend someone, we come down hard on the special topics of the *just* (the lawful) or the *unjust* (the illegal) ; in ceremonial discourse, where we are seeking to praise or blame someone, we come down hard on the special topics of *virtue* (moral good) or *vice* (moral evil).

To discover the available means of persuasion for an emotional or pathetic appeal, one must have a sense for the disposition of a particular audience, must be aware of the principal human emotions, and must know how to arouse or subdue those emotions. Aristotle devoted the major portion of Book II of his *Rhetoric* to an analysis of the basic human emotions and of the strategies for playing on those emotions. He was the only one of the classical rhetoricians to devote an extensive section of his rhetoric text to the strategies of emotional appeal. We shall see how in the eighteenth century, with the growth of interest in psychology, the British rhetoricians, especially George Campbell, made a significant contribution to the psychology of persuasion through the emotions.

Aristotle maintained that the ethical appeal could very well be the most significant of the appeals in the persuasive process, because if an audience did not trust or admire the speaker or writer, all of his logical and emotional appeals, however cogent they might be, would have little effect. Aristotle pointed out that the ethical appeal of a speaker or writer will be effective if in his discourse he creates an image of himself as being a man of good sense, good moral character, and good will toward his audience. The Latin rhetoricians, especially Quintilian, who defined an effective orator as "a good man speaking," reinforced this notion of the importance of the ethical appeal by insisting that to be an effective persuader one must give evidence of intelligence, learning, and moral integrity. This insistence on the *ethos* of the speaker was also Aristotle's way of answering Plato's charge that men skilled in the use of words could use that power for nefarious purposes.

This process of finding all the available means of persuasion was treated by the ancient rhetoricians under the first of the five "offices" of rhetoric—*inventio* or invention, in the sense of "discovery" or "finding." The second "office" of rhetoric in the classical system was *dispositio* or arrangement, which was concerned with the selection of the arguments discovered through invention and their organization in the most effective order. Arrangement was commonly dealt with in terms of the parts of an oration: (1) the *exordium* or introduction, in which the speaker oriented, conciliated, and gained the attention of his audience; (2) the *narratio* or statement of the issue to be argued; (3) the *confirmatio* or proof, the main body of the discourse, in which the speaker presented his positive arguments for his thesis; (4) the *confutatio* or refutation of the opposing arguments; (5) the *epilogue* or conclusion, in which the speaker recapitulated his arguments, reinforced his ethical appeal, and perhaps made a final pitch to the emotions. Rhetoric texts gave general instructions about the kinds of strategy that might be employed, in a variety of circumstances, in each of these parts of the discourse. For instance, they would advise when it would be better to advance one's strong arguments first or when it would be better to refute the opposing arguments first before arguing one's own case.

The third "office" of traditional rhetoric was *elocutio* or style. This was concerned with the actual expression or verbalization of the arguments that had been discovered and judiciously selected and organized. Here students were instructed in the choice of apt, precise, decorous diction, in the disposition of words into perspicuous, graceful, arresting, rhythmical patterns, and in the use of figures of speech. Some of the rhetoricians, like Gorgias, and Demetrius in his *On Style,* and Dionysius of Halicarnassus in his *De Compositione Verborum,* and even Longinus in his great work *On the Sublime,* and several of the Renaissance rhetoricians, devoted their attention either predominantly or exclusively to style, and this preoccupation with style brought on the charge, at some time in every age, that rhetoric was more concerned with words than with matter, that it merely produced a lot of sound and fury signifying nothing. We shall see what careful attention Blair gave to style in his lectures on rhetoric.

The fourth and fifth "offices" of rhetoric were *memoria* or memorization and *pronuntiatio* or delivery. Although a great deal of attention seems to have been devoted to these two divisions of rhetoric in the classroom, little or no space was devoted to them in the rhetoric texts. Treatment of memorization consisted largely of suggested mnemonic devices to help students commit their prepared speech to memory so that it could be more spontaneously and vigorously delivered. Treatment of delivery consisted of training and frequent practice in the management of the voice and gestures. The second half of the eighteenth century saw a surge of interest in *elocution*, a term which by then had changed its meaning from "style" to "delivery," and, as we shall see, men like Thomas Sheridan, John Walker, and Richard Whately gave a great impetus to the revived interest in the delivery aspects of rhetoric.

The system of rhetorical training outlined above was basically the one that prevailed in the schools throughout the Roman period, the Middle Ages, the Renaissance, and the seventeenth century. At different periods, of course, the system was subjected to retrenchments, amplifications, shifts of emphasis, revitalizations, innovations, and changes in terminology, sometimes to suit the whim of a particular teacher or group, at other times to make the system more relevant to the needs and moods of the times. After the invention of printing, for instance, and during periods when a great deal of political and mercantile business was carried on through the medium of letters, the emphasis both in the classroom and in the rhetoric texts shifted more and more from oral to written discourse. In the Roman period, such pedagogical devices as the *progymnasmata* or elementary finger exercises in a variety of short written compositions and the declamatory exercises called *suasoriae* and *controversiae* had some value in that they enabled the student to learn by doing but often they became so artificial and fantastic that they lost their value as practical training for the real world of give-and-take that the student would enter. The Middle Ages saw a great growth of interest in the sermon, a species of discourse which did not exactly fit in with any of the kinds of oration—deliberative, forensic, or ceremonial—that the Greek and Roman rhetoricians had classified, and so medieval rhetoricians like St. Augustine, in his *De Doctrina Christiana*, adapted Ciceronian rhetoric so that it could serve as a means of expounding the Scriptures for the enlightenment of the laity and of inducing congregations to follow the straight and narrow path of virtue. When the humanists of the English Renaissance were preparing rhetoric courses for their schools, they turned mainly to the rhetorics of Cicero and Quintilian because those Roman rhetoricians had conceived of rhetorical training in terms of a liberal arts course rather than simply as an art for the composition of persuasive discourse; when clergymen took over as schoolmasters they looked with favor upon Quintilian's insistence that the rhetorician should be concerned with the moral, as well as the intellectual, development of his pupils. When the vernacular rhetorics, like Thomas Wilson's *Arte of Rhetorique* (1553), began to appear in the sixteenth century, some of the authors of those texts sought to replace the foreboding Greek and Latin terminology with simpler English words or coinages.

Two developments in the late sixteenth century threatened the preeminence of rhetoric in the curriculum and eventually effected profound changes in the rationale of rhetorical training offered in the schools. One of these was the revolution in rhetorical studies that the French scholar Peter Ramus promoted by fostering a realignment of the provinces of logic and rhetoric. He assigned invention and arrangement to logic, because he saw those activities as functions primarily of reason, and he relegated to rhetoric only the provinces of style and delivery, which he regarded as the peculiar functions of the imagination. This breakup of the traditional five-part structure of rhetorical training was promoted in the schools through Ramus' influential logic text and the companion rhetoric text by his ardent disciple, Omer Talon. The effects of this Ramistic dichotomy are reflected in the titles of some of the most influential of the English vernacular texts: Dudley Fenner's *The Arts of Logic and Rhetoric* (1584), Abraham Fraunce's *The Lawyer's Logic* and *The Arcadian Rhetoric* (1588), Charles Butler's *The Two Books of Ramean Rhetoric* (1597), and Thomas Farnaby's *Index Rhetoricus* (1625). The most significant effect of this reassignment, however, was that the conceptualizing part of the composition process came to be regarded as an activity of private inquiry rather than one of the steps in the preparation for communicating with an audience.

This view of logic or dialectics as a tool for inquiry fitted in well with the growing interest in science, which was promoted by Francis Bacon early in the seventeenth century and by members of the Royal Society after 1660. In *The Advancement of Learning*, Francis Bacon proposed that the function of rhetoric was "to apply and recommend the dictates of reason to imagination in order to excite the appetite and will." In this distinctly Ramistic view, communication involves an interaction between reason and the imagination, but it is clear from Bacon's development of this notion that reason is the dominant faculty in the process. We are not surprised then to find Bacon and other men of science advocating that matter (*res*) should take precedence over words (*verba*) and eventually, through one of the programs of the Royal Society, the creation of a simple, unadorned prose style for the exposition of inductively derived discoveries. The ideal scientific style would be one as strictly denotative as mathematical symbols. Fortunately, the development of such a barren prose style was prevented by the development, in the Augustan Age, of an elegant middle style by such writers as John Dryden, Jonathan Swift, and Joseph Addison. The Royal Society's program to develop a "mathematical" style had at least one good effect therefore, in that it encouraged the development of a gracefully informal prose style that would counteract, on the one hand, the "barebones" prose of the scientist and, on the other hand, the kind of ornate, euphuistic prose that Thomas Hobbes dubbed a tissue of "windy blisters."

We are brought now, after a series of seven-league bounds through the long history of rhetoric, to the eve of the eighteenth century, when the future directions of rhetorical studies would be determined, for better or for worse.

From its beginning, the eighteenth century was virile and intellectually alive. It was a period characterized by intensive study of the classical tradition, a pervasive enthusiasm for the newly developing empirical method, a commitment to rationalism, a curiosity to understand human nature and man's relationship to God, a preoccupation with the origin and use of language, and an appreciation of the potentialities of persuasion as a force in a democracy and in a Christian society. These interests combined to create one of the most prolific eras in rhetorical history.

The eighteenth-century rhetoricians, most of whom were acquainted with the doctrines of the ancients, responded to these theories in different ways. Some writers, choosing to ignore contemporary ideas advanced in the natural and social sciences as well as in the humanities, held that there was no need to alter the teachings of Aristotle, Cicero, and Quintilian. Thus numerous continental classical works, such as Fènèlon's *Dialogues sur l' Eloquence* (1717), were translated into English. Of those British authors who produced volumes which strictly adhered to the classical framework, three were both representative and influential. These include John Holmes's *The Art of Rhetoric* (1739), John Lawson's *Lectures Concerning Oratory* (1752), and John Ward's *Systems of Oratory* (1759). The latter, which covers more than eight hundred pages, is, according to Douglas Ehninger, the most extensive restatement of ancient rhetorical theory in the English language. But despite the fact that *Systems of Oratory* contains a thorough and accurate interpretation of the classical rhetorical doctrines, and notwithstanding its immediate popularity, this work, like Holmes's *Art of Rhetoric* and Lawson's *Lectures Concerning Oratory*, was too sterile and unimaginative to constitute an important landmark in the evolution of rhetorical theory.

A second response to the classical rhetorical tradition was the development of the elocutionary movement. In theory the leaders of this movement accepted four of the five traditional canons of rhetoric: invention, disposition, style, and delivery. But, as Wilbur S. Howell has suggested, they were sensitive to the criticisms which science had leveled against the excessive preoccupation with style as expressed in such volumes as Leonard Cox's *The Arte or Crafte of Rhethoryke* (1530), Richard Sherry's *A Treatise of Schemes and Tropes* (1550), and Henry Peacham's *Garden of Eloquence* (1577). Moreover, they were aware of the unfavorable reaction produced by Peter Ramus when he sought to relegate invention and disposition to logic, and style and delivery to rhetoric. With enthusiasm, therefore, they turned to the one remaining canon which had not yet felt the full brunt of scientific criticism: delivery. In doing so, they expressed two rationalizations for explaining their decision to single out a particular rhetorical element. First, they had found ample support for emphasizing delivery in the celebrated, but apparently apocryphal, quotation of Demosthenes on the value of action, and in Quintilian's detailed analysis of voice control, eye contact, and bodily activity. Secondly, they shared Swift's and Chesterfield's concern with the carelessness in articulation, pronunciation, and action which all too often characterized the speaking of eighteenth-century Englishmen.

Among those treatises which best epitomize the elocutionary movement in England, perhaps the most significant were Thomas Sheridan's *Lectures on Elocution* (1763) and *Lectures on Reading* (1775), John Walker's *Elements of Elocution* (1781), and Gilbert Austin's *Chironomia, or a Treatise on Rhetorical Delivery* (1806). The principal merit of this movement found eloquent expression in Sheridan's recommendation that effective voice control and bodily activity utilize the conversational pattern of delivery. But the excesses, including Sheridan's development of a complex marking system to be used in oral reading and Walker's absurd and ludicrous classification and description of the emotions, brought a charge of artificiality. The elocutionists, nevertheless, won many converts, including James Boswell, a former student of Love, the actor, and a close friend of Thomas Sheridan. Not even the barbs of Johnson could persuade Boswell that this form of speech training was artificial and impotent. He rejoiced when elocution, after several years of decline, was revived in London. In April 1781 with fifty men and twenty women, he went to hear Sheridan discuss his favorite subject. There, he tells us in his *Private Papers,* he was impressed with the apparatus which was used to "clear and smooth and mellow" the voice.

The rise of the belletristic movement in the eighteenth century constitutes a third response to the classical rhetorical tradition. This approach was based upon the concept that rhetoric and related polite arts, poetry, drama, art, history, biography, philology, and so on should be joined under the broad heading of rhetoric and belles lettres. Since these disciplines share a common interest in taste, style, criticism, and sublimity, they seek to instruct the student to become an effective practitioner and judge in written and oral communication. The belletristic scholar, therefore, was not content to construct a rhetorical theory limited to the subject matter covered by Aristotle in his *Rhetoric.* Instead he, consciously or unconsciously, gave equal emphasis to another tradition initiated by Aristotle's *Poetics,* Isocrates' theory of culture, Longinus' *On the Sublime,* and Horace's *Ars Poetica.*

This wedding of rhetoric and its companion art poetics took place in the modern era on the European continent in the later part of the sixteenth and early part of the seventeenth centuries. The principal works demonstrating this approach included Gerardus Vossius' *De Philosophia* (1658), Bernard Lami's *L'Art de Parler* (1675), and Charles Rollin's *De La Maniere d'Enseigner et d'Etudier les Belles-Lettres* (1726–1728). Two decades after the publication of Rollin's work, Adam Smith became the first Englishman to give impetus to the belletristic movement. In 1748, Smith, a native of Scotland and a graduate of Oxford University, began, under the sponsorship of Lord Kames, a series of public lectures in Edinburgh on rhetoric and belles lettres which were repeated during the following two years. Among the regular attendants who heard these discussions was a youthful minister of the Presbyterian Church at St. Giles, Hugh Blair. As the first public lecturer in the British Isles to unite rhetoric and belles lettres, Smith taught his audience to appreciate the nature of style, eloquence, and literary forms, and the pedagogically attractive method of using modern and classical models. The popularity of the lectures won for Smith a Chair at the University of Glasgow where, for more than a decade, he continued to teach rhetoric and belles lettres, even in his courses in moral philosophy and political economy.

Probably the most revolutionary response to the classical tradition was the emergence of the psychological-philosophical theories of public address. Many scholars, applying the principles of rationalism and the empirical method, saw the strengths and shortcomings of classicism. The more they studied ancient science, philosophy, and rhetoric, the more they realized man's lack of meaningful insight concerning his basic nature. Thus with a desire to advance knowledge in a crucial area which they had come to believe was either misunderstood or neglected by the ancients, they set for themselves the task of unraveling the mystery of the human mind and soul. Despite the fact that these philosophers and psychologists were essentially nonrhetoricians, they profoundly influenced the direction which rhetoric was to take during the later half of the eighteenth century.

The writers who contributed the most elaborate theories describing man's mental and moral nature were John Locke, Francis Hutcheson, David Hume, David Hartley, Thomas Reid, and Adam Smith. In his celebrated *Essay on Human Understanding* (1689), Locke concluded that since the mind has the power to *perceive* and *prefer*, it must be comprised of two major faculties, the understanding and the will. In explaining the nature of the faculty of understanding, Locke developed his famous theory of ideas. Reflection upon sensory experience, he observed, produces ideas which are, in turn, held together in a meaningful pattern through the ability of the mind to trace relationships that show natural correspondence and connection. Similarly, reason enables us to unite ideas that are apparently unrelated by utilizing the laws of association. Here we may observe from past experiences that whenever a particular idea reaches the understanding an "associate appears with it." Under such circumstances, the doctrine of association permits us to connect these concepts so that they will form an inseparable unit in our minds.

Locke's reflections led him to reject the syllogism on the grounds that it neither demonstrates nor strengthens the connection that two ideas may have with each other. Nor does it advance an argument or lead to moral truth. The power of inference, a talent given to man by God, makes it possible for us to perceive associations and to determine whether or not ideas are coherent or incoherent. Thus the understanding, concludes Locke, "is not taught to reason" by the "methods of syllogizing." The far-reaching significance of this thesis may be seen when we turn later to Campbell's theory of logical proof.

As one of the early proponents of faculty psychology, Locke came to believe that an idea which reaches the understanding does not necessarily have the power to motivate the will. The rational process, he held, must be reinforced by an emotional appeal that ultimately becomes the principal determinant of action. All of the emotions have one common element which Locke called "uneasiness," and described as the absence of some good. Whenever the mind experiences "uneasiness," it feels pain and generates the compelling desire to remove it. The will, in short, may be influenced when the passions are stirred, for the arousal of an emotion inevitably causes pain. There is little chance for persuasion, however, if the mind is at ease since the desire for happiness has already been achieved.

Locke's discussion of the nature of ideas, his tendency to compartmentalize the mind into faculties, his analysis of the doctrine of association, and his recognition that the emotions are the prime movers of the will profoundly influenced Hume. Few eighteenth-century thinkers were better qualified than Hume to follow the lead of Locke and probe into the mental characteristics of man in order to explain human knowledge. Impressed by the achievements of Newton in natural science and convinced that his success was due largely to the experimental method, Hume became the first writer to construct a solid empirical base upon which to build a science of human nature.

Probably the most important contribution Hume made to subsequent rhetorical theory was his extension of Locke's views on the laws of association. In his *Treatise on Human Nature* (1739), Hume observed that the mind moves freely from one idea to another through the three qualities of "resemblance, contiguity in time or place, and cause and effect." The imagination stimulates the mind to see the connection between ideas that are similar. Moreover, as the senses choose to change their focus from one object to another, they may proceed along a continuum of space and time. Ideas which are in juxtaposition naturally have strong associations with each other. There was little new in this concept of resemblance and contiguity. As Hume discussed the third quality of association, cause and effect, he was, however, original and influential. The mind, which he strangely held to be nothing more than a bundle of perceptions united by association, may be subdivided into two faculties, impressions and ideas. Although these elements differ from each other only in the degree of force and vivacity, impressions constitute the cause and ideas the effect. Past experience recalled by memory and reinforced by imagination enables us to make causal inferences. From these premises Hume suggested that a belief may be defined as "a lively idea related to or associated with a present impression."

Hume's willingness to give impressions a priority ranking over ideas prompted him further to develop the thesis that all human motivation stems from man's emotional nature. Standing squarely in the tradition of Locke, he argued that appeals to the passions, especially those which produce pleasure or pain, are necessary to induce the will to act. But he went far beyond Locke when he claimed that "reason is and ought only to be the slave of the passions, and can never pretend to any other office than to serve and obey them." Hume diminished the value of deductive reasoning not only because of his belief in the superior power of impressions, but also because of his devotion to the experimental method. He found it easy, therefore, to exclude the syllogism as an effective tool in exploring human knowledge. Similarly he distrusted elaborate chains of reasoning designed to prove the existence of God, and testimonials supporting the authenticity of the biblical miracles on the grounds that they could not be corroborated by present experience.

The interest which Locke and Hume displayed in faculty psychology and associationism was shared by David Hartley, a physician who wrote a detailed and cumbersome book entitled, *Observations on Man, His Frame, His Duty, and His Expectations* (1749). To the mental faculties of understanding and will outlined by Locke, Hartley added memory, imagination or fancy, and affection. He agreed with both Locke and Hume in asserting that reason and emotions are dependent upon the law of assocation. But unlike his predecessors, he introduced a new idea which he called "vibrations." "All human actions," he stated, "proceed from Vibrations in the Nerves of the muscles." Thus when a man experiences pain or pleasure, he is responding to sensations which take the form of muscular vibrations. In holding this position, Hartley veered in the direction of Hume's views on the power of impressions and away from Locke's commitment to reflective thinking. Hartley's elaborate and partially traditional, yet innovative approach contributed significantly to Joseph Priestley's *Course of Lectures on Oratory and Criticism* (1777). Moreover, it kept alive the growing concern of eighteenth-century scholars to root knowledge in human nature.

If Locke, Hume, and Hartley focused primarily, though not exclusively, on man's mental nature, it was Francis Hutcheson, a Scottish philosopher and professor, who gave the most penetrating insights into man's moral sense. In the second edition of his *Short Introduction to Moral Philosophy* (1753), he observed that human nature consists of soul and body, and that the soul, in turn, is comprised of two faculties, understanding and the will. Content to leave principles of the body to physicians like Hartley, he dealt only with the constituent elements of the soul. Hutcheson charged his students to use their conscience as a guide in analyzing their own sentiments, and then to employ the principle of sympathy in evaluating the actions of others. This twofold attack of self-analysis and fellow-feeling will bring man closer to God's intended purpose for his life, and help him share in the joys and sorrows of others.

Among those who were influenced by Hutcheson's doctrine of sympathy was Adam Smith, who used this thesis as the basis of his popular book, *The Theory of Moral Sentiments* (1759). "We must look at ourselves," argued Smith, "with the same eyes with which we look at others: we must imagine ourselves not the actors, but the spectators of our own character and conduct." Through this practice we will, as Hutcheson also stated, come to an understanding of our sentiments and an appreciation of the feelings of others.

Still another psychological and epistemological theme with eighteenth-century rhetorical implications attracted the attention of the students of human nature. This was the doctrine of "common sense," a theory advocated by the Scottish School of Philosophy in general, and crystallized in the major works of Thomas Reid—*Inquiry into the Human Mind, on the Principles of Common Sense* (1764), and *Essays on the Power of the Human Mind* (1812). Reid interpreted "common sense" as a science which could be coded in self-evident laws of nature recognized and understood by men of all cultures. Further, he held that since it is equated with good common judgment and is "the first-born of reason," it is the final arbiter of disputes that occur between experts on matters of taste and judgment.

We have traced four major responses to the classical rhetorical tradition that occurred in the first half of the eighteenth century: (1) the uncritical acceptance of ancient doctrines; (2) the singling out by the elocutionists of the canon of delivery as the most defensible and urgent need in speech training; (3) the uniting of rhetoric and belles lettres to form a broader view of written and oral communication; and (4) the grounding of all human knowledge, including rhetoric, in human nature. The question which as yet has not been answered is how did Campbell, Blair, and Whately respond to these rhetorical trends?

First, Campbell, Blair and Whately, applying the yardstick of critical judgment to the classical rhetorical theories, endorsed some ideas but modified and rejected others. As a basic premise, they argued that no one can succeed as a speaker, writer, or critic unless he is acquainted with the ancient authors. Of those who deserve special attention, Blair recommended Aristotle, Demetrius, Dionysius of Halicarnassus, Cicero, and, most importantly, Quintilian. Campbell, moreover, found it necessary to remind his theological students to immerse themselves in such specific works as Quintilian's *Institutio Oratoria,* Cicero's *De Inventione* and *De Oratore,* the *Ad Herennium,* Longinus' *On the Sublime,* and the critical essays of Dionysius. Nor was Whately less enthusiastic about the classical writers. He praised the systematic approach of Aristotle, the practical advice of Cicero, and the sound sense of Quintilian. Not to be overlooked is the fact that Blair, Campbell, and Whately gave force to these recommendations by turning freely to the works of the ancients for source material used for the purpose of illustrating their own rhetorical principles. Blair, for instance, repeatedly inserted quotations from his favorite author, Quintilian. On forty-nine separate occasions, Campbell alluded to the classical authors; similarly, Whately made seventy-one references. What they liked most of all was the classical emphasis on rules as an art form. In his *Lectures on Pulpit Eloquence,* Campbell taunted his contemporaries for their inability to extend the highly artistic approach to rhetoric developed by the ancients. "As to the rhetorical art itself," he said, "in the particular the moderns appear to me to have made hardly any advance or improvement upon the ancients. I can say, at least, of most of the performances in the way of institute, which I have had an opportunity of reading on the subject, either in French or English, every thing valuable is servilely copied from Aristotle, Cicero, and Quintilian."

Campbell, Blair, and Whately, in sum, endorsed at least five basic premises which constitute a major emphasis in classical rhetorical theory: (1) they accepted the classical communication model which focused on the speaker, the speech, and the audience; (2) they recognized that effective ethical, logical, and emotional proof are essential to persuasion; (3) they felt that a well-organized address should have interest, unity, coherence, and progression; (4) they held that style should be characterized by perspicuity and vividness; and (5) above all, they suggested that while nature endows the orator with special talents, nurture or training is needed to improve and perfect these inborn traits.

Notwithstanding the fact that Campbell, Blair, and Whately borrowed heavily from the classical tradition, they deviated sharply from Aristotle, Cicero, and Quintilian in several important respects. Campbell, for example, did not attempt to present an elaborate analysis of each of the five canons of rhetoric containing practical rules for speech improvement. Convinced that this already had been achieved by the ancients, he concentrated instead on the task of formulating a philosophy of rhetoric which would answer Locke's celebrated indictment that rhetoric is a "powerful instrument of Error and Deceit." Blair likewise had a different aim, for he wanted to construct a rhetorical system which would not only help one become an effective speaker, but also a competent writer and critic in the broad field of literature. Whately, whose purpose was more narrow than that of both the ancients and of Campbell and Blair, chose to limit his discussion to "argumentative composition, *generally* and *exclusively*."

A second major modification of classical rhetorical theory occurs in the treatment of the ends of rhetoric. All of the ancient writers, with the possible exception of Cicero and Quintilian, restricted rhetoric to persuasion. But, as we shall note later, Campbell, Blair, and Whately gave equal emphasis to those speech purposes that appeal to the understanding.

A third and more significant alteration of the classical rhetorical tradition is seen in the handling of the canons of *inventio* and *dispositio*. The ancients had stressed the value of commonplaces or topics as useful aids in helping the speaker discover available means of persuasion. Blair's indictment of this practice is instructive. He rejected the doctrine of *loci communes* by pointing out that it has little effect on the improvement of invention. He supported the claim with the assertion that the inventive ability of a speaker is closely related to genius, and, therefore, cannot be materially affected by rhetorical rules. Then he posed the question: Can we imagine Demosthenes' use of artificial commonplaces in his eloquent attacks on Philip? This argument, echoed by Campbell and Whately, weakens a central position in classical inventional theory.

The ancient rhetoricians, further, had evolved a theory of proof which was compartmentalized into three distinctive forms: ethical, logical, and pathetic. Although these appeals may interact with one another, the boundaries are carefully delineated. Campbell, Blair, and Whately, as we have observed, recognized the persuasive power inherent in these forms of proof but chose, on the other hand, to blend them together, thereby blurring the lines of demarcation. Indeed, Whately goes so far as to treat the subject of "deference," which quite clearly belongs to ethos, as an aspect of the logical principle of presumption. In addition, Campbell's concept of sympathy is equally applicable to ethical and emotional proof.

These modifications of the canon of *inventio* could not help but affect the element of *dispositio*. By eliminating the role of discovery from *inventio*, Campbell, Blair, and Whately altered the starting point to be used in speech preparation. Speakers can assume that since arguments and proof are present from the outset, their principal challenge is to learn how to manage rather than invent or discover ideas. Blair illuminates this approach in his series of lectures entitled, "The Conduct of the Discourse in All Its Parts." Moreover, neither Campbell nor Whately deal with content and organization as separate entities. Thus the boundary lines between *inventio* and *dispositio,* as Ehninger has correctly observed, are blurred, just as they were in the forms of proof.

In dealing with the second rhetorical trend, the elocutionary movement, Campbell, Blair, and Whately supported the emphasis on the conversational pattern of delivery, but deplored the excesses of the elocutionists as a whole. In Blair's brief discussion of delivery, he acknowledged his debt to the movement by admitting that much of his material was taken from the writings of Thomas Sheridan who had stressed the importance of conversing with an audience in a genuine face-to-face manner. Campbell, who ignored delivery in his *Philosophy of Rhetoric,* presented practical rules on articulation and pronunciation in his *Lectures on Pulpit Eloquence* that were consistent with the recommendations of Sheridan. But while endorsing the suggestions of Sheridan, Blair, and Campbell could not condone the highly artificial teachings of other elocutionists such as Walker. Even less so could Whately, who felt constrained to devote Part IV of his *Elements of Rhetoric* to a stinging rebuke of the elocutionary movement for its violation of the natural method. Whately's attack, though not altogether discriminating or fair with respect to Sheridan, remains as the ablest critical analysis of one of the important trends in rhetorical history.

The belletristic movement, the third major rhetorical force operating in the eighteenth century, shaped the theories of Blair, but made little visible impact on the treatises of Campbell and Whately. Blair was impressed with the pedagogically attractive lectures of Adam Smith, which, in uniting the principles of rhetoric and belles lettres, relied on high-compulsion models drawn from classical and modern works. But, unlike Smith, Blair was not willing to limit his theory of criticism to the neoclassical doctrines of "refinement," "correctness," "strict unity," and "simple clarity." Indeed, he occasionally pushed aside these elements of decorum and propriety in order to make room in his system for some of the benchmarks of emerging romanticism, including disorder and irregularity as characteristics of the sublime, a belief that genius is a process in artistic creation, an acceptance of the supernatural elements in Shakespeare, and the general elevation of feeling and emotion. Blair's refusal to be identified with one school of thought contributed to the long-range effect of his work.

Campbell reacted cautiously to this tendency to combine rhetoric and polite literature in a single volume. Although he told his preministerial students to read "the lectures on eloquence lately published by the ingenious and truly eloquent Dr. Blair," he expressed concern about his friend Lord Kames's decision to incorporate discussions of sculpture, painting, music, architecture, gardening, poetry, and eloquence in his *Elements of Criticism.* Campbell, however, was strikingly similar to Blair and other belletristic scholars in his attempt to amplify rhetorical doctrines with literary examples. In addition to the forty-nine classical references previously mentioned, he made forty-six allusions to Milton, Shakespeare, and Johnson, and 113 to the Augustan authors, Pope, Addison, Swift, and Dryden. Partly because of his own lack of interest in studying the broad range of literature and partly because of his belief that the belletristic school was too eclectic to be original and too superficial and wide in scope to be useful, Whately rejected it as he had the elocutionary movement.

The fourth rhetorical trend in the first half of the eighteenth century, the psychological-philosophical theory of human communication behavior, significantly influenced the principles of Campbell, and to a lesser degree, those of Blair and Whately. Campbell was intrigued by the prospects of letting nature provide the substance out of which rhetoric could be demonstrated and explained. In the preface to his *Philosophy,* he pointed out that his purpose was to exhibit, on the one hand "a tolerable sketch of the human mind," and, "on the other hand, from the science of human nature, to ascertain with greater precision the radical principles of that art, whose object it is, by the use of language, to operate on the soul of the hearer, in the way of informing, convincing, pleasing, moving, or persuading." In grounding rhetoric in human nature, Campbell accepted the following tenets advanced by Locke, Hume, and Hartley: (1) the mind is separated into faculties; (2) the experimental method is superior to syllogistic reasoning; (3) ideas are held together by the laws of association; and (4) belief and persuasion are dependent upon the liveliness of an idea and the force of emotional appeals. From Hutcheson and Smith, Campbell borrowed the doctrine of sympathy and used it to explain the speaker's relationship with his hearers. Finally, he included Reid's philosophy of "common sense" as one of the three constituent elements of intuitive evidence.

Campbell's heavy reliance upon Locke, Hume, Hartley, and Reid did not prevent him from putting the stamp of his own original mind upon the psychological-epistemological theories of speech included in his text. He produced a new dimension to the faculties of the mind by inserting "imagination" and "passions" between "understanding" and the "will," and by arranging these faculties in an order of natural progression which culminates in the influencing of the will. Further, he attempted to fill in a gap created by Hume in his discussion of association by adding the quality of order in space and time to the other qualities of resemblance, contiguity, and causation. Lastly, he narrowed the meaning of "common sense" so that it would have greater relevance for rhetoric.

Some of the eighteenth-century views on the science of human nature are also present in the works of Blair and Whately. Both in his sermons and in his rhetorical lectures Blair expressed belief in the conviction-persuasion duality. In his sermon, "On Devotion," preached several years before the publication of his lectures, he supported the claim of the faculty psychologists that enlightening the understanding is only the first step in persuasion.

That religion is essential to the welfare of man, can be proved by the most convincing arguments. But these, however demonstrative soever, are insufficient to support its authority over human conduct. For arguments may convince the understanding, when they cannot conquer the passions. Irresistible they seem in the calm hours of retreat; but, in the season of action, they often vanish into smoke. There are other and more powerful springs, which influence the great movements of the human frame. In order to operate with success on the active powers, the heart must be gained. Sentiment and affection must be brought to the aid of reason. It is not enough that men believe religion to be a wise and rational rule of conduct, unless they relish it as agreeable, and find it to carry its own reward.

Later in the same address Blair echoed the sentiments of Hume when he said: "It is not the sight, so much as the strong conception, or deep impression of an object, which affects the passions. . . . Look abroad in the world, and observe how few act upon deliberate and rational views of their true interest. The bulk of mankind are impelled by their feelings." Blair also gleaned from Smith's *Theory of Moral Sentiments* and Reid's "common sense" philosophy ideas which helped formulate his theories of taste and criticism. Evidence of Whately's indebtedness to the science of human nature may be seen in his discussion of the methods of inquiry and proof, his treatment of the managerial nature of invention, and his four references to Smith's *Moral Sentiments*.

Campbell, Blair, and Whately, it would appear, owed much to the rhetorical trends and psychological-philosophical ideas which flourished in the eighteenth century. But they were equally affected by another source of knowledge, the Judaeo-Christian tradition. By profession they were Protestant divines who believed in a moderate but orthodox interpretation of the Bible and in God's potential role in the affairs of men. As practicing ministers and theologians, they held that the doctrines of religion cope with the noblest subjects confronting man and that they provide the most revealing insights into human nature. Rhetoric at its highest, therefore, becomes the means of conveying sublime themes for the purpose of redeeming man from his degenerate state and of preparing the Christian preacher or layman to defend his faith.

Several important innovations give to the rhetorics of Campbell, Blair, and Whately an ecclesiastical emphasis. First, they drew heavily upon the Scriptures for illustrative material. Campbell, for instance, quotes from the Bible on seventy-six occasions, while Whately alludes to the Scriptures and to his own ecclesiastical writings forty-one times. Secondly, all three rhetorics contain practical advice for religious speakers. Blair developed a lecture on pulpit eloquence, and Campbell covered similar ground when describing types of persons addressed, different forms of discourse, and various speaking occasions. Even more religious instruction is found in Whately's *Elements of Rhetoric*. The most significant aspects of his logical proof, presumption, burden of proof, and refutation, are designed primarily to help the Christian communicate his religious doctrines with precision and force.

Thirdly, the ecclesiastical nature of these rhetorics is evident in the extended discussions on testimony. In 1762, Campbell, with the approval of Blair, published his *Dissertation on Miracles* in response to Hume's treatise on the same subject which denied the authenticity of biblical testimony. Campbell sought to answer the scepticism of Hume by attempting to demonstrate that nothing in human nature, in recorded history, or in common sense has established a presumption which successfully negates the testimony of the Apostles concerning miracles. Campbell's arguments, later refined in numerous sermons before the Synod of Aberdeen and included in part in his *Philosophy of Rhetoric,* prompted Whately to write a pamphlet in 1819 entitled, *Historic Doubts to Napoleon Bonaparte.* In this popular and clever essay, Whately's purpose was to show how Hume's scepticism with respect to the value of testimony on miracles, if extended to its logical conclusion, could prove the premise that Napoleon Bonaparte never existed. This stress upon past fact rather than future fact elevated testimony to the level of artistic proof.

George Campbell, Hugh Blair, and Richard Whately then were the first rhetoricians of modern rhetoric. Anticipating present-day speech theory, they appreciated the multidisciplinary nature of communication. Thus they saw the relationships between rhetoric and literature, theology, psychology, philosophy, history, language, and natural science. What they borrowed from these and other related disciplines was modified to suit the needs of a developing, dynamic rhetoric with a strong ethical base. Although some of their conclusions can no longer be supported by recent scientific findings, the works of Campbell, Blair, and Whately have left their mark on twentieth-century rhetorical theory. Post-World War II courses combining units on reading, writing, speaking, and listening are directly traceable to Blair's lectures. The practice of assigning expository, persuasive, and entertaining speeches or themes adheres to Campbell's discussion on the ends of discourse. And current procedures in argumentation and in intercollegiate forensics are consistent with the recommendations of Whately. With such an influence, *The Lectures on Rhetoric and Belles Lettres,* the *Philosophy of Rhetoric,* and the *Elements of Rhetoric* can be profitably read by contemporary students of rhetorical theory.

General Bibliography

Abelson, Paul, *The Seven Liberal Arts: A Study in Medieval Culture* (New York, 1906).

Bacon, Wallace A., "The Elocutionary Career of Thomas Sheridan," *Speech Monographs,* XXXI (March 1964), 1–53.

Baldwin, Charles S., *Ancient Rhetoric and Poetic* (New York, 1924).

———, *Medieval Rhetoric and Poetic* (New York, 1928).

Baldwin, T. W., *William Shakspere's Small Latine & Lesse Greeke,* 2 vols. (Urbana, Illinois, 1944).

Bate, Walter Jackson, *From Classic to Romantic: Premises of Taste in Eighteenth-Century England* (Cambridge, Massachusetts, 1946).

Beck, Frederick A. G., *Greek Education 450–350 B.C.* (New York, 1964).

Bevilacqua, Vincent M., "Philosophical Influences in the Development of English Rhetorical Theory: 1748 to 1783," *Proceedings of the Leeds Philosophical and Literary Society, Literary and Historical Section,* Vol. XII, Part VI (April 1968), 191–215.

Bosker, A., *Literary Criticism in the Age of Johnson* (Groningen, 1930).

Boswell, James, *Private Papers of James Boswell from Malahide Castle,* 18 vols. (Mt. Vernon, New York, 1928–1934).

Bower, Alexander, *The History of the University of Edinburgh,* 3 vols. (Edinburgh, 1830).

Burton, John H., *Life and Correspondence of David Hume,* 2 vols. (Edinburgh, 1846).

Burwick, Frederick, "Associationist Rhetoric and Scottish Prose Style," *Speech Monographs,* XXXIV (March 1967), 21–34.

Carlyle, Alexander, *Autobiography of the Rev. Dr. Alexander Carlyle, Minister at Inveresk; containing memorials of the men and events of his time,* ed. J. H. Burton (Boston, 1861).

Chambers, Frank P., *The History of Taste* (New York, 1932).

Chambers, Robert, ed., *A Biographical Dictionary of Eminent Scotsmen,* 4 vols. (Glasgow, Edinburgh, and London, 1855).

Charvat, William, *The Origins of American Critical Thought: 1810–1835* (Philadelphia, 1936).

Clark, Donald L., *John Milton at St. Paul's School: A Study of Ancient Rhetoric in English Renaissance Education* (New York, 1948).

———, *Rhetoric in Greco-Roman Education* (New York, 1957).

Clarke, Martin L., *Rhetoric at Rome: A Historical Survey* (London, 1953).

Constable, John, *Archibald Constable and His Literary Correspondents,* 3 vols. (Edinburgh, 1873).

Corbett, Edward P. J., "A Survey of Rhetoric," *Classical Rhetoric for the Modern Student* (New York, 1965), pp. 535–568.

Crane, William G., *Wit and Rhetoric in the Renaissance* (New York, 1937).

Dargan, Edwin C., *A History of Preaching,* 2 vols. (New York, 1911).

Ehninger, Douglas, "Selected Theories of *Inventio* in English Rhetoric, 1759–1828." Unpublished Ph.D. dissertation, Ohio State University, 1949.

———, "Dominant Trends in English Rhetorical Thought, 1750–1800," *The Southern Speech Journal,* XVII (September 1952), 3–12.

———, "Campbell, Blair, and Whately: Old Friends in a New Light," *Western Speech,* XIX (October 1955), 263–269.

———, "Campbell, Blair, and Whately Revisited," *The Southern Speech Journal,* XXVIII (Spring 1963), 169–182.

———, "On Rhetoric and Rhetorics," *Western Speech,* XXXI (Fall 1967), 242–249.

Gerard, Alexander, *An Essay on Taste* (London and Edinburgh, 1759).

Golden, James L., "John Wesley on Rhetoric and Belles Lettres," *Speech Monographs,* XXVIII (November 1961), 250–264.

———, "James Boswell on Rhetoric and Belles Lettres," *Quarterly Journal of Speech,* L (October 1964), 266–276.

———, "The Rhetorical Theory of Adam Smith," *Southern Speech Journal,* XXXIII (Spring 1968), 200–215.

Gosse, Edmund, *A History of Eighteenth-Century Literature* (New York, 1927).

Graham, Henry G., *Scottish Men of Letters in the Eighteenth Century* (London, 1901).

Graves, S. A., *The Scottish Philosophy of Common Sense* (Oxford, 1960).

Greig, J. Y. T., *David Hume* (New York, 1931).

———, *The Letters of David Hume,* 2 vols. (Oxford, 1932).

Grene, Marjorie, "Gerard's Essay on Taste," *Modern Philology,* XLI (1943), 45–58.

Gwynn, A. O., *Roman Education from Cicero to Quintilian* (Oxford, 1926).

Haberman, Frederick W., "English Sources of American Elocution," *History of Speech Education in America,* ed. Karl R. Wallace (New York, 1954), pp. 105–126.

Harding, Harold F., "English Rhetorical Theory, 1750–1800." Unpublished Ph.D. dissertation, Cornell University, 1937.

Hartley, David, *Observations on Man, His Frame, His Duty, and His Expectations* (1749) (Gainesville, Florida, 1966).

Holmes, John, *The Art of Rhetoric Made Easy* (London, 1739).

Home, Henry Lord Kames, *Elements of Criticism,* 3 vols. (Edinburgh and London, 1762).

Hooker, Edward Niles, "The Discussion of Taste, from 1750 to 1770, and the New Trends in Literary Criticism," *Publications of the Modern Language Association,* XLIX (1934), 577–592.

Howell, Wilbur S., *Logic and Rhetoric in England, 1500–1700* (Princeton, 1956).

———, "Sources of the Elocutionary Movement in England," *Quarterly Journal of Speech,* XLV (February 1959), 1–18.

———, "Renaissance Rhetoric and Modern Rhetoric: A Study in Change," *The Rhetorical Idiom,* ed. Donald C. Bryant (Ithaca, New York, 1961).

———, "John Locke and the New Rhetoric," *Quarterly Journal of Speech,* LIII (December 1967), 319–333.

Hume, David, *A Treatise of Human Nature* (London, 1739).

———, "Of Eloquence," *Essays Moral and Political* (London, 1741).

———, "Of the Standard of Taste," *Essays by David Hume* (London, n.d.), pp. 165–182.

Hutcheson, Francis, *A Short Introduction to Moral Philosophy* (Glasgow, 1753).

Jaeger, Werner, *Paideia: the Ideals of Greek Culture,* trans. Gilbert Highet, Second Edition, 3 vols. (New York, 1945).

Jebb, R. C., "Rhetoric," *The Encyclopaedia Britannica*, Eleventh Edition, XXIII, 233–237.

Joseph, Sister Miriam, *Shakespeare's Use of the Arts of Language* (New York, 1947).

Kennedy, George, *The Art of Persuasion in Greece* (Princeton, 1963).

———, "Speech Education in Greece," *Western Speech*, XXXI (Winter 1967), 2–9.

Lami, Bernard, *L'Art de Parler* (Paris, 1675).

Lawson, John, *Lectures Concerning Oratory* (Dublin, 1758).

Locke, John, *An Essay on Human Understanding*, 2 vols. (London, 1760).

Marrou, H. I., *A History of Education in Antiquity*, trans. George Lamb (London, 1956; Mentor paperback edition, 1964).

Mason, John, *An Essay on Elocution* (London, 1748).

Mathieson, William L., *The Awakening of Scotland* (Glasgow, 1910).

McCosh, James, *Scottish Philosophy: Biographical, Expository, Critical, from Hutcheson to Hamilton* (New York, 1875).

McKeon, Richard, "Rhetoric in the Middle Ages," *Critics and Criticism*, ed. R. S. Crane (Chicago, 1952), pp. 260–296.

Meador, Prentice A., Jr., "Speech Education at Rome," *Western Speech*, XXXI (Winter 1967), 9–15.

Meikle, Henry W., "The Chair of Rhetoric and Belles Lettres at the University of Edinburgh," *University of Edinburgh Journal*, XIII (1946), 89–103.

Mitchell, W. F., *English Pulpit Oratory* (London, 1932).

Monk, Samuel H., *The Sublime: A Study of Critical Theories in XVIII-Century England* (New York, 1935).

Mossner, Ernest, *The Forgotten Hume* (New York, 1943).

Mozley, Rev. Thomas, *Reminiscences, Chiefly of Oriel College and the Oxford Movement* (Boston, 1882).

Murphy, James J., "Cicero's Rhetoric in the Middle Ages," *Quarterly Journal of Speech*, LIII (December 1967), 334–341.

Ong, Walter J., *Ramus, Method, and the Decay of Dialogue* (Cambridge, Massachusetts, 1958).

Paetow, Louis John, *The Arts Course at Medieval Universities with Special Reference to Grammar and Rhetoric* (Urbana, Illinois, 1910).

Perrin, Porter G., "The Teaching of Rhetoric in the American Colleges before 1750." Unpublished Ph.D. dissertation, University of Chicago, 1936.

Priestley, Joseph, *A Course of Lectures on Oratory and Criticism* (London, 1777).

Rae, John, *Life of Adam Smith* (London, 1895).

Ramsay, John, *Scotland and the Scotsmen of the Eighteenth Century*, 2 vols. (Edinburgh, 1888).

Randall, Helen W., *The Critical Theory of Lord Kames* (Northampton, Massachusetts, 1944).

Reid, Thomas, *Inquiry into the Human Mind on the Principles of Common Sense* (London, 1764).

———, *Essays on the Power of the Human Mind*, 3 vols. (Edinburgh, 1812).

Roberts, W. Rhys, *Greek Rhetoric and Literary Criticism* (New York, 1928).

Rollin, Charles, *The Method of Teaching and Studying the Belles Lettres*, 4 vols. (London, 1737).

Ross, Ian, "Unpublished Letters of Thomas Reid to Lord Kames, 1762–1782," *Texas Studies in Literature and Language*, VII (Spring 1965), 17–65.

Saintsbury, George, *A History of Criticism and Literary Taste in Europe*, 3 vols. (New York, 1902).

Sandford, William F., *English Theories of Public Address, 1530–1828* (Columbus, Ohio, 1931).

Schwartz, Joseph, and John A. Rycenga, eds., *The Province of Rhetoric* (New York, 1965).

Scott, William R., *Adam Smith as Student and Professor* (Glasgow, 1937).

Sheridan, Thomas, *A Discourse Being Introductory to a Course of Lectures on Elocution and the English Language* (London, 1759).

———, *Lectures on Elocution* (London, 1762).

———, *Lectures on the Art of Reading* (Dublin, 1775).

Smith, Adam, *Theory of Moral Sentiments* (London, 1759).

———, *Lectures on Rhetoric and Belles Lettres,* ed. John M. Lothian (London, 1963).

Somerville, Thomas, *My Own Life and Times: 1741–1814* (Edinburgh, 1861).

Stephen, Leslie, *History of English Thought in the Eighteenth Century,* 2 vols. (London, 1902).

Taylor, Harold, "Hume's Theory of Imagination," *University of Toronto Quarterly,* XII (1942), 180–190.

Thonssen, Lester, and A. Craig Baird, *Speech Criticism: The Development of Standards of Rhetorical Appraisal* (New York, 1948).

Tuckwell, W., *Pre-Tractarian Oxford* (London, 1909).

Tytler, Alexander Fraser, *Memoirs of the Life and Writings of Henry Home of Kames,* 2 vols. (Edinburgh, 1807).

Vossius, Gerardus, *De Philosophia* (The Hague, 1658).

Wallace, Karl R., *Francis Bacon on Communication and Rhetoric* (Chapel Hill, North Carolina, 1943).

———, "Aspects of Modern Rhetoric in Francis Bacon," *Quarterly Journal of Speech,* XLII (December 1946), 398–406.

Wallach, Luitpold, ed., *The Classical Tradition: Literary and Historical Studies in Honor of Harry Caplan* (Ithaca, New York, 1966).

Ward, John, *A System of Oratory,* 2 vols. (London, 1759).

Williams, A. M., "The Scottish School of Rhetoric," *Education,* XIII (1892–1893), 142–150; 220–227; 281–290; 344–354; 427–434; 488–496.

Addenda

Benzie, W., *The Dublin Orator: Thomas Sheridan's Influence on Eighteenth-Century Rhetoric and Belles Lettres* (Mentson and Yorkshire, 1972).

Bevilacqua, Vincent M., "Vico, Rhetorical Humanism, and The Study Method of our Time," *Quarterly Journal of Speech,* LVIII (February 1972), 70–83.

Bushnell, Nelson S., "Lord Kames and Eighteenth Century Scotland," *Studies in Scottish Literature,* 10 (April 1973), 241–254.

Cherwitz, Richard A. and Hikins, James W., "John Stuart Mill's *On Liberty*: Implications for the Epistemology of the New Rhetoric," *Quarterly Journal of Speech,* LXV (February 1979), 12–25.

Cohen, Ralph, "The Rationale of Hume's Literary Inquiries," in *David Hume, Many-Sided Genius.* Edited by Merill, Kenneth R. and Shahan, Robert W. (Norman, Oklahoma, 1976), pp. 97–117.

Durham, Weldon B., "The Elements of Thomas De Quincey's Rhetoric," *Speech Monographs,* XXXVII (November 1970), 240–248.

Golden, James L., "The Influence of Rhetoric on the Social Science Theories of Giambattista Vico and David Hume," *Western Speech,* XXXIV (Summer 1970), 170–180.

———, "Adam Smith as a Rhetorical Theorist and Literary Critic," *Costerus* (Amsterdam: Rodopi NV, 1972), I, 89–114.

Golden, James L., Berquist, Goodwin, and Coleman, William, *The Rhetoric of Western Thought,* Second Edition (Dubuque, Iowa, 1979).

Grover, David H., "John Walker: The Mechanical Man Revisited," *Southern Speech Journal,* XXXIV (Summer 1969), 288–297.

Hill, L. Brooks, "Lockean Influence in the Evolution of Rhetorical Theory," *Central States Speech Journal,* XXVI (Summer 1975), 107–114.

Howell, Wilbur Samuel, "Adam Smith's Lectures on Rhetoric: An Historical Assessment," *Speech Monographs,* XXXVI (November 1969), 393–418.

———, *Eighteenth-Century British Logic and Rhetoric* (Princeton, 1971).

Irvine, James R., "James Beattie's Psychology of Taste," *Western Speech,* XXXIV (Winter 1970), 21–28.

Kelley, William G., "Thomas Reid on Common Sense: Meta-Rational Approach to Truth," *Southern Speech Communication Journal,* XXXIX (Fall 1973), 40–54.

King, Andrew A., "Thomas De Quincey on Rhetoric and National Character," *Central States Speech Journal,* XXIV (Summer 1974), 128–134.

King, E. H., "James Beattie's Literary Essays (1776, 1783) and the Evolution of Romanticism," *Studies in Scottish Literature,* XI (April 1974), 199–216.

Kivy, Peter, "Introduction," in his *Thomas Reid's Lectures on the Fine Arts* (The Hague, 1973), pp. 1–18.

Lehmann, William C., *Henry Home, Lord Kames, and the Scottish Enlightenment: A Study in National Character and in the History of Ideas* (The Hague, 1971).

McGuinness, Arthur E., *Henry Home, Lord Kames* (New York, 1970).

Meersman, Roger, "Père René Rapin's Eloquence des Belles Lettres," *Speech Monographs,* XXXVIII (November 1971), 290–301.

Mohrmann, G. P., "The Real *Chironomia,*" *Southern Speech Journal,* XXXIV (Fall 1968), 17–27.

Patton, John H., "Experience and Imagination: Approaches to Rhetoric by John Locke and David Hume," *Southern Speech Communication Journal,* XLI (Fall 1975), 11–29.

Rewa, Michael, "Aspects of Rhetoric in Johnson's 'Professedly Serious' Rambler Essays," *Quarterly Journal of Speech,* LVI (February 1970), 75–84.

Ross, Ian Simpson, *Lord Kames and the Scotland of His Day* (Oxford, 1972).

Skopec, Eric William, "Thomas Reid's Fundamental Rules of Eloquence," *Quarterly Journal of Speech,* LXIV (December 1978), 400–408.

Skopec, Ernest, "Thomas Reid's Rhetorical Theory: A Manuscript Report," *Communication Monographs,* XLV (August 1978), 258–264.

Spence, Patricia R., "Sympathy and Propriety in Adam Smith's Rhetoric," *Quarterly Journal of Speech,* LX (February 1974), 92–99.

Stephens, James, "Bacon's New English Rhetoric and the Debt to Aristotle," *Speech Monographs,* XXXIX (November 1972), 248–259.

Thompson, Wayne N., "Aristotle as a Predecessor to Reid's 'Common Sense,' " *Speech Monographs,* XLII (August 1975), 209–220.

Wallace, Karl R., "Francis Bacon on Understanding, Reason, and Rhetoric," *Speech Monographs,* XXXVIII (June 1971), 79–91.

———, "Francis Bacon and Method Theory and Practice," *Speech Monographs,* XL (November 1973), 243–272.

Warnick, Barbara, "Fenelon's Recommendation to the French Academy Concerning Rhetoric," *Communication Monographs,* XLV (March 1978), 73–84.

Weedon, Jerry L., "Locke on Rhetoric and Rational Man," *Quarterly Journal of Speech,* LVI (December 1970), 378–387.

Weidner, Hal Rivers, "Three Models of Rhetoric: Traditional, Mechanical, and Vital," Ph.D. Dissertation, University of Michigan, 1975.

HUGH BLAIR

꩜꩜꩜꩜꩜꩜꩜꩜꩜

Hugh Blair (1718–1800) was born in Edinburgh on April 7, the only child of John Blair, a clerk in the Excise, and of Martha Ogston, the daughter of a bookseller. He received his early education in the family circle which included his scholarly uncle, James Bannatine, a minister of Trinity Church. He then went on to the noted High School of Edinburgh, where in his fifth and final year he was required to read heavily in the Roman rhetoricians. In 1730, at the age of twelve, he entered the University of Edinburgh, at a time when the curriculum and the quality of instruction were undergoing a radical revamping. Under the direction of John Stevenson, Professor of Logic, Blair wrote and publicly read an essay "On the Beautiful," an exercise that undoubtedly influenced his later lectures on taste and the sublime. The academic life so suited Blair's temperament that he did not move to take his M. A. degree until 1739, nine years after he entered the University. After he took his degree, he stayed on at the University for another three years, tutoring and preaching occasionally.

Blair's main vocation in life was settled in 1742, when he was ordained at his first pastorate at Collessee in Fife. A year after this appointment, he was elected to the coveted post at the Canongate Church in Edinburgh, where he first established his reputation as a preacher and a litterateur. In 1754, he moved to Lady Yester's Church, and four years later he won appointment to the most prestigious pulpit in Scotland, the High Church at St. Giles, where he remained until his retirement from the active ministry in the 1770s. Early in his ministry, Blair identified himself with the Moderates, a group of liberal, rationalistic, scholarly clergymen who were trying to counteract the influence of the strait-laced, dour, rather anti-intellectual ministers of the Scottish church. His defense of David Hume and Henry Home (Lord Kames) against the charge of heresy leveled by the so-called High Flying churchmen was indicative of his liberal and advanced thinking. In fact, it was his published defense of Hume that contributed to the early demise, after two issues, of the *Edinburgh Review,* which he and other members of the Edinburgh literati had launched in 1755. Despite a weak voice and a wooden style of delivery, Blair eventually became the most popular preacher in Edinburgh. His four volumes of sermons, published between 1777 and 1794, went into numerous editions. His sermons proved popular partly because they were short, well organized, and lucidly written and partly because they did not unsettle the congregation with constant reminders of such Calvinistic doctrines as those on original sin, total corruption, a priori election, and damnation.

In addition to his status as a respected and celebrated preacher, Blair soon came to be looked upon as a literary accoucheur in a city which in the second half of the eighteenth century was commonly referred to as the "Athens of the North." Students of literary history are not usually aware that Blair was the sixth in the line of eighteenth-century editors of Shakespeare, following Rowe, Pope, Theobald, Hanmer, and Warburton, and that in 1772 he supervised the publication, in forty-four volumes, of the first uniform edition of English poets to be produced in the British Isles. What students of literature do know about Blair, if they know anything at all, is that he was the most fervent promoter and defender of James Macpherson's translations of the Ossian epics, an enterprise that was eventually exposed as one of the greatest literary hoaxes of all time. The *Critical Dissertation* that Blair wrote for editions of the Ossian poems in the 1760s brought him a measure of international fame. From the vantage point of hindsight we can exult over Blair's naïvete and gullibility in this matter, but we must remember that at the time when Macpherson was one of the most lionized figures in Europe, Samuel Johnson was one of the few men of literary stature who expressed doubts about the authenticity of the Ossian poems. In this generally skeptical age, it did not occur to such close friends of Blair as David Hume, Adam Smith, William Robertson, Alexander Carlyle, and James Boswell that Macpherson might be a fraud, and indeed it was not until 1805 that the Highland Society of Scotland finally pronounced the Ossian poems as forgeries.

One of the reasons, perhaps, why Blair was so enraptured by the primitive rhapsodies of the "Scottish Homer" is that in the autumn of 1759, when Macpherson first brought his "translations" to Edinburgh, Blair was engaged in writing his lectures on "The Origin and Nature of Figurative Language," "The Sublime in Writing," and "Nature of Poetry—Its Origin and Progress" for a series he had been asked to give at the University of Edinburgh. It was this series of lectures, starting on December 9, 1759, which launched Blair's career as a teacher, a career in which he exerted his greatest influence and which resulted in his most enduring fame. The success of these lectures prompted the Town Council in the following year to appoint him officially as Professor of Rhetoric. In 1762, George III named Blair the first Regius Professor of Rhetoric and Belles Lettres at the University of Edinburgh, a chair which carried an annual stipend of seventy pounds and which in later years had such distinguished occupants as David Masson, George Saintsbury, H. J. C. Grierson, and J. Dover Wilson. Blair's rhetoric course proved to be so popular that during the twenty-one years that he served as Regius Professor, it regularly enrolled between fifty and sixty students each session. Although Blair occasionally made minor changes in the series of forty-seven lectures that he originally prepared for this course, the lectures remained fundamentally the same during the entire time of his tenure. So predictable were the lectures that students began to sell manuscript copies of notes that were taken in class. It was this circulation of notes that finally prompted Blair, on the eve of his retirement in 1783, to publish his lectures. As he said in the Preface to his *Lectures on Rhetoric and Belles Lettres,* "When the author saw them circulate so currently, as even to be quoted in print, and found himself often threatened with surreptitious publications of them, he judged it to be high time that they should proceed from his own hand, rather than come into public view under some very defective and erroneous form."

The *Lectures* had a phenomenal sale in Europe and the United States during the first century after publication. In the bibliography appended to his biography of Blair, Robert M. Schmitz listed twenty-six editions in Great Britain, thirty-seven editions in the United States, and fifty-two abridged editions of the *Lectures*. Besides these, there were two editions published in English on the continent and thirteen translations into French, Italian, Russian, and Spanish. In the final assessment of their contribution to rhetoric, Campbell and Whately will undoubtedly rate higher than Blair, but there is no question that of the three texts published by these men, Blair's enjoyed the widest sale and was written in the most lucid and charming style.

Blair spent his years of retirement playing host to the literary and political lights who visited Edinburgh and preparing volumes of his sermons for publication. As a solace for his grief over the death of his twenty-year-old daughter, an only child from his marriage to his cousin Katherine Bannatine in 1748, Blair adopted the eight-year-old orphaned daughter of his friend, David Hunter. Hugh Blair died in his eighty-third year, on December 27, 1800, leaving an estate valued at over 6000 pounds. There was probably more irony than compliment in Robert Burns's comment about the fellow Scotsman who had achieved such a high measure of fame in his day: "Dr. Blair is merely an astonishing proof of what industry and application can do."

Bibliography

Blair, Hugh, *A Critical Edition of the Poems of Ossian, the Son of Fingal* (London, 1763).

——, *Lectures on Rhetoric and Belles Lettres,* 2 vols. (London and Edinburgh, 1783).

——, *Sermons,* 5 vols. (Edinburgh, 1807).

——, Manuscript: Letters of Hugh Blair to Elizabeth Montague. Henry E. Huntington Library, San Marino, California.

Bowers, John Waite, "A Comparative Criticism of Hugh Blair's Essay on Taste," *Quarterly Journal of Speech,* XLVII (December 1961), 384–389.

Chapman, R. W., "Blair on Ossian," *Review of English Studies,* VII (1931), 80–83.

Cohen, Herman, "An Analysis of the Rhetoric of Hugh Blair." Unpublished Ph.D. dissertation, State University of Iowa, 1954.

——, "Hugh Blair's Theory of Taste," *Quarterly Journal of Speech,* XLIV (October 1958), 265–274.

——, "Hugh Blair on Speech Education," *Southern Speech Journal,* XXIX (1963), 1–11.

Corbett, Edward P. J., "Hugh Blair: A Study of His Rhetorical Theory." Unpublished Ph.D. dissertation, Loyola University, Chicago, 1956.

——, "Hugh Blair's Three (?) Critical Dissertations," *Notes and Queries,* New Series, I (November 1954), 478–480.

——, "Hugh Blair as an Analyzer of English Prose Style," *College Composition and Communication,* IX (May 1958), 98–103.

Cowling, G. H., "The English Teaching of Dr. Hugh Blair," *Palaestra,* CXLVIII (Brandl Festschrift, Band 110), 281–294.

Edney, Clarence W., "Blair's Theory of *Dispositio,*" *Speech Monographs,* XXIII (March 1956), 38–45.

Ehninger, Douglas and James Golden, "The Intrinsic Sources of Blair's Popularity," *The Southern Speech Journal,* XXI (Fall 1955), 12–30.

——, "The Extrinsic Sources of Blair's Popularity," *The Southern Speech Journal,* XXII (Fall 1956), 16–32.

Ferguson, J. DeLancey, "Burns and Hugh Blair," *Modern Language Notes,* XLV (1930), 440–446.

Finlayson, James, "A Short Account of the Life and Character of the Author," prefixed to *Sermons by Hugh Blair,* 3 vols. (New York, 1802).

Foster, John, Review of "An Account of the Life and Writings of Hugh Blair . . . by the late John Hill," *The Analectic Magazine,* V (1815), 188–203.

Golden, James L., "The Rhetorical Theory and Practice of Hugh Blair." Unpublished M.A. thesis, Ohio State University, 1948.

——, "Hugh Blair: Minister of St. Giles," *Quarterly Journal of Speech,* XXXVIII (April 1952), 155–160.

Harding, Harold F., ed., *Lectures on Rhetoric and Belles Lettres by Hugh Blair,* 2 vols. (Carbondale, Illinois, 1965).

Hawley, William N., "Hugh Blair: Moderate Preacher." Unpublished B.D. thesis, University of Chicago Divinity School, 1938.

Hill, John, *An Account of the Life and Writings of Hugh Blair* (Edinburgh, 1807).
Knowlton, E. C., "Wordsworth and Hugh Blair," *Philological Quarterly*, VI (July 1927), 277–281.
Mays, Morley J., "Johnson and Blair on Addison's Prose Style," *Studies in Philology*, XXXIX (1942), 638–649.
"The Ossian Controversy Stated," *London Magazine*, LI (1782), 511–512.
Schmitz, Robert M., *Hugh Blair* (New York, 1948).
———, "Scottish Shakespeare," *The Shakespeare Association Bulletin*, XVI (1941), 229–236.
———, "Dr. Johnson and Blair's Sermons," *Modern Language Notes*, LX (1945), 268–270.
Stephen, Leslie, "Hugh Blair," *Dictionary of National Biography* (London, 1882).
Tegg, William M., "Memoirs of the Rev. Hugh Blair." An Introduction to *The Beauties of Blair* (London, 1810).

Addenda

Golden, James L., Berquist, Goodwin F., and Coleman, William E., "Neoclassicism and Belles Lettres," in *The Rhetoric of Western Thought*, Second Edition (Dubuque, Iowa, 1979), pp. 89–106.
Howell, Wilbur Samuel, "Discordant Consensus: Hume, Lawson, Priestley, Blair, Witherspoon," in *Eighteenth-Century British Logic and Rhetoric* (Princeton, 1971), pp. 613–691.

Complete Table of Contents for
HUGH BLAIR
Lectures on Rhetoric and Belles Lettres

VOLUME I

VOLUME II

LECTURES ON RHETORIC AND BELLES LETTRES

Lecture I

INTRODUCTION

One of the most distinguished privileges which Providence has conferred upon mankind, is the power of communicating their thoughts to one another. Destitute of this power, reason would be a solitary, and, in some measure, an unavailable principle. Speech is the great instrument by which man becomes beneficial to man: and it is to the intercourse and transmission of thought, by means of speech, that we are chiefly indebted for the improvement of thought itself. Small are the advances which a single unassisted individual can make towards perfecting any of his powers. What we call human reason, is not the effort or ability of one, so much as it is the result of the reason of many, arising from lights mutually communicated, in consequence of discourse and writing.

It is obvious, then, that writing and discourse are objects entitled to the highest attention. Whether the influence of the speaker, or the entertainment of the hearer, be consulted; whether utility or pleasure be the principal aim in view, we are prompted, by the strongest motives, to study how we may communicate our thoughts to one another with most advantage. Accordingly we find, that in almost every nation, as soon as language had extended itself beyond that scanty communication which was requisite for the supply of men's necessities, the improvement of discourse began to attract regard. In the language even of rude uncultivated tribes, we can trace some attention to the grace and force of those expressions which they used, when they sought to persuade or to affect. They were early sensible of a beauty in discourse, and endeavoured to give it certain decorations, which experience had taught them it was capable of receiving, long before the study of those decorations was formed into a regular art.

But, among nations in a civilized state, no art has been cultivated with more care, than that of language, style, and composition. The attention paid to it may, indeed, be assumed as one mark of the progress of society towards its most improved period. For, according as society improves and flourishes, men acquire more influence over one another by means of reasoning and discourse; and in proportion as that influence is felt to enlarge, it must follow, as a natural consequence, that they will bestow more care upon the methods of expressing their conceptions with propriety and eloquence. Hence we find, that in all the polished nations of Europe, this study has been treated as highly important, and has possessed a considerable place in every plan of liberal education.

Indeed, when the arts of speech and writing are mentioned, I am sensible that prejudices against them are apt to rise in the minds of many. A sort of art is immediately thought of, that is ostentatious and deceitful; the minute and trifling study of words alone; the pomp of expression; the studied fallacies of rhetoric; ornament substituted in the room of use. We need not wonder, that, under such imputations, all study of discourse as an art, should have suffered in the opinion of men of understanding; and I am far from denying, that rhetoric and criticism have sometimes been so managed as to tend to the corruption, rather than to the improvement, of good taste and true eloquence. But sure it is equally possible to apply the principles of reason and good sense to this art, as to any other that is cultivated among men. If the following Lectures have any merit, it will consist in an endeavour to substitute the application of these principles in the place of artificial and scholastic rhetoric; in an endeavour to explode false ornament, to direct attention more towards substance than show, to recommend good sense as the foundation of all good composition, and simplicity as essential to all true ornament.

When entering on this subject, I may be allowed, on this occasion, to suggest a few thoughts concerning the importance and advantages of such studies, and the rank they are entitled to possess in academical education.[1] I am under no temptation, for this purpose, of extolling their importance at the expense of any other department of science. On the contrary, the study of Rhetoric and Belles Lettres supposes and requires a proper acquaintance with the rest of the liberal arts. It embraces them all within its circle, and recommends them to the highest regard. The first care of all such as wish either to write with reputation, or to speak in public so as to command attention, must be, to extend their knowledge; to lay in a rich store of ideas relating to those subjects of which the occasions of life may call them to discourse or to write. Hence, among the ancients, it was a fundamental principle, and frequently inculcated, "Quod omnibus disciplinis et artibus debet esse instructus orator;" that the orator ought to be an accomplished scholar, and conversant in every part of learning. It is indeed impossible to contrive an art, and very pernicious it were if it could be contrived, which should give the stamp of merit to any composition rich or splendid in expression, but barren or erroneous in thought. They are the wretched attempts towards an art of this kind, which have so often disgraced oratory, and debased it below its true standard. The graces of composition have been employed to disguise or to supply the want of matter; and the temporary applause of the ignorant has been courted, instead of the lasting approbation of the discerning. But such imposture can never

1 The author was the first who read lectures on this subject in the university of Edinburgh. He began with reading them in a private character in the year 1759. In the following year he was chosen Professor of Rhetoric by the magistrates and town-council of Edinburgh; and, in 1762, his Majesty was pleased to erect and endow a Profession of Rhetoric and Belles Lettres in that university, and the author was appointed the first Regius Professor.

maintain its ground long. Knowledge and science must furnish the materials that form the body and substance of any valuable composition. Rhetoric serves to add the polish; and we know that none but firm and solid bodies can be polished well.

Of those who peruse the following Lectures, some by the profession to which they addict themselves, or in consequence of their prevailing inclination, may have the view of being employed in composition, or in public speaking. Others, without any prospect of this kind, may wish only to improve their taste with respect to writing and discourse, and to acquire principles which will enable them to judge for themselves in that part of literature called the Belles Lettres.

With respect to the former, such as may have occasion to communicate their sentiments to the public, it is abundantly clear that some preparation of study is requisite for the end which they have in view. To speak or to write perspicuously and agreeably with purity, with grace and strength, are attainments of the utmost consequence to all who purpose, either by speech or writing, to address the public. For without being master of those attainments, no man can do justice to his own conceptions; but how rich soever he may be in knowledge and in good sense, will be able to avail himself less of those treasures, than such as possess not half his store, but who can display what they possess with more propriety. Neither are these attainments of that kind for which we are indebted to nature merely. Nature has, indeed, conferred upon some a very favourable distinction in this respect, beyond others. But in these, as in most other talents she bestows, she has left much to be wrought out by every man's own industry. So conspicuous have been the effects of study and improvement in every part of eloquence; such remarkable examples have appeared of persons surmounting, by their diligence, the disadvantages of the most untoward nature, that among the learned it has long been a contested, and remains still an undecided point, whether nature or art confer most towards excelling in writing or discourse.

With respect to the manner in which art can most effectually furnish assistance for such a purpose, there may be diversity of opinions. I by no means pretend to say that mere rhetorical rules, how just soever, are sufficient to form an orator. Supposing natural genius to be favourable, more by a great deal will depend upon private application and study, than upon any system of instruction that is capable of being publicly communicated. But at the same time, though rules and instructions cannot do all that is requisite, they may, however, do much that is of real use. They cannot, it is true, inspire genius; but they can direct and assist it. They cannot remedy barrenness; but they may correct redundancy. They point out proper models for imitation. They bring into view the chief beauties that ought to be studied, and the principal thoughts that ought to be avoided; and thereby tend to enlighten taste, and to lead genius from unnatural deviations, into its proper channel. What would not avail for the production of great excellencies, may at least serve to prevent the commission of considerable errors.

All that regards the study of eloquence and composition, merits the higher attention upon this account, that it is intimately connected with the improvement of our intellectual powers. For I must be allowed to say, that when we are employed, after a proper manner, in the study of composition, we are cultivating reason itself. True rhetoric and sound logic are very nearly allied. The study of arranging and expressing our thoughts with propriety, teaches to think as well as to speak accurately. By putting our sentiments into words, we always conceive them more distinctly. Every one who has the slightest acquaintance with composition knows, that when he expresses himself ill on any subject, when his arrangement is loose, and his sentences become feeble, the defects of his style can, almost on every occasion, be traced back to his indistinct conception of the subject: so close is the connexion between thoughts and the words in which they are clothed.

The study of composition, important in itself at all times, has acquired additional importance from the taste and manners of the present age. It is an age wherein improvements in every part of science, have been prosecuted with ardour. To all the liberal arts much attention has been paid; and to none more than to the beauty of language, and the grace and elegance of every kind of writing. The public ear is become refined. It will not easily bear what is slovenly and incorrect. Every author must aspire to some merit in expression, as well as in sentiment, if he would not incur the danger of being neglected and despised.

I will not deny that the love of minute elegance, and attention to inferior ornaments of composition, may at present have engrossed too great a degree of the public regard. It is indeed my opinion, that we lean to this extreme; often more careful of polishing style, than of storing it with thought. Yet hence arises a new reason for the study of just and proper composition. If it be requisite not to be deficient in elegance or ornament in times when they are in such high estimation, it is still more requisite to attain the power of distinguishing false ornament from true, in order to prevent our being carried away by that torrent of false and frivolous taste, which never fails, when it is prevalent, to sweep along with it the raw and ignorant. They who have never studied eloquence in its principles, nor have been trained to attend to the genuine and manly beauties of good writing, are always ready to be caught by the mere glare of language; and when they come to speak in public, or to compose, have no other standard on which to form themselves, except what chances to be fashionable and popular, how corrupted soever, or erroneous, that may be.

But as there are many who have no such objects as either composition or public speaking in view, let us next consider what advantages may be derived by them, from such studies as form the subject of these lectures. To them, rhetoric is not so much a practical art as a speculative science; and the same instructions which assist others in composing, will assist them in discerning and relishing the beauties of composition. Whatever enables genius to execute well, will enable taste to criticise justly.

When we name criticising, prejudices may perhaps arise, of the same kind with those which I mentioned before with respect to rhetoric. As rhetoric has been sometimes thought to signify nothing more than the scholastic study of words, and phrases, and tropes, so criticism has been considered as merely the art of finding faults; as the frigid application of certain technical terms, by means of which persons are taught to cavil and censure in a learned manner. But this is the criticism of pedants only. True criticism is a liberal and humane art. It is the offspring of good sense and refined taste. It aims at acquiring a just discernment of the real merit of authors. It promotes a lively relish of their beauties, while it preserves us from that blind and implicit veneration which would confound their beauties and faults in our esteem. It teaches us, in a word, to admire and to blame with judgment, and not to follow the crowd blindly.

In an age when works of genius and literature are so frequently the subjects of discourse, when every one erects himself into a judge, and when we can hardly mingle in polite society without bearing some share in such discussions; studies of this kind, it is not to be doubted, will appear to derive part of their importance from the use to which they may be applied in furnishing materials for those fashionable topics of discourse, and thereby enabling us to support a proper rank in social life.

But I should be sorry if we could not rest the merit of such studies on somewhat of solid and intrinsical use, independent of appearance and show. The exercise of taste and of sound criticism is, in truth, one of the most improving employments of the understanding. To apply the principles of good sense to composition and discourse; to examine what is beautiful and why it is so; to employ ourselves in distinguishing accurately between the specious and the solid, between affected and natural ornament, must certainly improve us not a little in the most valuable part of all philosophy, the philosophy of human nature. For such disquisitions are very intimately connected with the knowledge of ourselves. They necessarily lead us to reflect on the operations of the imagination, and the movements of the heart; and increase our acquaintance with some of the most refined feelings which belong to our frame.

Logical and ethical disquisitions move in a higher sphere; and are conversant with objects of a more severe kind; the progress of the understanding in its search after knowledge, and the direction of the will in the proper pursuit of good. They point out to man the improvement of his nature as an intelligent being; and his duties as the subject of moral obligation. Belles Lettres and criticism chiefly consider him as a being endowed with those powers of taste and imagination, which were intended to embellish his mind, and to supply him with rational and useful entertainment. They open a field of investigation peculiar to themselves. All that relates to beauty, harmony, grandeur, and elegance; all that can sooth the mind, gratify the fancy, or move the affections, belongs to their province. They present human nature under a different aspect from that which it assumes when viewed by other sciences. They bring to light various springs of action, which, without their aid, might have passed unobserved; and which, though of a delicate nature, frequently exert a powerful influence on several departments of human life.

Such studies have also this peculiar advantage, that they exercise our reason without fatiguing it. They lead to inquiries acute, but not painful; profound, but not dry nor abstruse. They strew flowers in the path of science; and while they keep the mind bent, in some degree, and active, they relieve it at the same time from that more toilsome labour to which it must submit in the acquisition of necessary erudition, or the investigation of abstract truth.

The cultivation of taste is farther recommended by the happy effects which it naturally tends to produce on human life. The most busy man, in the most active sphere, cannot be always occupied by business. Men of serious professions cannot always be on the stretch of serious thought. Neither can the most gay and flourishing situations of fortune afford any man the power of filling all his hours with pleasure. Life must always languish in the hands of the idle. It will frequently languish even in the hands of the busy, if they have not some employments subsidiary to that which forms their main pursuit. How then shall these vacant spaces, those unemployed intervals, which more or less, occur in the life of every one, be filled up? How can we contrive to dispose of them in any way that shall be more agreeable in itself, or more consonant to the dignity of the human mind, than in the entertainments of taste, and the study of polite literature? He who is so happy as to have acquired a relish for these, has always at hand an innocent and irreproachable amusement for his leisure hours, to save him from the danger of many a pernicious passion. He is not in hazard of being a burden to himself. He is not obliged to fly to low company, or to court the riot of loose pleasures, in order to cure the tediousness of existence.

Providence seems plainly to have pointed out this useful purpose to which the pleasures of taste may be applied, by interposing them in a middle station between the pleasures of sense, and those of pure intellect. We were not designed to grovel always among objects so low as the former; nor are we capable of dwelling constantly in so high a region as the latter. The pleasures of taste refresh the mind after the toils of the intellect, and the labours of abstract study; and they gradually raise it above the attachments of sense, and prepare it for the enjoyments of virtue.

So consonant is this to experience, that in the education of youth, no object has in every age appeared more important to wise men, than to tincture them early with a relish for the entertainments of taste. The transition is commonly made with ease from these to the discharge of the higher and more important duties of life. Good hopes may be entertained of those whose minds have this liberal and elegant turn. It is favourable to many virtues. Whereas to be entirely devoid of relish for eloquence, poetry, or any of the fine arts, is justly construed to be an unpromising symptom of youth; and raises suspicions of their being prone to low gratifications, or destined to drudge in the more vulgar and illiberal pursuits of life.

There are indeed few good dispositions of any kind with which the improvement of taste is not more or or less connected. A cultivated taste increases sensibility to all the tender and humane passions, by giving them frequent exercise while it tends to weaken the more violent and fierce emotions.

> These polish'd arts have humaniz'd mankind,
> Soften'd the rude, and calm'd the boist'rous mind

The elevated sentiments and high examples which poetry, eloquence, and history, are often bringing under our view, naturally tend to nourish in our minds public spirit, the love of glory, contempt of external fortune, and the admiration of what is truly illustrious and great.

I will not go so far as to say that the improvement of taste and of virtue is the same; or that they may always be expected to co-exist in an equal degree. More powerful correctives than taste can apply, are necessary for reforming the corrupt propensities which too frequently prevail among mankind. Elegant speculations are sometimes found to float on the surface of the mind, while bad passions possess the interior regions of the heart. At the same time this cannot but be admitted, that the exercise of taste is, in its native tendency, moral and purifying. From reading the most admired productions of genius, whether in poetry or prose, almost every one rises with some good impressions left on his mind; and though these may not always be durable, they are at least to be ranked among the means of disposing the heart to virtue. One thing is certain, and I shall hereafter have occasion to illustrate it more fully, that, without possessing the virtuous affections in a strong degree, no man can attain eminence in the sublime parts of eloquence. He must feel what a good man feels, if he expects greatly to move, or to interest mankind. They are the ardent sentiments of honour, virtue, magnanimity, and public spirit, that only can kindle that fire of genius, and call up into the mind those high ideas, which attract the admiration of ages; and if this spirit be necessary to produce the most distinguished efforts of eloquence, it must be necessary also to our relishing them with proper taste and feeling.

On these general topics I shall dwell no longer; but proceed directly to the consideration of the subjects which are to employ the following Lectures. They divide themselves into five parts. First, some introductory dissertations on the nature of taste, and upon the sources of its pleasures. Secondly, the consideration of language. Thirdly, of style. Fourthly of eloquence, properly so called, or public speaking in its different kinds. Lastly, a critical examination of the most distinguished species of composition, both in prose and verse.

Lecture II

TASTE

The nature of the present undertaking leads me to begin with some inquiries concerning taste, as it is this faculty which is always appealed to, in disquisitions concerning the merit of discourse in writing.

There are few subjects on which men talk more loosely and indistinctly than on taste; few which it is more difficult to explain with precision; and none which in this course of Lectures will appear more dry or abstract. What I have to say on the subject, shall be in the following order. I shall first explain the Nature of Taste as a power or faculty in the human mind. I shall next consider, how far it is an improveable faculty. I shall show the sources of its improvement, and the characters of taste in its most perfect state. I shall then examine the various fluctuations to which it is liable, and inquire whether there be any standard to which we can bring the different tastes of men, in order to distinguish the corrupted from the true.

Taste may be defined "The power of receiving pleasure from the beauties of nature and of art." The first question that occurs concerning it is, whether it is to be considered as an internal sense, or as an exertion of reason? Reason is a very general term; but if we understand by it, that power of the mind which in speculative matters discovers truth, and in practical matters judges of the fitness of means to an end, I apprehend the question may be easily answered. For nothing can be more clear, than that taste is not resolvable into any such operation of reason. It is not merely through a discovery of the understanding or a deduction of argument, that the mind receives pleasure from a beautiful prospect or a fine poem. Such objects often strike us intuitively, and make a strong impression, when we are unable to assign the reasons of our being pleased. They sometimes strike in the same manner the philosopher and the peasant; the boy and the man. Hence the faculty by which we relish such beauties, seems more nearly allied to a feeling of sense, than to a process of the understanding; and accordingly from an external sense it has borrowed its name; that sense by which we receive and distinguish the pleasures of food, having, in several languages, given rise to the word taste, in the metaphorical meaning under which we now consider it. However, as in all subjects which regard the operations of the mind, the inaccurate use of words is to be carefully avoided, it must not be inferred from what I have said, that reason is entirely excluded from the exertions of taste. Though taste, beyond doubt, be ultimately founded on a certain natural and instinctive sensibility to beauty, yet reason, as I shall show hereafter, assists taste in many of its operations, and serves to enlarge its power.[1]

Taste, in the sense in which I have explained it, is a faculty common in some degree to all men. Nothing that belongs to human nature is more general than the relish of beauty of one kind or other; of what is orderly, proportioned, grand, harmonious, new, or sprightly. In children, the rudiments of taste discover themselves very early in a thousand instances; in their fondness for regular bodies, their admiration of pictures and statues, and imitations of all kinds; and their strong attachment to whatever is new or marvellous. The most ignorant peasants are delighted with ballads and tales, and are struck with the beautiful appearance of nature in the earth and heavens. Even in the deserts of America, where human nature shows itself in its most uncultivated state, the savages have their ornaments of dress, their war and their death songs, their harangues and their orators. We must therefore conclude the principles of taste to be deeply founded in the human mind. It is no less essential to man to have some discernment of beauty, than it is to possess the attributes of reason and of speech.[2]

But although none be wholly devoid of this faculty, yet the degrees in which it is possessed are widely different. In some men only the feeble glimmerings of taste appear; the beauties which they relish are of the coarsest kind; and of these they have but a weak and confused impression; while in others, taste rises to an acute discernment, and a lively enjoyment of the most refined beauties. In general, we may observe, that in the powers and pleasures of taste, there is a more remarkable inequality among men than is usually found in point of common sense, reason, and judgment. The constitution of our nature in this, as in all other respects, discovers admirable wisdom. In the distribution of those talents which are necessary for man's well-being, nature hath made less distinction among her children. But in the distribution of those which belong only to the ornamental part of life, she hath bestowed her favours with more frugality. She hath both sown the seeds more sparingly; and rendered a higher culture requisite for bringing them to perfection.

This inequality of taste among men is owing, without doubt, in part, to the different frame of their natures; to nicer organs, and finer internal powers, with which some are endowed beyond others. But, if it be owing in part to nature, it is owing to education and culture still more. The illustration of this leads to my next remark on this subject, that taste is a most improveable faculty, if there be any such in human nature; a remark which gives great encouragement to such a course of study as we are now

---

1 See Dr. Gerard's *Essay on Tastes*—D'Alembert's Reflections on the use and abuse of Philosophy in matters which relate to Taste:—*Reflections Critiques sur la Poésie et sur la Peinture*, tome ii. ch. 22–31:—*Elements of Criticism*, chap. 25:—Mr. Hume's *Essay on the Standard of Taste*—Introduction to the *Essay on the Sublime and Beautiful*.
2 On the subject of taste, considered as a power or faculty of the mind, much less is to be found among the ancient, than among the modern rhetorical and critical writers.

proposing to pursue. Of the truth of this assertion we may easily be convinced, by only reflecting on that immense superiority which education and improvement give to civilized, above barbarous nations, in refinement of taste; and on the superiority which they give in the same nation to those who have studied the liberal arts, above the rude and untaught vulgar. The difference is so great, that there is perhaps no one particular in which these two classes of men are so far removed from each other, as in respect of the powers and the pleasures of taste: and assuredly for this difference no other general cause can be assigned, but culture and education. I shall now proceed to show what the means are by which taste becomes so remarkably susceptible of cultivation and progress.

Reflect first upon that great law of our nature, that exercise is the chief source of improvement in all our faculties. This holds both in our bodily, and in our mental powers. It holds even in our external senses, although these be less the subject of cultivation than any of our other faculties. We see how acute the senses become in persons whose trade or business leads to nice exertions of them. Touch, for instance, becomes infinitely more exquisite in men whose employment requires them to examine the polish of bodies, than it is in others. They who deal in microscopical observations, or are accustomed to engrave on precious stones, acquire surprising accuracy of sight in discerning the minutest objects; and practice in attending to different flavours and tastes of liquors, wonderfully improves the power of distinguishing them, and of tracing their composition. Placing internal taste therefore on the footing of a simple sense, it cannot be doubted that frequent exercise, and curious attention to its proper objects, must greatly heighten its power. Of this we have one clear proof in that part of taste, which is called an ear for music. Experience every day shows, that nothing is more improvable. Only the simplest and plainest compositions are relished at first; use and practice extend our pleasure; teach us to relish finer melody, and by degrees enable us to enter into the intricate and compounded pleasures of harmony. So an eye for the beauties of painting is never all at once acquired. It is gradually formed by being conversant among pictures, and studying the works of the best masters.

Precisely in the same manner, with respect to the beauty of composition and discourse, attention to the most approved models, study of the best authors, comparisons of lower and higher degrees of the same beauties, operate towards the refinement of taste. When one is only beginning his acquaintance with works of genius, the sentiment which attends them is obscure and confused. He cannot point out the several excellencies or blemishes of a performance which he peruses; he is at a loss on what to rest his judgment: all that can be expected is, that he should tell in general whether he be pleased or not. But allow him more experience in works of this kind, and his taste becomes by degrees more exact and enlightened. He begins to perceive not only the character of the whole, but the beauties and defects of each part; and is able to describe the peculiar qualities which he praises or blames. The mist dissipates which seemed formerly to hang over the object; and he can at length pronounce firmly, and without hesitation, concerning it. Thus in taste, considered as mere sensibility, exercise opens a great source of improvement.

But although taste be ultimately founded on sensibility, it must not be considered as instinctive sensibility alone. Reason and good sense, as I before hinted, have so extensive an influence on all the operations and decisions of taste, that a thorough good taste may well be considered as a power compounded of natural sensibility to beauty, and of improved understanding. In order to be satisfied of this, let us observe, that the greater part of the productions of genius are no other than imitations of nature; representations of the characters, actions, or manners of men. The pleasure we receive from such imitations or representations is founded on mere taste: but to judge whether they be properly executed, belongs to the understanding, which compares the copy with the original.

In reading, for instance, such a poem as the *Aeneid*, a great part of our pleasure arises from the plan or story being well conducted, and all the parts joined together with probability and due connexion; from the characters being taken from nature, the sentiments being suited to the characters, and the style to the sentiments. The pleasure which arises from a poem so conducted, is felt or enjoyed by taste as an internal sense; but the discovery of this conduct in the poem is owing to reason; and the more that reason enables us to discover such propriety in the conduct, the greater will be our pleasure. We are pleased, through our natural sense of beauty. Reason shows us why, and upon what grounds, we are pleased. Wherever in works of taste, any resemblance to nature is aimed at, wherever there is any reference of parts to a whole, or of means to an end, as there is indeed in almost every writing and discourse, there the understanding must always have a great part to act.

Here then is a wide field for reason's exerting its powers in relation to the objects of taste, particularly with respect to composition, and works of genius; and hence arises a second and a very considerable source of the improvement of taste, from the application of reason and good sense to such productions of genius. Spurious beauties, such as unnatural characters, forced sentiments, affected style, may please for a little; but they please only because their opposition to nature and to good sense has not been examined, or attended to. Once show how nature might have been more justly imitated or represented; how the writer might have managed his subject to greater advantage; the illusion will presently be dissipated, and these false beauties will please no more.

From these two sources then, first, the frequent exercise of taste, and next the application of good sense and reason to the objects of taste, taste as a power of the mind receives its improvement. In its perfect state, it is undoubtedly the result both of nature and of art. It supposes our natural sense of beauty to be refined by frequent attention to the most beautiful objects, and at the same time to be guided and improved by the light of the understanding.

I must be allowed to add, that as a sound head, so likewise a good heart, is a very material requisite to just taste. The moral beauties are not only themselves superior to all others, but they exert an influence, either more near, or more remote, on a great variety of other objects of taste. Wherever the affections, characters, or actions of men are concerned, (and these certainly afford the noblest subjects to genius,) there can be neither any just or affecting description of them, nor any thorough feeling of the beauty of that description, without our possessing the virtuous affections. He whose heart is indelicate or hard, he who has no admiration of what is truly noble or praise-worthy, nor the proper sympathetic sense of what is soft and tender, must have a very imperfect relish of the highest beauties of eloquence and poetry.

The characters of taste, when brought to its most improved state, are all reducible to two, Delicacy and Correctness.

Delicacy of taste respects principally the perfection of that natural sensibility on which taste is founded. It implies those finer organs or powers which enable us to discover beauties that lie hid from a vulgar eye. One may have strong sensibility, and yet be deficient in delicate taste. He may be deeply impressed by such beauties as he perceives; but he perceives only what is in some degree coarse, what is bold and palpable; while chaster and simpler ornaments escape his notice. In this state, taste generally exists among rude and unrefined nations. But a person of delicate taste both feels strongly, and feels accurately. He sees distinctions and differences where others see none; the most latent beauty does not escape him, and he is sensible of the smallest blemish. Delicacy of taste is judged of by the same marks that we use in judging of the delicacy of an external sense. As the goodness of the palate is not tried by strong flavours, but by a mixture of ingredients, where, notwithstanding the confusion, we remain sensible of each; in like manner delicacy of internal taste appears, by a quick and lively sensibility to its finest, most compounded, or most latent objects.

Correctness of taste respects chiefly the improvement which that faculty receives through its connexion with the understanding. A man of correct taste is one who is never imposed on by counterfeit beauties; who carries always in his mind that standard of good sense which he employs in judging of every thing. He estimates with propriety the comparative merit of the several beauties which he meets with in any work of genius; refers them to their proper classes; assigns the principles, as far as they can be traced, whence their power of pleasing flows, and is pleased himself precisely in that degree in which he ought, and no more.

It is true, that these two qualities of taste, delicacy and correctness, mutally imply each other. No taste can be exquisitely delicate without being correct; nor can be thoroughly correct without being delicate. But still a predominancy of one or other quality in the mixture is often visible. The power of delicacy is chiefly seen in discerning the true merit of a work; the power of correctness, in rejecting false pretensions to merit. Delicacy leans more to feeling; correctness, more to reason and judgment. The former is more the gift of nature; the latter, more the product of culture and art. Among the ancient critics, Longinus possessed most delicacy; Aristotle, most correctness. Among the moderns, Mr. Addison is a high example of delicate taste; Dean Swift, had he written on the subject of criticism, would perhaps have afforded the example of a correct one.

Having viewed taste in its most improved and perfect state, I come next to consider its deviations from that state, the fluctuations and changes to which it is liable; and to inquire whether, in the midst of these, there be any means of distinguishing a true from a corrupted taste. This brings us to the most difficult part of our task. For it must be acknowledged, that no principle of the human mind is, in its operations, more fluctuating and capricious than taste. Its variations have been so great and frequent, as to create a suspicion with some, of its being merely arbitrary; grounded on no foundation, ascertainable by no standard, but wholly dependent on changing fancy; the consequence of which would be, that all studies or regular inquiries concerning the objects of taste were vain. In architecture, the Grecian models were long esteemed the most perfect. In succeeding ages, the Gothic architecture alone prevailed, and afterwards the Grecian taste revived in all its vigour, and engrossed the public admiration. In eloquence and poetry, the Asiatics at no time relished any thing but what was full of ornament, and splendid in a degree that we should denominate gawdy; whilst the Greeks admired only chaste and simple beauties, and despised the Asiatic ostentation. In our own country, how many writings that were greatly extolled two or three centuries ago, are now fallen into entire disrepute and oblivion. Without going back to remote instances, how very different is the taste of poetry which prevails in Great Britain now, from what prevailed there no longer ago than the reign of king Charles II, which the authors too of that time deemed an Augustan age: when nothing was in vogue but an affected brilliancy of wit; when the simple majesty of Milton was overlooked, and *Paradise Lost* almost entirely unknown; when Cowley's laboured and unnatural conceits were admired as the very quintessence of genius; Waller's gay sprightliness was mistaken for the tender spirit of love poetry; and such writers as Suckling and Etheridge were held in esteem for dramatic composition?

The question is, what conclusion we are to form from such instances as these? Is there any thing that can be called a standard of taste, by appealing to which we may distinguish between a good and a bad taste? Or, is there in truth no such distinction? and are we to hold that, according to the proverb, there is no disputing of tastes; but that whatever pleases is right, for that reason that it does please? This is the question, and a very nice and subtle one it is, which we are now to discuss.

I begin by observing, that if there be no such thing as any standard of taste, this consequence must immediately follow, that all tastes are equally good; a position, which, though it may pass unnoticed in slight matters, and when we speak of the lesser differences among the tastes of men, yet when we apply it to the extremes, presently shows its absurdity. For is there any one who will seriously maintain that the taste of a Hottentot or a Laplander is as delicate and as correct as that of a Longinus or an Addison? or, that he can be charged with no defect or incapacity who thinks a common newswriter as excellent an historian as Tacitus? As it would be held downright extravagance to talk in this manner, we are led unavoidably to this conclusion, that there is some foundation for the preference of one man's taste to that of another; or, that there is a good and a bad, a right and a wrong in taste, as in other things.

But to prevent mistakes on this subject, it is necessary to observe next, that the diversity of tastes which prevails among mankind, does not in every case infer corruption of taste, or oblige us to seek for some standard in order to determine who are in the right. The tastes of men may differ very considerably as to their object, and yet none of them be wrong. One man relishes poetry most; another takes pleasure in nothing but history. One prefers comedy; another, tragedy. One admires the simple; another, the ornamented style. The young are amused with gay and sprightly compositions. The elderly are more entertained with those of a graver cast. Some nations delight in bold pictures of manners, and strong representations of passion. Others incline to more correct and regular elegance both in description and sentiment. Though all differ, yet all pitch upon some one beauty which peculiarly suits their turn of mind; and therefore no one has a title to condemn the rest. It is not in matters of taste, as in questions of mere reason, where there is but one conclusion that can be true, and all the rest are erroneous. Truth, which is the object of reason, is one; beauty, which is the object of taste, is manifold. Taste, therefore, admits of latitude and diversity of objects, in sufficient consistency with goodness or justness of taste.

But then, to explain this matter thoroughly, I must observe farther that this admissible diversity of tastes can only have place where the objects of taste are different. Where it is with respect to the same object that men disagree, when one condemns that as ugly, which another admires as highly beautiful; then it is no longer diversity, but direct opposition of taste that takes place; and therefore one must be in the right, and another in the wrong, unless that absurd paradox were allowed to hold, that all tastes are equally good and true. One man prefers Virgil to Homer. Suppose that I, on the other hand, admire Homer more than Virgil. I have as yet no reason to say that our tastes are contradictory. The other person is more struck with the elegance and tenderness which are the characteristics of Virgil; I, with the simplicity and fire of Homer. As long as neither of us deny that both Homer and Virgil have great beauties, our difference falls within the compass of that diversity of tastes, which I have showed to be natural and allowable. But if the other man shall assert that Homer has no beauties whatever; that he holds him to be a dull and spiritless writer, and that he would as soon peruse any old legend of knight-errantry as the

Iliad; then I exclaim, that my antagonist either is void of all taste, or that his taste is corrupted in a miserable degree; and I appeal to whatever I think the standard of taste, to show him that he is in the wrong.

What that standard is to which, in such opposition of tastes, we are obliged to have recourse, remains to be traced. A standard properly signifies, that which is of such undoubted authority as to be the test of other things of the same kind. Thus a standard weight or measure, is that which is appointed by law to regulate all other measures and weights. Thus the court is said to be the standard of good breeding; and the scripture of theological truth.

When we say that nature is the standard of taste, we lay down a principle very true and just, as far as it can be applied. There is no doubt, that in all cases where an imitation is intended of some object that exists in nature, as in representing human characters or actions, conformity to nature affords a full and distinct criterion of what is truly beautiful. Reason hath in such cases full scope for exerting its authority; for approving or condemning; by comparing the copy with the original. But there are innumerable cases in which this rule cannot be at all applied; and conformity to nature, is an expression frequently used, without any distinct or determinate meaning. We must therefore search for somewhat that can be rendered more clear and precise, to be the standard of taste.

Taste, as I before explained it, is ultimately founded on an internal sense of beauty, which is natural to men, and which, in its application to particular objects, is capable of being guided and enlightened by reason. Now were there any one person who possessed in full perfection all the powers of human nature, whose internal senses were in every instance exquisite and just, and whose reason was unerring and sure, the determinations of such a person concerning beauty, would, beyond doubt, be a perfect standard for the taste of all others. Wherever their taste differed from his, it could be imputed only to some imperfection in their natural powers. But as there is no such living standard, no one person to whom all mankind will allow such submission to be due, what is there of sufficient authority to be the standard of the various and opposite tastes of men? Most certainly there is nothing but the taste, as far as it can be gathered, of human nature. That which men concur the most in admiring, must be held to be beautiful. His taste must be esteemed just and true, which coincides with the general sentiments of men. In this standard we must rest. To the sense of mankind the ultimate appeal must ever lie, in all works of taste. If any one should maintain that sugar was bitter and tobacco was sweet, no reasonings could avail to prove it. The taste of such a person would infallibly be held to be diseased, merely because it differed so widely from the taste of the species to which he belongs. In like manner, with regard to the objects of sentiment or internal taste, the common feelings of men carry the same authority, and have a title to regulate the taste of every individual.

But have we then, it will be said, no other criterion of what is beautiful, than the approbation of the majority? Must we collect the voices of others, before we form any judgment for ourselves, of what deserves applause in eloquence or poetry? By no means; there are principles of reason and sound judgment which can be applied to matters of taste, as well as to the subjects of science and philosophy. He who admires or censures any work of genius, is always ready, if his taste be in any degree improved, to assign some reasons for his decision. He appeals to principles, and points out the grounds on which he proceeds. Taste is a sort of compound power, in which the light of the understanding always mingles, more or less, with the feelings of sentiment.

But though reason can carry us a certain length in judging concerning works of taste, it is not to be forgotten that the ultimate conclusions to which our reasonings lead, refer at last to sense and perception. We may speculate and argue concerning propriety of conduct in a tragedy, or an epic poem. Just reasonings on the subject will correct the caprice of unenlightened taste, and establish principles for judging of what deserves praise. But, at the same time, these reasonings appeal always in the last resort, to feeling. The foundation upon which they rest, is what has been found from experience to please mankind universally. Upon this ground we prefer a simple and natural, to an artificial and affected style; a regular and well-connected story, to loose and scattered narratives; a catastrophe which is tender and pathetic, to one which leaves us unmoved. It is from consulting our own imagination and heart, and from attending to the feelings of others, that any principles are formed which acquire authority in matters of taste.

When we refer to the concurring sentiments of men as the ultimate taste of what is to be accounted beautiful in the arts, this is to be always understood of men placed in such situations as are favourable to the proper exertions of taste. Every one must perceive, that among rude and uncivilized nations, and during the ages of ignorance and darkness, any loose notions that are entertained concerning such subjects, carry no authority. In those states of society, taste has no materials on which to operate. It is either totally suppressed, or appears in its lower and most imperfect form. We refer to the sentiments of mankind in polished and flourishing nations; when arts are cultivated and manners refined; when works of genius are subjected to free discussion, and taste is improved by science and philosophy.

Even among nations, at such a period of society, I admit that accidental causes may occasionally warp the proper operations of taste; sometimes the taste of religion, sometimes the form of government, may for a while pervert; a licentious court may introduce a taste for false ornaments, and dissolute writings. The usage of one admired genius may procure approbation for his faults, and even render them fashionable. Sometimes envy may have power to bear down, for a little, productions of great merit; while popular humour, or party spirit, may, at other times, exalt to a high, though short-lived reputation, what little deserved it. But though such casual circumstances give the appearance of caprice to the judgments of taste, that appearance is easily corrected. In the course of time, the genuine taste of human nature never fails to disclose itself and to gain the ascendant over any fantastic and corrupted modes of taste which may chance to have been introduced. These may have currency for a while, and mislead superficial judges; but being subjected to examination, by degrees they pass away; while that alone remains which is founded on sound reason, and the native feelings of men.

I by no means pretend, that there is any standard of taste, to which, in every particular instance, we can resort for clear and immediate determination. Where, indeed, is such a standard to be found for deciding any of those great controversies in reason and philosophy, which perpetually divide mankind? In the present case, there was plainly no occasion for any such strict and absolute provision to be made. In order to judge of what is morally good or evil, of what man ought, or ought not in duty to do, it was fit that the means of clear and precise determination should be afforded us. But to ascertain in every case with the utmost exactness what is beautiful or elegant, was not at all necessary to the happiness of man. And therefore some diversity in feeling was here allowed to take place; and room was left for discussion and debate, concerning the degree of approbation to which any work of genius is entitled.

The conclusion, which it is sufficient for us to rest upon, is, that taste is far from being an arbitrary principle, which is subject to the fancy of every individual, and which admits of no criterion for determining whether it be false or true. Its foundation is the same in all human minds. It is built upon sentiments and perceptions which belong to our nature; and which, in general, operate with the same uniformity as our other intellectual principles. When these sentiments are perverted by ignorance and prejudice, they are capable of being rectified by reason. Their sound and natural state is ultimately determined, by comparing them with the general taste of mankind. Let men declaim as much as they please concerning the caprice and the uncertainty of taste, it is found, by experience, that there are beauties, which, if they be displayed in a proper light, have power to command lasting and general admiration. In every composition, what interests the imagination, and touches the heart, pleases all ages and all nations. There is a certain string to which, when properly struck, the human heart is so made as to answer.

Hence the universal testimony which the most improved nations of the earth have conspired, throughout a long tract of ages, to give to some few works of genius; such as the Iliad of Homer, and the Aeneid of Virgil. Hence the authority which such works have acquired, as standards in some degree of poetical composition; since from them we are enabled to collect what the sense of mankind is, concerning those beauties which give them the highest pleasure, and which therefore poetry ought to exhibit. Authority or prejudice may, in one age or country, give a temporary reputation to an indifferent poet or a bad artist; but when foreigners, or when posterity examine his works, his faults are discerned, and the genuine taste of human nature appears. *Opinionum commenta delet dies; naturæ judicia confirmat.* (Time overthrows the illusions of opinion, but establishes the decisions of nature.)

~.~.~.~.~.~.~

Lecture III

CRITICISM—GENIUS—PLEASURES OF TASTE—SUBLIMITY IN OBJECTS

Taste, criticism, and genius, are words currently employed, without distinct ideas annexed to them. In beginning a course of lectures where such words must often occur, it is necessary to ascertain their meaning with some precision. Having in the last lecture treated of taste, I proceed to explain the nature and foundation of criticism. True criticism is the application of taste and of good sense to the several fine arts. The object which it proposes is, to distinguish what is beautiful and what is faulty in every performance; from particular instances to ascend to general principles; and so to form rules or conclusions concerning the several kinds of beauty in works of genius.

The rules of criticism are not formed by any induction a priori, as it is called; that is, they are not formed by a train of abstract reasoning, independent of facts and observations. Criticism is an art founded wholly on experience; on the observations of such beauties as have come nearest to the standard which I before established; that is, of such beauties as have been found to please mankind most generally. For example: Aristotle's rules concerning the unity of action in dramatic and epic composition, were not rules first discovered by logical reasoning, and then applied to poetry; but they were drawn from the practice of Homer and Sophocles: they were founded upon observing the superior pleasure which we receive from the relation of an action which is one and entire, beyond what we receive from the relation of scattered and unconnected facts. Such observations taking their rise at first from feeling and experience, were found on examination to be so consonant to reason and to the principles of human nature, as to pass into established rules, and to be conveniently applied for judging of the excellency of any performance. This is the most natural account of the origin of criticism.

A masterly genius, it is true, will of himself, untaught, compose in such a manner as shall be agreeable to the most material rules of criticism, for as these rules are founded in nature, nature will often suggest them in practice. Homer, it is more than probable, was acquainted with no systems of the art of poetry. Guided by genius alone, he composed in verse a regular story, which all posterity has admired. But this is no argument against the usefulness of criticism as an art. For as no human genius is perfect, there is no writer but may receive assistance from critical observations upon the beauties and faults of those who have gone before him. No observations or rules can indeed supply the defect of genius, or inspire it where it is wanting. But they may often direct it into its proper channel; they may correct its extravagances, and point out to it the most just and proper imitation of nature. Critical rules are designed chiefly to show the faults that ought to be avoided. To nature we must be indebted for the production of eminent beauties.

From what has been said, we are enabled to form a judgment concerning those complaints which it has long been fashionable for petty authors to make against critics and criticism. Critics have been represented as the great abridgers of the native liberty of genius; as the imposers of unnatural shackles and bonds upon writers, from whose cruel persecution they must fly to the public, and implore its protection. Such supplicatory prefaces are not calculated to give very favourable ideas of the genius of the author. For every good writer will be pleased to have his work examined by the principles of sound understanding and true taste. The declamations against criticism commonly proceed upon this supposition, that critics are such as judge by rule, not by feeling; which is so far from being true, that they who judge after this manner are pedants, not critics. For all the rules of genuine criticism I have shown to be ultimately founded on feeling; and taste and feeling are necessary to guide us in the application of these rules to every particular instance. As there is nothing in which all sorts of persons more readily affect to be judges than in works of taste, there is no doubt that the number of incompetent critics will always be great. But this affords no more foundation for a general invective against criticism, than the number of bad philosophers or reasoners affords against reason and philosophy.

An objection more plausible may be formed against criticism, from the applause that some performances have received from the public, which, when accurately considered, are found to contradict the rules established by criticism. Now, according to the principles laid down in the last lecture, the public is the supreme judge to whom the last appeal must be made in every work of taste; as the standard of taste is founded on the sentiments that are natural and common to all men. But with respect to this, we are to observe, that the sense of the public is often too hastily judged of. The genuine public taste does not always appear in the first applause given upon the publication of any new work. There are both a great vulgar and a small, apt to be catched and dazzled by very superficial beauties, the admiration of which in a little time passes away; and sometimes a writer may acquire great temporary reputation merely by his compliance with the passions or prejudices, with the party-spirit or superstitious notions that may chance to rule for a time almost a whole nation. In such cases, though the public may seem to praise, true criticism may with reason condemn; and it will in progress of time gain the ascendant: for the judgment of true criticism, and the voice of the public, when once become unprejudiced and dispassionate, will ever coincide at last.

Instances, I admit, there are of some works that contain gross transgressions of the laws of criticism, acquiring, nevertheless, a general, and even a lasting admiration. Such are the plays of Shakspeare, which, considered as dramatic poems, are irregular in the highest degree. But then we are to remark, that they have gained the public admiration, not by their being irregular, not by their transgressions of the rules of art, but in spite of such transgressions. They possess other beauties which are conformable to just rules; and the force of these beauties has been so great as to overpower all censure, and to give the public a degree of satisfaction superior to the disgust arising from their blemishes. Shakspeare pleases, not by his bringing the transactions of many years into one play; not by his grotesque mixtures of tragedy and comedy in one piece, nor by the strained thoughts and affected witticisms, which he sometimes employs. These we consider as blemishes, and impute them to the grossness of the age in which he lived. But he pleases by his animated and masterly representations of characters, by the liveliness of his descriptions, the force of his sentiments, and his possessing, beyond all writers, the natural language of passion: Beauties which true criticism no less teaches us to place in the highest rank, than nature teaches us to feel.

I proceed next to explain the meaning of another term, which there will be frequent occasion to employ in these lectures; that is, *genius*.

Taste and *genius* are two words frequently joined together; and therefore by inaccurate thinkers, confounded. They signify, however, two quite different things. The difference between them can be clearly pointed out; and it is of importance to remember it. Taste consists in the power of judging; genius, in the power of executing. One may have a considerable degree of taste in poetry, eloquence, or any of the fine arts, who has little or hardly any genius for composition or execution in any of these arts: but genius cannot be found without including taste also. Genius, therefore, deserves to be considered as a higher power of the mind than taste. Genius always imports something inventive or creative; which does not rest in mere sensibility to beauty where it is perceived, but which can, moreover, produce new beauties, and exhibit them in such a manner as strongly to impress the minds of others. Refined taste forms a good critic; but genius is farther necessary to form the poet, or the orator.

It is proper also to observe, that *genius* is a word, which, in common acceptation, extends much farther than to the objects of taste. It is used to signify that talent or aptitude which we receive from nature, for excelling in any one thing whatever. Thus we speak of a genius for mathematics, as well as a genius for poetry; of a genius for war, for politics, or for any mechanical employment.

This talent or aptitude for excelling in some one particular, is, I have said, what we receive from nature. By art and study, no doubt, it may be greatly improved; but by them alone it cannot be acquired. As genius is a higher faculty than taste, it is ever, according to the usual frugality of nature, more limited in the sphere of its operations. It is not uncommon to meet with persons who have an excellent taste in several of the polite arts, such as music, poetry, painting, and eloquence, altogether; but, to find one who is an excellent performer in all these arts, is much more rare; or rather, indeed, such an one is not to be looked for. A sort of universal genius, or one who is equally and indifferently turned towards several different professions and arts, is not likely to excel in any. Although there may be some few exceptions, yet in general it holds, that when the bent of the mind is wholly directed towards some one object, exclusive in a manner of others, there is the fairest prospect of eminence in that, whatever it be. The rays must converge to a point, in order to glow intensely. This remark I here choose to make, on account of its great importance to young people; in leading them to examine with care, and to pursue with ardour, the current and pointing of nature towards those exertions of genius in which they are most likely to excel.

A genius for any of the fine arts, as I before observed, always supposes taste; and it is clear, that the improvement of taste will serve both to forward and to correct the operations of genius. In proportion as the taste of a poet, or orator, becomes more refined with respect to the beauties of composition, it will certainly assist him to produce the more finished beauties in his work. Genius, however, in a poet or orator, may sometimes exist in a higher degree than taste; that is, genius may be bold and strong, when taste is neither very delicate, nor very correct. This is often the case in the infancy of arts; a period, when genius frequently exerts itself with great vigour, and executes with much warmth; while taste, which requires experience, and improves by slower degrees, hath not yet attained to its full growth. Homer and Shakspeare are proofs of what I now assert; in whose admirable writings are found instances of rudeness and indelicacy, which the more refined taste of later writers, who had far inferior genius to them, would have taught them to avoid. As all human perfection is limited, this may very probably be the law of our nature, that it is not given to one man to execute with vigour and fire, and, at the same time, to attend to all the lesser and more refined graces that belong to the exact perfection of his work; while, on the other hand, a thorough taste for those inferior graces is for the most part, accompanied with a diminution of sublimity and force.

Having thus explained the nature of taste, the nature and importance of criticism, and the distinction between taste and genius; I am now to consider the sources of the pleasures of taste. Here opens a very extensive field; no less than all the pleasures of the imagination, as they are commonly called, whether afforded us by natural objects, or by the imitations and descriptions of them. But it is not necessary to the purpose of my lectures, that all these should be examined fully; the pleasure which we receive from discourse, or writing, being the main object of them. All that I propose is to give some openings into the pleasures of taste in general; and to insist more particularly upon sublimity and beauty.

We are far from having yet attained to any system concerning this subject. Mr. Addison was the first who attempted a regular inquiry, in his Essay on the Pleasures of the Imagination, published in the sixth volume of the Spectator. He has reduced these pleasures under three heads—beauty, grandeur, and novelty. His speculations on this subject, if not exceedingly profound, are, however, very beautiful and entertaining; and he has the merit of having opened a track, which was before unbeaten. The advances made since his time in this curious part of philosophical criticism, are not very considerable; though some ingenious writers have pursued the subject. This is owing, doubtless, to that thinness and subtilty which are found to be properties of all the feelings of taste. They are engaging objects; but when we would lay firm hold of them, and subject them to a regular discussion, they are always ready to elude our grasp. It is difficult to make a full enumeration of the several objects that give pleasure to taste: it is more difficult to define all those which have been discovered, and to reduce them under proper classes; and, when we would go farther, and investigate the efficient causes of the pleasure which we receive from such objects, here, above all, we find ourselves at a loss. For instance, we all learn by experience, that certain figures of bodies appear to us more beautiful than others. On inquiring farther, we find that the regularity of some figures, and the graceful variety of others, are the foundation of the beauty which we discern in them; but when we attempt to go a step beyond this, and inquire what is the cause of regularity and variety producing in our minds the sensation of beauty, any reason we can assign is extremely imperfect. These first principles of internal sensation, nature seems to have covered with an inpenetrable veil.

It is some comfort, however, that although the efficient cause be obscure, the final cause of those sensations lies in many cases more open: and, in entering on this subject, we cannot avoid taking notice of the strong impression which the powers of taste and imagination are calculated to give us of the benignity of our Creator. By endowing us with such powers, he hath widely enlarged the sphere of the pleasure of human life; and those, too, of a kind the most pure and innocent. The necessary purposes of life might have been abundantly answered, though our senses of seeing and hearing had only served to distinguish external objects, without conveying to us any of those refined and delicate sensations of beauty and grandeur, with which we are now so much delighted. This additional embellishment and glory, which for promoting our entertainment, the Author of nature hath poured forth upon his works, is one striking testimony, among many others, of benevolence and goodness. This thought, which Mr. Addison first started, Dr. Akenside, in his poem on the Pleasures of the Imagination, has happily pursued.

> Not content
> With every food of life to nourish man,

> By kind illusions of the wondering sense,
> Thou mak'st all nature beauty to his eye,
> Or music to his ear.

I shall begin with considering the pleasure which arises from sublimity, or grandeur, which I propose to treat at some length; both, as this has a character more precise and distinctly marked than any other of the pleasures of the imagination, and as it coincides more directly with our main subject. For the greater distinctness I shall, first, treat of the grandeur or sublimity of external objects themselves, which will employ the rest of this lecture; and, afterwards, of the description of such objects, or, of what is called the sublime in writing, which shall be the subject of a following lecture. I distinguish these two things from one another, the grandeur of the objects themselves when they are presented to the eye, and the description of that grandeur in discourse or writing; though most critics, inaccurately I think, blend them together; and I consider *grandeur* and *sublimity* as .erms synonymous, or nearly so. If there be any distinction between them, it arises from sublimity's expressing grandeur in its highest degree.[1]

It is not easy to describe, in words, the precise impression which great and sublime objects make upon us, when we behold them; but everyone has a conception of it. It produces a sort of internal elevation and expansion; it raises the mind much above its ordinary state, and fills it with a degree of wonder and astonishment, which it cannot well express. The emotion is certainly delightful; but it is altogether of the serious kind; a degree of awfulness and solemnity, even approaching to severity, commonly attends it when at its height; very distinguishable from the more gay and brisk emotion raised by beautiful objects.

The simplest form of external grandeur appears in the vast and boundless prospects presented to us by nature; such as wide extended plains, to which the eye can see no limits; the firmament of heaven; or the boundless expanse of the ocean. All vastness produces the impression of sublimity. It is to be remarked, however, that space extended in length, makes not so strong an impression as height or depth. Though a boundless plain be a grand object, yet a high mountain, to which we look up, or an awful precipice or tower whence we look down on the objects which lie below, is still more so. The excessive grandeur of the firmament arises from its height joined to its boundless extent; and that of the ocean, not from its extent alone, but from the perpetual motion and irresistible force of that mass of waters. Wherever space is concerned, it is clear that amplitude or greatness of extent, in one dimension or other, is necessary to grandeur. Remove all bounds from any object, and you presently render it sublime. Hence infinite space, endless numbers, and eternal duration, fill the mind with great ideas.

From this some have imagined, that vastness, or amplitude of extent, is the foundation of all sublimity. But I cannot be of this opinion, because

---

1 See a Philosophical Inquiry into the Origin of Our Ideas of the Sublime and Beautiful:—Dr. Gerard on Taste, section ii:—*Elements of Criticism, chap. iv.*

many objects appear sublime which have no relation to space at all. Such, for instance, is great loudness of sound. The burst of thunder or of cannon, the roaring of winds, the shouting of multitudes, the sound of vast cataracts of water, are all incontestably grand objects. "I heard the voice of a great multitude, as the sound of many waters, and of mighty thunderings, saying, Allelujah." In general we may observe, that great power and strength exerted, always raise sublime ideas; and perhaps the most copious source of these is derived from this quarter. Hence the grandeur of earthquakes and burning mountains; of great conflagrations; of the stormy ocean, and overflowing waters; of tempests of wind; of thunder and lightning; and of all the uncommon violence of the elements. Nothing is more sublime than mighty power and strength. A stream that runs within its banks, is a beautiful object, but when it rushes down with the impetuosity and noise of a torrent, it presently becomes a sublime one. From lions and other animals of strength, are drawn sublime comparisons in poets. A race-horse is looked upon with pleasure; but it is the war-horse, "whose neck is clothed with thunder," that carries grandeur in its idea. The engagement of two great armies, as it is the highest exertion of human might, combines a variety of sources of the sublime; and has accordingly been always considered as one of the most striking and magnificent spectacles that can be either presented to the eye, or exhibited to the imagination in description.

For the farther illustration of this subject, it is proper to remark, that all ideas of the solemn and awful kind, and even bordering on the terrible, tend greatly to assist the sublime; such as darkness, solitude, and silence. What are the scenes of nature that elevate the mind in the highest degree, and produce the sublime sensation? Not the gay landscape, the flowery field, or the flourishing city; but the hoary mountain, and the solitary lake; the aged forest, and the torrent falling over the rock. Hence, too, night-scenes are commonly the most sublime. The firmament when filled with stars, scattered in such vast numbers, and with such magnificent profusion, strikes the imagination with a more awful grandeur, than when we view it enlightened by all the splendour of the sun. The deep sound of a great bell, or the striking of a great clock, are at any time grand; but when heard amid the silence and stillness of the night, they become doubly so. Darkness is very commonly applied for adding sublimity to all our ideas of the Deity. "He maketh darkness his pavilion; he dwelleth in the thick cloud." So Milton:

> How oft, amidst
> Thick clouds and dark, does heaven's all-ruling Sire
> Choose to reside, his glory unobscur'd,
> And with the majesty of darkness round
> Circles his throne.   *PL,* Book II. 263.

Observe, with how much art Virgil has introduced all those ideas of silence, vacuity, and darkness, when he is going to introduce his hero to the infernal regions, and to disclose the secrets of the great deep.

Dii, quibus imperium est animarum, umbræque silentes,
Et Chaos, et Phlegethon, loca nocte silentia late,
Sit mihi fas audita loqui; sit numine vestro
Pandere res altâ terrâ et caligine mersas.[2]

Ibant obscuri, sola sub nocte, per umbram,
Perque domos Ditis vacuos, et inania regna;
Quale per incertam lunam, sub luce malignâ
Est iter in Sylvis.[3]

These passages I quote at present, not so much as instances of sublime writing, though in themselves they truly are so, as to show, by the effect of them, that the objects which they present to us, belong to the class of sublime ones.

Obscurity, we are farther to remark, is not unfavourable to the sublime. Though it render the object indistinct, the impression, however, may be great; for as an ingenious author has well observed, it is one thing to make an idea clear, and another to make it affecting to the imagination; and the imagination may be strongly affected, and, in fact, often is so, by objects of which we have no clear conception. Thus we see, that almost all the descriptions given us of the appearances of supernatural beings, carry some sublimity, though the conceptions which they afford us be confused and indistinct. Their sublimity arises from the ideas, which they always convey, of superior power and might, joined with an awful obscurity. We may see this fully exemplified in the following noble passage of the book of Job. "In thoughts from the visions of the night, when deep sleep falleth upon men, fear came upon me, and trembling, which made all my bones to shake. Then a spirit passed before my face; the hair of my flesh stood up: it stood still; but I could not discern the form thereof; an image was before mine eyes; there was silence; and I heard a voice—Shall mortal man be more just than God?" (Job iv. 15.) No ideas, it is plain, are so sublime as those taken from the Supreme Being; the most unknown, but the greatest of all objects; the infinity of whose nature, and the eternity of whose duration, joined with the omnipotence of his power, though they surpass our concep-

[2]   Ye subterranean gods, whose awful sway
      The gliding ghosts and silent shades obey:
      O Chaos, hear! and Phlegethon profound!
      Whose solemn empire stretches wide around;
      Give me, ye great tremendous powers! to tell
      Of scenes and wonders in the depths of hell;
      Give me your mighty secrets to display,
      From those black realms of darkness to the day.   (trans., Pitt)

[3]   Obscure they went; through dreary shades that led
      Along the waste dominions of the dead;
      As wander travellers in woods by night,
      By the moon's doubtful and malignant light.   (trans., Dryden)

tions, yet exalt them to the highest. In general, all objects that are greatly
raised above us, or far removed from us, either in space or in time, are apt
to strike us as great. Our viewing them, as through the mist of distance or
antiquity, is favourable to the impressions of their sublimity.

As obscurity, so disorder too, is very compatible with grandeur; nay, frequently heightens it. Few things that are strictly regular and methodical,
appear sublime. We see the limits on every side; we feel ourselves confined;
there is no room for the mind's exerting any great effort. Exact proportion
of parts, though it enters often into the beautiful, is much disregarded in
the sublime. A great mass of rocks, thrown together by the hand of nature
with wildness and confusion, strike the mind with more grandeur, than if
they had been adjusted to one another with the most accurate symmetry.

In the feeble attempts, which human art can make towards producing
grand objects, (feeble, I mean, in comparison with the powers of nature,)
greatness of dimensions always constitutes a principal part. No pile of
building can convey any idea of sublimity, unless it be ample and lofty.
There is too, in architecture, what is called greatness of manner; which
seems chiefly to arise, from presenting the object to us in one full point of
view; so that it shall make its impression whole, entire, and undivided
upon the mind. A Gothic cathedral raises ideas of grandeur in our minds,
by its size, its height, its awful obscurity, its strength, its antiquity, and its
durability.

There still remains to be mentioned one class of sublime objects, which
may be called the moral, or sentimental sublime; arising from certain exertions of the human mind; from certain affections, and actions, of our
fellow-creatures. These will be found to be all, or chiefly, of that class,
which comes under the name of magnanimity or heroism: and they produce an effect extremely similar to what is produced by the view of grand
objects in nature; filling the mind with admiration, and elevating it above
itself. A noted instance of this, quoted by all the French critics, is the celebrated *Qu'il Mourut* of Corneille, in the tragedy of Horace. In the famous
combat between the Horatii and the Curiatii, the old Horatius being informed that two of his sons are slain, and that the third had betaken himself to flight, at first will not believe the report; but being thoroughly assured of the fact, is fired with all the sentiments of high honour and indignation at this supposed unworthy behaviour of his surviving son. He is re-
minded, that his son stood alone against three, and asked what he wished
him to have done? "To have died," he answers. In the same manner Porus,
taken prisoner by Alexander, after a gallant defence, and asked how he
wished to be treated? answering, "Like a king;" and Cæsar chiding the
pilot who was afraid to set out with him in the storm, *"Quid times? Cæsarem vehis"* [What are you afraid of? You carry Cæsar], are good instances of this sentimental sublime. Wherever, in some critical and high
situation, we behold a man uncommonly intrepid, and resting upon himself; superior to passion and to fear; animated by some great principle to the

contempt of popular opinion, of selfish interest, of dangers, or of death; there we are struck with a sense of the sublime.[4]

High virtue is the most natural and fertile source of this moral sublimity. However, on some occasions, where virtue either has no place, or is but imperfectly displayed, yet if extraordinary vigour and force of mind be discovered, we are not insensible to a degree of grandeur in the character; and from the splendid conqueror or the daring conspirator, whom we are far from approving, we cannot withhold our admiration.

I have now enumerated a variety of instances, both in inanimate objects and in human life, wherein the sublime appears. In all these instances, the emotion raised in us is of the same kind, although the objects that produce the emotion be of widely different kinds. A question next arises, whether we are able to discover some one fundamental quality in which all these different objects agree, and which is the cause of their producing an emotion of the same nature in our minds? Various hypotheses have been formed concerning this; but, as far as appears to me, hitherto unsatisfactory. Some have imagined that amplitude, or great extent, joined with simplicity, is either immediately, or remotely, the fundamental quality of whatever is sublime; but we have seen that amplitude is confined to one species of sublime objects, and cannot, without violent straining be applied to them all. The Author of "A Philosophical Inquiry into the Origin of Our Ideas of the Sublime and Beautiful" [Edmund Burke], to whom we are indebted for several ingenious and original thoughts upon this subject, proposes a formal theory upon this foundation, that terror is the source of the sublime, and that no objects have this character, but such as produce impressions of pain and danger. It is indeed true, that many terrible objects are highly sublime; and that grandeur does not refuse an alliance with the idea of danger. But though this is very properly illustrated by the author, (many of whose sentiments on that head I have adopted,) yet he seems to stretch his theory too far, when he represents the sublime as consisting wholly in modes of danger, or of pain. For the proper sensation of

---

[4] The sublime, in natural and in moral objects, is brought before us in one view, and compared together, in the following beautiful passage of Akenside's Pleasures of the Imagination:

> Look then abroad through nature to the range
> Of planets, suns, and adamantine spheres,
> Wheeling, unshaken, thro' the void immense;
> And speak, O man! does this capacious scene,
> With half that kindling majesty dilate
> Thy strong conception, as when Brutus rose,
> Refulgent, from the stroke of Cæsar's fate,
> Amid the crowd of patriots; and his arm
> Aloft extending, like eternal Jove,
> When guilt brings down the thunder, call'd aloud
> On Tully's name, and shook his crimson steel,
> And bade the father of his country hail?
> For, lo! the tyrant prostrate on the dust,
> And Rome again is free.   Book I.

sublimity appears to be distinguishable from the sensation of either of these; and on several occasions, to be entirely separated from them. In many grand objects, there is no coincidence with terror at all; as in the magnificent prospect of wide extended plains, and of the starry firmament; or in the moral dispositions and sentiments, which we view with high admiration; and in many painful and terrible objects also, it is clear there is no sort of grandeur. The amputation of a limb, or the bite of a snake, are exceedingly terrible; but are destitute of all claim whatever to sublimity. I am inclined to think, that mighty force or power, whether accompanied with terror or not, whether employed in protecting, or in alarming us, has a better title, than any thing that has yet been mentioned, to be the fundamental quality of the sublime; as, after the review which we have taken, there does not occur to me any sublime object, into the idea of which, power, strength, and force, either enter not directly, or are not at least intimately associated with the idea, by leading our thoughts to some astonishing power as concerned in the production of the object. However, I do not insist upon this as sufficient to found a general theory; it is enough, to have given this view of the nature and different kinds of sublime objects; by which I hope to have laid a proper foundation for discussing, with greater accuracy, the sublime in writing and composition.

Lecture IV

THE SUBLIME IN WRITING

Having treated of grandeur or sublimity in external objects, the way seems now to be cleared, for treating, with more advantage, of the descriptions of such objects; or, of what is called the sublime in writing. Though I may appear early to enter on the consideration of this subject, yet, as the sublime is a species of writing which depends less than any other on the artificial embellishments of rhetoric, it may be examined with as much propriety here, as in any subsquent part of the lectures.

Many critical terms have unfortunately been employed in a sense too loose and vague; none more so, than that of the *sublime*. Every one is acquainted with the character of Cæsar's Commentaries, and of the style in which they are written: a style remarkably pure, simple, and elegant; but the most remote from the sublime of any of the classical authors. Yet this author has a German critic, Johannes Gulielmus Bergerus, who wrote no longer ago than the year 1720, pitched upon as the perfect model of the sublime, and has composed a quarto volume, entitled *De naturali pulchri-*

tudine Orationis; the express intention of which is to show, that Cæsar's Commentaries contain the most complete exemplification of all Longinus' rules relating to sublime writing. This I mention as a strong proof of the confused ideas which have prevailed, concerning this subject. The true sense of sublime writing, undoubtedly, is such a description of objects, or exhibition of sentiments, which are in themselves of a sublime nature, as shall give us strong impressions of them. But there is another very indefinite, and therefore very improper, sense, which has been too often put upon it; when it is applied to signify any remarkable and distinguishing excellency of composition; whether it raise in us the ideas of grandeur, or those of gentleness, elegance, or any other sort of beauty. In this sense, Cæsar's Commentaries may, indeed, be termed sublime, and so may many sonnets, pastorals, and love elegies, as well as Homer's Iliad. But this evidently confounds the use of words, and marks no one species, or character, of composition whatever.

I am sorry to be obliged to observe, that the sublime is too often used in this last and improper sense, by the celebrated critic Longinus, in his treatise on this subject. He sets out, indeed, with describing it in its just and proper meaning; as something that elevates the mind above itself, and fills it with high conceptions, and a noble pride. But from this view of it he frequently departs; and substitutes in the place of it, whatever, in any strain of composition, pleases highly. Thus, many of the passages which he produces as instances of the sublime, are merely elegant, without having the most distant relation to proper sublimity; witness Sappho's famous ode, on which he descants at considerable length. He points out five sources of the sublime. The first is boldness or grandeur in the thoughts; the second is, the pathetic; the third, the proper application of figures; the fourth, the use of tropes and beautiful expressions; the fifth, musical structure and arrangement of words. This is the plan of one who was writing a treatise of rhetoric, or of the beauties of writing in general; not of the sublime in particular. For of these five heads, only the two first have any peculiar relation to the sublime; boldness and grandeur in the thoughts, and in some instances the pathetic, or strong exertions of passion; the other three, tropes, figures, and musical arrangement, have no more relation to the sublime, than to other kinds of good writing; perhaps less to the sublime, than to any other species whatever; because it requires less the assistance of ornament. From this it appears, that clear and precise ideas on this head are not to be expected from that writer. I would not, however, be understood, as if I meant, by this censure, to represent his treatise as of small value. I know no critic, ancient or modern, that discovers a more lively relish of the beauties of fine writing, than Longinus; and he has also the merit of being himself an excellent, and in several passages, a truly sublime, writer. But as his work has been generally considered as a standard on this subject, it was incumbent on me to give my opinion concerning the benefit to be derived from it. It deserves to be consulted, not so much for distinct instruction concerning the sublime, as for excellent general ideas concerning beauty in writing.

I return now to the proper and natural idea of the sublime in composition. The foundation of it must always be laid in the nature of the object described. Unless it be such an object as, if presented to our eyes, if exhibited to us in reality, would raise ideas of that elevating, that awful and magnificent kind, which we call sublime; the description, however finely drawn, is not entitled to come under this class. This excludes all objects that are merely beautiful, gay, or elegant. In the next place, the object must not only, in itself, be sublime, but it must be set before us in such a light as is most proper to give us a clear and full impression of it; it must be described with strength, with conciseness, and simplicity. This depends, principally, upon the lively impression which the poet, or orator, has of the object which he exhibits; and upon his being deeply affected, and warmed, by the sublime idea which he would convey. If his own feeling be languid, he can never inspire us with any strong emotion. Instances, which are extremely necessary on this subject, will clearly show the importance of all the requisites which I have just now mentioned.

It is, generally speaking, among the most ancient authors, that we are to look for the most striking instances of the sublime. I am inclined to think that the early ages of the world, and the rude unimproved state of society, are peculiarly favourable to the strong emotions of sublimity. The genius of men is then much turned to admiration and astonishment. Meeting with many objects, to them new and strange, their imagination is kept glowing, and their passions are often raised to the utmost. They think, and express themselves boldly, and without restraint. In the progress of society, the genius and manners of men undergo a change more favourable to accuracy, than to strength or sublimity. . . .

I have produced these instances, in order to demonstrate that conciseness and simplicity are essential to sublime writing. Simplicity I place in opposition to studied and profuse ornament: and conciseness, to superfluous expression. The reason why a defect, either in conciseness or simplicity, is hurtful in a peculiar manner to the sublime, I shall endeavour to explain. The emotion occasioned in the mind by some great or noble object, raises it considerably above its ordinary pitch. A sort of enthusiasm is produced, extremely agreeable while it lasts; but from which the mind is tending every moment to fall down into its ordinary situation. Now, when an author has brought us, or is attempting to bring us, into this state; if he multiplies words unnecessarily; if he decks the sublime object which he presents to us, round and round, with glittering ornaments; nay, if he throws in any one decoration that sinks in the least below the capital image, that moment he alters the key; he relaxes the tension of the mind; the strength of the feeling is emasculated, the beautiful may remain, but the sublime is gone. When Julius Cæsar said to the pilot who was afraid to put to sea with him in a storm, *"Quid times? Cæsarem vehis;"* we are struck with the daring magnanimity of one relying with such confidence on his cause and his fortune. These few words convey every thing necessary to give us the impression full. . . .

On account of the great importance of simplicity and conciseness, I conceive rhyme, in English verse, to be, if not inconsistent with the sublime, at least very unfavourable to it. The constrained elegance of this kind of verse, and studied smoothness of the sounds, answering regularly to each other at the end of the line, though they be quite consistent with gentle emotions, yet weaken the native force of sublimity; besides, that the superfluous words which the poet is often obliged to introduce in order to fill up the rhyme, tend farther to enfeeble it. Homer's description of the nod of Jupiter, as shaking the heavens, has been admired, in all ages, as highly sublime. Literally translated, it runs thus: "He spoke, and bending his sable brows, gave the awful nod; while he shook the celestial locks of his immortal head, all Olympus was shaken." Mr. Pope translates it thus:

> He spoke: and awful bends his sable brows,
> Shakes his ambrosial curls, and gives the nod,
> The stamp of fate, and sanction of a God.
> High heaven with trembling the dread signal took,
> And all Olympus to its centre shook.

The image is spread out, and attempted to be beautified; but it is, in truth, weakened. The third line—"The stamp of fate, and sanction of a God," is merely expletive, and introduced for no other reason but to fill up the rhyme; for it interrupts the description, and clogs the image. For the same reason, out of mere compliance with the rhyme, Jupiter is represented as shaking his locks before he gives the nod;—"Shakes his ambrosial curls, and gives the nod," which is trifling, and without meaning: whereas, in the original, the hair of his head shaken, is the effect of his nod, and makes a happy picturesque circumstance in the description.

The boldness, freedom, and variety of our blank verse, is infinitely more favourable than rhyme, to all kinds of sublime poetry. The fullest proof of this is afforded by Milton; an author whose genius led him eminently to the sublime. The whole first and second books of Paradise Lost, are continued instances of it. Take, for an example, the following noted description of Satan, after his fall, appearing at the head of the infernal hosts:

> He, above the rest,
> In shape and gesture proudly eminent,
> Stood like a tower; his form had not yet lost
> All her original brightness, nor appear'd
> Less than archangel ruin'd; and the excess
> Of glory obscur'd: as when the sun new risen,
> Looks through the horizontal misty air,
> Shorn of his beams; or, from behind the moon,
> In dim eclipse, disastrous twilight sheds
> On half the nations, and with fear of change
> Perplexes monarchs. Darken'd so, yet shone
> Above them all th' archangel.

Here concur a variety of sources of the sublime: the principal object eminently great; a high superior nature, fallen indeed, but erecting itself against distress; the grandeur of the principal object heightened, by associating it with so noble an idea as that of the sun suffering an eclipse; this picture shaded with all those images of change and trouble, of darkness and terror, which coincide so finely with the sublime emotion; and the whole expressed in a style and versification, easy, natural, and simple, but magnificent.

I have spoken of simplicity and conciseness, as essential to sublime writing. In my general description of it, I mentioned strength, as another necessary requisite. The strength of description arises, in a great measure, from a simple conciseness; but, it supposes also something more; namely, a proper choice of circumstances in the description, so as to exhibit the object in its full and most striking point of view. For every object has several faces, so to speak, by which it may be presented to us, according to the circumstances with which we surround it; and it will appear eminently sublime, or not, in proportion as all these circumstances are happily chosen, and of a sublime kind. Here lies the great art of the writer; and, indeed, the great difficulty of sublime description. If the description be too general, and divested of circumstances, the object appears in a faint light; it makes a feeble impression, or no impression at all, on the reader. At the same time, if any trivial or improper circumstances are mingled, the whole is degraded.

A storm or tempest, for instance, is a sublime object in nature. But to render it sublime in description, it is not enough either to give us mere general expressions concerning the violence of the tempest, or to describe its common vulgar effects, in overthrowing trees and houses. It must be painted with such circumstances as fill the mind with great and awful ideas. This is very happily done by Virgil, in the following passage:

Ipse Pater, media nimborum in nocte, coruscâ
Fulmina molitur dextrâ; quo maxima motu
Terra tremit; fugêre feræ; et mortalia corda
Per gentes humilis stravit pavor: Ille flagranti
Aut Atho, aut Rhodopen, aut alta Ceraunia telo
Dejicit.[1]   Georgics, I.

[1]
The father of the gods his glory shrouds,
Involv'd in tempests, and a night of clouds;
And from the middle darkness flashing out,
By fits he deals his fiery bolts about.
Earth feels the motions of her angry God,
Her entrails tremble, and her mountains nod,
And flying beasts in forests seek abode.
Deep horror seizes every human breast;
Their pride is humbled, and their fears confest:
While he, from high, his rolling thunder throws,
And fires the mountains with repeated blows;
The rocks are from their old foundations rent,
The winds redouble, and the rains augment.   (trans., Dryden)

Every circumstance in this noble description is the production of an imagination heated and astonished with the grandeur of the object. If there be any defect, it is in the words immediately following those I have quoted: *"Ingeminant Austri, et densissimus imber;"* where the transition is made too hastily, I am afraid, from the preceding sublime images, to a thick shower, and the blowing of the south wind; and shows how difficult it frequently is to descend with grace, without seeming to fall.

The high importance of the rule which I have been now giving, concerning the proper choice of circumstances, when description is meant to be sublime, seems to me not to have been sufficiently attended to. It has, however, such a foundation in nature, as renders the least deflexion from it fatal. When a writer is aiming at the beautiful only, his descriptions may have improprieties in them, and yet be beautiful still. Some trivial, or misjudged circumstances, can be overlooked by the reader; they make only the difference of more or less: the gay, or pleasing emotion, which he has raised, subsists still. But the case is quite different with the sublime. There, one trifling circumstance, one mean idea, is sufficient to destroy the whole charm. This is owing to the nature of the emotion aimed at by sublime description, which admits of no mediocrity, and cannot subsist in a middle state; but must either highly transport us, or, if unsuccessful in the execution, leave us greatly disgusted and displeased. We attempt to rise along with the writer; the imagination is awakened, and put upon the stretch; but it requires to be supported; and if, in the midst of its efforts, you desert it unexpectedly, down it comes with a painful shock. When Milton, in his battle of the angels, describes them as tearing up the mountains, and throwing them at one another: there are, in his description, as Mr. Addison has observed, no circumstances but what are properly sublime:

> From their foundations loos'ning to and fro,
> They pluck'd the seated hills, with all their load,
> Rocks, waters, woods; and by the shaggy tops
> Uplifting, bore them in their hands.

Whereas Claudian, in a fragment upon the wars of the giants, has contrived to render this idea of their throwing the mountains, which is in itself so grand, burlesque and ridiculous; by this single circumstance, of one of his giants with the mountain Ida upon his shoulders, and a river which flowed from the mountain, running down along the giant's back, as he held it up in that posture. There is a description too in Virgil, which, I think, is censurable; though more slightly in this respect. It is that of the burning mountain Ætna; a subject certainly very proper to be worked up by a poet into a sublime description:

> Horrificis juxta tonat Ætna ruinis.
> Interdumque atram prorumpit ad æthera nubem,
> Turbine fumantem piceo, et candente favilla;

Attollitque globos flammarum, et sidera lambit.
Interdum scopulos, avulsaque viscera montis
Erigit eructans, liquefactaque saxa sub auras
Cum gemitu glomerat, fundoque exæstuat imo.[2]

Aeneid, III, 571.

Here, after several magnificent images, the poet concludes with personifying the mountain under this figure, *"eructans viscera cum gemitu,"* (belching up its bowels with a groan) ; which, by likening the mountain to a sick or drunk person, degrades the majesty of the description. It is to no purpose to tell us, that the poet here alludes to the fable of the giant Enceladus lying under mount Ætna; and that he supposes his motions and tossings to have occasioned the fiery eruptions. He intended the description of a sublime object; and the natural ideas, raised by a burning mountain, are infinitely more lofty, than the belchings of any giant, how huge soever. The debasing effect of the idea which is here presented, will appear in a stronger light, by seeing what figure it makes in a poem of Sir Richard Blackmore's, who, through a monstrous perversity of taste, had chosen this for the capital circumstance in his description, and thereby (as Dr. Arbuthnot humourously observes, in his Treatise on the Art of Sinking,) had represented the mountain as in a fit of cholic.

> Ætna, and all the burning mountains, find
> Their kindled stores with inbred storms of wind
> Blown up to rage, and roaring out complain,
> As torn with inward gripes, and torturing pain;
> Labouring, they cast their dreadful vomit round,
> And with their melted bowels spread the ground.

Such instances show how much the sublime depends upon a just selection of circumstances; and with how great care every circumstance must be avoided, which by bordering in the least upon the mean or even upon the gay or the trifling, alters the tone of the emotion.

If it shall now be inquired, what are the proper sources of the sublime? my answer is, that they are to be looked for every where in nature. It is not by hunting after tropes, and figures, and rhetorical assistances, that we can expect to produce it. No: it stands clear, for the most part, of these la-

---

2   The port capacious, and secure from wind,
Is to the foot of thundering Ætna join'd.
By turns a pitchy cloud she rolls on high,
By turns hot embers from her entrails fly,
And flakes of mounting flames that lick the sky.
Oft from her bowels massy rocks are thrown,
And shiver'd by the force, come piece-meal down.
Oft liquid lakes of burning sulphur flow,
Fed from the fiery springs that boil below.

In this translation of Dryden's, the debasing circumstance to which I object in the original, is, with propriety, omitted.

boured refinements of art. It must come unsought, if it comes at all; and be the natural offspring of a strong imagination.

Wherever a great and awful object is presented in nature, or a very magnanimous and exalted affection of the human mind is displayed; thence, if you can catch the impression strongly, and exhibit it warm and glowing, you may draw the sublime. These are its only proper sources. In judging of any striking beauty in composition, whether it is, or is not, to be referred to this class, we must attend to the nature of the emotion which it raises; and only, if it be of that elevating, solemn, and awful kind, which distinguishes this feeling, we can pronounce it sublime.

From the account which I have given of the nature of the sublime, it clearly follows, that it is an emotion which can never be long protracted. The mind, by no force of genius, can be kept, for any considerable time, so far raised above its common tone; but will, of course, relax into its ordinary situation. Neither are the abilities of any human writer sufficient to furnish a long continuation of uninterrupted sublime ideas. The utmost we can expect is, that this fire of imagination should sometimes flash upon us like lightning from heaven, and then disappear. In Homer and Milton, this effulgence of genius breaks forth more frequently, and with greater lustre, than in most authors. Shakspeare also rises often into the true sublime. But no author whatever is sublime throughout. Some indeed, there are, who, by a strength and dignity in their conceptions, and a current of high ideas that runs through their whole composition, preserve the reader's mind always in a tone nearly allied to the sublime; for which reason they may, in a limited sense, merit the name of continued sublime writers; and, in this class, we may justly place Demosthenes and Plato.

As for what is called the sublime style, it is, for the most part, a very bad one; and has no relation, whatever, to the real sublime. Persons are apt to imagine, that magnificent words, accumulated epithets, and a certain swelling kind of expression, by rising above what is usual or vulgar, contributes to, or even forms, the sublime. Nothing can be more false. In all the instances of sublime writing, which I have given, nothing of this kind appears. "God said, let there be light; and there was light." This is striking and sublime. But put it into what is commonly called the sublime style: "The sovereign arbiter of nature, by the potent energy of a single word, commanded the light to exist;" and, as Boileau has well observed, the style indeed is raised, but the thought is fallen. In general, in all good writing, the sublime lies in the thought, not in the words; and when the thought is truly noble, it will for the most part, clothe itself in a native dignity of language. The sublime, indeed, rejects mean, low, or trivial expressions; but it is equally an enemy to such as are turgid. The main secret of being sublime, is to say great things in few and plain words. It will be found to hold without exception, that the most sublime authors are the simplest in their style; and wherever you find a writer, who affects a more than ordinary pomp and parade of words, and is always endeavouring to magnify his subject by epithets, there you may immediately suspect, that, feeble in sentiment, he is studying to support himself by mere expression.

The same unfavourable judgment we must pass, on all that laboured apparatus with which some writers introduce a passage, or description, which they intend shall be sublime; calling on their readers to attend, invoking their muse, or breaking forth into general, unmeaning exclamations, concerning the greatness, terribleness, or majesty of the object, which they are to describe. Mr. Addison, in his Campaign, has fallen into an error of this kind, when about to describe the battle of Blenheim.

> But O my muse! what numbers wilt thou find
> To sing the furious troops in battle join'd?
> Methinks, I hear the drum's tumultuous sound,
> The victor's shouts, and dying groans, confound;

Introductions of this kind, are a forced attempt in a writer, to spur up himself, and his reader, when he finds his imagination begin to flag. It is like taking artificial spirits in order to supply the want of such as are natural. By this observation, however, I do not mean to pass a general censure on Mr. Addison's Campaign, which in several places, is far from wanting merit; and in particular, the noted comparison of his hero to the angel who rides in the whirlwind and directs the storm, is a truly sublime image.

The faults opposite to the sublime are chiefly two: the frigid, and the bombast. The frigid consists, in degrading an object or sentiment, which is sublime in itself, by our mean conception of it; or by our weak, low, and childish description of it. This betrays entire absence, or at least great poverty of genius. Of this there are abundance of examples, and these commented upon with much humour, in the Treatise on the Art of Sinking, in Dean Swift's works; the instances taken chiefly from Sir Richard Blackmore. One of these, I had occasion already to give, in relation to mount Ætna, and it were needless to produce any more. The bombast lies, in forcing an ordinary or trivial object out of its rank, and endeavouring to raise it into the sublime; or, in attempting to exalt a sublime object beyond all natural and reasonable bounds. Into this error, which is but too common, writers of genius may sometimes fall, by unluckily losing sight of the true point of the sublime. This is also called fustian, or rant. Shakespeare, a great but incorrect genius, is not unexceptionable here. Dryden and Lee, in their tragedies, abound with it.

Thus far of the Sublime, of which I have treated fully, because it is so capital an excellency in fine writing, and because clear and precise ideas on this head are, as far as I know, not to be met with in critical writers.

Before I conclude this lecture, there is one observation which I choose to make at this time; I shall make it once for all, and hope it will be afterwards remembered. It is with respect to the instances of faults, or rather blemishes and imperfections, which, as I have done in this lecture, I shall hereafter continue to take, when I can, from writers of reputation. I have not the least intention thereby to disparage their character in the general.

I shall have other occasions of doing equal justice to their beauties. But it is no reflection on any human performance, that it is not absolutely perfect. The task would be much easier for me, to collect instances of faults from bad writers. But they would draw no attention, when quoted from books which nobody reads. And I conceive, that the method which I follow, will contribute more to make the best authors be read with pleasure, when one properly distinguishes their beauties from their faults; and is led to imitate and admire only what is worthy of imitation and admiration.

Lecture X

STYLE—PERSPICUITY AND PRECISION

Having finished the subject of language, I now enter on the consideration of style, and the rules that relate to it.

It is not easy to give a precise idea of what is meant by style. The best definition I can give of it, is, the peculiar manner in which a man expresses his conceptions, by means of language. It is different from mere language, or words. The words which an author employs, may be proper and faultless; and his style may, nevertheless, have great faults: it may be dry, or stiff, or feeble, or affected. Style has always some reference to an author's manner of thinking. It is a picture of the ideas which arise in his mind, and of the manner in which they rise there; and hence, when we are examining an author's composition, it is, in many cases, extremely difficult to separate the style from the sentiment. No wonder these two should be so intimately connected, as style is nothing else than that sort of expression which our thoughts most readily assume. Hence, different countries have been noted for peculiarities of style, suited to their different temper and genius. The eastern nations animated their style with the most strong and hyperbolical figures. The Athenians, a polished and acute people, formed a style accurate, clear, and neat. The Asiatics, gay and loose in their manners, affected a style florid and diffuse. The like sort of characteristical differences are commonly remarked in the style of the French, the English, and the Spaniards. In giving the general characters of style, it is usual to talk of a nervous, a feeble, or a spirited style; which are plainly the characters of a writer's manner of thinking, as well as of expressing himself: so difficult it is to separate these two things from one another. Of the general characters of style, I am afterwards to discourse; but it will be necessary to begin with examining the more simple qualities of it; from the assemblage of which, its more complex denominations, in a great measure, result.

All the qualities of good style may be ranged under two heads, perspicuity and ornament. For all that can possibly be required of language is, to convey our ideas clearly to the minds of others, and, at the same time, in such a dress, as by pleasing and interesting them, shall most effectually strengthen the impressions which we seek to make. When both these ends are answered, we certainly accomplish every purpose for which we use writing and discourse.

Perspicuity, it will be readily admitted, is the fundamental quality of style, a quality so essential in every kind of writing, that for the want of it, nothing can atone. Without this, the richest ornaments of style only glimmer through the dark; and puzzle, instead of pleasing the reader. This, therefore, must be our first object, to make our meaning clearly and fully understood, and understood without the least difficulty. *"Oratio,"* says Quintilian, *"debet negligenter quoque audientibus esse aperta; ut in animum audientis, sicut sol in oculos, etiamsi in eum non intendatur, occurat. Quare non solum ut intelligere possit, sed ne omnino possit non intelligere curandum."* [1] If we are obliged to follow a writer with much care, to pause, and read over his sentences a second time, in order to comprehend them fully, he will never please us long. Mankind are too indolent to relish so much labour. They may pretend to admire the author's depth, after they have discovered his meaning; but they will seldom be inclined to take up his work a second time.

Authors sometimes plead the difficulty of their subject as an excuse for the want of perspicuity. But the excuse can rarely, if ever, be admitted. For whatever a man conceives clearly, that, it is in his power, if he will be at the trouble, to put into distinct propositions, or to express clearly to others: and upon no subject ought any man to write, where he cannot think clearly. His ideas, indeed, may, very excusably, be on some subjects incomplete or inadequate; but still, as far as they go, they ought to be clear; and wherever this is the case, perspicuity in expressing them is always attainable. The obscurity which reigns so much among many metaphysical writers, is, for the most part, owing to the indistinctness of their own conceptions. They see the object but in a confused light; and, of course, can never exhibit it in a clear one to others.

Perspicuity in writing, is not to be considered as merely a sort of negative virtue, or freedom from defect. It has higher merit: it is a degree of positive beauty. We are pleased with an author, we consider him as deserving praise, who frees us from all fatigue of searching for his meaning; who carries us through his subject without any embarrassment or confusion; whose style flows always like a limpid stream, where we see to the very bottom.

The study of perspicuity requires attention, first, to single words and phrases, and then to the construction of sentences. I begin with treating of the first, and shall confine myself to it in this lecture.

1 "Discourse ought always to be obvious, even to the most careless and negligent hearer: so that the sense shall strike his mind, as the light of the sun does our eyes, though they are not directed upwards to it. We must study not only that every hearer may understand us, but that it shall be impossible for him not to understand us."

Perspicuity, considered with respect to words and phrases, requires these three qualities in them, *purity, propriety,* and *precision.*

Purity and propriety of language, are often used indiscriminately for each other; and, indeed, they are very nearly allied. A distinction, however, obtains between them. Purity is the use of such words, and such constructions, as belong to the idiom of the language which we speak; in opposition to words and phrases that are imported from other languages, or that are obsolete, or new coined, or used without proper authority. Propriety is the selection of such words in the language, as the best and most established usage has appropriated to those ideas which we intend to express by them. It implies the correct and happy application of them, according to that usage, in opposition to vulgarisms or low expressions; and to words and phrases, which would be less significant of the ideas that we mean to convey. Style may be pure, that is, it may all be strictly English, without Scoticisms or Gallicisms, or ungrammatical irregular expressions of any kind, and may, nevertheless, be deficient in propriety. The words may be ill chosen; not adapted to the subject, nor fully expressive of the author's sense. He has taken all his words and phrases from the general mass of English language; but he has made his selection among these words unhappily. Whereas, style cannot be proper without being also pure; and where both purity and propriety meet, besides making style perspicuous, they also render it graceful. There is no standard, either of purity or of propriety, but the practice of the best writers and speakers in the country.

When I mentioned obsolete or new coined words, as incongruous with purity of style, it will be easily understood, that some exceptions are to be made. On certain occasions, they may have grace. Poetry admits of greater latitude than prose, with respect to coining, or, at least, new compounding words; yet, even here, this liberty should be used with a sparing hand. In prose, such innovations are more hazardous, and have a worse effect. They are apt to give style an affected and conceited air; and should never be ventured upon, except by such, whose established reputation gives them some degree of dictatorial power over language.

The introduction of foreign and learned words, unless where necessity requires them, should always be avoided. Barren languages may need such assistances; but ours is not one of these. Dean Swift, one of our most correct writers, valued himself much on using no words but such as were of native growth: and his language may, indeed, be considered as a standard of the strictest purity and propriety, in the choice of words. At present, we seem to be departing from this standard. A multitude of Latin words have, of late, been poured in upon us. On some occasions, they give an appearance of elevation and dignity to style. But often, also, they render it stiff and forced: and, in general, a plain, native style, as it is more intelligible to all readers, so, by a proper management of words, it may be made equally strong and expressive with this Latinised English.

Let us now consider the import of precision in language, which, as it is the highest part of the quality denoted by perspicuity, merits a full explication; and the more, because distinct ideas are, perhaps, not commonly formed about it.

The exact import of precision, may be drawn from the etymology of the word. It comes from *"præcidere,"* to cut off: it imports retrenching all superfluities, and pruning the expression, so as to exhibit neither more nor less than an exact copy of his idea who uses it. I observed before, that it is often difficult to separate the qualities of style from the qualities of thought; and it is found so in this instance. For, in order to write with precision, though this be properly a quality of style, one must possess a very considerable degree of distinctness and accuracy in his manner of thinking.

The words which a man uses to express his ideas, may be faulty in three respects; they may either not express that idea which the author intends, but some other which only resembles, or is akin to it; or, they may express that idea, but not quite fully and completely; or, they may express it, together with something more than he intends. Precision stands opposed to all these three faults; but chiefly to the last. In an author's writing with propriety, his being free from the two former faults seems implied. The words which he uses are proper; that is, they express that idea which he intends, and they express it fully; but to be precise, signifies, that they express that idea, and no more. There is nothing in his words which introduces any foreign idea, any superfluous unseasonable accessory, so as to mix it confusedly with the principal object, and thereby to render our conception of that object loose and indistinct. This requires a writer to have, himself, a very clear apprehension of the object he means to present to us; to have laid fast hold of it in his mind; and never to waver in any one view he takes of it; a perfection to which, indeed, few writers attain.

The use and importance of precision, may be deduced from the nature of the human mind. It never can view, clearly and distinctly, above one object at a time. If it must look at two or three together, especially objects among which there is resemblance or connexion, it finds itself confused and embarrassed. It cannot clearly perceive in what they agree, and in what they differ. Thus, were any object, suppose some animal, to be presented to me, of whose structure I wanted to form a distinct notion, I would desire all its trappings to be taken off, I would require it to be brought before me by itself, and to stand alone, that there might be nothing to distract my attention. The same is the case with words. If, when you would inform me of your meaning, you also tell me more than what conveys it; if you join foreign circumstances to the principal object; if, by unnecessarily varying the expression, you shift the point of view, and make me see sometimes the object itself, and sometimes another thing that is connected with it; you thereby oblige me to look on several objects at once, and I lose sight of the principal. You load the animal you are showing me, with so many trappings and collars, and bring so many of the same species before me, somewhat resembling, and yet somewhat differing, that I see none of them clearly.

This forms what is called a loose style; and is the proper opposite to precision. It generally arises from using a superfluity of words. Feeble writers employ a multitude of words to make themselves understood, as they think, more distinctly; and they only confound the reader. They are sensible of not having caught the precise expression, to convey what they would signify; they do not, indeed, conceive their own meaning very precisely themselves; and therefore help it out, as they can, by this and the other word, which may, as they suppose, supply the defect, and bring you somewhat nearer to their idea: they are always going about it, and about it, but never just hit the thing. The image, as they set it before you, is always seen double; and no double image is distinct. When an author tells me of his hero's *courage* in the day of battle, the expression is precise, and I understand it fully. But if, from the desire of multiplying words, he will needs praise his *courage* and *fortitude;* at the moment he joins these words together, my idea begins to waver. He means to express one quality more strongly; but he is, in truth, expressing two. *Courage* resists danger; *fortitude* supports pain. The occasion of exerting each of these qualities is different; and being led to think of both together, when only one of them should be in my view, my view is rendered unsteady, and my conception of the object indistinct.

From what I have said, it appears that an author may, in a qualified sense, be perspicuous, while yet he is far from being precise. He uses proper words, and proper arrangement; he gives you the idea as clear as he conceives it himself; and so far he is perspicuous: but the ideas are not very clear in his own mind; they are loose and general; and, therefore, cannot be expressed with precision. All subjects do not equally require precision. It is sufficient, on many occasions, that we have a general view of the meaning. The subject, perhaps, is of the known and familiar kind; and we are in no hazard of mistaking the sense of the author, though every word which he uses be not precise and exact.

Few authors, for instance, in the English language, are more clear and perspicuous, on the whole, than Archbishop Tillotson, and Sir William Temple; yet neither of them are remarkable for precision. They are loose and diffuse; and accustomed to express their meaning by several words, which show you fully whereabouts it lies, rather than to single out those expressions, which would convey clearly the idea which they have in view, and no more. Neither, indeed, is precision the prevailing character of Mr. Addison's style; although he is not so deficient in this respect as the other two authors.

Lord Shaftesbury's faults, in point of precision, are much greater than Mr. Addison's; and the more unpardonable, because he is a professed philosophical writer; who, as such, ought, above all things, to have studied precision. His style has both great beauties and great faults; and, on the whole, is by no means a safe model for imitation. Lord Shaftesbury was well acquainted with the power of words; those which he employs are generally proper and well sounding; he has great variety of them; and his arrangement, as shall be afterwards shown, is commonly beautiful. His defect, in precision, is not owing so much to indistinct or confused ideas, as to perpetual affectation. He is fond, to excess, of the pomp and parade of language; he is never satisfied with expressing any thing clearly and simply; he must always give it the dress of state and majesty. Hence perpetual circumlocutions, and many words and phrases employed to describe somewhat, that would have been described much better by one of them. If he has occasion to mention any person or author, he very rarely mentions him by his proper name. In the treatise, entitled, Advice to an Author, he descants for two or three pages together upon Aristotle, without once naming him in any other way, than the master critic, the mighty genius and judge of art, the prince of critics, the grand master of art, and consummate philologist. In the same way, the grand poetic sire, the philosophical patriarch, and his disciple of noble birth and lofty genius, are the only names by which he condescends to distinguish Homer, Socrates, and Plato, in another passage of the same treatise. This method of distinguishing persons is extremely affected; but it is not so contrary to precision, as the frequent circumlocutions he employs for all moral ideas; attentive, on every occasion, more to the pomp of language, than to the clearness which he ought to have studied as a philosopher. The moral sense, for instance, after he had once defined it, was a clear term; but, how vague becomes the idea, when, in the next page, he calls it, "That natural affection, and anticipating fancy, which makes the sense of right and wrong?" Self examination, or reflection on our own conduct, is an idea conceived with ease; but when it is wrought into all the forms of "A man's dividing himself into two parties, becoming a self-dialogist, entering into partnership with himself, forming the dual number practically within himself;" we hardly know what to make of it. On some occasions, he so adorns, or rather loads with words, the plainest and simplest propositions, as, if not to obscure, at least, to enfeeble them.

In the following paragraph, for example, of the inquiry concerning virtue, he means to show, that, by every ill action we hurt our mind, as much as one who should swallow poison, or give himself a wound, would hurt his body. Observe what a redundancy of words he pours forth: "Now if the fabric of the mind or temper appeared to us such as it really is; if we saw it impossible to remove hence any one good or orderly affection, or to introduce any ill or disorderly one, without drawing on, in some degree, that dissolute state which, at its height, is confessed to be so miserable; it would then, undoubtedly, be confessed, that since no ill, immoral, or unjust action, can be committed, without either a new inroad and breach on the temper and passions, or a further advancing of that execution already done: whoever did ill, or acted in prejudice to his integrity, good nature, or worth, would, of necessity, act with greater cruelty towards himself, than he who scrupled not to swallow what was poisonous, or who, with his own hands, should voluntarily mangle or wound his outward form or constitution, natural limbs, or body." [2] Here, to commit a bad action, is, first, "To remove a good and orderly affection, and to introduce an ill or dis-

2 Characteristics, Vol. II, p. 85.

orderly one;" next, it is, "To commit an action that is ill, immoral, and unjust;" and in the next line, it is, "To do ill, or to act in prejudice of integrity, good nature, and worth;" nay, so very simple a thing as a man's wounding himself, is, "To mangle, or wound, his outward form or constitution, his natural limbs or body." Such superfluity of words is disgustful to every reader of correct taste; and serves no purpose but to embarrass and perplex the sense. This sort of style is elegantly described by Quintilian: "A crowd of unmeaning words is brought together by some authors, who, afraid of expressing themselves after a common and ordinary manner, and allured by an appearance of splendour, surround every thing which they mean to say with a certain copious loquacity."

The great source of a loose style, in opposition to precision, is the injudicious use of those words termed synonymous. They are called synonymous, because they agree in expressing one principal idea; but, for the most part, if not always, they express it with some diversity in the circumstances. They are varied by some accessary idea which every word introduces, and which forms the distinction between them. Hardly, in any language, are there two words that convey precisely the same idea; a person thoroughly conversant in the propriety of the language, will always be able to observe something that distinguishes them. As they are like different shades of the same colour, an accurate writer can employ them to great advantage, by using them, so as to heighten and to finish the picture which he gives us. He supplies by one, what was wanting in the other, to the force, or to the lustre of the image which he means to exhibit. But, in order to this end, he must be extremely attentive to the choice which he makes of them. For the bulk of writers are very apt to confound them with each other; and to employ them carelessly, merely for the sake of filling up a period, or of rounding and diversifying the language, as if their signification were exactly the same, while, in truth, it is not. Hence a certain mist and indistinctness is unwarily thrown over style.

From all that has been said on this head, it will now appear, that, in order to write or speak with precision, two things are especially requisite: one, that an author's own ideas be clear and distinct; and the other, that we have an exact and full comprehension of the force of those words which he employs. Natural genius is here required; labour and attention still more. Dean Swift is one of the authors, in our language, most distinguished for precision of style. In his writings, we seldom or never find vague expressions and synonymous words carelessly thrown together. His meaning is always clear, and strongly marked.

I had occasion to observe before, that though all subjects of writing or discourse demand perspicuity, yet all do not require the same degree of that exact precision which I have endeavoured to explain. It is, indeed, in every sort of writing, a great beauty to have, at least, some measure of precision, in distinction from that loose profusion of words which imprints no clear idea on the reader's mind. But we must, at the same time, be on our guard, lest too great a study of precision, especially in subjects where it is not strictly requisite, betray us into a dry and barren style; lest, from the desire of pruning too closely, we retrench all copiousness and ornament. Some degree of this failing may, perhaps, be remarked in Dean Swift's serious works. Attentive only to exhibit his ideas clear and exact, resting wholly on his sense and distinctness, he appears to reject, disdainfully, all embellishment, which, on some occasions, may be thought to render his manner somewhat hard and dry. To unite copiousness and precision, to be flowing and graceful, and at the same time correct and exact in the choice of every word, is, no doubt, one of the highest and most difficult attainments in writing. Some kinds of composition may require more of copiousness and ornament; others, more of precision and accuracy; nay, in the same composition, the different parts of it may demand a proper variation of manner. But we must study never to sacrifice, totally, any one of these qualities to the other; and by a proper management, both of them may be made fully consistent, if our own ideas be precise, and our knowledge and stock of words be, at the same time, extensive.

꙰꙰꙰꙰꙰꙰

Lecture XIV

ORIGIN AND NATURE OF FIGURATIVE LANGUAGE

Having now finished what related to the construction of sentences, I proceed to other rules concerning style. My general division of the qualities of style, was into perspicuity and ornament. Perspicuity, both in single words and sentences, I have considered. Ornament, as far as it arises from a graceful, strong, and melodious construction of words, has also been treated of. Another, and a great branch of the ornament of style, is, figurative language; which is now to be the subject of our consideration, and will require a full discussion.

Our first inquiry must be, what is meant by figures of speech?

In general, they always imply some departure from simplicity of expression; the idea which we intend to convey, not only enunciated to others, but enunciated, in a particular manner, and with some circumstance added, which is designed to render the impression more strong and vivid. When I say, for instance, "That a good man enjoys comfort in the midst of adversity;" I just express my thought in the simplest manner possible. But when I say, "To the upright there ariseth light in darkness;" the same sentiment is expressed in a figurative style; a new circumstance is introduced; light is put in the place of comfort, and darkness is used to suggest the idea of adversity. In the same manner, to say, "It is impossible, by any search we can make, to explore the divine nature fully," is to make a simple proposition. But when we say, "Canst thou, by searching, find out God? Canst thou find out the Almighty to perfection? It is high as heaven, what canst thou do? deeper than hell, what canst thou know?" This introduces a figure into style; the proposition being not only expressed, but admiration and astonishment being expressed together with it.

But, though figures imply a deviation from what may be reckoned the most simple form of speech, we are not thence to conclude, that they imply any thing uncommon, or unnatural. This is so far from being the case, that, on very many occasions, they are both the most natural, and the most common method of uttering our sentiments. It is impossible to compose any discourse without using them often; nay, there are few sentences of any length, in which some expression or other, that may be termed a figure, does not occur. From what causes this happens, shall be afterwards explained. The fact, in the meantime, shows, that they are to be accounted part of that language which nature dictates to men. They are not the inventions of the schools, nor the mere product of study: on the contrary, the most illiterate speak in figures, as often as the most learned. Whenever the imaginations of the vulgar are much awakened, or their passions inflamed against one another, they will pour forth a torrent of figurative language as forcible as could be employed by the most artificial declaimer.

What then is it, which has drawn the attention of critics and rhetoricians so much to these forms of speech? It is this: They remarked, that in them consists much of the beauty and the force of language; and found them always to bear some characters, or distinguishing marks, by the help of which they could reduce them under separate classes and heads. To this, perhaps, they owe their name of figures. As the figure, or shape of one body, distinguishes it from another, so these forms of speech have, each of them, a cast or turn peculiar to itself, which both distinguishes it from the rest, and distinguishes it from simple expression. Simple expression just makes our idea known to others; but figurative language, over and above, bestows a particular dress upon that idea; a dress, which both makes it to be remarked, and adorns it. Hence, this sort of language became early a capital object of attention to those who studied the powers of speech.

Figures, in general, may be described to be that language, which is prompted either by the imagination, or by the passions. The justness of this description will appear, from the more particular account I am afterwards to give of them. Rhetoricians commonly divide them into two great classes; figures of words, and figures of thought. The former, figures of words, are commonly called tropes, and consist in a word's being employed to signify something that is different from its original and primitive meaning; so that if you alter the word, you destroy the figure. Thus, in the instance I gave before; "Light ariseth to the upright in darkness." The trope consists in "light and darkness" being not meant literally, but substituted for comfort and adversity, on account of some resemblance or analogy which they are supposed to bear to these conditions of life. The other class, termed figures of thought, supposes the words to be used in their proper and literal meaning, and the figure to consist in the turn of the thought; as is the case in exclamations, interrogations, apostrophes, and comparisons; where, though you vary the words that are used, or translate them from one language into another, you may, nevertheless, still preserve the same figure in the thought. This distinction, however, is of no great use, as nothing can be built upon it in practice; neither is it always very clear. It is of little importance, whether we give to some particular mode of expression the name of a trope, or of a figure; provided we remember, that figurative language always imports some colouring of the imagination, or from some emotion of passion, expressed in our style: and, perhaps, figures of imagination, and figures of passion, might be a more useful distribution of the subject. But without insisting on any artificial divisions, it will be more useful, that I inquire into the origin and the nature of figures. Only, before I proceed to this, there are two general observations which it may be proper to premise.

The first is, concerning the use of rules with respect to figurative language. I admit, that persons may both speak and write with propriety, who know not the names of any of the figures of speech, nor ever studied any rules relating to them. Nature, as was before observed, dictates the use of figures; and, like Mons. Jourdain, in Molière, who had spoken for forty years in prose, without ever knowing it, many a one uses metaphorical expressions to good purpose, without any idea of what a metaphor is. It will not, however, follow thence, that rules are of no service. All science arises from observations on practice. Practice has always gone before method and rule; but method and rule have afterwards improved and perfected practice in every art. We every day meet with persons who sing agreeably without knowing one note of the gamut. Yet, it has been found of importance to reduce these notes to a scale, and to form an art of music; and it would be ridiculous to pretend, that the art is of no advantage, because the practice is founded in nature. Propriety and beauty of speech, are certainly as improveable as the ear or the voice; and to know the principles of this beauty, or the reasons which render one figure, or one manner of speech, preferable to another, cannot fail to assist and direct a proper choice.

But I must observe, in the next place, that although this part of style merits attention, and is a very proper object of science and rule; although much of the beauty of composition depends on figurative language; yet we must beware of imagining that it depends solely, or even chiefly, upon such language. It is not so. The great place which the doctrine of tropes and figures has occupied in systems of rhetoric; the over-anxious care which has been shown in giving names to a vast variety of them, and in ranging them under different classes, has often led persons to imagine, that if their composition was well bespangled with a number of these ornaments of speech, it wanted no other beauty: whence has arisen much stiffness and affectation. For it is, in truth, the sentiment or passion, which lies under the figured expression, that gives it any merit. The figure is only the dress; the sentiment is the body and the substance. No figures will render a cold or an empty composition interesting; whereas, if a sentiment be sublime or pathetic, it can support itself perfectly well, without any borrowed assistance. Hence, several of the most affecting and admired passages of the best authors, are expressed in the simplest language. The following sentiment from Virgil, for instance, makes its way at once to the heart, without the help of any figure whatever. He is describing an Argive, who falls in battle, in Italy, at a great distance from his native country:

> Sternitur, infelix, alieno vulnere, coelumque
> Aspicit, et dulcis moriens reminiscitur Argos.[1]
>
> Aeneid, X, 781.

A single stroke of this kind, drawn as by the very pencil of nature, is worth a thousand figures. In the same manner, the simple style of scripture: "He spoke, and it was done; he commanded, and it stood fast." "God said, let there be light; and there was light;" imparts a lofty conception, to much greater advantage, than if it had been decorated by the most pompous metaphors. The fact is, that the strong pathetic, and the pure sublime, not only have little dependence on figures of speech, but generally reject them. The proper region of these ornaments is, where a moderate degree of elevation and passion is predominant; and there they contribute to the embellishment of discourse, only when there is a basis of solid thought and natural sentiment; when they are inserted in their proper place; and when they rise, of themselves, from the subject without being sought after.

Having premised these observations, I proceed to give an account of the origin and nature of figures; principally of such as have their dependence on language; including that numerous tribe which the rhetoricians call tropes.

At the first rise of language, men would begin with giving names to the different objects which they discerned, or thought of. This nomenclature would, at the beginning, be very narrow. According as men's ideas multiplied, and their acquaintance with objects increased, their stock of names and words would increase also. But to the infinite variety of objects and ideas, no language is adequate. No language is so copious, as to have a separate word for every separate idea. Men naturally sought to abridge this labour of multiplying words *in infinitum;* and, in order to lay less burden on their memories, made one word, which they had already appropriated

---

1   "Anthares had from Argos travell'd far,
         Alcides' friend, and brother of the war;
         Now falling, by another's wound, his eyes
         He casts to Heaven, on Argos thinks, and dies."
In this translation, much of the beauty of the original is lost. "On Argos thinks, and dies," is by no means equal to *"dulcis moriens reminiscitur Argos"* "As he dies he remembers his beloved Argos." It is indeed observable, that in most of those tender and pathetic passages, which do so much honour to Virgil, that great poet expresses himself with the utmost simplicity.

to a certain idea or object, stand also for some other idea or object; between which and the primary one, they found, or fancied, some relation. Thus, the preposition, *in,* was originally invented to express the circumstance of place: "The man was killed *in* the wood." In progress of time, words were wanted to express men's being connected with certain conditions of fortune, or certain situations of mind; and some resemblance, or analogy, being fancied between these, and the place of bodies, the word *in,* was employed to express men's being so circumstanced; as, one's being *in* health, or *in* sickness, *in* prosperity, or *in* adversity, *in* joy or *in* grief, *in* doubt, or *in* danger, or *in* safety. Here we see this preposition, *in,* plainly assuming a tropical signification, or carried off from its original meaning, to signify something else which relates to, or resembles it.

Tropes of this kind abound in all languages, and are plainly owing to the want of proper words. The operations of the mind and affections, in particular, are, in most languages, described by words taken from sensible objects. The reason is plain. The names of sensible objects were, in all languages, the words most early introduced; and were, by degrees, extended to those mental objects, of which men had more obscure conceptions, and to which they found it more difficult to assign distinct names. They borrowed, therefore, the name of some sensible idea, where their imagination found some affinity. Thus, we speak of a *piercing* judgment, and a *clear* head; a *soft* or a *hard* heart; a *rough* or a *smooth* behaviour. We say, *inflamed* by anger, *warmed* by love; *swelled* with pride, *melted* into grief; and these are almost the only significant words which we have for such ideas.

But, although the barrenness of languages, and the want of words, be doubtless one cause of the invention of tropes; yet it is not the only, nor, perhaps, even the principal source of this form of speech. Tropes have arisen more frequently, and spread themselves wider, from the influence which imagination possesses over language. The train on which this has proceeded among all nations, I shall endeavour to explain.

Every object which makes any impression on the human mind, is constantly accompanied with certain circumstances and relations, that strike us at the same time. It never presents itself to our view *isolé,* as the French express it; that is, independent on, and separated from, every other thing; but always occurs as somehow related to other objects; going before them, or following them; their effect or their cause; resembling them, or opposed to them; distinguished by certain qualities, or surrounded with certain circumstances. By this means, every idea or object carries in its train some other ideas, which may be considered as its accessories. These accessories often strike the imagination more than the principal idea itself. They are, perhaps, more agreeable ideas; or they are more familiar to our conceptions; or they recall to our memory a greater variety of important circumstances. The imagination is more disposed to rest upon some of them; and therefore, instead of using the proper name of the principal idea which it means to express, it employs in its place the name of the accessory or correspondent idea; although the principal have a proper and well known name of its own. Hence a vast variety of topical or figurative words obtain currency in all languages, through choice, not necessity; and men of lively imaginations are every day adding to their number.

Thus, when we design to intimate the period at which a state enjoyed most reputation or glory, it were easy to employ the proper words for expressing this; but as this is readily connected, in our imagination, with the flourishing period of a plant or a tree, we lay hold of this correspondent idea, and say, "The Roman empire flourished most under Augustus." The leader of a faction is plain language: but because the head is the principal part of the human body, and is supposed to direct all the animal operations, resting upon this resemblance, we say, "Catiline was the head of the party." The word *voice,* was originally invented to signify the articulate sound, formed by the organs of the mouth; but, as by means of it men signify their ideas and their intentions to each other, *voice* soon assumed a great many other meanings, all derived from this primary effect. "To give our voice" for any thing, signified, to give our sentiment in favour of it. Not only so; but *voice* was transferred to signify any intimation of will or judgment, though given without the least interposition of voice in its literal sense, or any sound uttered at all. Thus we speak of listening to the *voice* of conscience, the *voice* of nature, the *voice* of God. This usage takes place, not so much from barrenness of language, or want of a proper word, as from an allusion which we choose to make to *voice* in its primary sense, in order to convey our idea, connected with a circumstance which appears to the fancy to give it more sprightliness and force.

The account which I have now given, and which seems to be a full and fair one, of the introduction of tropes into all languages, coincides with what Cicero briefly hints, in his third book, *De Oratore.* "The figurative usage of words is very extensive; an usage to which necessity first gave rise, on account of the paucity of words, and barrenness of language; but which the pleasure that was found in it afterwards rendered frequent. For as garments were first contrived to defend our bodies from the cold, and afterwards were employed for the purpose of ornament and dignity, so figures of speech, introduced by want, were cultivated for the sake of entertainment."

From what has been said, it clearly appears how that must come to pass, which I had occasion to mention in a former lecture, that all languages are most figurative in their early state. Both the causes to which I ascribed the origin of figures, concur in producing this effect at the beginnings of society. Language is then most barren: the stock of proper names which have been invented for things, is small; and, at the same time, imagination exerts great influence over the conceptions of men, and their method of uttering them; so that, both from necessity and from choice, their speech will, at that period, abound in tropes; for the savage tribes of men are always much given to wonder and astonishment. Every new object surprises, terrifies, and makes a strong impression on their mind; they are governed by imagination and passion, more than by reason; and of course, their speech must be deeply tinctured by their genius. In fact, we find, that this is the character of the American and Indian languages: bold, picturesque, and metaphorical; full of strong allusions to sensible qualities, and to such objects as struck them most in their wild and solitary life. An Indian chief makes a harangue to his tribe, in a style full of stronger metaphors than an European would use in an epic poem.

As language makes gradual progress towards refinement, almost every object comes to have a proper name given to it, and perspicuity and precision are more studied. But still, for the reasons before given, borrowed words, or as rhetoricians call them, tropes, must continue to occupy a considerable place. In every language, too, there are a multitude of words, which, though they were figurative in their first application to certain objects, yet, by long use, lose their figurative power wholly, and come to be considered as simple and literal expressions. In this case, are the terms which I remarked before, as transferred from sensible qualities to the operations or qualities of the mind, a *piercing* judgment, a *clear* head, a *hard* heart, and the like. There are other words which remain in a sort of middle state; which have neither lost wholly their figurative application, nor yet retain so much of it as to imprint any remarkable character of figured language on our style; such as these phrases, "apprehend one's meaning:" "enter on a subject:" "follow out an argument:" "stir up strife:" and a great many more, of which our language is full. In the use of such phrases, correct writers will always preserve a regard to the figure or allusion on which they are founded, and will be careful not to apply them in any way that is inconsistent with it. One may be "sheltered under the patronage of a great man:" but it were wrong to say, "sheltered under the mask of dissimulation," as a mask conceals, but does not shelter. An object, in description, may be "clothed," if you will, "with epithets;" but it is not so proper to speak of its being "clothed with circumstances:" as the word "circumstances" alludes to standing round, not to clothing. Such attentions as these to the propriety of language are requisite in every composition.

What has been said on this subject, tends to throw light on the nature of language in general, and will lead to the reasons, why tropes or figures contribute to the beauty and grace of style.

First, They enrich language, and render it more copious. By their means, words and phrases are multiplied for expressing all sorts of ideas; for describing even the minutest differences; the nicest shades and colours of thought; which no language could possibly do by proper words alone, without assistance from tropes.

Secondly, They bestow dignity upon style. The familiarity of common words, to which our ears are much accustomed, tends to degrade style. When we want to adapt our language to the tone of an elevated subject, we should be greatly at a loss, if we could not borrow assistance from figures; which, properly employed, have a similar effect on language, with what is produced by the rich and splendid dress of a person of rank; to create respect, and to give an air of magnificence to him who wears it. Assistance of this kind, is often needed in prose compositions; but poetry could not subsist without it. Hence figures form the constant language of poetry. To say, that "the sun rises," is trite and common; but it becomes a magnificent image when expressed, as Mr. Thomson has done:

> But yonder comes the powerful king of day,
> Rejoicing in the east.—

In the third place, figures give us the pleasure of enjoying two objects presented together to our view, without confusion; the principal idea, which is the subject of the discourse, along with its accessory, which gives it the figurative dress. We see one thing in another, as Aristotle expresses it; which is always agreeable to the mind. For there is nothing with which the fancy is more delighted, than with comparisons, and resemblances of objects; and all tropes are founded upon some relation or analogy between one thing and another. When, for instance, in place of "youth," I say the "morning of life;" the fancy is immediately entertained with all the resembling circumstances which presently occur between these two objects. At one moment, I have in my eye a certain period of human life, and a certain time of the day, so related to each other, that the imagination plays between them with pleasure, and contemplates two similar objects, in one view, without embarrassment or confusion.

In the fourth place, figures are attended with this farther advantage, of giving us frequently a much clearer and more striking view of the principal object, than we could have of it were it expressed in simple terms, and divested of its accessory idea. This is, indeed, their principal advantage, in virtue of which, they are very properly said to illustrate a subject, or to throw a light upon it. For they exhibit the object, on which they are employed, in a picturesque form; they can render an abstract conception, in some degree, an object of sense; they surround it with such circumstances, as enable the mind to lay hold of it steadily, and to contemplate it fully. "Those persons," says one, "who gain the hearts of most people, who are chosen as the companions of their softer hours, and their reliefs from anxiety and care, are seldom persons of shining qualities, or strong virtues: it is rather the soft green of the soul, on which we rest our eyes, that are fatigued with beholding more glaring objects." Here, by a happy allusion to a colour, the whole conception is conveyed clear and strong to the mind in one word. By a well-chosen figure, even conviction is assisted, and the impression of a truth upon the mind made more lively and forcible than it would otherwise be. As in the following illustration of Dr. Young's: "When we dip too deep in pleasure, we always stir a sediment that renders it impure and noxious;" or in this, "A heart boiling with violent passions, will always send up infatuating fumes to the head." An image that presents so much congruity between a moral and a sensible idea, serves like an argument from analogy, to enforce what the other asserts, and to induce belief.

Besides, whether we are endeavouring to raise sentiments of pleasure or aversion, we can always heighten the emotion by the figures which we in-

troduce; leading the imagination to a train, either of agreeable or disagreeable, of exalting or debasing ideas, correspondent to the impression
which we seek to make. When we want to render an object beautiful, or
magnificent, we borrow images from all the most beautiful or splendid
scenes of nature; we thereby naturally throw a lustre over our object; we
enliven the reader's mind, and dispose him to go along with us, in the gay
and pleasing impressions which we give him of the subject. This effect of
figures is happily touched in the following lines of Dr. Akenside, and illustrated by a very sublime figure:

> Then th' inexpressive strain
> Diffuses its enchantment. Fancy dreams
> Of sacred fountains and Elysian groves,
> And vales of bliss; the intellectual power,
> Bends from his awful throne, a wond'ring ear,
> And smiles.
>
> Pleasures of Imagination, I. 124

What I have now explained, concerning the use and effects of figures,
naturally leads us to reflect on the wonderful power of language; and, indeed, we cannot reflect on it without the highest admiration. What a fine
vehicle is it now become for all the conceptions of the human mind; even
for the most subtile and delicate workings of the imagination! What a pli-
able and flexible instrument in the hand of one who can employ it skilfully; prepared to take every form which he chooses to give it! Not content
with a simple communication of ideas and thoughts, it paints those ideas to
the eye; it gives colouring and relievo, even to the most abstract conceptions. In the figures which it uses, it sets mirrors before us, where we may
behold objects, a second time, in their likeness. It entertains us, as with a
succession of the most splendid pictures; disposes in the most artificial
manner, of the light and shade, for viewing every thing to the best advantage: in fine, from being a rude and imperfect interpreter of men's wants
and necessities, it has now passed into an instrument of the most delicate
and refined luxury.

To make these effects of figurative language sensible, there are few authors in the English language to whom I can refer with more advantage
than Mr. Addison, whose imagination is at once remarkably rich, and remarkably correct and chaste. When he is treating, for instance, of the effect
which light and colours have to entertain the fancy, considered in Mr.
Locke's view of them as secondary qualities, which have no real existence
in matter, but are only ideas of the mind, with what beautiful painting has
he adorned this philosophic speculation! "Things," says he, "would make
but a poor appearance to the eye, if we saw them only in their proper figures and motions. Now, we are everywhere entertained with pleasing shows
and apparitions; we discover imaginary glories in the heavens, and in the
earth, and see some of this visionary beauty poured out upon the whole
creation. But what a rough unsightly sketch of nature should we be enter-

tained with, did all her colouring disappear, and the several distinctions of light and shade vanish? In short, our souls are at present delightfully lost, and bewildered in a pleasing delusion: and we walk about like the enchanted hero of a romance, who sees beautiful castles, woods, and meadows: and at the same time hears the warbling of birds, and the purling of streams; but, upon the finishing of some secret spell, the fantastic scene breaks up, and the disconsolate knight finds himself on a barren heath, or in a solitary desert. It is not improbable, that something like this may be the state of the soul after its first separation, in respect of the images it will receive from matter" (No. 413, Spectator).

Having thus explained, at sufficient length, the origin, the nature, and the effects of tropes, I should proceed next to the several kinds and divisions of them. But, in treating of these, were I to follow the common tract of the scholastic writers on rhetoric, I should soon become tedious, and, I apprehend, useless at the same time. Their great business has been, with a most patient and frivolous industry, to branch them out under a vast number of divisions, according to all the several modes in which a word may be carried from its literal meaning, into one that is figurative, without doing any more; as if the mere knowledge of the names and classes of all the tropes that can be formed, could be of any advantage towards the proper, or graceful use of language. All that I purpose is, tò give, in a few words, before finishing this lecture, a general view of the several sources whence the tropical meaning of words is derived: after which I shall, in subsequent lectures, descend to a more particular consideration of some of the most considerable figures of speech, and such as are in most frequent use; by treating of which, I shall give all the instruction I can, concerning the proper employment of figurative language, and point out the errors and abuses which are apt to be committed in this part of style.

All tropes, as I before observed, are founded on the relation which one object bears to another; in virtue of which, the name of the one can be substituted instead of the name of the other, and by such a substitution, the vivacity of the idea is commonly meant to be increased. These relations, some more, some less intimate, may all give rise to tropes. One of the first and most obvious relations, is that between a cause and its effect. Hence, in figurative language, the cause is sometimes put for the effect. Thus, Mr. Addison, writing of Italy:

> Blossoms, and fruits, and flowers, together rise,
> And the whole year in gay confusion lies.

Where the "whole year" is plainly intended, to signify the effects or productions of all the seasons of the year. At other times, again, the effect is put for the cause; as, "gray hairs" frequently for old age, which causes gray hairs; and "shade," for trees that produce the shade. The relation between the container and the thing contained, is also so intimate and obvious, as naturally to give rise to tropes:

> Ille impiger hausit
> Spumantem pateram et pleno se proluit auro.

Where everyone sees, that the cup and the gold are put for the liquor that was contained in the golden cup. In the same manner, the name of any country is often used to denote the inhabitants of that country; and Heaven, very often employed to signify God, because he is conceived as dwelling in Heaven. To implore the assistance of Heaven, is the same as to implore the assistance of God. The relation betwixt any established sign and the thing signified, is a further source of tropes. Hence,

> Cedant arma togæ; concedat laurea linguæ.

The "toga," being the badge of the civil professions, and the "laurel" of military honours, the badge of each is put for the civil and military characters themselves. To "assume the sceptre," is a common phrase for entering on royal authority. To tropes, founded on these several relations, of cause and effect, container and contained, sign and thing signified, is given the name of Metonymy.

When the trope is founded on the relation between an antecedent and a consequent, or what goes before, and immediately follows, it is then called a Metalepsis; as in the Roman phrase of *"Fuit,"* or *"Vixit,"* to express that one was dead. *"Fuit Ilium et ingens gloria Dardanidum,"* signifies, that the glory of Troy is now no more.

When the whole is put for a part, or a part for the whole; a genus for a species, or a species for a genus; the singular for the plural, or the plural for the singular number; in general when any thing less, or any thing more, is put for the precise object meant; the figure is then called a Synecdoche. It is very common, for instance, to describe a whole object by some remarkable part of it; as when we say, "a fleet of so many sail," in the place of "ships;" when we use the "head" for the "person," the "pole" for the "earth," the "waves" for the "sea." In like manner, an attribute may be put for a subject; as, "youth and beauty," for "the young and beautiful;" and sometimes a subject for its attribute. But it is needless to insist longer on this enumeration, which serves little purpose. I have said enough, to give an opening into that great variety of relations between objects, by means of which, the mind is assisted to pass easily from one to another; and understands, by the name of the one, the other to be meant. It is always some accessory idea, which recalls the principal to the imagination; and commonly recalls it with more force, than if the principal idea had been expressed.

The relation which is far the most fruitful of tropes I have not yet mentioned; that is, the relation of similitude and resemblance. On this is founded what is called the metaphor; when, in place of using the proper name of any object, we employ, in its place, the name of some other which is like it; which is a sort of picture of it, and which thereby awakens the conception of it with more force or grace. This figure is more frequent than all the rest put together; and the language, both of prose and verse, owes to it much of its elegance and grace. This, therefore, deserves very full and particular consideration; and shall be the subject of the next lecture.

From Lecture XIX

DIRECTIONS FOR FORMING A STYLE

It will be more to the purpose, that I conclude these dissertations upon style, with a few directions concerning the proper method of attaining a good style, in general; leaving the particular character of that style to be either formed by the subject on which we write, or prompted by the bent of genius.

The first direction which I give for this purpose, is, to study clear ideas on the subject concerning which we are to write or speak. This is a direction which may at first appear to have small relation to style. Its relation to it, however, is extremely close. The foundation of all good style, is good sense, accompanied with a lively imagination. The style and thoughts of a writer are so intimately connected, that, as I have several times hinted, it is frequently hard to distinguish them. Wherever the impressions of things upon our minds are faint and indistinct, or perplexed and confused, our style in treating of such things will infallibly be so too. Whereas, what we conceive clearly and feel strongly, we shall naturally express with clearness and with strength. This, then, we may be assured, as a capital rule as to style, to think closely of the subject, till we have attained a full and distinct view of the matter which we are to clothe in words, till we become warm and interested in it; then and not till then, shall we find expression begin to flow. Generally speaking, the best and most proper expressions, are those which a clear view of the subject suggests, without much labour or inquiry after them. This is Quintilian's observation, Bk. VIII, chap. 1: "The most proper words for the most part adhere to the thoughts which are to be expressed by them, and may be discovered as by their own light. But we hunt after them, as if they were hidden, and only to be found in a corner. Hence instead of conceiving the words to lie near the subject, we go in quest of them to some other quarter, and endeavour to give force to the expressions we have found out."

In the second place, in order to form a good style, the frequent practice of composing is indispensably necessary. Many rules concerning style I have delivered, but no rules will answer the end, without exercise and habit. At the same time, it is not every sort of composing that will improve style. This is so far from being the case, that by frequent, careless, and hasty composition, we shall acquire certainly a very bad style; we shall have more trouble afterwards in unlearning faults, and correcting negligences, than if we had not been accustomed to composition at all. In the beginning, therefore, we ought to write slowly and with much care. Let the facility and speed of writing, be the fruit of longer practice. Says Quintilian, with the greatest reason, "I enjoin, that such as are beginning the practice of composition, write slowly and with anxious deliberation. Their great object at first should be, to write as well as possible; practice will enable them to write speedily. By degrees, matter will offer itself still more readily; words will be at hand; composition will flow; every thing as in the arrangement of a well-ordered family, will present itself in its proper place. The sum of the whole is this; by hasty composition, we shall never acquire the art of composing well; by writing well, we shall come to write speedily."

We must observe, however, that there may be an extreme, in too great and anxious care about words. We must not retard the course of thought, nor cool the heat of imagination, by pausing too long on every word we employ. There is, on certain occasions, a glow of composition which should be kept up, if we hope to express ourselves happily, though at the expense of allowing some inadvertencies to pass. A more severe examination of these must be left to be the work of correction. For, if the practice of composition be useful, the laborious work of correcting is no less so: it is indeed absolutely necessary to our reaping any benefit from the habit of composition. What we have written, should be laid by for some little time, till the ardour of composition be past, till the fondness for the expressions we have used be worn off, and the expressions themselves be forgotten; and then, reviewing our work with a cool and critical eye, as if it were the performance of another, we shall discern many imperfections which at first escaped us. Then is the season for pruning redundances; for weighing the arrangement of sentences; for attending to the juncture and connecting particles; and bring style into a regular, correct, and supported form. This "Limæ Labor," must be submitted to by all who would communicate their thoughts with proper advantage to others; and some practice in it will soon sharpen their eye to the most necessary objects of attention, and render it a much more easy and practicable work than might at first be imagined.

In the third place, with respect to the assistance that is to be gained from the writings of others, it is obvious, that we ought to render ourselves well acquainted with the style of the best authors. This is requisite both in order to form a just taste in style, and to supply us with a full stock of words on every subject. In reading authors with a view to style, attention should be given to the peculiarities of their different manners; and in this, and former lectures, I have endeavoured to suggest several things that may be useful in this view. I know no exercise that will be found more useful for acquiring a proper style, than to translate some passages from an eminent English author, into our own words. What I mean is, to take, for instance, some page of one of Mr. Addison's Spectators, and read it carefully over two or three times, till we have got a firm hold of the thoughts contained in it; then to lay aside the book; to attempt to write out the passage from memory, in the best way we can; and having done so, next to open the book, and compare what we have written with the style of the author. Such an exercise will, by comparison, show us where the defects of our style lie; will lead us to the proper attentions for rectifying them, and, among the different ways in which the same thought may be expressed, will make us perceive that which is the most beautiful.

In the fourth place, I must caution, at the same time, against a servile imitation of any author whatever. This is always dangerous. It hampers genius; it is likely to produce a stiff manner; and those who are given to close imitation, generally imitate an author's faults as well as his beauties. No man will ever become a good writer or speaker, who has not some degree of confidence to follow his own genius. We ought to beware, in particular, of adopting any author's noted phrases, or transcribing passages from him. Such a habit will prove fatal to all genuine composition. Infinitely better it is to have something that is our own, though of moderate beauty, than to affect to shine in borrowed ornaments, which will, at last, betray the utter poverty of our genius. On these heads of composing, correcting, reading, and imitating, I advise every student of oratory to consult what Quintilian has delivered in the tenth book of his Institutions, where he will find a variety of excellent observations and directions, that well deserve attention.

In the fifth place, it is an obvious, but material rule, with respect to style, that we always study to adapt it to the subject, and also to the capacity of our hearers, if we are to speak in public. Nothing merits the name of eloquent or beautiful, which is not suited to the occasion, and to the persons to whom it is addressed. It is to the last degree awkward and absurd, to attempt a poetical florid style, on occasions when it should be our business only to argue and reason; or to speak with elaborate pomp of expression, before persons who comprehend nothing of it, and who can only stare at our unseasonable magnificence. These are defects not so much in point of style, as, what is much worse, in point of common sense. When we begin to write or speak, we ought previously to fix in our minds a clear conception of the end to be aimed at; to keep this steadily in our view, and to suit our style to it. If we do not sacrifice to this great object every ill-timed ornament that may occur to our fancy, we are unpardonable; and though children and fools may admire, men of sense will laugh at us and our style.

In the last place, I cannot conclude the subject without this admonition, that in any case, and on any occasion, attention to style must not engross us so much, as to detract from a higher degree of attention to the thoughts. "*Curam verborum,*" says the great Roman critic, "rerum volo esse solicitudinem." (To your expressions be attentive: but about your matter be solicitous.) A direction the more necessary, as the present taste of the age in writing, seems to lean more to style than to thought. It is much easier to dress up trivial and common sentiments with some beauty of expression, than to afford a fund of vigorous, ingenious, and useful thoughts. The latter, requires true genius; the former may be attained by industry, with the help of very superficial parts. Hence, we find so many writers frivolously rich in style, but wretchedly poor in sentiment. The public ear is now so much accustomed to a correct and ornamented style, that no writer can, with safety, neglect the study of it. But he is a contemptible one who does not look to something beyond it; who does not lay the chief stress upon his matter, and employ such ornaments of style to recommend it, as are manly, not foppish. As Quintilian says, "A higher spirit ought to animate those who study eloquence. They ought to consult the health and soundness of the whole body, rather than bend their attention to such trifling objects as paring the nails, and dressing the hair. Let ornament be manly and chaste, without effeminate gayety, or artificial colouring; let it shine with the glow of health and strength."

꙾.꙾.꙾.꙾.꙾.꙾.

Lecture XXIV

CRITICAL EXAMINATION OF THE STYLE IN A PASSAGE OF DEAN SWIFT'S WRITINGS

My design in the four preceding lectures, was not merely to appreciate the merit of Mr. Addison's style, by pointing out the faults and the beauties that are mingled in the writings of that great author. They were not composed with any view to gain the reputation of a critic: but intended for the assistance of such as are desirous of studying the most proper and elegant construction of sentences in the English language. To such, it is hoped, that they may be of advantage; as the proper application of rules respecting style, will always be best learned by means of the illustration which examples afford. I conceive that examples, taken from the writings of an author so justly esteemed, would on that account, not only be more attended to, but would also produce this good effect, of familarizing those who study composition with the style of a writer, from whom they may, upon the whole, derive great benefit. With the same view, I shall, in this lecture, give one critical exercise more of the same kind, upon the style of an author, of a different character, Dean Swift; repeating the intimation I gave formerly, that such as stand in need of no assistance of this kind, and who, therefore, will naturally consider such minute discussions concerning the propriety of words, and structure of sentences, as beneath their attention, had best pass over what will seem to them a tedious part of the work.

I formerly gave the general character of Dean Swift's style. He is esteemed one of our most correct writers. His style is of the plain and simple kind; free from all affectation, and all superfluity; perspicuous, manly, and pure. These are its advantages. But we are not to look for much ornament and grace in it.[1] On the contrary, Dean Swift seems to have slighted and despised the ornaments of language, rather than to have studied them. His arrangement is often loose and negligent. In elegant, musical, and figurative language, he is much inferior to Mr. Addison. His manner of writing carries in it the character of one who rests altogether upon his sense, and aims at no more than giving his meaning in a clear and concise manner.

That part of his writings which I shall now examine, is the beginning of his treatise, entitled, "A Proposal for correcting, improving and ascertaining the English Tongue," in a letter addressed to the Earl of Oxford, then Lord High Treasurer. I was led, by the nature of the subject, to choose this treatise; but, in justice to the Dean, I must observe, that, after having examined it, I do not esteem it one of his most correct productions; but am apt to think it has been more hastily composed than some other of them. It bears the title and form of a letter; but it is, however, in truth, a treatise designed for the public; and therefore, in examining it, we cannot proceed upon the indulgence due to an epistolary correspondence. When a man addresses himself to a friend only, it is sufficient if he makes himself fully understood by him; but when an author writes for the public, whether he employ the form of an epistle or not, we are always entitled to expect, that he shall express himself with accuracy and care. Our author begins thus:

"What I had the honour of mentioning to your Lordship, some time ago, in conversation, was not a new thought, just then started by accident or occasion, but the result of long reflection; and I have been confirmed in my sentiments by the opinion of some very judicious persons with whom I consulted."

The disposition of circumstances in a sentence, such as serve to limit or to qualify some assertion, or to denote time and place, I formerly showed to be a matter of nicety; and I observed, that it ought to be always held a rule, not to crowd such circumstances together, but rather to intermix them with more capital words, in such different parts of the sentence as can admit them naturally. Here are two circumstances of this kind placed together, which had better had been separated; *Sometime ago in conversation*—better thus: *What I had the honour, sometime ago, of mentioning to your lordship in conversation—was not a new thought,* proceeds our author, *started by accident or occasion:* the different meaning of these two words may not at first occur. They have, however, a distinct meaning, and

---

[1] I am glad to find that, in my judgment concerning this author's composition I have coincided with the opinion of a very able critic. "This easy and safe conveyance of meaning, it was Swift's desire to attain, and for having attained, he certainly deserves praise, though perhaps, not the highest praise. For purposes merely didactic, when something is to be told that was not known before, it is in the highest degree proper; but against that inattention by which known truths are suffered to be neglected, it makes no provision; it instructs, but does not persuade." Johnson's *Lives of the Poets.*

are properly used: for it is one very laudable property of our author's style, that it is seldom encumbered with superfluous, synonymous words. *Started by accident,* is, fortuitously, or at random; started *by occasion,* is by some incident, which at that time gave birth to it. His meaning is, that it was not a new thought which either casually sprung up in his mind, or was suggested to him for the first time, by the train of the discourse: but, as he adds, *was the result of long reflection.* He proceeds:

"They all agreed, that nothing would be of greater use towards the improvement of knowledge and politeness, than some effectual method for correcting, enlarging, and ascertaining our language; and they think it a work very possible to be compassed under the protection of a prince, the countenance and encouragement of a ministry, and the care of proper persons chosen for such an undertaking."

This is an excellent sentence; clear, and elegant. The words are all simple, well chosen, and expressive; and are arranged in the most proper order. It is a harmonious period too, which is a beauty not frequent in our author. The last part of it consists of three members, which gradually rise and swell one above another, without any affected or unsuitable pomp; *under the protection of a prince, the countenance and encouragement of a ministry, and the care of proper persons chosen for such an undertaking.* We may remark, in the beginning of the sentence, the proper use of the preposition *towards—greater use towards the improvement of knowledge and politeness*—importing the pointing or tendency of anything to a certain end; which could not have been so well expressed by the preposition *for,* commonly employed in place of *towards,* by authors who are less attentive, than Dean Swift was, to the force of words.

One fault might, perhaps, be found, both with this and the former sentence, considered as introductory ones. We expect, that an introduction is to unfold, clearly and directly, the subject that is to be treated of. In the first sentence, our author has told us, of a thought he mentioned to his Lordship in conversation, which had been the result of long reflection, and concerning which he had consulted judicious persons. But what that thought was, we are never told directly. We gather it indeed from the second sentence, wherein he informs us, in what these judicious persons agreed; namely, that some method for improving the language was both useful and practicable. But this indirect method of opening the subject, would have been very faulty in a regular treatise; though the ease of the epistolary form, which our author here assumes in addressing his patron, may excuse it in the present case.

"I was glad to find your Lordship's answer in so different a style from what hath commonly been made use of, on the like occasions, for some years past; *that all such thoughts must be deferred to a time of peace;* a topic which some have carried so far, that they would not have us, by any means, think of preserving our civil and religious constitution, because we are engaged in a war abroad."

This sentence also is clear and elegant; only there is one inaccuracy, when he speaks of his Lordship's *answer* being in so different a style from what had formerly been used. His *answer* to what? or to whom? For from anything going before, it does not appear that any application or address had been made to his Lordship by those persons, whose opinion was mentioned in the preceding sentence; and to whom the answer, here spoken of, naturally refers. There is a little indistinctness, as I before observed, in our author's manner of introducing his subject here. We may observe too that the phrase, *glad to find your answer in so different a style,* though abundantly suited to the language of conversation, or of a familiar letter, yet, in regular composition, requires an additional word—*glad to find your answer run in so different a style.*

"It will be among the distinguishing marks of your ministry, my Lord, that you have a genius above all such regards, and that no reasonable proposals, for the honour, the advantage, or ornament of your country, however foreign to your immediate office, was ever neglected by you."

The phrase, *a genius above all such regards,* both seems somewhat harsh, and does not clearly express what the author means, namely, the *confined views* of those who neglected every thing that belonged to the arts of peace in the time of war. Except this expression, there is nothing that can be subject to the least reprehension in this sentence, nor in all that follows, to the end of the paragraph.

"I confess, the merit of this candour and condescension is very much lessened, because your Lordship hardly leaves us room to offer our good wishes; removing all our difficulties, and supplying our wants, faster than the most visionary projector can adjust his schemes. And therefore, my Lord, the design of this paper is not so much to offer you ways and means, as to complain of a grievance, the redressing of which is to be your own work, as much as that of paying the nation's debts, or opening a trade into the South sea; and, though not of such immediate benefit as either of these, or any other of your glorious actions, yet, perhaps, in future ages, not less to your honour."

The compliments which the Dean here pays to his patron, are very high and strained; and show that, with all his surliness, he was as capable, on some occasions, of making his court to a great man by flattery, as other writers. However, with respect to the style, which is the sole object of our present consideration, everything here, as far as appears to me, is faultless. In these sentences, and, indeed, throughout this paragraph, in general, which we have now ended, our author's style appears to great advantage. We see that ease and simplicity, that correctness and distinctness, which particularly characterize it. It is very remarkable, how few Latinised words Dean Swift employs. No writer, in our language, is so purely English as he is, or borrows so little assistance from words of foreign derivation. From none can we take a better model of the choice and proper significancy of words. It is remarkable, in the sentences we have now before us, how plain all the expressions are, and yet, at the same time, how significant; and, in the midst of that high strain of compliment into which he rises, how little there is of pomp, or glare of expression. How very few writers can preserve this manly temperance of style; or would think of compliment of this nature supported with sufficient dignity, unless they had embellished it with some of those high-sounding words, whose chief effect is no other than to give their language a stiff and forced appearance?

"My Lord, I do here, in the name of all the learned and polite persons of the nation, complain to your Lordship, as first minister, that our language is extremely imperfect; that its daily improvements are by no means in proportion to its daily corruptions; that the pretenders to polish and refine it, have chiefly multiplied abuses and absurdities; and that, in many instances, it offends against every part of grammar."

The turn of this sentence is extremely elegant. He had spoken before of a grievance for which he sought redress, and he carries on the allusion, by entering here directly on his subject, in the style of a public representation presented to the minister of state. One imperfection, however, there is in this sentence, which luckily for our purpose, serves to illustrate a rule before given, concerning the position of adverbs, so as to avoid ambiguity. It is in the middle of the sentence; *that the pretenders to polish and refine it, have chiefly multiplied abuses and absurdities.* Now, concerning the import of this adverb, *chiefly*, I ask, whether it signifies that these pretenders to polish the language, have been the *chief persons* who have multiplied its abuses, in distinction *from others,* or, that the *chief thing* which these pretenders have done, is to multiply the abuses of our language in opposition to their *doing any thing to refine it?* These two meanings are really different; and yet, by the position which the word *chiefly* has in the sentence, we are left at a loss in which to understand it. The construction would lead us rather to the latter sense; that the chief thing which these pretenders have done, is to multiply the abuses of our language. But it is more than probable, that the former sense was what the Dean intended, as it carries more of his usual satirical edge; "that the pretended refiners of our language were, in fact, its chief corrupters;" on which supposition, his words ought to have run thus: *that the pretenders to polish and refine it, have been the chief persons to multiply its abuses and absurdities;* which would have rendered the sense perfectly clear.

Perhaps, too, there might be ground for observing farther upon this sentence, that as language is the object with which it sets out; *that our language is extremely imperfect;* and as there follows an enumeration concerning language, in three particulars, it had been better if language had been kept the ruling word, or the nominative to every verb, without changing the construction; by making *pretenders* the ruling word, as is done in the second member of the enumeration, and then, in the third, returning again to the former word, *language. That the pretenders to polish—and that, in many instances, it offends*—I am persuaded, that the structure of the sentence would have been more neat and happy, and its unity more complete, if the members of it had been arranged thus: "That our language is extremely imperfect; that its daily improvements are by no means in proportion to its daily corruptions; that, in many instances, it offends against every part of grammar: and that the pretenders to polish and refine it, have been the chief persons to multiply its abuses and absurdities." This degree of attention seemed proper to be bestowed on such a sentence as this, in order to show how it might have been conducted after the most perfect manner. Our author, after having said,

"Lest your Lordship should think my censure too severe, I shall take leave to be more particular;" proceeds in the following paragraph:

"I believe your Lordship will agree with me, in the reason why our language is less refined than those of Italy, Spain, or France."

I am sorry to say, that now we shall have less to commend in our author. For the whole of this paragraph, on which we are entering, is in truth, perplexed and inaccurate. Even in this short sentence, we may discern an inaccuracy—*why our language is less refined than those of Italy, Spain, or France;* putting the pronoun *those* in the plural, when the antecedent substantive to which it refers is in the singular, *our language.* Instances of this kind may sometimes be found in English authors; but they sound harsh to the ear, and are certainly contrary to the purity of grammar. By a very little attention, this inaccuracy might have been remedied; and the sentence have been made to run much better in this way; "why our language is less refined than the Italian, Spanish, or French."

"It is plain, that the Latin tongue, in its purity, was never in this island; towards the conquest of which, few or no attempts were made till the time of Claudius; neither was that language ever so vulgar in Britain, as it is known to have been in Gaul and Spain."

To say that *the Latin tongue, in its purity, was never in this island,* is very careless style; it ought to have been, *was never spoken in this island.* In the progress of the sentence, he means to give a reason why the Latin was never spoken in its purity amongst us, because our island was not conquered by the Romans till after the purity of their tongue began to decline. But this reason ought to have been brought out more clearly. This might easily have been done, and the relation of the several parts of the sentence to each other much better pointed out by means of a small variation; thus: "It is plain that the Latin tongue in its purity was never spoken in this island, as few or no attempts towards the conquest of it were made till the time of Claudius." He adds, *neither was that language ever so vulgar in Britain. Vulgar* was one of the worst words he could have chosen for expressing what he means here: namely, that the Latin tongue was at no time so *general,* or so much in *common use,* in Britain, as it is known to have been in Gaul and Spain. *Vulgar,* when applied to language, commonly signifies impure, or debased language, such as is spoken by the low people, which is quite opposite to the author's sense here; for, instead of meaning to say, that the Latin spoken in Britain was not so debased, as what was spoken in Gaul and Spain; he means just the contrary, and had been telling us, that we never were acquainted with the Latin at all, till its purity began to be corrupted.

"Further, we find that the Roman legions here, were at length all recalled to help their country against the Goths and other barbarous invaders."

The chief scope of this sentence is, to give a reason why the Latin tongue did not strike any deep root in this island, on account of the short continuance of the Romans in it. He goes on:

"Meantime the Britons, left to shift for themselves, and daily harassed by cruel inroads from the Picts, were forced to call in the Saxons for their defence; who, consequently, reduced the greatest part of the island to their own power, drove the Britons into the most remote and mountainous parts, and the rest of the country, in customs, religion, and language, became wholly Saxon."

This is a very exceptionable sentence. First, the phrase *left to shift for themselves,* is rather a low phrase, and too much in the familiar style to be proper in a grave treatise. Next as the sentence advances—*forced to call in the Saxons for their defence, who consequently reduced the greatest part of the island to their own power.* What is the meaning of *consequently* here? If it means "afterwards," or, "in progress of time," this, certainly, is not a sense in which *consequently* is often taken; and therefore the expression is chargeable with obscurity. The adverb, *consequently,* in its most common acceptation, denotes one thing following from another, as an effect from a cause. If he uses it in this sense, and means that the Britons being subdued by the Saxons, was a necessary consequence of their having called in these Saxons to their assistance, this consequence is drawn too abruptly, and needed more explanation. For though it has often happened, that nations have been subdued by their own auxiliaries, yet this is not a consequence of such a nature that it can be assumed, as it seems here to be done, for a first and self-evident principle. But further, what shall we say to this phrase, *reduced the greatest part of the island to their own power?* we say, *reduce to rule, reduce to practice;* we can say, that *one nation reduces another to subjection.* But when *dominion* or *power* is used, we always, as far as I know, say, *reduce under their power. Reduce to their power,* is so harsh and uncommon an expression, that, though Dean Swift's authority in language be very great, yet in the use of this phrase, I am of opinion that it would not be safe to follow his example.

Besides these particular inaccuracies, this sentence is chargeable with want of unity in the composition of the whole. The persons and the scene are too often changed upon us. First, the Britons are mentioned, who are harassed by inroads from the Picts; next, the Saxons appear, who subdue the greatest part of the island, and drive the Britons into the mountains; and, lastly, the rest of the country is introduced, and a description given of the change made upon it. All this forms a group of various objects, presented in such quick succession, that the mind finds it difficult to comprehend them under one view. Accordingly, it is quoted in the Elements of Criticism, as an instance of a sentence rendered faulty by the breach of unity.

"This I take to be the reason why there are more Latin words remaining in the British than the old Saxon; which, excepting some few variations in the orthography, is the same in most original words with our present English, as well as with the German and other northern dialects."

This sentence is faulty, somewhat in the same manner with the last. It is loose in the connexion of its parts; and besides this, it is also too loosely connected with the preceding sentence. What he had there said, concerning the Saxons expelling the Britons, and changing the customs, the religion, and the language of the country, is a clear and good reason for our present language being Saxon rather than British. This is the inference which we would naturally expect him to draw from the premises just before laid down: but when he tells us, that *this is the reason why there are more Latin words remaining in the British tongue than in the old Saxon,* we are presently at a stand. No reason for this inference appears. If it can be gathered at all from the foregoing deduction, it is gathered only imperfectly. For, as he had told us, that the Britons had *some* connexion with the Romans, he should have also told us, in order to make out his inference, that the Saxons never had *any.* The truth is, the whole of this paragraph concerning the influence of the Latin tongue upon ours, is careless, perplexed, and obscure. His argument required to have been more fully unfolded, in order to make it be distinctly apprehended, and to give it its due force. In the next paragraph, he proceeds to discourse concerning the influence of the French tongue upon our language. The style becomes more clear, though not remarkable for great beauty or elegance.

"Edward the Confessor having lived long in France, appears to be the first who introduced any mixture of the French tongue with the Saxon; the court affecting what the Prince was fond of, and others taking it up for a fashion, as it is now with us. William the Conqueror proceeded much further, bringing over with him vast numbers of that nation, scattering them in every monastery, giving them great quantities of land, directing all pleadings to be in that language, and endeavouring to make it universal in the kingdom."

On these two sentences, I have nothing of moment to observe. The sense is brought out clearly, and in simple, unaffected language.

"This, at least, is the opinion generally received; but your Lordship hath fully convinced me, that the French tongue made yet a greater progress here under Harry the Second, who had large territories on that continent both from his father and his wife; made frequent journeys and expeditions thither; and was always attended with a number of his countrymen, retainers at court."

In the beginning of this sentence, our author states an opposition between an opinion generally received, and that of his Lordship; and in compliment to his patron, he tells us, that his Lordship had convinced him of somewhat that differed from the general opinion. Thus one must naturally understand his words: *This, at least, is the opinion generally received; but your Lordship hath fully convinced me.*—Now here there must be an inaccuracy of expression. For on examining what went before, there appears no sort of opposition betwixt the generally received opinion, and that of the author's patron. The general opinion was, that William the Conqueror had proceeded much farther than Edward the Confessor, in propagating the French language, and had endeavoured to make it universal. Lord Oxford's opinion was, that the French tongue had gone on to make a yet greater progress under Harry the Second, than it had done under his predecessor William: which two opinions are as entirely consistent with each other, as any can be; and therefore the opposition here affected to be stated between them, by the adversative particle *but,* was improper and groundless.

"For some centuries after, there was a constant intercourse between France and England by the dominions we possessed there, and the conquests we made; so that our language, between two and three hundred years ago, seems to have had a greater mixture with French than at present; many words having been afterwards rejected, and some since the days of Spenser; although we have still retained not a few, which have been long antiquated in France."

This is a sentence too long and intricate, and liable to the same objection that was made to a former one, of the want of unity. It consists of four members, each divided from the subsequent by a semicolon. In going along, we naturally expect the sentence is to end at the second of these, or at farthest, at the third: when, to our surprise, a new member of the period makes its appearance, and fatigues our attention in joining all the parts together. Such a structure of a sentence is always the mark of careless writing. In the first member of the sentence, *a constant intercourse between France and England, by the dominions we possessed there, and the conquests we made,* the construction is not sufficiently filled up. In place of *intercourse by the dominions we possessed,* it should have been—*by reason of the dominions we possessed*—or—*occasioned by the dominions we possessed*—and in place of—*the dominions we possessed there, and the conquests we made,* the regular style is—*the dominions which we possessed there and the conquests which we made.* The relative pronoun *which,* is, indeed, in phrases of this kind, sometimes omitted. But, when it is omitted the style becomes elliptic; and though in conversation, or in the very light and easy kinds of writing, such elliptic style may not be improper, yet in grave and regular writing, it is better to fill up the construction, and insert the relative pronoun. After having said, *I could produce several instances of both kinds, if it were of any use or entertainment,* our author begins the next paragraph thus:

"To examine into the several circumstances by which the language of a country may be altered, would force me to enter into a wide field."

There is nothing remarkable in this sentence, unless that here occurs the first instance of a metaphor since the beginning of this treatise; *entering into a wide field,* being put for beginning an extensive subject. Few writers deal less in figurative language than Swift. I before observed, that he appears to despise ornaments of this kind; and though this renders his style somewhat dry on serious subjects, yet his plainness and simplicity, I must not forbear to remind my readers, is far preferable to an ostentatious and affected parade of ornament.

"I shall only observe, that the Latin, the French, and the English, seem to have undergone the same fortune. The first from the days of Romulus to those of Julius Cæsar, suffered perpetual changes; and by what we meet in those authors who occasionally speak on that subject, as well as from certain fragments of old laws, it is manifest that the Latin, three hundred years before Tully, was as unintelligible in his time, as the French and English of the same period are now; and these two have changed as much since William the Conqueror (which is but little less than 700 years) as the Latin appears to have done in the like term."

The Dean plainly appears to be writing negligently here. This sentence is one of that involved and intricate kind, of which some instances have occurred before; but none worse than this. It requires a very distinct head to comprehend the whole meaning of the period at first reading. In one part of it we find extreme carelessness of expression. He says, *It is manifest that the Latin, 300 years before Tully was as unintelligible in his time, as the English and French of the same period are now.* By the English and French *of the same period* must naturally be understood, *The English and French that were spoken three hundred years before Tully.* This is the only grammatical meaning his words will bear; and yet assuredly what he means, and what it would have been easy for him to have expressed with more precision, is, *the English and French that were spoken 300 years ago;* or at a period equally distant from our age as the old Latin, which he had mentioned, was from the age of Tully. But when an author writes hastily, and does not review with proper care what he has written, many such inaccuracies will be apt to creep into his style.

"Whether our language or the French will decline as fast as the Roman did, is a question that would perhaps admit more debate than it is worth. There were many reasons for the corruptions of the last; as the change of their government to a tyranny, which ruined the study of eloquence, there being no further use or encouragement for popular orators: their giving not only the freedom of the city, but capacity for employments, to several towns in Gaul, Spain, and Germany, and other distant parts, as far as Asia, which brought a great number of foreign pretenders to Rome; the slavish disposition of the senate and people, by which the wit and eloquence of the age where wholly turned into panegyric, the most barren of all subjects; the great corruption of manners, and introduction of foreign luxury, with foreign terms to express it, with several others that might be assigned; not to mention the invasions from the Goths and Vandals, which are too obvious to insist on."

In the enumeration here made of the causes contributing towards the corruption of the Roman language, there are many inaccuracies—*the change of their government to a tyranny:* Of whose government? He had indeed been speaking of the Roman language, and therefore we guess at his meaning; but his style is ungrammatical; for he had not mentioned the Romans themselves; and therefore, when he says *their government,* there is no antecedent in the sentence to which the pronoun *their* can refer with any propriety. *Giving the capacity for employments to several towns in Gaul,* is a questionable expression. For though towns are sometimes put for the people who inhabit them, yet to give a town *the capacity for employments,* sounds harsh and uncouth. *The wit and eloquence of the age wholly turned into panegyric,* is a phrase which does not well express the meaning. Neither wit nor eloquence can be turned into panegyric; but they may be turned *towards panegyric,* or, *employed in panegyric,* which was the sense the author had in view.

The conclusion of the enumeration is visibly incorrect—*the great corruption of manners, and introduction of foreign luxury with foreign terms to express it, with several others that might be assigned*—He means, *with several other reasons.* The word *reasons,* had indeed been mentioned before; but as it stands, at the distance of thirteen lines backward, the repetition of it here became indispensable in order to avoid ambiguity. *Not to mention,* he adds, *the invasions from the Goths and Vandals, which are too obvious to insist on.* One would imagine him to mean, that the invasions from the Goths and Vandals, are *historical facts* too well known and obvious to be insisted on. But he means quite a different thing, though he has not taken the proper method of expressing it, through his haste, probably, to finish the paragraph; namely, that these invasions from the Goths and Vandals, *were causes of the corruption of the Roman language too obvious to be insisted on.*

I shall not pursue this criticism any farther. I have been obliged to point out many inaccuracies in the passage which we have considered. But, in order that my observations may not be construed as meant to depreciate the style or the writings of Dean Swift below their just value, there are two remarks which I judge it necessary to make before concluding this lecture. One is, that it were unfair to estimate an author's style on the whole, by some passage in his writings, which chances to be composed in a careless manner. This is the case with respect to this treatise, which has much the appearance of a hasty production: though, as I before observed, it was by no means on that account that I pitched upon it for the subject of this exercise. But after having examined it, I am sensible that in many other of his writings, the Dean is more accurate.

My other observation, which is equally applicable to Dean Swift and Mr. Addison, is, that there may be writers much freer from such inaccuracies, as I have had occasion to point out in these two, whose style, however, upon the whole, may not have half their merit. Refinement in language has, of late years, begun to be much attended to. In several modern productions of very small value, I should find it difficult to point out many errors in language. The words might, probably, be all proper words, correctly and clearly arranged; and the turn of the sentence sonorous and musical; whilst yet the style, upon the whole, might deserve no praise. The fault often lies in what may be called the general cast, or complexion of the style; which a person of a good taste discerns to be vicious; to be feeble, for instance, and diffuse; flimsy or affected; petulant or ostentatious; though the faults cannot be so easily pointed out and particularized, as when they lie in some erroneous or negligent construction of a sentence. Whereas such writers as Addison and Swift, carry always those general characters of good style, which in the midst of their occasional negligences, every person of good taste must discern and approve. We see their faults overbalanced by higher beauties. We see a writer of sense and reflection expressing his sentiments without affectation, attentive to thoughts as well as to words; and, in the main current of his language, elegant and beautiful; and, therefore, the only proper use to be made of the blemishes which occur in the writings of such authors, is to point out to those who apply themselves to the study of composition, some of the rules which they ought to observe for avoiding such errors; and to render them sensible of the necessity of strict attention to language and to style. Let them imitate the ease and simplicity of those great authors; let them study to be always natural, and, as far as they can, always correct in their expressions: let them endeavour to be, at some times, lively and striking; but carefully avoid being at any time ostentatious and affected.

Lecture XXVII

DIFFERENT KINDS OF PUBLIC SPEAKING— ELOQUENCE OF POPULAR ASSEMBLIES— EXTRACTS FROM DEMOSTHENES

After the preliminary views which have been given of the nature of eloquence in general, and of the state in which it has subsisted in different ages and countries, I am now to enter on the consideration of the different kinds of public speaking, the distinguishing characters of each, and the rules which relate to them. The ancients divided all orations into three kinds; the demonstrative, the deliberative, and the judicial. The scope of the demonstrative was to praise or to blame; that of the deliberative, to advise or to dissuade; that of the judicial, to accuse or to defend. The chief subjects of demonstrative eloquence, were panegyrics, invectives, gratulatory and funeral orations. The deliberative was employed in matters of public concern, agitated in the senate, or before the assemblies of the people. The judicial is the same with the eloquence of the bar, employed in addressing judges, who have power to absolve or to condemn. This division runs through all the ancient treatises on rhetoric; and is followed by the moderns, who copy them. It is a division not inartificial; and comprehends most, or all, of the matters which can be the subject of public discourse. It will, however, suit our purpose better, and be found, I imagine, more useful to follow that division which the train of modern speaking naturally points out to us, taken from the three great scenes of eloquence, popular assemblies, the bar, and the pulpit; each of which has a distinct character that particularly suits it. This division coincides in part with the ancient one. The eloquence of the bar is precisely the same with what the ancients called the judicial. The eloquence of popular assemblies, though mostly of what they term the deliberative species, yet admits also of the demonstrative. The eloquence of the pulpit is altogether of a distinct nature, and cannot be properly reduced under any of the heads of the ancient rhetoricians.

To all the three, pulpit, bar, and popular assemblies, belong, in common, the rules concerning the conduct of a discourse in all its parts. Of these rules I purpose afterwards to treat at large. But before proceeding to them, I intend to show, first, what is peculiar to each of these three kinds of oratory, in their spirit, character, or manner. For every species of public speaking has a manner or character peculiarly suited to it; of which it is highly material to have a just idea, in order to direct the application of general rules. The eloquence of a lawyer is fundamentally different from that of a divine, or a speaker in parliament: and to have a precise and proper idea of the distinguishing character which any kind of public speaking requires, is the foundation of what is called a just taste in that kind of speaking.

Laying aside any question concerning the pre-eminence in point of rank, which is due to any one of the three kinds before mentioned, I shall begin with that which tends to throw most light upon the rest, viz. the eloquence of popular assemblies. The most august theatre for this kind of eloquence, to be found in any nation of Europe, is, beyond doubt, the parliament of Great Britain. In meetings, too, of less dignity, it may display itself. Wherever there is a popular court, or wherever any number of men are assembled for debate or consultation, there, in different forms, this species of eloquence may take place.

Its object is, or ought always to be, persuasion. There must be some end proposed; some point, most commonly of public utility or good, in favour of which we seek to determine the hearers. Now, in all attempts to persuade men, we must proceed upon this principle, that it is necessary to convince their understanding. Nothing can be more erroneous than to imagine, that, because speeches to popular assemblies admit more of a declamatory style than some other discourses, they therefore stand less in need of being supported by sound reasoning. When modelled upon this false idea, they may have the show, but never can produce the effect, of real eloquence. Even the show of eloquence which they make, will please only the trifling and superficial. For, with all tolerable judges, indeed almost with all men, mere declamation soon becomes insipid. Of whatever rank the hearers be, a speaker is never to presume, that by a frothy and ostentatious harangue, without solid sense and argument, he can either make impression on them, or acquire fame to himself. It is, at least, a dangerous experiment; for, where such an artifice succeeds once, it will fail ten times. Even the common people are better judges of argument and good sense, than we sometimes think them; and upon any question of business, a plain man, who speaks to the point without art, will generally prevail over the most artful speaker, who deals in flowers and ornament, rather than in reasoning. Much more, when public speakers address themselves to any assembly where there are persons of education and improved understanding, they ought to be careful not to trifle with their hearers.

Let it be ever kept in view, that the foundation of all that can be called eloquence, is good sense, and solid thought. As popular as the orations of Demosthenes were, spoken to all the citizens of Athens, every one who looks into them, must see how fraught they are with argument; and how important it appeared to him, to convince the understanding, in order to persuade, or to work on the principles of action. Hence their influence in his own time; hence their fame at this day. Such a pattern as this, public speakers ought to set before them for imitation, rather than follow the track of those loose and frothy declaimers, who have brought discredit on eloquence. Let it be their first study, in addressing any popular assembly to be previously masters of the business on which they are to speak; to be well provided with matter and argument; and to rest upon these the chief stress. This will always give to their discourse an air of manliness and strength, which is a powerful instrument of persuasion. Ornament, if they have genius for it, will follow of course: at any rate, it demands only their secondary study: *"Cura sit verborum; solicitudo rerum."* (To your expression be attentive; but about your matter be solicitous) is an advice of Quintilian, which cannot be too often recollected by all who study oratory.

In the next place, in order to be persuasive speakers in a popular assembly, it is, in my opinion, a capital rule, that we be ourselves persuaded of whatever we recommend to others. Never, when it can be avoided, ought we to espouse any side of the argument, but what we believe to be the true and the right one. Seldom or never will a man be eloquent, but when he is in earnest, and uttering his own sentiments. They are only the *"veræ voces ab imo pectore,"* the unassumed language of the heart or head, that carry the force of conviction. In a former lecture, when entering on this subject, I observed, that all high eloquence must be the offspring of passion, or warm emotion. It is this which makes every man persuasive; and gives a force to his genius, which it possesses at no other time. Under what disadvantage then is he placed, who, not feeling what he utters, must counterfeit a warmth to which he is a stranger.

I know, that young people, on purpose to train themselves to the art of speaking, imagine it useful to adopt that side of the question under debate, which, to themselves, appears the weakest, and to try what figure they can make upon it. But, I am afraid, this is not the most improving education for public speaking; and that it tends to form them to a habit of flimsy and trivial discourse. Such a liberty they should, at no time, allow themselves, unless in meetings where no real business is carried on, but where declamation and improvement of speech is the sole aim. Nor even in such meetings, would I recommend it as the most useful exercise. They will improve themselves to more advantage, and acquit themselves with more honour, by choosing always that side of the debate to which, in their own judgment, they are most inclined, and supporting it by what seems to themselves most solid and persuasive. They will acquire the habit of reasoning closely, and expressing themselves with warmth and force, much more when they are adhering to their own sentiments, than when they are speaking in contradiction to them. In assemblies where any real business is carried on, whether that business be of much importance or not, it is always of dangerous consequence for young practitioners to make trial of this sort of play of speech. It may fix an imputation on their characters before they are aware; and what they intended merely as amusement, may be turned to the discredit, either of their principles or their understanding.

Debate in popular courts, seldom allows the speaker that full and accurate preparation beforehand, which the pulpit always, and the bar sometimes, admits. The arguments must be suited to the course which the debate takes; and as no man can exactly foresee this, one who trusts to a set speech, composed in his closet, will, on many occasions, be thrown out of the ground which he had taken. He will find it pre-occupied by others, or his reasonings superseded by some new turn of the business; and, if he ventures to use his prepared speech, it will be frequently at the hazard of making an awkward figure. There is a general prejudice with us, and not wholly an unjust one, against set speeches in public meetings. The only occasion, when they have any propriety, is, at the opening of a debate, when the speaker has it in his power to choose his field. But as the debate advances, and parties warm, discourses of this kind become more unsuitable. They want the native air; the appearance of being suggested by the business that is going on; study and ostentation are apt to be visible; and, of course, though applauded as elegant, they are seldom so persuasive as more free and unconstrained discourses.

This, however, does not by any means conclude against premeditation of what we are to say; the neglect of which, and the trusting wholly to extemporaneous efforts, will unavoidably produce the habit of speaking in a loose and undigested manner. But the premeditation which is of most advantage, in the case which we now consider, is of the subject or argument in general, rather than of nice composition in any particular branch of it. With regard to the matter, we cannot be too accurate in our preparation, so as to be fully masters of the business under consideration; but with regard to words and expression, it is very possible so far to overdo, as to render our speech stiff and precise. Indeed, till once persons acquire that firmness, that presence of mind, and command of expression, in a public meeting, which nothing but habit and practice can bestow, it may be proper for a young speaker to commit to memory the whole of what he is to say. But after some performances of this kind shall have given him boldness, he will find it the better method not to confine himself so strictly; but only to write, beforehand, some sentences with which he intends to set out, in order to put himself fairly in the train; and, for the rest, to set down short notes of the topics, or principal thoughts upon which he is to insist, in their order, leaving the words to be suggested by the warmth of discourse. Such short notes of the substance of the discourse, will be found of considerable service, to those, especially, who are beginning to speak in public. They will accustom them to some degree of accuracy, which, if they speak frequently, they are in danger too soon of losing. They will even accustom them to think more closely on the subject in question; and will assist them greatly in arranging their thoughts with method and order.

This leads me next to observe, that in all kinds of public speaking, nothing is of greater consequence than a proper and clear method. I mean not that formal method of laying down heads and subdivisions, which is commonly practised in the pulpit; and which, in popular assemblies, unless the speaker be a man of great authority and character, and the subject of great importance, and the preparation too very accurate, is rather in hazard of disgusting the hearers; such an introduction is presenting always the melancholy prospect of a long discourse. But though the method be not laid down in form, no discourse, of any length, should be without method; that is, every thing should be found in its proper place. Every one who speaks, will find it of the greatest advantage to himself to have previously arranged his thoughts, and classed under proper heads, in his own mind, what he is to deliver. This will assist his memory, and carry him through his discourse without that confusion to which one is every moment subject who has fixed no distinct plan of what he is to say. And with respect to the hearers, order in discourse is absolutely necessary for making any proper impression. It adds both force and light to what is said. It makes them accompany the speaker easily and readily, as he goes along; and makes them feel the full effect of every argument which he employs. Few things, therefore, deserve more to be attended to, than distinct arrangement; for eloquence, however great, can never produce entire conviction without it. Of the rules of method, and the proper distribution of the several parts of a discourse, I am hereafter to treat.

Let us now consider the style and expression suited to the eloquence of popular assemblies. Beyond doubt, these give scope for the most animated manner of public speaking. The very aspect of a large assembly, engaged in some debate of moment, and attentive to the discourse of one man, is sufficient to inspire that man with such elevation and warmth, as both gives rise to strong impressions, and gives them propriety. Passion easily rises in a great assembly, where the movements are communicated by mutual sympathy between the orator and the audience. Those bold figures, of which I treated formerly as the native language of passion, have then their proper place. That ardour of speech, that vehemence and glow of sentiment, which arise from a mind animated and inspired by some great and public object, form the peculiar characteristics of popular eloquence, in its highest degree of perfection.

The liberty, however, which we are now giving of the strong and passionate manner to this kind of oratory, must be always understood with certain limitations and restraints, which, it will be necessary to point out distinctly, in order to guard against dangerous mistakes on this subject.

As, first, the warmth which we express must be suited to the occasion and the subject; for nothing can be more preposterous, than an attempt to introduce great vehemence into a subject, which is either of slight importance, or which, by its nature, requires to be treated of calmly. A temperate tone of speech, is that for which there is most frequent occasion; and he who is, on every subject, passionate and vehement, will be considered as a blusterer, and meet with little regard.

In the second place, we must take care never to counterfeit warmth without feeling it. This always betrays persons into an unnatural manner, which exposes them to ridicule. For, as I have often suggested, to support the appearance, without the real feeling of passion, is one of the most difficult things in nature. The disguise can almost never be so perfect, as not to be discovered. The heart can only answer to the heart. The great rule here, as indeed in every other case, is, to follow nature; never to attempt a strain of eloquence which is not seconded by our own genius. One may be a speaker, both of much reputation and much influence, in the calm argumentative manner. To attain the pathetic, and the sublime of oratory, requires those strong sensibilities of mind, and that high power of expression, which are given to few.

In the third place, even when the subject justifies the vehement manner, and when genius prompts it; when warmth is felt, not counterfeited; we must still set a guard on ourselves, not to allow impetuosity to transport us too far. Without emotion in the speaker, eloquence, as was before observed, will never produce its highest effects; but at the same time, if the speaker lose command of himself, he will soon lose command of his audience too. He must never kindle too soon: he must begin with moderation; and study to carry his hearers along with him, as he warms in the progress of his discourse. For, if he runs before in the course of passion, and leaves them behind; if they are not tuned, if we may speak so, in unison to him, the discord will presently be felt, and be very grating. Let a speaker have ever so good reason to be animated and fired by his subject, it is always expected of him, that the awe and regard due to his audience should lay a decent restraint upon his warmth, and prevent it from carrying him beyond certain bounds. If, when most heated by the subject, he can be so far master of himself as to preserve close attention to argument, and even to some degree of correct expression, this self-command, this exertion of reason, in the midst of passion, has a wonderful effect both to please, and to persuade. It is indeed the master-piece, the highest attainment of eloquence; uniting the strength of reason, with the vehemence of passion; affording all the advantages of passion for the purpose of persuasion, without the confusion and disorder which are apt to accompany it.

In the fourth place, in the highest and most animated strain of popular speaking, we must always preserve regard to what the public ear will bear. This direction I give, in order to guard against an injudicious imitation of ancient orators, who, both in their pronunciation and gesture, and in their figures of expression, used a bolder manner than what the greater coolness of modern taste will readily suffer. This may, perhaps, as I formerly observed, be a disadvantage to modern eloquence. It is no reason why we should be too severe in checking the impulse of genius, and continue always creeping on the ground; but it is a reason, however, why we should avoid carrying the tone of declamation to a height that would now be reckoned extravagant. Demosthenes, to justify the unsuccessful action of Cheronæa, calls up the manes of those heroes who fell in the battle of Marathon and Platæa, and swears by them, that their fellow-citizens had done well, in their endeavours to support the same cause. Cicero, in his oration for Milo, implores and obtests the Alban hills and groves, and makes a long address to them: and both passages, in these orators, have a fine effect. But how few modern orators could venture on such apostrophes? and what a power of genius would it require to give such figures now their proper grace, or make them produce a due effect upon the hearers?

In the fifth and last place, in all kinds of public speaking, but especially in ̇popular assemblies, it is a capital rule to attend to all the decorums of time, place, and character. No warmth of eloquence can atone for the neglect of these. That vehemence, which is becoming in a person of character and authority, may be unsuitable to the modesty expected from a young speaker. That sportive and witty manner which may suit one subject and one assembly, is altogether out of place in a grave cause, and a solemn meeting. *"Caput artis est,"* says Quintilian, *"decere."* (The first principle of art, is to observe decorum.) No one should ever rise to speak in public, without forming to himself a just and strict idea of what suits his own age and character; what suits the subject, the hearers, the place, the occasion: and adjusting the whole train and manner of his speaking on this idea. All the ancients insist much on this. Consult the first chapter of the eleventh book of Quintilian, which is employed wholly on this point, and is full of good sense. Cicero's admonitions, in his Orator ad Brutum, I shall give in his own words, which should never be forgotten by any who speak in public: "Good sense is the foundation of eloquence, as it is of all other things that are valuable. It happens in oratory exactly as it does in life, that frequently nothing is more difficult than to discern what is proper and becoming. In consequence of mistaking this, the grossest faults are often committed. For to the different degrees of rank, fortune, and age among men, to all the varieties of time, place, and auditory, the same style of language, and the same strain of thought, cannot agree. In every part of a discourse, just as in every part of life, we must attend to what is suitable and decent:

whether that be determined by the nature of the subject of which we treat, or by the characters of those who speak, or of those who hear." So much for the considerations that require to be attended to, with respect to the vehemence and warmth which is allowed in popular eloquence.

The current of style should in general be full, free, and natural. Quaint and artificial expressions are out of place here; and always derogate from persuasion. It is a strong and manly style which should chiefly be studied; and metaphorical language, when properly introduced, produces often a happy effect. When the metaphors are warm, glowing, and descriptive, some inaccuracy in them will be overlooked, which, in a written composition, would be remarked and censured. Amidst the torrent of declamation, the strength of the figure makes impression; the inaccuracy of it escapes.

With regard to the degree of conciseness or diffuseness suited to popular eloquence, it is not easy to fix any exact bounds. I know that it is common to recommend a diffuse manner as the most proper. I am inclined, however, to think, that there is danger of erring in this respect; and that by indulging too much in the diffuse style, public speakers often lose more in point of strength, than they gain by the fullness of their illustration. There is no doubt, that in speaking to a multitude, we must not speak in sentences and apothegms: care must be taken to explain and to inculcate; but this care may be, and frequently is, carried too far. We ought always to remember, that how much soever we may be pleased with hearing ourselves speak, every audience is very ready to be tired; and the moment they begin to be tired, all our eloquence goes for nothing. A loose and verbose manner never fails to create disgust; and, on most occasions, we had better run the risk of saying too little than too much. Better place our thought in one strong point of view, and rest it there, than by turning it into every light, and pouring forth a profusion of words upon it, exhaust the attention of our hearers, and leave them flat and languid.

Of pronunciation and delivery, I am hereafter to treat apart. At present it is sufficient to observe, that in speaking to mixt assemblies, the best manner of delivery is the firm and the determined. An arrogant and overbearing manner is indeed always disagreeable; and the least appearance of it ought to be shunned: but there is a certain decisive tone, which may be assumed even by a modest man, who is thoroughly persuaded of the sentiments he utters; and which is calculated for making a general impression. A feeble and hesitating manner bespeaks always some distrust of a man's own opinion; which is, by no means, a favourable circumstance for his inducing others to embrace it

These are the chief thoughts which have occurred to me from reflection and observation, concerning the peculiar distinguishing characters of the eloquence proper for popular assemblies. The sum of what has been said, is this: the end of popular speaking is persuasion; and this must be founded on conviction. Argument and reasoning must be the basis, if we would be speakers of business, and not mere declaimers. We should be engaged in earnest on the side which we espouse; and utter, as much as possible, our own, and not counterfeited sentiments. The premeditation should be of things, rather than of words. Clear order and method should be studied; the manner and expression warm and animated; though still, in the midst of that vehemence, which may at times be suitable, carried on under the proper restraints which regard to the audience, and to the decorum of character, ought to lay on every public speaker: the style free and easy; strong and descriptive, rather than diffuse; and the delivery determined and firm. To conclude this head, let every orator remember, that the impression made by fine and artful speaking is momentary; that made by argument and good sense, is solid and lasting.

Lecture XXXI

CONDUCT OF A DISCOURSE IN ALL ITS PARTS—INTRODUCTION, DIVISION, NARRATION, AND EXPLICATION

I have, in the four preceding lectures, considered what is peculiar to each of the three great fields of public speaking, popular assemblies, the bar, and the pulpit. I am now to treat of what is common to them all; of the conduct of a discourse or oration, in general. The previous view which I have given of the distinguishing spirit and character of different kinds of public speaking, was necessary for the proper application of the rules which I am about to deliver; and as I proceed, I shall further point out, how far any of these rules may have a particular respect to the bar, to the pulpit, or to popular courts.

On whatever subject any one intends to discourse, he will most commonly begin with some introduction, in order to prepare the minds of his hearers; he will then state his subject, and explain the facts connected with it; he will employ arguments for establishing his own opinion, and overthrowing that of his antagonist; he may, perhaps, if there be room for it, endeavour to touch the passions of his audience; and after having said all he thinks proper, he will bring his discourse to a close by some peroration or conclusion. This being the natural train of speaking, the parts that compose a regular formal oration, are these six; first, the exordium or introduction; secondly, the state, and the division of the subject; thirdly, narration or explication; fourthly, the reasoning or arguments; fifthly, the pathetic part; and lastly, the conclusion. I do not mean that each of these must enter into every public discourse, or that they must enter always in this order. There is no reason for being so formal on every occasion; nay, it would often be a fault, and would render a discourse pedantic and stiff.

There may be many excellent discourses in public, where several of these parts are altogether wanting; where the speaker, for instance, uses no introduction, but enters directly on his subject; where he has no occasion either to divide or explain; but simply reasons on one side of the question, and then finishes. But as the parts which I have mentioned are the natural constituent parts of a regular oration; and as in every discourse whatever, some of them must be found, it is necessary to our present purpose, that I should treat of each of them distinctly.

I begin, of course, with the exordium or introduction. This is manifestly common to all the three kinds of public speaking. It is not a rhetorical invention. It is founded upon nature, and suggested by common sense. When one is going to counsel another; when he takes upon him to instruct, or to reprove, prudence will generally direct him not to do it abruptly, but to use some preparation; to begin with somewhat that may incline the persons to whom he addresses himself, to judge favourably of what he is about to say, and may dispose them to such a train of thought as will forward and assist the purpose which he has in view. This is, or ought to be, the main scope of an introduction. Accordingly, Cicero and Quintilian mention three ends, to one or other of which it should be subservient: *"Reddere auditores benevolos, attentos, dociles."*

First, to conciliate the good will of the hearers; to render them benevolent, or well-affected to the speaker and to the subject. Topics for this purpose may, in causes at the bar, be sometimes taken from the particular situation of the speaker himself, or of his client, or from the character or behaviour of his antagonists, contrasted with his own; on other occasions, from the nature of the subject, as closely connected with the interest of the hearers: and, in general, from the modesty and good intention with which the speaker enters upon his subject. The second end of an introduction is, to raise the attention of the hearers; which may be effected, by giving them some hints of the importance, dignity, or novelty of the subject; or some favourable view of the clearness and precision with which we are to treat it; and of the brevity with which we are to discourse. The third end, is to render the hearers docile, or open to persuasion; for which end, we must begin with studying to remove any particular prepossessions they may have contracted against the cause, or side of the argument, which we espouse.

Some one of these ends should be proposed by every introduction. When there is no occasion for aiming at any of them; when we are already secure of the good will, the attention, and the docility of the audience, as may often be the case, formal introductions may, without any prejudice, be omitted. And indeed, when they serve for no purpose but mere ostentation, they had, for the most part, better be omitted; unless as far as respect to the audience makes it decent, that a speaker should not break in upon them too abruptly, but by a short exordium prepare them for what he is going to say. Demosthenes' introductions are always short and simple; Cicero's are fuller and more artful.

The ancient critics distinguished two kinds of introductions, which they call *"principium,"* and *"insinuatio."* *"Principium"* is, where the orator plainly and directly professes his aim in speaking. *"Insinuatio"* is, where a larger compass must be taken; and where, presuming the disposition of the audience to be much against the orator, he must gradually reconcile them to hearing him, before he plainly discovers the point which he has in view.

Of this latter sort of introduction, we have an admirable instance in Cicero's second oration against Rullus. This Rullus was tribune of the people, and had proposed an Agrarian law; the purpose of which was to create a decemvirate, or ten commissioners, with absolute power for five years, over all the lands conquered by the republic, in order to divide them among the citizens. Such laws had often been proposed by factious magistrates, and were always greedily received by the people. Cicero is speaking to the people; he had lately been made consul by their interest; and his first attempt is to make them reject this law. The subject was extremely delicate, and required much art. He begins with acknowledging all the favours which he had received from the people, in preference to the nobility. He professes himself the creature of their power, and of all men the most engaged to promote their interest. He declares, that he held himself to be the consul of the people; and that he would always glory in preserving the character of a popular magistrate. But to be popular, he observes, is an ambiguous word. He understood it to import a steady attachment to the real interest of the people, to their liberty, their ease, and their peace; but by some, he saw it was abused, and made a cover to their own selfish and ambitious designs. In this manner, he begins to draw gradually nearer to his purpose of attacking the proposal of Rullus; but still with great management and reserve. He protests, that he is far from being an enemy to Agrarian laws; he gives the highest praises to the Gracchi, those zealous patrons of the people; and assures them, that when he first heard of Rullus's law, he had resolved to support it if he found it for their interest; but that, upon examining it, he found it calculated to establish a dominion that was inconsistent with liberty, and to aggrandize a few men at the expense of the public: and then terminates his exordium, with telling them that he is going to give his reasons for being of this opinion; but that if his reasons shall not satisfy them, he will give up his own opinion and embrace theirs. In all this there was great art. His eloquence produced the intended effect; and the people, with one voice, rejected this Agrarian law.

Having given these general views of the nature and end of an introduction, I proceed to lay down some rules for the proper composition of it. These are the more necessary, as this is a part of the discourse which requires no small care. It is always of importance to begin well; to make a favourable impression at first setting out; when the minds of the hearers, vacant as yet and free, are most disposed to receive any impression easily. I must add, too, that a good introduction is often found to be extremely difficult. Few parts of the discourse give the composer more trouble, or are attended with more nicety in the execution.

The first rule is, that the introduction should be easy and natural. The subject must always suggest it. It must appear, as Cicero beautifully expresses it, *"Effloruisse penitus ex re de qua tum agitur"* (To have sprung up, of its own accord, from the matter which is under consideration.) It is too common a fault in introductions, that they are taken from some common-place topic, which has no peculiar relation to the subject in hand; by which means they stand apart, like pieces detached from the rest of the discourse. Of this kind are Sallust's introductions, prefixed to his Catilinarian and Jugurthine wars. They might as well have been introductions to any other history, or to any other treatise whatever: and, therefore, though elegant in themselves, they must be considered as blemishes in the work, from want of due connexion with it. Cicero, though abundantly correct in this particular in his orations, yet is not so in his other works. It appears from a letter of his to Atticus, (L. xvi. 6.) that it was his custom to prepare, at his leisure, a collection of different introductions or prefaces, ready to be prefixed to any work that he might afterwards publish. In consequence of this strange method of composing, it happened to him, to employ the same introduction twice without remembering it; prefixing it to two different works. Upon Atticus informing him of this, he acknowledges the mistake, and sends him a new introduction.

In order to render introductions natural and easy, it is, in my opinion, a good rule, that they should not be planned till after one has meditated in his own mind the substance of his discourse. Then, and not till then, he should begin to think of some proper and natural introduction. By taking a contrary course, and labouring in the first place on an introduction, every one who is accustomed to composition will often find, that either he is led to lay hold of some common-place topic, or that, instead of the introduction being accommodated to the discourse, he is obliged to accommodate the whole discourse to the introduction which he had previously written. Cicero makes this remark; though, as we have seen, his practice was not always conformable to his own rule: "When I have planned and digested all the materials of my discourse, it is my custom to think, in the last place, of the introduction with which I am to begin. For if at any time I have endeavoured to invent an introduction first, nothing has ever occurred to me for that purpose, but what was trifling, nugatory, and vulgar." After the mind has been once warmed and put in train, by close meditation on the subject, materials for the preface will then suggest themselves much more readily.

In the second place, in an introduction, correctness should be carefully studied in the expression. This is requisite on account of the situation of the hearers. They are then more disposed to criticise than at any other period; they are, as yet, unoccupied with the subject or the arguments; their attention is wholly directed to the speaker's style and manner. Something must be done, therefore, to prepossess them in his favour; though, for the same reasons, too much art must be avoided; for it will be more easily detected at that time than afterwards, and will derogate from persuasion in all that follows. A correct plainness, and elegant simplicity, is the proper character of an introduction: *"Ut videamur,"* says Quintilian, *"accuratè non callidè dicere."* (That we might seem to speak accurately not heatedly.)

In the third place, modesty is another character which it must carry. All appearances of modesty are favourable and prepossessing. If the orator set out with an air of arrogance and ostentation, the self-love and pride of the hearers will be presently awakened, and will follow him with a very suspicious eye throughout all his progress. His modesty should discover itself not only in his expressions at the beginning, but in his whole manner; in his looks, in his gestures, in the tone of his voice. Every auditory takes in good part those marks of respect and awe, which are paid to them by one who addresses them. Indeed, the modesty of an introduction should never betray anything mean or abject. It is always of great use to an orator, that together with modesty and deference to his hearers, he should show a certain sense of dignity, arising from a persuasion of the justice or importance of the subject on which he is to speak.

The modesty of an introduction requires, that it promise not too much. *"Non fumum ex fulgore, sed ex fumo dare lucem."* (Not to give smoke from lightning but from smoke to give light.) This certainly is the general rule, that an orator should not put forth all his strength at the beginning, but should rise and grow upon us, as his discourse advances. There are cases, however, in which it is allowable for him to set out from the first in a high and bold tone; as, for instance, when he rises to defend some cause which has been much run down, and decried by the public. Too modest a beginning might be then like a confession of guilt. By the boldness and strength of his exordium, he must endeavour to stem the tide that is against him, and to remove prejudices, by encountering them without fear. In subjects, too, of a declamatory nature, and in sermons, where the subject is striking, a magnificent introduction has sometimes a good effect, if it be properly supported in the sequel. Thus Bishop Atterbury, in beginning an eloquent sermon, preached on the 30th of January, the anniversary of what is called King Charles's Martyrdom, sets out in this pompous manner: "This is a day of trouble, of rebuke, and of blasphemy; distinguished in the calendar of our church, and the annals of our nation, by the sufferings of an excellent prince, who fell a sacrifice to the rage of his rebellious subjects; and, by his fall, derived infamy, misery, and guilt on them, and their sinful posterity." Bossuet, Flechier, and the other celebrated French preachers, very often begin their discourses with laboured and sublime introductions. These raise attention, and throw a lustre on the subject; but let every speaker be much on his guard against striking a higher note at the beginning, than he is able to keep up in his progress.

In the fourth place, an introduction should usually be carried on in the calm manner. This is seldom the place for vehemence and passion. Emotions must rise as the discourse advances. The minds of the hearers must be gradually prepared, before the speaker can venture on strong and passionate sentiments. The exceptions to this rule are, when the subject is such, that the very mention of it naturally awakens some passionate emotion; or when the unexpected presence of some person or object, in a popular assembly, inflames the speaker, and makes him break forth with unusual warmth. Either of these will justify what is called the *Exordium ab abrupto*. Thus the appearance of Catiline in the senate renders the vehement beginning of Ciciero's first oration against him very natural and proper: "*Quousque tandem, Catilina, abutêre patientia nostra?*" And thus Bishop Atterbury, in preaching from this text, "Blessed is he, whosoever shall not be offended in me," ventures on breaking forth with this bold exordium: "And can any man then be offered in thee, blessed Jesus?" which address to our Savior he continues for a page or two, till he enters on the division of his subject. But such introductions as these should be hazarded by very few, as they promise so much vehemence and unction through the rest of the discourse, that it is very difficult to fulfill the expectations of the hearers.

At the same time, though the introduction is not the place in which warm emotions are usually to be attempted, yet I must take notice, that it ought to prepare the way for such as are designed to be raised in subsequent parts of the discourse. The orator should, in the beginning, turn the minds of his hearers towards those sentiments and feelings which he seeks to awaken in the course of his speech. According, for instance, as it is compassion, or indignation, or contempt, on which his discourse is to rest, he ought to sow the seeds of these in his introduction; he ought to begin with breathing that spirit which he means to inspire. Much of the orator's art and ability is shown, in thus striking properly at the commencement, the key note, if we may so express it, of the rest of his oration.

In the fifth place, it is a rule in introductions, not to anticipate any material part of the subject. When topics, or arguments, which are afterwards to be enlarged upon, are hinted at, and, in part, brought forth in the introduction, they lose the grace of novelty upon their second appearance. The impression intended to be made by any capital thought, is always made with the greatest advantage, when it is made entire, and in its proper place.

In the last place, the introduction ought to be proportioned, both in length and in kind, to the discourse that is to follow: in length, as nothing can be more absurd than to erect a very great portico before a small building; and in kind, as it is no less absurd to overcharge, with superb ornaments, the portico of a plain dwelling-house, or to make the entrance to a monument as gay as that to an arbour. Common sense directs that every part of a discourse should be suited to the strain and spirit of the whole.

These are the principal rules that relate to introductions. They are adapted, in a great measure, equally, to discourses of all kinds. In pleadings at the bar, or speeches in public assemblies, particular care must be taken not to employ any introduction of that kind, which the adverse party may lay hold of, and turn to his advantage. To this inconvenience all those introductions are exposed, which are taken from general and common-place topics; and it never fails to give an adversary a considerable triumph, if, by giving a small turn to something we had said in our exordium, he can appear to convert, to his own favour, the principles with which we had set out, in beginning our attack upon him. In the case of replies, Quintilian makes an observation which is very worthy of notice; that introductions, drawn from something that has been said in the course of the debate, have always a peculiar grace; and the reason he gives for it is just and sensible: "An introduction, which is founded upon the pleading of the opposite party, is extremely graceful; for this reason, that it appears not to have been meditated at home, but to have taken rise from the business, and to have been composed on the spot. Hence, it gives to the speaker the reputation of a quick invention, and adds weight likewise to his discourse, as art-less and unlaboured: insomuch, that though all the rest of his oration should be studied and written, yet the whole discourse has the appearance of being extemporary, as it is evident that the introduction to it was unpremeditated."

In sermons, such a practice as this cannot take place; and, indeed, in composing sermons, few things are more difficult than to remove an appearance of stiffness from an introduction, when a formal one is used. The French preachers, as I before observed, are often very splendid and lively in their introductions; but, among us, attempts of this kind are not always so successful. When long introductions are formed upon some common-place topic, as the desire of happiness being natural to man, or the like, they never fail of being tedious. Variety should be studied in this part of composition as much as possible; often it may be proper to begin without any introduction at all, unless, perhaps, one or two sentences. Explanatory introductions from the context, are the most simple of any, and frequently the best that can be used; but as they are in hazard of becoming dry, they should never be long. A historical introduction has, generally, a happy effect to rouse attention, when one can lay hold upon some noted fact that is connected with the text or the discourse, and, by a proper illustration of it, open the way to the subject that is to be treated of.

After the introduction, what commonly comes next in order, is the proposition, or enunciation of the subject; concerning which there is nothing to be said, but that it should be as clear and distinct as possible, and expressed in few and plain words, without the least affectation. To this generally succeeds the division, or the laying down the method of the discourse; on which it is necessary to make some observations. I do not mean, that in every discourse, a formal division, or distribution of it into parts, is requisite. There are many occasions of public speaking, when this is neither requisite nor would be proper; when the discourse, perhaps, is to be short, or only one point is to be treated of; or when the speaker does not choose to warn his hearers of the method he is to follow, or of the conclusion to which he seeks to bring them. Order of one kind or other is, indeed, essential to every good discourse; that is, every thing should be so arranged, as that what goes before may give light and force to what follows. But this may be accomplished by means of a concealed method. What we call division is, when the method is propounded in form to the hearers.

The discourse in which this sort of division most commonly takes place, is a sermon; and a question has been moved, whether this method of laying down heads, as it is called, be the best method of preaching. A very able judge, the Archbishop of Cambray, in his Dialogues on Eloquence, declares strongly against it. He observes, that it is a modern invention; that it was never practised by the Fathers of the church: and, what is certainly true, that it took its rise from the schoolmen, when metaphysics began to be introduced into preaching. He is of opinion, that it renders a sermon stiff; that it breaks the unity of the discourse; and that, by the natural connexion of one part with another, the attention of the hearers would be carried along the whole with more advantage.

But notwithstanding his authority and his arguments, I cannot help being of opinion, that the present method of dividing a sermon into heads, ought not to be laid aside. Established practice has now given it so much weight, that, were there nothing more in its favour, it would be dangerous for any preacher to deviate so far from the common track. But the practice itself has also, in my judgment, much reason on its side. If formal partitions give a sermon less of the oratorical appearance, they render it, however, more clear, more easily apprehended, and, of course, more instructive to the bulk of hearers, which is always the main object to be kept in view. The heads of a sermon are great assistances to the memory and recollection of a hearer. They serve also to fix his attention. They enable him more easily to keep pace with the progress of the discourse; they give him pauses and resting places, where he can reflect on what has been said, and look forward to what is to follow. They are attended with this advantage too, that they give the audience the opportunity of knowing, beforehand, when they are to be released from the fatigue of attention, and thereby make them follow the speaker more patiently. "*Reficit audientem,*" says Quintilian, taking notice of this very advantage of divisions in other discourses, "*Reficit audientem certo singularum partium fine; non aliter quam facientibus iter, multum detrahunt fatigationis notata spatia inscriptis lapidibus: nam et exhausti laboris nosse mensuram voluptati est; et hortatur ad reliqua fortius exequenda, scire quantum supersit.*" [1] With regard to breaking the unity of a discourse, I cannot be of opinion that there arises, from that quarter, any argument against the method I am defending. If the unity be broken, it is to the nature of the heads, or topics of which the speaker treats, that this is to be imputed; not to his laying them down in form. On the contrary, if his heads be well chosen, his marking them out, and distinguishing them, in place of impairing the unity of the whole,

---

[1] "The conclusion of each head is a relief to the hearers; just as, upon a journey, the mile-stones which are set up on the road, serve to diminish the traveller's fatigue. For we are always pleased with seeing our labour begin to lessen; and, by calculating how much remains, are stirred up to finish our task more cheerfully."

renders it more conspicuous and complete; by showing how all the parts of a discourse hang upon one another, and tend to one point.

In a sermon, or in a pleading, or any discourse, where division is proper to be used, the most material rules are,

First, That the several parts into which the subject is divided be really distinct from one another; that is, that no one include another. It were a very absurd division, for instance, if one should propose to treat, first, of the advantages of virtue, and next, of those of justice or temperance; because, the first head evidently comprehends the second, as a genus does the species; which method of proceeding involves the subject in indistinctness and disorder.

Secondly, In division, we must take care to follow the order of nature; beginning with the simplest points, such as are easiest apprehended, and necessary to be first discussed; and proceeding thence to those which are built upon the former, and which suppose them to be known. We must divide the subject into those parts, into which most easily and naturally it is resolved; that it may seem to split itself, and not to be violently torn asunder: *"Dividere,"* as is commonly said, *"non frangere."* (To divide, not to break.)

Thirdly, The several members of a division ought to exhaust the subject; otherwise we do not make a complete division; we exhibit the subject by pieces and corners only, without giving any such plan as displays the whole.

Fourthly, The terms in which our partitions are expressed, should be as concise as possible. Avoid all circumlocution here. Admit not a single word but what is necessary. Precision is to be studied, above all things, in laying down a method. It is this which chiefly makes a division appear neat and elegant; when the several heads are propounded in the clearest, most expressive, and, at the same time, the fewest words possible. This never fails to strike the hearers agreeably; and is, at the same time, of great consequence towards making the divisions be more easily remembered.

Fifthly, Avoid an unnecessary multiplication of heads. To split a subject into a great many minute parts, by divisions and subdivisions without end, has always a bad effect in speaking. It may be proper in a logical treatise; but it makes an oration appear hard and dry, and unnecessarily fatigues the memory. In a sermon, there may be from three to five or six heads, including subdivisions; seldom should there be more.

In a sermon, or in pleading at the bar, few things are of greater consequence, than a proper or happy division. It should be studied with much accuracy and care; for if one take a wrong method at first setting out, it will lead him astray in all that follows. It will render the whole discourse either perplexed or languid; and though the hearers may not be able to tell where the fault or disorder lies, they will be sensible there is a disorder somewhere, and find themselves little affected by what is spoken. The French writers of sermons study neatness and elegance in laying down their heads, much more than the English do; whose distributions, though sensible and just, yet are often inartificial and verbose. Among the French, however, too much quaintness appears in their divisions, with an affectation of always setting out either with two, or with three, general heads of discourse. A division of Massillon's on this text, "It is finished," has been much extolled by the French critics:—"This imports," says the preacher, "the consummation, first, of justice on the part of God; secondly, of wickedness on the part of men; thirdly, of love on the part of Christ." This also of Bourdaloue's has been much praised, from these words: "My peace I give unto you." "Peace," says he, "first to the understanding, by submission to faith; secondly, to the heart, by submission to the law."

The next constituent part of a discourse, which I mentioned, was narration or explication. I put these two together, both because they fall nearly under the same rules, and because they commonly answer the same purpose; serving to illustrate the cause or the subject of which the orator treats, before he proceeds to argue either on one side or other; or to make any attempt for interesting the passions of the hearers.

In pleadings at the bar, narration is often a very important part of the discourse, and requires to be particularly attended to. Besides its being in any case no easy matter to relate with grace and propriety; there is in narrations at the bar, a peculiar difficulty. The pleader must say nothing but what is true; and, at the same time, he must avoid saying any thing that will hurt his cause. The facts which he relates are to be the ground-work of all his future reasoning. To recount them so as to keep strictly within the bounds of truth, and yet to present them under the colours most favourable to his cause; to place, in the most striking light, every circumstance which is to his advantage, and to soften and weaken such as make against him, demand no small exertion of skill and dexterity. He must always remember, that if he discovers too much art, he defeats his own purpose, and creates a distrust of his sincerity. Quintilian very properly directs, "In this part of discourse, the speaker must be very careful to shun every appearance of art and cunning. For there is no time at which the judge is more upon his guard, than when the pleader is relating facts. Let nothing then seem feigned: nothing anxiously concealed. Let all that is said, appear to arise from the cause itself, and not to be the work of the orator."

To be clear and distinct, to be probable, and to be concise, are the qualities which critics chiefly require in narration; each of which carries sufficiently the evidence of its importance. Distinctness belongs to the whole train of the discourse, but is especially requisite in narration, which ought to throw light on all that follows. A fact, or a single circumstance left in obscurity, and misapprehended by the judge, may destroy the effect of all the argument and reasoning which the speaker employs. If his narration be improbable, the judge will not regard it; and if it be tedious and diffuse, he will be tired of it, and forget it. In order to produce distinctness, besides the study of the general rules of perspicuity which were formerly given, narration requires a particular attention to ascertain clearly the names, the dates, the places, and every other material circumstance of the facts recounted. In order to be probable in narration, it is material to enter into the characters of the persons of whom we speak, and to show, that their actions proceeded from such motives as are natural, and likely to gain belief. In order to be as concise as the subject will admit, it is necessary to throw out all superfluous circumstances; the rejection of which will likewise tend to make our narration more forcible, and more clear.

Cicero is very remarkable for his talent of narration; and from the examples in his orations much may be learned. The narration, for instance, in the celebrated oration *pro Milone*, has been often and justly admired. His scope is to show, that though in fact Clodius was killed by Milo or his servants, yet that it was only in self-defence; and that the design had been laid, not by Milo against Clodius, but by Clodius against Milo's life. All the circumstances for rendering this probable are painted with wonderful art. In relating the manner of Milo's setting out from Rome, he gives the most natural description of a family excursion to the country, under which it was impossible that any bloody design could be concealed. "He remained," says he, "in the senate house that day, till all the business was over. He came home, changed his clothes deliberately, and waited for some time, till his wife had got all her things ready for going with him in his carriage to the country. He did not set out, till such time as Clodius might easily have been in Rome, if he had not been lying in wait for Milo by the way. By and by, Clodius met him on the road, on horse-back, like a man prepared for action; no carriage, not his wife, as was usual, nor any family equipage along with him: whilst Milo, who is supposed to be meditating slaughter and assassination, is travelling in a carriage with his wife, wrapped up in his cloak, embarrassed with baggage, and attended by a great train of women-servants, and boys." He goes on describing the rencounter that followed; Clodius's servants attacking those of Milo, and killing the driver of his carriage; Milo jumping out, throwing off his cloak, and making the best defence he could, while Clodius's servants endeavoured to surround him; and then concludes his narration with a very delicate and happy stroke. He does not say in plain words, that Milo's servants killed Clodius, but that "in the midst of the tumult, Milo's servants, without the orders, without the knowledge, without the presence of their master, did what every master would have wished his servants, in like conjuncture, to have done."

In sermons, where there is seldom any occasion for narration, explication of the subject to be discoursed on, comes in the place of narration at the bar, and is to be taken up much on the same tone; that is, it must be concise, clear, and distinct: and in a style correct and elegant, rather than highly adorned. To explain the doctrine of the text with propriety; to give a full and perspicuous account of the nature of that virtue or duty which forms the subject of the discourse, is properly the didactic part of preaching; on the right execution of which much depends for all that comes afterwards in the way of persuasion. The great art of succeeding in it, is to meditate profoundly on the subject, so as to be able to place it in a clear and strong point of view. Consider what light other passages of scripture throw upon it; consider whether it be a subject nearly related to some other from which it is proper to distinguish it; consider whether it can be illustrated to advantage by comparing it with, or opposing it to, some other thing; by inquiring into causes, or tracing effects; by pointing out examples, or appealing to the feelings of the hearers; that thus, a definite, precise, circumstantial view may be afforded of the doctrine to be inculcated. Let the preacher be persuaded, that by such distinct and apt illustrations of the known truths of religion, he may both display great merit in the way of composition, and, what he ought to consider as far more valuable, render his discourses weighty, instructive, and useful.

.෯.෯.෯.෯.෯.෯.

Lecture XXXII

CONDUCT OF A DISCOURSE—
THE ARGUMENTATIVE PART—
THE PATHETIC PART—
THE PERORATION

In treating of the constituent parts of a regular discourse or oration, I have already considered the introduction, the division, and the narration or explication. I proceed next to treat of the argumentative or reasoning part of a discourse. In whatever place, or on whatever subject one speaks, this, beyond doubt, is of the greatest consequence. For the great end for which men speak on any serious occasion, is to convince their hearers of something being either true, or right, or good; and, by means of this conviction, to influence their practice. Reason and argument make the foundation, as I have often inculcated, of all manly and persuasive eloquence.

Now, with respect to arguments, three things are requisite. First, the invention of them; secondly, the proper disposition and arrangement of them; and thirdly, the expressing of them in such a style and manner, as to give them their full force.

The first of these, invention, is, without doubt, the most material, and the ground-work of the rest. But, with respect to this, I am afraid it is beyond the power of art to give any real assistance. Art cannot go so far as to supply a speaker with arguments on every cause, and every subject; though it may be of considerable use in assisting him to arrange and express those, which his knowledge of the subject has discovered. For it is one thing to discover the reasons that are most proper to convince men, and another to manage these reasons with the most advantage. The latter is all that rhetoric can pretend to.

The ancient rhetoricians did indeed attempt to go much farther than this. They attempted to form rhetoric into a more complete system; and professed not only to assist public speakers in setting off their arguments to most advantage; but to supply the defect of their invention, and to teach them where to find arguments on every subject and cause. Hence their doctrine of topics, or *"Loci Communes,"* and *"Sedes Argumentorum,"* which makes so great a figure in the writings of Aristotle, Cicero, and Quintilian. These topics, or *loci,* were no other than general ideas applicable to a great many different subjects, which the orator was directed to consult, in order to find out materials for his speech. They had their intrinsic and extrinsic *loci;* some *loci,* that were common to all the different kinds of public speaking, and some that were peculiar to each. The common or general *loci,* were such as genus and species, cause and effect, antecedents and consequents, likeness and contrariety, definition, circumstances of time and place; and a great many more of the same kinds. For each of the different kinds of public speaking, they had their *"Loci Personarum,"* and *"Loci Rerum."* As in demonstrative orations, for instance, the heads from which any one could be decried or praised; his birth, his country, his education, his kindred, the qualities of his body, the qualities of his mind, the fortune he enjoyed, the stations he had filled, &c.; and in deliberative orations, the topics that might be used in recommending any public measure, or dissuading from it; such as, honesty, justice, facility, profit, pleasure, glory, assistance from friends, mortifications to enemies, and the like.

The Grecian sophists were the first inventors of this artificial system of oratory; and they showed a prodigious subtilty and fertility in the contrivance of these *loci.* Succeeding rhetoricians, dazzled by the plan, wrought them up into so regular a system, that one would think they meant to teach how a person might mechanically become an orator, without any genius at all. They gave him receipts for making speeches on all manner of subjects. At the same time, it is evident, that though this study of common places might produce very showy academical declamations, it could never produce discourses on real business. The *loci* indeed supplied a most exuberant fecundity of matter. One who had no other aim, but to talk copiously and plausibly, by consulting them on every subject, and laying hold of all that they suggested, might discourse without end; and that, too, though he had none but the most superficial knowledge of his subject. But such discourse could be no other than trivial. What is truly solid and persuasive, must be drawn *"ex visceribus causæ,"* from a thorough knowledge of the subject, and profound meditation on it. They who would direct students of oratory to any other sources of argumentation, only delude them; and by attempting to render rhetoric too perfect an art, they render it, in truth, a trifling and childish study.

On this doctrine, therefore, of the rhetorical *loci,* or topics, I think it superfluous to insist. If any think that the knowledge of them may contribute to improve their invention, and extend their views, they may consult Aristotle and Quintilian, or what Cicero has written on this head, in his

Treatise *De Inventione,* his *Topica,* and second book *De Oratore*. But when they are to prepare a discourse, by which they purpose to convince a judge, or to produce any considerable effect upon an assembly, I would advise them to lay aside their common places, and to think closely of their subject. Demosthenes, I dare say, consulted none of the *loci,* when he was inciting the Athenians to take arms against Philip; and where Cicero has had recourse to them, his orations are so much the worse on that account.

I proceed to what is of more real use, to point out the assistance that can be given, not with respect to the invention, but with respect to the disposition and conduct of arguments.

Two different methods may be used by orators, in the conduct of their reasoning; the terms of art for which are, the analytic, and the synthetic method. The analytic is, when the orator conceals his intention concerning the point he is to prove, till he has gradually brought his hearers to the designed conclusion. They are led on step by step, from one known truth to another, till the conclusion be stolen upon them, as the natural consequence of a chain of propositions. As, for instance, when one intending to prove the being of a God, sets out with observing, that every thing which we see in the world has had a beginning; that whatever has had a beginning, must have a prior cause; that in human productions, art shown in the effect, necessarily infers design in the cause: and proceeds leading you on from one cause to another, till you arrive at one supreme first cause, from whom is derived all the order and design visible in his works. This is much the same with the Socratic method, by which that philosopher silenced the sophists of his age. It is a very artful method of reasoning; may be carried on with much beauty, and is proper to be used when the hearers are much prejudiced against any truth, and by imperceptible steps must be led to conviction.

But there are few subjects that will admit this method, and not many occasions on which it is proper to be employed. The mode of reasoning more generally used, and most suited to the train of popular speaking, is what is called the synthetic; when the point to be proved is fairly laid down, and one argument upon another is made to bear upon it, till the hearers be fully convinced.

Now, in all arguing, one of the first things to be attended to is, among the various arguments which may occur upon a cause, to make a proper selection of such as appear to one's self the most solid; and to employ these as the chief means of persuasion. Every speaker should place himself in the situation of a hearer, and think how he would be affected by those reasons which he purposes to employ for persuading others. For he must not expect to impose on mankind by mere arts of speech. They are not so easily imposed on, as public speakers are sometimes apt to think. Shrewdness and sagacity are found among all ranks; and the speaker may be praised for his fine discourse, while yet the hearers are not persuaded of the truth of any one thing he has uttered.

Supposing the arguments properly chosen, it is evident that their effect will, in some measure, depend on the right arrangement of them; so as they shall not justle and embarrass one another, but give mutual aid; and bear with the fairest and fullest direction on the point in view. Concerning this, the following rules may be taken:

In the first place, avoid blending arguments confusedly together, that are of a separate nature. All arguments whatever are directed to prove one or other of these three things; that something is true; that it is morally right or fit; or that it is profitable and good. These make the three great subjects of discussion among mankind; truth, duty, and interest. But the arguments directed towards any one of them are generically distinct; and he who blends them all under one topic, which he calls his argument, as in sermons, especially, is too often done, will render his reasoning indistinct and inelegant. Suppose, for instance, that I am recommending to an audience benevolence or the love of our neighbour, and that I take my first argument, from the inward satisfaction which a benevolent temper affords; my second, from the obligation which the example of Christ lays upon us to this duty; and my third, from its tendency to procure us the good will of all around us: my arguments are good, but I have arranged them wrong; for, my first and third arguments are taken from considerations of interest, internal peace, and external advantages; and between these, I have introduced one which rests wholly upon duty. I should have kept those classes of arguments which are addressed to different principles in human nature, separate and distinct.

In the second place, with regard to the different degrees of strength in arguments, the general rule is to advance in the way of climax, *"ut augeatur semper, et increscat oratio"* (so that the speech might constantly grow and become stronger) . This especially is to be the course, when the speaker has a clear cause, and is confident that he can prove it fully. He may then adventure to begin with feeble arguments; rising gradually, and not putting forth his whole strength till the last, when he can trust to his making a successful impression on the minds of hearers, prepared by what has gone before. But this rule is not to be always followed. For, if he distrusts his cause, and has but one material argument on which to lay the stress, putting less confidence in the rest, in this case, it is often proper for him to place this material argument in the front; to pre-occupy the hearers early, and make the strongest effort at first; that, having removed prejudices, and disposed them to be favourable, the rest of his reasoning may be listened to with more candour. When it happens, that amidst a variety of arguments, there are one or two which we are sensible are more inconclusive than the rest, and yet proper to be used, Cicero advises to place these in the middle, as a station less conspicuous than either the beginning or the end of the train of reasoning.

In the third place, when our arguments are strong and satisfactory, the more they are distinguished and treated apart from each other, the better. Each can then bear to be brought out by itself, placed in its full light, amplified and rested upon. But when our arguments are doubtful, and only of the presumptive kind, it is safer to throw them together in a crowd, and to run them into one another: *"ut quæ sunt naturâ imbecilla,"* as Quintilian speaks, *"mutuo auxilio sustineantur"* (that though infirm of themselves, they may serve mutually to prop each other). He gives a good example, in the case of one who had been accused of murdering a relation, to whom he was heir. Direct proof was wanting; but, "you expected a succession, and a great succession; you were in distrest circumstances; you were pushed to the utmost by your creditors; you had offended your relation, who had made you his heir; you knew that he was just then intending to alter his will; no time was to be lost. Each of these particulars by itself," says the author, "is inconclusive; but when they are assembled in one group, they have effect."

Of the distinct amplification of one persuasive argument, we have a most beautiful example, in Cicero's oration for Milo. The argument is taken from a circumstance of time. Milo was candidate for the consulship; and Clodius was killed a few days before the election. He asks, if any one could believe that Milo would be mad enough at such a critical time, by a most odious assassination, to alienate from himself the favour of people, whose suffrages he was so anxiously courting? This argument, the moment it is suggested, appears to have considerable weight. But it was not enough, simply to suggest it; it could bear to be dwelt upon, and brought out into full light. The orator, therefore, draws a just and striking picture of that solicitous attention with which candidates, at such a season, always found it necessary to cultivate the good opinion of the people: "Well do I know to what length the timidity goes of such as are candidates for public offices, and how many anxious cares and attentions, a canvass for the consulship necessarily carries along with it. On such an occasion, we are afraid not only of what we may openly be reproached with, but of what others may think of us in secret. The slightest rumour, the most improbable tale that can be devised to our prejudice, alarms and disconcerts us. We study the countenance, and the looks, of all around us: for nothing is so delicate, so frail, uncertain, as the public favour. Our fellow-citizens not only are justly offended with the vices of candidates, but even on occasions of meritorious actions, are apt to conceive capricious disgusts. Is there then the least credibility, that Milo, after having so long fixed his attention on the important and wished-for day of election, would dare to have any thoughts of presenting himself before the august assembly of the people, as a murderer and assassin, with his hands imbrued in blood?" But though such amplifications as this be extremely beautiful, I must add a caution.

In the fourth place, against extending arguments too far, and multiplying them too much. This serves rather to render a cause suspected, than to give it weight. An unnecessary multiplicity of arguments both burdens the memory, and detracts from the weight of that conviction which a few well chosen arguments carry. It is to be observed too, that in the amplification of arguments, a diffuse and spreading method, beyond the bounds of reasonable illustration, is always enfeebling. It takes off greatly from that *"vis et acumen,"* which should be the distinguishing character of the argumentative part of a discourse. When a speaker dwells long on a favourite argument, and seeks to turn it into every possible light, it almost always happens, that, fatigued with the effort, he loses the spirit with which he set out, and concludes with feebleness what he began with force. There is a proper temperance in reasoning, as there is in other parts of a discourse.

After due attention given to the proper arrangement of arguments, what is next requisite for their success is, to express them in such a style, and to deliver them in such a manner, as shall give them full force. On these heads I must refer the reader to the directions I have given in treating of style, in former lectures; and to the directions I am afterwards to give concerning pronunciation and delivery.

I proceed, therefore, next, to another essential part of discourse, which I mentioned as the fifth in order, that is, the pathetic; in which, if anywhere, eloquence reigns, and exerts its power. I shall not, in beginning this head, take up time in combating the scruples of those who have moved a question, whether it be consistent with fairness and candour in a public speaker, to address the passions of his audience? This is a question about words alone, and which common sense easily determines. In inquiries after mere truth, in matters of simple information and instruction, there is no question that the passions have no concern, and that all attempts to move them are absurd. Wherever conviction is the object, it is the understanding alone that is to be applied to. It is by argument and reasoning, that one man attempts to satisfy another of what is true, or right, or just; but if persuasion be the object, the case is changed. In all that relates to practice, there is no man who seriously means to persuade another, but addresses himself to his passions more or less; for this plain reason, that passions are the great springs of human action. The most virtuous man, in treating of the most virtuous subject, seeks to touch the heart of him to whom he speaks; and makes no scruple to raise his indignation at injustice, or his pity to the distressed, though pity and indignation be passions.

In treating of this part of eloquence, the ancients made the same sort of attempt as they employed with respect to the argumentative part, in order to bring rhetoric into a more perfect system. They inquired metaphysically into the nature of every passion; they gave a definition, and a description of it; they treated of its causes, its effects, and its concomitants; and thence deduced rules for working upon it. Aristotle in particular has, in his treatise upon rhetoric, discussed the nature of the passions with much profoundness and subtilty; and what he has written on that head, may be read with no small profit, as a valuable piece of moral philosophy; but whether it will have any effect in rendering an orator more pathetic, is to me doubtful. It is not, I am afraid, any philosophical knowledge of the passions, that can confer this talent. We must be indebted for it to nature, to a certain strong and happy sensibility of mind; and one may be a most thorough adept in all the speculative knowledge that can be acquired concerning the passions, and remain, at the same time, a cold and dry speaker. The use of rules and instructions on this, or any other part of oratory, is not to supply the want of genius, but to direct it where it is found, into its proper channel; to assist it in exerting itself with most advantage, and to prevent the errors and extravagances into which it is sometimes apt to run. On the head of the pathetic, the following directions appear to me to be useful.

The first is, to consider carefully, whether the subject admit the pathetic, and render it proper: and if it does, what part of the discourse is the most proper for attempting it. To determine these points belongs to good sense; for it is evident, that there are many subjects which admit not the pathetic at all, and that even in those that are susceptible of it, an attempt to excite the passions in the wrong place, may expose an orator to ridicule. All that can be said in general is, that if we expect any emotion which we raise to have a lasting effect, we must be careful to bring over to our side, in the first place, the understanding and judgment. The hearers must be convinced that there are good and sufficient grounds for their entering with warmth into the cause. They must be able to justify to themselves the passion which they feel; and remain satisfied that they are not carried away by mere delusion. Unless their minds be brought into this state, although they may have been heated by the orator's discourse, yet, as soon as he ceases to speak, they will resume their ordinary tone of thought; and the emotion which he has raised will die entirely away. Hence most writers assign the pathetic to the peroration, or conclusion, as its natural place; and, no doubt, all other things being equal, this is the impression that one would choose to make last, leaving the minds of the hearers warmed with the subject, after argument and reasoning had produced their full effect: but wherever it is introduced, I must advise,

In the second place, never to set apart a head of a discourse in form, for raising any passion; never give warning that you are about to be pathetic; and call upon your hearers, as is sometimes done, to follow you in the attempt. This almost never fails to prove a refrigerant to passion. It puts the hearers immediately on their guard and disposes them for criticising, much more than for being moved. The indirect method of making an impression is likely to be more successful; when you seize the critical moment that is favourable to emotion, in whatever part of the discourse it occurs; and then, after due preparation, throw in such circumstances, and present such glowing images, as may kindle their passions before they are aware. This can often be done more happily, in a few sentences inspired by natural warmth, than in a long and studied address.

In the third place, it is necessary to observe, that there is a great difference between showing the hearers that they ought to be moved, and actually moving them. This distinction is not sufficiently attended to, especially by preachers, who, if they have a head in their sermon to show how much we are bound to be grateful to God, or to be compassionate to the distrest, are apt to imagine this to be a pathetic part. Now all the arguments you produce to show me, why it is my duty, why it is reasonable and fit, that I should be moved in a certain way, go no farther than to dispose or prepare me for entering into such an emotion; but they do not actually excite it. To every emotion or passion, nature has adapted a set of corresponding objects; and, without setting these before the mind, it is not in the power of any orator to raise that emotion. I am warmed with gratitude, I am touched with compassion, not when a speaker shows me that these are noble dispositions, and that it is my duty to feel them; or when he exclaims against me for my indifference and coldness. All this time, he is speaking only to my reason or conscience. He must describe the kindness and tenderness of my friend; he must set before me the distress suffered by the person for whom he would interest me; then, and not till then, my heart begins to be touched, my gratitude or my compassion begins to flow. The foundation, therefore, of all successful execution in the way of pathetic oratory is, to paint the object of that passion which we wish to raise, in the most natural and striking manner; to describe it with such circumstances as are likely to awaken it in the minds of others. Every passion is most strongly excited by sensation; as anger, by the feeling of an injury, or the presence of the injurer. Next to the influence of sense, is that of memory; and next to memory, is the influence of the imagination. Of this power, therefore, the orator must avail himself, so as to strike the imagination of the hearers with circumstances which, in lustre and steadiness, resemble those of sensation and remembrance. In order to accomplish this,

In the fourth place, the only effectual method is, to be moved yourselves. There are a thousand interesting circumstances suggested by real passion, which no art can imitate, and no refinement can supply. There is obviously a contagion among the passions.

> Ut ridentibus, arrident, sic flentibus adflent,
> Humani vultus.[1]

The internal emotion of the speaker adds a pathos to his words, his looks, his gestures, and his whole manner, which exerts a power almost irresistible over those who hear him. But on this point, though the most material of all, I shall not now insist, as I have often had occasion before to show, that all attempts towards becoming pathetic, when we are not moved ourselves, expose us to certain ridicule.

Quintilian, who discourses upon this subject with much good sense, takes pains to inform us of the method which he used, when he was a public speaker, for entering into those passions which he wanted to excite in others; setting before his own imagination what he calls, "Phantasiæ" or "Visiones," strong pictures of the distress or indignities which they had suffered, whose cause he had to plead, and for whom he was to interest his hearers; dwelling upon these, and putting himself in their situation, till he was affected by a passion similar to that which the persons themselves had felt. To this method he attributes all the success he ever had in public speaking; and there can be no doubt, that whatever tends to increase an orator's sensibility, will add greatly to his pathetic powers.

[1] The countenance should laugh with those who are laughing and weep with those who are weeping.

In the fifth place, it is necessary to attend to the proper language of the passions. We should observe in what manner any one expresses himself, who is under the power of a real and a strong passion; and we shall always find his language unaffected and simple. It may be animated, indeed, with bold and strong figures, but it will have no ornament or finery. He is not at leisure to follow out the play of imagination. His mind being wholly seized by one object which has heated it, he has no other aim, but to represent that, in all its circumstances, as strongly as he feels it. This must be the style of the orator, when he would be pathetic; and this will be his style, if he speaks from real feeling; bold, ardent, simple. No sort of description will then succeed, but what is written *"fervente calamo"* (with a glowing pen). If he stay till he can work up his style, and polish and adorn it, he will infallibly cool his own ardour, and then he will touch the heart no more. His composition will become frigid; it will be the language of one who describes, but who does not feel. We must take notice, that there is a great difference between painting to the imagination, and painting to the heart. The one may be done coolly, and at leisure; the other must always be rapid and ardent. In the former, art and labour may be suffered to appear; in the latter, no effect can follow, unless it seem to be the work of nature only.

In the sixth place, avoid interweaving any thing of a foreign nature with the pathetic part of a discourse. Beware of all digressions, which may interrupt or turn aside the natural course of the passion, when once it begins to rise and swell. Sacrifice all beauties, however bright and showy, which would divert the mind from the principal object, and which would amuse the imagination, rather than touch the heart. Hence comparisons are always dangerous, and generally quite improper, in the midst of passion. Beware even of reasoning unseasonably; or, at least, of carrying on a long and subtile train of reasoning, on occasions when the principal aim is to excite warm emotions.

In the last place, never attempt prolonging the pathetic too much. Warm emotions are too violent to be lasting. Study the proper time of making a retreat; of making a transition from the passionate to the calm tone; in such a manner, however, as to descend without falling, by keeping up the same strain of sentiment that was carried on before, though now expressing it with more moderation. Above all things, beware of straining passion too far; of attempting to raise it to unnatural heights. Preserve always a due regard to what the hearers will bear; and remember, that he who stops not at the proper point; who attempts to carry them farther in passion than they will follow him, destroys his whole design. By endeavouring to warm them too much, he takes the most effectual method of freezing them completely.

Having given these rules concerning the pathetic, I shall give one example from Cicero, which will serve to illustrate several of them, particularly the last. It shall be taken from his oration against Verres, wherein he describes the cruelty exercised by Verres, when governor of Sicily, against one Gavius, a Roman citizen. This Gavius had made his escape from prison, into which he had been thrown by the governor; and when just embarking at Messina, thinking himself now safe, had uttered some threats, that when he had once arrived at Rome, Verres should hear of him, and be brought to account for having put a Roman citizen in chains. The chief magistrate of Messina, a creature of Verres's, instantly apprehends him, and gives information of his threatenings. The behaviour of Verres, on this occasion, is described in the most picturesque manner, and with all the colours which are proper, in order to excite against him the public indignation. He thanks the magistrate of Messina for his diligence. Filled with rage, he comes into the forum; orders Gavius to be brought forth, the executioners to attend, and against the laws, and contrary to the well-known privileges of a Roman citizen, commands him to be stripped naked, bound, and scourged publicly in a cruel manner. Cicero then proceeds thus: "In the midst of the market-place of Messina, a Roman citizen, O Judges! was cruelly scourged with rods; when, in the mean time, amidst the noise of the blows which he suffered, no voice, no complaint of this unhappy man was heard, except this exclamation, remember that I am a Roman citizen! By pleading this privilege of his birthright, he hoped to have stopped the strokes of the executioner. But his hopes were vain; for, so far was he from being able to obtain thereby any mitigation of his torture, that when he continued to repeat this exclamation, and to plead the rights of a citizen, a cross, a cross, I say, was preparing to be set up for the execution of this unfortunate person, who never before had beheld that instrument of cruel death. O sacred and honoured name of liberty! O boasted and revered privilege of a Roman citizen! O ye Porcian and Sempronian laws! to this issue have ye all come, that a citizen of Rome, in a province of the Roman empire, within an allied city, should publicly in a market-place be loaded with chains, and beaten with rods, at the command of one who, from the favour of the Roman people alone, derived all his authority and ensigns of power!"

Nothing can be finer, nor better conducted, than this passage. The circumstances are well chosen for exciting both the compassion of his hearers for Gavius, and their indignation against Verres. The style is simple; and the passionate exclamation, the address to liberty and the laws, is well timed, and in the proper style of passion. The orator goes on to exaggerate Verres's cruelty still farther, by another very striking circumstance. He ordered a gibbet to be erected for Gavius, not in the common place of execution, but just by the sea-shore, over against the coast of Italy. "Let him," said he "who boasts so much of his being a Roman citizen, take a view from his gibbet of his own country. This insult over a dying man is the least part of his guilt. It was not Gavius alone that Verres meant to insult; but it was you, O Romans! it was every citizen who now hears me; in the person of Gavius, he scoffed at your rights, and showed in what contempt he held the Roman name, and Roman liberties."

Hitherto all is beautiful, animated, pathetic; and the model would have been perfect, if Cicero had stopped at this point. But his redundant and florid genius carried him further. He must needs interest, not his hearers only, but the beasts, the mountains, and the stones, against Verres: "Were I employed in lamenting those instances of an atrocious oppression and cruelty, not among an assembly of Roman citizens, not among the allies of our state, not among those who had ever heard the name of the Roman people, not even among human creatures, but in the midst of the brute creation; and to go farther, were I pouring forth my lamentations to the stones, and to the rocks, in some remote and desert wilderness, even those mute and inanimate beings would, at the recital of such shocking indignities, be thrown into commotion." This, with all the deference due to so eloquent an orator, we must pronounce to be declamatory, not pathetic. This is straining the language of passion too far. Every hearer sees this immediately to be a studied figure of rhetoric; it may amuse him, but instead of inflaming him more, it, in truth, cools his passion. So dangerous it is to give scope to a flowery imagination, when one intends to make a strong and passionate impression.

No other part of the discourse remains now to be treated of, except the peroration, or conclusion. Concerning this, it is needless to say much, because it must vary considerably, according to the strain of the preceding discourse. Sometimes, the whole pathetic part comes in most properly at the peroration. Sometimes, when the discourse has been entirely argumentative, it is fit to conclude with summing up the arguments, placing them in one view, and leaving the impression of them, full and strong, on the mind of the audience. For the great rule of a conclusion, and what nature obviously suggests, is, to place that last on which we choose that the strength of our cause should rest.

In sermons, inferences from what has been said, make a common conclusion. With regard to these, care should be taken not only that they rise naturally, but, (what is less commonly attended to) that they should so much agree with the strain of sentiment throughout the discourse, as not to break the unity of the sermon. For inferences, how justly soever they may be deduced from the doctrine of the text, yet have a bad effect, if, at the conclusion of a discourse, they introduce a subject altogether new, and turn off our attention from the main object to which the preacher may have directed our thoughts. They appear, in this case, like excrescences jutting out from the body, which form an unnatural addition to it; and tend to enfeeble the impression which the composition, as a whole, is calculated to make.

The most eloquent of the French, perhaps, indeed, of all modern orators, Bossuet, bishop of Meaux, terminates in a very moving manner, his funeral oration on the great prince of Condé, with this return upon himself, and his old age: "Accept, O prince! these last efforts of a voice which you once well knew. With you, all my funeral discourses are now to end. Instead of deploring the death of others, henceforth, it shall be my study to learn from you, how my own may be blessed. Happy, if warned by those gray hairs, of the account which I must soon give of my ministry, I reserve, solely, for that flock whom I ought to feed with the word of life, the feeble remains of a voice which now trembles, and of an ardour which is now on the point of being extinct."

In all discourses, it is a matter of importance to hit the precise time of concluding, so as to bring our discourse just to a point; neither ending abruptly and unexpectedly; nor disappointing the expectation of the hearers, when they look for the close, and continuing to hover round and round the conclusion, till they become heartily tired of us. We should endeavour to go off with a good grace; not to end with a languishing and drawling sentence; but to close with dignity and spirit, that we may leave the minds of the hearers warm, and dismiss them with a favourable impression of the subject, and of the speaker.

Lecture XXXIV

MEANS OF IMPROVING IN ELOQUENCE

I have now treated fully of the different kinds of public speaking, of the composition, and of the delivery of a discourse. Before I finish this subject, it may be of use to suggest some things concerning the proper means of improvement in the art of public speaking, and the most necessary studies for that purpose.

To be an eloquent speaker, in the proper sense of the word, is far from being either a common or an easy attainment. Indeed, to compose a florid harangue on some popular topic, and to deliver it so as to amuse an audience, is a matter not very difficult. But though some praise be due to this, yet the idea which I have endeavoured to give of eloquence, is much higher. It is a great exertion of the human powers. It is the art of being persuasive and commanding; the art, not of pleasing the fancy merely, but of speaking both to the understanding and to the heart; of interesting the hearers in such a degree, as to seize and carry them along with us; and to leave them with a deep and strong impression of what they have heard. How many talents, natural and acquired, must concur for carrying this to perfection? A strong, lively, and warm imagination; quick sensibility of heart, joined with solid judgment, good sense, and presence of mind; all improved by great and long attention to style and composition; and supported also by the exterior, yet important qualifications of a graceful manner, a presence not ungainly, and a full and tunable voice. How little reason to wonder, that a perfect and accomplished orator, should be one of the characters that is most rarely to be found?

Let us not despair, however. Between mediocrity and perfection, there is a very wide interval. There are many intermediate spaces, which may be filled up with honour; and the more rare and difficult that complete perfection is, the greater is the honour of approaching to it, though we do not fully attain it. The number of orators who stand in the highest class is, perhaps, smaller than the number of poets who are foremost in poetic fame; but the study of oratory has this advantage above that of poetry, that, in poetry, one must be an eminently good performer, or he is not supportable. In eloquence this does not hold. There, one may possess a moderate station with dignity. Eloquence admits of a great many different forms; plain and simple, as well as high and pathetic; and a genius that cannot reach the latter, may shine with much reputation and usefulness in the former.

Whether nature or art contribute most to form an orator, is a trifling inquiry. In all attainments whatever, nature must be the prime agent. She must bestow the original talents. She must sow the seeds; but culture is requisite for bringing these seeds to perfection. Nature must always have done somewhat: but a great deal will always be left to be done by art. This is certain, that study and discipline are more necessary for the improvement of natural genius in oratory, than they are in poetry. What I mean is, that though poetry be capable of receiving assistance from critical art, yet a poet, without any aid from art, by the force of genius alone, can rise higher than a public speaker can do, who has never given attention to the rules of style, composition, and delivery. Homer formed himself; Demosthenes and Cicero were formed by the help of much labour, and of many assistances derived from the labour of others. After these preliminary observations, let us proceed to the main design of this lecture; to treat of the means to be used for improving in eloquence.

In the first place, what stands highest in the order of means, is personal character and disposition. In order to be a truly eloquent or persuasive speaker, nothing is more necessary than to be a virtuous man. This was a favourite position among the ancient rhetoricians: *"Non posse oratorem esse nisi virum bonum."* (It is not possible to be an orator unless one is a good man). To find any such connexion between virtue and one of the highest liberal arts, must give pleasure; and it can, I think, be clearly shown, that this is not a mere topic of declamation, but that the connexion here alleged, is undoubtedly founded in truth and reason.

For, consider first, whether anything contribute more to persuasion, than the opinion which we entertain of the probity, disinterestedness, candour, and other good moral qualities of the person who endeavours to persuade? These give weight and force to everything which he utters; nay, they add a beauty to it; they dispose us to listen with attention and pleasure; and create a secret partiality in favour of that side which he espouses. Whereas, if we entertain a suspicion of craft and disingenuity, of a corrupt, or a base mind, in the speaker, his eloquence loses all its real effect. It may entertain and amuse; but it is viewed as artifice, as trick, as the play only of speech; and viewed in this light, whom can it persuade? We can even read a book with more pleasure, when we think favourably of its author; but when we have the living speaker before our eyes, addressing us personally on some subject of importance, the opinion we entertain of his character must have a much more powerful effect.

But, lest it should be said, that this relates only to the character of virtue, which one may maintain, without being at the bottom a truly worthy man, I must observe farther, that besides the weight which it adds to character, real virtue operates also, in other ways, to the advantage of eloquence.

First, nothing is so favourable as virtue to the prosecution of honourable studies. It prompts a generous emulation to excel; it inures to industry; it leaves the mind vacant and free, master of itself, disencumbered of those bad passions and disengaged from those mean pursuits, which have ever been found the greatest enemies to true proficiency. Quintilian has touched this consideration very properly: "If the management of an estate, if anxious attention to domestic economy, a passion for hunting, or whole days given up to public places of amusements, consume so much time that is due to study, how much greater waste must be occasioned by licentious desires, avarice, or envy? Nothing is so much hurried and agitated, so contradictory to itself, or so violently torn and shattered by conflicting passions, as a bad heart. Amidst the distractions which it produces, what room is left for the cultivation of letters, or the pursuit of any honourable art? No more, assuredly, than there is for the growth of corn in a field that is overrun with thorns and brambles."

But, besides this consideration, there is another of still higher importance, though I am not sure of its being attended to as much as it deserves; namely, that from the fountain of real and genuine virtue, are drawn those sentiments which will ever be most powerful in affecting the hearts of others. Bad as the world is, nothing has so great and universal a command over the minds of men as virtue. No kind of language is so generally understood, and so powerfully felt, as the native language of worthy and virtuous feelings. He only, therefore, who possesses these full and strong, can speak properly, and in its own language, to the heart. On all great subjects and occasions, there is a dignity, there is an energy in noble sentiments, which is overcoming and irresistible. They give an ardour and a flame to one's discourse, which seldom fails to kindle a like flame in those who hear; and which, more than any other cause, bestows on eloquence that power, for which it is famed, of seizing and transporting an audience. Here, art and imitation will not avail. An assumed character conveys none of this powerful warmth. It is only a native and unaffected glow of feeling, which can transmit the emotion to others. Hence, the most renowned orators, such as Cicero and Demosthenes, were no less distinguished for some of the high virtues, as public spirit and zeal for their country, than for eloquence. Beyond doubt, to these virtues their eloquence owed much of its effect; and those orations of theirs, in which there breathes most of the virtuous and magnanimous spirit, are those which have most attracted the admiration of ages.

Nothing, therefore, is more necessary for those who would excel in any of the higher kinds of oratory, than to cultivate habits of the several virtues, and to refine and improve all their moral feelings. Whenever these become dead, or callous, they may be assured, that, on every great occasion, they will speak with less power, and less success. The sentiments and dispositions particularly requisite for them to cultivate, are the following: The love of justice and order and indignation at insolence and oppression; the love of honesty and truth, and detestation of fraud, meanness, and corruption; magnanimity of spirit; the love of liberty, of their country, and the public; zeal for all great and noble designs, and reverence for all worthy and heroic characters. A cold and skeptical turn of mind, is extremely adverse to eloquence; and no less so, is that cavilling disposition which takes pleasure in depreciating what is great, and ridiculing what is generally admired. Such a disposition bespeaks one not very likely to excel in any thing: but least of all in oratory. A true orator should be a person of generous sentiments, of warm feelings, and a mind turned towards the admiration of all those great and high objects, which mankind are naturally formed to admire. Joined with the manly virtues, he should, at the same time, possess strong and tender sensibility to all the injuries, distresses, and sorrows of his fellow-creatures; a heart that can easily relent; that can readily enter into the circumstances of others, and can make their case his own. A proper mixture of courage, and of modesty, must also be studied by every public speaker. Modesty is essential; it is always and justly supposed to be a concomitant of merit; and every appearance of it is winning and prepossessing. But modesty ought not to run into excessive timidity. Every public speaker should be able to rest somewhat on himself; and to assume that air, not of self-complacency, but of firmness, which bespeaks a consciousness of his being thoroughly persuaded of the truth or justice of what he delivers; a circumstance of no small consequence for making an impression on those who hear.

Next to moral qualifications, what in the second place is most necessary to an orator, is a fund of knowledge. Much is this inculcated by Cicero and Quintilian: *"Quod omnibus disciplinis et artibus debet esse instructus orator."* By which they mean, that he ought to have what we call, a liberal education; and to be formed by a regular study of philosophy, and the polite arts. We must never forget that,

Scribendi recte, sapere est et principium et fons.

(Good sense and knowledge, are the foundation of all good speaking.) There is no art that can teach one to be eloquent, in any sphere, without a sufficient acquaintance with what belongs to that sphere; or if there were an art that made such pretensions, it would be mere quackery, like the pretensions of the sophists of old to teach their disciples to speak for and against every subject; and would be deservedly exploded by all wise men. Attention to style, to composition, and all the arts of speech, can only assist an orator in setting off to advantage, the stock of materials which he possesses; but the stock, the materials themselves, must be brought from other quarters than from rhetoric. He who is to plead at the bar, must make himself thoroughly master of the knowledge of the law; of all the learning and experience that can be useful in his profession, for supporting a cause or convincing a judge. He who is to speak from the pulpit, must apply himself closely to the study of divinity, of practical religion, of morals, of human nature; that he may be rich in all the topics, both of instruction and of persuasion. He who would fit himself for being a member of the supreme council of the nation, or of any public assembly, must be thoroughly acquainted with the business that belongs to such assembly; he must study the forms of court, the course of procedure; and must attend minutely to all the facts that may be the subject of question or deliberation.

Besides the knowledge that properly belongs to his profession, a public speaker, if ever he expects to be eminent, must make himself acquainted, as far as his necessary occupations allow, with the general circle of polite literature. The study of poetry may be useful to him, on many occasions, for embellishing his style, for suggesting lively images, or agreeable allusions. The study of history may be still more useful to him; as the knowledge of facts, of eminent characters, and of the course of human affairs, finds place on many occasions. There are few great occasions of public speaking in which one will not derive assistance from cultivated taste, and extensive knowledge. They will often yield him materials for proper ornament; sometimes for argument and real use. A deficiency of knowledge, even in subjects that belong not directly to his own profession, will expose him to many disadvantages, and give better qualified rivals a great superiority over him.

Allow me to recommend, in the third place, not only the attainment of useful knowledge, but a habit of application and industry. Without this, it is impossible to excel in any thing. We must not imagine, that it is by a sort of mushroom growth, that one can rise to be a distinguished pleader, or preacher, or speaker in any assembly. It is not by starts of application, or by a few years preparation of study afterwards discontinued, that eminence can be attained. No; it can be attained only by means of regular industry, grown up into a habit, and ready to be exerted on every occasion that calls for industry. This is the fixed law of our nature; and he must have a very high opinion of his own genius indeed, that can believe himself an exception to it. A very wise law of our nature it is; for industry is, in truth, the great *"condimentum,"* the seasoning of every pleasure; without which life is doomed to languish. Nothing is so great an enemy both to honourable attainments, and to the real, to the brisk, and spirited enjoyment of life, as that relaxed state of mind which arises from indolence and dissipation. One that is destined to excel in any art, especially in the arts of speaking and writing, will be known by this more than by any other mark whatever, an enthusiasm for that art; an enthusiasm, which firing his mind with the object he has in view, will dispose him to relish every labour which the means require. It was this that characterized the great men of antiquity; it is this, which must distinguish the moderns who would tread in their steps.

This honourable enthusiasm, it is highly necessary for such as are studying oratory to cultivate. If youth wants it, manhood will flag miserably.

In the fourth place, attention to the best models will contribute greatly towards improvement. Every one who speaks, or writes, should, indeed, endeavour to have somewhat that is his own, that is peculiar to himself, and that characterizes his composition and style. Slavish imitation depresses genius, or rather betrays the want of it. But withal, there is no genius so original, but may be profited and assisted by the aid of proper examples, in style, composition, and delivery. They always open some new ideas; they serve to enlarge and correct our own. They quicken the current of thought, and excite emulation.

Much, indeed, will depend on the right choice of models which we purpose to imitate; and supposing them rightly chosen, a farther care is requisite, of not being seduced by a blind, universal admiration. For, *"decipit exemplar, vitiis imitabile."* (For a model whose faults are imitated can deceive.) Even in the most finished models we can select, it must not be forgotten, that there are always some things improper for imitation. We should study to acquire a just conception of the peculiar characteristic beauties of any writer, or public speaker, and imitate these only. One ought never to attach himself too closely to any single model; for he who does so, is almost sure of being seduced into a faulty and affected imitation. His business should be, to draw from several the proper ideas of perfection. Living examples of public speaking, in any kind, it will not be expected that I should here point out. As to the writers, ancient and modern, from whom benefit may be derived in forming composition and style, I have spoken so much of them in former lectures, that it is needless to repeat what I have said of their virtues and defects. I own it is to be regretted, that the English language, in which there is much good writing, furnishes us, however, with but very few recorded examples of eloquent public speaking. Among the French there are more. Saurin, Bourdaloue, Flechier, Massillon, particularly the last, are eminent for the eloquence of the pulpit. But the most nervous and sublime of all their orators is Bossuet, the famous Bishop of Meaux; in whose *Oraisons Funèbres,* there is a high spirit of oratory. Some of Fontenelle's harangues to the French Academy, are elegant and agreeable. And at the bar, the printed pleadings of Cochin and D'Aguesseau, are highly extolled by the late French critics.

There is one observation which it is of importance to make, concerning imitation of the style of any favourite author, when we would carry his style into public speaking. We must attend to a very material distinction, between written and spoken language. These are, in truth, two different manners of communicating ideas. A book that is to be read, requires one sort of style: a man that is to speak, must use another. In books, we look for correctness, precision, all redundancies pruned, all repetitions avoided, language completely polished. Speaking admits a more easy, copious style, and less fettered by rule; repetitions may often be necessary, parentheses may sometimes be graceful, the same thought must often be placed in different views; as the hearers can catch it only from the mouth of the speaker, and have not the advantage, as in reading a book, of turning back again, and of dwelling on what they do not fully comprehend. Hence the style of many good authors, would appear stiff, affected, and even obscure, if, by too close an imitation, we should transfer it to a popular oration. How awkward, for example, would Lord Shaftesbury's sentences sound in the mouth of a public speaker? Some kinds of public discourse, it is true, such as that of the pulpit, where more exact preparation, and more studied style are admitted, would bear such a manner better than others, which are expected to approach more to extemporaneous speaking. But still there is, in general, so much difference between speaking, and composition designed only to be read, as should guard us against a close and injudicious imitation.

Some authors there are, whose manner of writing approaches nearer to the style of speaking than others; and who, therefore, can be imitated with more safety. In this class, among the English authors, are Dean Swift, and Lord Bolingbroke. The Dean, throughout all his writings, in the midst of much correctness maintains the easy natural manner of an unaffected speaker; and this is one of his chief excellencies. Lord Bolingbroke's style is more splendid, and more declamatory than Dean Swift's; but still it is the style of one who speaks, or rather who harangues. Indeed, all his political writings (for it is to them only, and not to his philosophical ones, that this observation can be applied,) carry much more the appearance of one declaiming with warmth in a great assembly, than of one writing in a closet, in order to be read by others. They have all the copiousness, the fervour, the inculcating method that is allowable and graceful in an orator; perhaps too much of it for a writer: and it is to be regretted, as I have formerly observed, that the matter contained in them, should have been so trivial or so false; for, from the manner and style, considerable advantage might be reaped.

In the fifth place, besides attention to the best models, frequent exercise both in composing and speaking, will be admitted to be a necessary mean of improvement. That sort of composition is, doubtless, most useful, which relates to the profession, or kind of public speaking, to which persons addict themselves. This, they should keep ever in their eye, and be gradually inuring themselves to it. But let me also advise them, not to allow themselves in negligent composition of any kind. He who has it for his aim to write or to speak correctly, should, in the most trivial kind of composition, in writing a letter, nay, even in common discourse, study to acquit himself with propriety. I do not at all mean, that he is never to write, or to speak a word, but in elaborate and artificial language. This would form him to a stiffness and affectation, worse, by ten thousand degrees, than the greatest negligence. But it is to be observed, that there is, in every thing, a manner which is becoming, and has propriety; and opposite to it, there is a clumsy and faulty performance of the same thing. The becoming manner is very often the most light, and seemingly careless manner; but it requires taste and attention to seize the just idea of it. That idea, when acquired, we should keep in our eye, and form upon it whatever we write or say.

Exercises of speaking have always been recommended to students, in order that they may prepare themselves for speaking in public, and on real business. The meetings, or societies, into which they sometimes form themselves for this purpose, are laudable institutions; and, under proper conduct, may serve many valuable purposes. They are favourable to knowledge and study, by giving occasion to inquiries, concerning those subjects which are made the ground of discussion. They produce emulation; and gradually inure those who are concerned in them, to somewhat that resembles a public assembly. They accustom them to know their own powers, and to acquire a command of themselves in speaking; and what is, perhaps, the greatest advantage of all, they give them a facility and fluency of expression, and assist them in procuring that *"Copia verborum,"* which can be acquired by no other means but frequent exercise in speaking.

But the meetings which I have now in my eye, are to be understood of those academical associations, where a moderate number of young gentlemen, who are carrying on their studies, and are connected by some affinity in the future pursuits which they have in view, assemble privately, in order to improve one another, and to prepare themselves for those public exhibitions which may afterwards fall to their lot. As for those public and promiscuous societies, in which multitudes are brought together, who are often of low stations and occupations, who are joined by no common bond of union, except an absurd rage for public speaking, and have no other object in view, but to make a show of their supposed talents, they are institutions not merely of an useless, but of an hurtful nature. They are in great hazard of proving seminaries of licentiousness, petulance, faction, and folly. They mislead those who, in their own callings, might be useful members of society, into fantastic plans of making a figure on subjects, which divert their attention from their proper business, and are widely remote from their sphere in life.

Even the allowable meetings into which students of oratory form themselves, stand in need of direction, in order to render them useful. If their subjects of discourse be improperly chosen; if they maintain extravagant or indecent topics; if they indulge themselves in loose and flimsy declamation, which has no foundation in good sense; or accustom themselves to speak pertly on all subjects without due preparation, they may improve one another in petulance, but in no other thing; and will infallibly form themselves to a very faulty and vicious taste in speaking. I would, therefore, advise all who are members of such societies, in the first place, to attend to the choice of their subjects; that they be useful and manly, either formed on the course of their studies, or on something that has relation to morals and taste, to action and life. In the second place, I would advise them to be temperate in the practice of speaking; not to speak too often, nor on subjects where they are ignorant or unripe; but only, when they have proper materials for a discourse, and have digested and thought of the subject beforehand. In the third place, when they do speak, they should study always to keep good sense and persuasion in view, rather than an ostentation of eloquence; and for this end I would, in the fourth place, repeat the advice which I gave in a former lecture, that they should always choose that side of the question to which, in their own judgment, they are most inclined, as the right and the true side; and defend it by such arguments as seem to them most solid. By these means, they will take the best method of forming themselves gradually to a manly, correct, and persuasive manner of speaking.

It now only remains to inquire, of what use may the study of critical and rhetorical writers be, for improving one in the practice of eloquence? These are certainly not to be neglected; and yet I dare not say that much is to be expected from them. For professed writers on public speaking, we must look chiefly among the ancients. In modern times, for reasons which were before given, popular eloquence, as an art, has never been very much the object of study; it has not the same powerful effects among us that it had in more democratical states; and therefore has not been cultivated with the same care. Among the moderns, though there has been a great deal of good criticism on the different kinds of writing, yet much has not been attempted on the subject of eloquence, or public discourse; and what has been given us of that kind, has been drawn mostly from the ancients. Such a writer as Joannes Gerardus Vossius, who has gathered into one heap of ponderous lumber, all the trifling, as well as the useful things, that are to be found in the Greek and Roman writers, is enough to disgust one with the study of eloquence. Among the French, there has been more attempted, on this subject, than among the English. The Bishop of Cambray's writings on eloquence, I before mentioned with honour; Rollin, Batteux, Crevier, Gibert, and several other French critics, have also written on oratory; but though some of them may be useful, none of them are so considerable as to deserve particular recommendation.

It is to the original ancient writers that we must chiefly have recourse; and it is a reproach to any one, whose profession calls him to speak in public, to be unacquainted with them. In all the ancient rhetorical writers, there is, indeed, this defect, that they are too systematical, as I formerly showed; they aim at doing too much; at reducing rhetoric to a complete and perfect art, which may even supply invention with materials on every subject; insomuch, that one would imagine they expected to form an orator by rule, in as mechanical a manner as one would form a carpenter. Whereas, all that can, in truth, be done, is to give openings for assisting and enlightening taste, and for pointing out to genius the course it ought to hold.

Aristotle laid the foundation for all that was afterwards written on the subject. That amazing and comprehensive genius, which does honour to human nature, and which gave light unto so many different sciences, has investigated the principles of rhetoric with great penetration. Aristotle appears to have been the first who took rhetoric out of the hands of sophists, and introduced reasoning and good sense into the art. Some of the profoundest things which have been written on the passions and manners of men, are to be found in his Treatise on Rhetoric; though in this, as in all his writings, his great brevity often renders him obscure. Succeeding Greek rhetoricians, most of whom are now lost, improved on the foundation which Aristotle had laid. Two of them still remain, Demetrius Phalereus, and Dionysius of Halicarnassus; both write on the construction of sentences, and deserve to be perused; especially Dionysius, who is a very accurate and judicious critic.

I need scarcely recommend the rhetorical writings of Cicero. Whatever, on the subject of eloquence, comes from so great an orator, must be worthy of attention. His most considerable work on that subject is that *De Oratore,* in three books. None of Cicero's writings are more highly finished than this treatise. The dialogue is polite; the characters well supported, and the conduct of the whole is beautiful and agreeable. It is, indeed, full of digressions, and his rules and observations may be thought sometimes too vague and general. Useful things, however, may be learned from it; and it is no small benefit to be made acquainted with Cicero's own idea of eloquence. The *Orator ad M. Brutum,* is also a considerable treatise: and, in general, throughout Cicero's rhetorical works there run those high and sublime ideas of eloquence, which are fitted both for forming a just taste, and for creating that enthusiasm for the art, which is of the greatest consequence for excelling in it.

But of all the ancient writers on the subject of oratory, the most instructive, and most useful, is Quintilian. I know few books which abound more with good sense, and discover a greater degree of just and accurate taste, than Quintilian's *Institutions.* Almost all the principles of good criticism are to be found in them. He has digested into excellent order all the ancient ideas concerning rhetoric; and is, at the same time, himself an eloquent writer. Though some parts of his work contain too much of the technical and artificial system then in vogue, and for that reason may be dry and tedious, yet I would not advise the omitting to read any part of his *Institutions.* To pleaders at the bar, even these technical parts may prove of much use. Seldom has any person, of more sound and distinct judgment than Quintilian, applied himself to the study of the art of oratory.

GEORGE CAMPBELL

⌇⌇⌇⌇⌇⌇⌇⌇⌇⌇⌇

George Campbell (1719–1796) was born in Aberdeen, Scotland, educated at Kings and Marischal College, and ordained as a minister in the Presbyterian Church. Licensed to preach in 1746, he secured his first pastorate two years later and continued to deliver sermons regularly until his retirement in 1795. Throughout most of his career Campbell served not only as a practicing minister but as an educational administrator and theologian. In 1759, he became Principal of Marischal College, and in 1771 was elected Professor of Divinity at the same institution.

Campbell came into prominence in 1761 following the publication of his *Dissertation on Miracles,* a treatise designed to answer the scepticism of David Hume. As a religious moderate, he, like Blair, rejected both the religious emphasis of the "enthusiasts" who stressed dogmatism and emotionalism, and the liberal doctrines of the rationalistic theologians and philosophers who doubted the authenticity of the Scriptures. In defending the biblical account of the miracles first in the celebrated treatise and later in numerous sermons before the Presbyterian Synod at Aberdeen, Campbell used closely reasoned discourse and a wide variety of evidence. These principles of argumentation became a trademark of his pulpit oratory.

Campbell began his systematic study of rhetoric in 1750. After composing two essays which ultimately became the first two chapters of his *Philosophy of Rhetoric,* he put aside his writing for five years. In 1757, after reading his essays to a literary society in Aberdeen which he helped form, he was encouraged by the warm response. He thus decided to continue his project of constructing a theory of rhetoric based upon the principles of human nature. By 1760, he had completed most of Book I. When Campbell finished rough drafts of additional chapters during the next fifteen years, he submitted them to his friends for criticism before revising them.

Shortly after the volume was published in 1776, Blair, after quickly perusing a copy forwarded to him, expressed an attitude of guarded optimism concerning the impact the book might produce. In a letter to Elizabeth Montagu on June 8, he said:

You may perhaps have looked into Dr. Campbell's *Philosophy of Rhetoric;* I am persuaded you will not be displeased with it. I know the author to be a most ingenious and acute man and I am convinced his book will carry that Character. I have as yet, just only seen it; and can form no judgment from perusal. I wish only it may not be so acute as to border on the abstruse: but that it will convey instruction of a profound nature I make no doubt.

The *Philosophy of Rhetoric,* perhaps the most comprehensive and original treatment of rhetoric since the classical period, probes deeply into the nature, foundations, and essential and discriminating properties of eloquence. As we have seen, the best psychological, philosophical, epistemological, and literary thoughts of the eighteenth century are brought to bear on the subject of informing, pleasing, convincing, and moving a hearer. In describing the ends of speaking, the types of oratory, the nature of speech content and style, and audience analysis, he demonstrates that the purpose of oral communication is to express sentiments, passions, and moods as well as ideas.

The significance of Campbell's *Philosophy of Rhetoric* cannot be measured in terms of popular response. In the first one hundred years following its publication, it reached the public through twenty-one major editions. During the same period, however, Blair's *Lectures on Rhetoric and Belles Lettres,* as noted earlier, was produced in sixty-two complete editions and fifty-one abridgements.

Although Campbell's rhetorical views are best summarized in his major text, he wrote two other works which are similarly important to the student of public address. The first was a sermon preached before the Synod of Aberdeen in 1752 and entitled, "The Character of a Minister of the Gospel as a Teacher and Pattern." Standing squarely in the tradition of Quintilian's "good man" theory, Campbell urged all ministers to live an exemplary life. Since persuasion depends largely upon the listener's attitude toward the speaker, sincerity and moral integrity are essential requisites of the pulpit orator. That speaker, therefore, whose doctrine and practice correspond will treble his effectiveness. Campbell's other contribution to speech education was his more extensive *Lectures on Systematic Theology and Pulpit Eloquence,* published posthumously in 1807. These addresses, most of which were presented to the students at Marischal College before the publication of *The Philosophy of Rhetoric,* provide a handbook for inexperienced preachers who have had little training in public address. They are essentially lessons in voice control, elocution, and organization. Thus they serve as an excellent supplement to the *Philosophy of Rhetoric.*

In addition to his *Dissertation on Miracles,* his published sermons, and his works on rhetoric and homiletics, Campbell produced two other volumes which reflected his lifelong interest in theology. The first was the *New Testament Gospels; The Four Gospels Translated from Greek, with Preliminary Dissertations and Notes* (1789); the other, published posthumously, was entitled *Lectures on Ecclesiastical History* (1800).

Campbell, in sum, was a convincing pulpit speaker, an able educational administrator and professor, and a productive scholar. Despite his commitment to the pulpit and to theology, Campbell is best remembered as a rhetorician. His writings on this subject, taken together, provide a remarkable analysis of the speaker, the speech, and the audience. It is an analysis which stems from both the author's grasp of book knowledge and from his long career as a practitioner. If these discussions were less popular with the reading public than those of Blair, they perhaps have exerted a greater influence on contemporary rhetorical theory.

Bibliography

Bevilacqua, Vincent M., "Philosophical Origins of George Campbell's Philosophy of Rhetoric," *Speech Monographs,* XXXII (March 1965), 1–12.

Bitzer, Lloyd F., "The Lively Idea: A Study of Hume's Influence on George Campbell's *Philosophy of Rhetoric.*" Unpublished Ph.D. dissertation, State University of Iowa, 1962.

——, ed., *The Philosophy of Rhetoric by George Campbell* (Carbondale, Illinois, 1963).

——, "A Re-Evaluation of Campbell's Doctrine of Evidence," *Quarterly Journal of Speech,* XLVI (April 1960), 135–140.

Campbell, George, *The Philosophy of Rhetoric,* 2 vols. (London, 1776).

——, "The Character of a Minister of the Gospel as a Teacher and Pattern," A Sermon preached before the Synod of Aberdeen at Aberdeen, April 7, 1752 (Aberdeen, 1752).

——, *A Dissertation on Miracles,* . . . 3d edition. With a correspondence on the subject by Mr. Hume, Dr. Campbell, and Dr. Blair, 2 vols. (Edinburgh, 1797).

——, *Lectures on Systematic Theology and Pulpit Eloquence* (Boston, 1832).

Crawford, John, "The Rhetoric of George Campbell." Unpublished Ph.D. dissertation, Northwestern University, 1947.

Edney, Clarence W., "George Campbell's Theory of Public Address." Unpublished Ph.D. dissertation, State University of Iowa, 1946.

——, "Campbell's Theory of Logical Truth," *Speech Monographs,* XV (March 1948), 19–32.

——, "Campbell's Lectures on Pulpit Eloquence," *Speech Monographs,* XIX (March 1952), 1–10.

Ehninger, Douglas, "George Campbell and the Revolution in Inventional Theory," *The Southern Speech Journal,* XV (May 1950), 270–276.

Ettlich, Ernest, Dominic La Russo, Herman Cohen, G. P. Mohrmann, and Phil Dolph, "Symposium: The Rhetorical Theory of George Campbell," *Western Speech,* XXXII (Spring 1968), 84–113.

Hall, Alta, "George Campbell's *Philosophy of Rhetoric.*" Unpublished Ph.D. dissertation, Cornell University, 1934.

McDermott, Douglas, "George Campbell and the Classical Tradition," *Quarterly Journal of Speech,* XLIX (December 1963), 403–409.

Stephen, Leslie, "George Campbell," *Dictionary of National Biography* (London, 1882).

Addenda

Bitzer, Lloyd, "Hume's Philosophy in George Campbell's Philosophy of Rhetoric," *Philosophy & Rhetoric*, 2 (Summer 1969), 139–166.

Cohen, Herman, "William Leechman's Anticipation of Campbell," *Western Speech*, XXXII (Spring 1968), 92–99.

Ettlich, Ernest, LaRusso, Dominick, Cohen, Herman, Mohrmann, G. P., and Dolph, Phil, "Symposium: The Rhetorical Theory of George Campbell," *Western Speech* XXXII (Spring 1968), 84–113.

Golden, James L., Berquist, Goodwin F., and Coleman, William E., "The Rhetorics of Campbell and Whately," in *The Rhetoric of Western Thought*, Second Edition (Dubuque, Iowa, 1979), pp. 123–143.

Howell, Wilbur Samuel, "George Campbell and the Philosophical Rhetoric of the New Learning," in *Eighteenth-Century British Logic and Rhetoric* (Princeton, 1971), pp. 577–612.

La Russo, Dominick, "Root or Branch? A Re-examination of Campbell's 'Rhetoric,'" *Western Speech*, XXXII (Spring 1968), 85–91.

McKerrow, Ray E., "Campbell, Whately on the Utility of Syllogistic Logic," *Western Speech Communication*, XL (Winter 1976), 3–13.

Mohrmann, G. P., "George Campbell: The Psychological Background," *Western Speech*, XXXII (Spring 1968), 99–104.

Rasmussen, Karen, "Inconsistency in Campbell's Rhetoric," *Quarterly Journal of Speech*, LX (April 1974), 190–200.

Complete Table of Contents for
GEORGE CAMPBELL
The Philosophy of Rhetoric

BOOK III
THE DISCRIMINATING PROPERTIES OF ELOCUTION

THE
PHILOSOPHY OF RHETORIC

Book I   The Nature and Foundations
of Eloquence

CHAPTER I

Eloquence in the largest acceptation defined, its more general forms exhibited, with their different objects, ends, and characters.

In speaking there is always some end proposed, or some effect which the speaker intends to produce on the hearer. The word *eloquence* in its greatest latitude denotes, "That art or talent by which the discourse is adapted to its end." [1]

All the ends of speaking are reducible to four; every speech being intended to enlighten the understanding, to please the imagination, to move the passions, or to influence the will.

Any one discourse admits only one of these ends as the principal. Nevertheless, in discoursing on a subject, many things may be introduced, which are more immediately and apparently directed to some of the other ends of speaking, and not to that which is the chief intent of the whole. But then these other and immediate ends are in effect but means, and must be rendered conducive to that which is the primary intention. Accordingly, the propriety or the impropriety of the introduction of such secondary ends, will always be inferred from their subserviency or want of subserviency to that end, which is, in respect of them, the ultimate. For example, a discourse addressed to the understanding, and calculated to illustrate or evince some point purely speculative, may borrow aid from the imagination, and admit metaphor and comparison, but not the bolder and more striking figures, as that called vision or fiction, prosopopœia, and the like, which are not so much intended to elucidate a subject, as to excite admiration. Still less will it admit an address to the passions, which, as it never fails to disturb the operation of the intellectual faculty, must be regarded by every intelligent hearer as foreign at least, if not insidious. It is obvious, that either of these, far from being subservient to the main design, would distract the attention from it.

There is indeed one kind of address to the understanding, and only one,

---

[1] *"Dicere secundum virtutem orationis. Scientia bene dicendi."* (Quintilian) The word *eloquence,* in common conversation, is seldom used in such a comprehensive sense. I have, however, made choice of this definition on a double account: 1st. It exactly corresponds to Tully's idea of a perfect orator; *"Optimus est orator qui dicendo animos audientium et docet, et delectat, et permovet."* 2dly. It is best adapted to the subject of these papers.

which, it may not be improper to observe, disdains all assistance whatever from the fancy. The address I mean is mathematical demonstration. As this does not, like moral reasoning, admit degrees of evidence, its perfection, in point of eloquence, if so uncommon an application of the term may be allowed, consists in perspicuity. Perspicuity here results entirely from propriety and simplicity of diction, and from accuracy of method, where the mind is regularly, step by step, conducted forwards in the same track, the attention no way diverted, nothing left to be supplied, no one unnecessary word or idea introduced.[2] On the contrary, an harangue framed for affecting the hearts or influencing the resolves of an assembly, needs greatly the assistance both of intellect and of imagination.

In general it may be asserted, that each preceding species, in the order above exhibited, is preparatory to the subsequent; that each subsequent species is founded on the preceding; and that thus they ascend in a regular progression. Knowledge, the object of the intellect, furnisheth materials for the fancy; the fancy culls, compounds, and, by her mimic art, disposes these materials so as to affect the passions; the passions are the natural spurs to volition or action, and so need only to be right directed. This connexion and dependency will better appear from the following observations.

When a speaker addresseth himself to the understanding, he proposes the *instruction* of his hearers, and that, either by explaining some doctrine unknown, or not distinctly comprehended by them, or by proving some position disbelieved or doubted by them.—In other words, he proposes either to dispel ignorance or to vanquish error. In the one, his aim is their *information;* in the other, their *conviction.* Accordingly the predominant quality of the former is *perspicuity;* of the latter, *argument.* By that we are made to know, by this to believe.

The imagination is addressed by exhibiting to it a lively and beautiful representation of a suitable object. As in this exhibition, the task of the orator may, in some sort, be said, like that of the painter, to consist in imitation, the merit of the work results entirely from these two sources; dignity, as well in the subject or thing imitated, as in the manner of imitation; and resemblance, in the portrait or performance. Now the principal scope for this class being in narration and description, poetry, which is one mode of oratory, especially epic poetry, must be ranked under it. The effect of the dramatic, at least of tragedy, being upon the passions, the drama falls under another species, to be explained afterwards. But that kind of address of which I am now treating, attains the summit of perfection in the *sublime,* or those great and noble images, which, when in suitable colouring pre-

2 Of this kind Euclid hath given us the most perfect models, which have not, I think, been sufficiently imitated by later mathematicians. In him you find the exactest arrangement inviolably observed, the properest and simplest, and by consequence the plainest expressions constantly used, nothing deficient, nothing superfluous; in brief, nothing which in more, or fewer, or other words, or words otherwise disposed, could have been better expressed.

sented to the mind, do, as it were, distend the imagination with some vast conception, and quite ravish the soul.

The sublime, it may be urged, as it raiseth admiration, should be considered as one species of address to the passions. But this objection, when examined, will appear superficial. There are few words in any language (particularly such as relate to the operations and feelings of the mind) which are strictly univocal. Thus admiration, when persons are the object, is commonly used for a high degree of esteem; but when otherwise applied, it denotes solely an internal taste. It is that pleasurable sensation which instantly ariseth on the perception of magnitude, or of whatever is great and stupendous in its kind. For there is a greatness in the degrees of quality in spiritual subjects, analogous to that which subsists in the degrees of quantity in material things. Accordingly, in all tongues, perhaps without exception, the ordinary terms, which are considered as literally expressive of the latter, are also used promiscuously to denote the former. Now admiration, when thus applied, doth not require to its production, as the passions generally do, any reflex view of motives or tendencies, or of any relation either to private interest, or to the good of others; and ought therefore to be numbered among those original feelings of the mind, which are denominated by some the reflex senses, being of the same class with a taste for beauty, an ear for music, or our moral sentiments. Now, the immediate view of whatever is directed to the imagination (whether the subject be things inanimate or animal forms, whether characters, actions, incidents, or manner) terminates in the gratification of some internal taste: as a taste for the wonderful, the fair, the good; for elegance, for novelty, or for grandeur.

But it is evident, that this creative faculty, the fancy, frequently lends her aid in promoting still nobler ends. From her exuberant stores most of those tropes and figures are extracted, which, when properly employed, have such a marvellous efficacy in rousing the passions, and by some secret, sudden, and inexplicable association, awakening all the tenderest emotions of the heart. In this case, the address of the orator is not ultimately intended to astonish by the loftiness of his images, or to delight by the beauteous resemblance which his painting bears to nature; nay, it will not permit the hearers even a moment's leisure for making the comparison, but as it were by some magical spell, hurries them, ere they are aware, into love, pity, grief, terror, desire, aversion, fury, or hatred. It therefore assumes the denomination of *pathetic*,[3] which is the characteristic of the third species of discourse, that addressed to the passions.

Finally, as that kind, the most complex of all, which is calculated to influence the will, and persuade to a certain conduct, is in reality an artful mixture of that which proposes to convince the judgment, and that which interests the passions, its distinguished excellency results from these two, the

---

3 I am sensible that this word is commonly used in a more limited sense, for that which only excites commiseration. *Perhaps* the word *impassioned* would answer better.

argumentative and the pathetic incorporated together. These acting with united force, and, if I may so express myself, in concert, constitute that passionate eviction, that *vehemence* of contention, which is admirably fitted for persuasion, and hath always been regarded as the supreme qualification in an orator.[4] It is this which bears down every obstacle, and procures the speaker an irresistible power over the thoughts and purposes of his audience. It is this which hath been so justly celebrated as giving one man an ascendant over others, superior even to what despotism itself can bestow; since by the latter the more ignoble part only, the body and its members are enslaved; whereas from the dominion of the former, nothing is exempted, neither judgment nor affection, not even the inmost recesses, the most latent movements of the soul. What opposition is he not prepared to conquer, on whose arms reason hath conferred solidity and weight, and passion such a sharpness as enables them, in defiance of every obstruction, to open a speedy passage to the heart?

It is not, however, every kind of pathos, which will give the orator so great an ascendancy over the minds of his hearers. All passions are not alike capable of producing this effect. Some are naturally inert and torpid; they deject the mind, and indispose it for enterprise. Of this kind are sorrow, fear, shame, humility. Others, on the contrary, elevate the soul, and stimulate to action. Such are hope, patriotism, ambition, emulation, anger. These, with the greatest facility, are made to concur in direction with arguments exciting to resolution and activity: and are, consequently, the fittest for producing, what for want of a better term in our language, I shall hence-

4 This animated reasoning the Greek rhetoricians termed δεινοτης, which from signifying the principal excellency in an orator, came at length to denote oratory itself. And as vehemence and eloquence became synonymous, the latter, suitably to this way of thinking, was sometimes defined the *art of persuasion*. But that this definition is defective, appears even from their own writings, since in a consistency with it, their rhetorics could not have comprehended those orations called *demonstrative*, the design of which was not to persuade but to please. Yet it is easy to discover the origin of this defect, and that both from the nature of the thing, and from the customs which obtained among both Greeks and Romans. First, from the nature of the thing, for to persuade presupposes in some degree, and therefore may be understood to imply, all the other talents of an orator, to enlighten, to evince, to paint, to astonish, to inflame; but this doth not hold inversely; one may explain with clearness, and prove with energy, who is incapable of the sublime, the pathetic, and the vehement: besides, this power of persuasion, or, as Cicero calls it, "*Posse voluntates hominum impellere quo velis, unde velis, deducere*," as it makes a man master of his hearers, is the most considerable in respect of consequences. Secondly, from ancient customs. All their public orations were ranked under three classes, the demonstrative, the judiciary, and the deliberative. In the two last it was impossible to rise to eminence, without that important talent, the power of persuasion. These were in much more frequent use than the first, and withal the surest means of advancing both the fortune and the fame of the orator; for as on the judiciary the lives and estates of private persons depended, on the deliberative hung the resolves of senates, the fate of kingdoms, nay, of the most renowned republics the world ever knew. Consequently, to excel in these, must have been the direct road to riches, honours, and preferment. No wonder, then, that persuasion should almost wholly engross the rhetorician's notice.

forth denominate the *vehement*. There is, besides, an intermediate kind of passions, which do not so congenially and directly either restrain us from acting, or incite us to act; but, by the art of the speaker, can, in an oblique manner, be made conducive to either. Such are joy, love, esteem, compassion. Nevertheless, all these kinds may find a place in suasory discourses, or such as are intended to operate on the will. The first is properest for dissuading; the second, as hath been already hinted, for persuading; the third is equally accommodated to both.

Guided by the above reflections, we may easily trace that connexion in the various forms of eloquence, which was remarked on, distinguishing them by their several objects. The imagination is charmed by a finished picture, wherein even drapery and ornament are not neglected; for here the end is pleasure. Would we penetrate further, and agitate the soul, we must exhibit only some vivid strokes, some expressive features, not decorated as for show (all ostentation being both despicable and hurtful here), but such as appear the natural exposition of those bright and deep impressions, made by the subject upon the speaker's mind; for here the end is not pleasure, but emotion. Would we not only touch the heart, but win it entirely to cooperate with our views, those affecting lineaments must be so interwoven with our argument, as that, from the passion excited our reasoning may derive importance, and so be fitted for commanding attention; and by the justness of the reasoning the passion may be more deeply rooted and enforced; and that thus both may be made to conspire in effectuating that persuasion which is the end proposed. For here, if I may adopt the schoolmen's language, we do not argue to gain barely the assent of the understanding, but, which is infinitely more important, the consent of the will.

To prevent mistakes, it will not be beside my purpose further to remark, that several of the terms above explained are sometimes used by rhetoricians and critics in a much larger and more vague signification, than has been given them here. Sublimity and vehemence, in particular, are often confounded, the latter being considered as a species of the former. In this manner has this subject been treated by that great master Longinus, whose acceptation of the term *sublime* is extremely indefinite, importing an eminent degree of almost any excellence of speech, of whatever kind. Doubtless, if things themselves be understood, it does not seem material what names are assigned them. Yet it is both more accurate, and proves no inconsiderable aid to the right understanding of things, to discriminate by different signs such as are truly different. And that the two qualities above mentioned are of this number is undeniable, since we can produce passages full of vehemence, wherein no image is presented, which, with any propriety, can be termed great or sublime. In matters of criticism, as in the abstract sciences, it is of the utmost consequence to ascertain, with precision, the meanings of words, and, as nearly as the genius of the language in which one writes will permit, to make them correspond to the boundaries assigned by Nature to the things signified. That the lofty and the vehement, though still distinguishable, are sometimes combined, and act with united force, is not to be denied. It is then only that the orator can be said to fight with weapons which are at once sharp, massive, and refulgent, which, like heaven's artillery, dazzle while they strike, which overpower the sight and the heart at the same instant. How admirably do the two forenamed qualities, when happily blended, correspond in the rational, to the thunder and lightning in the natural world, which are not more awfully majestical in sound and aspect, then irresistible in power.

Thus much shall suffice for explaining the spirit, the intent, and the distinguishing qualities of each of the forementioned sorts of address; all of which agree in this, an accommodation to affairs of a serious and important nature.

CHAPTER II

Of wit, humour, and ridicule

This article, concerning eloquence in its largest acceptation, I cannot properly dismiss without making some observations on another genus of oratory, in many things similar to the former, but which is naturally suited to light and trivial matters.

This also may be branched into three sorts, corresponding to those already discussed, directed to the fancy, the passions, and the will; for that which illuminates the understanding serves as a common foundation to both, and has here nothing peculiar. This may be styled the eloquence of conversation, as the other is more strictly the eloquence of declamation.[1] Not, indeed, but that wit, humour, ridicule, which are the essentials of the former, may often be successfully admitted into public harangues. And, on the other hand, sublimity, pathos, vehemence, may sometimes enter the precincts of familiar converse. To justify the use of such distinctive appellations, it is enough that they refer to those particulars which are predominant in each, though not peculiar to either.

SECTION I—OF WIT

To consider the matter more nearly, it is the design of wit to excite in the mind an agreeable surprise, and that arising, not from any thing marvellous in the subject, but solely from the imagery she employs, or the strange assemblage of related ideas presented to the mind. This end is effected in one or other of these three ways: first in debasing things pompous or seemingly grave: I say *seemingly* grave, because to vilify what is *truly* grave has

[1] In the latter of these the ancients excel; in the former the moderns. Demosthenes and Cicero, not to say Homer and Virgil, to this day remain unrivalled; and in all antiquity, Lucian himself not excepted, we cannot find a match for Swift and Cervantes.

something shocking in it, which rarely fails to counteract the end: secondly, in aggrandizing things little and frivolous: thirdly, in setting ordinary objects, by means not only remote, but apparently contrary, in a particular and uncommon point of view.[2] This will be better understood from the following observations and examples.

The materials employed by wit in the grotesque pieces she exhibits, are partly derived from those common fountains of whatever is directed to the imaginative powers, the ornaments of elocution, and the oratorical figures, simile, apostrophe, antithesis, metaphor; partly from those she in a manner appropriates to herself, irony, hyperbole, allusion, parody, and (if the reader will pardon my descending so low) paronomasia,[3] and pun. The limning of wit differs from the rhetorical painting above described in two respects. One is, that in the latter there is not only a resemblance requisite in that particular on which the comparison is founded, but there must also be a general similitude, in the nature and quality of that which is the basis of the imagery, to that which is the theme of discourse. In respect of dignity, or the impression they make upon the mind, they must be things homogeneous. What has magnificence, must invariably be portrayed by what is magnificent; objects of importance by objects important; such as have grace by things graceful: Whereas the witty, though requiring an exact likeness in the first particular, demands, in the second, a contrariety rather, or remoteness. This enchantress exults in reconciling contradictions, and in hitting on that special light and attitude, wherein you can discover an unexpected similarity in objects, which, at first sight, appear the most dissimilar and heterogeneous. Thus high and low are coupled, humble and superb, momentous and trivial, common and extraordinary. Addison, indeed, observes,[4] that wit is often produced, not by the resemblance, but by the opposition of ideas. But this, of which, however, he hath not given us an instance, doth not constitute a different species, as the repugnancy in that

2 I know no language which affords a name for this species of imagery, but the English. The French *esprit* or *bel esprit*, though on some occasions rightly translated *wit*, hath commonly a signification more extensive and generical. It must be owned, indeed, that in conformity to the style of French critics, the term *wit*, in English writings, hath been sometimes used with equal latitude. But this is certainly a perversion of the word from its ordinary sense, through an excessive deference to the manner and idiom of our ingenious neighbours. Indeed, when an author varies the meaning in the same work, he not only occasions perplexity to his reader, but falls himself into an apparent inconsistency. An error of this kind, in Mr. Pope, has been lately pointed out by a very ingenious and judicious critic. "In the Essay on Criticism it is said,
> True wit is nature to advantage dress'd:

But immediately after this the poet adds,
> For works may have more wit than does 'em good.

Now let us substitute the definition in the place of the thing, and it will stand thus: A work may have more of *nature dressed to advantage*, than will do it good. This is impossible; and it is evident, that the confusion arises from the poet's having annexed two different ideas to the same word." Webb's Remarks on the Beauties of Poetry, Dialogue ii.

3 Paronomasia is properly that figure which the French call *jeu de mots*.

4 *Spectator.*

case will always be found between objects in other respects resembling; for it is to the contrast of dissimilitude and likeness, remoteness and relation, in the same objects, that its peculiar effect is imputable. Hence we hear of the flashes and the sallies of wit, phrases which imply suddenness, surprise, and contrariety. These are illustrated in the first by a term which implies an instantaneous emergence of light in darkness: in the second, by a word which denotes an abrupt transition to things distant. For we may remark in passing, that though language be older than criticism, those expressions adopted by the former, to elucidate matters of taste, will be found to have a pretty close conformity to the purest discoveries of the latter.

Nay, of so much consequence here are surprise and novelty, that nothing is more tasteless, and sometimes disgusting, than a joke that has become stale by frequent repetition. For the same reason, even a pun or a happy allusion will appear excellent when thrown out extempore in conversation, which would be deemed execrable in print. In like manner, a witty repartee is infinitely more pleasing than a witty attack. For though, in both cases, the thing may be equally new to the reader or hearer, the effect on him is greatly injured, when there is ground to suppose that it may be the slow production of study and premediation. This, however, holds most with regard to the inferior tribes of witticisms, of which their readiness is the best recommendation.

The other respect in which wit differs from the illustrations of the graver orator, is the way wherein it affects the hearer. Sublimity elevates, beauty charms, wit diverts. The first, as hath been already observed, enraptures, and as it were, dilates the soul; the second diffuseth over it a serene delight; the third tickles the fancy, and throws the spirits into an agreeable vibration.

To these reflections I shall subjoin examples in each of the three sorts of wit above explained.

It will, however, be proper to premise, that if the reader should not at first be sensible of the justness of the solutions and explications to be given, he ought not hastily to form an unfavourable conclusion. Wherever there is taste, the witty and the humorous make themselves perceived, and produce their effect instantaneously; but they are of so subtle a nature, that they will hardly endure to be touched, much less to undergo a strict analysis and scrutiny. They are like those volatile essences, which, being too delicate to bear the open air, evaporate almost as soon as they are exposed to it. Accordingly, the wittiest things will sometimes be made to appear insipid, and the most ingenious frigid, by scrutinizing them too narrowly. Besides, the very frame of spirit proper for being diverted with the laughable in objects, is so different from that which is necessary for philosophizing on them, that there is a risk, that when we are most disposed to inquire into the cause, we are least capable of feeling the effect; as it is certain, that when the effect hath its full influence on us, we have little inclination for investigating the cause. For these reasons, I have resolved to be brief in my illustrations, having often observed that, in such nice and abstract inquiries, if a proper hint do not suggest the matter to the reader, he will be but more perplexed by long and elaborate discussions.

Of the first sort, which consists in the debasement of things great and eminent, Butler, amongst a thousand other instances, hath given us those which follow:

> And now had Phœbus in the lap
> Of Thetis taken out his nap;
> And, like a lobster boil'd, the morn
> From black to red began to turn.[5]

Here the low allegorical style of the first couplet, and the simile used in the second, afford us a just notion of this lowest species, which is distinguished by the name of *the ludicrous*. Another specimen from the same author you have in these lines:

> Great on the bench, great in the saddle,
> That could as well bind o'er as swaddle,
> Mighty he was at both of these,
> And styled of *war,* as well as *peace:*
> So some rats of amphibious nature,
> Are either for the *land* or *water*.[6]

In this coarse kind of drollery, those laughable translations or paraphrases of heroic and other serious poems, wherein the authors are said to be travestied, chiefly abound.

To the same class those instances must be referred, in which, though there is no direct comparison made, qualities of real dignity and importance are degraded, by being coupled with things mean and frivolous, as in some respect standing in the same predicament. An example of this I shall now give from the same hand.

> For when the restless Greeks sat down
> So many years, before Troy town,
> And were renown'd, as Homer writes,
> For well-soled boots, no less than fights.[7]

I shall only observe further, that this sort, whose aim is to debase, delights in the most homely expressions, provincial idioms, and cant phrases.

The second kind, consisting of the aggrandizement of little things, which is by far the most splendid, and displays a soaring imagination, these lines of Pope will serve to illustrate:

> As Berecynthia, while her offspring vie
> In homage to the mother of the sky,
> Surveys around her in the blest abode,
> An hundred sons, and every son a god:
> Not with less glory mighty Dulness crown'd,

5 *Hudibras,* Part ii. Canto 3.
6 Ibid. Part i. Canto 1.
7 *Hudibras,* Part i. Canto 2.

> Shall take thro' Grub-street her triumphant round;
> And her Parnassus glancing o'er at once,
> Behold an hundred sons, and each a dunce.[8]

This whole similitude is spirited. The parent of the celestials is contrasted by the daughter of Night and Chaos; heaven by Grub-street; gods by dunces. Besides, the parody it contains on a beautiful passage in Virgil, adds a particular lustre to it. This species we may term *the thrasonical*, or *the mock-majestic*. It affects the most pompous language, and sonorous phraseology, as much as the other affects the reverse, the vilest and most grovelling dialect.

I shall produce another example from the same writer, which is, indeed, inimitably fine. It represents a lady employed at her toilet, attended by her maid, under the allegory of the celebration of some solemn and religious ceremony. The passage is rather long for a quotation, but as the omission of any part would be a real mutilation, I shall give it entire.

> And now unveil'd the toilet stands display'd,
> Each silver vase in mystic order laid.
> First, rob'd in white, the nymph intent adores,
> With head uncovered, the cosmetic powers.
> A heavenly image in the glass appears,
> To that she bends, to that her eyes she rears;
> Th' inferior priestess, at her altar's side,
> Trembling begins the sacred rites of pride;
> Unnumbered treasures ope at once, and here
> The various offerings of the world appear;
> From each she nicely culls with curious toil,
> And decks the goddess with the glittering spoil.
> This casket India's glowing gems unlocks,
> And all Arabia breathes from yonder box.
> The tortoise here and elephant unite,
> Transform'd to combs, the speckled and the white.
> Here files of pins extend their shining rows,
> Puffs, powders, patches, bibles, billet-doux.
> Now awful beauty puts on all its arms,
> The fair each moment rises in her charms,
> Repairs her smiles, awakens every grace,
> And calls forth all the wonders of her face;
> Sees by degrees a purer blush arise,
> And keener lightnings quicken in her eyes.[9]

To this class also we must refer the application of grave reflections to mere trifles. For that *great* and *serious* are naturally associated by the mind, and likewise little and trifling, is sufficiently evinced by the common modes of expression on these subjects used in every tongue. An apposite instance of such an application we have from Philips,

8 *Dunciad*, B.
9 *Rape of the Lock*, Canto 1.

> My galligaskins, that have long withstood
> The winter's fury and encroaching frosts,
> By time subdued, (*what will not time subdue?*)
> A horrid chasm disclose.[10]

Like to this, but not equal, is that of Young,

> One day his wife (*for who can wives reclaim?*)
> Levell'd her barbarous needle at his fame.[11]

To both the preceding kinds the term *burlesque* is applied, but especially to the first.

Of the third species of wit, which is by far the most multifarious, and which results from what I may call the queerness or singularity of the imagery, I shall give a few specimens that will serve to mark some of its principal varieties. To illustrate all would be impossible.

The first I shall exemplify is where there is an apparent contrariety in the things she exhibits as connected. This kind of contrast we have in these lines of Garth,

> Then Hydrops next appears amongst the throng;
> Bloated and big she slowly sails along;
> But, like a miser, in excess she's poor;
> And pines for thirst amidst her watery store.[12]

The wit in these lines doth not so much arise from the comparison they contain of the dropsy to a miser, (which falls under the description that immediately succeeds,) as from the union of contraries they present to the imagination, poverty in the midst of opulence, and thirst in one who is already drenched in water.

A second sort is where the things compared are what with dialecticians would come under the denomination of *disparates,* being such as can be ranked under no common genus. Of this I shall subjoin an example from Young,

> Health chiefly keeps an Atheist in the dark,
> A fever argues better than a *Clarke:*
> Let but the logic in his pulse decay,
> The Grecian he'll renounce, and learn to pray.[13]

Here, by implication, health is compared to a sophister, or darkener of the understanding, a fever to a metaphysical disputant, a regular pulse to false logic, for the word logic in the third line is used ironically. In other words, we have here modes and substances, the affections of body, and the exercise of reason, strangely, but not insignificantly linked together; strangely, else the sentiment, however just, could not be denominated witty; significantly,

---

10 *Splendid Shilling.*
11 *Universal Passion.*
12 *Dispensary.*
13 *Universal Passion.*

because an unmeaning jumble of things incongruous would not be wit, but nonsense.

A third variety in this species springs from confounding artfully the proper and metaphorical sense of an expression. In this way, one would assign as a motive what is discovered to be perfectly absurd, when but ever so little attended to; and yet, from the ordinary meaning of the words, hath a specious appearance on a single glance. Of this kind you have an instance in the subsequent lines,

> While thus the lady talk'd, the knight
> Turn'd th' outside of his eyes to white,
> As men of inward light are wont
> To turn their optics in upon't.[14]

For whither can they turn their eyes more properly than to the light?

A fourth variety, much resembling the former, is when the argument or comparison (for all argument is a kind of comparison) is founded on the supposal of corporeal or personal attributes in what is strictly not susceptible of them, as in this,

> But Hudibras gave him a twitch
> As quick as lightning in the breech,
> Just in the place where honour's lodg'd,
> As wise philosophers have judg'd;
> Because a kick in that place more
> Hurts honour than deep wounds before.[15]

Is demonstration itself more satisfactory? Can any thing be hurt, but where it is? However, the mention of this as the sage deduction of philosophers, is no inconsiderable addition to the wit. Indeed, this particular circumstance belongs properly to the first species mentioned, in which high and low, great and little, are coupled. Another example, not unlike the preceding, you have in these words,

> What makes morality a crime,
> The most notorious of the time;
> Morality which both the saints
> And wicked too cry out against?
> 'Cause grace and virtue are within
> Prohibited decrees of kin:
> And therefore no true saint allows
> They shall be suffer'd to espouse.[16]

When the two foregoing instances are compared together we should say of the first, that it has more of simplicity and nature, and is therefore more pleasing; of the second, that it has more of ingenuity and conceit, and is consequently more surprising.

---

14 *Hudibras,* Part iii. Canto 1.
15 Ibid. Part ii. Canto 2.
16 *Hudibras,* Part iii. Canto 1.

The fifth and only other variety I shall observe, is that which ariseth from a relation not in the things signified, but in the sign, of all relations, no doubt, the slightest. Identity here gives rise to puns and clinches: resemblance to quibbles, cranks, and rhymes: Of these, I imagine, it is quite unnecessary to exhibit specimens. The wit here is so dependent on the sound, that it is commonly incapable of being transfused into another language, and as, among persons of taste and discernment, it is in less request than the other sorts above enumerated, those who abound in this, and never rise to anything superior, are distinguished by the diminutive appellation of witlings.

Let it be remarked in general, that from one or more of the three last-mentioned varieties, those plebeian tribes of witticism, the conundrums, the rebuses, the riddles, and some others, are lineally, though perhaps not all legitimately descended. I shall only add, that I have not produced the forenamed varieties as an exact enumeration of all the subdivisions of which the third species of wit is susceptible. It is capable, I acknowledge, of being almost infinitely diversified; and it is principally to its various exhibitions that we apply the epithets *sportive, sprightly, ingenious,* according as they recede more or less from those of the declaimer.

SECTION II—OF HUMOUR

As wit is the painting, humour is the pathetic, in this inferior sphere of eloquence. The nature and efficacy of humour may be thus unravelled. A just exhibition of any ardent or durable passion, excited by some adequate cause, instantly attacheth sympathy, the common tie of human souls, and thereby communicates the passion to the breast of the hearer. But when the emotion is either not violent or not durable, and the motive not any thing real, but imaginary, or at least quite disproportionate to the effect; or when the passion displays itself preposterously, so as rather to obstruct than to promote its aim, in these cases a natural representation, instead of fellow-feeling, creates amusement, and universally awakens contempt. The portrait in the former case we call *pathetic,* in the latter *humorous.*[17] It was said that the emotion must be either not violent or not durable. This limitation is necessary, because a passion extreme in its degree, as well as lasting, cannot

[17] It ought to be observed, that this term is also used to express any lively strictures of such specialties in temper and conduct, as have neither moment enough to interest sympathy, nor incongruity enough to excite contempt. In this case, humour, not being addressed to passion, but to fancy, must be considered as a kind of moral painting, and differs from wit only in these two things; first, in that character alone is the subject of the former, whereas all things whatever fall within the province of the latter; secondly, humour paints more simply by direct imitation, wit more variously by illustration and imagery. Of this kind of humour, merely graphical, Addison hath given us numberless examples in many of the characters he hath so finely drawn, and little incidents he hath so pleasantly related in his Tatlers and Spectators. I might remark of the word *humour,* as I did of the term *wit,* that we scarcely find in other languages a word exactly corresponding. The Latin *facetiæ* seems to come the nearest.

yield diversion to a well-disposed mind, but generally affects it with pity, not seldom with a mixture of horror and indignation. The sense of the ridiculous, though invariably the same, is in this case totally surmounted by a principle of our nature, much more powerful.

The passion which humour addresseth as its object, is, as hath been signified above, contempt. But it ought carefully to be noted, that every address, even every pertinent address to contempt, is not humorous. This passion is not less capable of being excited by the severe and tragic, than by the merry and comic manner. The subject of humour is always character, but not every thing in character; its foibles generally, such as caprices, little extravagances, weak anxieties, jealousies, childish fondness, pertness, vanity, and self-conceit. One finds the greatest scope for exercising this talent in telling familiar stories, or in acting any whimsical part in an assumed character. Such an one, we say, has the talent of humouring a tale, or any queer manner which he chooseth to exhibit. Thus we speak of the passions in tragedy, but of the humours in comedy; and even to express passion as appearing in the more trivial occurrences of life, we commonly use this term, as when we talk of good humour, ill humour, peevish or pleasant humour; hence it is that a capricious temper we call humorsome, the person possessed of it a humorist, and such facts or events as afford subject for the humours, we denominate comical.

Indeed, comedy is the proper province of humour. Wit is called in solely as an auxiliary, humour predominates. The comic poet bears the same analogy to the author of the mock-heroic, that the tragic poet bears to the author of the epic. The epos recites, and advancing with a step majestic and sedate, engageth all the nobler powers of imagination, a sense of grandeur, of beauty, and of order; tragedy personates, and thus employing a more rapid and animated diction, seizeth directly upon the heart. The little epic, a narrative intended for amusement, and addressed to all the lighter powers of fancy, delights in the excursions of wit: the production of the comic muse, being a representation, is circumscribed by narrower bounds, and is all life and activity throughout. Thus Buckingham says with the greatest justness, of comedy,

> *Humour is all. Wit* should be only brought
> To turn agreeably some proper thought.[18]

The pathetic and facetious differ not only in subject and effect, as will appear upon the most superficial review of what hath been said, but also in the manner of imitation. In this the man of humour descends to a minuteness which the orator disdains. The former will often successfully run into downright mimicry, and exhibit peculiarities in voice, gesture, and pronunciation, which in the other would be intolerable. The reason of the difference is this: That we may divert, by exciting scorn and contempt, the individual must be exposed; that we may move, by interesting the more

---

18 *Essay on Poetry.*

generous principles of humanity, the language and sentiments, not so much of the individual, as of human nature, must be displayed. So very different, or rather opposite, are these two in this respect, that there could not be a more effectual expedient for undoing the charm of the most affecting representation, than an attempt in the speaker to mimic the personal singularities of the man for whom he desires to interest us. On the other hand, in the humorous, where the end is diversion, even overacting, if moderate, is not improper.

It was observed already, that though contempt be the only passion addressed by humour, yet this passion may with propriety and success be assailed by the severer eloquence, where there is not the smallest tincture of humour. This it will not be beside our purpose to specify, in order the more effectually to show the difference.—Lord Bolingbroke, speaking of the state of these kingdoms from the time of Restoration, has these words: "The two brothers, Charles, and James, when in exile, became infected with popery to such degrees as their different characters admitted of. Charles had parts; and his good understanding served as an antidote to repel the poison. James, the simplest man of his time, drank off the whole chalice. The poison met, in his composition, with all the fear, all the credulity, and all the obstinacy of temper proper to increase its virulence, and to strengthen its effect.—Drunk with superstitious, and even enthusiastic zeal, he ran headlong into his own ruin, whilst he endeavoured to precipitate ours. His parliament and his people did all they could to save themselves, by winning him. But all was vain. He had no principle on which they could take hold. Even his good qualities worked against them; and his love of his country went halves with his bigotry. How he succeeded we have heard from our fathers. The Revolution of one thousand six hundred and eighty-eight saved the nation, and ruined the king." [19] —Nothing can be more contemptuous, and, at the same time, less derisive, than this representation. We should readily say of it, that it is strongly animated, and happily expressed; but no man who understands English would say it is humorous. I shall add one example from Dr. Swift. "I should be exceedingly sorry to find the legislature make any new laws against the practice of duelling, because the methods are easy and many for a wise man to avoid a quarrel with honour, or engage in it with innocence. And I can discover no political evil in suffering bullies, sharpers, and rakes, to rid the world of each other by a method of their own, where the law hath not been able to find an expedient." [20]

For a specimen of the humorous, take as a contrast to the two last examples, the following delineation of a fop:

> Sir Plume (of amber snuff-box justly vain,
> And the nice conduct of a clouded cane)
> With earnest eyes and round unthinking face,

[19] A Letter to Sir William Wyndham.
[20] Swift on Good Manners.

> He first the snuff-box open'd, then the case,
> And thus broke out, "My Lord, why,—what the devil?
> Z—ds!—damn the lock!—'fore Gad, you must be civil!
> Plague on't!—'tis past a jest,—nay prithee,—pox!
> Give her the hair."—He spoke and rapp'd his box.
> "It grieves me much," replied the peer again,
> "Who speaks so well, should ever speak in vain:
> But"———— 21

This, both in the descriptive and the dramatic part, particularly in the draught it contains of the baronet's mind, aspect, manner, and eloquence, (if we except the sarcastic term *justly*, the double sense of the word *open'd*, and the fine irony couched in the reply) is purely facetious. An instance of wit and humour combined, where they reciprocally set off and enliven each other, Pope hath also furnished us with in another part of the same exquisite performance.

> Whether the nymph shall break Diana's law,
> Or some frail china jar receive a flaw;
> Or stain her honour, or her new brocade;
> Forget her prayers, or miss a masquerade;
> Or lose her heart, or necklace, at a ball;
> Or whether heaven has doom'd that Shock must fall.22

This is humorous, in that it is a lively sketch of the female estimate of mischances, as our poet's commentator rightly terms it, marked out by a few striking lineaments. It is likewise witty, for, not to mention the play on words like that remarked in the former example, a trope familiar to this author, you have here a comparison of—a woman's chastity to a piece of porcelain,—her honour to a gaudy robe,—her prayers to a fantastical disguise,—her heart to a trinket; and all these together to her lap-dog, and that founded on one lucky circumstance (a malicious critic would perhaps discern or imagine more) by which these things, how unlike soever in other respects, may be compared, the impression they make on the mind of a fine lady.

Hudibras, so often above quoted, abounds in wit in almost all its varieties; to which the author's various erudition hath not a little contributed. And this, it must be owned, is more suitable to the nature of his poem. At the same time, it is by no means destitute of humour, as appears particularly in the different exhibitions of character given by the knight and his squire. But in no part of the story is this talent displayed to greater advantage than in the consulation of the lawyer,23 to which I shall refer the reader, as the passage is too long for my transcribing. There is, perhaps, no book in any language, wherein the humorous is carried to a higher pitch of perfection, than in the adventures of the celebrated knight of La Mancha. As to our

21 *Rape of the Lock*, Canto 4.
22 *Rape of the Lock*, Canto 2.
23 Part iii. Canto 3.

English dramatists, who does not acknowledge the transcendent excellence of Shakespeare in this province, as well as in the pathetic? Of the later comic writers, Congreve has an exuberance of wit, but Farquhar has more humour. It may, however, with too much truth, be affirmed of English comedy in general, (for there are some exceptions,) that, to the discredit of our stage, as well as of the national delicacy and discernment, obscenity is made too often to supply the place of wit, and ribaldry the place of humour.

Wit and humour, as above explained, commonly concur in a tendency to provoke laughter, by exhibiting a curious and unexpected affinity; the first generally by comparison, either direct or implied, the second by connecting in some other relation, such as causality or vicinity, objects apparently the most dissimilar and heterogeneous; which incongruous affinity, we may remark by the way, gives the true meaning of the word *oddity*, and is the proper object of laughter.

The difference between these and that grander kind of eloquence treated in the first part of this chapter, I shall, if possible, still further illustrate, by a few similitudes borrowed from the optical science. The latter may be conceived as a plane mirror, which faithfully reflects the object, in colour, figure, size, and posture. Wit, on the contrary, Proteus-like, transforms itself into a variety of shapes. It is now a convex speculum, which gives a just representation in form and colour, but withal reduces the greatest objects to the most despicable littleness: now a concave speculum, which swells the smallest trifles to an enormous magnitude; now again a speculum of a cylindrical, a conical, or an irregular make, which, though in colour, and even in attitude, it reflects a pretty strong resemblance, widely varies the proportions. Humour, when we consider the contrariety of its effects, contempt and laughter, (which constitute what in one word is termed *derision*,) to that sympathy and love often produced by the pathetic, may in respect of these be aptly compared to a concave mirror, when the object is placed beyond the focus; in which case it appears, by reflection, both diminished and inverted, circumstances which happily adumbrate the contemptible and the ridiculous.

SECTION III—OF RIDICULE

The intention of raising a laugh is either merely to divert by that grateful titillation which it excites, or to influence the opinions and purposes of the hearers. In this also, the risible faculty, when suitably directed, hath often proved a very potent engine. When this is the view of the speaker, as there is always an air of reasoning conveyed under that species of imagery, narration, or description, which stimulates laughter, these, thus blended, obtain the appellation of *ridicule*, the poignancy of which hath a similar effect in futile subjects, to that produced by what is called *the vehement* in solemn and important matters.

Nor doth all the difference between these lie in the dignity of the subject. Ridicule is not only confined to questions of less moment, but is fitter for

refuting error than for supporting truth, for restraining from wrong conduct, than for inciting to the practice of what is right. Nor are these the sole
restrictions; it is not properly levelled at the false, but at the *absurd* in
tenets; nor can the edge of ridicule strike with equal force every species of
misconduct: it is not the criminal part which it attacks, but that which we
denominate silly or foolish. With regard to doctrine, it is evident that it is
not falsity or mistake, but palpable error or absurdity (a thing hardly
confutable by mere argument), which is the object of contempt; and consequently those dogmas are beyond the reach of cool reasoning which are
within the rightful confines of ridicule. That they are generally conceived to
be so, appears from the sense universally assigned to expressions like these,
"Such a position is ridiculous—It doth not deserve a serious answer." Every
body knows that they import more than "It is false," being, in other words,
"This is such an extravagance as is not so much a subject of argument as of
laughter." And that we may discover what it is, with regard to conduct, to
which ridicule is applicable, we need only consider the different departments of tragedy and of comedy. In the last, it is of mighty influence; into
the first it never legally obtains admittance. Those things which principally
come under its lash are awkwardness, rusticity, ignorance, cowardice, levity, foppery, pedantry, and affectation of every kind. But against murder,
cruelty, parricide, ingratitude, perfidy,[24] to attempt to raise a laugh, would
show such an unnatural insensibility in the speaker as would be excessively
disgustful to any audience. To punish such enormities the tragic poet must
take a very different route.

Now, from this distinction of vices or faults into two classes, there hath
sprung a parallel division in all the kinds of poesy which relate to manners.
The epopée, a picturesque, or graphical poem, is either heroic, or what is
called mock-heroic, and by Aristotle iambic,[25] from the measure in which
poems of this kind were at first composed. The drama, an animated poem, is
either in the buskin or in the sock; for farce deserves not a place in the
subdivision, being at most but a kind of dramatical apologue, whereof the
characters are monstrous, the intrigue unnatural, the incidents often impossible, and which, instead of humour, has adopted a spurious bantling called
fun. To satisfy us that satire, whose end is persuasion, admits also the like
distribution, we need only recur to the different methods pursued by the
two famous Latin satirists, Juvenal and Horace. The one declaims, the
other derides. Accordingly, as Dryden justly observes,[26] vice is the quarry of

---

[24] To this black catalogue an ancient Pagan of Athens or of Rome would have added
adultery, but the modern refinements of us Christians (if without profanation we can so
apply the name) absolutely forbid it, as nothing on our theatre is a more common subject
of laughter than this. Nor is the laugh raised against the adulterer, else we might have
some plea for our morals, if none for our taste; but, to the indelible reproach of the
taste, the sense, and the virtue of the nation, in his favour.

[25] *Poetics.*

[26] *Origin and Progress of Satire.*

the former, folly of the latter.[27] Thus, of the three graver forms, the aim, whether avowed or latent, always is, or ought to be, the improvement of the three lighter, the refinement of manners.[28] But though the latter have for their peculiar object manners, in the limited and distinctive sense of that word, they may, with propriety, admit many things which directly conduce to the advancement of morals, and ought never to admit any thing which hath a contrary tendency. Virtue is of primary importance, both for the happiness of individuals, and for the well-being of society; an external polish is at best but a secondary accomplishment, ornamental indeed when it adds a lustre to virtue, pernicious when it serves only to embellish profligacy, and in itself comparatively of but little consequence, either to private or to public felicity.[29]

Another remarkable difference, the only one which remains to be ob-

[27] The differences and relations to be found in the several forms of poetry mentioned, may be more concisely marked by the following scheme, which brings them under the view at once.

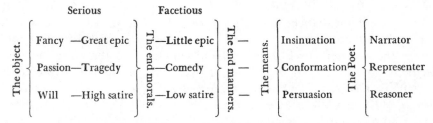

[28] These observations will enable us to understand that of the poet,

———Ridiculum acri

Fortius et melius magnas plerumque secat res.　　　　　Hor.

Great and signal, it must be owned, are the effects of ridicule; but the subject must always appear to the ridiculer, and to those affected by his pleasantry, under the notion of littleness and futility, two essential requisites in the object of contempt and risibility.

[29] Whether this attention has been always given to morals, particularly in comedy, must be left to the determination of those who are most conversant in that species of scenic representations. One may, however, venture to prognosticate, that if in any period it shall become fashionable to show no regard to virtue in such entertainments, if the hero of the piece, a fine gentleman to be sure, adorned as usual with all the superficial and exterior graces which the poet can confer, and crowned with success in the end, shall be an unprincipled libertine, a man of more spirit, forsooth, than to be checked in his pursuits by the restraints of religion, by a regard to the common rights of mankind, or by the laws of hospitality and private friendship, which were accounted sacred among the Pagans and those whom we denominate Barbarians; then, indeed, the stage will become merely the school of gallantry and intrigue; thither the youth of both sexes will resort, and will not resort in vain, in order to get rid of that troublesome companion modesty, intended by Providence as a guard to virtue, and a check against licentiousness; there vice will soon learn to provide herself in a proper stock of effrontery, and a suitable address for effecting her designs, and triumphing over innocence; then, in fine, if religion, virtue, principle, equity, gratitude, and good faith, are not empty sounds, the stage will prove the greatest of nuisances, and deserve to be styled the principal corrupter of the age. Whether such an era hath ever happened in the history of the theatre, in this or any other country, or is likely to happen, I do not take upon me to decide.

served, between the vehement or contentious and the derisive, consists in
the manner of conducting them. As in each there is a mixture of argument,
this in the former ought, in appearance at least, to have the ascendant, but
not in the latter. The attack of the declaimer is direct and open; argument
therefore is his avowed aim. On the contrary, the passions which he excites
ought never to appear to the auditors as the effects of his intention and
address, but both in him and them, as the native, the unavoidable consequences of the subject treated, and of that conviction which his reasoning
produces in the understanding. Although, in fact, he intends to move his
auditory, he only declares his purpose to convince them. To reverse this
method, and profess an intention to work upon their passions, would be in
effect to tell them that he meant to impose upon their understandings, and
to bias them by his art, and consequently, would be to warn them to be on
their guard against him. Nothing is better founded than the famous apho-
rism of rhetoricians, that the perfection of art consists in concealing art. On
the other hand, the assault of him who ridicules is, from its very nature,
covert and oblique. What we profess to contemn, we scorn to confute. It
is on this account that the reasoning in ridicule, if at all delicate, is always
conveyed under a species of disguise. Nay, sometimes, which is more astonishing, the contempt itself seems to be dissembled, and the rallier assumes
an air of arguing gravely in defence of that which he actually exposeth as
ridiculous. Hence, undoubtedly, it proceeds, that a serious manner commonly adds energy to a joke. The fact, however, is, that in this case the
very dissimulation is dissembled. He would not have you think him in
earnest, though he affects the appearance of it; knowing that otherwise his
end would be frustrated. He wants you should perceive that he is dis-
sembling, which no real dissembler ever wanted. It is, indeed, this
circumstance alone, which distinguishes an ironical expression from a lie.
Accordingly, through the thinness of the veil employed, he takes care that
the sneer shall be discovered. You are quickly made to perceive his aim, by
means of the strange arguments he produces, the absurd consequences he
draws, the odd embarrassments which in his personated character he is
involved in, and the still odder methods he takes to disentangle himself. In
this manner doctrines and practices are treated, when exposed to a continued run of irony; a way of refutation which bears a strong analogy to
that species of demonstration termed by mathematicians apagogical, as reducing the adversary to what is contradictory or impracticable. This method
seems to have been first introduced into moral subjects, and employed with
success, by the father of ancient wisdom, Socrates. As the attack of ridicule,
whatever form it adopts, is always indirect, that of irony may be said to be
reverted. It resembles the manner of fighting ascribed to the ancient Par-
thians, who were ever more formidable in flight than in onset; who looked
towards one quarter, and fought towards the opposite; whose bodies moved
in one direction, and their arrows in the contrary.

It remains now to confirm and illustrate this branch of the theory, by
suitable examples. And, not to encumber the reader with a needless multi-

plicity of excerptions, I shall first recur to those already produced. The first, second, and the fifth passages from Butler, the first from Young, and the quotation from the Dispensary, though witty, have no ridicule in them. Their whole aim is to divert by the oddness of the imagery. This merits a careful and particular attention, as on the accuracy of our conceptions here, depends, in a great measure, our forming a just notion of the relation which ridicule bears to wit, and of the distinction that subsists between them. Let this, therefore, be carefully remembered, that where nothing reprehensible, or supposed to be reprehensible, either in conduct or in sentiment, is struck at, there is properly no satire (or as it is sometimes termed emphatically enough, pointed wit) , and consequently no ridicule.

The example that first claims particular notice here is one from Young's *Satires,*

> Health chiefly keeps an Atheist in the dark, &c.

The wittiness of this passage was already illustrated: I shall now endeavour to show the argument couched under it, both which together constitute the ridicule. "Atheism is unreasonable." Why? "The Atheist neither founds his unbelief on reason, nor will attend to it. Was ever an Infidel in health convinced by reasoning; or did he ever in sickness need to be reasoned with on this subject? The truth then is that the daring principles of the libertine are solely supported by the vigour and healthiness of his constitution, which incline him to pleasure, thoughtlessness, and presumption; accordingly you find that, when this foundation is subverted, the whole fabric of infidelity falls to pieces." There is rarely, however, so much of argument in ridicule as may be discovered in this passage. Generally, as was observed already, it is but hinted in a single word or phrase, or appears to be glanced at occasionally, without any direct intention. Thus, in the third quotation from Butler, there is an oblique thrust at Homer, for his manner of recurring so often, in poems of so great dignity, to such mean and trifling epithets. The fourth and sixth satirize the particular fanatical practice, and fanatical opinion, to which they refer. To assign a preposterous motive to an action, or to produce an absurd argument for an opinion, is an innuendo, that no good motive or argument can be given.[30] The citations from the *Rape of the Lock* are no otherwise to be considered as ridicule, than as a lively exhibition of some follies, either in disposition or in behaviour, is the strongest dissuasive from imitating them. In this way, humour rarely fails to have some raillery in it, in like manner as the pathetic often persuades without argument, which, when obvious, is supplied by the judgment of the hearer.[31] The second example seems intended to disgrace the petty quaint-

---

[30] We have an excellent specimen of this sort of ridicule in Montesquieu's *Spirit of Laws*, b. xv. c. 5, where the practice of Europeans, in enslaving the negroes, is ironically justified, in a manner which does honour to the author's humanity and love of justice, at the same time that it displays a happy talent in ridicule.

[31] Ridicule resulting from a simple, but humorous narration, is finely illustrated in the first ten or twelve Provincial Letters.

ness of a fop's manner, and the emptiness of his conversation, as being a huddle of oaths and nonsense. The third finely satirizes the value which the ladies too often put upon the merest trifles. To these I shall add one instance more from *Hudibras,* where it is said of priests and exorcists,

> Supplied with spiritual provision,
> And magazines of ammunition,
> With crosses, relics, crucifixes,
> Beads, pictures, rosaries, and pixes,
> The tools of working our salvation,
> By mere mechanic operation.[32]

The reasoning here is sufficiently insinuated by the happy application of a few words, such as mechanic tools to the work of salvation; crosses, relics, beads, pictures, and other such trumpery, to spiritual provision. The justness of the representation of their practice, together with the manifest incongruity of the things, supply us at once with the wit and the argument. There is in this poem a great deal of ridicule; but the author's quarry is the frantic excesses of enthusiasm, and the base artifices of hypocrisy; he very rarely, as in the above passage, points to the idiot gewgaws of superstition. I shall only add one instance from Pope, which has something peculiar in it,

> Then sighing thus, "And am I now threescore?
> Ah! why, ye gods! should two and two make four?" [33]

This, though not in the narrative, but in the dramatic style, is more witty than humorous. The absurdity of the exclamation in the second line is too gross to be natural to any but a madman, and therefore hath not humour. Nevertheless, its resemblance to the common complaint of old age, contained in the first, of which it may be called the analysis, renders it at once both an ingenious exhibition of such complaint in its real import, and an argument of its folly. But notwithstanding this example, it holds in general, that when anything nonsensical in principle is to be assailed by ridicule, the natural ally of reason is wit; when any extravagance or impropriety in conduct, humour seldom fails to be of the confederacy. It may be further observed, that the words *banter* and *raillery* are also used to signify ridicule of a certain form, applied, indeed, more commonly to practices than to opinions, and oftener to the little peculiarities of individuals, than to the distinguishing customs or usages of sects and parties. The only difference in meaning, as far as I have remarked, between the two terms, is, that the first generally denotes a coarser, the second a finer sort of ridicule; the former prevails most among the lower classes of the people, the latter only among persons of breeding.

I shall conclude this chapter with observing, that though the gayer and more familiar eloquence, now explained, may often properly, as was remarked before, be admitted into public orations on subjects of consequence,

---

[32] Part iii. Canto 1.
[33] *Dunciad.*

such, for instance, as are delivered in the senate or at the bar, and even sometimes, though more sparingly, on the bench; it is seldom or never of service in those which come from the pulpit. It is true, that an air of ridicule in disproving or dissuading, by rendering opinions or practices contemptible, hath occasionally been attempted, with approbation, by preachers of great name. I can only say, that when this airy manner is employed, it requires to be managed with the greatest care and delicacy, that it may not degenerate into a strain but ill adapted to so serious an occupation. For the reverence of the place, the gravity of the function, the solemnity of worship, the severity of the precepts, and the importance of the motives of religion; above all, the awful presence of God, with a sense of which the mind, when occupied in religious exercises, ought eminently to be impressed; all these seem utterly incompatible with the levity of ridicule. They render jesting impertinence, and laughter madness. Therefore, any thing in preaching which might provoke this emotion, would justly be deemed an unpardonable offence against both piety and decorum.

In the two preceding chapters I have considered the nature of oratory in general, its various forms, whether arising from difference in the object, understanding, imagination, passion, will; or in the subject, eminent and severe, light and frivolous, with their respective ends and characters. Under these are included all the primary and characteristical qualities of whatever can pertinently find a place either in writing or in discourse, or can truly be termed fine in the one, or eloquent in the other.

CHAPTER III

The Doctrine of the preceding Chapter defended

Before I proceed to another topic, it will perhaps be thought proper to inquire how far the theory, now laid down and explained, coincides with the doctrines on this article to be found in the writings of philosophers and critics. Not that I think such inquiries and discussions always necessary; on the contrary, I imagine they often tend but to embarrass the reader, by distracting his attention to a multiplicity of objects, and so to darken and perplex a plain question. This is particularly the case on those points on which there hath been a variety of jarring sentiments. The simplest way and the most perspicuous, and generally that which best promotes the discovery of truth, is to give as distinct and methodical a delineation as possible of one's own ideas, together with the grounds on which they are founded, and to leave it to the doubtful reader (who thinks it worth the trouble) to compare the theory with the systems of other writers, and then to judge for himself. I am not, however, so tenacious of this method, as not to allow that it may sometimes, with advantage, be departed from. This holds especially when the sentiments of an author are opposed by inveterate prejudices in the reader, arising from contrary opinions early imbibed, or from an excessive deference to venerable names and ancient authorities.

SECTION I—ARISTOTLE'S ACCOUNT OF THE RIDICULOUS EXPLAINED

Some, on a superficial view, may imagine that the doctrine above expounded is opposed by no less authority than that of Aristotle. If it were, I should not think that equivalent to a demonstration of its falsity. But let us hear; Aristotle hath observed, that "the ridiculous implies something deformed, and consists in those smaller faults, which are neither painful nor pernicious, but unbeseeming: thus a face excites laughter wherein there is deformity and distortion without pain." For my part, nothing can appear more coincident than this, as far as it goes, with the principles which I have endeavoured to establish. The Stagyrite here speaks of ridicule, not of laughter in general, and not of every sort of ridicule, but solely of the ridiculous in manners, of which he hath in few words given a very apposite description. To take notice of any other laughable object, would have been foreign to his purpose. Laughter is not his theme, but comedy, and laughter only so far as comedy is concerned with it. Now, the concern of comedy reaches no further than that kind of ridicule which, as I said, relates to manners. The very words, with which the above quotation is introduced, evince the truth of this. "Comedy," says he, "is, as we remarked, an imitation of things that are amiss; yet it does not level at every vice." He had remarked in the preceding chapter, that its means of correction are "not reproach, but ridicule." Nor does the clause in the end of the sentence, concerning a countenance which raises laughter, in the least invalidate what I have now affirmed; for it is plain that this is suggested in the way of similitude, to illustrate what he had advanced, and not as a particular instance of the position he had laid down. For we can never suppose that he would have called distorted features "a certain fault or slip," and still less that he would have specified this, as what might be corrected by the art of the comedian. As an instance, therefore, it would have confuted his definition, and shown that his account of the object of laughter must be erroneous, since this emotion may be excited, as appears from the example produced by himself, where there is nothing faulty or vicious in any kind or degree. As an illustration it was extremely pertinent. It showed that the ridiculous in manners (which was all that his definition regarded) was, as far as the different nature of the things would permit, analogous to the laughable in other subjects, and that it supposed an incongruous combination, where there is nothing either calamitous or destructive. But that in other objects, unconnected with either character or conduct, with either the body or the soul, there might not be images or exhibitions presented to the mind which would naturally provoke laughter, the philosopher has nowhere, as far as I know, so much as insinuated.

SECTION II—HOBBES'S ACCOUNT OF LAUGHTER EXAMINED

From the founder of the peripatetic school, let us descend to the philosopher of Malmesbury, who hath defined laughter "a sudden glory, arising from a sudden conception of some eminency in ourselves, by comparison with the infirmity of others, or with our own formerly." [1] This account is, I acknowledge, incompatible with that given in the preceding pages, and, in my judgment, results entirely from a view of the subject, which is in some respect partial, and in some respect false. It is in some respect partial. When laughter is produced by ridicule, it is, doubtless, accompanied with some degree of contempt. Ridicule, as hath been observed already, has a double operation, first on the fancy, by presenting to it such a group as constitutes a laughable object; secondly, on the passion mentioned, by exhibiting absurdity in human character, in principles or in conduct: and contempt always implies a sense of superiority. No wonder then that one likes not to be ridiculed or laughed at. Now, it is this union which is the great source of this author's error, and of his attributing to one of the associated principles, from an imperfect view of the subject, what is purely the effect of the other.

For that the emotion called laughter doth not result from the contempt, but solely from the perception of oddity, with which the passion is occasionally, not necessarily, combined, is manifest from the following considerations. First, contempt may be raised in a very high degree, both suddenly and unexpectedly, without producing the least tendency to laugh. Of this instances have been given already from Bolingbroke and Swift, and innumerable others will occur to those who are conversant in the writings of those authors. Secondly, laughter may be, and is daily, produced by the perception of incongruous association, when there is no contempt. And this shows that Hobbes's view of the matter is false as well as partial. "Men," says he, "laugh at jests, the wit whereof always consisteth in the elegant discovering and conveying to our minds some absurdity of another." [2] I maintain, that men also laugh at jests, the wit whereof doth not consist in discovering any absurdity of another; for all jests do not come within his description. On a careful perusal of the foregoing sheets, the reader will find that there have been several instances of this kind produced already, in which it hath been observed that there is wit, but no ridicule. I shall bring but one other instance. Many have laughed at the queerness of the comparison of these lines,

> For rhyme the rudder is of verses,
> With which like ships they steer their courses; [3]

who never dreamt that there was any person or party, practice or opinion, derided in them. But as people are often very ingenious, in their manner of defending a favourite hypothesis, if any admirer of the Hobbesian philosophy should pretend to discover some class of men whom the poet here meant to ridicule, he ought to consider that if any one hath been tickled with the passage, to whom the same thought never occurred, that single instance would be sufficient to subvert the doctrine, as it would show that there may

1 *Human Nature*, Chap. ix. § 13.
2 *Human Nature*, Chap. ix. § 13.
3 *Hudibras*, Part i. Canto 1.

be laughter, where is no triumph or glorying over any body, and consequently no conceit of one's own superiority. So that there may be, and often is, both contempt without laughter, and laughter without contempt.

Besides, where wit is really pointed, which constitutes ridicule, that it is not from what gives the conceit of our own eminence by comparison, but purely from the odd assemblage of ideas, that the laughter springs, is evident from this, that if you make but a trifling alteration in the expression, so as to destroy the wit (which often turns on a very little circumstance), without altering the real import of the sentence (a thing not only possible but easy), you will produce the same opinion, and the same contempt; and consequently will give the same subject of triumph, yet without the least tendency to laugh: and conversely, in reading a well written satire, a man may be much diverted by the wit, whose judgment is not convinced by the ridicule or insinuated argument, and whose former esteem of the object is not in the least impaired. Indeed, men's telling their own blunders, even blunders recently committed, and laughing at them, a thing not uncommon in very risible dispositions, is utterly inexplicable on Hobbes's system. For, to consider the thing only with regard to the laugher himself, there is to him no subject of glorying, that is not counter-balanced by an equal subject of humiliation (he being both the person laughing, and the person laughed at), and these two subjects must destroy one another. With regard to others, he appears solely under the notion of inferiority, as the person triumphed over. Indeed, as in ridicule, agreeably to the doctrine here propounded, there is always some degree, often but a very slight degree, of contempt, it is not every character, I acknowledge, that is fond of presenting to others such subjects of mirth. Wherever one shows a proneness to it, it is demonstrable that on that person sociality and the love of laughter have much greater influence than vanity or self-conceit: since for the sake of sharing with others in the joyous entertainment, he can submit to the mortifying circumstance of being the subject. This, however, is in effect no more than enjoying the sweet which predominates, notwithstanding a little of the bitter with which it is mingled. The laugh in this case is so far from being expressive of the passion, that it is produced in spite of the passion which operates against it, and if strong enough would effectually restrain it.

But it is impossible that there could be any enjoyment to him on the other hypothesis, which makes a laughter merely the expression of a triumph, occasioned by the sudden display of one's own comparative excellence, a triumph in which the person derided could not partake. In this case, on the contrary, he must undoubtedly sustain the part of the weeper, (according to the account which the same author hath given of that opposite passion,[4] as he calls it,) and "suddenly fall out with himself, on the sudden conception of defect." To suppose that a person in laughing enjoys the contempt of himself as a matter of exultation over his own infirmity, is

4 Hobbes's *Human Nature,* Chap. ix. § 14.

of a piece with Cowley's description of envy exaggerated to absurdity, wherein she is said

> To envy at the praise herself had won.[5]

In the same way, a miser may be said to grudge the money that himself hath got, or a glutton the repast; for the lust of praise as much terminates in self, as avarice or gluttony. It is a strange sort of theory, which makes the frustration of a passion and the gratification the same thing.

As to the remark, that wit is not the only cause of this emotion, that men laugh at indecencies and mischances; nothing is more certain. A well-dressed man falling into the kennel, will raise in the spectators a peal of laughter. But this confirms, instead of weakening, the doctrine here laid down. The genuine object is always things grouped together, in which there is some striking unsuitableness. The effect is much the same, whether the things themselves are presented to the senses by external accident, or the ideas of them are presented to the imagination by wit and humour; though it is only with the latter that the subject of eloquence is concerned.

In regard to Hobbes's system, I shall only remark further, that according to it, a very risible man, and a very self-conceited supercilious man, should imply the same character, yet, in fact, perhaps, no two characters more rarely meet in the same person. Pride, and contempt, its usual attendant, considered in themselves, are unpleasant passions, and tend to make men fastidious, always finding ground to be dissatisfied with their situation and their company. Accordingly, those who are most addicted to these passions are not generally the happiest of mortals. It is only when the last of these hath gotten for an alloy a considerable share of sensibility in regard to wit and humour, which serves both to moderate and to sweeten the passion, that it can be termed in any degree sociable or agreeable. It hath been often remarked of very proud persons, that they disdain to laugh, as thinking that it derogates from their dignity, and levels them too much with the common herd. The merriest people, on the contrary, are the least suspected of being haughty and contemptuous people. The company of the former is generally as much courted as that of the latter is shunned. To refer ourselves to such universal observations, is to appeal to the common sense of mankind. How admirably is the height of pride and arrogance touched in the character which Caesar gives to Cassius!

> ——— He loves no plays
> As thou dost, Antony; he hears no music;
> Seldom he smiles, and smiles in such a sort,
> As if he mock'd himself, and scorn'd his spirit,
> That could be mov'd to smile at any thing.[6]

I should not have been so particular in the refutation of the English philosopher's system in regard to laughter, had I not considered a careful discus-

[5] *Davideis,* Book i.
[6] Shakspeare's *Julius Caesar.*

sion of this question as one of the best means of developing some of the radical principles of this inquiry.

CHAPTER IV

Of the relation which eloquence bears to logic and to grammar

In contemplating a human creature, the most natural division of the subject is the common division into soul and body, or into the living principle of perception and of action, and that system of material organs by which the other receives information from without, and is enabled to exert its powers, both for its own benefit and for that of the species. Analogous to this, there are two things in every discourse which principally claim our attention, the sense and the expression; or in other words, the thought and the symbol by which it is communicated. These may be said to constitute the soul and the body of an oration, or indeed of whatever is signified to another by language. For, as in man, each of these constituent parts hath its distinctive attributes, and as the perfection of the latter consisteth in its fitness for serving the purposes of the former, so it is precisely with those two essential parts of every speech, the sense and the expression. Now, it is by the sense that rhetoric holds of logic, and by the expression that she holds of grammar.

The sole and ultimate end of logic is the eviction of truth; one important end of eloquence, though, as appears from the first chapter, neither the sole, nor always the ultimate, is the conviction of the hearers. Pure logic regards only the subject, which is examined solely for the sake of information. Truth, as such, is the proper aim of the examiner. Eloquence not only considers the subject, but also the speaker and the hearers, and both the subject and the speaker for the sake of the hearers, or rather for the sake of the effect intended to be produced in them. Now, to convince the hearers is always either proposed by the orator, as his end in addressing them, or supposed to accompany the accomplishment of his end. Of the five sorts of discourses above mentioned, there are only two wherein conviction is the avowed purpose. One is that addressed to the understanding, in which the speaker proposeth to prove some position disbelieved or doubted by the hearers; the other is that which is calculated to influence the will, and persuade to a certain conduct; for it is by convincing the judgment that he proposeth to interest the passions and fix the resolution. As to the three other kinds of discourses enumerated, which address the understanding, the imagination, and the passions, conviction, though not the end, ought ever to accompany the accomplishment of the end. It is never formally proposed as an end where there are not supposed to be previous doubts or errors to conquer. But when due attention is not paid to it, by a proper management of the subject, doubts, disbelief, and mistake will be raised by the discourse itself, where there were none before, and these will not fail to obstruct the speaker's end, whatever it be. In explanatory discourses, which are of all kinds the simplest, there is a certain precision of manner which ought to pervade the whole, and which, though not in the form of argument, is not the less satisfactory, since it carries internal evidence along with it. In harangues pathetic or panegyrical, in order that the hearers may be moved or pleased, it is of great consequence to impress them with the belief of the reality of the subject. Nay, even in those performances where truth, in regard to the individual facts related, is neither sought nor expected, as in some sorts of poetry, and in romance, truth still is an object to the mind, the general truths regarding character, manners, and incidents. When these are preserved, the piece may justly be denominated true, considered as a picture of life; though false, considered as a narrative of particular events. And even these untrue events must be counterfeits of truth, and bear its image; for in cases wherein the proposed end can be rendered consistent with unbelief, it cannot be rendered compatible with incredibility. Thus, in order to satisfy the mind, in most cases, truth, and in every case, what bears the semblance of truth, must be presented to it. This holds equally, whatever be the declared aim of the speaker. I need scarcely add, that to prove a particular point is often occasionally necessary in every sort of discourse, as a subordinate end conducive to the advancement of the principal. If then it is the business of logic to evince the truth, to convince an auditory, which is the province of eloquence, is but a particular application of the logician's art. As logic therefore forges the arms which eloquence teacheth us to wield, we must first have recourse to the former, that being made acquainted with the materials of which her weapons and armour are severally made, we may know their respective strength and temper, and when and how each is to be used.

Now, if it be by the sense or soul of the discourse that rhetoric holds of logic, or the art of thinking and reasoning, it is by the expression or body of the discourse that she holds of grammar, or the art of conveying our thoughts in the words of a particular language. The observation of one analogy naturally suggests another. As the soul is of heavenly extraction and the body of earthly, so the sense of the discourse ought to have its source in the invariable nature of truth and right, whereas the expression can derive its energy only from the arbitrary conventions of men, sources as unlike, or rather as widely different, as the breath of the Almighty and the dust of the earth. In every region of the globe we may soon discover, that people feel and argue in much the same manner, but the speech of one nation is quite unintelligible to another. The art of the logician is accordingly, in some sense, universal; the art of the grammarian is always particular and local. The rules of argumentation laid down by Aristotle, in his Analytics, are of as much use for the discovery of truth in Britain or China as they were in Greece; but Priscian's rules of inflection and construction can assist us in learning no language but Latin. In propriety there cannot be such a thing as an universal grammar, unless there were such a thing as an universal language. The term hath sometimes, indeed, been applied to a collection of observations on the similar analogies that have been discovered in all tongues, ancient and modern, known to the authors of such collections. I do not mention this liberty in the use of the term with a view to censure it. In the application of technical or learned words, an author hath greater scope than in the application of those which are in more frequent use, and is only then thought censurable when he exposeth himself to be misunderstood. But it is to my purpose to observe that, as such collections convey the knowledge of no tongue whatever, the name *grammar,* when applied to them, is used in a sense quite different from that which it has in the common acceptation; perhaps as different, though the subject be language, as when it is applied to a system of geography.

Now, the grammatical art hath its completion in syntax; the oratorical, as far as the body or expression is concerned, in style. Syntax regards only the composition of many words into one sentence; style, at the same time that it attends to this, regards further the composition of many sentences into one discourse. Nor is this the only difference; the grammarian, with respect to what the two arts have in common, the structure of sentences, requires only purity; that is, that the words employed belong to the language, and that they be construed in the manner, and used in the signification, which custom hath rendered necessary for conveying the sense. The orator requires also beauty and strength. The highest aim of the former is the lowest aim of the latter; where grammar ends eloquence begins.

Thus the grammarian's department bears much the same relation to the orator's which the art of the mason bears to that of the architect. There is, however, one difference that well deserves our notice. As in architecture it is not necessary that he who designs should execute his own plans, he may be an excellent artist in this way who would handle very awkwardly the hammer and the trowel. But it is alike incumbent on the orator to design and to execute. He must, therefore, be master of the language he speaks or writes, and must be capable of adding to grammatic purity those higher qualities of elocution which will render his discourse graceful and energetic.

So much for the connexion that subsists between rhetoric and these parent arts, logic and grammar.

CHAPTER V

Of the different sources of Evidence, and the different Subjects to which they are respectively adapted

Logical truth consisteth in the conformity of our conceptions to their archetypes in the nature of things. This conformity is perceived by the mind, either immediately on a bare attention to the ideas under review, or mediately by a comparison of these with other related ideas. Evidence of the former kind is called intuitive; of the latter, deductive.

SECTION I—OF INTUITIVE EVIDENCE

Part I—Mathematical Axioms

Of intuitive evidence there are different sorts. One is that which results purely from *intellection*.[1] Of this kind is the evidence of these propositions: "One and four make five—Things equal to the same thing are equal to one another—The whole is greater than a part"; and, in brief, all axioms in arithmetic and geometry. These are, in effect, but so many different expositions of our own general notions, taken in different views. Some of them are no other than definitions, or equivalent to definitions. To say, "One and four make *five*," is precisely the same as to say, "We give the name of *five* to one added to four." In fact, they are all, in some respect, reducible to this axiom, "Whatever is, is." I do not say they are deduced from it, for they have in like manner that original and intrinsic evidence, which makes them, as soon as the terms are understood, to be perceived intuitively. And if they are not thus perceived, no deduction of reason will ever confer on them any additional evidence. Nay, in point of time, the discovery of the less general truths has the priority, not from their superior evidence, but solely from this consideration, that the less general are sooner objects of perception to us, the natural progress of the mind, in the acquisition of its ideas, being from particular things to universal notions, and not inversely. But I affirm that, though not deduced from that axiom, they may be considered as particular exemplifications of it, and coincident with it, inasmuch as they are all implied in this, that the properties of our clear and adequate ideas can be no other than what the mind clearly perceives them to be.

But, in order to prevent mistakes, it will be necessary further to illustrate this subject. It might be thought that if axioms were propositions perfectly identical, it would be impossible to advance a step, by their means, beyond the simple ideas first perceived by the mind. And it must be owned, if the predicate of the proposition were nothing but a repetition of the subject, under the same aspect, and in the same or synonymous terms, no conceivable advantage could be made of it for the furtherance of knowledge. Of such propositions as these for instance, "Seven are seven," "eight are eight," and "ten added to eleven, are equal to ten added to eleven," it is manifest, that we could never avail ourselves of them for the improvement of science.

---

[1] I have here adopted the term *intellection* rather than *perception*, because, though not so usual, it is both more apposite and less equivocal. *Perception* is employed alike to denote every immediate object of thought, or whatever is apprehended by the mind, our sensations themselves, and those qualities in body suggested by our sensations, the ideas of these upon reflection, whether remembered or imagined, together with those called general notions, or abstract ideas. It is only the last of these kinds which are considered as peculiarly the object of the understanding, and which, therefore, require to be distinguished by a peculiar name. Obscurity arising from an uncommon word is easily surmounted, whereas ambiguity, by misleading us, ere we are aware, confounds our notion of the subject altogether.

Nor does the change of the name make any alteration in point of utility. The propositions, "Twelve are a dozen," "twenty are a score," unless considered as explications of the words *dozen* and *score,* are equally insignificant with the former. But when the thing, though in effect coinciding, is considered under a different aspect; when what is single in the subject is divided in the predicate, and conversely; or when what is a whole in the one is regarded as a part of something else in the other; such propositions lead to the discovery of innumerable and apparently remote relations. One added to four may be accounted no other than a definition of the word *five,* as was remarked above. But when I say, "Two added to three are equal to five," I advance a truth, which, though equally clear, is quite distinct from the preceding. Thus, if one should affirm, "Twice fifteen make thirty," and again, "Thirteen added to seventeen make thirty," nobody would pretend that he had repeated the same proposition in other words. The cases are entirely similar. In both, the same thing is predicated of ideas which, taken severally, are different. From these again result other equations, as, "One added to four are equal to two added to three," and "twice fifteen are equal to thirteen added to seventeen."

Now, it is by the aid of such simple and elementary principles, that the arithmetician and the algebraist proceed to the most astonishing discoveries. Nor are the operations of the geometrician essentially different. By a very few steps you are made to perceive the equality, or rather the coincidence, of the sum of the two angles formed by one straight line falling on another, with two right angles. By a process equally plain you are brought to discover, first, that if one side of a triangle be produced, the external angle will be equal to both the internal and opposite angles, and then, that all the angles of a triangle are equal to two right angles. So much for the nature and use of the first kind of intuitive evidence, resulting from pure intellection.

Part II—Consciousness

The next kind is that which ariseth from *consciousness.* Hence every man derives the perfect assurance that he hath his own existence. Nor is he only in this way assured that he exists, but that he thinks, that he feels, that he sees, that he hears, and the like. Hence his absolute certainty in regard to the reality of his sensations and passions, and of every thing whose essence consists in being perceived. Nor does this kind of intuition regard only the truth of the original feelings or impressions, but also many of the judgments that are formed by the mind, on comparing these one with another. Thus the judgments we daily and hourly form, concerning resemblances or disparities in visible objects, or size in things tangible, where the odds is considerable, darker or lighter tints in colours, stronger or weaker tastes or smells, are all self-evident, and discoverable at once. It is from the same principle that, in regard to ourselves, we judge infallibly concerning the feelings, whether pleasant or painful, which we derive from what are called the internal senses, and pronounce concerning beauty or deformity, harmony or discord, the elegant or the ridiculous. The difference between this kind of intuition and the former will appear on the slightest reflection. The former concerns only abstract notions and ideas, particularly in regard to number and extension, the objects purely of the understanding; the latter concerns only the existence of the mind itself, and its actual feelings, impressions or affections, pleasures or pains, the immediate subjects of sense, taking that word in the largest acceptation. The former gives rise to those universal truths, first principles or axioms, which serve as the foundation of abstract science; whereas the latter, though absolutely essential to the individual, yet as it only regards particular perceptions, which represent no distinct genus or species of objects, the judgments resulting thence cannot form any general positions to which a chain of reasoning may be fastened, and consequently are not of the nature of axioms, though both similar and equal in respect of evidence.

Part III—Common Sense

The third sort is that which ariseth from what hath been termed properly enough, *common sense*,[2] as being an original source of knowledge common

2 The first among the moderns who took notice of this principle, as one of the genuine springs of our knowledge, was Buffier, a French philosopher of the present century, in a book entitled *Traité des Premières Vérités;* one who to an uncommon degree of acuteness in matters of abstraction added that solidity of judgment which hath prevented in him, what had proved the wreck of many great names in philosophy, his understanding becoming the dupe of his ingenuity. This doctrine hath lately, in our own country, been set in the clearest light, and supported by invincible force of argument, by two very able writers in the science of man, Dr. Reid, in his *Inquiry into the Human Mind,* and Dr. Beattie, in his *Essay on the Immutability of Truth.* I beg leave to remark in this place, that, though for distinction's sake, I use the term *common sense* in a more limited signification than either of the authors last mentioned, there appears to be no real difference in our sentiments of the thing itself. I am not ignorant that this doctrine has been lately attacked by Dr. Priestley in a most extraordinary manner, a manner which no man, who has any regard to the name either of Englishman or of philosopher, will ever desire to see imitated, in this or any other country. I have read the performance, but have not been able to discover the author's sentiments in relation to the principal point in dispute. He says expressly, [Examination of Dr. Reid's Inquiry, &c. p. 119,] "Had these writers," Messieurs Reid, Beattie, and Oswald, "assumed as the elements of their common sense certain truths which are so plain that no man could doubt of them, (without entering into the ground of our assent to them,) their conduct would have been liable to very little objection." And is not this the very thing which these writers have done? What he means to signify by the parenthesis, " (without entering into the ground of our assent to them,) " it is not easy to guess. By a ground of assent to any proposition is commonly understood a reason or argument in support of it. Now, by his own hypothesis, there are truths so plain, that no man can doubt of them. If so, what ground of assent beyond their own plainness ought we to seek; what beside this can we ever hope to find, or what better reason needs be given for denominating such truths the dictates of common sense? If something plainer could be found to serve as evidence of any of them, then this plainer truth would be admitted as the first principle, and the other would be considered as deduced by reasoning. But notwithstanding the mistake in the instance, the general doctrine

to all mankind. I own, indeed, that in different persons it prevails in different degrees of strength; but no human creature hath been found originally and totally destitute of it, who is not accounted a monster in his kind; for

---

of primary truths would remain unhurt. It seems, however, that though their conduct would have been liable to very little, it would have been liable to some objection. "All that could have been said would have been, that, without any necessity, they had made an innovation in the received use of the term." I have a better opinion of these gentlemen than to imagine, that if the thing which they contend for be admitted, they will enter into a dispute with any person about the name: though, in my judgment, even as to this, it is not they, but he, who is the innovator. He proceeds, "For no person ever denied that there are self-evident truths, and that these must be assumed, as the foundation of all our reasoning. I never met with any person who did not acknowledge this, or heard of any argumentative treatise that did not go on the supposition of it." Now, if this be the case, I would gladly know what is the great point he controverts. Is it, whether such self-evident truths shall be denominated principles of Common Sense, or be distinguished by some other appellation? Was it worth any man's while to write an octavo of near 400 pages, for the discussion of such a question as this? And if, as he assures us, they have said more than is necessary, in proof of a truth which he himself thinks indisputable, was it no more than necessary in Dr. Priestley to compose so large a volume, in order to convince the world that too much had been said already on the subject? I do not enter into the examination of his objections to some of the particular principles produced as primary truths. An attempt of this kind would be foreign to my purpose; besides that the authors he has attacked are better qualified for defending their own doctrine, and no doubt will do it, if they think there is occasion. I shall only subjoin two remarks on this book. The first is, that the author, through the whole, confounds two things totally distinct, certain associations of ideas, and certain judgments implying belief, which, though in some, are not in all cases, and therefore not necessarily, connected with the association. And if so, merely to account for the association is in no case to account for the belief with which it is attended. Nay, admitting his plea, [page 86,] that by the principle of association not only the ideas but the concomitant belief may be accounted for, even this does not invalidate the doctrine he impugns. For, let it be observed that it is one thing to assign a cause which, from the mechanism of our nature, has given rise to a particular tenet or belief, and another thing to produce a reason by which the understanding has been convinced. Now, unless this be done as to the principles in question, they must be considered as primary truths, in respect of the understanding, which never deduced them from other truths, and which is under a necessity, in all moral reasonings, of founding upon them. In fact, to give any other account of our conviction of them is to confirm instead of confuting the doctrine, that in all argumentation they must be regarded as primary truths, or truths which reason never inferred, through any medium, from other truths previously perceived. My second remark is, that though this examiner has, from Dr. Reid, given us a catalogue of first principles, which he deems unworthy of the honourable place assigned them, he has no where thought proper to give us a list of those self-evident truths which, by his own account, and in his own express words, "must be assumed as the foundation of all our reasoning." How much light might have been thrown upon the subject by the contrast! Perhaps we should have been enabled, on the comparison, to discover some distinctive characters in his genuine axioms, which would have preserved us from the danger of confounding them with their spurious ones. Nothing is more evident than that, in whatever regards matter of fact, the mathematical axioms will not answer. These are purely fitted for evolving the abstract relations of quantity. This he in effect owns himself [page 39]. It would have been obliging, then, and would have greatly contributed to shorten the controversy, if he had given us at least a specimen of those self-evident principles, which, in his estimation, are the *ne plus ultra* of moral reasoning.

such, doubtless, are all idiots and changelings. By madness, a disease which makes terrible havoc on the faculties of the mind, it may be in a great measure, but is never entirely lost.

It is purely hence that we derive our assurance of such truths as these: "Whatever has a beginning has a cause"—"When there is in the effect a manifest adjustment of the several parts to a certain end, there is intelligence in the cause." "The course of nature will be the same to-morrow that it is to-day; or, the future will resemble the past"—"There is such a thing as body; or, there are material substances independent of the mind's conceptions"—"There are other intelligent beings in the universe besides me"— "The clear representations of my memory, in regard to past events, are indubitably true." These, and a great many more of the same kind, it is impossible for any man by reasoning to evince, as might easily be shown, were this a proper place for the discussion. And it is equally impossible, without a full conviction of them, to advance a single step in the acquisition of knowledge, especially in all that regards mankind, life, and conduct.

I am sensible that some of these, to men not accustomed to inquiries of this kind, will appear at first not to be primary principles, but conclusions from other principles; and some of them will be thought to coincide with the other kinds of intuition above mentioned. Thus the first, "Whatever hath a beginning hath a cause," may be thought to stand on the same footing with mathematical axioms. I acknowledge that in point of evidence they are equal, and it is alike impossible, in either case, for a rational creature to withhold his assent. Nevertheless, there is a difference in kind. All the axioms in mathematics are but the enunciations of certain properties in our abstract notions, distinctly perceived by the mind, but have no relation to any thing without themselves, and can never be made the foundation of any conclusion concerning actual existence; whereas, in the axiom last specified, from the existence of one thing we intuitively conclude the existence of another. This proposition, however, so far differs, in my apprehension, from others of the same order, that I cannot avoid considering the opposite assertion as not only false but contradictory; but I do not pretend to explain the ground of this difference.

The faith we give to memory may be thought, on a superficial view, to be resolvable into consciousness, as well as that we give to the immediate impressions of sense. But on a little attention one may easily perceive the difference. To believe the report of our senses doth indeed commonly imply to believe the existence of certain external and corporeal objects, which give rise to our particular sensations. This, I acknowledge, is a principle which doth not spring from consciousness, (for consciousness cannot extend beyond sensation,) but from common sense, as well as the assurance we have in the report of memory. But this was not intended to be included under the second branch of intuitive evidence. By that firm belief in sense, which I there resolved into consciousness, I meant no more than to say, I am certain that I see, and feel, and think, what I actually see, and feel, and think. As in this I pronounce only concerning my own present feelings, whose essence consists in being felt, and of which I am at present conscious, my conviction is reducible to this axiom, or coincident with it, "It is impossible for a thing to be and not to be at the same time." Now when I say, I trust entirely to the clear report of my memory, I mean a good deal more than, "I am certain that my memory gives such a report, or represents things in such a manner," for this conviction I have indeed from consciousness; but I mean, "I am certain that things happened heretofore at such a time, in the precise manner in which I now remember that they then happened." Thus there is a reference in the ideas of memory to former sensible impressions, to which there is nothing analogous in sensation. At the same time it is evident, that remembrance is not always accompanied with this full conviction. To describe, in words, the difference between those lively signatures of memory, which command an unlimited assent, and those fainter traces which raise opinion only, or even doubt, is perhaps impracticable; but no man stands in need of such assistance to enable him in fact to distinguish them, for the direction of his own judgment and conduct. Some may imagine that it is from experience we come to know what faith in every case is due to memory. But it will appear more fully afterwards, that unless we had implicitly relied on the distinct and vivid informations of that faculty, we could not have moved a step towards the acquisition of experience. It must, however, be admitted, that experience is of use in assisting us to judge concerning the more languid and confused suggestions of memory; or, to speak more properly, concerning the reality of those things, of which we ourselves are doubtful whether we remember them or not.

In regard to the primary truths of this order, it may be urged that it cannot be affirmed of them all at least, as it may of the axioms in mathematics, or the assurances we have from consciousness, that the denial of them implies a manifest contradiction. It is, perhaps, physically possible that the course of nature will be inverted the very next moment; that my memory is no other than a delirium, and my life a dream; that all is mere illusion; that I am the only being in the universe, and that there is no such thing as body. Nothing can be juster than the reply given by Buffier, "It must be owned," says he,[3] "that to maintain propositions, the reverse of the primary truths of common sense, doth not imply a contradiction; it only implies insanity." But if any person, on account of this difference in the nature of these two classes of axioms, should not think the term intuitive so properly applied to the evidence of the last mentioned, let him denominate it, if he please, instinctive: I have no objection to the term; nor do I think it derogates in the least from the dignity, the certainty, or the importance of the truths themselves. Such instincts are no other than the oracles of eternal wisdom.

For, let it be observed further, that axioms of this last kind are as essential to moral reasoning, to all deductions concerning life and existence, as those of the first kind are to the sciences of arithmetic and geometry. Perhaps it

[3] *Premières Vérités,* Part i. Chap. xi.

will appear afterwards that, without the aid of some of them, these sciences themselves would be utterly inaccessible to us. Besides, the mathematical axioms can never extend their influence beyond the precincts of abstract knowledge, in regard to number and extension, or assist us in the discovery of any matter of fact: whereas, with knowledge of the latter kind, the whole conduct and business of human life is principally and intimately connected. All reasoning necessarily supposes that there are certain principles in which we must acquiesce, and beyond which we cannot go—principles clearly discernible by their own light, which can derive no additional evidence from any thing besides. On the contrary supposition, the investigation of truth would be an endless and a fruitless task; we should be eternally proving, whilst nothing could ever be proved; because, by the hypothesis, we could never ascend to premises which require no proof. "If there be no first truths," says the author lately quoted, "there can be no second truths, nor third, nor indeed any truth at all."

So much for intuitive evidence, in the extensive meaning which hath here been given to that term, as including every thing whose evidence results from the simple contemplation of the ideas or perceptions which form the proposition under consideration, and requires not the intervention of any third idea as a medium of proof. This, for order's sake, I have distributed into three classes, the truths of pure intellection, of consciousness, and of common sense. The first may be denominated metaphysical, the second physical, the third moral; all of them natural, original, and unaccountable.

SECTION II—OF DEDUCTIVE EVIDENCE

Part I—Division of the Subject into Scientific and Moral
with the Principal Distinctions between Them

All rational or deductive evidence is derived from one or other of these two sources: from the invariable properties or relations of general ideas; or from the actual, though perhaps variable connexions subsisting among things. The former we call demonstrative, the latter moral. Demonstration is built on pure intellection, and consisteth in an uninterrupted series of axioms. That propositions formerly demonstrated are taken into the series, doth not in the least invalidate this account; inasmuch as these propositions are all resolvable into axioms, and are admitted as links in the chain; not because necessary, but merely to avoid the useless prolixity which frequent and tedious repetition of proofs formerly given would occasion. Moral evidence is founded on the principles we have from consciousness and common sense, improved by experience; and as it proceeds on this general presumption or moral axiom, that the course of nature in time to come will be similar to what it hath been hitherto, it decides, in regard to particulars, concerning the future from the past, and concerning things unknown from things familiar to us. The first is solely conversant about number and extension, and about those other qualities which are measurable by these. Such are duration, velocity, and weight. With regard to such qualities as pleasure and pain, virtue and vice, wisdom and folly, beauty and deformity, though they admit degrees, yet, as there is no standard or common measure, by which their differences and proportions can be ascertained and expressed in numbers, they can never become the subject of demonstrative reasoning. Here rhetoric, it must be acknowledged, hath little to do. Simplicity of diction, and precision in arrangement, whence results perspicuity, are, as was observed already (Chap. I), all the requisites. The proper province of rhetoric is the second, or moral evidence; for to the second belong all decisions concerning fact, and things without us.

But that the nature of moral evidence may be better understood, it will not be amiss to remark a few of the most eminent differences between this and the demonstrative.

The first difference that occurs is in their subjects. The subject of the one is, as hath been observed, abstract independent truth, or the unchangeable and necessary relations of ideas; that of the other, the real but often changeable and contingent connexions that subsist among things actually existing. Abstract truths, as the properties of quantity, have no respect to time or to place, no dependence on the volition of any being, or on any cause whatever, but are eternally and immutably the same. The very reverse of all this generally obtains with regard to fact. In consequence of what has been now advanced, assertions opposite to truths of the former kind, are not only false, but absurd. They are not only not true, but it is impossible they should be true, whilst the meanings of the words (and consequently the ideas compared) remain the same. This doth not hold commonly in any other kind of evidence. Take, for instance, of the first kind, the following affirmations, "The cube of two is the half of sixteen,"—"The square of the hypothenuse is equal to the sum of the squares of the sides,"—"If equal things be taken from equal things, the remainders will be equal." Contrary propositions, as, "The cube of two is more than the half of sixteen,"—"The square of the hypothenuse is less than the sum of the squares of the sides," —"If equal things be taken from equal things, the remainders will be unequal," are chargeable, not only with falsity, but with absurdity, being inconceivable and contradictory. Whereas, to these truths which we acquire by moral evidence, "Cæsar overcame Pompey,"—"The sun will rise to-morrow,"—"All men will die,"—the opposite assertions, though untrue, are easily conceivable without changing, in the least, the import of the words, and therefore do not imply a contradiction.

The second difference I shall remark is, that moral evidence admits degrees, demonstration doth not. This is a plain consequence of the preceding difference. Essential or necessary truth, the sole object of the latter, is incompatible with degree. And though actual truth, or matter of fact, be the ultimate aim of the former, likelihood alone, which is susceptible of degree, is usually the utmost attainment. Whatever is exhibited as demonstration is either mere illusion, and so no evidence at all, or absolutely perfect. There is no medium. In moral reasoning we ascend from possibility, by an insensible gradation, to probability, and thence, in the same manner, to the summit of moral certainty. On this summit, or on any of the steps leading to it, the conclusion of the argument may rest. Hence the result of that is, by way of eminence, denominated science, and the evidence itself is termed scientific; the result of this is frequently (not always) entitled to no higher denomination than opinion. Now, in the mathematical sciences, no mention is ever made of opinions.

The third difference is, that in the one there never can be any contrariety of proofs; in the other, there not only may be, but almost always is. If one demonstration were ever capable of being refuted, it could be solely by another demonstration, this being the only sort of evidence adapted to the subject, and the only sort by which the former could be matched. But to suppose that contraries are demonstrable, is to suppose that the same proposition is both true and false, which is a manifest contradiction. Consequently, if there should ever be the appearance of demonstration on opposite sides, that on one side must be fallacious and sophistical. It is not so with moral evidence, for, unless in a few singular instances, there is always real, not apparent evidence on both sides. There are contrary experiences, contrary presumptions, contrary testimonies, to balance against one another. In this case, the probability, upon the whole, is in the proportion which the evidence on the side that preponderates bears to its opposite. We usually say, indeed, that the evidence lies on such a side of the question, and not on the reverse; but by this expression is only meant the overplus of evidence, on comparing both sides. In like manner, when we affirm of an event, that it is probable, we say the contrary is only possible, although, when they are severally considered, we do not scruple to say, This is more probable than that; or, The probabilities on one side outweigh those on the other.

The fourth and last difference I shall observe is, that scientific evidence is simple, consisting of only one coherent series, every part of which depends on the preceding, and, as it were, suspends the following: moral evidence is generally complicated, being in reality a bundle of independent proofs. The longest demonstration is but one uniform chain, the links whereof, taken severally, are not to be regarded as so many arguments, and consequently when thus taken, they conclude nothing; but taken together, and in their proper order, they form one argument, which is perfectly conclusive. It is true, the same theorem may be demonstrable in different ways, and by different mediums; but as a single demonstration, clearly understood, commands the fullest conviction, every other is superfluous. After one demonstrative proof, a man may try a second, purely as an exercise of ingenuity, or the better to assure himself that he hath not committed an oversight in the first. Thus it may serve to warrant the regular procedure of his faculties, but not to make an addition to the former proof, or supply any deficiency perceived in it. So far is it from answering this end, that he is no sooner sensible of a defect in an attempt of this nature, than the whole is rejected as good for nothing, and carrying with it no degree of evidence whatever. In moral reasoning, on the contrary, there is often a combination of many distinct topics of argument, no way dependent on one another. Each hath a certain portion of evidence belonging to itself, each bestows on the conclusion a particular degree of likelihood, of all which accumulated the credibility of the fact is compounded. The former may be compared to an arch, no part of which can subsist independently of the rest. If you make any breach in it, you destroy the whole. The latter may be compared to a tower, the height whereof is but the aggregate of the heights of the several parts reared above one another, and so may be gradually diminished, as it was gradually raised.

So much for the respective natures of scientific and of moral evidence, and those characteristical qualities which discriminate them from each other. On a survey of the whole, it seems indubitable, that if the former is infinitely superior in point of authority, the latter no less excels in point of importance. Abstract truth, as far as it is the object of our faculties, is almost entirely confined to quantity, concrete or discrete. The sphere of Demonstration is narrow, but within her sphere she is a despotic sovereign, her sway is uncontrollable. Her rival, on the contrary, hath less power but wider empire. Her forces, indeed, are not always irresistible; but the whole world is comprised in her dominions. Reality or fact comprehends the laws and the works of nature, as well as the arts and the institutions of men; in brief, all the beings which fall under the cognizance of the human mind, with all their modifications, operations, and effects. By the first, we must acknowledge, when applied to things, and combined with the discoveries of the second, our researches into nature in a certain line are facilitated, the understanding is enlightened, and many of the arts, both elegant and useful, are improved and perfected. Without the aid of the second, society must not only suffer but perish. Human nature itself could not subsist. This organ of knowledge, which extends its influence to every precinct of philosophy, and governs in most, serves also to regulate all the ordinary but indispensable concernments of life. To these it is admirably adapted, notwithstanding its inferiority in respect of dignity, accuracy, and perspicuity. For it is principally to the acquisitions procured by experience that we owe the use of language, and the knowledge of almost every thing that makes the soul of a man differ from that of a new-born infant. On the other hand, there is no despot so absolute as not to be liable to a check on some side or other; and that the prerogatives of demonstration are not so very considerable, as on a cursory view one is apt to imagine; and this, as well as every other operation of the intellect, must partake in the weakness incident to all our mental faculties, and inseparable from our nature, I shall afterwards take an opportunity particularly to evince.

Part II—The Nature and Origin of Experience

I should now consider the principal tribes comprehended under the general name of moral evidence; but, that every difficulty may be removed, which might retard our progress in the proposed discussion, it will be necessary, in the first place, to explore more accurately those sources in our nature which give being to experience, and consequently to all those attainments, moral and intellectual, that are derived from it. These sources are two, sense and memory. The senses, both external and internal, are the original inlets of perception. They inform the mind of the facts, which in the present instant are situated within the sphere of their activity, and no sooner discharge their office in any particular instance than the articles of information exhibited by them are devolved on the memory. Remembrance instantly succeeds sensation, insomuch that the memory becomes the sole repository of the knowledge received from sense; knowledge which, without this repository, would be as instantaneously lost as it is gotten, and could be of no service to the mind. Our sensations would be no better than the fleeting pictures of a moving object on a camera obscura, which leave not the least vestige behind them. Memory, therefore, is the only original voucher extant of those past realities for which we had once the evidence of sense. Her ideas are, as it were, the prints that have been left by sensible impressions. But from these two faculties, considered in themselves, there results to us the knowledge only of individual facts, and only of such facts as either heretofore have come, or at present do come, under the notice of our senses.

Now, in order to render this knowledge useful to us, in discovering the nature of things, and in regulating our conduct, a further process of the mind is necessary, which deserves to be carefully attended to, and may be thus illustrated. I have observed a stone fall to the ground when nothing intervened to impede its motion. This single fact produces little or no effect on the mind beyond a bare remembrance. At another time, I observe the fall of a tile, at another of an apple, and so of almost every kind of body in the like situation. Thus my senses first, and then my memory, furnish me with numerous examples, which, though different in every other particular, are similar in this, that they present a body moving downwards, till obstructed either by the ground or by some intervenient object. Hence my first notion of gravitation. For, with regard to the similar circumstances of different facts, as by the repetition such circumstances are more deeply imprinted, the mind acquires a habit of retaining them, omitting those circumstances peculiar to each wherein their differences consist. Hence, if objects of any kind, in a particular manner circumstanced, are remembered to have been usually, and still more if uniformly, succeeded by certain particular consequences, the idea of the former, in the supposed circumstance introduced into the mind, immediately associates the idea of the latter; and if the object itself, so circumstanced, be presented to the senses, the mind instantly anticipates the appearance of the customary consequence. This holds also inversely. The retention and association above explained are called Experience. The anticipation is in effect no other than a particular conclusion from that experience. Here we may remark by the way, that though memory gives birth to experience, which results from the comparison of facts remembered, the experience or habitual association remains, when the individual facts on which it is founded are all forgotten. I know from an experience which excludes all doubt, the power of fire in melting silver, and yet may not be able at present to recollect a particular instance in which I have seen this effect produced, or even in which I have had the fact attested by a credible witness.

Some will perhaps object that the account now given makes our experimental reasoning look like a sort of mechanism, necessarily resulting from the very constitution of the mind. I acknowledge the justness of the remark, but do not think that it ought to be regarded as an objection. It is plain that our reasoning in this way, if you please to call it so, is very early, and precedes all reflection on our faculties, and the manner of applying them. Those who attend to the progress of human nature through its different stages, and through childhood in particular, will observe that children make great acquisitions in knowledge from experience long before they attain the use of speech. The beasts also, in their sphere, improve by experience, which hath in them just the same foundations of sense and memory as in us, and hath, besides, a similar influence on their actions. It is precisely in the same manner, and with the same success, that you might train a dog, or accustom a child to expect food on your calling to him in one tone of voice, and to dread your resentment when you use another. The brutes have evidently the rudiments of this species of rationality, which extends as far in them as the immediate purposes of self-preservation require, and which, whether you call it reason or instinct, they both acquire and use in the same manner as we do. That it reaches no further in them, seems to arise from an original incapacity of classing, and (if I may use the expression) generalizing their perceptions; an exercise which to us very quickly becomes familiar, and is what chiefly fits us for the use of language. Indeed, in the extent of this capacity, as much, perhaps, as in any thing, lies also the principal natural superiority of one man over another.

But that we may be satisfied, that to this kind of reasoning, in its earliest or simplest form, little or no reflection is necessary, let it be observed, that it is now universally admitted by opticians, that it is not purely from sight, but from sight aided by experience, that we derive our notions of the distance of visible objects from the eye. The sensation, say they, is instantaneously followed by a conclusion or judgment founded on experience. The point is determined from the different phases of the object found, in former trials, to be connected with different distances, or from the effort that accompanies the different conformations we are obliged to give the organs of sight, in order to obtain a distinct vision of the object. Now, if this be the case, as I think hath been sufficiently evinced of late, it is manifest that this judgment is so truly instantaneous, and so perfectly the result of feeling and association, that the forming of it totally escapes our notice. Perhaps in no period of life will you find a person, that, on the first mention of it, can be easily persuaded that he derives this knowledge from experience. Every man will be ready to tell you that he needs no other witnesses than his eyes, to satisfy him that objects are not in contact with his body, but are at different distances from him as well as from one another. So passive is the mind in this matter, and so rapid are the transitions which, by this ideal attraction, she is impelled to make, that she is, in a manner, unconscious of her own operations. There is some ground to think, from the exact analogy which their organs bear to ours, that the discovery of distance from the eye is attained by brutes in the same manner as by us. As to this, however, I will not be positive. But though, in this way, the mind acquires an early perception of the most obvious and necessary truths, without which the bodily organs would be of little use; in matters less important her procedure is much slower, and more the result of voluntary application; and as the exertion is more deliberate, she is more conscious of her own activity, or, at least, remembers it longer. It is then only that in common style we honour her operation with the name of *reasoning;* though there is no essential difference between the two cases. It is true, indeed, that the conclusions in the first way, by which also in infancy we learn language, are commonly more to be regarded as infallible, than those effected in the second.

Part III—The Subdivisions of Moral Reasoning

But to return to the proposed distribution of moral evidence. Under it I include these three tribes, experience, analogy, and testimony. To these I shall subjoin the consideration of a fourth, totally distinct from them all, but which appears to be a mixture of the demonstrative and the moral; or rather a particular application of the former, for ascertaining the precise force of the latter. The evidence I mean is that resulting from calculations concerning chances.

I—EXPERIENCE

The first of these I have named peculiarly the evidence of experience, not with philosophical propriety, but in compliance with common language, and for distinction's sake. Analogical reasoning is surely reasoning from a more indirect experience. Now, as to this first kind, our experience is either uniform or various. In the one case, provided the facts on which it is founded be sufficiently numerous, the conclusion is said to be morally certain. In the other, the conclusion, built on the greater number of instances, is said to be probable, and more or less so, according to the proportion which the instances on that side bear to those on the opposite. Thus we are perfectly assured that iron thrown into the river will sink, that deal will float; because these conclusions are built on a full and uniform experience. That in the last week of December next, it will snow in any part of Britain specified, is perhaps probable; that is, if, on inquiry or recollection, we are satisfied that this hath more frequently happened than the contrary; that some time in that month it will snow, is more probable, but not certain, because, though this conclusion is founded on experience, that experience is not uniform; lastly, that it will snow some time during winter will, I believe, on the same principles, be pronounced certain.

It was affirmed that experience, or the tendency of the mind to associate ideas under the notion of causes, effects, or adjuncts, is never contracted by one example only. This assertion, it may be thought, is contradicted by the principle on which physiologists commonly proceed, who consider one accurate experiment in support of a particular doctrine as sufficient evidence. The better to explain this phenomenon, and the further to illustrate the nature of experience, I shall make the following observations. First, whereas sense and memory are conversant only about individuals, our earliest experiences imply, or perhaps generate, the notion of a species, including all those individuals which have the most obvious and universal resemblance. From Charles, Thomas, William, we ascend to the idea of man; from Britain, France, Spain, to the idea of kingdom. As our acquaintance with nature enlarges, we discover resemblances, of a striking and important nature, between one species and another, which naturally begets the notion of a genus. From comparing men with beasts, birds, fishes, and reptiles, we perceive that they are all alike possessed of life, or a principle of sensation and action, and of an organized body, and hence acquire the idea of animal: in like manner, from comparing kingdoms with republics and aristocracies, we obtain the idea of nation, and thence again rise in the same track to ideas still more comprehensive. Further, let it be remembered, that by experience we not only decide concerning the future from the past, but concerning things uncommon from things familiar which resemble them.

Now, to apply this observation: a botanist, in traversing the fields, lights on a particular plant, which appears to be of a species he is not acquainted with. The flower, he observes, is monopetalous, and the number of flowers it carries is seven. Here are two facts that occur to his observation; let us consider in what way he will be disposed to argue from them. From the first he does not hesitate to conclude, not only as probable, but as certain, that this individual, and all of the same species, invariably produce monopetalous flowers. From the second, he by no means concludes, as either certain, or even probable, that the flowers which either this plant, or others of the same species, carry at once, will always be seven. This difference, to a superficial inquirer, might seem capricious, since there appears to be one example, and but one in either case, on which the conclusion can be founded. The truth is, that it is not from this example only that he deduces these inferences. Had he never heretofore taken the smallest notice of any plant, he could not have reasoned at all from these remarks. The mind recurs instantly from the unknown to all the other known species of the same genus, and thence to all the known genera of the same order or tribe; and having experienced in the one instance, a regularity in every species, genus, and tribe, which admits no exception; in the other a variety as boundless as that of season, soil, and culture, it learns hence to mark the difference.

Again, we may observe that, on a closer acquaintance with those objects wherewith we are surrounded, we come to discover that they are mostly of a compound nature, and that not only as containing a complication of those qualities called accidents, as gravity, mobility, colour, extension, figure, solidity, which are common almost to all matter, not only as consisting of different members, but as comprehending a mixture of bodies, often very different in their nature and properties, as air, fire, water, earth, salt, oil, spirit, and the like. These, perhaps, on deeper researches, will be found to consist of materials still simpler. Moreover, as we advance in the study of nature, we daily find more reason to be convinced of her constancy in all her operations, that like causes, in like circumstances, always produce like effects, and inversely, like effects always flow from like causes. The inconstancy which appears at first in some of nature's works, a more improved experience teacheth us to account for in this manner. As most of the objects we know are of a complex nature, on a narrower scrutiny we find, that the effects ascribed to them ought often solely to be ascribed to one or more of the component parts; that the others noway contribute to the production: that, on the contrary, they sometimes tend to hinder it. If the parts in the composition of similar objects were always in equal quantity, their being compounded would make no odds; if the parts, though not equal, bore always the same proportion to the whole, this would make a difference: but such as in many cases might be computed. In both respects, however, there is an immense variety. Perhaps every individual differs from every other individual of the same species, both in the quantities and in the proportions of its constituent members and component parts. This diversity is also found in other things, which, though hardly reducible to species, are generally known by the same name. The atmosphere in the same place at different times, or at the same time in different places, differs in density, heat, humidity, and the number, quality, and proportion of the vapours or particles with which it is loaden. The more then we become acquainted with elementary natures, the more we are ascertained by a general experience of the uniformity of their operations. And though perhaps it be impossible for us to attain the knowledge of the simplest elements of any body, yet when any thing appears so simple, or rather so exactly uniform, as that we have observed it invariably to produce similar effects; on discovering any new effects, though but by one experiment, we conclude, from the general experience of the efficient, a like constancy in this energy as in the rest. Fire consumes wood, melts copper, and hardens clay. In these instances it acts uniformly, but not in these only. I have always experienced hitherto, that whatever of any species is consumed by it once, all of the same species it will consume upon trial at any time. The like may be said of what is melted, or hardened, or otherwise altered by it. If then, for the first time, I try the influence of fire on any fossil, or other substance, whatever be the effect, I readily conclude that fire will always produce a similar effect on similar bodies. This conclusion is not founded on this single instance, but on this instance compared with a general experience of the regularity of this element in all its operations.

So much for the first tribe, the evidence of experience, on which I have enlarged the more, as it is, if not the foundation, at least the criterion of all moral reasoning whatever. It is, besides, the principal organ of truth in all the branches of physiology (I use the word in its largest acceptation), including natural history, astronomy, geography, mechanics, optics, hydrostatics, meteorology, medicine, chemistry. Under the general term I also comprehend natural theology and psychology, which, in my opinion, have been most unnaturally disjoined by philosophers. Spirit, which here comprises only the Supreme Being and the human soul, is surely as much included under the notion of natural object as body is, and is knowable to the philosopher purely in the same way, by observation and experience.

II—ANALOGY

The evidence of analogy, as was hinted above, is but a more indirect experience, founded on some remote similitude. As things, however, are often more easily comprehended by the aid of example than by definition, I shall in that manner illustrate the difference between experimental evidence and analogical. The circulation of the blood in one human body is, I shall suppose, experimentally discovered. Nobody will doubt of this being a sufficient proof from experience, that the blood circulates in every human body. Nay, further, when we consider the great similarity which other animal bodies bear to the human body, and that both in the structure and in the destination of the several organs and limbs; particularly when we consider the resemblance in the blood itself, and blood-vessels, and in the fabric and pulsation of the heart and arteries, it will appear sufficient experimental evidence of the circulation of the blood in brutes, especially in quadrupeds. Yet, in this application, it is manifest, that the evidence is weaker than in the former. But should I from the same experiment infer the circulation of the sap in vegetables, this would be called an argument only from analogy. Now, all reasonings from experience are obviously weakened in proportion to the remoteness of the resemblance subsisting between that on which the argument is founded, and that concerning which we form the conclusion.

The same thing may be considered in a different way. I have learnt from experience, that like effects sometimes proceed from objects which faintly resemble, but not near so frequently as from objects which have a more perfect likeness. By this experience I have been enabled to determine the degrees of probability from the degrees of similarity in the different cases. It is presumable that the former of these ways has the earliest influence, when the mind, unaccustomed to reflection, forms but a weak association, and consequently but a weak expectation of a similar event from a weak resemblance. The latter seems more the result of thought, and is better adapted to the ordinary forms of reasoning.

It is allowed that an analogical evidence is at best but a feeble support, and is hardly ever honoured with the name of proof. Nevertheless, when the analogies are numerous, and the subject admits not evidence of another kind, it doth not want efficacy. It must be owned, however, that it is generally more successful in silencing objections than in evincing truth, and on this account may more properly be styled the defensive arms of the orator than the offensive. Though it rarely refutes, it frequently repels refutation, like those weapons which, though they cannot kill the enemy, will ward his blows.[4]

III—TESTIMONY

The third tribe is the evidence of testimony, which is either oral or written. This also hath been thought by some, but unjustly, to be solely and originally derived from the same source, experience.[5] The utmost in regard to this, that can be affirmed with truth, is that the evidence of testimony is to be considered as strictly logical, no further than human veracity in general, or the veracity of witnesses of such a character, and in such circumstances in particular, is supported, or perhaps more properly, hath not been refuted, by experience. But that testimony, antecedently to experience, hath a natural influence on belief, is undeniable. In this it resembles memory; for though the defects and misrepresentations of memory are corrected by experience, yet that this faculty hath an innate evidence of its own we know from this, that if we had not previously given an implicit faith to memory, we had never been able to acquire experience. This will appear from the revisal of its nature, as explained above. Nay, it must be owned, that in what regards single facts, testimony is more adequate evidence than any conclusions from experience. The immediate conclusions from experience are general, and run thus: "This is the ordinary course of nature;"—"Such an event may reasonably be expected, when all the attendant circumstances are similar." When we descend to particulars, the conclusion necessarily becomes weaker, being more indirect. For though all the *known* circumstances be similar, all the *actual* circumstances may not be similar; nor is it possible in any case to be assured, that all the actual circumstances are known to us. Accordingly, experience is the foundation of philosophy; which consists in a collection of general truths, systematically digested. On the contrary, the direct conclusion from testimony is particular, and runs thus: "This is the fact in the instance specified." Testimony, therefore, is the foundation of history, which is occupied about individuals. Hence we derive our acquaintance with past ages, as from experience we derive all that we can discover of the future. But the former is dignified with the name of knowledge, whereas the latter is regarded as matter of conjecture only. When experience is applied to the discovery of the truth in a particular incident, we call the evidence presumptive; ample testimony is accounted a positive proof of the fact. Nay, the strongest conviction built merely on the former is sometimes overturned by the slightest attack of the latter. Testimony is capable of giving us absolute certainty (Mr. Hume himself being

[4] Dr. Butler, in his excellent treatise called *The Analogy of Religion Natural and Revealed, to the Constitution and Course of Nature,* hath shown us how useful this mode of reasoning may be rendered, by the application he hath so successfully made of it for refuting the cavils of infidelity.

[5] I had occasion to make some reflections on this subject formerly. See *Dissertation on Miracles,* Part i. Sect. 1. There are several ingenious observations on the same subject in Reid's *Inquiry,* Ch. vi. Sect. 23.

judge [6]) even of the most miraculous fact, or of what is contrary to uniform experience. For, perhaps, in no other instance can experience be applied to individual events with so much certainty, as in what relates to the revolutions of the heavenly bodies. Yet, even this evidence, he admits, may not only be counterbalanced, but destroyed by testimony.

But to return. Testimony is a serious intimation from another, of any fact or observation, as being what he remembers to have seen or heard or experienced. To this, when we have no positive reasons of mistrust or doubt, we are, by an original principle of our nature (analogous to that which compels our faith in memory), led to give an unlimited assent. As on memory alone is founded the merely personal experience of the individual, so on testimony in concurrence with memory is founded the much more extensive experience which is not originally our own, but derived from others.[7] By the first, I question not, a man might acquire all the knowledge necessary for mere animal support, in that rudest state of human nature (if ever such a state existed) which was without speech and without society; to the last, in conjunction with the other, we are indebted for every thing which distinguishes the man from the brute, for language, arts, and civilization. It hath been observed, that from experience we learn to confine our belief in human testimony within the proper bounds. Hence we are taught to consider many attendant circumstances, which serve either to corroborate or to invalidate its evidence. The reputation of the attester, his manner of address, the nature of the fact attested, the occasion of giving the testimony, the possible or probable design in giving it, the disposition of the hearers to whom it was given, and several other circumstances, have all considerable influence in fixing the degree of credibility. But of these I shall have occasion to take notice afterwards. It deserves likewise to be attended to on this subject, that in a number of concurrent testimonies (in cases wherein there could have been no previous concert), there is a probability distinct from that which may be termed the sum of the probabilities resulting from the testimonies of the witnesses, a probability which would remain even though the witnesses were of such a character as to merit no faith at all. This probability arises purely from the concurrence itself. That such a concurrence should spring from chance is as one to infinite; that is, in other words, morally impossible. If therefore concert be excluded, there remains no other cause but the reality of the fact.

Now to this species of evidence, testimony, we are first immediately indebted for all the branches of philology, such as, history, civil, ecclesiastic, and literary; grammar, languages, jurisprudence, and criticism; to which I may add revealed religion, as far as it is to be considered as a subject of historical and critical inquiry, and so discoverable by natural means: and secondly, to the same source we owe, as was hinted above, a great part of that light which is commonly known under the name of experience, but

6 *Essay on Miracles,* p. 2.
7 *Dissertation on Miracles,* Part i. Sect. 2.

which is, in fact, not founded on our own personal observations, or the notices originally given by our own senses, but on the attested experiences and observations of others. So that as hence we derive entirely our knowledge of the actions and productions of men, especially in other regions and in former ages, hence also we derive, in a much greater measure than is commonly imagined, our acquaintance with Nature and her works.—Logic, rhetoric, ethics, economics, and politics are properly branches of pneumatology, though very closely connected with the philological studies above enumerated.

IV—CALCULATIONS OF CHANCES

The last kind of evidence I proposed to consider, was that resulting from calculations of chances. Chance is not commonly understood, either in philosophic or in vulgar language, to imply the exclusion of a cause, but our ignorance of the cause. It is often employed to denote a bare possibility of an event, when nothing is known either to produce or to hinder it. But in this meaning it can never be made the subject of calculation. It then only affords scope to the calculator, when a cause is known for the production of an effect, and when that effect must necessarily be attended with this or that or the other circumstance; but no cause is known to determine us to regard one particular circumstance in preference to the rest, as that which shall accompany the supposed effect. The effect is then considered as necessary, but the circumstance as only casual or contingent. When a die is thrown out of the hand, we know that its gravity will make it fall; we know also that this, together with its cubical figure, will make it lie so, when intercepted by the table, as to have one side facing upwards. Thus far we proceed on the certain principles of a uniform experience; but there is no principle which can lead me to conclude that one side rather than another will be turned up. I know that this circumstance is not without cause; but is, on the contrary, as really effected by the previous tossing which it receives in the hand or in the box, as its fall and the manner of its lying are by its gravity and figure. But the various turns or motions given it, in this manner, do inevitably escape my notice; and so are held for nothing. I say, therefore, that the chance is equal for every one of the six sides. Now, if five of these were marked with the same figure, suppose a dagger [†], and only one with an asterisk [*], I should in that case say, there were five chances that the die would turn up the dagger, for one that it would turn up the asterisk. For the turning up each of the six sides being equally possible, there are five cases in which the dagger, and only one in which the asterisk would be uppermost.

This differs from experience, inasmuch as I reckon the probability here, not from numbering and comparing the events after repeated trials, but without any trial, from balancing the possibilities on both sides. But though different from experience, it is so similar, that we cannot wonder that it should produce a similar effect upon the mind. These different positions being considered as equal, if any of five shall produce a similar effect, and but the sixth another, the mind, weighing the different events, resteth in an expectation of that in which the greater number of chances concur; but still accompanied with a degree of hesitancy, which appears proportioned to the number of chances on the opposite side. It is much after the same manner that the mind, on comparing its own experiences, when five instances favour one side to one that favours the contrary, determines the greater credibility of the former. Hence, in all complicated cases, the very degree of probability may be arithmetically ascertained. That two dice marked in the common way will turn up seven, is thrice as probable as that they will turn up eleven, and six times as probable as that they will turn up twelve.[8] The degree of probability is here determined demonstratively. It is indeed true that such mathematical calculations may be founded on experience, as well as upon chances. Examples of this we have in the computations that have been made of the value of annuities, insurances, and several other commercial articles. In such cases a great number of instances is necessary, the greatest exactness in collecting them on each side, and due care that there be no discoverable peculiarity in any of them, which would render them unfit for supporting a general conclusion.

Part IV—The Superiority of Scientific Evidence Re-examined

After the enumeration made in the first part of this section, of the principal differences between scientific evidence and moral, I signified my intention of resuming the subject afterwards, as far at least as might be necessary to show, that the prerogatives of demonstration are not so considerable, as on a cursory view one is apt to imagine. It will be proper now to execute this intention. I could not attempt it sooner, as the right apprehension of what is to be advanced will depend on a just conception of those things which have lately been explained. In the comparison referred to, I contrasted the two sorts of evidence, as they are in themselves, without considering the influence which the necessary application of our faculties in using both, has, and ought to have, on the effect. The observations then made in that abstracted view of the subject, appear to be well founded. But that view, I acknowledge, doth not comprehend the whole with which we are concerned.

It was observed of memory, that as it instantly succeeds sensation, it is the repository of all the stores from which our experience is collected, and that

---

[8] Call one die A, the other B. The chances for 7 are

A 1.	B 6.	A 4.	B 3.
A 2.	B 5.	A 5.	B 2.
A 3.	B 4.	A 6.	B 1.

The chances for eleven are

A 6. B 5.

A 5. B 6.

The only chance for 12 is A 6. B 6. The 1st is to the 2nd as 6 to 2; to the 3rd, as 6 to 1.

without an implicit faith in the clear representations of that faculty, we could not advance a step in the acquisition of experimental knowledge. Yet we know that memory is not infallible: nor can we pretend that in any case there is not a physical possibility of her making a false report. Here, it may be said, is an irremediable imbecility in the very foundation of moral reasoning. But is it less so in demonstrative reasoning? This point deserves a careful examination.

It was remarked concerning the latter, that it is a proof consisting of an uninterrupted series of axioms. The truth of each is intuitively perceived as we proceed. But this process is of necessity gradual, and these axioms are all brought in succession. It must then be solely by the aid of memory, that they are capable of producing conviction in the mind. Nor by this do I mean to affirm, that we can remember the preceding steps with their connexions, so as to have them all present to our view at one instant; for then we should, in that instant, perceive the whole intuitively. Our remembrance, on the contrary, amounts to no more than this, that the perception of the truth of the axiom to which we are advanced in the proof, is accompanied with a strong impression on the memory of the satisfaction that the mind received from the justness and regularity of what preceded. And in this we are under a necessity of acquiescing; for the understanding is no more capable of contemplating and perceiving at once the truth of all the propositions in the series, than the tongue is capable of uttering them at once. Before we make progress in geometry, we come to demonstrations, wherein there is a reference to preceding demonstrations; and in these perhaps to others that preceded them. The bare reflection, that as to these we once were satisfied, is accounted by every learner, and teacher too, as sufficient. And if it were not so, no advancement at all could be made in this science. Yet, here again, the whole evidence is reduced to the testimony of memory. It may be said that, along with the remembrance now mentioned, there is often in the mind a conscious power of recollecting the several steps, whenever it pleases; but the power of recollecting them severally, and successively, and the actual instantaneous recollection of the whole, are widely different. Now, what is the consequence of this induction? It is plainly this, that, in spite of the pride of mathesis, no demonstration whatever can produce, or reasonably ought to produce, a higher degree of certainty than that which results from the vivid representations of memory, on which the other is obliged to lean. Such is here the natural subordination, however rational and purely intellectual the former may be accounted, however mysterious and inexplicable the latter. For it is manifest, that without a perfect acquiescence in such representations, the mathematician could not advance a single step beyond his definitions and axioms. Nothing therefore is more certain, however inconceivable it appeared to Dr. Priestley, than what was affirmed by Dr. Oswald, that *the possibility of error attends the most complete demonstration.*

If from theory we recur to fact, we shall quickly find, that those most deeply versed in this sort of reasoning are conscious of the justness of the remark now made. A geometrician, I shall suppose, discovers a new theorem, which, having made a diagram for the purpose, he attempts to demonstrate, and succeeds in the attempt. The figure he hath constructed is very complex, and the demonstration long. Allow me now to ask, Will he be so perfectly satisfied on the first trial as not to think it of importance to make a second, perhaps a third, and a fourth? Whence arises this diffidence? Purely from the consciousness of the fallibility of his own faculties. But to what purpose, it may be said, the reiterations of the attempt, since it is impossible for him, by any efforts, to shake off his dependence on the accuracy of his attention and fidelity of his memory? Or, what can he have more than reiterated testimonies of his memory, in support of the truth of its former testimony? I acknowledge, that after a hundred attempts he can have no more. But even this is a great deal. We learn from experience, that the mistakes or oversights committed by the mind in one operation, are sometimes, on a review, corrected on the second, or perhaps on a third. Besides, the repetition, when no error is discovered, enlivens the remembrance, and so strengthens the conviction. But, for this conviction, it is plain that we are in a great measure indebted to memory, and in some measure even to experience.

Arithmetical operations, as well as geometrical, are in their nature scientific; yet the most accurate accountants are very sensible of the possibility of committing a blunder, and therefore rarely fail, for securing the matter, when it is of importance, to prove what they have done, by trying to effect the same thing another way. You have employed yourself, I suppose, in resolving some difficult problem by algebra, and are convinced that your solution is just. One whom you know to be an expert algebraist, carefully peruses the whole operation, and acquaints you that he hath discovered an error in your procedure. You are that instant sensible that your conviction was not of such an impregnable nature, but that his single testimony, in consequence of the confidence you repose in his experienced veracity and skill, makes a considerable abatement in it.

Many cases might be supposed, of belief founded only on moral evidence, which it would be impossible thus to shake. A man of known probity and good sense, and (if you think it makes an addition of any moment in this case) an astronomer and philosopher, bids you look at the sun as it goes down, and tells you, with a serious countenance, that the sun which sets today will never again rise upon the earth. What would be the effect of this declaration? Would it create in you any doubts? I believe it might, as to the soundness of the man's intellects, but not as to the truth of what he said. Thus, if we regard only the effect, demonstration itself doth not always produce such immovable certainty, as is sometimes consequent on merely moral evidence. And if there are, on the other hand, some well known demonstrations, of so great authority, that it would equally look like lunacy to impugn, it may deserve the attention of the curious to inquire how far, with respect to the bulk of mankind, these circumstances, their having stood the test of ages, their having obtained the universal suffrage of those who are qualified to examine them (things purely of the nature of moral evidence), have contributed to that unshaken faith with which they are received.

The principal difference then, in respect of the result of both kinds, is reduced to this narrow point. In mathematical reasoning, provided you are ascertained of the regular procedure of the mind, to affirm that the conclusion is false implies a contradiction; in moral reasoning, though the procedure of the mind were quite unexceptionable, there still remains a physical possibility of the falsity of the conclusion. But how small this difference is in reality, any judicious person who but attends a little may easily discover. The geometrician, for instance, can no more doubt whether the book called Euclid's Elements is a human composition, whether its contents were discovered and digested into the order in which they are there disposed, by human genius and art, than he can doubt the truth of the propositions therein demonstrated. Is he in the smallest degree surer of any of the properties of the circle, than that if he take away his hand from the compasses with which he is describing it on the wall, they will immediately fall to the ground. These things affect his mind, and influence his practice, precisely in the same manner.

So much for the various kinds of evidence, whether intuitive or deductive; intuitive evidence, as divided into that of pure intellection, of consciousness, and of common sense, under the last of which that of memory is included; deductive evidence, as divided into scientific and moral, with the subdivisions of the latter into experience, analogy, and testimony, to which hath been added the consideration of a mixed species concerning chances. So much for the various subjects of discourse, and the sorts of eviction of which they are respectively susceptible. This, though peculiarly the logician's province, is the foundation of all conviction, and consequently of persuasion too. To attain either of these ends, the speaker must always assume the character of the close candid reasoner: for though he may be an acute logician who is no orator, he will never be a consummate orator who is no logician.

CHAPTER VI

Of the Nature and Use of the scholastic art of Syllogizing

Having in the preceding chapter endeavoured to trace the outlines of natural logic, perhaps with more minuteness than in such an inquiry as this was strictly necessary, it might appear strange to pass over in silence the dialectic of the schools; an art which, though now fallen into disrepute, maintained, for a tract of ages, the highest reputation among the learned. What was so long regarded as teaching the only legitimate use and application of our rational powers in the acquisition of knowledge, ought not surely, when we are employed in investigating the nature and the different sorts of evidence, to be altogether overlooked.

It is long since I was first convinced, by what Mr. Locke had said on the subject, that the syllogistic art, with its figures and moods, serves more to display the ingenuity of the inventor, and to exercise the address and fluency of the learner, than to assist the diligent inquirer in his researches after truth. The method of proving by syllogism, appears, even on a superficial review, both unnatural and prolix. The rules laid down for distinguishing the conclusive from the inconclusive forms of argument, the true syllogism from the various kinds of sophism, are at once cumbersome to the memory, and unnecessary in practice. No person, one may venture to pronounce, will ever be made a reasoner, who stands in need of them. In a word, the whole bears the manifest indications of an artificial and ostentatious parade of learning, calculated for giving the appearance of great profundity to what in fact is very shallow. Such, I acknowledge, have been, for a long time, my sentiments on the subject. On a nearer inspection, I cannot say I have found reason to alter them, though I think I have seen a little further into the nature of this disputative science, and consequently into the grounds of its futility. I shall, therefore, as briefly as possible, lay before the reader a few observations on the subject, and so dismiss this article.

Permit me only to premise in general, that I proceed all along on the supposition, that the reader hath some previous acquaintance with school logic. It would be extremely superfluous, in a work like this, to give even the shortest abridgment that could be made of an art so well known, and which is still to be found in many thousand volumes. On the other hand, it is not necessary that he be an adept in it; a mere smattering will sufficiently serve the present purpose.

My first observation is, that this method of arguing has not the least affinity to moral reasoning, the procedure in the one being the very reverse of that employed in the other. In moral reasoning we proceed by analysis, and ascend from particulars to universals; in syllogizing we proceed by synthesis, and descend from universals to particulars. The analytic is the only method which we can follow, in the acquisition of natural knowledge, or whatever regards actual existences; the synthetic is more properly the method that ought to be pursued, in the application of knowledge already acquired. It is for this reason it has been called the didactic method, as being the shortest way of communicating the principles of a science. But even in teaching, as often as we attempt, not barely to inform, but to convince, there is a necessity of recurring to the track in which the knowledge we would convey was first attained. Now, the method of reasoning by syllogism more resembles mathematical demonstration, wherein, from universal principles, called axioms, we deduce many truths, which, though general in their nature, may, when compared with those first principles, be justly styled particular. Whereas in all kinds of knowledge, wherein experience is our only guide, we can proceed to general truths solely by an induction of particulars.

Agreeably to this remark, if a syllogism be regular in mood and figure, and if the premises be true, the conclusion is infallible. The whole foundation of the syllogistic art lies in these two axioms: "Things which coincide with the same thing, coincide with one another;" and "Two things, whereof one does, and one does not coincide with the same thing, do not coincide with one another." On the former rest all the affirmative syllogisms, on the latter all the negative. Accordingly, there is no more mention here of probability and of degrees of evidence, than in the operations of geometry and algebra. It is true, indeed, that the term *probable* may be admitted into a syllogism, and make an essential part of the conclusion, and so it may also in an arithmetical computation; but this does not in the least affect what was advanced just now; for in all such cases, the probability itself is assumed in one of the premises: whereas, in the inductive method of reasoning, it often happens, that from certain facts we can deduce only probable consequences.

I observe secondly, that though this manner of arguing has more of the nature of scientific reasoning than of moral, it has, nevertheless, not been thought worthy of being adopted by mathematicians, as a proper method of demonstrating their theorems. I am satisfied that mathematical demonstration is capable of being moulded into the syllogistic form, having made the trial with success on some propositions. But that this form is a very incommodious one, and has many disadvantages, but not one advantage of that commonly practised, will be manifest to every one who makes the experiment. It is at once more indirect, more tedious, and more obscure. I may add, that if into those abstract sciences one were to introduce some specious fallacies, such fallacies could be much more easily sheltered under the awkward verbosity of this artificial method, than under the elegant simplicity of that which has hitherto been used.

My third remark, which, by the way, is directly consequent on the two former, shall be, that in the ordinary application of this art to matters with which we can be made acquainted only by experience, it can be of little or no utility. So far from leading the mind, agreeably to the design of all argument and investigation, from things known to things unknown, and by things evident to things obscure; its usual progress is, on the contrary, from things less known to things better known, and by things obscure to things evident. But that it may not be thought that I do injustice to the art by this representation, I must entreat that the few following considerations may be attended to.

When, in the way of induction, the mind proceeds from individual instances to the discovery of such truths as regard a species, and from these again to such as comprehend a genus, we may say with reason, that as we advance, there may be in every succeeding step, and commonly is, less certainty than in the preceding; but in no instance whatever can there be more. Besides, as the judgment formed concerning the less general was anterior to that formed concerning the more general, so the conviction is more vivid arising from both circumstances, that, being less general, it is more distinctly conceived, and being earlier, it is more deeply imprinted.

Now, the customary procedure in the syllogistic science is, as was remarked, the natural method reversed, being from general to special, and consequently from less to more obvious. In scientific reasoning the case is very different, as the axioms, or universal truths from which the mathematician argues, are so far from being the slow result of induction and experience, that they are self-evident. They are no sooner apprehended than necessarily assented to.

But to illustrate the matter by examples, take the following specimen in *Barbara,* the first mood of the first figure:—

> All animals feel;
> All horses are animals;
> Therefore all horses feel.

It is impossible that any reasonable man, who really doubts whether a horse has feeling or is a mere automaton, should be convinced by this argument. For, supposing he uses the names *horse* and *animal,* as standing in the same relation of species and genus which they bear in the common acceptation of the words, the argument you employ is, in effect, but an affirmation of the point which he denies, couched in such terms as include a multitude of other similar affirmations, which, whether true or false, are nothing to the purpose. Thus *all animals feel,* is only a compendious expression, for *all horses feel, all dogs feel, all camels feel, all eagles feel,* and so through the whole animal creation. I affirm, besides, that the procedure here is from things less known to things better known. It is possible that one may believe the conclusion who denies the major: but the reverse is not possible; for, to express myself in the language of the art, that may be predicated of the species, which is not predicable of the genus; but that can never be predicated of the genus, which is not predicable of the species. If one, therefore, were under such an error in regard to the brutes, true logic, which is always coincident with good sense, would lead our reflections to the indications of perception and feeling, given by these animals, and the remarkable conformity which in this respect, and in respect to their bodily organs, they bear to our own species.

It may be said, that if the subject of the question were a creature much more ignoble than the horse, there would be no scope for this objection to the argument. Substitute, then, the word *oysters* for horses in the minor, and it will stand thus,

> All animals feel;
> All oysters are animals;
> Therefore all oysters feel.

In order to give the greater advantage to the advocate for this scholastic art, let us suppose the antagonist does not maintain the opposite side from any favour to Descartes' theory concerning brutes, but from some notion entertained of that particular order of beings which is the subject of dispute. It is evident, that though he should admit the truth of the major, he would regard the minor as merely another manner of expressing the conclusion; for he would conceive an animal no otherwise than as a body endowed with sensation or feeling.

Sometimes, indeed, there is not in the premises any position more generic, under which the conclusion can be comprised. In this case you always find that the same proposition is exhibited in different words; insomuch that the stress of the argument lies in a mere synonyma or something equivalent. The following is an example:—

> The Almighty ought to be worshippèd;
> God is the Almighty;
> Therefore God ought to be worshipped.

It would be superfluous to illustrate that this argument could have no greater influence on the Epicurean, than the first mentioned one would have on the Cartesian. To suppose the contrary is to suppose the conviction effected by the charm of a sound, and not by the sense of what is advanced. Thus also the middle term and the subject frequently correspond to each other, as the definition, description, or circumlocution, and the name. Of this I shall give an example in *Disamis,* as in the technical dialect the third mood of the third figure is denominated,—

> Some men are rapacious;
> All men are rational animals;
> Therefore some rational animals are rapacious.

Who does not perceive that "rational animals" is but a periphrasis for men?

It may be proper to subjoin one example at least, in negative syllogisms. The subsequent is one in *Celarent,* the second mood of the first figure:—

> Nothing violent is lasting;
> But tyranny is violent;
> Therefore tyranny is not lasting.

Here a *thing violent* serves for the genus of which *tyranny* is a species; and nothing can be clearer than that it requires much less experience to discover whether shortness of duration be justly attributed to tyranny the species, than whether it be justly predicated of every violent thing. The application of what was said on the first example, to that now given, is so obvious that it would be losing time to attempt further to illustrate it.

Logicians have been at pains to discriminate the regular and consequential combinations of the three terms, as they are called, from the irregular and inconsequent. A combination of the latter kind, if the defect be in the form, is called a paralogism; if in the sense, a sophism; though sometimes these two appellations are confounded. Of the latter, one kind is denominated *petitio principii,* which is commonly rendered in English, *a begging of the question,* and is defined the proving of a thing by itself, whether expressed in the same or in different words, or which amounts to the same thing, assuming in the proof the very opinion or principle proposed to be proved. It is surprising that this should ever have been by those artists styled a sophism, since it is in fact so essential to the art, that there is always some radical defect in a syllogism which is not chargeable with this. The truth of what I now affirm will appear to any one, on the slightest review of what has been evinced in the preceding part of this chapter.

The fourth and last observation I shall make on this topic is, that the proper province of the syllogistical science is rather the adjustment of our language, in expressing ourselves on subjects previously known, than the acquisition of knowledge in things themselves. According to M. du Marsais, "Reasoning consists in deducing, inferring, or drawing a judgment from other judgments already known; or rather in showing that the judgment in question has been already formed implicitly, insomuch that the only point is to develope it, and show its identity with some anterior judgment." Now I affirm that the former part of this definition suits all deductive reasoning, whether scientifical or moral, in which the principle deduced is distinct from, however closely related to, the principles from which the deduction is made. The latter part of the definition, which begins with the words *or rather,* does not answer as an explication of the former, as the author seems to have intended, but exactly hits the character of syllogistic reasoning, and indeed of all sorts of controversy merely verbal. If you regard only the thing signified, the argument conveys no instruction, nor does it forward us in the knowledge of things a single step. But if you regard principally the signs, it may serve to correct misapplications of them, through inadvertency or otherwise.

In evincing the truth of this doctrine, I shall begin with a simple illustration from what may happen to any one in studying a foreign tongue. I learn from an Italian and French dictionary, that the Italian word *pecora* corresponds to the French word *brebis,* and from a French and English dictionary, that the French *brebis* corresponds to the English *sheep.* Hence I form this argument,

> *Pecora* is the same with *brebis;*
> *Brebis* is the same with *sheep;*
> Therefore *pecora* is the same with *sheep.*

This, though not in mood and figure, is evidently conclusive. Nay, more, if the words *pecora, brebis,* and *sheep,* under the notion of signs, be regarded as the terms, it has three distinct terms, and contains a direct and scientifical deduction from this axiom, "Things coincident with the same thing are coincident with one another." On the other hand, let the things signified be solely regarded, and there is but one term in the whole, namely, the species of quadruped denoted by the three names above mentioned. Nor is there, in this view of the matter, another judgment in all the three propositions, but this identical one, "A sheep is a sheep."

Nor let it be imagined that the only right application can be in the acquisition of strange languages. Every tongue whatever gives scope for it, inasmuch as in every tongue the speaker labours under great inconveniences, especially on abstract questions, both from the paucity, obscurity, and ambiguity of the words on the one hand; and from his own misapprehensions, and imperfect acquaintance with them on the other. As a man may, therefore, by an artful and sophistical use of them, be brought to admit, in certain terms, what he would deny in others, this disputatious discipline may, under proper management, by setting in a stronger light the inconsistencies occasioned by such improprieties, be rendered instrumental in correcting them. It was remarked above,[9] that such propositions as these, "Twelve are a dozen," "Twenty are a score," unless considered as explications of the words *dozen* and *score,* are quite insignificant. This limitation, however, it was necessary to add; for those positions which are identical when considered purely as relating to the things signified, are nowise identical when regarded purely as explanatory of the names. Suppose that through the imperfection of a man's knowledge in the language, aided by another's sophistry, and perhaps his own inattention, he is brought to admit of the one term, what he would refuse of the other, such an argument as this might be employed,

> Twelve, you allow, are equal to the fifth part of sixty;
> Now a dozen are equal to twelve;
> Therefore a dozen are equal to the fifth part of sixty.

I mark the case rather strongly, for the sake of illustration; for I am sensible, that in what regards things so definite as all names of number are, it is impossible for any one, who is not quite ignorant of the tongue, to be misled. But the intelligent reader will easily conceive, that in abstruse and metaphysical subjects, wherein the terms are often both extensive and indefinite in their signification, and sometimes even equivocal, the most acute and wary may be entangled in them.

In further confirmation of my fourth remark, I shall produce an example in *Camestres,* the second mood of the second figure:

> All animals are mortal;
> But angels are not mortal;
> Therefore angels are not animals.

When the antagonist calls an angel an animal, it must proceed from one or other of these two causes, either from an error in regard to the nature of the angelic order, or from a mistake as to the import of the English word *animal.* If the first be the case,—namely, some erroneous opinion about angels, as that they are embodied spirits, generated and corruptible like ourselves,—it is evident that the forementioned syllogism labours under the common defect of all syllogisms. It assumes the very point in question. But if the difference between the disputants be, as it frequently happens, merely verbal, and the opponent uses the word *animal* as another name for living

9 Chap. v. Sect. 1. Part 1.

creature, and as exactly corresponding to the Greek term, (Ζῶον) arguments of this sort may be of service, for setting the impropriety of such a mis-application of the English name in a clearer light. For let it be observed, that though Nature hath strongly marked the principal differences to be found in different orders of beings, a procedure which hath suggested to men the manner of classing things into genera and species, this does not hold equally in every case. Hence it is, that the general terms in different languages do not always exactly correspond. Some nations, from particular circumstances, are more affected by one property in objects, others by an-other. This leads to a different distribution of things under their several names. Now, though it is not of importance that the words in one tongue exactly correspond to those in another, it is of importance that in the same tongue uniformity in this respect be, as much as is possible, observed. Errors in regard to the signs tend not only to retard the progress of knowledge, but to introduce errors in regard to the things signified. Now, by suggesting the different attributes comprised in the definition of the term, as so many mediums in the proof, an appeal is made to the adversary's practice in the language. In this way such mediums may be presented as will satisfy a candid adversary, that the application he makes of the term in question is not conformable to the usage of the tongue.

On the other hand, it is certain, that in matters of an abstract and complex nature, where the terms are comprehensive, indefinite, not in fre-quent use, and consequently not well ascertained, men may argue together eternally, without making the smallest impression on each other, not sensi-ble, all the while, that there is not at bottom any difference between them, except as to the import of words and phrases. I do not say, however, that this is a consequence peculiar to this manner of debating, though perhaps oftener resulting from it, on account of its many nice distinctions, unmean-ing subtleties, and mazy windings, than from any other manner. For it must be owned, that the syllogistic art has at least as often been employed for imposing fallacies on the understanding, as for detecting those imposed. And though verbal controversy seems to be its natural province, it is neither the only method adapted to such discussions, nor the most expeditious.

To conclude then; what shall we denominate the artificial system, or organ of truth, as it has been called, of which we have been treating? Shall we style it the art of reasoning? So honourable an appellation it by no means merits, since, as hath been shown, it is ill adapted to scientific mat-ters, and for that reason never employed by the mathematician; and is utterly incapable of assisting us in our researches into nature. Shall we then pronounce it the science of *logomachy,* or in plain English, the art of fight-ing with words, and about words? And in this wordy warfare, shall we say that the rules of syllogizing are the tactics? This would certainly hit the matter more nearly; but I know not how it happens, that to call any thing *logomachy* or *altercation,* would be considered as giving bad names; and when a good use may be made of an invention, it seems unreasonable to fix an odious name upon it, which ought only to discriminate the abuse. I shall therefore only title it the scholastic art of disputation. It is the schoolmen's science of defence.

When all erudition consisted more in an acquaintance with words, and an address in using them, than in the knowledge of things, dexterity in this exercitation conferred as much lustre on the scholar, as agility in the tilts and tournaments added glory to the knight. In proportion as the attention of mankind has been drawn off to the study of nature, the honours of this contentious art have faded, and it is now almost forgotten. There is no reason to wish its revival, as eloquence seems to have been very little benefited by it, and philosophy still less.

Nay, there is but good reason to affirm, that there are two evils at least which it has gendered. These are, first, an itch of disputing on every subject, however uncontrovertible; the other, a sort of philosophic pride, which will not permit us to think that we believe any thing, even a self-evident principle, without a previous reason or argument. In order to gratify this passion, we invariably recur to words, and are at immense pains to lose ourselves in clouds of our own raising. We imagine we are advancing and making wonderful progress, while the mist of words in which we have involved our intellects, hinders us from discerning that we are moving in a circle all the time.

CHAPTER VII

Of the Consideration which the Speaker ought to have of the Hearers, as men in general

Rhetoric, as was observed already, not only considers the subject, but also the hearers and the speaker (Chap. IV). The hearers must be considered in a twofold view, as men in general, and as such men in particular.

As men in general, it must be allowed there are certain principles in our nature, which, when properly addressed and managed, give no inconsiderable aid to reason in promoting belief. Nor is it just to conclude from this concession, as some have hastily done, that oratory may be defined, "The art of deception." The use of such helps will be found, on a stricter examination, to be in most cases quite legitimate, and even necessary, if we would give reason herself that influence which is certainly her due. In order to evince the truth considered by itself, conclusive arguments alone are requisite; but in order to convince me by these arguments, it is moreover requisite that they be understood, that they be attended to, that they be remembered by me; and in order to persuade me by them to any particular action or conduct, it is further requisite, that by interesting me in the subject, they may, as it were, be felt. It is not therefore the understanding alone that is here concerned. If the orator would prove successful, it is necessary that he engage in his service all these different powers of the mind, the imagination, the memory, and the passions. These are not the supplanters of reason, or even rivals in her sway; they are her handmaids, by whose ministry she is enabled to usher truth into the heart, and procure it there a favourable reception. As handmaids they are liable to be seduced by sophistry in the garb of reason, and sometimes are made ignorantly to lend their aid in the introduction of falsehood. But their service is not on this account to be dispensed with; there is even a necessity of employing it, founded on our nature. Our eyes and hands and feet will give us the same assistance in doing mischief as in doing good; but it would not therefore be better for the world, that all mankind were blind and lame. Arms are not to be laid aside by honest men, because carried by assassins and ruffians; they are to be used the rather for this very reason. Nor are those mental powers, of which eloquence so much avails herself, like the art of war or other human arts, perfectly indifferent to good and evil, and only beneficial as they are rightly employed. On the contrary, they are by nature, as will perhaps appear afterwards, more friendly to truth than to falsehood, and more easily retained in the cause of virtue, than in that of vice.

SECTION I—MEN CONSIDERED AS ENDOWED WITH UNDERSTANDING

But to descend to particulars; the first thing to be studied by the speaker is, that his arguments may be understood. If they be unintelligible, the cause must be either in the sense or in the expression. It lies in the sense if the mediums of proof be such as the hearers are unacquainted with; that is, if the ideas introduced be either without the sphere of their knowledge, or too abstract for their apprehension and habits of thinking. It lies in the sense likewise, if the train of reasoning (though no unusual ideas should be introduced) be longer, or more complex, or more intricate, than they are accustomed to. But as the fitness of the arguments, in these respects, depends on the capacity, education, and attainments of the hearers, which in different orders of men are different, this properly belongs to the consideration which the speaker ought to have of his audience, not as men in general, but as men in particular. The obscurity which ariseth from the expression will come in course to be considered in the sequel.

SECTION II—MEN CONSIDERED AS ENDOWED WITH IMAGINATION

The second thing requisite is that his reasoning be attended to; for this purpose the imagination must be engaged. Attention is prerequisite to every effect of speaking, and without some gratification in hearing, there will be no attention, at least of any continuance. Those qualities in ideas which principally gratify the fancy, are vivacity, beauty, sublimity, novelty. Nothing contributes more to vivacity than striking resemblances in the imagery, which convey, besides, an additional pleasure of their own.

But there is still a further end to be served by pleasing the imagination, than that of awakening and preserving the attention, however important this purpose alone ought to be accounted. I will not say with a late subtle metaphysician,[1] that "Belief consisteth in the liveliness of our ideas." That this doctrine is erroneous, it would be quite foreign to my purpose to attempt here to evince.[2] Thus much however is indubitable, that belief commonly enlivens our ideas; and that lively ideas have a stronger influence than faint ideas to induce belief. But so far are these two from being coincident, that even this connexion between them, though common, is not necessary. Vivacity of ideas is not always accompanied with faith, nor is faith always able to produce vivacity. The ideas raised in my mind by the Oedipus Tyrannus of Sophocles, or the Lear of Shakespeare, are incomparably more lively than those excited by a cold but faithful historiographer. Yet I may give full credit to the languid narrative of the latter, though I believe not a single sentence in those tragedies. If a proof were asked of the greater vivacity in the one case than in the other (which, by the way, must be finally determined by consciousness), let these effects serve for arguments. The ideas of the poet give greater pleasure, command closer attention, operate more strongly on the passions, and are longer remembered. If these be not sufficient evidences of greater vivacity, I own I have no apprehension of the meaning which that author affixes to the term. The connexion, however, that generally subsisteth between vivacity and belief will appear less marvellous, if we reflect that there is not so great a difference between argument and illustration as is usually imagined. The same ingenious writer says, concerning moral reasoning, that it is but a kind of comparison. The truth of this assertion any one will easily be convinced of, who considers the preceding observations on that subject.

Where then lies the difference between addressing the judgment and addressing the fancy? and what hath given rise to the distinction between ratiocination and imagery? The following observations will serve for an answer to this query. It is evident, that though the mind receives a considerable pleasure from the discovery of resemblance, no pleasure is received when the resemblance is of such a nature as is familiar to every body. Such are those resemblances which result from the specific and generic qualities of ordinary objects. What gives the principal delight to the imagination, is the exhibition of a strong likeness, which escapes the notice of the generality of people. The similitude of man to man, eagle to eagle, sea to sea, or in brief, of one individual to another individual of the same species, affects not the fancy in the least. What poet would ever think of comparing a combat between two of his heroes to a combat between other two? Yet no where else will he find so strong a resemblance. Indeed, to the faculty of imagination, this resemblance appears rather under the notion of identity; although it be the foundation of the strongest reasoning from experience. Again, the similarity of one species to another of the same genus, as of the lion to the tiger, of the alder to the oak, though this too be a considerable fund of argumen-

1 The author of a *Treatise of Human Nature*, in 3 vols.
2 If one is desirous to see a refutation of this principle, let him consult Reid's *Inquiry*, Chap. ii. Sect. 5.

tation, hardly strikes the fancy more than the preceding, inasmuch as the generical properties, whereof every species participates, are also obvious. But if from the experimental reasoning we descend to the analogical, we may be said to come upon a common to which reason and fancy have an equal claim. "A comparison," says Quintilian, "hath almost the effect of an example." But what are rhetorical comparisons, when brought to illustrate any point inculcated on the hearers,—what are they, I say, but arguments from analogy? In proof of this let us borrow an instance from the forementioned rhetorician, "Would you be convinced of the necessity of education for the mind, consider of what importance culture is to the ground: the field which, cultivated, produceth a plentiful crop of useful fruits, if neglected, will be overrun with briars and brambles, and other useless or noxious weeds." It would be no better than trifling to point out the argument couched in this passage. Now if comparison, which is the chief, hath so great an influence upon conviction, it is no wonder that all those other oratorical tropes and figures addressed to the imagination, which are more or less nearly related to comparison, should derive hence both life and efficacy. Even antithesis implies comparison. Simile is a comparison in epitome.[3] Metaphor is an allegory in miniature. Allegory and prosopopeia are comparisons conveyed under a particular form.

SECTION III—MEN CONSIDERED AS ENDOWED WITH MEMORY

Further, vivid ideas are not only more powerful than languid ideas in commanding and preserving attention, they are not only more efficacious in producing conviction, but they are also more easily retained. Those several powers, understanding, imagination, memory, and passion, are mutually subservient. That it is necessary for the orator to engage the help of memory, will appear from many reasons, particularly from what was remarked above, on the fourth difference between moral reasoning and demonstrative.[4] It was there observed, that in the former the credibility of the fact is the sum of the evidence of all the arguments, often independent of one another, brought to support it. And though it was shown that demonstration itself, without the assistance of this faculty, could never produce conviction; yet here it must be owned, that the natural connexion of the several links in the chain renders the remembrance easier. Now, as nothing can operate on the mind which is not in some respect present to it, care must be taken by the orator that, in introducing new topics, the vestiges left by the former on the minds of the hearers may not be effaced. It is the sense of this necessity which hath given rise to the rules of composition.

3 Simile and comparison are in common language frequently confounded. The difference is this: Simile is no more than a comparison suggested in a word or two; as, He fought like a lion: His face shone as the sun. Comparison is a simile circumstantiated and included in one or more separate sentences.
4 Chap. v. Sect. ii. P. 1.

Some will perhaps consider it as irregular, that I speak here of addressing the memory, of which no mention at all was made in the first chapter, wherein I considered the different forms of eloquence, classing them by the different faculties of the mind addressed. But this apparent irregularity will vanish, when it is observed, that, with regard to the faculties there mentioned, each of them may not only be the direct, but even the ultimate object of what is spoken. The whole scope may be at one time to inform or convince the understanding, at another to delight the imagination, at a third to agitate the passions, and at a fourth to determine the will. But it is never the ultimate end of speaking to be remembered, when what is spoken tends neither to instruct, to please, to move, nor to persuade. This therefore is of necessity no more on any occasion than a subordinate end; or, which is precisely the same thing, the means to some further end; and as such, it is more or less necessary on every occasion. The speaker's attention to this subserviency of memory is always so much the more requisite, the greater the difficulty of remembrance is, and the more important the being remembered is to the attainment of the ultimate end. On both accounts, it is of more consequence in those discourses whose aim is either instruction or persuasion, than in those whose design is solely to please the fancy, or to move the passions. And if there are any which answer none of those ends, it were better to learn to forget them than to teach the method of making them to be retained.

The author of the treatise above quoted hath divided the principles of association in ideas into resemblance, contiguity, and causation. I do not here inquire into all the defects of this enumeration, but only observe that, even on his own system, order both in space and time ought to have been included. It appears at least to have an equal title with causation, which, according to him, is but a particular modification and combination of the other two. Causation, considered as an associating principle, is, in his theory, no more than the contiguous succession of two ideas, which is more deeply imprinted on the mind by its experience of a similar contiguity and succession of the impressions from which they are copied. This therefore is the result of resemblance and vicinity united. Order in place is likewise a mode of vicinity, where this last tie is strengthened by the regularity and simplicity of figure; which qualities arise solely from the resemblance of the corresponding parts of the figure; or the parts similarly situated. Regular figures, besides the advantages they derive from simplicity and uniformity, have this also, that they are more familiar to the mind than irregular figures, and are therefore more easily conceived. Hence the influence which order in place hath upon the memory. If any person question this influence, let him but reflect, how much easier it is to remember a considerable number of persons, whom one hath seen ranged on benches or chairs, round a hall, than the same number seen standing promiscuously in a crowd: and how natural it is, for assisting the memory in recollecting the persons, to recur to the order wherein they were placed.

As to order in time, which in composition is properly styled Method, it consisteth principally in connecting the parts in such a manner as to give vicinity to things in the discourse which have an affinity; that is, resemblance, causality, or other relation in nature; and thus making their customary association and resemblance, as in the former case, co-operate with their contiguity in duration, or immediate succession in the delivery. The utility of method for aiding the memory, all the world knows. But besides this, there are some parts of the discourse, as well as figures of speech, peculiarly adapted to this end. Such are the division of the subject, the rhetorical repetitions of every kind, the different modes of transition and recapitulation.

SECTION IV—MEN CONSIDERED AS ENDOWED WITH PASSIONS

To conclude; when persuasion is the end, passion also must be engaged. If it is fancy which bestows brilliancy on our ideas, if it is memory which gives them stability, passion doth more, it animates them. Hence they derive spirit and energy. To say that it is possible to persuade without speaking to the passions, is but at best a kind of specious nonsense. The coolest reasoner always in persuading addresseth himself to the passions some way or other. This he cannot avoid doing, if he speak to the purpose. To make me believe it is enough to show me that things are so; to make me act, it is necessary to show that the action will answer some end. That can never be an end to me which gratifies no passion or affection in my nature. You assure me, "It is for my honour." Now you solicit my pride, without which I had never been able to understand the word. You say, "It is for my interest." Now you bespeak my self-love. "It is for the public good." Now you rouse my patriotism. "It will relieve the miserable." Now you touch my pity. So far therefore it is from being an unfair method of persuasion to move the passions, that there is no persuasion without moving them.

But if so much depend on passion, where is the scope for argument? Before I answer this question, let it be observed that, in order to persuade, there are two things which must be carefully studied by the orator. The first is, to excite some desire or passion in the hearers; the second is satisfy their judgment that there is a connexion between the action to which he would persuade them, and the gratification of the desire or passion which he excites. This is the analysis of persuasion. The former is effected by communicating lively and glowing ideas of the object; the latter, unless so evident of itself as to supersede the necessity, by presenting the best and most forcible arguments which the nature of the subject admits. In the one lies the pathetic, in the other the argumentative. These incorporated together (as was observed in the first chapter) constitute that vehemence of contention, to which the greatest exploits of eloquence ought doubtless to be ascribed. Here then is the principal scope for argument, but not the only scope, as will appear in the sequel. When the first end alone is attained, the pathetic without the rational, the passions are indeed roused from a disagreeable languor by the help of the imagination, and the mind is thrown into a state which, though accompanied with some painful emotions, rarely fails, upon the whole, to affect it with pleasure. But, if the hearers are judicious, no practical effect is produced. They cannot by such declamation be influenced to a particular action, because not convinced that that action will conduce to the gratifying of the passion raised. Your eloquence hath fired my ambition, and makes me burn with public zeal. The consequence is, there is nothing which at present I would not attempt for the sake of fame, and the interest of my country. You advise me to such a conduct; but you have not shown me how that can contribute to gratify either passion. Satisfy me in this, and I am instantly at your command. Indeed, when the hearers are rude and ignorant, nothing more is necessary in the speaker than to inflame their passions. They will not require that the connexion between the conduct he urges and the end proposed be evinced to them. His word will satisfy. And therefore bold affirmations are made to supply the place of reasons. Hence it is that the rabble are ever the prey of quacks and impudent pretenders of every denomination.

On the contrary, when the other end alone is attained, the rational without the pathetic, the speaker is as far from his purpose as before. You have proved, beyond contradiction, that acting thus is the sure way to procure such an object. I perceive that your reasoning is conclusive: but I am not affected by it. Why? I have no passion for the object. I am indifferent whether I procure it or not. You have demonstrated that such a step will mortify my enemy. I believe it; but I have no resentment, and will not trouble myself to give pain to another. Your arguments evince that it would gratify my vanity. But I prefer my ease. Thus passion is the mover to action, reason is the guide. Good is the object of the will, truth is the object of the understanding.[5]

It may be thought that when the motive is the equity, the generosity, or the intrinsic merit of the action recommended, argument may be employed to evince the reasonableness of the end, as well as the fitness of the means. But this way of speaking suits better the popular dialect than the philosophical. The term *reasonableness,* when used in this manner, means nothing but the goodness, the amiableness, or moral excellency. If therefore the hearer hath no love of justice, no benevolence, no regard to right, although he were endowed with the perspicacity of a cherub, your harangue could never have any influence on his mind. The reason is, when you speak of the fitness of the means, you address yourself only to the head; when you speak of the goodness of the end, you address yourself to the heart, of which we supposed him destitute. Are we then to class the virtues among the passions? By no means. But without entering into a discussion of the difference, which would be foreign to our purpose, let it suffice to observe, that they have this

[5] Several causes have contributed to involve this subject in confusion. One is the ambiguity and imperfection of language. Motives are often called arguments, and both motives and arguments are promiscuously styled reasons. Another is, the idle disputes that have arisen among philosophers concerning the nature of good, both physical and moral.

in common with passion. They necessarily imply an habitual propensity to a certain species of conduct, an habitual aversion to the contrary: a veneration for such a character, an abhorrence of such another. They are, therefore, though not passions, so closely related to them, that they are properly considered as motives to action, being equally capable of giving an impulse to the will. The difference is akin to that, if not the same, which rhetoricians observe between *pathos* and *ethos,* passion and disposition.[6] Accordingly, what is addressed solely to the moral powers of the mind, is not so properly denominated the pathetic, as the *sentimental.* The term, I own, is rather modern, but is nevertheless convenient, as it fills a vacant room, and doth not, like most of our newfangled words, justle out older and worthier occupants, to the no small detriment of the language. It occupies, so to speak, the middle place between the pathetic and that which is addressed to the imagination, and partakes of both, adding to the warmth of the former the grace and attractions of the latter.

Now, the principal questions on this subject are these two:—How is a passion or disposition that is favourable to the design of the orator, to be excited in the hearers? How is an unfavourable passion or disposition to be calmed? As to the first it was said already in general, that passion must be awakened by communicating lively ideas of the object. The reason will be obvious from the following remarks: A passion is most strongly excited by sensation. The sight of danger, immediate or near, instantly rouseth fear; the feeling of an injury, and the presence of the injurer, in a moment kindle anger. Next to the influence of sense is that of memory, the effect of which upon passion, if the fact be recent, and remembered distinctly and circumstantially, is almost equal. Next to the influence of memory is that of imagination; by which is here solely meant the faculty of apprehending what is neither perceived by the senses, nor remembered. Now, as it is this power of which the orator must chiefly avail himself, it is proper to inquire what those circumstances are, which will make the ideas he summons up in the imaginations of his hearers, resemble, in lustre and steadiness, those of sensation and remembrance. For the same circumstances will infallibly make them resemble also in their effects; that is, in the influence they will have upon the passions and affections of the heart.

SECTION V—THE CIRCUMSTANCES THAT ARE CHIEFLY INSTRUMENTAL IN OPERATING ON THE PASSIONS

These are perhaps all reducible to the seven following, probability, plausibility, importance, proximity of time, connexion of place, relation of the actors or sufferers to the hearers or speaker, interest of the hearers or speaker in the consequences.[7]

---

[6] This seems to have been the sense which Quintilian had of the difference between *pathos* and *ethos,* when he gave *amor* for an example of the first, and *caritas* of the second. The word *ethos* is also sometimes used for moral sentiment.

[7] I am not quite positive as to the accuracy of this enumeration, and shall therefore freely permit my learned and ingenious friend Dr. Reid, to annex the *et cœtera* he pro-

Part I—Probability

The first is *probability*, which is now considered only as an expedient for enlivening passion. Here again there is commonly scope for argument.[8] Probability results from evidence, and begets belief. Belief invigorates our ideas. Belief raised to the highest becomes certainty. Certainty flows either from the force of the evidence, real or apparent, that is produced: or without any evidence produced by the speaker, from the previous notoriety of the fact. If the fact be notorious, it will not only be superfluous in the speaker to attempt to prove it, but it will be pernicious to his design. The reason is plain. By proving he supposeth it questionable, and by supposing actually renders it so to his audience: he brings them from viewing it in the stronger light of certainty, to view it in the weaker light of probability: in lieu of sunshine he gives them twilight. Of the different means and kinds of probation I have spoken already.

Part II—Plausibility

The second circumstance is *plausibility*, a thing totally distinct from the former, as having an effect upon the mind quite independent of faith or probability. It ariseth chiefly from the consistency of the narration, from its being what is commonly called natural and feasible. This the French critics have aptly enough denominated in their language *vraisemblance,* the English critics more improperly in theirs *probability*. In order to avoid the manifest ambiguity there is in this application of the word, it had been better to retain the word *verisimilitude,* now almost obsolete. That there is a relation between those two qualities must, notwithstanding, be admitted. This, however, is an additional reason for assigning them different names. An homonymous term, whose different significations have no affinity to one another, is very seldom liable to be misunderstood.

But as to the nature and extent of this relation, let it be observed, that the want of plausibility implies an internal improbability, which it will require the stronger external evidence to surmount. Nevertheless, the implausibility may be surmounted by such evidence, and we may be fully ascertained of what is in itself exceedingly implausible. Implausibility is, in a certain degree, positive evidence against a narrative; whereas plausibility implies no positive evidence for it. We know that fiction may be as plausible as truth. A narration may be possessed of this quality to the highest degree,

---

poses in such cases, in order to supply all defects. See *Sketches of the History of Man,* B. iii. Sk. 1. Appendix, c. ii. sect. 2.

8 In the judiciary orations of the ancients, this was the principal scope for argument. That to condemn the guilty, and to acquit the innocent, would gratify their indignation against the injurious, and their love of right, was too manifest to require a proof. The fact that there was guilt in the prisoner, or that there was innocence, did require it. It was otherwise in deliberative orations, as the conduct recommended was more remotely connected with the emotions raised.

which we not only regard as improbable, but know to be false. Probability is a light darted on the object, from the proofs, which for this reason are pertinently enough styled *evidence*. Plausibility is a native lustre issuing directly from the object. The former is the aim of the historian, the latter of the poet. That every one may be satisfied that the second is generally not inferior to the first, in its influence on the mind, we need but appeal to the effects of tragedy, of epic, and even of romance, which, in its principal characters, participates of the nature of poesy, though written in prose.

It deserves, however, to be remarked, that though plausibility alone hath often greater efficacy in rousing the passions than probability, or even certainty; yet, in any species of composition wherein truth, or at least probability, is expected, the mind quickly nauseates the most plausible tale, which is unsupported by proper arguments. For this reason it is the business of the orator, as much as his subject will permit, to avail himself of both qualities. There is one case, and but one, in which plausibility itself may be dispensed with; that is, when the fact is so incontestible that it is impossible to entertain a doubt of it; for when implausibility is incapable of impairing belief, it hath sometimes, especially in forensic causes, even a good effect. By presenting us with something monstrous in its kind, it raiseth astonishment, and thereby heightens every passion which the narrative is fitted to excite.

But to return to the explication of this quality. When I explained the nature of experience, I showed that it consisteth of all the general truth collected from particular facts remembered; the mind forming to itself, often insensibly, and as it were mechanically, certain maxims, from comparing, or rather associating the similar circumstances of different incidents.[9] Hence it is, that when a number of ideas relating to any fact or event are successively introduced into my mind by a speaker; if the train he deduceth coincide with the general current of my experience; if in nothing it thwart those conclusions and anticipations which are become habitual to me, my mind accompanies him with facility, glides along from one idea to another, and admits the whole with pleasure. If, on the contrary, the train he introduceth run counter to the current of my experience; if in many things it shock those conclusions and anticipations which are become habitual to me, my mind attends him with difficulty, suffers a sort of violence in passing from one idea to another, and rejects the whole with disdain:

> For while upon such monstrous scenes we gaze,
> They shock our faith, our indignation raise.
> (Horace, *The Art of Poetry*, trans. Francis)

In the former case I pronounce the narrative natural and credible, in the latter I say it is unnatural and incredible, if not impossible; and, which is particularly expressive of the different appearances in respect of connexion made by the ideas in my mind, the one tale I call coherent, the other incoherent. When therefore the orator can obtain no direct aid from the memory of his hearers, which is rarely to be obtained, he must, for the sake

9 Chap. V. Sect. ii. Part 2.

of brightening, and strengthening, and if I may be permitted to use so bold a metaphor, cementing his ideas, bespeak the assistance of experience. This, if properly employed, will prove a potent ally, by adding the grace of *verisimilitude* to the whole. It is therefore first of all requisite, that the circumstances of the narration, and the order in which they are exhibited, be what is commonly called natural, that is, congruous to general experience.

Where passion is the end, it is not a sufficient reason for introducing any circumstance that it is natural; it must also be pertinent. It is pertinent, when either necessary for giving a distinct and consistent apprehension of the object, at least for obviating some objection that may be started, or doubt that may be entertained concerning it; or when such as, in its particular tendency, promotes the general aim. All circumstances, however plausible, which serve merely for decoration, never fail to divert the attention, and so become prejudicial to the proposed influence on passion.

But I am aware that, from the explication I have given of this quality, it will be said, that I have run into the error, if it be an error, which I intended to avoid, and have confounded it with probability, by deriving it solely from the same origin, experience. In answer to this, let it be observed, that in every plausible tale which is unsupported by external evidence, there will be found throughout the whole, when duly canvassed, a mixture of possibilities and probabilities, and that not in such a manner as to make one part or incident probable, another barely possible, but so blended as equally to affect the whole, and every member. Take the Iliad for an example. That a haughty, choleric, and vindictive hero, such as Achilles is represented to have been, should, upon the public affront and injury he received from Agamemnon, treat that general with indignity, and form a resolution of withdrawing his troops, remaining thenceforth an unconcerned spectator of the calamities of his countrymen, our experience of the baleful influences of pride and anger renders in some degree probable; again, that one of such a character as Agamemnon, rapacious, jealous of his pre-eminence as commander-in-chief, who envied the superior merit of Achilles, and harboured resentment against him—that such a one, I say, on such an occurrence as is related by the poet, should have given the provocation, will be acknowledged also to have some probability. But that there were such personages, of such characters, in such circumstances, is merely possible. Here there is a total want of evidence. Experience is silent. Properly indeed the case comes not within the verge of its jurisdiction. Its general conclusions may serve in confutation, but can never serve in proof of particular or historical facts. Sufficient testimony, and that only, will answer here. The testimony of the poet in this case goes for nothing. His object we know is not truth but likelihood. Experience, however, advances nothing against those allegations of the poet, therefore we call them possible; it can say nothing for them, therefore we do not call them probable. The whole at most amounts to this—if such causes existed, such effects probably followed. But we have no evidence of the existence of the causes; therefore we have no evidence of the existence of the effects. Consequently, all the probability implied in this quality is a hypothetical probability, which is in effect none at all. It is an axiom among dialecticians, in relation to the syllogistic art, that the conclusion always follows the weaker of the premises. To apply this to the present purpose, an application not illicit, though unusual,—if one of the premises, suppose the major, contain an affirmation that is barely possible, the minor, one that is probable, possibility only can be deduced in the conclusion.

These two qualities, therefore, PROBABILITY and PLAUSIBILITY, (if I may be indulged a little in the allegoric style) , I shall call sister-graces, daughter of the same father *Experience,* who is the progeny of *Memory,* the first-born and heir of *Sense.* These daughters *Experience* had by different mothers. The elder is the offspring of *Reason,* the younger is the child of *Fancy.* The elder, regular in her features, and majestic both in shape and mien, is admirably fitted for commanding esteem, and even a religious veneration: the younger, careless, blooming, sprightly, is entirely formed for captivating the heart, and engaging love. The conversation of each is entertaining and instructive, but in different ways. Sages seem to think that there is more instruction to be gotten from the just observations of the elder; almost all are agreed that there is more entertainment in the lively sallies of the younger. The principal companion and favourite of the first is *Truth,* but whether *Truth* or *Fiction* share most in the favour of the second it were often difficult to say. Both are naturally well-disposed, and even friendly to *Virtue,* but the elder is by much the more steady of the two; the younger, though perhaps not less capable of doing good, is more easily corrupted, and hath sometimes basely turned procuress to *Vice.* Though rivals, they have a sisterly affection to each other, and love to be together. The elder, sensible that there are but few who can for any time relish her society alone, is generally anxious that her sister be of the party; the younger, conscious of her own superior talents in this respect, can more easily dispense with the other's company. Nevertheless, when she is discoursing on great and serious subjects in order to add weight to her words, she often quotes her sister's testimony, which she knows is better credited than her own, a compliment that is but sparingly returned by the elder. Each sister hath her admirers. Those of the younger are more numerous, those of the elder more constant. In the retinue of the former you will find the young, the gay, the dissipated; but these are not her only attendants. The middle-aged, however, and the thoughtful, more commonly attach themselves to the latter. To conclude; as something may be learned of characters from the invectives of enemies, as well as from the encomiums of friends, those who have not judgment to discern the good qualities of the first-born, accuse her of dulness, pedantry, and stiffness; those who have not taste to relish the charms of the second, charge her with folly, levity, and falseness. Meantime, it appears to be the universal opinion of the impartial, and such as have been best acquainted with both, that though the attractives of the younger be more irresistible at sight, the virtues of the elder will be longer remembered.

So much for the two qualities *probability* and *plausibility,* on which I have expatiated the more, as they are the principal, and in some respect, indispensable. The others are not compatible with every subject; but as they are of real moment, it is necessary to attend to them, that so they may not be overlooked in cases wherein the subject requires that they be urged.

Part III—Importance

The third circumstance I took notice of was *importance,* the appearance of which always tends, by fixing attention more closely, to add brightness and strength to the ideas. The importance in moral subjects is analogous to the quantity of matter in physical subjects, as on quantity the moment of moving bodies in a great degree depends. An action may derive importance from its own nature, from those concerned in it as acting or suffering, or from its consequences. It derives importance from its own nature, if it be stupendous in its kind, if the result of what is uncommonly great, whether good or bad, passion or invention, virtue or vice, as what in respect of generosity is godlike, what in respect of atrocity is diabolical: it derives importance from those concerned in it, when the actors or the sufferers are considerable, on account either of their dignity or of their number, or of both: it derives importance from its consequences, when these are remarkable in regard to their greatness, their multitude, their extent, and that either as to the many and distant places affected by them, or as to the future and remote periods to which they may reach, or as to both.

All the four remaining circumstances derive their efficacy purely from one and the same cause, the connexion of the subject with those occupied, as speaker or hearers, in the discourse. *Self* is the centre here, which hath a similar power in the ideal world to that of the sun in the material world, in communicating both light and heat to whatever is within the sphere of its activity, and in a greater or less degree according to the nearness or remoteness.

Part IV—Proximity of Time

First, as to *proximity of time,* every one knows that any melancholy incident is the more affecting that it is recent. Hence it is become common with storytellers, that they may make a deeper impression on the hearers, to introduce remarks like these; that the tale which they relate is not old, that it happened but lately, or in their own time, or that they are yet living who had a part in it, or were witnesses of it. Proximity of time regards not only the past but the future. An event that will probably soon happen hath greater influence upon us than what will probably happen a long time hence. I have hitherto proceeded on the hypothesis, that the orator rouses the passions of his hearers by exhibiting some past transaction; but we must acknowledge that passion may be as strongly excited by his reasonings concerning an event yet to come. In the judiciary orations there is greater scope for the former, in the deliberative for the latter; though in each kind there may occasionally be scope for both. All the seven circumstances enumerated are applicable, and have equal weight, whether they relate to the future or to the past. The only exception that I know of is, that probability and plausibility are scarcely distinguishable, when used in reference to events in futurity. As in these there is no access for testimony, what constitutes the principal distinction is quite excluded. In comparing the influence of the past upon our minds, with that of the future, it appears in general, that if the evidence, the importance, and the distance of the objects be equal, the latter will be greater than the former. The reason, I imagine, is, we are conscious that as every moment, the future, which seems placed before us, is approaching; and the past, which lies, as it were, behind, is retiring, our nearness or relation to the one constantly increaseth as the other decreaseth. There is something like attraction in the first case, and repulsion in the second. This tends to interest us more in the future than in the past, and consequently to the present view aggrandizes the one and diminishes the other.

What, nevertheless, gives the past a very considerable advantage, is its being generally susceptible of much stronger evidence than the future. The lights of the mind are, if I may so express myself, in an opposite situation to the lights of the body. These discover clearly the prospect lying before us, but not the ground we have already passed. By the memory, on the contrary, that great luminary of the mind, things past are exhibited in retrospect: we have no correspondent faculty to irradiate the future: and even in matters which fall not within the reach of our memory, past events are often clearly discoverable by testimony, and by effects at present existing; whereas we have nothing equivalent to found our arguments upon in reasoning about things to come. It is for this reason, that the future is considered as the province of conjecture and uncertainty.

Part V—Connexion of Place

Local *connexion,* the fifth in the above enumeration, hath a more powerful effect than proximity of time. Duration and space are two things, (call them entities or attributes, or what you please,) in some respects the most like, and in some respects the most unlike to one another. They resemble in continuity, divisibility, infinity, in their being deemed essential to the existence of other things, and in the doubts that have been raised as to their having a real or independent existence of their own. They differ, in that the latter is permanent, whereas the very essence of the former consisteth in transitoriness; the parts of the one are all successive, of the other all co-existent. The greater portions of time are all distinguished by the memorable things which have been transacted in them, the smaller portions by the revolutions of the heavenly bodies: the portions of place, great and small, (for we do not here consider the regions of the fixed stars and planets,) are distinguished by the various tracts of land and water, into which the earth is divided and subdivided; the one distinction intelligible, the other sensible; the one chiefly known to the inquisitive, the other in a great measure obvious to all.

Hence perhaps it arises, that the latter is considered as a firmer ground of relation than the former. Who is not more curious to know the notable transactions which have happened in his own country from the earliest antiquity, than to be acquainted with those which have happened in the remotest regions of the globe, during the century wherein he lives? It must be owned, however, that the former circumstance is more frequently aided by that of personal relation than the latter. Connexion of place not only includes vicinage, but every other local relation, such as being in a province under the same government with us, in a state that is in alliance with us, in a country well known to us, and the like. Of the influence of this connexion in operating on our passions we have daily proofs. With how much indifference, at least with how slight and transient emotion, do we read in newspapers the accounts of the most deplorable accidents in countries distant and unknown! How much, on the contrary, are we alarmed and agitated on being informed that any such accident hath happened in our neighbourhood, and that even though we be totally unacquainted with the persons concerned!

Part VI—Relation to the Persons Concerned

Still greater is the power of *relation* to the persons concerned, which was the sixth circumstance mentioned, as this tie is more direct than that which attacheth us to the scene of action. It is the persons, not the place, that are the immediate objects of the passions love or hatred, pity or anger, envy or contempt. Relation to the actors commonly produces an effect contrary to that produced by relation to the sufferers, the first in extenuation, the second in aggravation of the crime alleged. The first makes for the apologist, the second for the accuser. This I say is commonly the case, not always. A remote relation to the actors, when the offence is heinous, especially if the sufferers be more nearly related, will sometimes rather aggravate than extenuate the guilt in our estimation. But it is impossible with any precision to reduce these effects to rules; so much depending on the different tempers and sentiments of different audiences. Personal relations are of various kinds. Some have generally greater influence than others; some again have greater influence with one person, others with another. They are consanguinity, affinity, friendship, acquaintance, being fellow-citizens, countrymen, of the same surname, language, religion, occupation, and innumerable others.

Part VII—Interest in the Consequences

But of all the connective circumstances, the most powerful is *interest*, which is the last. Of all relations, personal relation, by bringing the object very near, most enlivens that sympathy which attacheth us to the concerns of others; interest in the effects brings the object, if I may say so, into contact with us, and makes the mind cling to it as a concern of its own. Sympathy is but a reflected feeling, and therefore, in ordinary cases, must be weaker than the original. Though the mirror be ever so true, a lover will not be obliged to it for presenting him with the figure of his mistress when he hath an opportunity of gazing on her person. Nor will the orator place his chief confidence in the assistance of the social and sympathetic affections, when he hath it in his power to arm the selfish.

Men universally, from a just conception of the difference, have, when self is concerned, given a different name to what seems originally the same passion in a higher degree. Injury, to whomsoever offered, is to every man that observes it, and whose sense of right is not debauched by vicious practice, the natural object of *indignation.* Indignation always implies *resentment,* or a desire of retaliating on the injurious person, so far at least as to make him repent the wrong he hath committed. This indignation in the person injured is, from our knowledge of mankind, supposed to be, not indeed universally, but generally so much stronger, that it ought to be distinguished by another appellation, and is, accordingly, denominated *revenge.* In like manner beneficence, on whomsoever exercised, is the natural object of our *love;* love always implies *benevolence,* or a desire of promoting the happiness of the beneficent person; but this passion in the person benefited is conceived to be so much greater, and to infer so strong an obligation to a return of good offices to his benefactor, that it merits to be distinguished by the title *gratitude.* Now by this circumstance of *interest* in the effects, the speaker, from engaging *pity* in his favour, can proceed to operate on a more powerful principle, *self-preservation.* The *benevolence* of his hearers he can work up into *gratitude,* their *indignation* into *revenge.*

The two last-mentioned circumstances, personal relation and interest, are not without influence, as was hinted in the enumeration, though they regard the speaker only, and not the hearers. The reason is, a person present with us, whom we see and hear, and who, by words, and looks, and gestures, gives the liveliest signs of his feelings, has the surest and most immediate claim upon our sympathy. We become infected with his passions. We are hurried along by them, and not allowed leisure to distinguish between his relation and our relation, his interest and our interest.

SECTION VI—OTHER PASSIONS, AS WELL AS MORAL SENTIMENTS, USEFUL AUXILIARIES

So much for those circumstances in the object presented by the speaker, which serve to awaken and inflame the passions of the hearers. But when a passion is once raised, there are also other means by which it may be kept alive, and even augmented. Other passions or dispositions may be called in as auxiliaries. Nothing is more efficacious in this respect than a sense of justice, a sense of public utility, a sense of glory; and nothing conduceth more to operate on these, than the sentiments of sages whose wisdom we venerate, the example of heroes whose exploits we admire. I shall conclude what relates to the exciting of passion when I have remarked, that pleading the importance and the other pathetic circumstances, or pleading the authority of opinions or precedents, is usually considered, and aptly enough, as being likewise a species of reasoning.

This concession, however, doth not imply, that by any reasoning we are ever taught that such an object ought to awaken such a passion. This we must learn originally from feeling, not from argument. No speaker attempts to prove it; though he sometimes introduceth moral considerations, in order to justify the passion when raised, and to prevent the hearers from attempting to suppress it. Even when he is enforcing their regard to the pathetic circumstances above mentioned, it is not so much his aim to show that these circumstances ought to augment the passion, as that these circumstances are in the object. The effect upon their minds he commonly leaves to nature; and is not afraid of the conclusion, if he can make every aggravating circumstance be, as it were, both perceived and felt by them. In the enthymeme, (the syllogism of orators, as Quintilian terms it,) employed in such cases, the sentiment that such a quality or circumstance ought to rouse such a passion, though the foundation of all, is generally assumed without proof, or even without mention. This forms the major proposition, which is suppressed as obvious. His whole art is exerted in evincing the minor, which is the antecedent in his argument, and which maintains the reality of those attendant circumstances in the case in hand. A careful attention to the examples of vehemence in the first chapter, and the quotation in the foregoing note, will sufficiently illustrate this remark.

SECTION VII—HOW AN UNFAVOURABLE PASSION MUST BE CALMED

I come now to the second question on the subject of passion. How is an unfavourable passion, or disposition, to be calmed? The answer is, either, first, by annihilating, or at least diminishing the object which raised it; or secondly, by exciting some other passion which may counterwork it.

By proving the falsity of the narration, or the utter incredibility of the future event, on the supposed truth of which the passion was founded, the object is annihilated. It is diminished by all such circumstances as are contrary to those by which it is increased. These are, improbability, implausibility, insignificance, distance of time, remoteness of place, the persons concerned such as we have no connexion with, the consequences such as we have no interest in. The method recommended by Gorgias, and approved by Aristotle, though peculiar in its manner, is, in those cases wherein it may properly be attempted, coincident in effect with that now mentioned. "It was a just opinion of Gorgias, that the serious argument of an adversary should be confounded by ridicule, and his ridicule by serious argument." For this is only endeavouring, by the aid of laughter and contempt, to diminish, or even quite undo, the unfriendly emotions that have been raised in the minds of the hearers; or, on the contrary, by satisfying them of the seriousness of the subject, and of the importance of its consequences, to extinguish the contempt, and make the laughter, which the antagonist wanted to excite, appear when examined, no better than madness.

The second way of silencing an unfavourable passion or disposition, is by conjuring up some other passion or disposition, which may overcome it. With regard to conduct, whenever the mind deliberates, it is conscious of contrary motives impelling it in opposite directions; in other words, it finds that acting thus would gratify one passion; not acting, or acting otherwise, would gratify another. To take such a step, I perceive, would promote my interest, but derogate from my honour. Such another will gratify my resentment, but hurt my interest. When this is the case, as the speaker can be at no loss to discover the conflicting passions, he must be sensible that whatever force he adds to the disposition that favours his design, is in fact so much subtracted from the disposition that opposeth it, and conversely; as in the two scales of a balance, it is equal in regard to the effect, whether you add so much weight to one scale, or take it from the other.

Thus we have seen in what manner passion to an absent object may be excited by eloquence, which, by enlivening and invigorating the ideas of imagination, makes them resemble the impressions of sense and the traces of memory; and in this respect hath an effect on the mind similar to that produced by a telescope on the sight; things remote are brought near, things obscure rendered conspicuous. We have seen also in what manner a passion already excited may be calmed; how, by the oratorical magic, as by inverting the telescope, the object may be again removed and diminished.

It were endless to enumerate all the rhetorical figures that are adapted to the pathetic. Let it suffice to say, that most of those already named may be successfully employed here. Of others the principal are these, correction, climax, vision, exclamation, apostrophe, and interrogation. The three first, correction, climax, and vision, tend greatly to enliven the ideas, by the implicit, but animated comparison and opposition conveyed in them. Implicit and indirect comparison is more suitable to the disturbed state of mind required by the pathetic, than that which is explicit and direct. The latter implies leisure and tranquillity, the former rapidity and fire. Exclamation and apostrophe operate chiefly by sympathy, as they are the most ardent expressions of perturbation in the speaker. It at first sight appears more difficult to account for the effect of interrogation, which, being an appeal to the hearers, though it might awaken a closer attention, yet could not, one would imagine, excite in their minds any emotion that was not there before. This, nevertheless, it doth excite, through an oblique operation of the same principle. Such an appeal implies in the orator the strongest confidence in the rectitude of his sentiments, and in the concurrence of every reasonable being. The auditors, by sympathizing with this frame of spirit, find it impracticable to withhold an assent which is so confidently depended on. But there will be occasion afterwards for discussing more particularly the rhetorical tropes and figures, when we come to treat of elocution.

Thus I have finished the consideration which the speaker ought to have of his hearers as men in general; that is, as thinking beings endowed with understanding, imagination, memory, and passions, such as we are conscious of in ourselves, and learn from the experience of their effects to be in others. I have pointed out the arts to be employed by him in engaging all those faculties in his service, that what he advanceth may not only be understood, not only command attention, not only be remembered, but, which is the chief point of all, may interest the heart.

CHAPTER VIII

Of the Consideration which the Speaker ought to have of the Hearers, as such men in particular

It was remarked in the beginning of the preceding chapter, that the hearers ought to be considered in a twofold view, as men in general, and as such men in particular. The first consideration I have despatched, I now enter on the second.

When it is affirmed that the hearers are to be considered as such men in particular, no more is meant, than that regard ought to be had by the speaker to the special character of the audience, as composed of such individuals; that he may suit himself to them, both in his style and in his arguments. Now, the difference between one audience and another is very great, not only in intellectual but in moral attainments. That may be clearly intelligible to a House of Commons, which would appear as if spoken in an unknown tongue to a conventicle of enthusiasts. That may kindle fury in the latter, which would create no emotion in the former but laughter and contempt. The most obvious difference that appears in different auditories, results from the different cultivation of the understanding; and the influence which this, and their manner of life, have both upon the imagination and upon the memory.

But even in cases wherein the difference in education and moral culture hath not been considerable, different habits afterwards contracted, and different occupations in life, give different propensities, and make one incline more to one passion, another to another. They consequently afford the intelligent speaker an easier passage to the heart, through the channel of the favourite passion. Thus liberty and independence will ever be prevalent motives with republicans, pomp and splendour with those attached to monarchy. In mercantile states, such as Carthage among the ancients, or Holland among the moderns, interest will always prove the most cogent argument; in states solely or chiefly composed of soldiers, such as Sparta and ancient Rome, no inducement will be found a counterpoise to glory. Similar differences are also to be made in addressing different classes of men. With men of genius the most successful topic will be fame; with men of industry, riches; with men of fortune, pleasure.

But as the characters of audiences may be infinitely diversified, and as the influence they ought to have respectively upon the speaker must be obvious to a person of discernment, it is sufficient here to have observed thus much in the general concerning them.

CHAPTER IX

Of the Consideration which the Speaker ought to have of Himself

The last consideration I mentioned, is that which the speaker ought to have of himself. By this we are to understand, not that estimate of himself which is derived directly from consciousness or self-acquaintance, but that which is obtained reflexively from the opinion entertained of him by the hearers, or the character which he bears with them. Sympathy is one main engine by which the orator operates on the passions.

> With them who laugh, our social joy appears;
> With them who mourn, we sympathize in tears;
> If you would have me weep, begin the strain,
> Then I shall feel your sorrows, feel your pain.
> (Horace, *The Art of Poetry,* trans. FRANCIS)

Whatever, therefore, weakens that principle of sympathy, must do the speaker unutterable prejudice in respect of his power over the passions of his audience, but not in this respect only. One source, at least, of the primary influence of testimony on faith, is doubtless to be attributed to the same communicative principle. At the same time it is certain, as was remarked above, that every testimony doth not equally attack this principle; that in this particular the reputation of the attester hath a considerable power. Now, the speaker's apparent conviction of the truth of what he advanceth, adds to all his other arguments an evidence, though not precisely the same, yet near akin to that of his own testimony. This hath some weight even with the wisest hearers, but is every thing with the vulgar. Whatever therefore lessens sympathy, must also impair belief.

Sympathy in the hearers to the speaker may be lessened several ways, chiefly by these two; by a low opinion of his intellectual abilities, and by a bad opinion of his morals. The latter is the more prejudicial of the two. Men generally will think themselves in less danger of being seduced by a man of weak understanding, but of distinguished probity, than by a man of the best understanding who is of a profligate life. So much more powerfully do the qualities of the heart attach us, than those of the head. This preference, though it may be justly called untaught and instinctive, arising purely from the original frame of the mind, reason, or the knowledge of mankind acquired by experience, instead of weakening, seems afterwards to corroborate. Hence it hath become a common topic with rhetoricians, that, in order to be a successful orator, one must be a good man; for to be good is the only sure way of being long esteemed good, and to be esteemed good is previously necessary to one's being heard with due attention and regard. Consequently, the topic hath a foundation in human nature. There are indeed other things in the character of the speaker, which, in a less degree, will hurt his influence; youth, inexperience of affairs, former want of success, and the like.

But of all the prepossessions in the minds of the hearers which tend to impede or counteract the design of the speaker, party-spirit, where it happens to prevail, is the most pernicious, being at once the most inflexible and the most unjust. This prejudice I mention by itself, as those above recited may have place at any time, and in any national circumstances. This hath place only when a people is so unfortunate as to be torn by faction. In that case, if the speaker and the hearers, or the bulk of the hearers, be of contrary parties, their minds will be more prepossessed against him, though his life were ever so blameless, than if he were a man of the most flagitious manners, but of the same party. This holds but too much alike of all parties, religious and political. Violent party-men not only lose all sympathy with those of the opposite side, but contract an antipathy to them. This, on some occasions, even the divinest eloquence will not surmount.

As to personal prejudices in general, I shall conclude with two remarks. The first is, the more gross the hearers are, so much the more suceptible they are of such prejudices. Nothing exposes the mind more to all their baneful influences than ignorance and rudeness; the rabble chiefly consider who speaks, men of sense and education what is spoken. Nor are the multitude, to do them justice, less excessive in their love than in their hatred, in their attachments than in their aversions. From a consciousness, it would seem, of their own incapacity to guide themselves, they are ever prone blindly to submit to the guidance of some popular orator, who hath had the address first, either to gain their approbation by his real or pretended virtues, or, which is the easier way, to recommend himself to their esteem by a flaming zeal for their favourite distinctions, and afterwards by his eloquence to work upon their passions. At the same time it must be acknowledged, on the other hand, that even men of the most improved intellects, and most refined sentiments, are not altogether beyond the reach of preconceived opinion, either in the speaker's favour or to his prejudice.

The second remark is, that when the opinion of the audience is unfavourable, the speaker hath need to be much more cautious in every step he takes, to show more modesty, and greater deference to the judgment of his hearers; perhaps in order to win them, he may find it necessary to make some concessions in relation to his former principles or conduct, and to entreat their attention from pure regard to the subject; that, like men of judgment and candour, they would impartially consider what is said, and give a welcome reception to truth, from what quarter soever it proceed. Thus he must attempt, if possible, to mollify them, gradually to insinuate himself into their favour, and thereby imperceptibly to transfuse his sentiments and passions into their minds.

The man who enjoys the advantage of popularity needs not this caution. The minds of his auditors are perfectly attuned to his. They are prepared for adopting implicitly his opinions, and accompanying him in all his most passionate excursions. When the people are willing to run with you, you may run as fast as you can, especially when the case requires impetuosity and despatch. But if you find in them no such ardour, if it is not even without reluctance that they are induced to walk with you, you must slacken your pace and keep them company, lest they either stand still or turn back. Different rules are given by rhetoricians as adapted to different circumstances. Differences in this respect are numberless. It is enough here to have observed those principles in the mind on which the rules are founded.

CHAPTER X

The different kinds of public speaking in use among the moderns compared, with a view to their different advantages in respect of eloquence

The principal sorts of discourses which here demand our notice, and on which I intend to make some observations, are the three following: orations delivered at the bar, those pronounced in the senate, and those spoken from the pulpit. I do not make a separate article of the speeches delivered by judges to their colleagues on the bench; because, though there be something peculiar here, arising from the difference in character that subsists between the judge and the pleader, in all the other material circumstances, the persons addressed, the subject, the occasion, and the purpose in speaking, there is in these two sorts a perfect coincidence. In like manner, I forbear to mention the theatre, because so entirely dissimilar, both in form and in kind, as hardly to be capable of a place in the comparison. Besides, it is only a cursory view of the chief differences, and not a critical examination of them all, that is here proposed; my design being solely to assist the mind both in apprehending rightly, and in applying properly, the principles above laid down. In this respect, the present discussion will serve to exemplify and illustrate those principles. Under these five particulars, therefore, the speaker, the hearers or persons addressed, the subject, the occasion, and the end in view, or the effect intended to be produced by the discourse, I shall arrange, for order's sake, the remarks I intend to lay before the reader.

SECTION I—IN REGARD TO THE SPEAKER

The first consideration is that of the character to be sustained by the speaker. It was remarked in general, in the preceding chapter, that for promoting the success of the orator, (whatever be the kind of public speaking in which he is concerned,) it is a matter of some consequence that, in the opinion of those whom he addresseth, he is both a wise and a good man. But though this in some measure holds universally, nothing is more certain than that the degree of consequence which lies in their opinion, is exceedingly different in the different kinds. In each it depends chiefly on two circumstances, the nature of his profession as a public speaker, and the character of those to whom his discourses are addressed.

As to the first, arising from the nature of the profession, it will not admit a question, that the preacher hath in this respect the most difficult task; inasmuch as he hath a character to support, which is much more easily injured than that either of the senator, or the speaker at the bar. No doubt the reputation of capacity, experience in affairs, and as much integrity as is thought attainable by those called men of the world, will add weight to the words of the senator; that of skill in his profession, and fidelity in his representation, will serve to recommend what is spoken by the lawyer at the bar; but if these characters in general remain unimpeached, the public will be sufficiently indulgent to both in every other respect. On the contrary, there is little or no indulgence, in regard to his own failings, to be expected by the man who is professedly a sort of authorized censor, who hath it in charge to mark and reprehend the faults of others. And even in the execution of this so ticklish a part of his office, the least excess on either hand exposeth him to censure and dislike. Too much lenity is enough to stigmatize him as lukewarm in the cause of virtue, and too much severity as a stranger to the spirit of the gospel.

But let us consider more directly what is implied in the character, that we may better judge of the effect it will have on the expectations and demands of the people, and consequently on his public teaching. First, then, it is a character of some authority, as it is of one educated for a purpose so important as that of a teacher of religion. This authority, however, from the nature of the function, must be tempered with moderation, candour, and benevolence. The preacher of the gospel, as the very terms import, is the minister of grace, the herald of divine mercy to ignorant, sinful, and erring men. The magistrate, on the contrary, (under which term may be included secular judges and counsellors of every denomination,) is the minister of divine justice and of wrath. *He beareth not the sword in vain.*[1] He is on the part of heaven the avenger of the society with whose protection he is intrusted, against all who invade its rights. The first operates chiefly on our love, the second on our fear. *Minister of religion,* like angel of God, is a name that ought to convey the idea of something endearing and attractive; whereas the title *minister of justice* invariably suggests the notion of something awful and unrelenting. In the former, even his indignation against sin ought to be surmounted by his pity of the condition, and concern for the recovery, of the sinner. Though firm in declaring the will of God, though steady in maintaining the cause of truth, yet mild in his addresses to the

[1] Romans xiii. 4.

people, condescending to the weak, using rather entreaty than command, beseeching them by the lowliness and gentleness of Christ, knowing that "the servant of the Lord must not strive, but be gentle to all men, apt to teach, patient, in meekness instructing those that oppose themselves." [2] He must be grave without moroseness, cheerful without levity. And even in setting before his people the terrors of the Lord, affection ought manifestly to predominate in the warning which he is compelled to give. From these few hints it plainly appears, that there is a certain delicacy in the character of a preacher, which he is never at liberty totally to overlook, and to which, if there appear any thing incongruous, either in his conduct or in his public performances, it will never fail to injure their effect. On the contrary, it is well known, that as, in the other professions, the speaker's private life is but very little minded, so there are many things which, though they would be accounted nowise unsuitable from the bar or in the senate, would be deemed altogether unbefitting the pulpit.

It ought not to be overlooked, on the other hand, that there is one pecularity in the lawyer's professional character, which is unfavourable to conviction, and consequently gives him some disadvantage both of the senator and the preacher. We know that he must defend his client, and argue on the side on which he is retained. We know also that a trifling and accidental circumstance, which nowise affects the merit of the cause, such as a prior application from the adverse party, would probably have made him employ the same acuteness, and display the same fervour, on the opposite side of the question. This circumstance, though not considered as a fault in the character of the man, but a natural, because an ordinary, consequent of the office, cannot fail, when reflected on, to make us shyer of yielding our assent. It removes entirely what was observed in the preceding chapter to be of great moment, our belief of the speaker's sincerity. This belief can hardly be rendered compatible with the knowledge that both truth and right are so commonly and avowedly sacrificed to interest. I acknowledge that an uncommon share of eloquence will carry off the minds of most people from attending to this circumstance, or at least from paying any regard to it. Yet Antony is represented by Cicero, as thinking the advocate's reputation so delicate, that the practice of amusing himself in philosophical disputations with his friends is sufficient to hurt it, and consequently to affect the credibility of his pleadings. Surely the barefaced prostitution of his talents, (and in spite of his commonness, what else can we call it?) in supporting indifferently, as pecuniary considerations determine him, truth or falsehood, justice or injustice, must have a still worse effect on the opinion of his hearers.

It was affirmed that the consequence of the speaker's own character, in furthering or hindering his success, depends in some measure on the character of those whom he addresseth. Here indeed it will be found, on inquiry, that the preacher labours under a manifest disadvantage. Most congregations are of that kind, as will appear from the article immediately succeeding, which, agreeably to an observation made in the former chapter, very much considers who speaks; those addressed from the bar, or in the senate, consider more what is spoken.

SECTION II—IN REGARD TO THE PERSONS ADDRESSED

The second particular mentioned as a ground of comparison, is the consideration of the character of the hearers, or more properly the persons addressed. The necessity which a speaker is under of suiting himself to his audience, both that he may be understood by them, and that his words may have influence upon them, is a maxim so evident as to need neither proof nor illustration.

Now, the first remark that claims our attention here is, that the more mixed the auditory is, the greater is the difficulty of speaking to them with effect. The reason is obvious—what will tend to favour your success with one, may tend to obstruct it with another. The more various therefore the individuals are, in respect of age, rank, fortune, education, prejudices, the more delicate must be the art of preserving propriety in an address to the whole. The pleader has, in this respect, the simplest and the easiest task of all; the judges, to whom his oration is addressed, being commonly men of the same rank, of similar education, and not differing greatly in respect of studies or attainments. The difference in these respects is much more considerable when he addresses the jury. A speaker in the house of peers hath not so mixed an auditory as one who harangues in the house of commons. And even here, as all the members may be supposed to have been educated as gentlemen, the audience is not nearly so promiscuous as were the popular assemblies of Athens and of Rome, to which their demagogues declaimed with so much vehemence, and so wonderful success. Yet, even of these, women, minors, and servants made no part.

We may therefore justly reckon a Christian congregation in a populous and flourishing city, where there is a great variety in rank and education, to be of all audiences the most promiscuous. And though it is impossible that, in so mixed a multitude, every thing that is advanced by the speaker should, both in sentiment and in expression, be adapted to the apprehension of every individual hearer, and fall in with his particular prepossessions, yet it may be expected, that whatever is advanced shall be within the reach of every class of hearers, and shall not unnecessarily shock the innocent prejudices of any. This is still, however, to be understood with the exception of mere children, fools, and a few others who, through the total neglect of parents or guardians in their education, are grossly ignorant. Such, though in the audience, are not to be considered as constituting a part of it. But how great is the attention requisite in the speaker in such an assembly, that, whilst on the one hand he avoids, either in style or in sentiment, soaring above the capacity of the lower class, he may not, on the other, sink below the regard of the higher. To attain simplicity without flatness, delicacy without refinement, perspicuity without recurring to low idioms and similitudes, will require his utmost care.

Another remark on this article that deserves our notice is, that the less improved in knowledge and discernment the hearers are, the easier it is for the speaker to work upon their passions, and by working on their passions, to obtain his end. This, it must be owned, appears, on the other hand, to give a considerable advantage to the preacher, as in no congregation can the bulk of the people be regarded as on a footing, in point of improvement, with either house of parliament, or with the judges in a court of judicature. It is certain, that the more gross the hearers are, the more avowedly may you address yourself to their passions, and the less occasion there is for argument; whereas, the more intelligent they are, the more covertly must you operate on their passions, and the more attentive must you be in regard to the justness, or at least the speciousness of your reasoning. Hence some have strangely concluded, that the only scope for eloquence is in haranguing the multitude; that in gaining over to your purpose men of knowledge and breeding, the exertion of oratorical talents hath no influence. This is precisely as if one should argue, because a mob is much easier subdued than regular troops, there is no occasion for the art of war, nor is there a proper field for the exertion of military skill, unless when you are quelling an undisciplined rabble. Every body sees in this case, not only how absurd such a way of arguing would be, but that the very reverse ought to be the conclusion. The reason why people do not so quickly perceive the absurdity in the other case is, that they affix no distinct meaning to the word *eloquence*, often denoting no more by that term than simply the power of moving the passions. But even in this improper acceptation, their notion is far from being just; for wherever there are men, learned or ignorant, civilized or barbarous, there are passions; and the greater the difficulty is in affecting these, the more art is requisite. The truth is, eloquence, like every other art, proposeth the accomplishment of a certain end. Passion is for the most part but the means employed for effecting the end, and therefore, like all other means, will no further be regarded in any case, than it can be rendered conducible to the end.

Now the preacher's advantage even here, in point of facility, at least in several situations, will not appear, on reflection, to be so great as on a superficial view it may be thought. Let it be observed, that in such congregations as were supposed, there is a mixture of superior and inferior ranks. It is therefore the business of the speaker, so far only to accommodate himself to one class, as not wantonly to disgust another. Besides, it will scarcely be denied that those in the superior walks of life, however much by reading and conversation improved in all genteel accomplishments, often have as much need of religious instruction and moral improvement, as those who in every other particular are acknowledged to be their inferiors. And doubtless the reformation of such will be allowed to be, in one respect, of greater importance, (and therefore never to be overlooked,) that in consequence of such an event, more good may redound to others, from the more extensive influence of their authority and example.

SECTION III—IN REGARD TO THE SUBJECT

The third particular mentioned was the subject of discourse. This may be considered in a twofold view; first, as implying the topics of argument, motives, and principles, which are suited to each of the different kinds, and must be employed in order to produce the intended effect on the hearers; secondly, as implying the person or things in whose favour, or to whose prejudice, the speaker purposes to excite the passions of the audience, and thereby to influence their determinations.

On the first of these articles, I acknowledge the preacher hath incomparably the advantage of every other public orator. At the bar, critical explications of dark and ambiguous statutes, quotations of precedents sometimes contradictory, and comments on jarring decisions and reports, often necessarily consume the great part of the speaker's time. Hence the mixture of a sort of metaphysics and verbal criticism, employed by lawyers in their pleadings, hath come to be distinguished by the name *chicane,* a species of reasoning too abstruse to command attention of any continuance even from the studious, and consequently not very favourable to the powers of rhetoric. When the argument doth not turn on the common law, or on nice and hypercritical explications of the statute, but on the great principles of natural right and justice, as sometimes happens, particularly in criminal cases, the speaker is much more advantageously situated for exhibiting his rhetorical talents than in the former case. When, in consequence of the imperfection of the evidence, the question happens to be more question of fact than either of municipal law or of natural equity, the pleader hath more advantages than in the first case, and fewer than in the second.

Again, in the deliberations in the senate, the utility or the disadvantages that will probably follow on a measure proposed, if it should receive the sanction of the legislature, constitute the principal topics of debate. This, though it sometimes leads to a kind of reasoning rather too complex and involved for ordinary apprehension, is in the main more favourable to the display of pathos, vehemence, and sublimity than the much greater part of the forensic causes can be said to be. That these qualities have been sometimes found in a very high degree in the orations pronounced in a British senate, is a fact incontrovertible.

But beyond all question, the preacher's subject of argument, considered in itself, is infinitely more lofty and more affecting. The doctrines of religion are such as relate to God, the adorable Creator and Ruler of the world, his attributes, government, and law. What science to be compared with it in sublimity? It teaches also the origin of man, his primitive dignity, the source of his degeneracy, the means of his recovery, the eternal happiness that awaits the good, and the future misery of the impenitent. Is there any kind of knowledge in which human creatures are so deeply interested? In a word, whether we consider the doctrines of religion or its documents, the examples it holds forth to our imitation, or its motives, promises, and threatenings, we see on every hand a subject that gives scope for the exertion of all the highest powers of rhetoric. What are the sanctions of any human laws, compared with the sanctions of the divine law, with which we are brought acquainted by the gospel? Or where shall we find instructions, similitudes, and examples, that speak so directly to the heart, as the parables and the divine lessons of our blessed Lord?

In regard to the second thing which I took notice of as included under the general term *subject,* namely the persons or things in whose favour, or to whose prejudice the speaker intends to excite the passions of the audience, and thereby to influence their determinations, the other two have commonly the advantage of the preacher. The reason is, that his subject is generally things; theirs, on the contrary, is persons. In what regards the painful passions, indignation, hatred, contempt, abhorrence, this difference invariably obtains. The preacher's business is solely to excite your detestation of the crime; the pleader's business is principally to make you detest the criminal. The former paints vice to you in all its odious colours; the latter paints the vicious. There is a degree of abstraction, and consequently a much greater degree of attention, requisite to enable us to form just conceptions of the ideas and sentiments of the former; whereas, those of the latter, referring to an actual, perhaps a living, present, and well-known subject, are much more level to common capacity, and therefore not only are more easily apprehended by the understanding, but take a stronger hold of the imagination. It would have been impossible even for Cicero to inflame the minds of the people to so high a pitch against *oppression,* considered in the abstract, as he actually did inflame them against Verres the *oppressor;* nor could he have incensed them so much against *treason* and *conspiracy,* as he did incense them against Catiline the *traitor* and *conspirator.* The like may be observed of the effects of his orations against Antony, and in a thousand other instances.

Though the occasions in this way are more frequent at the bar, yet, as the deliberations in the senate often proceed on the reputation and past conduct of individuals, there is commonly here also a much better handle for rousing the passions than that enjoyed by the preacher. How much advantage Demosthenes drew from the known character and insidious arts of Philip king of Macedon, for influencing the resolves of the Athenians, and other Grecian states, those who are acquainted with the Philippics of the orator, and the history of that period, will be very sensible. In what concerns the pleasing affections, the preacher may sometimes, not often, avail himself of real human characters, as in funeral sermons, and in discourses on the patterns of virtue given us by our Saviour, and by those saints of whom we have the history in the sacred code. But such examples are comparatively few.

SECTION IV—IN REGARD TO THE OCCASION

The fourth circumstance mentioned as a ground of comparison, is the particular occasion of speaking. And in this I think it evident, that both the pleader and the senator have the advantage of the preacher. When any important cause comes to be tried before a civil judicatory, or when any important question comes to be agitated in either house of parliament, as the point to be discussed hath generally for some time before been a topic of conversation in most companies, perhaps throughout the kingdom, (which of itself is sufficient to give consequence to any thing,) people are apprized beforehand of the particular day fixed for the discussion. Accordingly, they come prepared with some knowledge of the case, a persuasion of its importance, and a curiosity which sharpens their attention, and assists both their understanding and their memory.

Men go to church without any of these advantages. The subject of the sermon is not known to the congregation, till the minister announces it just as he begins, by reading the text. Now, from our experience of human nature, we may be sensible that whatever be the comparative importance of the things themselves, the generality of men cannot here be wrought up, in an instant, to the like anxious curiosity about what is to be said, nor can be so well prepared for hearing it. It may indeed be urged, in regard to those subjects which come regularly to be discussed at stated times, as on public festivals, as well as in regard to assize-sermons, charity-sermons, and other occasional discourses, that these must be admitted as exceptions. Perhaps in some degree they are, but not altogether: for first, the precise point to be argued, or proposition to be evinced, is very rarely known. The most that we can say is, that the subject will have a relation (sometimes remote enough) to such an article of faith, or to the obligations we lie under to the practice of such a duty. But further, if the topic were ever so well known, the frequent recurrence of such occasions, once a year at least, hath long familiarized us to them, and, by destroying their novelty, hath abated exceedingly of that ardour which ariseth in the mind for hearing a discussion, conceived to be of importance, which one never had access to hear before, and probably never will have access to hear again.

I shall here take notice of another circumstance, which, without great stretch, may be classed under this article, and which likewise gives some advantage to the counsellor and the senator. It is the opposition and contradiction which they expect to meet with. Opponents sharpen one another, as iron sharpeneth iron. There is not the same spur either to exertion in the speaker, or to attention in the hearer, where there is no conflict, where you have no adversary to encounter with equal terms. Mr. Bickerstaff would have made but small progress in the science of defence, by pushing at the human figure which he had chalked upon the wall, in comparison of what he might have made by the help of a fellow combatant of flesh and blood. I do not, however, pretend that these cases are entirely parallel. The whole of an adversary's plea may be perfectly known, and may, to the satisfaction of every reasonable person, be perfectly confuted, though he hath not been heard by the counsel at the bar.

SECTION V—IN REGARD TO THE END IN VIEW

The fifth and last particular mentioned, and indeed the most important of them all, is the effect in each species intended to be produced. The primary intention of preaching is the reformation of mankind. "The grace of God, that bringeth salvation, hath appeared to all men, teaching us that, denying ungodliness and worldly lusts, we should live soberly, righteously, and godly in this present world." [3] Reformation of life and manners—of all things that which is the most difficult by any means whatever to effectuate; I may add, of all tasks ever attempted by persuasion, that which has the most frequently baffled its power.

What is the task of any other orator compared with this? It is really as nothing at all, and hardly deserves to be named. An unjust judge, gradually worked on by the resistless force of human eloquence, may be persuaded, against his inclination, perhaps against a previous resolution, to pronounce an equitable sentence. All the effect on him, intended by the pleader, was merely momentary. The orator hath had the address to employ the time allowed him in such a manner as to secure the happy moment. Notwithstanding this, there may be no real change wrought upon the judge. He may continue the same obdurate wretch he was before. Nay, if the sentence had been delayed but a single day after hearing the cause, he would perhaps have given a very different award.

Is it to be wondered at, that when the passions of the people were agitated by the persuasive powers of a Demosthenes, whilst the thunder of his eloquence was yet sounding in their ears, the orator should be absolute master of their resolves? But an apostle or evangelist (for there is no anachronism in a bare supposition) might have thus addressed the celebrated Athenian, "You do, indeed, succeed to admiration, and the address and genius which you display in speaking justly entitle you to our praise. But however great the consequences may be of the measures to which, by your eloquence, they are determined, the change produced in the people is nothing, or next to nothing. If you would be ascertained of the truth of this, allow the assembly to disperse immediately after hearing you; give them time to cool, and then collect their votes, and it is a thousand to one you shall find that the charm is dissolved."

But very different is the purpose of the Christian orator. It is not a momentary, but a permanent effect at which he aims. It is not an immediate and favourable suffrage, but a thorough change of heart and disposition, that will satisfy his view. That man would need to be possessed of oratory superior to human, who would effectually persuade him that stole to steal

3 Tit. ii. 11, 12.

no more, the sensualist to forego his pleasures, and the miser his hoards, the insolent and haughty to become meek and humble, the vindictive forgiving, the cruel and unfeeling merciful and humane.

I may add to these considerations, that the difficulty lies not only in the permanency, but in the very nature of the change to be effected. It is wonderful, but it is too well vouched to admit of a doubt, that by the powers of rhetoric you may produce in mankind almost any change more easily than this. It is not unprecedented that one should persuade a multitude, from mistaken motives of religion, to act the part of ruffians, fools, or madmen; to perpetrate the most extravagant, nay, the most flagitious actions; to steel their hearts against humanity, and the loudest calls of affection: but where is the eloquence that will gain such an ascendant over a multitude, as to persuade them, for the love of God, to be wise, and just, and good? Happy the preacher whose sermons, by the blessing of Heaven, have been instrumental in producing even a few such instances! Do but look into the annals of church history, and you will soon be convinced of the surprising difference there is in the two cases mentioned—the amazing facility of the one, and the almost impossibility of the other.

As to the foolish or mad extravagances, hurtful only to themselves, to which numbers may be excited by the powers of persuasion, the history of the flagellants, and even the history of monachism, afford many unquestionable examples. But what is much worse, at one time you see Europe nearly depopulated at the persuasion of a fanatical monk, its inhabitants rushing armed into Asia, in order to fight for Jesus Christ, as they termed it, but as it proved in fact, to disgrace, as far as lay in them, the name of Christ and of Christian amongst infidels; to butcher those who never injured them, and to whose lands they had at least no better title than those whom they intended, by all possible means, to dispossess; and to give the world a melancholy proof, that there is no pitch of brutality and rapacity to which the passions of avarice and ambition, consecrated and inflamed by religious enthusiasm, will not drive mankind. At another time you see multitudes, by the like methods, worked up into a fury against innocent countrymen, neighbours, friends, and kinsmen, glorying in being most active in cutting the throats of those who were formerly held dear to them.

Such were the crusades preached up but too effectually, first against the Mahometans in the East, and next against Christians whom they called heretics, in the heart of Europe. And even in our own time, have we not seen new factions raised by popular declaimers, whose only merit was impudence, whose only engine of influence was calumny and self-praise, whose only moral lesson was malevolence? As to the dogmas whereby such have at any time affected to discriminate themselves, these are commonly no other than the *shibboleth*, the watchword of the party, worn, for distinction's sake, as a badge, a jargon unintelligible alike to the teacher and to the learner. Such apostles never fail to make proselytes. For who would not purchase heaven at so cheap rate? There is nothing that people can more easily afford. It is only to think very well of their leader and of themselves, to think very ill of their neighbour, to calumniate him freely, and to hate him heartily.

I am sensible that some will imagine that this account itself throws an insuperable obstacle in our way, as from it one will naturally infer, that oratory must be one of the most dangerous things in the world, and much more capable of doing ill than good. It needs but some reflection to make this mighty obstacle entirely vanish.—Very little eloquence is necessary for persuading people to a conduct to which their own depravity hath previously given them a bias. How soothing is it to them not only to have their minds made easy under the indulged malignity of their disposition, but to have that very malignity sanctified with a good name! So little of the oratorical talent is required here, that those who court popular applause, and look upon it as the pinnacle of human glory to be blindly followed by the multitude, commonly recur to defamation, especially of superiors and brethren, not so much for a subject on which they may display their eloquence, as for a succedaneum to supply their want of eloquence, a succedaneum which never yet was found to fail. I knew a preacher who, from this expedient alone, from being long the aversion of the populace, on account of his dulness, awkwardness, and coldness, all of a sudden became their idol. Little force is necessary to push down heavy bodies placed on the verge of a declivity, but much force is requisite to stop them in their progress, and push them up.

If a man should say, that because the first is more frequently effected than the last, it is the best trial of strength, and the only suitable use to which it can be applied, we should at least not think him remarkable for distinctness in his ideas. Popularity alone, therefore, is no test at all of the eloquence of the speaker, no more than velocity alone would be of the force of the external impulse originally given to the body moving. As in this the direction of the body, and other circumstances, must be taken into the account; so in that, you must consider the tendency of the teaching, whether it favours or opposes the vices of the hearers. To head a sect, to infuse party-spirit, to make men arrogant, uncharitable, and malevolent, is the easiest task imaginable, and to which almost any blockhead is fully equal. But to produce the contrary effect, to subdue the spirit of faction, and that monster spiritual pride, with which it is invariably accompanied, to inspire equity, moderation, and charity into men's sentiments and conduct with regard to others, is the genuine test of eloquence. Here its triumph is truly glorious, and in its application to this end lies its great utility:

> The gates of hell are open night and day;
> Smooth the descent, and easy is the way:
> But to return and view the cheerful skies,
> In this the task and mighty labour lies.
>
> (Virgil, *Aeneid,* Bk. VI, trans. DRYDEN)

Now in regard to the comparison, from which I fear I shall be thought to have digressed, between the forensic and senatorian eloquence, and that of the pulpit, I must not omit to observe, that in what I say of the difference of the effect to be produced by the last mentioned species, I am to be understood as speaking of the effect intended by preaching in general, and even of that which, in whole or in part, is, or ought to be, either more immediately or more remotely, the scope of all discourses proceeding from the pulpit. I am, at the same time, sensible that in some of these, beside the ultimate view, there is an immediate and outward effect which the sermon is intended to produce. This is the case particularly in charity-sermons, and perhaps some other occasional discourses. Now of these few, in respect of such immediate purpose, we must admit, that they bear a pretty close analogy to the pleadings of the advocate, and the orations of the senator.

Upon the whole of the comparison I have stated, it appears manifest that, in most of the particulars above enumerated, the preacher labours under a very great disadvantage. He hath himself a more delicate part to perform than either the pleader or the senator, and a character to maintain which is much more easily injured. The auditors, though rarely so accomplished as to require the same accuracy of composition, or acuteness of reasoning, as may be expected in the other two, are more various in age, rank, taste, inclinations, sentiments, prejudices, to which he must accommodate himself. And if he derives some advantages from the richness, the variety, and the nobleness of the principles, motives, and arguments with which his subject furnishes him, he derives also some inconveniences from this circumstance, that almost the only engine by which he can operate on the passions of his hearers, is the exhibition of abstract qualities, virtues, and vices, whereas that chiefly employed by other orators is the exhibition of real persons, the virtuous and the vicious. Nor are the occasions of his addresses to the people equally fitted with those of the senator and of the pleader for exciting their curiosity and riveting their attention. And, finally, the task assigned him, the effect which he ought ever to have in view, is so great, so important, so durable, as seems to bid defiance to the strongest efforts of oratorical genius.

Nothing is more common than for people, I suppose without reflecting, to express their wonder that there is so little eloquence amongst our preachers, and that so little success attends their preaching. As to the last, their success, it is a matter not to be ascertained with so much precision as some appear fondly to imagine. The evil prevented, as well as the good promoted, ought here, in all justice, to come into the reckoning. And what that may be, it is impossible in any supposed circumstances to determine. As to the first, their eloquence, I acknowledge that for my own part, considering how rare the talent is among men in general, considering all the disadvantages preachers labour under, not only those above enumerated, but others, arising from their different situations, particularly considering the frequency of this exercise, together with the other duties of their office, to which the fixed pastors are obliged, I have been for a long time more disposed to wonder, that we hear so many instructive and even eloquent sermons, than that we hear so few.

CHAPTER XI

Of the cause of that pleasure which we receive from objects or representations that excite pity and other painful feelings

It hath been observed already (Chap. IV), that without some gratification in hearing, the attention must inevitably flag. And it is manifest from experience that nothing tends more effectually to prevent this consequence, and keep our attention alive and vigorous, than the pathetic, which consists chiefly in exhibitions of human misery. Yet that such exhibitions should so highly gratify us, appears somewhat mysterious. Every body is sensible, that of all qualities in a work of genius, this is that which endears it most to the generality of readers. One would imagine, on the first mention of this, that it were impossible to account for it otherwise than from an innate principle of malice, which teacheth us to extract delight to ourselves from the sufferings of others, and as it were to enjoy their calamities. A very little reflection, however, would suffice for correcting this error; nay, without any reflection, we may truly say, that the common sense of mankind prevents them effectually from falling into it. Bad as we are, and prone as we are to be hurried into the worst of passions by self-love, partiality, and pride, malice is a disposition which, either in the abstract, or as it discovers itself in the actions of an indifferent person, we can never contemplate without feeling a just detestation and abhorrence, being ready to pronounce it the ugliest of objects. Yet this sentiment is not more universal than is the approbation and even love that we bestow on the tender-hearted, or those who are most exquisitely susceptible of all the influence of the pathetic. Nor are there any two dispositions of which human nature is capable, that have ever been considered as further removed from each other, than the malicious and the compassionate are. The fact itself, that the mind derives pleasure from representations of anguish, is undeniable: the question about the cause is curious, and hath a manifest relation to my subject.

I purposed, indeed, at first, to discuss this point in that part of the sixth chapter which relates to the means of operating on the passions, with which the present inquiry is intimately connected. Finding afterwards that the discussion would prove rather too long an interruption, and that the other points which came naturally to be treated in that place could be explained with sufficient clearness independently of this, I judged it better to reserve this question for a separate chapter. Various hypotheses have been devised by the ingenious, in order to solve the difficulty. These I shall first briefly examine, and then lay before the reader what appears to me to be the true solution. Of all that have entered into the subject, those who seem most to merit our regard are two French critics and one of our own country.

SECTION I—THE DIFFERENT SOLUTIONS HITHERTO GIVEN BY PHILOSOPHERS EXAMINED

Part I—The First Hypothesis

Abbé du Bos begins his excellent reflections on poetry and painting, with that very question which is the subject of this chapter, and in answer to it supports at some length [1] a theory, the substance of which I shall endeavour to comprise in a few words. Few things, according to him, are more disagreeable to the mind, than that listlessness into which it falls, when it has nothing to occupy it, or to awake the passions. In order to get rid of this most painful situation, it seeks with avidity every amusement and pursuit; business, gaming, news, shows, public executions, romances; in short, whatever will rouse the passions, and take off the mind's attention from itself. It matters not what the emotion be, only the stronger it is, so much the better. And for this reason, those passions which, considered in themselves, are the most afflicting and disagreeable, are preferable to the pleasant, inasmuch as they most effectually relieve the soul from that oppressive languor which preys upon it in a state of inactivity. They afford it ample occupation, and, by giving play to its latent movements and springs of action, convey a pleasure which more than counterbalances the pain.

I admit, with Mr. Hume,[2] that there is some weight in these observations, which may sufficiently account for the pleasure taken in gaming, hunting, and several other diversions and sports. But they are not quite satisfactory, as they do not assign a sufficient reason why poets, painters, and orators, exercise themselves more in actuating the painful passions, than in exciting the pleasant. These, one would think, ought in every respect to have the advantage, because, at the same time that they preserve the mind from a state of inaction, they convey a feeling that is allowed to be agreeable. And though it were granted, that passions of the former kind are stronger than those of the latter (which doth not hold invariably, there being perhaps more examples of persons who have been killed with joy, than those who have died of grief), strength alone will not account for the preference. It by no means holds here, that the stronger the emotion is, so much the fitter for this purpose. On the contrary, if you exceed but ever so little a certain measure, instead of that sympathetic delightful sorrow, which makes affliction itself wear a lovely aspect, and engages the mind to hug it, not only with tenderness, but with transport, you only excite horror and aversion. "It is certain," says the author last quoted, very justly, "that the same object of distress which pleases in a tragedy, were it really set before us, would give the most unfeigned uneasiness, though it be then the most effectual cure of languor and indolence." And it is more than barely possible, even in the representa-

1 *Reflexions critiques sur la Poesie et sur la Peinture,* Sect. i, ii, iii,
2 "Essay on Tragedy."

tions of the tragedian, or in the descriptions of the orator or the poet, to exceed that measure. I acknowledge, indeed, that this measure or degree is not the same to every temper. Some are much sooner shocked with mournful representations than others. Our mental, like our bodily appetites and capacities, are exceedingly various. It is, however, the business of both the speaker and the writer, to accommodate himself to what may be styled the common standard; for there is a common standard, in what regards the faculties of the mind, as well as in what concerns the powers of the body. Now, if there be any quality in the afflictive passions, besides their strength, that renders them peculiarly adapted to rescue the mind from that torpid but corrosive rest which is considered as the greatest of evils, that quality ought to have been pointed out: for till then the phenomenon under examination is not accounted for. The most that can be concluded from the Abbé's premises is the utility of exciting passion of some kind or other, but nothing that can evince the superior fitness of the distressful affections.

Part II—The Second Hypothesis

The next hypothesis is Fontenelle's.[3] Not having the original at hand at present, I shall give Mr. Hume's translation of the passage, in his Essay on Tragedy above quoted. "Pleasure and pain, which are two sentiments so different in themselves, differ not so much in their cause. From the instance of tickling it appears that the movement of pleasure, pushed a little too far, becomes pain; and that the movement of pain, a little moderated, becomes pleasure. Hence it proceeds, that there is such a thing as a sorrow soft and agreeable. It is a pain weakened and diminished. The heart likes naturally to be moved and affected. Melancholy objects suit it, and even disastrous and sorrowful, provided they are softened by some circumstance. It is certain that, on the theatre, the representation has almost the effect of reality; but yet it has not altogether that effect. However we may be hurried away by the spectacle, whatever dominion the senses and imagination may usurp over the reason, there still lurks at the bottom a certain idea of falsehood in the whole of what we see. This idea, though weak and disguised, suffices to diminish the pain which we suffer from the misfortunes of those whom we love, and to reduce that affliction to such a pitch as converts it into a pleasure. We weep for the misfortunes of a hero to whom we are attached. In the same instant we comfort ourselves by reflecting that it is nothing but a fiction: and it is precisely that mixture of sentiments which composes an agreeable sorrow, and tears that delight us. But as that affliction which is caused by exterior and sensible objects is stronger than the consolation which arises from an internal reflection, they are the effects and symptoms of sorrow which ought to prevail in the composition."

I cannot affirm that this solution appears to me so just and convincing as

---

3 *Reflexions sur la Poetique*, Sect. xxxvi.

it seems it did to Mr. Hume. If this English version, like a faithful mirror, reflect the true image of the French original, I think the author in some degree chargeable with what in that language is emphatically enough styled *verbiage,* a manner of writing very common with those of his nation, and with their imitators in ours. The only truth that I can discover in his hypothesis, lies in one small circumstance, which is so far from being applicable to the whole case under consideration, that it can properly be applied but to a very few particular instances, and is therefore no solution at all. That there are at least many cases to which it cannot be applied, the author last mentioned declares himself to be perfectly sensible.

But let us examine the passage more narrowly. He begins with laying it down as a general principle, that however different the feelings of pleasure and of pain are in themselves, they differ not much in their cause; that the movement of pleasure pushed a little too far becomes pain; and that the movement of pain a little moderated becomes pleasure. For an illustration of this he gives an example in tickling. I will admit that there are several other similar instances, in which the observation to appearance holds. The warmth received from sitting near the fire, by one who hath been almost chilled with cold, is very pleasing; yet you may increase this warmth, first to a disagreeable heat, and then to burning, which is one of the greatest torments. It is nevertheless extremely hazardous, on a few instances, and those not perfectly parallel to the case in hand, to found a general theory. Let us make the experiment, how the application of this doctrine to the passions of the mind will answer. And for our greater security against mistake, let us begin with the simplest cases in the direct, and not in the reflex or sympathetic passions, in which hardly ever any feeling or affection comes alone. A merchant loseth all his fortune by a shipwreck, and is reduced at one stroke from opulence to indigence. His grief, we may suppose, will be very violent. If he had lost half his stock only, it is natural to think he would have borne the loss more easily, though still he would have been affected; perhaps the loss of fifty pounds he would have scarcely felt: but I should be glad to know how much the movement or passion must be moderated; or, in other words, as the difference ariseth solely from the different degrees of the cause, how small the loss must be when the sentiment of feeling of it begins to be converted into a real pleasure: for to me it doth not appear natural that any the most trifling loss, were it of a single shilling, should be the subject of positive delight.

But to try another instance, a gross and public insult commonly provokes a very high degree of resentment, and gives a most pungent vexation to a person of sensibility. I would gladly know whether a smaller affront, or some slight instance of neglect or contempt, gives such a person any pleasure. Try the experiment also on friendship and hatred, and you will find the same success. As the warmest friendship is highly agreeable to the mind, the slightest liking is also agreeable, though in a less degree. Perfect hatred is a kind of torture to the breast that harbours it, which will not be found capable of being mitigated into pleasure; for there is no degree of ill-will without pain. The gradation in the cause and in the effect are entirely correspondent.

Nor can any just conclusion be drawn from the affections of the body, as in these the consequence is often solely imputable to a certain proportion of strength, in the cause that operates, to the present disposition of the organs. But though I cannot find that in any uncompounded passion the most remote degrees are productive of such contrary effects, I do not deny that when different passions are blended, some of them pleasing and some painful, the pleasure or the pain of those which predominate may, through the wonderful mechanism[4] of our mental frame, be considerably augmented by the mixture.

The only truth which, as I hinted already, I can discover in the preceding hypothesis, is, that the mind in certain cases avails itself of the notion of falsehood, in order to prevent the representation or narrative from producing too strong an effect upon the imagination, and consequently to relieve itself from such an excess of passion as could not otherwise fail to be painful. But let it be observed, that this notion is not a necessary concomitant of the pleasure that results from pity and other such affections, but is merely accidental. It was remarked above, that if the pathetic exceeds a certain measure, from being very pleasant it becomes very painful. Then the mind recurs to every expedient, and to disbelief amongst others, by which it may be enabled to disburden itself of what distresseth it. And, indeed, whenever this recourse is had by any, it is a sure indication that, with regard to such, the poet, orator, or historian hath exceeded the proper measure.

But that this only holds when we are too deeply interested by the sympathetic sorrow, will appear from the following considerations: first, from the great pains often taken by writers (whose design is certainly not to shock, but to please their readers) to make the most moving stories they relate be firmly believed; secondly, from the tendency, nay fondness, of the generality of mankind to believe what moves them, and their averseness to be convinced that it is a fiction. This can result only from the consciousness that, in ordinary cases, disbelief, by weakening their pity, would diminish, instead of increasing, their pleasure. They must be very far then from entertaining Fontenelle's notion, that it is necessary to the producing of that pleasure; for we cannot well suspect them of a plot against their own enjoyment. Thirdly, and lastly, from the delight which we take in reading or hearing the most tragical narrations of orators and historians, of the reality of which we entertain no doubt; I might add, in revolving in our own minds, and in relating to others, disastrous incidents which have fallen

---

4 The word *mechanism*, applied to the mind, ought not reasonably to give offence to any. I only use the term metaphorically, for those effects in the operation of the mental faculties produced in consequence of such fixed laws as are independent of the will. It hath here therefore no reference to the doctrine of the materialist, a system which, in my opinion, is not only untenable, but absurd.

within the compass of our own knowledge, and as to which, consequently, we have an absolute assurance of the fact.

Part III—The Third Hypothesis

The third hypothesis which I shall produce on this subject, is Mr. Hume's. Only it ought to be remarked previously, that he doth not propose it as a full solution of the question, but rather as a supplement to the former two, in the doctrine of both which he, in a great measure, acquiesces. Take his theory in his own words. He begins with putting the question, "What is it, then, which, in this case," that is, when the sorrow is not softened by fiction, "raises a pleasure from the bosom of uneasiness, so to speak; and a pleasure which still retains all the features and outward symptoms of distress and sorrow?" I answer: "This extraordinary effect proceeds from that very eloquence with which the melancholy scene is represented. The genius required to paint objects in a lively manner, the art employed in collecting all the pathetic circumstances, the judgment displayed in disposing them; the exercise, I say, of these noble talents, together with the force of expression, and beauty of oratorical numbers, diffuse the highest satisfaction on the audience, and excite the most delightful movements. By this means, the uneasiness of the melancholy passions is not only overpowered and effaced by something stronger of an opposite kind, but the whole movement of those passions is converted into pleasure, and swells the delight which the eloquence raises in us. The same force of oratory, employed on an uninteresting subject, would not please half so much, or rather would appear altogether ridiculous; and the mind, being left in absolute calmness and indifference, would relish none of those beauties of imagination or expression which, if joined to passion, give it such exquisite entertainment. The impulse or vehemence arising from sorrow, compassion, indignation, receives a new direction from the sentiments of beauty. The latter, being the predominant emotion, seize the whole mind, and convert the former into themselves, or at least tincture them so strongly, as totally to alter their nature: and the soul being, at the same time, roused by passion and charmed by eloquence, feels on the whole a strong movement which is altogether delightful."

I am sorry to say, but truth compels me to acknowledge, that I have reaped no more satisfaction from this account of the matter, than from those which preceded it. I could have wished, indeed, that the author had been a little more explicit in his manner of expressing himself; for I am not certain that I perfectly comprehend his meaning. At one time he seems only to intend to say, that it is the purpose of eloquence, to the promoting of which its tropes and figures are wonderfully adapted, to infuse into the mind of the hearer such compassion, sorrow, indignation, and other passions, as are, notwithstanding their original character, when abstractly considered, accompanied with pleasure. At another time it appears rather his design to signify, though he doth not plainly speak it out, that the discovery made by the hearer, of the admirable art and ingenuity of the speaker, and of the elegance and harmony of what is spoken, gives that peculiar pleasure to the mind which makes even the painful passions become delightful.

If the first of these be all that he intended to affirm, he hath told us indeed a certain truth, but nothing new or uncommon; nay more, he hath told us nothing that can serve in the smallest degree for a solution of the difficulty. Who ever doubted, that it is the design and work of eloquence to move the passions, and to please? The question which this naturally gives rise to is, How doth eloquence produce this effect? This, I believe, it will be acknowledged to do principally, if not solely, agreeably to the doctrine explained above (Chap. VI), by communicating lively, distinct, and strong ideas of the distress which it exhibits. By a judicious yet natural arrangement of the most affecting circumstances, by a proper selection of the most suitable tropes and figures, it enlivens the ideas raised in the imagination to such a pitch as makes them strongly resemble the perceptions of the senses, or the transcripts of the memory. The question, then, with which we are immediately concerned, doth obviously recur, and seems, if possible, more mysterious than before: for how can the aggravating of all the circumstances of misery in the representation, make it be contemplated with pleasure? One would naturally imagine that this must be the most effectual method for making it give still greater pain. How can the heightening of grief, fear, anxiety, and other uneasy sensations, render them agreeable?

Besides, this ingenious author has not adverted, that his hypothesis, instead of being supplementary to Fontenelle's, as he appears to have intended, is subversive of the principles on which the French critic's theory is founded. The effect, according to the latter, results from moderating, weakening, softening, and diminishing the passion: according to the former, it results from what is directly opposite, from the arts employed by the orator for the purpose of exaggerating, strengthening, heightening, and inflaming the passion. Indeed, neither of these writers seems to have attended sufficiently to one particular, which of itself might have shown the insufficiency of their systems. The particular alluded to is, that pity, if it exceed not a certain degree, gives pleasure to the mind, when excited by the original objects in distress, as well as by the representations made by poets, painters, and orators: and, on the contrary, if it exceed a certain degree, it is on the whole painful, whether awakened by the real objects of pity, or roused by the exhibitions of the historian or of the poet. Indeed, as sense operates much more strongly on the mind than imagination does, the excess is much more frequent in the former case than in the latter.

Now, in attempting to give a solution of the difficulty, it is plain, that all our theorists ought regularly and properly to begin with the former case. If in that, which is the original and the simplest, the matter is sufficiently accounted for, it is accounted for in every case, it being the manifest design both of painting and of oratory, as nearly as possible, to produce the same affections which the very objects represented would have produced in our minds: whereas, though Mr. Hume should be admitted to have accounted fully for the impression made by the poet and the orator, we are as far as ever from the discovery of the cause why pity excited by the objects themselves, when it hath no eloquence to recommend it, is on the whole, if not excessive, a pleasant emotion.

But if this celebrated writer intended to assert that the discovery of the oratory, that is, of the address and talents of the speaker, is what gives the hearer a pleasure, which, mingling itself with pity, fear, indignation, converts the whole, as he expresseth it, into one strong movement, which is altogether delightful: if this be his. sentiment, he hath indeed advanced something extraordinary, and entirely new. And that this is his opinion, appears, I think, obliquely, from the expressions which he useth. "The genius required, the art employed, the judgment displayed, along with force of expression, and beauty of oratorial numbers, diffuse the highest satisfaction on the audience."—Again, "The impulse or vehemence arising from sorrow, compassion, indignation, receives a new direction from the sentiments of beauty." If this then be a just solution of the difficulty, and the detection of the speaker's talents and address be necessary to render the hearer susceptible of this charming sorrow, this delightful anguish, how grossly have all critics and rhetoricians been deceived hitherto. These, in direct opposition to this curious theory, have laid it down in their rhetorics as a fundamental maxim, that "it is essential to the art to conceal the art;" a maxim, too, which, in their estimation, the orator, in no part of his province, is obliged to such a scrupulous observance of, as in the pathetic. In this the speaker, if he would prove successful, must make his subject totally engross the attention of the hearers; insomuch that he himself, his genius, his art, his judgment, his richness of language, his harmony of numbers, are not minded in the least.

Never does the orator obtain a nobler triumph by his eloquence than when his sentiments and style and order appear so naturally to arise out of the subject, that every hearer is inclined to think, he could not have either thought or spoken otherwise himself; when every thing, in short, is exhibited in such a manner,

> As all might hope to imitate with ease;
> Yet while they strive the same success to gain,
> Should find their labour and their hopes are vain.
>
> (Horace, *The Art of Poetry*, trans. FRANCIS)

As to the harmony of numbers, it ought no further to be the speaker's care, than that he may avoid an offensive dissonance or halting in his periods, which, by hurting the ear, abstracts the attention from the subject, and must by consequence serve to obstruct the effect. Yet, even this, it may be safely averred, will not tend half so much to counteract the end, as an elaborate harmony, or a flowing elocution, which carries along with it the evident marks of address and study.

Our author proceeds all along on the supposition that there are two distinct effects produced by the eloquence on the hearers; one the sentiment of beauty, or (as he explains it more particularly) of the harmony of oratorial numbers, of the exercise of these noble talents, genius, art, and judgment; the other the passion which the speaker purposeth to raise in their minds. He maintains, that when the first predominates, the mixture of the two effects becomes exceedingly pleasant, and the reverse when the second is superior. At least, if this is not what he means to assert and vindicate, I despair of being able to assign a meaning to the following expressions: "The genius required to paint,—the art employed in collecting,—the judgment displayed in disposing—diffuse the highest satisfaction on the audience, and excite the most delightful movements. By this means the uneasiness of the melancholy passions is not only overpowered and effaced by something stronger of an opposite kind, but the whole movement of those passions is converted into pleasure, and swells the delight which the eloquence raises in us." Again, "The impulse or vehemence arising from sorrow—receives a new direction from the sentiments of beauty. The latter being the predominant emotion, seize the whole mind, and convert the former—." Again, "The soul, being at the same time roused with passion and charmed by eloquence, feels on the whole—." And in the paragraph immediately succeeding, "It is thus the fiction of tragedy softens the passion, by an infusion of a new feeling, not merely by weakening or diminishing the sorrow—." Now to me it is manifest, that this notion of two distinguishable, and even opposite effects, as he terms them, produced in the hearer by the eloquence, is perfectly imaginary; that, on the contrary, whatever charm or fascination, if you please to call it so, there is in the pity excited by the orator, it ariseth not from any extrinsic sentiment of beauty blended with it, but intimately from its own nature, from those passions which pity necessarily associates, or, I should rather say, includes.

But do we not often hear people speak of eloquence as moving them greatly, and pleasing them highly at the same time? Nothing more common. But these are never understood by them as two original, separate, and independent effects, but as essentially connected. Push your inquiries but ever so little, and you will find all agree in affirming, that it is by being moved, and by that solely, that they are pleased: in philosophical strictness, therefore, the pleasure is the immediate effect of the passion, and the passion the immediate effect of the eloquence.

But is there then no pleasure in contemplating the beauty of composition, the richness of fancy, the power of numbers, and the energy of expression? There is undoubtedly. But so far is this pleasure from commixing with the pathos, and giving a direction to it, that, on the contrary, they seem to be in a great measure incompatible. Such indeed is the pleasure which the artist or the critic enjoys, who can cooly and deliberately survey the whole; upon whose passions the art of the speaker hath little or no influence, and that purely for this reason, because he discovers that art. The bulk of hearers know no further than to approve the man who affects them, who speaks to their heart, as they very properly and emphatically term it, and to commend the performance by which this is accomplished. But how it is accomplished, they neither give themselves the trouble to consider, nor attempt to explain.[5]

Part IV—The Fourth Hypothesis

Lastly, To mention only one other hypothesis; there are those who maintain that compassion is "an example of unmixed selfishness and malignity," and may be "resolved into that power of imagination by which we apply the misfortunes of others to ourselves;" that we are said "to pity no longer than we fancy ourselves to suffer, and to be pleased only by reflecting that our sufferings are not real; thus indulging a dream of distress, from which we can awake whenever we please, to exult in our security, and enjoy the comparison of the fiction with truth." [6]

This is no other than the antiquated doctrine of the philosopher of Malmesbury, rescued from oblivion, to which it had been fast descending, and republished with improvements. Hobbes indeed thought it a sufficient stretch, in order to render the sympathetic sorrow purely selfish, to define it, "imagination or fiction of future calamity to ourselves, proceeding from the sense of another man's calamity." [7] But in the first quotation we have another kind of fiction; namely, that we are at present the very sufferers ourselves, the identical persons whose cases are exhibited as being so deplorable, and whose calamities we so sincerely lament. There were some things hinted in the beginning of the chapter, in relation to this paradoxical conceit, which I should not have thought it necessary to resume, had it not been adopted by a late author, whose periodical essays seemed to entitle him to the character of an ingenious, moral, and instructive writer.[8] For though he hath declined entering formally into the debate, he hath sufficiently

[5] The inquiry contained in this chapter was written long before I had an opportunity of perusing a very ingenious English commentary and notes on Horace's Epistles to the Pisos and to Augustus, in which Mr. Hume's sentiments on this subject are occasionally criticized. The opinions of that commentator, in regard to Mr. Hume's theory, coincide in every thing material with mine. This author considers the question no further than it relates to the representations of tragedy, and hath, by confining his view to this single point, been led to lay greater stress on Fontenelle's hypothesis than, for the solution of the general phenomenon, it is entitled to. It is very true that our theatrical entertainments commonly exhibit a degree of distress which we could not bear to witness in the objects represented. Consequently the consideration that it is but a picture, and not the original, a fictitious exhibition, and not the reality, which we contemplate, is essential for rendering the whole, I may say, supportable as well as pleasant. But even in this case, when it is necessary to our repose to consider the scenical misery before us as mere illusion, we are generally better pleased to consider the things represented as genuine fact. It requires, indeed, but a further degree of affliction to make us even pleased to think that the copy never had any archetype in nature. But when this is the case we may truly say, that the poet hath exceeded and wrought up pity to a kind of horror.

[6] Adventurer, No. 110.

[7] Human Nature, chap. ix. sect. 10.

[8] Hawkesworth.

shown his sentiments on his article, and hath endeavoured indirectly to support them.

I doubt not that it will appear to many of my readers as equally silly to refute this hypothesis and to defend it. Nothing could betray reasonable men into such extravagances, but the dotage with which one is affected towards every appendage of a favourite system. And this is an appendage of that system which derives all the affections and springs of action in the human mind from self-love. In almost all system-builders of every denomination, there is a vehement desire of simplifying their principles, and reducing all to one. Hence in medicine, the passion for finding a catholicon, or cure of all diseases; and in chemistry, for discovering the true alcahest, or universal dissolvent. Nor have our moralists entirely escaped the contagion. One reduceth all the virtues to *prudence,* and is ready to make it clear as sunshine that there neither is nor can be another source of moral good, but a right conducted self-love: another is equally confident that all the virtues are but different modifications of disinterested *benevolence:* a third will demonstrate to you that *veracity* is the whole duty of man: a fourth, with more ingenuity, and much greater appearance of reason, assures you that the true system of ethics is comprised in one word, *sympathy.*

But to the point in hand: it appears a great objection to the selfish system, that in pity we are affected with a real sorrow for the sufferings of others, or at least that men have universally understood this to be the case, as appears from the very words and phrases expressive of this emotion to be found in all known languages. But to one who has thoroughly imbibed the principles and spirit of a philosophic sect, which hath commonly as violent an appetite for mystery (though under different name, for with the philosopher it is paradox) as any religious sect whatever, how paltry must an objection appear, which hath nothing to support it but the conviction of all mankind, those only excepted whose minds have been perverted by scholastic sophistry!

It is remarkable, that though so many have contended that some fiction of the imagination is absolutely necessary to the production of pity, and though the examples of this emotion are so frequent (I hope, in the theorists themselves no less than in others) as to give ample scope for examination, they are so little agreed what this fiction is. Some contend only, that in witnessing a tragedy one is under a sort of momentary deception, which a very little reflection can correct, and imagines that he is actually witnessing those distresses and miseries which are only represented in borrowed characters, and that the actors are the very persons whom they exhibit. This supposition, I acknowledge, is the most admissible of all. That children and simple people, who are utter strangers to theatrical amusements, are apt at first to be deceived in this manner, is undeniable. That, therefore, through the magical power (if I may call it so) of natural and animated action, a transient illusion somewhat similar may be produced in persons of knowledge and experience, I will not take upon me to controvert. But this hypothesis is not necessarily connected with any particular theory of the passions. The persons for whom we grieve, whether the real objects or only their representatives mistaken for them, are still other persons, and not ourselves. Besides, this was never intended to account but for the degree of emotion in one particular case only.

Others, therefore, who refer every thing to self, will have it, that by a fiction of the mind we instantly conceive some future and similar calamity as coming upon ourselves; and that it is solely this conception, and this dread, which call forth all our sorrow and our tears. Others, not satisfied with this, maintain boldly, that we conceive ourselves to be the persons suffering the miseries related or represented, at the very instant that our pity is raised. When nature is deserted by us, it is no wonder that we should lose our way in the devious tracks of imagination, and not know where to settle.

The first would say, "When I see Garrick in the character of King Lear in the utmost agony of distress, I am so transported with the passions raised in my breast, that I quite forget the tragedian, and imagine that my eyes are fixed on that much injured and most miserable monarch." Says the second, "I am not in the least liable to so gross a blunder; but I cannot help, in consequence of the representation, being struck with the impression that I am soon to be in the same situation, and to be used with the like ingratitude and barbarity." Says the third, "The case is still worse with me; for I conceive myself, and not the player, to be that wretched man at the very time that he is acted. I fancy that I am actually in the midst of the storm, suffering all his anguish, that my daughters have turned me out of doors, and treated me with such unheard-of cruelty and injustice." It is exceeding lucky that there do not oftener follow terrible consequences from these misconceptions. It will be said, "They are transient, and quickly cured by recollection." But however transient, if they really exist, they must exist for some time. Now, if unhappily a man had two of his daughters sitting near him at the very instant he was under this delusion, and if, by a very natural and consequential fiction, he fancied them to be Goneril and Regan, the effects might be fatal to the ladies, though they were the most dutiful children in the world.

It hath never yet been denied (for it is impossible to say what will be denied) that pity influences a person to contribute to relieve the object when it is in his power. But if there is a mistake in the object, there must of necessity be a mistake in the direction of the relief. For instance, you see a man perishing with hunger, and your compassion is raised; now you will pity no longer, say these acute reasoners, than you fancy yourself to suffer. You yourself properly are the sole object of your own pity, and as you desire to relieve the person only whom you pity, if there be any food within your reach, you will no doubt devour it voraciously, in order to allay the famine which you fancy you are enduring; but you will not give one morsel to the wretch who really needs your aid, but who is by no means the object of your regret, for whom you can feel no compunction, and with whose distress (which is quite a foreign matter to you) it is impossible you should be

affected, especially when under the power of a passion consisting of unmixed selfishness and malignity. For though, if you did not pity him, you
would, on cool reflection, give him some aid, perhaps from principle, perhaps from example, or perhaps from habit, unluckily this accursed pity, this
unmixed malignant selfishness, interposeth, to shut your heart against him,
and to obstruct the pious purpose.

I know no way of eluding this objection but one, which is indeed a very
easy way. It is to introduce another fiction of the imagination, and to say,
that when this emotion is raised, I lose all consciousness of my own existence
and identity, and fancy that the pitiable object before me is my very self;
and that the real I, or what I formerly mistook for myself, is some other
body, a mere spectator of my misery, or perhaps nobody at all. Thus un-
knowingly I may contribute to his relief, when under the strange illusion
which makes me fancy that, instead of giving to another, I am taking to
myself. But if the man be scrupulously honest, he will certainly restore to
me, when I am awake, what I gave him unintentionally in my sleep.

That such fictions may sometimes take place in madness, which almost
totally unhinges our mental faculties, I will not dispute; but that such are
the natural operations of the passions in a sound state, when the intellectual
powers are unimpaired, is what no man would have ever either conceived or
advanced, that had not a darling hypothesis to support. And by such arguments, it is certain that every hypothesis whatever may equally be supported. Suppose I have taken it into my head to write a theory of the mind:
and, in order to give unity and simplicity to my system, as well as to
recommend it by the grace of novelty, I have resolved to deduce all the
actions, all the pursuits, and all the passions of men from self-hatred, as the
common fountain. If to degrade human nature be so great a recommendation as we find it is to many speculators, as well as to all atheists and
fanatics, who happen, on this point, I know not how, to be most cordially
united, the theory now suggested is by no means deficient in that sort of
merit from which one might expect to it the very best reception. Self-love
is certainly no vice, however justly the want of love to our neighbour be
accounted one; but if any thing can be called vicious, self-hatred is undoubtedly so.

Let it not be imagined that nothing specious can be urged in favour of
this hypothesis; what else, it may be pleaded, could induce the miser to deny
himself not only the comforts, but even almost the necessaries of life, to pine
for want in the midst of plenty, to live in unintermitted anxiety and terror?
All the world sees that it is not to procure his own enjoyment, which he
invariably and to the last repudiates. And can any reasonable person be so
simple as to believe that it is for the purpose of leaving a fortune to his heir,
a man whom he despises, for whose deliverance from perdition he would not
part with half-a-crown, and whom of all mankind next to himself he hates
the most? What else could induce the sensualist to squander his all in
dissipation and debauchery; to rush on ruin certain and foreseen? You call
it pleasure. But is he ignorant that his pleasures are more than ten times

counterbalanced by the plagues and even torments which they bring? Does the conviction, or even the experience of this deter him? On the contrary, with what steady perseverance, with what determined resolution doth he proceed in his career, not intimidated by the haggard forms which stare him in the face, poverty and infamy, disease and death? What else could induce the man who is reputed covetous, not of money but of fame, that is of wind, to sacrifice his tranquillity, and almost all the enjoyments of life; to spend his days and nights in fruitless disquietude and endless care? Has a bare name, think you, an empty sound, such inconceivable charms? Can a mere nothing serve as a counterpoise to solid and substantial good? Are we not rather imposed upon by appearances, when we conclude this to be his motive? Can we be senseless enough to imagine that it is the bubble reputation (which, were it any thing, a dead man surely cannot enjoy) that the soldier is so infatuated as to seek even in the cannon's mouth? Are not these, therefore, but the various ways of self-destroying, to which, according to their various tastes, men are prompted, by the same universal principle of self-hatred?

If you should insist on certain phenomena, which appear to be irreconcilable to my hypothesis, I think I am provided with an answer. You urge our readiness to resent an affront or injury, real or imagined, which we receive, and which ought to gratify instead of provoking us, on the supposition that we hate ourselves. But may it not be retorted, that its being a gratification is that which excites our resentment, inasmuch as we are enemies to every kind of self-indulgence? If this answer will not suffice, I have another which is excellent. It lies in the definition of the word revenge. Revenge, I pronounce, may be justly "deemed an example of unmixed self-abhorrence and benignity, and may be resolved into that power of imagination, by which we apply the sufferings that we inflict on others to ourselves; we are said to wreak our vengeance no longer than we fancy ourselves to suffer, and to be satiated by reflecting that the sufferings of others are not really ours; that we have been but indulging a dream of self-punishment, from which, when we awake and discover the fiction, our anger instantly subsides, and we are meek as lambs." Is this extravagant? Compare it, I pray you, with the preceding explication of compassion, to which it is a perfect counterpart. Consider seriously, and you will find that it is not in the smallest degree more manifest, that another and not ourselves is the object of our resentment when we are angry, than it is that another and not ourselves is the object of our compassion when we are moved with pity. Both indeed have a self-evidence in them, which, whilst our minds remain unsophisticated by the dogmatism of system, extorts from us an unlimited assent.

SECTION II—THE AUTHOR'S HYPOTHESIS ON THIS SUBJECT

Where so many have failed of success, it may be thought presumptuous to attempt a decision. But despondency in regard to a question which seems to fall within the reach of our faculties, and is entirely subjected to our observation and experience, must appear to the inquisitive and philosophic mind a still greater fault than even presumption. The latter may occasion the introduction of a false theory, which must necessarily come under the review and correction of succeeding philosophers. And the detection of error proves often instrumental to the discovery of truth. Whereas the former quashes curiosity altogether, and influences one implicitly to abandon an inquiry as utterly undeterminable. I shall therefore now offer a few observations concerning the passions, which, if rightly apprehended and weighed, will, I hope, contribute to the solution of the present question.

My first observation shall be, that almost all the simple passions of which the mind is susceptible may be divided into two classes, the *pleasant* and the *painful*. It is at the same time acknowledged, that the pleasures and the pains created by the different passions, differ considerably from one another, both in kind and degree. Of the former class are love, joy, hope, pride, gratitude; of the latter, hatred, grief, fear, shame, anger. Let it be remarked, that by the name *pride* in the first class, (which I own admits a variety of acceptations,) no more is meant here than the feeling which we have on obtaining the merited approbation of other men, in which sense it stands in direct opposition to *shame* in the second class, or the feeling which we have when conscious of incurring the deserved blame of others. In like manner *gratitude,* or the resentment of favour, is opposed to *anger,* or the resentment of injury. To the second class I might have added *desire* and *aversion,* which give the mind some uneasiness or dissatisfaction with its present state; but these are often the occasion of pleasure, as they are the principal spurs to action, and perhaps more than any other passion relieve the mind from that languor which, according to the just remark of Abbé du Bos, is perfectly oppressive. Besides, as they are perpetually accompanied with some degree of either *hope* or *fear,* generally with both, they are either pleasant or painful as the one or the other preponderates. For these reasons they may be considered as in themselves of an indifferent or intermediate kind.

The second observation is, that there is an attraction or association among the passions, as well as among the ideas of the mind. Rarely any passion comes alone. To investigate the laws of this attraction would be indeed a matter of curious inquiry, but it doth not fall within the limits of the present question. Almost all the other affections attract or excite desire or aversion of some sort or other. The passions which seem to have the least influence on these are joy and grief; and of the two, joy, I believe, will be acknowledged to have less of the attractive power than grief. Joy is the end of desire and the completion of hope; therefore when attained, it not only excludes occasion for the others, but seems, for a while at least, to repel them, as what would give an impertinent interruption to the pleasure resulting from the contemplation of present felicity, with which the mind, under the influence of joy, is engrossed. Grief hath a like tendency. When the mind is overwhelmed by this gloomy passion, it resists the instigations of desire, as what would again, to no purpose, rouse its activity; it disdains hope, it even loathes it as a vain and a delusive dream. The first suggestions of these passions seem but as harbingers to the cutting recollection of former flattering prospects, once too fondly entertained, now utterly extinct, and succeeded by an insupportable and irremediable disappointment, which every recollection serves but to aggravate. Nay, how unaccountable soever it may appear, the mind seems to have a mournful satisfaction in being allowed to indulge its anguish, and to immerse itself wholly in its own afflictions. But this can be affirmed of sorrow only in the extreme. When it begins to subside, or when originally but in a weak degree, it leads the mind to seek relief from desire, and hope, and other passions.—Love naturally associates to it benevolence, which is one species of desire, for here no more is meant by it than a desire of the happiness of the person loved. Hatred as naturally associates malevolence or malice, which is the desire of evil to the person hated.[9]

My third observation is, that pain of every kind generally makes a deeper impression on the imagination than pleasure does, and is longer retained by the memory. It is a common remark of every people and of every age, and consequently hath some foundation in human nature, that benefits are sooner forgotten than injuries, and favours than affronts. Those who are accustomed to attend the theatre will be sensible, that the plots of the best tragedies which they have witnessed are better remembered by them than those of the most celebrated comedies. And indeed every body that reflects may be satisfied that no story takes a firmer hold of the memory than a tale of woe. In civil history, as well as in biography, it is the disastrous, and not the joyous events, which are oftenest recollected and retailed.

The fourth observation is, that from a group of passions (if I may so express myself) associated together, and having the same object, some of which are of the pleasant, others of the painful kind, if the present predominate, there ariseth often a greater and a more durable pleasure to the mind than would result from these, if alone and unmixed. That the case is so, will, I believe, on a careful inquiry, be found to be a matter of experience;

9 The ambiguity and even penury of all languages, in relation to our internal feelings, make it very difficult, in treating of them, to preserve at once perspicuity and accuracy. Benevolence is sometimes used, perhaps with little variation from its most common import, for charity or universal love; and love itself will be thought by some to be properly defined by the desire or wish of the happiness of its object. As to the first, it is enough that I have assigned the precise meaning in which I use the term; and in regard to the second, those who are duly attentive to what passes within their own breasts will be sensible, that by love, in the strictest acceptation, is meant a certain pleasurable emotion excited in the mind by a suitable object, to which the desire of the happiness of the object is generally consequent. The felicity of the object may however be such as to leave no room for any desire or wish of ours in regard to it. This holds particularly in our love to God. Besides, there may be a desire of the happiness of others, arising from very different causes, where there is nothing of that sentiment or feeling which is strictly called *love*. I own, at the same time, that the term *love* is also often used to denote simply benevolence or good-will; as when we are commanded to love all men, known and unknown, good and bad, friendly and injurious. To that tender emotion which qualities supposed amiable alone can excite, the precept surely doth not extend. These things I thought it necessary to observe, in order to prevent mistakes in a case which requires so much precision.

how it happens to be so, I am afraid human sagacity will never be able to investigate.

This observation holds especially when the emotions and affections raised in us are derived from sympathy, and have not directly self for the object. Sympathy is not a passion, but that quality of the soul which renders it susceptible of almost any passion, by communication from the bosom of another. It is by sympathy we *rejoice with them that rejoice, and weep with them that weep*. This faculty, however, doth not act with equal strength in these opposite cases, but is much weaker in the first than in the second. It would perhaps be easier to assign the intention of nature in this difference, than the cause of the difference. The miserable need the aid and sympathy of others; the happy do not. I must further observe on this subject, what I believe was hinted once already, that sympathy may be greatly strengthened or weakened by the influence of connected passions. Thus love associates to it benevolence, and both give double force to sympathy. Hatred, on the contrary, associates to it malice, and destroys sympathy.

There are consequently several reasons why a scene of pure unmixed joy, in any work of genius, cannot give a great or lasting pleasure to the mind. First, sympathetic joy is much fainter and more transient than sympathetic grief, and they are generally the sympathetic passions which are infused by poets, orators, painters, and historians: secondly, joy is the least attractive of all the affections. It perhaps can never properly be said to associate to it desire, the great spring of action. The most we can say is, that when it begins to subside it again gives place to desire, this passion being of such a nature, as that it can hardly for any time be banished from the soul. Hence it is that the joy, which has no other foundation but sympathy, quickly tires the mind and runs into satiety. Hence it is, also, that dramatic writers, and even romance writers, make a scene of pure joy always the last scene of the piece, and but a short one. It may just be mentioned, thirdly, not indeed as an argument, (for of its weakness in this respect I am very sensible,) but as an illustration from analogy, that every thing in nature is heightened and set off by its contrary, which, by giving scope for comparison, enhances every excellence. The colours in painting acquire a double lustre from the shades; the harmony in music is greatly improved by a judicious mixture of discords. The whole conduct of life, were it necessary, might exemplify the position. A mixture of pain, then, seems to be of consequence to give strength and stability to pleasure.

The fifth observation is, that under the name *pity* may be included all the emotions excited by tragedy. In common speech all indeed are included under this name that are excited by that species of eloquence which is denominated the pathetic. The passions moved by tragedy have been commonly said to be *pity* and *terror*. This enumeration is more popular than philosophical, even though adopted by the Stagyrite himself. For what is pity but a participation by sympathy in the woes of others, and the feelings naturally consequent upon them, of whatever kind they be, their fears as well as sorrows? whereas, this way of contradistinguishing terror from pity, would make one who knew nothing of tragedy but from the definition, imagine that it were intended to make us compassionate others in trouble, and dread mischief to ourselves. If this were really the case, I believe there are few or none who would find any pleasure in this species of entertainment. Of this there occurs an example, when, as hath sometimes happened, in the midst of the performance, the audience are alarmed with the sudden report that the house hath taken fire, or when they hear a noise which makes them suspect that the roof or walls are falling. Then, indeed, terror stares in every countenance; but such a terror as gives no degree of pleasure, and is so far from coalescing with the passions raised by the tragedy, that, on the contrary, it expels them altogether, and leaves not in the mind, for some time at least, another idea or reflection but what concerns personal safety.

On the other hand, if all the sympathetic affections excited by the theatrical representation were to be severally enumerated, I cannot see why hope, indignation, love and hatred, gratitude and resentment, should not be included as well as fear. To account then for the pleasure which we find in pity, is, in a great measure, to give a solution of the question under review. I do not say that this will satisfy in every case. On the contrary, there are many cases in which Abbé du Bos's account above recited, of the pleasure arising from the agitation and fluctuation of the passions, is the only solution that can be given.

My sixth and last observation on this head is, that pity is not a simple passion, but a group of passions, strictly united by association, and as it were blended by centring in the same object. Of these some are pleasant, some painful; commonly the pleasant preponderate. It hath been remarked already, that love attracts benevolence, benevolence quickens sympathy. The same attraction takes place inversely, though not, perhaps, with equal strength. Sympathy engages benevolence, and benevolence love. That benevolence, or the habit of wishing happiness to another, from whatever motive it hath originally sprung, will at length draw in love, might be proved from a thousand instances.

In the party divisions which obtain in some countries, it often happens, that a man is at first induced to take a side, purely from a motive of interest; for some time, from this motive solely, he wishes the success of the party with which he is embarked. From a habit of wishing this, he will continue to wish it, when, by a change of circumstances, his own interest is no longer connected with it; nay, which is more strange, he will even contract such a love and attachment to the party, as to promote their interest in direct opposition to his own. That commiseration or sympathy in woe hath still a stronger tendency to engage our love is evident.

This is the only rational account that can be given, why mothers of a humane disposition generally love most the sickliest child in the family, though perhaps far from being the loveliest in respect either of temper or of other qualities. The habit of commiseration habituates them to the feeling and exertion of benevolence. Benevolence, habitually felt and exerted, confirms and augments their love. "Nothing," says Mr. Hume,[10] "endears so much a friend as sorrow for his death. The pleasure of his company hath not so powerful an influence." Distress to the pitying eye diminishes every fault, and sets off every good quality in the brightest colours. Nor is it a less powerful advocate for the mistress than for the friend: often does the single circumstance of misfortune subdue all resentment of former coldness and ill usage, and make a languid and dying passion revive and flame out with a violence which it is impossible any longer to withstand. Every body acknowledges that beauty is never so irresistible as in tears. Distress is commonly sufficient, with those who are not very hard-hearted or pitiless (for these words are nearly of the same import), to make even enmity itself relent.

There are, then, in *pity* these three different emotions, first, *commiseration,* purely painful; secondly, *benevolence,* or a desire of the relief and happiness of the object pitied, a passion, as was already observed, of the intermediate kind; thirdly, *love,* in which is always implied one of the noblest and most exquisite pleasures whereof the sole is susceptible, and which is itself, in most cases, sufficient to give a counterpoise of pleasure to the whole.

For the further confirmation of this theory, let it be remarked, that orators and poets, in order to strengthen this association and union, are at pains to adorn the character of him for whom they would engage our pity, with every amiable quality which, in a consistency with probability, they can crowd into it. On the contrary, when the character is hateful, the person's misfortunes are unpitied. Sometimes they even occasion a pleasure of a very different kind; namely, that which the mind naturally takes in viewing the just punishment of demerit. When the character has such a mixture of good and odious qualities, as that we can neither withhold our commiseration, nor bestow our love; the mind is then torn opposite ways at once, by passions which, instead of uniting, repel one another. Hence the piece becomes shocking and disgustful. Such, to a certain degree, in my judgment, the tragedy of *Venice Preserved,* wherein the hero, notwithstanding several good qualities, is a villain and a traitor, will appear to every well disposed mind. All the above cases, if attended to, will be found exactly to tally with the hypothesis here suggested.

All the answer then which I am able to produce, upon the whole, and which results from the foregoing observations, is this: the principal pleasure in pity ariseth from its own nature, or from the nature of those passions of which it is compounded, and not from any thing extrinsic or adventitious. The tender emotions of love which enter into the composition, sweeten the commiseration or sympathetic sorrow; the commiseration gives a stability to those emotions, with which otherwise the mind would soon be cloyed, when

10 "Essay on Tragedy."

directed towards a person, imaginary, unknown, or with whom we are to-tally unacquainted. The very benevolence or wish of contributing to his relief, affords an occupation to the thoughts, which agreeably rouses them. It impels the mind to devise expedients by which the unhappy person (if our pity is excited by some calamitous incident) may be, or (if it is awak-ened by the art of the poet, the orator, or the historian) might have been, relieved from his distress. Yet the whole movement of the combined affec-tions is not converted into pleasure; for though the uneasiness of the melan-choly passions be overpowered, it is not effaced by something stronger of an opposite kind.

Mr. Hume, indeed, in his manner of expressing himself on this article, hath not observed either an entire uniformity, or his usual precision. I should rather say, from some dubiousness in relation to the account he was giving, he seems to have, in part, retracted what he had been establishing, and thus leaves the reader with an alternative in the decision. First he tells us, that "the whole movement of those [melancholy] passions is converted into pleasure." Afterwards, "the latter [the sentiments of beauty] being the predominate emotion, seize the whole mind, and convert the former [the impulse or vehemence arising from sorrow, compassion, indignation] into themselves;" he adds, by way of correction, "or at least tincture them so strongly, as totally to alter their nature." Again, "the soul feels, on the whole, a strong movement, which is altogether delightful." All this, I ac-knowledge, appears to me to be neither sufficiently definite, nor quite intel-ligible.

But passing that, I shall only subjoin, that the combination of the pas-sions in the instance under our examination, is not like the blending of colours, two of which will produce a third, wherein you can discern nothing of the original hues united in producing it; but it rather resembles a mix-ture of tastes, when you are quite sensible of the different savours of the ingredient. Thus blue and yellow mingled make green, in which you dis-cover no tint of either; and all the colours of a rainbow, blended, constitute a white, which appears to the eye as simple and original as any of them, and perfectly unlike to each. On the other hand, in eating meat with salt, for instance, we taste both distinctly; and though the latter singly would be disagreeable, the former is rendered more agreeable by the mixture than it would otherwise have been.

I own, indeed, that certain adventitious circumstances may contribute to heighten the effect. But these cannot be regarded as essential to the passion. They occur occasionally. Some of them actually occur but seldom. Of this sort is the satisfaction which ariseth from a sense of our own ease and security, compared with the calamity and the danger of another.

> 'Tis pleasant, safely to behold from shore
> The rolling ship, and hear the tempest roar:
> Not that another's pain is our delight,

But pains unfelt produce the pleasing sight.
'Tis pleasant also to behold from far
The moving legions mingled in the war.

(Lucretius, 1.2.)

The poet hath hit here on some of the very few circumstances in which it would be natural to certain tempers, not surely the most humane, to draw comfort in the midst of sympathetic sorrow, from such a comparison. The reflection, in my opinion, occurs almost only when a very small change in external situation, as a change in place to the distance of a few furlongs, would put us into the same lamentable circumstances which we are commiserating in others. Even something of this kind will present itself to our thoughts, when there is no particular object to demand our pity. A man who, in tempestuous weather, sits snug in a close house, near a good fire, and hears the wind and rain beating upon the roof and windows, will naturally think of his own comfortable situation, compared with that of a traveller, who, perhaps, far from shelter, is exposed to all the violence of the tempest. But in such cases, a difference, as I said, in a single accidental circumstance, which may happen at any time, is all that is necessary to put a man in the same disastrous situation, wherein he either sees or conceives others to be. And the very slightness of the circumstance which would have been sufficient to reverse the scene, makes him so ready to congratulate with himself on his better luck. Whereas nothing is less natural, and I will venture to say, less common, than such a reflection, when the differences are many, and of a kind which cannot be reckoned merely accidental; as when the calamity is what the person pitying must consider himself as not liable to, or in the remotest hazard of. A man who, with the most undissembled compassion, bewails the wretched and undeserved fate of Desdemona, is not apt to think of himself, how fortunate he is in not being the wife of a credulous, jealous, and revengeful husband; though perhaps a girl who hath lately rejected a suitor of this character, will reflect with great complacency on the escape she has made.

Another adventitious source of pleasure is the satisfaction that results from the conscious exercise of the humane affections, which it is our duty to cherish and improve. I mention this as adventitious, because, though not unnatural, I do not imagine that the sensations of sympathetic sorrow, either always or immediately, give rise to this reflection. Children, and even savages, are susceptible of pity, who think no more of claiming any merit to themselves on this score, than they think of claiming merit from their feeling the natural appetites of hunger and thirst. Nay, it is very possible that persons may know its power and sweetness too, when, through the influence of education and bad example, they consider it as a weakness or blemish in their disposition, and as such endeavour to conceal and stifle it. A certain degree of civilization seems to be necessary to make us thoroughly sensible of its beauty and utility, and consequently that it ought to be cultivated. Bigotry may teach a man to think inhumanity, in certain circumstances, a virtue. Yet nature will reclaim, and may make him, in spite of the dictates of a misguided conscience, feel all the tenderness of pity to the heretic, who, in his opinion, has more than merited the very worst that can be inflicted on him.

I acknowledge that, on the other hand, when the sentiment comes generally to prevail, that compassion is in itself praiseworthy, it may be rendered a source of much more self-satisfaction to the vain-glorious, than reasonably it ought to yield. Such persons gladly lay hold of every handle which serves to raise them in their own esteem. And I make no doubt that several, from this very motive, have exalted this principle as immoderately as others have vilified it. Every good man will agree, that this is the case when people consider it as either a veil for their vices, or an atonement for the neglect of their duty. For my own part, I am inclined to think, that those who are most ready to abuse it thus, are not the most remarkable for any exercise of it by which society can be profited. There is a species of deception in the case, which it is not beside the purpose briefly to unravel.

It hath been observed that sense invariably makes a stronger impression than memory, and memory a stronger than imagination; yet there are particular circumstances which appear to form an exception, and to give an efficacy to the ideas of imagination, beyond what either memory or sense can boast. So great is the anomaly which sometimes displays itself in human characters, that it is not impossible to find persons who are quickly made to cry at seeing a tragedy, or reading a romance, which they know to be fictions, and yet are both inattentive and unfeeling in respect of the actual objects of compassion who live in their neighbourhood, and are daily under their eye. Nevertheless, this is an exception from the rule, more in appearance than in reality. The cases are not parallel: there are certain circumstances which obtain in the one, and have no place in the other; and to these peculiarities the difference in the effect is solely imputable. What follows will serve fully to explain my meaning.

Men may be of a selfish, contracted, and even avaricious disposition, who are not what we should denominate hard-hearted, or insusceptible of sympathetic feeling. Such will gladly enjoy the luxury of pity (as Hawkesworth terms it) when it nowise interferes with their more powerful passions; that is, when it comes unaccompanied with a demand upon their pockets. With the tragic or the romantic hero or heroine they most cordially sympathize, because the only tribute which wretches of their dignity exact from them is sighs and tears. And of these their consciences inform them, to their inexpressible consolation, that they are no niggards. But the case is totally different with living objects. Barren tears and sighs will not satisfy these. Hence it is that people's avarice, a most formidable adversary to the unhappy, is interested to prevent their being moved by such, and to make them avoid, as much as possible, every opportunity of knowing or seeing them.[11] But as that cannot always be done, as commiseration is attended

11 In the parable of the compassionate Samaritan, Luke x. 30, &c. this disposition to shun the sight of misery, which one is resolved not to redress, is finely touched in the conduct

with benevolence, and as benevolence itself, if not gratified, by our giving relief when it is in our power, embitters the pleasure which would otherwise result from pity, as the refusal is also attended with self-reproach; a person of such a temper, strongly, and for the most part effectually, resists his being moved. He puts his ingenuity to the rack, in order to satisfy himself that he ought not to be affected. He is certain that the person is not a proper object of beneficence, he is convinced that his distress is more pretended than real; or, if that cannot be alleged, the man hath surely brought it on by his vices, therefore he deserves to suffer, and is nowise entitled to our pity; or at least he makes not a good use of what may charitably, but injudiciously, be bestowed upon him. Such are the common shifts by which selfishness eludes the calls of humanity, and chooses to reserve all its worthless stock of pity for fictitious objects, or for those who, in respect of time, or place, or eminence, are beyond its reach.

For these reasons, I am satisfied that compassion alone, especially that displayed on occasion of witnessing public spectacles, is at best but a very weak evidence of philanthropy. The only proof that is entirely unequivocal, is actual beneficence, when one seeks out the real objects of commiseration, not as a matter of self-indulgence, but in order to bring relief to those who need it, to give hope to the desponding, and comfort to the sorrowful, for the sake of which one endures the sight of wretchedness, when, instead of giving pleasure, it distresseth every feeling heart. Such, however, enjoy at length a luxury far superior to that of pity, the godlike luxury of dispelling grief, communicating happiness, and doing good.

.ॐ.ॐ.ॐ.ॐ.ॐ.ॐ.

Book II   The Foundations and Essential Properties of Elocution

CHAPTER I

The Nature and Characters of the Use which gives Law to Language

Eloquence hath always been considered, and very justly, as having a particular connexion with language. It is the intention of eloquence to convey our sentiments into the minds of others, in order to produce a certain effect upon them. Language is the only vehicle by which this conveyance can be made. The art of speaking, then, is not less necessary to the

---

of the priest and the Levite, who, when they espied a person naked, wounded, and almost expiring on the road, are said to have "passed by on the other side."

orator than the art of thinking. Without the latter, the former could not have existed. Without the former, the latter would be ineffective. Every tongue whatever is founded in use or custom,

——— Whose arbitrary sway
Words and the forms of language must obey.
(Horace, *The Art of Poetry,* trans. FRANCIS)

Language is purely a species of fashion (for this holds equally of every tongue) in which, by the general but tacit consent of the people of a particular state or country, certain sounds come to be appropriated to certain things, as their signs, and certain ways of inflecting and combining those sounds come to be established, as denoting the relations which subsist among the things signified.

It is not the business of grammar, as some critics seem preposterously to imagine, to give law to the fashions which regulate our speech. On the contrary, from its conformity to these, and from that alone, it derives all its authority and value. For, what is the grammar of any language? It is no other than a collection of general observations methodically digested, and comprising all the modes previously and independently established, by which the significations, derivations, and combinations of words in that language are ascertained. It is of no consequence here to what causes originally these modes or fashions owe their existence, to imitation, to reflection, to affectation, or to caprice; they no sooner obtain and become general, than they are laws of the language, and the grammarian's only business is to note, collect, and methodize them. Nor does this truth concern only those more comprehensive analogies or rules, which affect whole classes of words, such as nouns, verbs, and the other parts of speech; but it concerns every individual word, in the inflecting or the combining of which a particular mode hath prevailed. Every single anomaly, therefore, though departing from the rule assigned to the other words of the same class, and on that account called an exception, stands on the same basis on which the rules of the tongue are founded, custom having prescribed for it a separate rule.[1]

The truth of this position hath never, for aught I can remember, been directly controverted by anybody; yet it is certain, that both critics and grammarians often argue in such a way as is altogether inconsistent with it. What, for example, shall we make of that complaint of Doctor Swift, "that our language, in many instances, offends against every part of grammar?" [2] Or what could the doctor's notion of grammar be, when expressing himself in this manner? Some notion, possibly, he had of grammar in the abstract,

[1] Thus in the two verbs *call* and *shall,* the second person singular of the former is *callest,* agreeably to the general rule, the second person singular of the latter is *shalt,* aggreably to a particular rule affecting that verb. To say *shallest* for *shalt,* would be as much a barbarism, though according to the general rule, as to say *calt* for *callest,* which is according to no rule.

[2] Letter to the Lord High Treasurer, &c.

an universal archetype by which the particular grammars of all different tongues ought to be regulated. If this was his meaning, I cannot say whether he is in the right or in the wrong in this accusation. I acknowledge myself to be entirely ignorant of this ideal grammar; nor can I form a conjecture where its laws are to be learnt. One thing, indeed, every smatterer in philosophy will tell us, that there can be no natural connexion between the sounds of any language, and the things signified, or between the modes of inflection and combination and the relations they are intended to express. Perhaps he meant the grammar of some other language; if so, the charge was certainly true, but not to the purpose, since we can say with equal truth, of every language, that it offends against the grammar of every other language whatsoever. If he meant the English grammar, I would ask, whence has that grammar derived its laws? If from general use, (and I cannot conceive another origin,) then it must be owned, that there is a general use in that language as well as in others; and it were absurd to accuse the language which is purely what is conformable to general use in speaking and writing, as offending against general use. But if he meant to say, that there is no fixed, established, or general use in the language, that it is quite irregular, he hath been very unlucky in his manner of expressing himself. Nothing is more evident, than that where there is no law there is no transgression. In that case, he ought to have said that it is not susceptible of grammar; which, by the way, would not have been true of English, or indeed of any the most uncultivated language on the earth.

It is easy then to assign the reason, why the justness of the complaint, as Doctor Lowth observes,[3] has never yet been questioned; it is purely because, not being understood, it hath never been minded. But if, according to this ingenious gentleman, the words *our language,* have, by a new kind of trope, been used to denote those who speak and write English, and no more have been intended than to signify, that our best speakers and most approved authors frequently offend against the rules of grammar, that is, against the general use of language, I shall not here enter on a discussion of the question. Only let us rest in these as fixed principles, that use, or the custom of speaking, is the sole original standard of conversation, as far as regards the expression, and the custom of writing is the sole standard of style: that the latter comprehends the former, and something more; that to the tribunal of use, as to the supreme authority, and consequently, in every grammatical controversy, the last resort, we are entitled to appeal from the laws and the decisions of grammarians; and that this order of subordination ought never, on any account, to be reversed.

But if use be here a matter of such consequence, it will be necessary, before advancing any further, to ascertain precisely what it is. We shall otherwise be in danger, though we agree about the name, of differing widely in the notion that we assign to it.

3 Preface to his *Introduction to English Grammar.*

SECTION I—REPUTABLE USE

In what extent then must the word be understood? It is sometimes called *general use;* yet is it not manifest that the generality of people speak and write very badly? Nay, is not this a truth that will be even generally acknowledged? It will be so; and this very acknowledgment shows that many terms and idioms may be common, which nevertheless, have not the general sanction, no, nor even the suffrage of those that use them. The use here spoken of, implies not only *currency,* but *vogue.* It is properly *reputable custom.*

This leads to a distinction between good use and bad use in language, the former of which will be found to have the approbation of those who have not themselves attained it. The far greater part of mankind, perhaps ninety-nine of a hundred, are, by reason of poverty and other circumstances, deprived of the advantages of education, and condemned to toil for bread, almost incessantly, in some narrow occupation. They have neither the leisure nor the means of attaining any knowledge, except what lies within the contracted circle of their several professions. As the ideas which occupy their minds are few, the portion of the language known to them must be very scanty. It is impossible that our language of words should outstrip our knowledge of things. It may, and often doth, come short of it. Words may be remembered as sounds, but cannot be understood as signs, whilst we remain unacquainted with the things signified.

Hence it will happen, that in the lower walks of life, from the intercourse which all ranks occasionally have with one another, the people will frequently have occasion to hear words of which they never had occasion to learn the meaning. These they will pick up and remember, produce and misapply. But there is rarely any uniformity in such blunders, or any thing determinate in the senses they give to words which are not within their sphere. Nay, they are not themselves altogether unconscious of this defect. It often ariseth from an admiration of the manner of their superiors, and from an ill-judged imitation of their way of speaking, that the greatest errors of the illiterate, in respect of conversation, proceed. And were they sensible how widely different their use and application of such words is, from that of those whom they affect to imitate, they would renounce their own immediately.

But it may be said, and said with truth, that in such subjects as are within their reach, many words and idioms prevail among the populace which, notwithstanding a use pretty uniform and extensive, are considered as corrupt, and like counterfeit money, though common, not valued. This is the case particularly with those terms and phrases which critics have denominated *vulgarisms.* Their use is not reputable. On the contrary, we always associate with it such notions of meanness, as suit those orders of men amongst whom chiefly the use is found. Hence it is that many, who have contracted a habit of employing such idioms, do not approve them; and though, through negligence, they frequently fall into them in conversation, they carefully avoid them in writing, or even in a solemn speech on any important occasion. Their currency, therefore, is without authority and weight. The tattle of children hath a currency, but, however universal their manner of corrupting words may be among themselves, it can never establish what is accounted use in language. Now, what children are to men, that precisely the ignorant are to the knowing.

From the practice of those who are conversant in any art, elegant or mechanical, we always take the sense of the terms and phrases belonging to that art; in like manner, from the practice of those who have had a liberal education, and are therefore presumed to be best acquainted with men and things, we judge of the general use in language. If in this particular there be any deference to the practice of the great and rich, it is not ultimately because they are greater and richer than others, but because, from their greatness and riches, they are imagined to be wiser and more knowing. The source, therefore, of that preference which distinguisheth good use from bad in language, is a natural propension of the human mind to believe that those are the best judges of the proper signs, and of the proper application of them, who understand best the things which they represent.

But who are they that in the public estimation are possessed of this character? This question is of the greatest moment for ascertaining that use which is entitled to the epithets reputable and good. Vaugelas makes them in France to be "the soundest part of the court, and the soundest part of the authors of the age." With us Britons, the first part at least of this description will not answer. In France, which is a pure monarchy, as the dependence of the inferior orders is much greater, their submission to their superiors, and the humble respect which in every instance they show them, seem, in our way of judging, to border even upon adoration. With us, on the contrary, who in our spirit, as well as in the constitution of our government, have more of the republican than of the monarchical, there is no remarkable partiality in favour of courtiers. At least their being such rarely enhanceth our opinion either of their abilities or of their virtues.

I would not by this be understood to signify, that the primary principle which gives rise to the distinction between good use and bad in language, is different in different countries. It is not originally, even in France, a deference to power, but to wisdom. Only it must be remarked, that the tendency of the imagination is to accumulate all great qualities into the same character. Wherever we find one or two of these, we naturally presume the rest. This is particularly true of those qualities, which by their immediate consequences strongly affect the external senses. We are in a manner dazzled by them.—Hence it happens, that it is difficult even for a man of discernment, till he be better instructed by experience, to restrain a veneration for the judgment of a person of uncommon splendour and magnificence; as if one who is more powerful and opulent than his neighbours were of necessity wiser too. Now, this original bias of the mind some political constitutions serve to strengthen, others to correct.

But without resting the matter entirely on the difference in respect of government between France and Britain, the British court is commonly too fluctuating an object. Use in language requires firmer ground to stand upon. No doubt, the conversation of men of rank and eminence, whether of the court or not, will have its influence. And in what concerns merely the pronunciation, it is the only rule to which we can refer the matter in every doubtful case; but in what concerns the words themselves, their construction and application, it is of importance to have some certain, steady, and well-known standard to recur to, a standard which every one hath access to canvass and examine.

And this can be no other than authors of reputation. Accordingly, we find that these are, by universal consent, in actual possession of this authority; as to this tribunal, when any doubt arises, the appeal is always made.

I choose to name them authors of reputation, rather than good authors, for two reasons: first, because it is more strictly conformable to the truth of the case. It is solely the esteem of the public, and not their intrinsic merit (though these two go generally together), which raises them to this distinction, and stamps a value on their language. Secondly, this character is more definitive than the other, and therefore more extensively intelligible. Between two or more authors, different readers will differ exceedingly, as to the preference in point of merit, who agree perfectly as to the respective places they hold in the favour of the public. You may find persons of a taste so particular as to prefer Parnell to Milton; but you will hardly find a person that will dispute the superiority of the latter in the article of fame. For this reason, I affirm that Vaugelas' definition labours under an essential defect; inasmuch as it may be difficult to meet with two persons whose judgments entirely coincide in determining who are the sounder part of the court, or of the authors of the age. I need scarcely add, that when I speak of reputation, I mean not only in regard to knowledge, but in regard to the talent of communicating knowledge. I could name writers, who, in respect of the first, have been justly valued by the public, but who, on account of a supposed deficiency in respect of the second, are considered as of no authority in language.

Nor is there the least ground to fear that we should be cramped here within too narrow limits. In the English tongue there is a plentiful supply of noted writings in all the various kinds of composition, in prose and verse, serious and ludicrous, grave and familiar. Agreeably then to this first qualification of the term, we must understand to be comprehended under general use, *whatever modes of speech are authorized as good by the writings of a great number, if not the majority, of celebrated authors.*

SECTION II—NATIONAL USE

Another qualification of the term *use* which deserves our attention, is that it must be *national*. This I consider in a twofold view, as it stands opposed both to *provincial* and to *foreign*.

In every province there are peculiarities of dialect which affect not only the pronunciation and the accent, but even the inflection and the combination of words, whereby their idiom is distinguished both from that of the nation and from that of every other province. The narrowness of the circle to which the currency of the words and phrases of such dialects is confined, sufficiently discriminates them from that which is properly styled the language, and which commands a circulation incomparably wider. This is one reason, I imagine, why the term *use,* on this subject, is commonly accompanied with the epithet *general.* In the use of provincial idioms, there is, it must be acknowledged, a pretty considerable concurrence both of the middle and of the lower ranks. But still this use is bounded by the province, county, or district, which gives name to the dialect, and beyond which its peculiarities are sometimes unintelligible, and always ridiculous. But the language, properly so called, is found current, especially in the upper and the middle ranks, over the whole British empire. Thus, though in every province they ridicule the idiom of every other province, they all vail to the English idiom, and scruple not to acknowledge its superiority over their own.

For example, in some parts of Wales (if we may credit Shaskpeare [4]) , the common people say *goot* for good; in the south of Scotland they said *gude,* and in the north *gueed.* Wherever one of these pronunciations prevails, you will never hear from a native either of the other two; but the word *good* is to be heard every where from natives as well as strangers; nor do the people ever dream that there is any thing laughable in it, however much they are disposed to laugh at the county-accents and idioms which they discern in one another. Nay more, though the people of distant provinces do not understand one another, they mostly all understand one who speaks properly. It is a just and curious observation of Dr. Kenrick, that "the case of languages, or rather speech, being quite contrary to that of science, in the former the ignorant understand the learned better than the learned do the ignorant; in the latter, it is otherwise." [5]

Hence it will perhaps be found true, upon inquiry, notwithstanding its paradoxical appearance, that though it be very uncommon to speak or write pure English, yet, of all the idioms subsisting amongst us, that to which we give the character of purity is the commonest. The faulty idioms do not jar more with true English, than they do with one another; so that, in order to our being satisfied of the truth of the apparent paradox, it is requisite only that we remember that these idioms are diverse one from another, though they come under the common denomination of *impure.* Those who wander from the road may be incomparably more than those who travel in it; and yet, if it be into a thousand different bypaths that they deviate, there may not in any one of these be found so many as those whom you will meet upon the king's highway.

4 Fluellen in *Henry V.*
5 *Rhet. Gram.* chap. ii. sect. 4.

What hath been now said of provincial dialects, may, with very little variation, be applied to professional dialects, or the cant which is sometimes observed to prevail among those of the same profession or way of life. The currency of the latter cannot be so exactly circumscribed as that of the former, whose distinction is purely local; but their use is not on that account either more extensive or more reputable. Let the following serve as instances of this kind. *Advice,* in the commercial idiom, means information or intelligence; *nervous,* in open defiance of analogy, doth in the medical cant, as Johnson expresseth it, denote, having weak nerves; and the word *turtle,* though pre-occupied time immemorial by a species of dove, is, as we learn from the same authority, employed by sailors and gluttons to signify a tortoise.[6]

It was remarked, that national might also be opposed to foreign. I imagine it is too evident to need illustration, that the introduction of extraneous words and idioms, from other languages and foreign nations, cannot be a smaller transgression against the established custom of the English tongue, than the introduction of words and idioms peculiar to some precincts of England, or at least somewhere current within the British pale. The only material difference between them is, that the one is more commonly the error of the learned, the other of the vulgar. But if, in this view, the former is entitled to greater indulgence from the respect paid to learning; in another view, it is entitled to less, as it is much more commonly the result of affectation. Thus two essential qualities of usage, in regard to language, have been settled, that it be both *reputable* and *national.*

SECTION III—PRESENT USE

But there will naturally arise here another question, "Is not use, even good and national use, in the same country, different in different periods? And if so, to the usage of what period shall we attach ourselves, as the proper rule? If you say *the present,* as it may reasonably be expected that you will, the difficulty is not entirely removed. In what extent of signification must we understand the word *present?* How far may we safely range in quest of authorities? or, at what distance backwards from this moment are authors still to be accounted as possessing a legislative voice in language?" To this I own it is difficult to give an answer with all the precision that might be desired. Yet it is certain, that when we are in search of precedents for any word or idiom, there are certain mounds which we cannot overleap with safety. For instance, the authority of Hooker or of Raleigh, however great their merit and their fame be, will not now be admitted in support of a term or expression not to be found in any good writer of a later date.

In truth, the boundary must not be fixed at the same distance in every subject. Poetry hath ever been allowed a wider range than prose; and it is but just that, by an indulgence of this kind, some compensation should be

6 See those words in the *English Dictionary.*

made for the peculiar restraints she is laid under by the measure. Nor is this only a matter of convenience to the poet; it is also a matter of gratification to the reader. Diversity in the style relieves the ear, and prevents its being tired with the too frequent recurrence of the rhymes, or sameness of the metre. But still there are limits to this diversity. The authority of Milton and of Waller, on this article, remains as yet unquestioned. I should not think it prudent often to introduce words or phrases of which no example could be produced since the days of Spenser and of Shakspeare.

And even in prose, the bounds are not the same for every kind of composition. In matters of science, for instance, whose terms, from the nature of the thing, are not capable of such a currency as those which belong to ordinary subjects, and are within the reach of ordinary readers, there is no necessity of confining an author within a very narrow circle. But in composing pieces which come under this last denomination, as history, romance, travels, moral essays, familiar letters, and the like, it is safest for an author to consider those words and idioms as obsolete, which have been disused by all good authors for a longer period than the age of man extends to. It is not by ancient, but by present use, that our style must be regulated. And that use can never be denominated present, which hath been laid aside time immemorial, or, which amounts to the same thing, falls not within the knowledge or remembrance of any now living.

This remark not only affects terms and phrases, but also the declension, combination, and the construction of words. Is it not then surprising to find, that one of Lowth's penetration should think a single person entitled to revive a form of inflection in a particular word, which had been rejected by all good writers, of every denomination, for more than a hundred and fifty years? [7] But if present use is to be denounced for ancient, it will be necessary to determine at what precise period antiquity is to be regarded as a rule. One inclines to remove the standard to the distance of a century and a half; another may, with as good reason, fix it three centuries backwards, and another six. And if the language of any of these periods is to be judged by the use of any other, it will be found, no doubt, entirely barbarous. To me it is so evident, either that the present use must be the standard of the present language, or that the language admits no standard whatsoever, that I cannot conceive a clearer or more indisputable principle, from which to bring an argument to support it.

Yet it is certain, that even some of our best critics and grammarians talk

[7] Introd. &c. In a note on the irregular verb *sit,* he says, "Dr. Middleton hath, with great propriety, restored the true participle *sitten.*" Would he not have acted with as great propriety, had he restored the true participles, *pight* for *pitched, raught* for *reached, blent* for *blended,* and *shright* for *shrieked,* on full as good authority, the authority of Spenser, one of the sweetest of our ancient bards? And why might not Dr. Lowth himself have, with great propriety, restored the true participles *hitten, casten, letten, putten, setten, shutten, slitten, splitten, founden, grounden,* of the verbs *hit, cast, let, put, set, shut, slit, split, find, grind:* for it would not be impossible to produce antiquated authors in support of all these.—Besides, they are all used to this day in some provincial dialects.

occasionally as if they had a notion of some other standard, though they never give us a single hint) to direct us where to search for it. Dr. Johnson, for example, in the preface to his very valuable dictionary, acknowledges properly the absolute dominion of custom over language, and yet, in the explanation of particular words, expresseth himself sometimes in a manner that is inconsistent with this doctrine, "This word," says he in one place, "though common, and used by the best writers, is perhaps barbarous." [8] I have always understood a barbarism in speech to be a term or expression totally unsupported by the present usage of good writers in the language. A meaning very different is suggested here, but what that meaning is it will not be easy to conjecture. Nor has this celebrated writer given us, on the word *barbarous,* any definition of the term which will throw light on his application of it in the passage quoted. I entirely agree with Doctor Priestley, that it will never be the arbitrary rules of any man, or body of men whatever, that will ascertain the language,[9] there being no other dictator here but use.

It is indeed easier to discover the aim of our critics in their observations on this subject, than the meaning of the terms which they employ. These are often employed without precision; their aim, however, is generally good. It is, as much as possible, to give a check to innovation. But the means which they use for this purpose have sometimes even a contrary tendency. If you will replace what hath been long since expunged from the language, and extirpate what is firmly rooted, undoubtedly you yourself become an innovator. If you desert the present use, and by your example at least, establish it as a maxim, that every critic may revive at pleasure old-fashioned terms, inflections, and combinations, and make such alterations on words as will bring them nearer to what he supposeth to be the etymon, there can be nothing fixed or stable on the subject. Possibly you prefer the usage that prevailed in the reign of Queen Elizabeth; another may, with as good reason, have a partiality for that which subsisted in the days of Chaucer. And with regard to etymology, about which grammarians make so much useless bustle, if every one hath a privilege of altering words, according to his own opinion of their origin, the opinions of the learned being on this subject so various, nothing but a general chaos can ensue.

On the other hand, it may be said, "Are we to catch at every new-fashioned term and phrase which whim or affectation may invent, and folly circulate? Can this ever tend to give either dignity to our style, or permanency to our language?" It cannot, surely. This leads to a further explanation and limitation of the term *present use,* to prevent our being misled by a mere name. It is possible, nay, it is common, for men, in avoiding one error, to run into another and a worse. There is a mean in every thing. I have purposely avoided the expressions *recent use* and *modern use,* as these

8 See the word *Nowadays.*
9 Preface to his *Rudiments of English Grammar.*

seem to stand in direct opposition to what is *ancient*. But I have used the word *present* which, in respect of place, is always opposed to *absent,* and in respect of time, to *past* or *future,* that now have no existence. When, therefore, the word is used of language, its proper contrary is not ancient but *obsolete.* Besides, though I have acknowledged language to be a species of *mode* or *fashion,* as doubtless it is, yet, being much more permanent than articles of apparel, furniture, and the like, that, in regard to their form, are under the dominion of that inconstant power, I have avoided also using the words *fashionable* and *modish,* which but too generally convey the ideas of novelty and levity. Words, therefore, are by no means to be accounted the worse for being old, if they are not obsolete; neither is any word the better for being new. On the contrary, some time is absolutely necessary to constitute that custom or use, on which the establishment of words depends.

If we recur to the standard already assigned, namely, the writings of a plurality of celebrated authors; there will be no scope for the comprehension of words and idioms which can be denominated novel and upstart. It must be owned that we often meet with such terms and phrases in newspapers, periodical pieces, and political pamphlets. The writers to the times rarely fail to have their performances studded with a competent number of these fantastic ornaments. A popular orator in the House of Commons hath a sort of patent from the public, during the continuance of his popularity, for coining as many as he pleases. And they are no sooner issued, than they obtrude themselves upon us from every quarter, in all the daily papers, letters, essays, addresses, &c. But this is of no significancy. Such words and phrases are but the insects of a season at the most. The people, always fickle, are just as prompt to drop them, as they were to take them up. And not one of a hundred survives the particular occasion or party-struggle which gave it birth. We may justly apply to them what Johnson says of a great number of the terms of the laborious and mercantile part of the people, "This fugitive cant cannot be regarded as any part of the durable materials of a language, and therefore must be suffered to perish, with other things unworthy of preservation." [10]

As use, therefore, implies duration, and as even a few years are not sufficient for ascertaining the characters of authors, I have, for the most part, in the following sheets, taken my prose examples, neither from living authors, nor those who wrote before the Revolution; not from the first, because an author's fame is not so firmly established in his lifetime; nor from the last, that there may be no suspicion that the style is super-annuated. The vulgar translation of the Bible I must indeed except from this restriction. The continuance and universality of its use throughout the British dominions affords an obvious reason for the exception.

Thus I have attempted to explain what that *use* is, which is the sole mistress of language, and to ascertain the precise import and extent of these

[10] Preface to his *English Dictionary.*

her essential attributes, *reputable, national,* and *present,* and to give the directions proper to be observed in searching for the laws of this empress. In truth, grammar and criticism are but her ministers; and though, like other ministers, they would sometimes impose the dictates of their own humour upon the people, as the commands of their sovereign, they are not so often successful in such attempts as to encourage the frequent repetition of them.

RICHARD WHATELY

᠊ᢌ᠊ᢌ᠊ᢌ᠊ᢌ᠊ᢌ᠊ᢌ᠊ᢌ᠊ᢌ᠊ᢌ᠊

Richard Whately (1787–1863) was born in London on February 1. As a child, he was confined to the house owing to delicate health, and as often happens in such circumstances, he turned to books to occupy the lonely hours. It was not all reading for entertainment that he indulged in at this period of his life; he developed an interest in mathematics, ethics, and politics, which stood him in good stead later on in life when he developed professional interests in logic, ecclesiastical affairs, and political economy. After he was sent away to a private school near Bristol, his health improved so remarkably that by the time he was ready to go off to the university, he was a tall, robust young man with a fondness for fishing and for taking long walks through the countryside.

He was admitted to Oriel College, Oxford, in 1805, when that college was striving to emerge from the doldrums into which Oxford had fallen during the last half of the eighteenth century. There he fell in with that remarkable group of men whose names dot the pages of John Henry Newman's *Apologia Pro Vita Sua*—Edward Copleston, Nassau William Senior, Thomas Arnold, Edward Hawkins, and John Keble. Members of this group eventually became identified with the Noetics and the Tractarians, who figured so prominently in the Oxford Movement. After taking his B.A. degree in 1808, Whately was elected Fellow of Oriel, then on to take his M.A. in 1812, and soon after, was ordained as an Anglican clergyman.

In 1821, after he married Elizabeth Pope, by whom he eventually had a son and a daughter, he accepted a pastorate at Halesworth in Suffolk. He returned to Oxford in 1825 as principal of St. Alban Hall, with Newman as his first vice-principal. It was during this time, while he was engaged in a rigorous refurbishing of the intellectual life at St. Alban's, that he wrote for Coleridge's *Encyclopaedia Metropolitana* the long articles on Logic and Rhetoric that were the basis for his *Elements of Logic* (1826) and *Elements of Rhetoric* (1828) . In the next twenty-five years, the *Logic* enjoyed an even brisker sale than the *Rhetoric,* going into its ninth edition by 1850, but it was the *Rhetoric* that gave him his most enduring fame and influence. With each successive edition of the *Rhetoric,* Whately substantially revised and enlarged various parts, so that by the time it reached its seventh edition in 1846, Part I and Part II were more than two and a half times longer than they had been in the original encyclopedia article. What is ironic about the ultimate success of the *Elements of Rhetoric* is that rhetoric was not Whately's primary professional interest.

In 1829, Whately was named as Professor of Political Economy at Oxford, but he resigned that post two years later when he was called to be arch-bishop of St. Patrick's Cathedral in Dublin. This episcopal post engaged Whately in the political, social, and religious ferment that was stirring in Ireland and England at the time. Although as a member of the House of Lords he supported the movement for Catholic emancipation and many of the reforms designed to improve the lot of the Irish poor, Whately was never a popular figure in Dublin, as that earlier alien Englishman, Dean Swift, had been. Nor was he a popular preacher, as Hugh Blair had been at St. Giles. His dry, systematic, unimpassioned sermons failed to stir his congregation. He was active, too, on the academic side while in Ireland, founding a chair of political economy at Trinity College and serving as a member of the Royal Irish Academy.

Politically, Whately was an independent liberal. Ecclesiastically, he was, like the Tractarians, an anti-Erastian, one of that group who furiously resisted the attempts to subordinate the church to the secular arm of the Establishment. Although he was a close friend of most of the Tractarians in the early days of the Oxford Movement, he gradually drifted away from them ideologically and finally broke with them over the affair of the famous Tract XC. Though he had earlier worked closely and amicably with Newman (Newman, for instance, had helped him with the article on logic), Whately manifested his growing estrangement by befriending Joseph Blanco White, the apostate Roman Catholic priest who was causing Newman so much embarrassment, and by publishing in 1830 his polemical tract, *The Errors of Romanism Traced to Their Origin in Human Nature*. Part of his disaffection with the whole Oxford Movement was due to his congenital antipathy for metaphysical and theological speculations. The principle that governed the stand he took in all religious controversies was Chillingworth's premise that "the Bible, and the Bible alone, is the religion of Protestants." And it was this allegiance to the Scriptures that accounts for the emphasis he puts on testimony in his *Elements of Rhetoric*.

Of the three rhetoricians represented in this book, Whately was the most prolific. He published almost one hundred separate works during his lifetime. Most of these were religious books, but from time to time he published his disquisitions on various political and social questions of the times. He found it a labor of love to edit Copleston's *Remains* in 1854, and in 1856, he indulged his own boyhood interest by publishing an annotated edition of Francis Bacon's *Essays*. He published several volumes of his sermons, but there seems never to have been the demand for these that there had been for Blair's.

In his declining years, Whately retreated to the privacy of his study and his garden. He was always an accommodating host, but he never took easily to conversation or company. For all his liberal leanings, he found it difficult to be tolerant of those who differed with him on religious matters. Despite the exemplary piety that manifests itself in his religious writings and the rigorous intellectual integrity that characterizes his academic writings, Whately does not come through as a very prepossessing personality.

After a protracted illness, Whately died in Dublin, at the age of 76, on October 1, 1863. He was buried in St. Patrick's Cathedral. Visitors to the British Museum today can see an engraved portrait of him. There it hangs in the city of his birth, the portrait of a man who had devoted the main energies of his life to the service of the church but whose principal legacy to the intellectual life of Great Britain was the book he wrote on rhetoric.

Bibliography

Ehninger, Douglas, ed., *Elements of Rhetoric by Richard Whately* (Carbondale, Illinois, 1963).

———, "Whately on *Dispositio*," *Quarterly Journal of Speech*, XL (December 1954), 439–441.

Fitzpatrick, W. J., *Memoirs of R. Whately, Archbishop of Dublin* (London, 1864).

Parrish, Wayland M., "Richard Whately's *Elements of Rhetoric*." Unpublished Ph.D. dissertation, Cornell University, 1929.

———, "Whately and His Rhetoric," *Quarterly Journal of Speech*, XV (December 1929), 58–79.

Pence, Orville L., "The Concept and Function of Logical Proof in the Rhetorical System of Richard Whately." Unpublished Ph.D. dissertation, University of Iowa, 1946.

———, "The Concept and Function of Logical Proof in the Rhetorical System of Richard Whately," *Speech Monographs*, XX (March 1953), 23–38.

Pomeroy, Ralph S., "Whately's *Historic Doubts*: Argument and Origin," *Quarterly Journal of Speech*, XLIX (February 1963), 62–74.

Whately, Jane E., ed., *Miscellaneous Remains from the Commonplace Book of Richard Whately, D.D., Late Archbishop of Dublin* (London, 1864).

———, *Life and Correspondence of Richard Whately, D.D.*, 2 vols. (London, 1866).

Whately, Richard, *Elements of Logic* (London, 1826).

———, *Elements of Rhetoric* (London, 1828).

"Whately, Richard," *Dictionary of National Biography* (London, 1882).

Winans, James A., "Whately on Elocution," *Quarterly Journal of Speech*, XXXI (February 1945), 1–8.

Addenda

Berlin, James, "Richard Whately and Current-Traditional Rhetoric," accepted for publication in *College English*.

Freeman, William, "Whately and Stanislovski: Complementary Paradigms of Naturalness," *Quarterly Journal of Speech*, LVI (February 1970), 61–66.

Golden, James L., Berquist, Goodwin F., and Coleman, William E., "The Rhetorics of Campbell and Whately," in *The Rhetoric of Western Thought*, Second Edition (Dubuque, Iowa, 1979), pp. 123–143.

Howell, Wilbur Samuel, "Conclusion," in *Eighteenth-Century British Logic and Rhetoric* (Princeton, 1971), pp. 695–717.

Leathers, Dale G., "Whately's Logically Derived Rhetoric: A Stranger in Its Time," *Western Speech*, XXXIII (Winter 1969), 48–58.

McKerrow, Ray E., "Whately's Theory of Rhetoric," Ph.D. Dissertation, University of Iowa, 1974.

———, "Probable Argument and Proof in Whately's Theory of Rhetoric," *Central States Speech Journal*, XXVI (Winter 1975), 259–266.

———, "Campbell, Whately on the Utility of Syllogistic Logic," *Western Speech Communication*, XL (Winter 1976), 3–13.

———, " 'Method of Composition': Whately's Earliest 'Rhetoric,' " *Philosophy & Rhetoric*, 11 (Winter 1978), 43–58.

Sproule, J. Michael, "The Psychological Burden of Proof: On the Development of Richard Whately's Theory of Presumption," *Communication Monographs*, XLIII (June 1976), 115–129.

Complete Table of Contents for
RICHARD WHATELY
Elements of Rhetoric

PART IV
OF ELOCUTION, OR DELIVERY

ELEMENTS OF RHETORIC

Introduction

1

Various Definitions of Rhetoric

Of Rhetoric various definitions have been given by different writers; who, however, seem not so much to have disagreed in their conceptions of the nature of the same thing, as to have had different things in view while they employed the same term. Not only the word Rhetoric itself, but also those used in defining it, have been taken in various senses; as may be observed with respect to the word "Art" in Cicero's *De Oratore,* where a discussion is introduced as to the applicability of that term to Rhetoric; manifestly turning on the different senses in which "Art" may be understood.

To enter into an examination of all the definitions that have been given, would lead to much uninteresting and uninstructive verbal controversy. It is sufficient to put the reader on his guard against the common error of supposing that a general term has some real object, properly corresponding to it, independent of our conceptions;—that, consequently, some one definition in every case is to be found which will comprehend everything that is rightly designated by that term;—and that all others must be *erroneous:* whereas, in fact, it will often happen, as in the present instance, that both the wider, and the more restricted sense of a term, will be alike sanctioned by use (the only competent authority), and that the consequence will be a corresponding variation in the definitions employed; none of which perhaps may be fairly chargeable with error, though none can be framed that will apply to every acceptation of the term.

It is evident that in its primary signification, Rhetoric had reference to public *Speaking* alone, as its etymology implies. But as most of the rules for Speaking are of course applicable equally to Writing, an extension of the term naturally took place; and we find even Aristotle, the earliest systematic writer on the subject whose works have come down to us, including in his Treatise rules for such compositions as were not intended to be publicly recited.[1] And even as far as relates to Speeches, properly so called, he takes, in the same Treatise, at one time, a wider, and at another, a more restricted view of the subject; including under the term Rhetoric, in the opening of his work, nothing beyond the finding of topics of Persuasion, as far as regards the *matter* of what is spoken; and afterwards embracing the consideration of Style, Arrangement, and Delivery.

The invention of Printing, by extending the sphere of operation of the Writer, has of course contributed to the extension of those terms which, in

---

[1] Aristotle, *Rhetoric,* Bk. III.

their primary signification, had reference to Speaking alone. Many objects are now accomplished through the medium of the Press, which formerly came under the exclusive province of the Orator; and the qualifications requisite for success are so much the same in both cases, that we apply the term "Eloquent" as readily to a Writer as to a Speaker; though, etymologically considered, it could only belong to the latter. Indeed "Eloquence" is often attributed even to such compositions,—*e. g.* Historical works,—as have in view an object entirely different from any that could be proposed by an Orator; because *some part* of the rules to be observed in Oratory, or rules analogous to these, are applicable to such compositions. Conformably to this view, therefore, some writers have spoken of Rhetoric as the Art of Composition, universally; or, with the exclusion of Poetry alone, as embracing all Prose-composition.

A still wider extension of the province of Rhetoric has been contended for by some of the ancient writers; who, thinking it necessary to include, as belonging to the Art, everything that could conduce to the attainment of the object proposed, introduced into their systems, Treatises on Law, Morals, Politics, &c., on the ground that a knowledge of these subjects was requisite to enable a man to speak well on them: and even insisted on Virtue [2] as an essential qualification of a perfect Orator; because a good character, which can in no way be so surely established as by deserving it, has great weight with the audience.

Aristotle's Censure of His Predecessors

These notions are combated by Aristotle; who attributes them either to the ill-cultivated understanding of those who maintained them, or to their arrogant and pretending disposition *i. e.* a desire to extol and magnify the Art they professed. In the present day, the extravagance of such doctrines is so apparent to most readers, that it would not be worth while to take much pains in refuting them. It is worthy of remark, however, that the very same erroneous view is, even now, often taken of Logic; [3] which has been considered by some as a kind of system of universal knowledge, on the ground that Argument may be employed on all subjects, and that no one can argue well on a subject which he does not understand; and which has been complained of by others for not supplying any such universal instruction as its unskilful advocates have placed within its province; such as in fact no one Art or System can possibly afford.

The error is precisely the same in respect of Rhetoric and of Logic; both being *instrumental* arts; and, as such, *applicable* to various kind of subject-matter, which do not properly *come under* them.

So judicious an author as Quintilian would not have failed to perceive, had he not been carried away by an inordinate veneration for his own Art,

[2] See Quintilian.
[3] Whately, *Elements of Logic*, Introd.

that as the possession of building materials is no part of the art of Architecture, though it is impossible to build without materials, so, the knowledge of the subjects on which the Orator is to speak, constitutes no part of the art of Rhetoric, though it be essential to its successful employment; and though virtue, and the good reputation it procures, add materially to the Speaker's influence, they are no more to be, for that reason, considered as belonging to the Orator, as such, than wealth, rank, or a good person, which manifestly have a tendency to produce the same effect.

Extremes in the Limitation and Extension of the Province of Rhetoric

In the present day, however, the province of Rhetoric, in the widest acceptation that would be reckoned admissible, comprehends all "Composition in Prose;" in the narrowest sense, it would be limited to "Persuasive Speaking."

Object of the Present Treatise

I propose in the present work to adopt a middle course between these two extreme points; and to treat of "Argumentative Composition," *generally,* and *exclusively;* considering Rhetoric (in conformity with the very just and philosophical view of Aristotle) as an off-shoot from Logic.

See "Antistophos" in Aristotle – Answering or Compliment more than Subdivision or secondary off shoot

Philosophy and Rhetoric Compared

I remarked in treating of that Science, that Reasoning may be considered as applicable to two purposes, which I ventured to designate respectively by the terms "Inferring," and "Proving;" *i. e.* the *ascertainment* of the truth by investigation, and the *establishment* of it to the satisfaction of *another:* and I there remarked, that Bacon, in his *Organon,* has laid down rules for the conduct of the former of these processes, and that the latter belongs to the province of Rhetoric: and it was added, that to *infer* is to be regarded as the proper office of the Philosopher, or the Judge;—to *prove,* of the Advocate. It is not however to be understood that Philosophical works are to be excluded from the class to which Rhetorical rules are applicable; for the Philosopher who undertakes, by writing or speaking, to convey his notions to others, assumes, for the time being, the character of Advocate of the doctrines he maintains. The process of *investigation* must be supposed completed, and certain conclusions arrived at by that process, *before* he begins to impart his ideas to others in a treatise or lecture; the object of which must of course be to *prove* the justness of those conclusions. And in doing this, he will not always find it expedient to adhere to the same course of reasoning by which his own discoveries were originally made; other arguments may occur to him afterwards, more clear, or more concise, or better adapted to the understanding of those he addresses. In explaining therefore, and establishing the truth, he may often have occasion for rules of a different kind from those employed in its discovery. Accordingly, when I remarked, in the work above alluded to, that it is a common fault, for those engaged in Philosophical and Theological inquiries, to forget their own peculiar office, and assume that of the Advocate, improperly, this caution is to be understood as applicable to the process of *forming their own opinions;* not, as excluding them from advocating by all fair arguments, the conclusions at which they have arrived by candid investigation. But if this candid investigation do not take place in the first instance, no pains that they may bestow in searching for arguments, will have any tendency to ensure their attainment of truth. If a man begins (as is too plainly a frequent mode of proceeding) by hastily adopting, or strongly leaning to, some opinion which suits his inclination, or which is sanctioned by some authority that he blindly venerates, and then studies with the utmost dilgence, not as an Investigator of Truth, but as an Advocate labouring to prove his point, his talents and his researches, whatever effect they may produce in making converts to his notions, will avail nothing in enlightening his own judgment, and securing him from error.[4]

Composition, however, of the Argumentative kind, may be considered (as has been above stated) as coming under the province of Rhetoric. And this view of the subject is the less open to objection, inasmuch as it is not likely to lead to discussions that can be deemed superfluous, even by those who may choose to consider Rhetoric in the most restricted sense, as relating only to "Persuasive Speaking;" since it is evident that *Argument* must be, in most cases at least, the basis of Persuasion.

Plan of the Present Treatise

I propose then to treat, first and principally, of the Discovery of ARGUMENTS, and of their Arrangement; secondly, to lay down some Rules respecting the excitement and management of what are commonly called the *Passions,* (including every kind of Feeling, Sentiment, or Emotion,) with a view to the attainment of any object proposed,—principally, Persuasion, in the strict sense, *i. e.* the influencing of the WILL; thirdly, to offer some remarks on STYLE; and, fourthly, to treat of ELOCUTION.

2

History of Rhetoric

It may be expected that, before I proceed to treat of the Art in question, I should present the reader with a sketch of its history. Little however is required to be said on this head, because the present is not one of those branches of study in which we can trace with interest a progressive improvement from age to age. It is one, on the contrary, to which more attention appears to have been paid, and in which greater proficiency is supposed to have been made, in the earliest days of Science and Literature, than at any subsequent period.

4 See "Essay on the Love of Truth," 2nd Series.

Aristotle

Among the ancients, Aristotle, the earliest whose works are extant, may safely be pronounced to be also the best of the systematic writers on Rhetoric.

Cicero

Cicero is hardly to be reckoned among the number; for he delighted so much more in the practice, than in the theory, of his art, that he is perpetually drawn off from the rigid philosophical analysis of its principles, into discursive declamations, always eloquent indeed, and often highly interesting, but adverse to regularity of system, and frequently as unsatisfactory to the practical student as to the Philosopher. He abounds indeed with excellent practical remarks; though the best of them are scattered up and down his works with much irregularity: but his precepts, though of great weight, as being the result of experience, are not often traced up by him to first principles; and we are frequently left to guess, not only on what basis his rules are grounded, but in what cases they are applicable. Of this latter defect a remarkable instance will be hereafter cited.[5]

Quintilian

Quintilian *is* indeed a systematic writer; but cannot be considered as having much extended the philosophical views of his predecessors in this department. He possessed much good sense, but this was tinctured with pedantry;—with that *pretension,* as Aristotle calls it, which extends to an extravagant degree the province of the art which he professes. A great part of his work indeed is a Treatise on Education, generally; in the conduct of which he was no mean proficient; for such was the importance attached to public speaking, even long after the downfall of the Republic had cut off the Orator from the hopes of attaining, through the means of this qualification, the highest political importance, that he who was nominally a Professor of Rhetoric, had in fact the most important branches of instruction entrusted to his care.

Many valuable maxims however are to be found in this author; but he wanted the profundity of thought and power of analysis which Aristotle possessed.

The writers on Rhetoric among the ancients whose works are lost, seem to have been numerous; but most of them appear to have confined themselves to a very narrow view of the subject; and to have been occupied, as Aristotle complains, with the minor details of style and arrangement, and with the sophistical tricks and petty artifices of the Pleader, instead of giving a masterly and comprehensive sketch of the essentials.

[5] See Part I. ch. 3. § v.

Bacon

Among the moderns, few writers of ability have turned their thoughts to the subject; and but little has been added, either in respect of matter, or of system, to what the ancients have left us. Bacon's "Antitheta" however,—the Rhetorical common-places,—are a wonderful specimen of acuteness of thought and pointed conciseness of expression. I have accordingly placed a selection of them in the Appendix.[6]

Campbell

It were most unjust in this place to leave unnoticed Dr. Campbell's *Philosophy of Rhetoric:* a work which has not obtained indeed so high a degree of popular favour as Dr. Blair's once enjoyed, but is incomparably superior to it, not only in depth of thought and ingenious original research, but also in practical utility to the student. The title of Dr. Campbell's work has perhaps deterred many readers, who have concluded it to be more abstruse and less popular in its character than it really is. Amidst much however that is readily understood by any moderately intelligent reader, there is much also that calls for some exertion of thought, which the indolence of most readers refuses to bestow. And it must be owned that he also in some instances perplexes his readers by being perplexed himself, and bewildered in the discussion of questions through which he does not clearly see his way. His great defect, which not only leads him into occasional errors, but leaves many of his best ideas but imperfectly developed, is his ignorance and utter misconception of the nature and object of Logic; on which some remarks are made in my Treatise on that Science. Rhetoric being in truth an off-shoot of Logic, that Rhetorician must labour under great disadvantages who is not only ill-acquainted with that system, but also utterly unconscious of his deficiency.

3

From a general view of the history of Rhetoric, two questions naturally suggest themselves, which, on examination, will be found very closely connected together: first, what is the cause of the careful and extensive cultivation, among the ancients, of an Art which the moderns have comparatively neglected; and secondly, whether the former or the latter are to be regarded as the wiser in this respect;—in other words, whether Rhetoric be *worth* any diligent cultivation.

6 See Appendix, [A.]

Assiduous Cultivation of Rhetoric by the Ancients

With regard to the first of these questions, the answer generally given is, that the nature of the Government in the ancient democratical States caused a demand for public speakers, and for such speakers as should be able to gain influence not only with educated persons in dispassionate deliberation, but with a promiscuous multitude; and accordingly it is remarked that the extinction of liberty brought with it, or at least brought after it, the decline of Eloquence; as is justly remarked (though in a courtly form) by the author of the dialogue on Oratory, which passes under the name of Tacitus: "What need is there of long discourses in the Senate, when the best of its members speedily come to an agreement? or of numerous harangues to the people, when deliberations on public affairs are conducted, not by a multitude of unskilled persons, but by a single individual, and that, the wisest?"

The Ancients Hearers Rather than Readers

This account of the matter is undoubtedly correct as far as it goes; but the importance of public speaking is so great, in our own, and all other countries that are not under a despotic Government, that the apparent neglect of the study of Rhetoric seems to require some further explanation. Part of this explanation may be supplied by the consideration that the difference in this respect between the ancients and ourselves is not so great in reality as in appearance. When the *only* way of addressing the Public was by orations, and when all political measures were debated in popular assemblies, the characters of Orator, Author, and Politician, almost entirely coincided; he who would communicate his ideas to the world, or would gain political power, and carry his legislative schemes into effect, was necessarily a Speaker; since, as Pericles is made to remark by Thucydides, "one who forms a judgment on any point, but cannot explain himself clearly to the people, might as well have never thought at all on the subject." [7] The consequence was, that almost all who sought, and all who professed to give, instruction, in the principles of Government, and the conduct of judicial proceedings, combined these, in their minds and in their practice, with the study of Rhetoric, which was necessary to give effect to all such attainments; and in time the Rhetorical writers (of whom Aristotle makes that complaint) came to consider the Science of Legislation and of Politics in general, as part of their own Art.

Much therefore of what was formerly studied under the name of Rhetoric, is still, under other names, as generally and as diligently studied as ever. Much of what we now call Literature or "Belles Lettres," was formerly included in what the ancients called Rhetorical studies.

[7] Thucydides, book ii. See the Motto.

Disavowal of Rhetorical Studies among the Moderns

It cannot be denied however that a great difference, though less, as I have said, than might at first sight appear, does exist between the ancients and the moderns in this point;—that what is strictly and properly called Rhetoric, is much less studied, at least less systematically studied, now, than formerly. Perhaps this also may be in some measure accounted for from the circumstances which have been just noticed. Such is the distrust excited by any suspicion of Rhetorical artifice, that every speaker or writer who is anxious to carry his point, endeavours to disown or to keep out of sight any superiority of skill; and wishes to be considered as relying rather on the strength of his cause, and the soundness of his views, than on his ingenuity and expertness as an advocate. Hence it is, that even those who have paid the greatest and the most successful attention to the study of Composition and of Elocution, are so far from encouraging others by example or recommendation to engage in the same pursuit, that they labour rather to conceal and disavow their own proficiency; and thus theoretical rules are decried, even by those who owe the most to them. Whereas among the ancients, the same cause did not, for the reasons lately mentioned, operate to the same extent; since, however careful any speaker might be to disown the artifices of Rhetoric, properly so called, he would not be ashamed to acknowledge himself, generally, a student, or a proficient, in an Art which was understood to include the elements of Political wisdom.

4

Utility of Rhetoric

With regard to the other question proposed, viz. concerning the utility of Rhetoric, it is to be observed that it divides itself into two; first, whether Oratorical skill be, on the whole, a public benefit, or evil; and secondly, whether any artificial system of Rules is conducive to the attainment of that skill.

The former of these questions was eagerly debated among the ancients; on the latter, but little doubt seems to have existed. With us, on the contrary, the state of these questions seems nearly reversed. It seems generally admitted that skill in Composition and in speaking, liable as it evidently is to abuse, is to be considered, on the whole, as advantageous to the Public; because that liability to abuse is, neither in this, nor in any other case, to be considered as conclusive against the utility of any kind of art, faculty, or profession;—because the evil effects of misdirected power require that equal powers should be arrayed on the opposite side;—and because truth, having an intrinsic superiority over falsehood, may be expected to prevail when the skill of the contending parties is equal; which will be the more likely to take place, the more widely such skill is diffused.[8]

Eloquence Supposed to Be Something that Cannot Be Taught

But many, perhaps most persons, are inclined to the opinion that Eloquence, either in writing or speaking, is either a natural gift, or, at least, is to be acquired by mere practice, and is not to be attained or improved by any system of rules. And this opinion is favoured not least by those (as has been just observed) whose own experience would enable them to decide very differently; and it certainly seems to be in a great degree practically adopted. Most persons, if not left entirely to the disposal of chance in respect of this branch of education, are at least left to acquire what they can by *practice*, such as school or college-exercises afford, without much care being taken to initiate them systematically into the principles of the Art; and that, frequently, not so much from negligence in the conductors of education, as from their doubts of the utility of any such regular system.

Erroneous Systems of Rules

It certainly must be admitted, that rules not constructed on broad philosophical principles, are more likely to cramp than to assist the operations of our faculties;—that a pedantic display of technical skill is more detrimental in this than in any other pursuit, since by exciting distrust, it counteracts the very purpose of it;—that a system of rules imperfectly comprehended, or not familiarized by practice, will (while that continues to be the case) prove rather an impediment than a help; as indeed will be found in all other arts likewise;—and that no system can be expected to equalize men whose natural powers are different. But none of these concessions at all invalidate the positions of Aristotle; that some succeed better than others in explaining their opinions, and bringing over others to them; and that, not merely by superiority of natural gifts, but by acquired habit; and that consequently if we can discover the causes of this superior success,—the means by which the desired end is attained by all who *do* attain it,—we shall be in possession of rules capable of general application; which is, says he, the proper office of an Art. Experience so plainly evinces, what indeed we might naturally be led antecedently to conjecture, that a right judgment on any subject is not necessarily accompanied by skill in effecting conviction,—nor the ability to discover truth, by a facility in explaining it,—that it might be matter of

---

8 Aristotle, *Rhetoric* ch. 1. He might have gone further; for it will very often happen that, before a popular audience, a *greater* degree of skill is requisite for maintaining the cause of truth than of falsehood. There are cases in which the arguments which lie most on the surface, and are, to superficial reasoners, the most easily set forth in a plausible form, are those on the wrong side. It is often difficult to a Writer, and still more, to a Speaker, to point out and exhibit, in their full strength, the delicate distinctions on which truth sometimes depends.

wonder how any doubt should ever have existed as to the possibility of devising, and the utility of employing, a System of Rules for "Argumentative Composition" generally; distinct from any system conversant about the subject-matter of each composition.

Knowledge of Facts No Remedy for Logical Inaccuracy

I have remarked in the Lectures on Political Economy (Lect. 9.) that "some persons complain, not altogether without reason, of the prevailing *ignorance* of facts, relative to this and to many other subjects; and yet it will often be found that the parties censured, though possessed of less knowledge than they ought to have, yet possess more than they know what to do with. Their deficiency in arranging and applying their knowledge,—in combining facts,—and correctly deducing and employing general principles, shall be greater than their ignorance of facts. Now to attempt remedying this fault by imparting to them additional knowledge,—to confer the advantage of wider experience on those who have not the power of profiting by experience,—is to attempt enlarging the prospect of a short-sighted man by bringing him to the top of a hill.

"In the tale of Sandford and Merton, where the two boys are described as amusing themselves with building a hovel with their own hands, they lay poles horizontally on the top, and cover them with straw, so as to make a flat roof: of course the rain comes through; and Master Merton then advises to *lay on more straw:* but Sandford, the more intelligent boy, remarks that as long as the roof is flat, the rain must, sooner or later, soak through; and that the remedy is to make a new *arrangement,* and form the roof sloping. Now the idea of enlightening incorrect reasoners by additional knowledge, is an error similar to that of the flat roof; it is merely laying on *more straw:* they ought first to be taught the right way of raising the roof. Of course knowledge is necessary; so is straw to thatch the roof: but no quantity of materials will supply the want of knowing how to build.

✓ "I believe it to be a prevailing fault of the present day, not indeed to seek too much for knowledge, but to trust to accumulation of facts as a *substitute* for accuracy in the logical processes. Had Bacon lived in the present day, I am inclined to think he would have made his chief complaint against unmethodized inquiry and illogical reasoning. Certainly he would *not* have complained of *Dialectics* as corrupting Philosophy. To guard *now* against the evils prevalent in *his* time, would be to fortify a town against battering-rams, instead of against cannon. But it is remarkable that even that abuse of Dialectics which he complains of, was rather an error connected with the reasoning-process than one arising from a want of knowledge. Men were led to false conclusions, not through mere ignorance, but from hastily assuming the correctness of the data they reasoned from, without sufficient grounds. And it is remarkable that the revolution brought about in philosophy by Bacon, was not the *effect,* but the *cause,* of increased knowledge of physical facts: it was not that men were taught to think correctly by having new phenomena brought to light; but on the contrary, they discovered new phenomena in *consequence* of a new system of philosophizing."

It is probable that the existing prejudices on the present subject may be traced in great measure to the imperfect or incorrect notions of some writers, who have either confined their attention to trifling minutiæ of style, or at least have in some respect failed to take a sufficiently comprehensive view of the principles of the Art. One distinction especially is to be clearly laid down and carefully borne in mind by those who would form a correct idea of those principles; viz. the distinction already noticed in the *Elements of Logic,* between *an* Art, and *the* Art. "*An* Art of Reasoning" would imply, "a Method or System of Rules by the observance of which one may reason correctly;" "*the* Art of Reasoning" would imply a System of Rules to which every one *does* conform (whether knowingly, or not,) who reasons correctly: and such is Logic, considered as an Art.

A Rightly-Formed System Does Not Cramp the Natural Powers

In like manner "*an* Art of Composition" would imply "a System of Rules by which a good Composition may be produced;" "*the* Art of Composition," —"such rules as *every* good Composition must conform to," whether the author of it had them in his mind or not. Of the former character appear to have been (among others) many of the Logical and Rhetorical Systems of Aristotle's predecessors in those departments. He himself evidently takes the other and more philosophical view of both branches: as appears (in the case of Rhetoric) both from the plan he sets out with, that of investigating the causes of the success of *all* who do succeed in effecting conviction, and from several passages occurring in various parts of his treatise; which indicate how sedulously he was on his guard to conform to that plan. Those who have not attended to the important distinction just alluded to, are often disposed to feel wonder, if not weariness, at his reiterated remarks, that "*all* men effect persuasion either in this way or in that;" "it is *impossible* to attain such and such an object in any other way," &c.; which doubtless were intended to remind his readers of the nature of his design; viz. not to teach *an* Art of Rhetoric, but *the* Art; not to instruct them merely how conviction *might* be produced, but how it *must*.[9]

If this distinction were carefully kept in view by the teacher and by the learner of Rhetoric, we should no longer hear complaints of the natural powers being fettered by the formalities of a System; since no such complaint can lie against a System whose rules are drawn from the invariable practice of all who succeed in attaining their proposed object.

No one would expect that the study of Sir Joshua Reynolds's lectures would cramp the genius of the painter. No one complains of the rules of

9 See Appendix, note (AA.).

Grammar as fettering Language; because it is understood that correct use is not founded on Grammar, but Grammar on correct use. A just system of Logic or of Rhetoric is analogous, in this respect, to Grammar.

Popular Objections

One may still however sometimes hear—though less, now, than a few years back—the hackneyed objections against Logic and Rhetoric, and even Grammar also. Cicero has been gravely cited (as Aristotle might have been also, in the passage just above alluded to, in his very treatise on Rhetoric) to testify that rhetorical rules are derived from the practice of Oratory, and not *vice versâ;* and that consequently there must have been—as there still is—such a thing as a speaker ignorant of those rules. A drayman, we are told, will taunt a comrade by saying, "you're a pretty fellow," without having learnt that he is employing the figure called Irony; and may employ "will" and "shall" correctly, without being able to explain the principle that guides him. And it might have been added, that perhaps he will go home whistling a tune, though he does not know the name of a Note; that he will stir his fire, without knowing that he is employing the first kind of Lever; and that he will set his kettle on it to boil, though ignorant of the theory of Caloric, and of all the technical vocabulary of Chemistry. In short, of the two premises requisite for the conclusion contended for, the one about which there can be no possible doubt, is dwelt on, and elaborately proved; and the other, which is very disputable, is tacitly assumed. That the systems of Logic, Rhetoric, Grammar, Music, Mechanics, &c. must have been preceded by the practice of speaking, singing, &c., which no one ever did or can doubt, is earnestly insisted on; but that every system of which this can be said must consequently be mere useless trifling, which is at least a paradox, is quietly taken for granted; or, at least, is supposed to be sufficiently established, by repeating, in substance, the poet's remark, that

> ". . . all a Rhetorician's rules
> But teach him how to name his tools:"

and by observing that, for the most difficult points of all, natural genius and experience must do everything, and Systems of Art nothing.

To this latter remark it might have been added, that in *no* department can Systems of Art equalize men of different degrees of original ability and of experience; or teach us to accomplish all that is aimed at. No system of Agriculture can create Land; nor can the Art Military teach us to produce, like Cadmus, armed soldiers out of the Earth; though Land, and Soldiers, are as essential to the practice of these Arts, as the well-known preliminary admonition in the Cookery-book, "first take your carp," is to the culinary art. Nor can all the books that ever were written bring to a level with a man of military genius and experience, a person of ordinary ability who has never seen service.

As for the remark about "naming one's tools," which—with fair allowance for poetical exaggeration—may be admitted to be near the truth, it should be remembered, that if an inference be thence drawn of the uselessness of being thus provided with *names,* we must admit, by parity of reasoning, that it would be no inconvenience to a carpenter, or any other mechanic, to have no names for the several operations of *sawing, planing, boring,* &c. in which he is habitually engaged, or for the tools with which he performs them; and in like manner, that it would also be no loss to be without names—or without precise, appropriate, and brief names—for the various articles of dress and furniture that we use,—for the limbs and other bodily organs, and the plants, animals, and other objects around us;—in short, that it would be little or no evil to have a Language as imperfect as Chinese, or no Language at all.

Technical Terms

The simple truth is, TECHNICAL TERMS are a PART OF LANGUAGE. Now any portion of one's Language that relates to employments and situations foreign from our own, there is little need to be acquainted with. Nautical terms, *e. g.* it is little loss to a land-man to be ignorant of; though, to a sailor, they are as needful as any part of Language is to any one. And again, a deficiency in the proper Language of some *one* department, even though one we are not wholly unconcerned in, is not felt as a very heavy inconvenience. But if it were absolutely no disadvantage at all, then, it is plain the same might be said of a still *further* deficiency of a like character; and ultimately we should arrive at the absurdity above noticed,—the uselessness of Language altogether.

Real Use of Language

But though this is an absurdity which all would perceive,—though none would deny the importance of Language,—the full extent and real character of that importance is far from being universally understood. There are still (as is remarked in the Logic, Introd. § 5.) many,—though I believe not near so many as a few years back,—who, if questioned on the subject, would answer that the use of Language is to *communicate* our thoughts to each other; and that it is peculiar to Man: the truth being that *that* use of Language is *not* peculiar to Man, though enjoyed by him in a much higher degree than by the Brutes; while that which does distinguish Man from Brute, is another, and quite distinct, use of Language, viz. as an *instrument* of *thought,*—a system of General-Signs, without which the Reasoning-process could not be conducted. The full importance, consequently, of Language, and of precise technical Language,—of having accurate and well-defined "names for one's tools,"—can never be duly appreciated by those who still cling to the theory of "Ideas;" those imaginary objects of thought in the mind, of which "Common-terms" are merely the names, and by means of which we are supposed to be able to do what I am convinced is impossible; to carry on a train of Reasoning without the use of Language, or of any General-Signs whatever.

But each, in proportion as he the more fully embraces the doctrine of *Nominalism,* and consequently understands the real character of Language, will become the better qualified to estimate the importance of an accurate system of nomenclature.

5

Exercises in Composition

The chief reason probably for the existing prejudice against technical systems of composition, is to be found in the cramped, meagre, and feeble character of most of such essays, &c. as are *avowedly* composed according to the rules of any such system. It should be remembered, however, in the first place, that these are almost invariably the productions of *learners;* it being usual for those who have attained proficiency, either to write without thinking of any rules, or to be desirous (as has been said) , and, by their increased expertness, able, to conceal their employment of art. Now it is not fair to judge of the value of any system of rules,—those of a drawing-master for instance,—from the first awkward sketches of tyros in the art.

Still less would it be fair to judge of one system from the ill-success of another, whose rules were framed (as is the case with those ordinarily laid down for the use of students in Composition) on narrow, unphilosophical, and erroneous principles.

Choice of Subjects for the Composition of Exercises

But the circumstance which has mainly tended to produce the complaint alluded to, is, that in this case, the reverse takes place of the plan pursued in the learning of other arts; in which it is usual to begin, for the sake of practice, with what is *easiest:* here, on the contrary, the tyro has usually a *harder* task assigned him, and one in which he is less likely to succeed, than he will meet with in the actual business of life. For it is undeniable that it is much the most difficult to find either propositions to maintain, or arguments to prove them—to know, in short, what to say, or how to say it—on any subject on which one has hardly any information, and no interest; about which he knows little, and cares still less.

Now the subjects usually proposed for School or College-exercises are (to the learners themselves) precisely of this description. And hence it commonly happens, that an exercise composed with diligent care by a young student, though it will have cost him far more pains than a *real* letter written by him to his friends, on subjects that interest him, will be very greatly inferior to it. On the *real occasions* of after life (I mean, when the object proposed is, not to fill up a sheet, a book, or an hour, but to communicate his thoughts, to convince, or persuade) ,—on these real occasions, for which such exercises were designed to prepare him, he will find that he writes both better, and with more facility, than on the *artificial* occasion, as it may be called, of composing a Declamation;—that he has been attempting to learn the easier, by practising the harder.

Ill Effects Often Resulting from Exercises

But what is worse, it will often happen that such exercises will have formed a habit of stringing together empty common-places, and vapid declamations,—of multiplying words and spreading out the matter thin,—of composing in a stiff, artificial, and frigid manner: and that this habit will more or less cling through life to one who has been thus trained, and will infect all his future compositions.

So strongly, it should seem, was Milton impressed with a sense of this danger, that he was led to condemn the use altogether of exercises in Composition. In this opinion he stands perhaps alone among all writers on education. I should perhaps agree with him, if there were absolutely no other remedy for the evil in question; for I am inclined to think that this part of education, if conducted as it often is, does in general more harm than good. But I am convinced, that practice in Composition, both for boys and young men, may be so conducted as to be productive of many and most essential advantages.

Selection of Subjects

The obvious and the only preventive of the evils which I have been speaking of is, a most scrupulous care in the selection of such *subjects* for exercises as are likely to be *interesting* to the student, and on which he has (or may, with pleasure, and without much toil, acquire) sufficient information. Such subjects will of course vary, according to the learner's age and intellectual advancement; but they had better be rather below, than much above him; that is, they should never be such as to induce him to string together vague general expressions, conveying no distinct ideas to his own mind, and second-hand sentiments which he does not feel. He may freely transplant indeed from other writers such thoughts as will take root in the soil of his own mind; but he must never be tempted to collect *dried specimens*. He must also be encouraged to express himself (in correct language indeed, but) in a free, natural, and simple style; which of course implies (considering who and what the writer is supposed to be) such a style as, in itself, would be open to severe criticism, and certainly very unfit to appear in a book.

Compositions on such subjects, and in such a style, would probably be regarded with a disdainful eye, as puerile, by those accustomed to the opposite mode of teaching. But it should be remembered that the compositions of boys *must* be puerile, in one way or the other: and to a person of unsophisticated and sound taste, the truly contemptible kind of puerility would be found in the other kind of exercises. Look at the letter of an intelligent youth to one of his companions, communicating intelligence of such petty matters as are interesting to both—describing the scenes he has visited, and the recreations he has enjoyed during a vacation; and you will see a picture of the youth himself—boyish indeed in looks and in stature—in dress and in demeanour; but lively, unfettered, natural, giving a fair promise for manhood, and, in short, what a boy should be. Look at a theme composed by the same youth, on "Virtus est medium vitiorum," or "Natura beatis omnibus esse dedit," and you will see a picture of the same boy, dressed up in the garb, and absurdly aping the demeanour, of an elderly man. Our ancestors (and still more recently, I believe, the continental nations) were guilty of the absurdity of dressing up children in wigs, swords, huge buckles, hoops, ruffles, and all the elaborate full-dressed finery of grown-up people of that day.[10] It is surely reasonable that the analogous absurdity in greater matters also,—among the rest in that part of education I am speaking of,—should be laid aside; and that we should in all points consider what is appropriate to each different period of life.

Classes of Subjects for Exercises

The subjects for Composition to be selected on the principle I am recommending, will generally fall under one of three classes: first, subjects drawn from the studies the learner is engaged in; relating, for instance, to the characters or incidents of any history he may be reading; and sometimes, perhaps, leading him to forestall by conjecture, something which he will hereafter come to, in the book itself: secondly, subjects drawn from any conversation he may have listened to (*with interest*) from his seniors, whether addressed to himself, or between each other: or, thirdly, relating to the amusements, familiar occurrences, and every-day-transactions, which are likely to have formed the topics of easy conversation among his familiar friends. The student should not be confined exclusively to any one of these three classes of subjects. They should be intermingled in as much variety as possible. And the teacher should frequently recall to his own mind these two considerations; first, that since the benefit proposed does not consist in the intrinsic value of the composition, but in the *exercise* to the pupil's mind, it matters not how insignificant the subject may be, if it will but interest him, and thereby afford him such exercise; secondly, that the younger and backwarder each student is, the more unfit he will be for *abstract* speculations; and the less remote must be the subjects proposed from those *individual* objects and occurrences which always form the first beginnings of the furniture of the youthful mind.[11]

10 See "Sanford and Merton," *passim.*

11 For some observations relative to the learning of Elocution, see Part IV. chap. ii. § 5, and iv. § 2. See also some valuable remarks on the subject of exercises in composition in Mr. Hill's ingenious work on Public Education. It may be added, that if the teacher will, after pointing out any faults in the learner's exercise, and making him alter or re-write

Drawing Up of Outlines or Skeletons

It should be added, as a practical rule for all cases, whether it be an exercise that is written for practice' sake, or a composition on some real occasion, that an outline should be first drawn out,—a *skeleton* as it is sometimes called,—of the substance of what is to be said. The more *briefly* this is done, so that it does but exhibit clearly the several heads of the composition, the better: because it is important that the whole of it be placed before the eye and the mind in a small compass, and be taken in as it were at a glance: and it should be written therefore not in *sentences,* but like a table of contents. Such an outline should not be allowed to *fetter* the writer, if, in the course of the actual composition, he find any reason for deviating from his original plan. It should serve merely as a *track* to mark out a path for him, not as a *groove* to confine him. But the practice of drawing out such a skeleton will give a coherence to the Composition, a due *proportion* of its several parts, and a clear and easy arrangement of them; such as can rarely be attained if one begins by *completing* one portion before thinking of the rest. And it will also be found a most useful exercise for a beginner, to practise—if possible under the eye of a judicious lecturer—the drawing out of a great number of such skeletons, more than he subsequently fills up; and likewise to practise the analysing in the same way, the Compositions of another, whether read or heard.

If the system which I have been recommending be pursued, with the addition of sedulous care in correction—encouragement from the teacher—and inculcation of such general rules as each occasion calls for; then, *and not otherwise,* Exercises in Composition will be of the most important and lasting advantage; not only in respect of the object *immediately* proposed, but in producing clearness of thought, and in giving play to all the faculties. And if this branch of education be thus conducted, then, *and not otherwise,* the greater part of the present treatise will, it is hoped, be found not much less adapted to the use of those who are writing for practice' sake, than of those engaged in meeting the occasions of real life.

---

it, if necessary, then put before him a composition on the same subject written by *himself,* or by some approved writer,—such a practice, if both learner and teacher have patience and industry enough to follow it up, will be likely to produce great improvement.

☙☙☙☙☙☙

Part I   Of the Invention, Arrangement, and Introduction of Propositions and Arguments

CHAP. I—OF PROPOSITIONS

1

Inquiry after Truth and after Arguments Distinguished

It was remarked in the Treatise on LOGIC, that in the process of *Investigation* properly so called, viz. that by which we endeavour to discover Truth, it must of course be uncertain to him who is entering on that process, what the conclusion will be to which his researches will lead; but that in the process of *conveying truth* to others by reasoning, (*i. e.* in what may be termed, according to the view I have at present taken, the *Rhetorical process,*) the conclusion or conclusions which are to be established must be present to the mind of him who is conducting the Argument, and whose business is to find *Proofs* of a given proposition.

It is evident, therefore, that the first step to be taken by him, is to lay down distinctly in his own mind the proposition or propositions to be proved. It might indeed at first sight appear superfluous even to mention so obvious a rule; but experience shows that it is by no means uncommon for a young or ill-instructed writer to content himself with such a vague and indistinct view of the point he is to aim at, that the whole train of his reasoning is in consequence affected with a corresponding perplexity, obscurity, and looseness. It may be worth while therefore to give some hints for the conduct of this preliminary process,—the choice of propositions. Not, of course, that I am supposing the author to be in doubt what opinion he shall adopt: the process of Investigation [1] (which does not fall within the province of Rhetoric) being supposed to be concluded; but still there will often be room for deliberation as to the form in which an opinion shall be stated, and, when several propositions are to be maintained, in what order they shall be placed.

Conviction and Instruction

On this head therefore I shall proceed to propose some rules; after having premised (in order to anticipate some objections or doubts which might arise) one remark relative to the object to be effected. This is, of course, what may be called, in the widest sense of the word, Conviction; but under

[1] Whately, *Logic*, book iv. chap. 3. § 2.

that term are comprehended, first, what is strictly called *Instruction;* and, secondly, *Conviction* in the narrower sense; *i. e.* the Conviction of those who are either of a *contrary opinion* to the one maintained, or who are *in doubt* whether to admit or deny it. By instruction, on the other hand, is commonly meant the conviction of those who have neither formed an opinion on the subject, nor are deliberating whether to adopt or reject the proposition in question, but are merely desirous of ascertaining *what* is the truth in respect of the case before them. The former are supposed to have before their minds the *terms* of the proposition maintained, and are called upon to consider *whether that particular proposition* be true or false; the latter are not supposed to know the terms of the conclusion, but to be inquiring *what proposition* is to be received as true. The former may be described, in logical language, as doubting respecting the *Copula;* the latter, respecting the *Predicate.* It is evident that the speaker or writer is, relatively to these last, (though not to himself,) conducting a process of Investigation; as is plain from what has been said of that subject, in the treatise on Logic.

The distinction between these two objects gives rise in some points to corresponding differences in the mode of procedure, which will be noticed hereafter; these differences however are not sufficient to require that Rhetoric should on that account be divided into two distinct branches; since, generally speaking, though not universally, the same rules will be serviceable for attaining each of these objects.

2

The first step is, as I have observed, to lay down (in the author's mind) the proposition or propositions to be maintained, clearly, and in a suitable form.

One Subject Does not Imply Unity of Composition

He who strictly observes this rule, and who is thus brought to view steadily the point he is aiming at, will be kept clear, in a great degree, of some common faults of young writers; viz. entering on too wide a field of discussion, and introducing many propositions not sufficiently connected; an error which destroys the unity of the composition. This last error those are apt to fall into, who place before themselves a *Term* instead of a *Proposition;* and imagine that because they are *treating of one thing,* they are *discussing one question.* In an ethical work, for instance, one may be *treating of virtue,* while discussing all or any of these questions; "Wherein virtue consists?" "Whence our notions of it arise?" "Whence it derives its obligations?" &c.; but if these questions were confusedly blended together, or if all of them were treated of, within a short compass, the most just remarks and forcible arguments would lose their interest and their utility, in so perplexed a composition.

Copiousness of Matter Furnished by a Restricted View

Nearly akin to this fault is the other just mentioned, that of entering on too wide a field for the length of the work; by which means the writer is confined to barren and uninteresting generalities; as *e. g.* general exhortations to virtue (conveyed, of course, in very general terms) in the space of a discourse only of sufficient length to give a characteristic description of some one branch of duty, or of some one particular motive to the practice of it. Unpractised composers are apt to fancy that they shall have the greater abundance of matter, the wider extent of subject they comprehend; but experience shows that the reverse is the fact: the more general and extensive view will often suggest nothing to the mind but vague and trite remarks; when, upon narrowing the field of discussion, many interesting questions of detail present themselves. Now a writer who is accustomed to state to himself precisely, in the first instance, the conclusions to which he is tending, will be the less likely to content himself with such as consist of very general statements; and will often be led, even where an extensive view is at first proposed, to distribute it into several branches, and, waiving the discussion of the rest, to limit himself to the full development of one or two; and thus applying, as it were, a microscope to a small space, will present to the view much that a wider survey would not have exhibited.

3

Inquiry after Propositions

It may be useful for one who is about thus to lay down his propositions, to ask himself these three questions: first, What is the fact? secondly, Why [2] (*i. e.* from what Cause) is it so? or, in other words, how is it accounted for? and thirdly, What Consequence results from it?

The last two of these questions, though they will not in every case suggest such answers as are strictly to be called the Cause and the Consequence of the principal truth to be maintained, may, at least, often furnish such propositions as bear a somewhat similar relation to it.

It is to be observed, that in recommending the writer to begin by laying down in his own mind the propositions to be maintained, it is not meant to be implied that they are always to be *stated* first; that will depend upon the nature of the case; and rules will hereafter be given on that point.

It is to be observed also, that by the words "Proposition" or "Assertion," throughout this Treatise, is to be understood some *conclusion* to be established *for itself;* not, with a view to an ulterior conclusion: those propositions which are intended to serve as *premises,* being called, in allowable conformity with popular usage, *Arguments;* it being customary to argue in the enthymematic form, and to call, for brevity's sake, the expressed premises of an enthymeme, the *argument* by which the conclusion of it is proved.[3]

[2] See Whately, *Logic.* Appendix. Article "WHY."
[3] *Logic,* book i. § 2.

CHAP. II—OF ARGUMENTS

1

Proper Province of Rhetoric

The *finding* of suitable ARGUMENTS to prove a given point, and the skilful *arrangement* of them, may be considered as the immediate and proper province of Rhetoric, and of that alone.[1]

The business of Logic is, as Cicero complains, to *judge* of arguments, not to *invent* them: ("in inveniendis argumentis muta nimium est; in judicandis, nimium loquax)." [2] The knowledge, again, in each case, of the subject in hand, is essential; but it is evidently borrowed from the science or system conversant about that subject-matter, whether Politics, Theology, Law, Ethics, or any other. The art of addressing the feelings, again, does not belong exclusively to Rhetoric; since Poetry has at least as much to do with that branch. Nor are the considerations relative to Style and Elocution confined to argumentative and persuasive compositions. The art of *inventing* and *arranging Arguments* is, as has been said, the only province that Rhetoric can claim entirely and exclusively.

Various Divisions of Arguments

Arguments are divided according to several different principles; *i. e.* logically speaking, there are *several divisions* of them. And these *cross-divisions* have proved a source of endless perplexity to the Logical and Rhetorical student, because there is perhaps no writer on either subject that has been aware of their character. Hardly any thing perhaps has contributed so much to lessen the interest and the utility of systems of Rhetoric, as the indistinctness hence resulting. When in any subject the members of a division are not *opposed,* [contradistinguished,] but are in fact members of *different* divisions, *crossing* each other, it is manifestly impossible to obtain any clear notion of the Species treated of; nor will any labour or ingenuity bestowed on the subject be of the least avail, till the original source of perplexity is removed;—till, in short, the cross-division is detected and explained.

Arguments then may be divided.

First, into Irregular, and Regular, *i. e.* Syllogisms; these last into Categor-

---

1 Aristotle's division of Persuasives into "artificial" and "inartificial," including under the latter head, "Witnesses, Laws, Contracts," &c., is strangely unphilosophical. The one class, he says, the Orator is to make use of; the other, to devise. But it is evident that, in all cases alike, the *data* we argue *from* must be something already existing, and which we are not to make, but to use; and that the *arguments* derived from these data are the work of Art. Whether these data are general maxims or particular testimony—Laws of Nature, or Laws of the Land—makes, in this respect, no difference.

2 Cicero, *De Oratore.*

ical and Hypothetical; and the Categorical, into Syllogisms in the first Figure, and in the other Figures, &c. &c.

Secondly, They are frequently divided into "Probable," [or "Moral,"] and "Demonstrative," [or "Necessary."]

Thirdly, into the "Direct," and the "Indirect;" [or *reductio ad absurdum,*]—the Deictic, and the Elenctic, of Aristotle.

Fourthly, into Arguments from "Example," from "Testimony," from "Cause to Effect," from "Analogy," &c. &c.

It ill be perceived, on attentive examination, that several of the different species just mentioned will occasionally *contain* each other; *e. g.* a Probable Argument may be at the same time a Categorical Argument, a Direct Argument, and an Argument from Testimony, &c.; this being the consequence of Arguments having been divided on *several different principles;* a circumstance so obvious the moment it is distinctly stated, that I apprehend such of my readers as have not been conversant in these studies will hardly be disposed to believe that it could have been (as in the fact) generally overlooked, and that eminent writers should in consequence have been involved in inextricable confusion. I need only remind them however of the anecdote of Columbus breaking the egg. That which is perfectly obvious to any man of common sense, as soon as it is mentioned, may nevertheless fail to occur, even to men of considerable ingenuity.

Division of Forms of Arguments

It will also be readily perceived, on examining the principles of these several divisions, that the last of them alone is properly and strictly a division of *Arguments as such.* The First is evidently a division of the *Forms of stating them;* for every one would allow that the *same* Argument may be either stated as an enthymeme, or brought into the strict syllogistic form; and that, either categorically or hypothetically, &c.; *e. g.* "Whatever has a beginning has a cause; the earth had a beginning, therefore it had a cause; or, *If* the earth had a beginning, it had a cause: it had a beginning," &c. every one would call the *same* Argument, differently stated. This, therefore, evidently is not a division of Arguments *as such.*

Subject-Matter of Arguments

The Second is plainly a division of Arguments according to their *subject-matter,* whether Necessary or Probable, [certain or uncertain.] In Mathematics, *e. g.* every proposition that can be stated is either an immutable truth, or an absurdity and self-contradiction; while in human affairs the propositions which we assume are only true for the most part, and as general rules; and in Physics, though they must be true as long as the laws of nature remain undisturbed, the contradiction of them does not imply an absurdity; and the conclusions, of course, in each case, have the same degree and kind of certainty with the premises. This therefore is properly a division, not of *Arguments* as such, but of the *Propositions* of which they consist.

Purposes of Arguments

The Third is a division of Arguments according to the purpose for which they are employed; according to the *intention* of the reasoner; whether that be to establish "directly" [or "ostensively"] the conclusion drawn, or ["indirectly"] by means of an absurd conclusion to disprove one of the premises; (*i. e.* to prove its contradictory:) since the alternative proposed in *every* valid Argument is, *either* to admit the Conclusion, or to deny one of the Premises. Now it may so happen that in some cases, one person will choose the former, and another the latter, of these alternatives. It is probable, *e. g.* that many have been induced to admit the doctrine of Transubstantiation, from its clear connexion with the infallibility of the Romish Church; and many others, by the very same Argument, have surrendered their belief in that infallibility. Again, Berkeley and Reid seem to have alike admitted that the non-existence of matter was a necessary consequence of Locke's Theory of Ideas: but the former was hence led, *bonâ fide,* to admit and advocate that non-existence; while the latter was led by the very same Argument to reject the Ideal Theory. Thus, we see it is possible for the very same Argument to be Direct to one person, and Indirect to another; leading them to different results, according as they judge the original conclusion, or the contradictory of a premise, to be the more probable. This, therefore, is not properly a division of Arguments as such, but a division of *the purposes for which* they are on each occasion employed.

Division of Arguments as Such

The Fourth, which alone is properly a division of Arguments *as such,* and accordingly will be principally treated of, is a division according to the "relation of the subject-matter of the premises to that of the conclusion." I say, "of the subject-matter," because the *logical* connexion between the premises and conclusion is independent of the meaning of the terms employed, and may be exhibited with letters of the alphabet substituted for the terms; but the relation I am now speaking of between the premises and conclusion, (and the varieties of which form the several species of Arguments,) is in respect of their *subject-matter:* as *e. g.* an "Argument from Cause to Effect" is so called and considered, in reference to the relation existing between the premise, which is the Cause, and the conclusion, which is the Effect; and an "Argument from Example," in like manner, from the relation between a *known* and an *unknown* instance, both belonging to the same class. And it is plain that the present division, though it has a reference to the subject-matter of the premises, is yet not a division of *propositions* considered by themselves, (as in the case with the division into "probable" and "demonstrative,") but of *Arguments* considered as such; for when we say, *e. g.* that the premise is a Cause, and the conclusion the Effect, these expressions are evidently *relative,* and have no meaning, except in reference to each other; and so also when we say that the premise and the conclusion are two *parallel* cases, that very expression denotes their relation to each other.

In the Table [on the next page] I have sketched an outline of the several divisions of arguments here treated of.

2

Two Classes of Arguments

In distributing, then, the several kinds of Arguments, according to this division, it will be found convenient to lay down first two great classes, under one or other of which all can be brought; viz. first, such Arguments as might have been employed—not *as* arguments, but—to *account for* the fact or principle maintained, supposing its truth granted: secondly, such as could *not* be so employed. The former class (to which in this Treatise the name of *"A priori"* Argument will be confined) is manifestly Argument from *Cause* to Effect; since to *account* for any thing, signifies, to assign the Cause of it. The other class, of course, comprehends all other Arguments; of which there are several kinds, which will be mentioned hereafter.

The two sorts of proof which have been just spoken of, Aristotle seems to have intended to designate by the titles of ὅτι for the latter, and διότι for the former; but he has not been so clear as could be wished in observing the distinction between them. The only decisive test by which to distinguish the Arguments which belong to the one, and to the other, of these classes, is, to ask the question, "Supposing the proposition in question to be admitted, would this statement here used as an Argument, serve to *account* for and explain the truth, or not?" It will then be readily referred to the former or to the latter class, according as the answer is in the affirmative or the negative; as, *e.g.* if a murder were imputed to any one on the grounds of his "having a hatred to the deceased, and an interest in his death," the Argument would belong to the former class; because, *supposing* his guilt to be *admitted,* and an inquiry to be made how he can commit the murder, the circumstances just mentioned would serve to *account* for it; but not so, with respect to such an Argument as his "having blood on his clothes;" which would therefore be referred to the other class.

And here let it be observed, once for all, that when I speak of arguing from Cause to Effect, it is not intended to maintain the real and proper efficacy of what are called Physical Causes to produce their respective Effects, nor to enter into any discussion of the controversies which have been raised on that point; which would be foreign from the present purpose. The word "Cause," therefore, is to be understood as employed in the popular sense; as well as the phrase of "accounting for" any fact.

TABLE

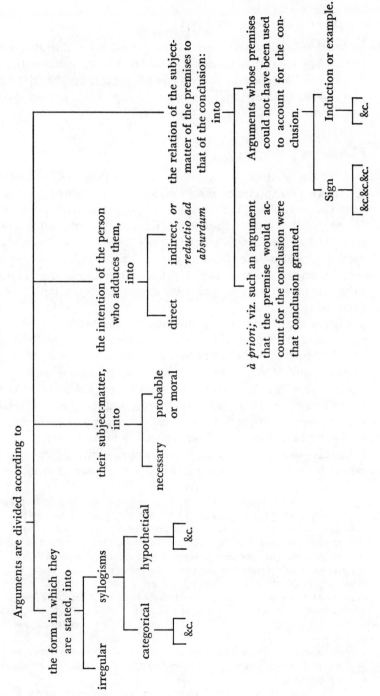

Arguments are divided according to

the form in which they are stated, into

- irregular
- syllogisms
  - categorical
    - &c.
  - hypothetical
    - &c.

their subject-matter, into

- necessary
- probable or moral

the intention of the person who adduces them, into

- direct
- indirect, *or reductio ad absurdum*

the relation of the subject-matter of the premises to that of the conclusion: into

- *à priori*; viz. such an argument that the premise would account for the conclusion were that conclusion granted.
- Arguments whose premises could not have been used to account for the conclusion.
  - Sign
    - &c. &c. &c.
  - Induction or example.
    - &c.

Argument from Cause to Effect

As far, then, as any Cause, popularly speaking, has a tendency to produce a certain Effect, so far its existence is an Argument for that of the Effect. If the Cause be fully *sufficient,* and no *impediments* intervene, the Effect in question follows certainly; and the nearer we approach to this, the stronger the Argument.

Plausibility

This is the kind of Argument which produces (when short of absolute certainty) that species of the Probable which is usually called the *"Plausible."* On this subject Dr. Campbell has some valuable remarks in his *"Philosophy of Rhetoric,"* (book i. § 5. ch. vii.) though he has been led into a good deal of perplexity, partly by not having logically analysed the two species of probabilities he is treating of, and partly by departing, unnecessarily, from the ordinary use of terms, in treating of the Plausible as something *distinct from* the Probable, instead of regarding it as a *species* of Probability.[3]

This is the chief kind of Probability which poets, or other writers of fiction, aim at; and in such works it is often designated by the term "natural." [4] Writers of this class, as they aim not at producing belief, are allowed to take their "Causes" for granted, (*i. e.* to assume any hypothesis they please,) provided they make the Effects follow naturally; representing, that is, the personages of the fiction as acting, and the events as resulting, in the same manner as might have been expected, supposing the assumed circumstances to have been real. And hence, the great Father of Criticism establishes his paradoxical maxim, that impossibilities which appear probable, are to be preferred to possibilities which appear improbable. For, as he

---

[3] I do not mean, however, that *every thing* to which the term "plausible" would apply would be in strict propriety called "probable"; as *e. g.* if we had fully ascertained some story that had been told us to be an imposition, we might still say, it was a "plausible" tale; though, subsequent to the detection, the word "probable" would not be so properly applied. But certainly common usage warrants the use of "probable" in many cases, on the ground of this plausibility alone; viz. the adequacy of some cause, known, or likely to exist, to produce the effect in question. I could have wished that there had been some other word to designate what I have called, after Dr. Campbell's example, the "plausible," because it sometimes suggests the idea of "untrue." But *"likely,"* which, according to etymology, ought to be the suitable term, is often used to denote the "probable," generally.

When however we have clearly *defined* the technical sense in which we propose to employ a certain term, it may fairly be so taken, even though not invariably bearing that sense in common usage.

[4] It is also important for them, though not so essential, to keep clear of the improbable air produced by the introduction of events, which, though not unnatural, have a great *preponderance of chances* against them. The distinction between these two kinds of faults is pointed out in a passage in the *Quarterly Review,* for which see Appendix, [B.]

justly observes, the impossibility of the hypothesis, as *e. g.* in Homer, the familiar intercourse of gods with mortals, is no bar to the kind of Probability (*i. e.* Verisimilitude) required, if those mortals are represented as acting in the manner men naturally would have done under those circumstances.

The Probability, then, which the writer of fiction aims at, has, for the reason just mentioned, no tendency to produce a *particular,* but only a *general,* belief; *i. e.* not that these particular events actually took place, but that *such* are likely, generally, to take place under such circumstances: [5] this kind of belief (unconsciously entertained) being necessary, and all that is necessary, to produce that sympathetic feeling which is the writer's object. In Argumentative Compositions, however, as the object of course is to produce conviction as to the particular point in question, the Causes from which our Arguments are drawn must be such as are either admitted, or may be proved, to be actually existing, or likely to exist.

The Unnatural Mistaken for Natural

It is worthy of remark, in reference to this kind of Probability—the "Plausible" or "Natural"—that men are apt to judge amiss of situations, persons, and circumstances, concerning which they have no exact knowledge, by applying to these the measure of their own feelings and experience: [6] the result of which is, that a correct account of these will often appear to them unnatural, and an erroneous one, natural. *E. G.* A person born with the usual endowments of the senses, is apt to attribute to the blind-born, and the deaf-mutes, such habits of thought, and such a state of mind, as his own would be, if he were to *become* deaf or blind, or to be left in the dark: which would be very wide of the truth. That a man born blind would not, on obtaining sight, know apart, on seeing them, a ball, and a cube, which he had been accustomed to handle, nor distinguish the dog from the cat, would appear to most persons unacquainted with the result of experiments, much less "natural" than the reverse. So it is also with those brought up free, in reference to the feelings and habits of thought of born-slaves; [7] with civilized men, in reference to Savages; and of men living in Society, in reference to one who passes whole years in total solitude. I have no doubt that the admirable fiction of Robinson Crusoe would have been not only much less amusing, but, to most readers less apparently *natural,* if Friday and the other Savages had been represented with the indocility and other qualities which really belong to such Beings as the Brazilian Cannibals; and if the hero himself had been represented with that half-brutish apathetic despondency, and carelessness about all comforts demanding steady exertion, which are the really natural results of a life of utter solitude: and if he

[5] On which ground Aristotle contends that the end of Fiction is more Philosophical than that of History, since it aims at general, instead of particular, Truth.
[6] See Part II. ch. ii. § 2.
[7] This has, in various ways, proved an obstacle to the abolition of Slavery. It has also caused great difficulty to some readers of the Book of Exodus.

had been described as almost losing the use of his own language, instead of remembering the Spanish.

Again, I remember mentioning to a very intelligent man the description given by the earliest Missionaries to New Zealand, of their introduction of the culture of wheat; which he derided as an absurd fabrication, but which appeared to me what might have been reasonably conjectured. The Savages were familiar with bread, in the form of ship-biscuit; and accordingly, *roots* being alone cultivated by them, and furnishing their chief food, they expected to find at the roots of the wheat, tubers which could be made into biscuits. They accordingly dug up the wheat; and were mortified at the failure of their hopes. The idea of collecting small seeds, pulverizing these, and making the powder into a paste which was to be hardened by fire, was quite foreign from all their experience. Yet here, an unnatural representation would, to many, have appeared the more natural.

Much pains therefore must in many cases be taken in giving such explanations as may put men on their guard against this kind of mistake, and enable them to see the improbability, and sometimes utter impossibility, of what at the first glance they will be apt to regard as perfectly natural; and to satisfy them that something which they were disposed to regard as extravagantly unnatural, is just what might have been reasonably anticipated.

One way in which the unnatural is often made to appear, for a time, natural, is, by giving a lively and striking description which is correct in its several *parts,* and unnatural only when these are combined into a *whole;* like a painter who should give an exact picture of an English country-house, of a grove of Palm-trees, an Elephant and an Iceberg, all in the same Landscape. Thus, a vivid representation of a den of infamy and degradation, and of an ingenuous and well-disposed youth, may each be, in itself, so natural, as to draw off, for a time, the attention from the absurdity of making the one arise out of the other.

Employment of the Phrase a Priori

On the appropriate use of the kind of Argument now before us, (which is probably the εἰκὸς of Aristotle, though unfortunately he has not furnished any example of it,) some Rules will be laid down hereafter; my object at present having been merely to ascertain the nature of it. And here it may be worth while to remark, that though I have applied to this mode of Reasoning the title of "*a priori,*" it is not meant to be maintained that all such arguments as have been by other writers so designated correspond precisely with what has been just described. The phrase, "*a priori*" Argument, is not indeed employed by all in the same sense; it would, however, generally be understood to extend to any argument drawn from an *antecedent* or *forerunner,* whether a Cause or not; *e. g.* "the mercury sinks, therefore it will rain." Now this Argument being drawn from a circumstance which, though an antecedent, is in no sense a Cause, would fall not under the former, but the latter, of the classes laid down; since when rain comes, no one would *account* for the phenomenon by the falling of the mercury; which they would call a *Sign* of rain; and yet most, perhaps, would class this among "*a priori*" Arguments. In like manner the expression, "*a posteriori*" Arguments, would not in its ordinary use coincide precisely, though it would very nearly, with the second class of Arguments.

The division, however, which has here been adopted, appears to be both more philosophical, and also more precise, and consequently more practically useful, than any other; since there is so easy and decisive a test by which an Argument may be at once referred to the one or to the other of the classes described.

3

The second, then, of these classes, (viz. "Arguments drawn from such topics as could not be used to account for the fact, &c. in question, supposing it granted,") may be subdivided into two kinds; which will be designated by the terms "Sign" and "Example."

Sign

By "Sign" is meant, what may be described as an "argument from an *Effect* to a *Condition:*"—a species of Argument of which the analysis is as follows: As far as any circumstance is, what may be called a *Condition* of the existence of a certain effect or phenomenon, so far it may be inferred from the existence of that Effect: if it be a Condition *absolutely essential,* the Argument is, of course, demonstrative; and the probability is the stronger in proportion as we approach to that case.

Of this kind is the Argument in the instance lately given: a man is suspected as the perpetrator of the supposed murder, from the circumstance of his clothes being bloody; the murder being considered as in a certain degree a probable *condition* of that appearance; *i. e.* it is presumed that his clothes would *not otherwise* have been bloody. Again, from the appearance of ice, we infer, decidedly, the existence of a temperature not above freezing-point; that temperature being an essential Condition of the crystallization of water.

Proof of a Cause

Among the circumstances which are conditional to any Effect, must evidently come the Cause or Causes; and if there be only one possible Cause, this being absolutely essential, may be demonstratively proved from the Effect: if the same Effect might result from other Causes, then the Argument is, at best, but probable. But it is to be observed, that there are also many circumstances which have no tendency to *produce* a certain Effect, though it cannot exist *without* them, and from which Effect, consequently, they may be inferred, as Conditions, though not Causes; *e. g.* a man's "being alive one day," is a circumstance necessary, as a Condition, to his "dying the next;" but has no tendency to produce it; his having been alive, therefore, on the former day, may be proved from his subsequent death, but not *vice versa.*[8]

It is to be observed, therefore, that though it is very common for the Cause to be proved from its Effect, it is never so proved, *so far forth as* it is a *Cause,* but so far forth as it is a *condition,* or necessary circumstance.

A Cause, again, may be employed to prove an Effect, (this being the first class of Arguments already described,) so far as it *has a tendency* to produce the Effect, even though it be not at all *necessary* to it; (*i. e.* when other Causes may produce the same Effect;) and in this case, though the Effect may be inferred from the Cause, the Cause cannot be inferred from the Effect: *e. g.* from a mortal wound you may infer death; but not *vice versâ.*

Lastly, when a Cause is also a necessary or probable *condition, i. e.* when it is the *only* possible or only likely Cause, then we may argue both ways: *e. g.* we may infer a General's success from his known skill, or, his skill, from his known success: (in this, as in all cases, assuming what is the *better known* as a proof of what is less-known, denied, or doubted,) these two Arguments belonging, respectively, to the two classes originally laid down.

Logical and Physical Sequence

And it is to be observed, that, in such Arguments from Sign as this last, the conclusion which *follows, logically,* from the premise, being the Cause from which the premise *follows,* physically, (*i. e.* as a natural Effect,) there are in this case two different kinds of *Sequence* opposed to each other; *e. g.* "With many of them God was not well pleased; for they were overthrown in the wilderness." In Arguments of the first class, on the contrary, these two kinds of Sequence are combined, *i. e.* the Conclusion which follows logically from the premise, is also the Effect following physically from it as a Cause; a General's skill, *e. g.* being both the Cause and the Proof of his being likely to succeed.

Importance of Distinguishing the Two Kinds of Sequence

It is most important to keep in mind the distinction between these two kinds of Sequence, which are, in Argument, sometimes *combined,* and some-

---

[8] It is however very common, in the carelessness of ordinary language, to mention, as the Causes of phenomena, circumstances which every one would allow, on consideration, to be not Causes, but only conditions, of the Effects in question: *e. g.* it would be said of a tender plant, that it was destroyed in consequence of not being covered with a mat; though every one would mean to imply that the *frost* destroyed it; this being a Cause too well known to need being mentioned; and that which is spoken of as the Cause, viz. the absence of a covering, being only the Condition, without which the real Cause could not have operated.

How common it is to confound a Sign with a Cause is apparent in the resentment men are prone to feel against the prophets of evil; as Ahab "hated" the Prophet Micaiah, and gave as a reason "he doth not prophesy good concerning me, but evil."

times *opposed*. There is no more fruitful source of confusion of thought than that ambiguity of the language employed on these subjects, which tends to confound together these two things, so entirely distinct in their nature. There is hardly any argumentative writer on subjects involving a discussion of the Causes or Effects of anything, who has clearly perceived and steadily kept in view the distinction I have been speaking of, or who has escaped the errors and perplexities thence resulting. The wide extent accordingly, and the importance, of the mistakes and difficulties arising out of the ambiguity complained of, is incalculable. Of all the "Idola Fori" [9] none is perhaps more important in its results. To dilate upon this point as fully as might be done with advantage, would exceed my present limits; but it will not be irrelevant to offer some remarks on the origin of the ambiguity complained of, and on the cautions to be used in guarding against being misled by it.

Logical Sequence

The Premise by which anything is proved, is not necessarily the Cause of the fact's *being* such as it is; but it is the cause of our *knowing*, or being convinced, that it is so; *e. g.* the wetness of the earth is not the Cause of rain, but it is the Cause of our knowing that it has rained. These two things, —the Premise which produces *our conviction*, and the Cause which produces that *of which* we are convinced,—are the more likely to be confounded together, in the looseness of colloquial language, from the circumstance that (as has been above remarked) they frequently coincide; as, *e. g.* when we *infer* that the ground will be wet, from the fall of rain which *produces* that wetness. And hence it is that the same words have come to be applied, in common, to each kind of Sequence; *e. g.* an Effect is said to "follow" from a Cause, and a Conclusion to "follow" from the Premises; the words "Cause" and "Reason," are each applied indifferently, both to a Cause, properly so called, and to the Premise of an Argument; though "Reason," in strictness of speaking, should be confined to the latter. "Therefore," "hence," "consequently," &c., and also, "since," "because," and "why," have likewise a corresponding ambiguity.

Ambiguity of "Because," "Therefore," &c

The multitude of the words which bear this double meaning (and that, in all languages) greatly increases our liability to be misled by it; since thus the very means men resort to for ascertaining the sense of any expression, are infected with the very same ambiguity; *e. g.* if we inquire what is meant by a "Cause," we shall be told that it is that from which something "follows;" or, which is indicated by the words "therefore," "consequently," &c., all which expressions are as equivocal and uncertain in their signification as

[9] Bacon's *"Idols of the Marketplace."*

the original one. It is in vain to attempt ascertaining by the balance the true amount of any commodity, if uncertain weights are placed in the opposite scale. Hence it is that so many writers, in investigating the Cause to which any fact or phenomenon is to be attributed, have assigned that which is not a *Cause*, but only a *Proof* that the fact is so; and have thus been led into an endless train of errors and perplexities.

Several, however, of the words in question, though employed indiscriminately in both significations, seem (as was observed in the case of the word ("Reason") in their primary and strict sense to be confined to one. "Δή," in Greek, and "ergo," [10] or "itaque," in Latin, seem originally and properly to denote the Sequence of Effect from Cause; "ἄρα," [11] and "igitur," that of conclusion from premises. The English word *"accordingly,"* will generally be found to correspond with the Latin "itaque."

Ambiguity of "Why"

The interrogative "why," is employed to inquire, either, first, the "Reasons," (or "Proof;") secondly, the "Cause;" or thirdly, the "object proposed," or Final-Cause: *e. g.* first, Why are the angles of a triangle equal to two right angles? secondly, Why are the days shorter in winter than in summer? thirdly, Why are the works of a watch constructed as they are? [12]

It is to be observed that the discovery of *Causes* belongs properly to the province of the Philosopher; that of "Reasons," strictly so called, (*i. e.* Arguments,) to that of the Rhetorician; and that, though each will have frequent occasion to assume the character of the other, it is most important that these two objects should not be confounded together.

4

Of Signs then there are some which from a certain Effect or phenomenon, infer the "Cause" of it; and others which, in like manner, infer some "Condition" which is not the Cause.

Testimony a Kind of Sign

Of these last, one species is the Argument from Testimony: the premise being the existence of the Testimony; the Conclusion, the truth of what is attested; which is considered as a "Condition" of the Testimony having been given: since it is evident that so far only as this allowed, (*i. e.* so far only as it is allowed, that the Testimony would not have been given, had it not been true,) can this Argument have any force. Testimony is of various

---

[10] Most Logical writers seem not to be aware of this, as they generally, in Latin Treatises, employ "ergo" in the other sense. It is from the Greek ἔργῳ *i. e.* "in fact."

[11] "Αρα having a signification of *fitness* or *coincidence;* whence ἄρω.

[12] See the article WHY, in the Appendix to the Treatise on Logic.

kinds; and may possess various degrees of force,[13] not only in reference to its own intrinsic character, but in reference also to the kind of conclusion that it is brought to support.

Matters of Fact, and of Opinion

In respect of this latter point, the first and great distinction is, between Testimony to *matters of Fact*, and, to *matters of Opinion*, or Doctrines.

The expressions "Matter [or Question] of Fact," and "Matter of Opinion," are not employed by all persons with precision and uniformity. But the notion most nearly conformable to ordinary usage seems to be this: by a "Matter of Fact" is meant, something which might, *conceivably*, be submitted to the *senses;* and about which it is supposed there could be no disagreement among persons who should be *present*, and to whose senses it should be submitted: and by a "Matter [or Question] of Opinion" is understood, anything respecting which an exercise of *judgment* would be called for on the part of those who should have certain objects before them, and who might conceivably disagree in their judgment thereupon.

No Greater Certainty about Facts, than Opinions

This, I think, is the description of what people in general intend to denote (though often without having themselves any very clear notion of it) by these phrases. Decidedly it is *not* meant, by those at least who use language with any precision, that there is greater *certainty*, or more general and ready *agreement*, in the one case than in the other. *E. G.* That one of Alexander's friends did, or did not, administer poison to him, every one would allow to be a question of *fact;* though it may be involved in inextricable doubt: while the question, *what sort of an act* that was, supposing it to have taken place, all would allow to be a question of *opinion;* though probably all would agree in their opinion thereupon.

A Question of Fact, One which Might Conceivably Be Submitted to the Senses

Again, it is not, apparently, necessary that a "Matter of Fact," in order to constitute it such, should have ever been actually submitted—or likely to be so—to the senses of any human Being; only, that it should be one which *conceivably might* be so submitted. *E. G.* Whether there is a lake in the centre of New Holland,—whether there is land at the South Pole—whether the Moon is inhabited,—would generally be admitted to be questions of

---

[13] Locke has touched on this subject, though slightly and scantily. He says, "In the testimony of others, is to be considered,—1. The number. 2. The integrity. 3. The skill of the witnesses. 4. The design of the author, where it is a testimony out of a book cited. 5. The consistency of the parts and circumstances of the relation. 6. Contrary testimonies."

fact; although no one has been able to bear testimony concerning them; and, in the last case, we are morally certain that no one ever will.

Questions of Opinion May Relate to Facts

The circumstance that chiefly tends to produce indistinctness and occasional inconsistency in the use of these phrases, is, that there is often much room for the exercise of judgment, and for difference of *opinion,* in *reference* to things which are, *themselves,* matters of *fact.* E. G. The degree of *credibility* of the *witnesses* who attest any fact, is, itself, a matter of Opinion; and so, in respect of the degree of weight due to any other kind of probabilities. That there *is,* or *is not,* land at the South Pole, is a matter of Fact; that the existence of land there is *likely,* or *unlikely,* is a matter of Opinion.

And in this, and many other cases, *different* questions very closely connected, are very apt to be confounded together,[14] and the proofs belonging to one of them brought forward as pertaining to the other. E. G. A case of alleged prophecy shall be in question: the event, said to have been foretold, shall be established as a fact; and also, the utterance of the supposed prediction *before* the event; and this will perhaps be assumed as proof of that which is in reality another question, and a "question of opinion;" whether the supposed prophecy *related* to the event in question; and again, whether it were merely a *conjecture* of human sagacity, or such as to imply superhuman prescience.

Again, whether a certain passage occurs in certain MSS. of the Greek Testament, is evidently a question of Fact; but whether the words imply *such and such a doctrine,*—however indubitable it may justly appear to us,—is evidently a "matter of opinion." [15]

Facts May Relate to Opinions

It is to be observed also, that, as there may be (as I have just said) questions of Opinion *relative* to Facts, so, there may also be questions of Fact, relative to Opinions: *i.e.* that such and such Opinions were, or were not, *maintained* at such a time and place, by such and such persons, is a question of Fact.

When the question is as to a Fact, it is plain we have to look chiefly to the *honesty* of a witness, his accuracy, and his means of gaining information. When the question is about a matter of Opinion, it is equally plain that his *ability to form a judgment* is no less to be taken into account.[16] But though this is admitted by all, it is very common with inconsiderate persons to overlook, in practice, the distinction, and to mistake as to, *what it is,* that,

[14] See Treatise on Fallacies, "Irrelevant Conclusion."
[15] See Preface to vol. ii. of *Translation of Neander.*
[16] Testimony to matters of opinion usually receives the name of *Authority;* which term however is also often applied when facts are in question; as when we say, indifferently, "the account of this transaction rests on the Authority"—or "on the Testimony—of such and such an historian." See *Logic,* Appendix, Art. "Authority."

in each case, is attested. *Facts,* properly so called, are, we should remember, *individuals;* though the term is often extended to *general* statements; especially when these are well established. And again, the *causes* or other circumstances connected with some event or phenomenon, are often stated as a part of the very fact attested. If, for instance, a person relates his having found coal in a certain stratum; or if he states, that in the East Indies he saw a number of persons who had been sleeping exposed to the moon's rays, afflicted with certain symptoms, and that after taking a certain medicine they recovered,—he is bearing testimony as to simple matters of fact: but if he declares that the stratum in question *constantly* contains coal;—or, that the patients in question were so affected in *consequence* of the moon's rays,—that such is the *general* effect of them in that climate,[17] and that that medicine is a *cure* for such symptoms, it is evident that his testimony,—however worthy of credit—is borne to a *different kind of conclusion;* namely, not an individual, but a *general,* conclusion, and one which must rest, not solely on the veracity, but also on the judgment, of the witness.

Character of Witnesses

Even in the other case, however,—when the question relates to what is strictly a matter of fact,—the intellectual character of the witness is not to be wholly left out of the account. A man strongly influenced by prejudice, to which the weakest men are ever the most liable, may even fancy he sees what he does not. And some degree of suspicion may thence attach to the testimony of prejudiced, though honest men, when *their prejudices are on the same side with their testimony:* for otherwise their testimony may even be the stronger. *E. G.* The early disciples of Jesus were, mostly, ignorant, credulous, and prejudiced men; but all their expectations,—all their early prejudices,—ran counter to almost every thing that they attested. They were, in that particular case, harder to be convinced than more intelligent and enlightened men would have been. It is most important, therefore, to remember—what is often forgotten—that Credulity and Incredulity are the *same* habit considered in *reference to different things.* The more easy of belief any one is in respect of what falls in with his wishes or preconceived notions, the harder of belief he will be of anything that opposes these.[18]

Number of Witnesses

Again, in respect of the *number* of witnesses, it is evident that,—other points being equal,—many must have more weight than one, or a few; but it is no uncommon mistake to imagine many witnesses to be bearing *concurrent* testimony to the *same* thing, when in truth they are attesting different things. One or two men may be bearing original testimony to some fact or transaction; and one or two hundred, who are repeating what they have

[17] Such is the prevailing, if not universal, belief of those who have resided in the East Indies.
[18] See *Logic,* b. ii. c. 2. §.

heard from these, may be, in reality, only bearing witness to their *having heard it,* and to their own belief. Multitudes may agree in maintaining some system or doctrine, which perhaps one out of a million may have convinced himself of by research and reflection; while the rest have assented to it in implicit reliance on authority. These are not, in reality, attesting the same thing. The one is, in reality, declaring that so and so is, as he conceives, a conclusion fairly established by *reasons* pertaining to the subject-matter; the rest, that so and so is the established belief; or is held by persons on whose authority they rely. These last may indeed have very good ground for their belief: for no one would say that a man who is not versed in Astronomy is not justified in believing the Earth's motion; or that the many millions of persons who have never seen the sea, are credulous in believing, on testimony, its existence: but still it is to be remembered that they are not, in reality, bearing witness to the *same* thing as the others.

Undesigned Testimony

Undesigned testimony is manifestly, so far, the stronger; the suspicion of fabrication being thus precluded. Slight incidental hints therefore, and oblique allusions to any fact, have often much more weight than distinct formal assertions of it. And, moreover, such allusions will often go to indicate not only that the fact is *true,* but that it was, at the time when so alluded to, *notorious* and undisputed. The account given by Herodotus, of Xerxes's cutting a canal through the isthmus of Athos, which is ridiculed by Juvenal, is much more strongly attested by Thucydides in an incidental mention of a place "near which some remains of the canal might be seen," than if he had distinctly recorded his conviction of the truth of the narrative.

So also, the many slight allusions in the Apostolic Epistles to the sufferings undergone, and the miracles wrought, by Disciples, as things familiar to the readers, are much more decisive than distinct descriptions, narratives, or assertions, would have been.

Small Circumstances May Have Great Weight

Paley, in that most admirable specimen of the investigation of this kind of evidence, the *"Horæ Paulinæ,"* puts in a most needful caution against supposing that because it is on very *minute points* this kind of argument turns, therefore the *importance* of these points in establishing the conclusion, is *small.*[19] The reverse, as he justly observes, is the truth; for the more minute,

[19] Thus Swift endeavoured (in Gulliver's Voyage to Laputa, and in some of his poems,) to cast ridicule on some of the evidence on which Bishop Atterbury's treasonable correspondence was brought home to him; the medium of proof being certain allusions, in some of the letters, to a lame lap-dog; as if the importance of the *evidence* were to be measured by the intrinsic importance of the *dog.* But Swift was far too acute a man probably to have fallen himself into such an error as he was endeavouring, for party-purposes, to lead his readers into.

and intrinsically trifling, and likely to escape notice, any point is, the more does it preclude the idea of design and fabrication. Imitations of natural objects,—flowers, for instance,—when so skilfully made as to deceive the naked eye, are detected by submitting the natural and the artificial to a *microscope*.

The same remarks will apply to other kinds of Sign also. The number and position of the nails in a man's shoe, corresponding with a foot-mark, or a notch in the blade of a knife, have led to the detection of a murderer.

Testimony of Adversaries

The Testimony of Adversaries,[20]—including under this term all who would be unwilling to admit the conclusion to which their testimony tends,—has, of course, great weight derived from that cirmumstance. And as it will, of-tener than not, fall under the head of "undesigned," much minute research will often be needful, in order to draw it out.

Cross-Examination

In oral examination of witnesses, a skilful cross-examiner will often elicit from a reluctant witness most important truths, which the witness is desir-ous of concealing or disguising. There is another kind of skill, which consists in so alarming, misleading, or bewildering an honest witness as to throw discredit on his testimony, or pervert the effect of it.[21] Of this kind of art, which may be characterised as the most, or one of the most, base and depraved of all possible employments of intellectual power, I shall only make one further observation. I am convinced that the most effectual mode of eliciting *truth*, is quite different from that by which an honest, simple-minded witness is most easily baffled and confused. I have seen the experi-ment tried, of subjecting a witness to such a kind of cross-examination by a practised lawyer, as would have been, I am convinced, the most likely to alarm and perplex many an honest witness; without any effect in shaking the testimony: and afterwards, by a totally opposite mode of examination, such as would not have at all perplexed one who was honestly telling the truth, that same witness was drawn on, step by step, to acknowledge the utter falsity of the whole.

Generally speaking, I believe that a quiet, gentle, and straightforward, though full and careful examination, will be the most adapted to elicit *truth;* and that the manœuvres, and the brow-beating, which are the most adapted to confuse an honest witness, are just what the dishonest one is the best prepared for. The more the storm blusters, the more carefully he wraps

20 E. G. I have seen in a professedly argumentative Work, a warning inserted against the alleged unsound doctrine contained in the Article "Person" in Appendix to the *Logic;* which being unaccompanied by any *proofs* of unsoundness, may be regarded as a strong testimony to the unanswerable character of the reasons I have there adduced.

21 See an extract from a valuable pamphlet on the "License of Counsel," cited in the Lec-ture appended to Part II.

round him the cloak, which a warm sunshine will often induce him to throw off.

Testimony of Adversaries Usually Incidental

In any testimony (whether oral or written) that is unwillingly borne, it will more frequently consist in something *incidentally implied,* than in a distinct statement. For instance, the generality of men, who are accustomed to cry up Common-sense as preferable to Systems of Art, have been brought to bear witness, collectively, (see Preface to "Elements of Logic,") on the opposite side; inasmuch as each of them gives the preference to the latter, in the subject,—whatever it may be,—in which he is most conversant.

Sometimes, however, an adversary will be compelled distinctly to admit something that makes against him, in order to contest some other point. Thus, the testimony of the Evangelists, that the miracles of Jesus were acknowledged by the unbelievers, and attributed to magic, is confirmed by the Jews, in a Work called "Toldoth Jeschu;" (the "Generation of Jesus;") which must have been compiled (at whatever period) from *traditions existing from the very first;* since it is incredible that if those *contemporaries* of Jesus who opposed Him, had denied the *fact* of the miracles having been wrought, their *descendants* should have admitted the facts, and resorted to the hypothesis of magic.

Negative Testimony

The *negative* testimony, either of adversaries, or of indifferent persons, is often of great weight. When statements or arguments, publicly put forth, and generally known, remain *uncontradicted,* an appeal may fairly be made to this circumstance, as a confirmatory testimony on the part of those acquainted with the matter, and interested in it; especially if they are likely to be unwilling to admit the conclusion.[22]

Concurrent Testimony

It is manifest that the concurrent testimony, positive or negative, of several witnesses, when there can have been no concert, and especially when there is any rivalry or hostility between them, carries with it a weight independent of that which may belong to each of them considered separately. For though, in such a case, each of the witnesses should be even considered as wholly undeserving of credit, still the chances might be incalculable against their all agreeing in the *same* falsehood. It is in this kind of testimony that the generality of mankind believe in the motions of the earth, and of the heavenly bodies, &c. Their belief is not the result of their own observations and calculations; nor yet again of their implicit reliance on the skill and the

22 See Hinds on the "Inspiration of Scripture."

good-faith of any one or more astronomers; but it rests on the agreement of many independent and rival astronomers; who want neither the ability nor the will to detect and expose each other's errors. It is on similar grounds, as Dr. Hinds has justly observed, that all men, except about two or three in a million, believe in the existence and in the genuineness of manuscripts of ancient books, such as the Scriptures. It is not that they have themselves examined these; or again, (as some represent) that they rely implicitly on the good faith of those who profess to have done so; but they rely on the *concurrent* and *uncontradicted* testimony of all who have made, or who *might make,* the examination; both unbelievers, and believers of various hostile sects; any one of whom would be sure to seize any opportunity to expose the forgeries or errors of his opponents.

This observation is the more important, because many persons are liable to be startled and dismayed on its being pointed out to them that they have been believing something—as they are led to suppose—on very insufficient reasons; when the truth is perhaps that they have been mis-stating their reasons.[23]

A remarkable instance of the testimony of adversaries,—both positive and negative,—has been afforded in the questions respecting penal-colonies. The pernicious character of the system was proved in various publications, and subsequently, before two committees of the House of Commons, from the testimony of persons who were *friendly* to that system: the report and evidence taken before those committees was published; and all this remained uncontradicted for years; till, on motions being made for the abolition of the system,[24] persons had the effrontery to come forward at the eleventh hour and deny the truth of the representations given: thus pronouncing on themselves a heavy condemnation, for having either left that representation—supposing they thought it false,—so long unrefuted, or else, denying what they knew to be true.

Misrepresentation, again, of argument,—attempts to suppress evidence, or to silence a speaker by clamour,—reviling and personality, and false charges—all these are presumptions of the same kind; that the cause against which they are brought, is,—in the opinion of adversaries at least,—unassailable on the side of truth.

Character of Things Attested

As for the character of the particular things that in any case may be attested, it is plain that we have to look to the probability or improbability, on the one hand, of their being real, and, on the other hand, of their having been either imagined or invented by the persons attesting them.

[23] See Appendix, [D.].
[24] See "Substance of a Speech on Transportation, delivered in the House of Lords, on the 19th of May, 1840," &c.

Things Intrinsically Improbable, the Less Likely to Be Feigned

Anything unlikely to *occur*, is, so far, the less likely to have been feigned or fancied: so that its antecedent improbability may sometimes add to the credibility of those who bear witness to it.[25] And again, anything which, however likely to *take place*, would not have been likely, *otherwise*, to enter the mind of *those particular* persons who attest to it, or would be at variance with their interest or prejudices, is thereby rendered the more credible. Thus, as has been above remarked, when the disciples of Jesus record occurrences and discourses, such as were both foreign to all the notions, and at variance with all the prejudices, of any man living in those days, and of Jews more especially, this is a strong confirmation of their testimony.

Things Not Understood, or Not Believed, by Those Who Attest Them

It is also, in some cases, a strongly confirmatory circumstance that the witness should appear not to *believe*, himself, or not to *understand*, the thing he is reporting, when it is such as is, to *us, not* unintelligible nor incredible. E. G. When an ancient historian records a report of certain voyagers having sailed to a distant country in which they found the shadows falling on the opposite side to that which they had been accustomed to, and regards the account as incredible, from not being able to understand how such a phenomenon could occur, *we*—recognising at once what we know takes place in the Southern Hemisphere, and perceiving that *he* could not have *invented* the account—have the more reason for believing it. The report thus becomes analogous to the copy of an inscription in a language unknown to him who copied it.

The negative circumstance also, of a witness's *omitting* to mention such things as it is morally certain he *would* have mentioned had he been inventing, adds great weight to what he does say.

Superior Force of Negative Probabilities

And it is to be observed [26] that, in many cases, silence, omission, absence of certain statements, &c. will have even greater weight than much that we do find stated. E. G. Suppose we meet with something in a passage of one of Paul's Epistles, which indicates with a certain degree of probability the existence of such and such a custom, institution, &c., and suppose there is just the same degree of probability that such and such another custom, institution, or event, which he does *not* mention anywhere, *would* have been mentioned by him in the same place, supposing it to have really existed, or occurred; this omission, and the *negative* argument resulting, has incomparably the more weight than the other, *if we also find* that same

---

[25] See Sermon IV on "A Christian Place of Worship."
[26] See Essay on the "Omission of Creeds," &c.

omission in *all the other* epistles, and in every one of the Books of the New Testament.

E. G. The universal omission of all notice of the office of Hiereus (a sacerdotal priest) among the Christian ministers [27]—of all reference to one supreme Church bearing rule over all the rest [28]—of all mention of any transfer of the Sabbath from the seventh day to the first [29]—are instances of decisive negative arguments of this kind.

So also, the omission of all allusion to a Future State, in those parts of the writings of Moses in which he is urging the Israelites to obedience by appeals to their hopes and fears; and again, in the whole of the early part of the Book of Job, in which that topic could not have failed to occur to persons believing in the doctrine,—this is a plain indication that no revelation of the doctrine was intended to be given in those Books; and that the passage, often cited, from the Book of Job, as having reference to the resurrection, must be understood as relating to that *temporal* deliverance which is narrated immediately after: since else it would (as Bishop Warburton has justly remarked) make all the rest of the Book unintelligible and absurd.[30]

Again, "although we do not admit the *positive* authority of antiquity in favour of any doctrine or practice which we do not find sanctioned by Scripture, we may yet, without inconsistency, appeal to it *negatively,* in refutation of many errors. . . . It is no argument in favour of the Millennium, that it was a notion entertained by Justin Martyr, since we do not believe him to have been inspired, and he may therefore have drawn erroneous inferences from certain texts of Scripture: but it is an argument against the doctrine of Transubstantiation, that we find no traces of it for above six centuries; and against the adoration of the Virgin Mary, that in like manner it does not appear to have been inculcated till the sixth century. It is very credible that the first Christian writers, who were but men, should have made mistakes to which all men are liable, in their interpretation of Scripture: but it is not credible that such important doctrines as Transubstantiation and the adoration of the Virgin Mary should have been transmitted from the Apostles, if we find no trace of them for five or six centuries after the birth of our Saviour." [31]

Absence of All Records of Savages Having Civilized Themselves

To take another instance: I have remarked in the Lectures on Political Economy (Lect. 5), that the descriptions some writers give of the Civilization of Mankind, by the spontaneous origin, among tribes of Savages, of the various arts of life, one by one, are to be regarded as wholly imaginary, and

[27] See Discourse on the Christian Priesthood appended to the Bampton Lectures. Also, Bernard's translation of Vitringa on the "Synagogue and the Church."
[28] See Essay II on the "Kingdom of Christ."
[29] See "Thoughts on the Sabbath."
[30] See "Essay on a Future State" (First Series).
[31] Bishop Pepys's Charge, 1845.

not agreeing with anything that ever did, or can, actually take place; inasmuch as there is no record or tradition of any race of savages having ever civilized themselves without external aid. Numerous as are the accounts we have, of Savages who have *not* received such aid, we do not hear, in any one instance, of their having ceased to be Savages. And again, abundant as are the traditions (though mostly mixed up with much that is fabulous) of the origin of civilization in various nations, all concur in tracing it up to some foreign, or some superhuman, instructor. If ever a nation did emerge, unassisted, from the savage state, all memory of such an event is totally lost.

Now the *absence* of all such records or traditions, in a case where there is every reason to expect that an instance could be produced if any had ever occurred,—this *negative* circumstance (in conjunction with the other indications there adduced) led me, many years ago, to the conclusion, that it is impossible for mere Savages to civilize themselves—that consequently Man must at some period have received the rudiments of civilization from a *superhuman* instructor,—and that Savages are probably the descendants of civilized men, whom wars and other afflictive visitations have degraded.[32]

It might seem superfluous to remark that none but very general rules, such as the above, can be profitably laid down; and that to attempt to supersede the discretion to be exercised on each individual case, by *fixing precisely* what degree of weight is to be allowed to the testimony of such and such persons, would be, at least, useless trifling, and, if introduced in practice, a most mischievous hindrance of a right decision. But attempts of this kind have actually been made, in the systems of Jurisprudence of some countries; and with such results as might have been anticipated. The reader will find an instructive account of some of this unwise legislation in an article on "German Jurisprudence" in the Edinburgh Review; from which an extract is subjoined in the Appendix.[33]

Testimony on *Oath* is commonly regarded as far more to be relied on—other points being equal—than any that is not sworn to. This however holds good, not universally, but only in respect of certain *intermediate* characters between the truly respectable and the worthless. For, these latter will either not scruple to take a false Oath, or, if they do, will satisfy their conscience by various *evasions* and *equivocations,* such as are vulgarly called "cheating the Devil"; so as to give, substantially, false testimony, while they cheat (in reality) *themselves,* by avoiding literal perjury. An upright man, again, considers himself as, virtually, on his Oath, whenever he makes a deliberate solemn assertion; and feels bound to guard against conveying any false impression.

But, even in respect of those intermediate characters, the influence of an Oath in securing veracity, is, I conceive, far less than some suppose. Let any one compare the evidence given on Oath, with that of those religionists who

---

[32] See an extract in the Appendix DD from the Lecture above alluded to.
[33] Appendix DDD.

are allowed by law to substitute a "solemn Affirmation," and he will find no signs of the advantage of Sworn-testimony. Or, if he consider these religionists as, generally, more conscientious than the average, let him compare the evidence (of which we have such voluminous records) given before Committees of the House of *Lords*, which is on Oath, with that before Committees of the *Commons*, which is not; and he will find about the same proportion of honest and of dishonest testimony in each.

Still, there doubtless are persons who would scruple to swear to a falsehood which they would not scruple deliberately to affirm. But I doubt whether this proves much, in favour of the practice of requiring Oaths;— whether its chief effect is not to lower men's sense of the obligations to veracity on occasions when they are *not* on Oath. The expressions which the practice causes to be so much in use, of *"calling* God to witness," and of *"invoking* the Divine judgment," tend to induce men to act as if they imagined that God does *not* witness their conduct *unless* specially "called on"; and that He will not judge false testimony unless with our permission: and thus an habitual disregard for veracity is fostered. If Oaths were abolished—leaving the *penalties* for false-witness (no unimportant part of our security) unaltered—I am convinced that, on the whole, Testimony would be more trust-worthy than it is.

Still, since there are, as I have said, persons whose Oath—as matters now stand—is more worthy of credit than their Word, this circumstance must be duly considered in weighing the value of Testimony.[34]

Concurrent Signs of Other Kinds

The remark above made, as to the force of *concurrent* testimonies, even though each, separately, might have little or none,[35] but whose *accidental* agreement in a falsehood would be extremely improbable, is not solely applicable to the Argument from *Testimony*, but may be extended to many arguments of other kinds also; in which a similar calculation of chances will enable us to draw a conclusion, sometimes even amounting to moral certainty, from a combination of data which singly would have had little or no weight. *E. G.* If any one out of a hundred men throw a stone which strikes a certain object,[36] there is but a slight probability, from that fact alone, that

[34] See Appendix, Note DDD.

[35] It is observed by Dr. Campbell that "It deserves likewise to be attended to on this subject, that in a number of concurrent testimonies, (in cases wherein there could have been no previous concert,) there is a probability distinct from that which may be termed the sum of the probabilities resulting from the testimonies of the witnesses, a probability which would remain even though the witnesses were of such a character as to merit no faith at all. This probability arises purely from the concurrence itself. That such a concurrence should spring from chance, is as one to infinite; that is, in other words, morally impossible. If therefore concert be excluded, there remains no other cause but the reality of the fact."—Campbell's *Philosophy of Rhetoric,* chap. V, bk. i, part 3.

[36] If I recollect rightly, these are the words of Mr. Dugald Stewart.

he aimed at that object; but if all the hundred threw stones which struck the *same* object, no one would doubt that they aimed at it. It is from such a combination of arguments that we infer the existence of an intelligent Creator, from the marks of contrivance visible in the Universe, though many of these are such as, taken singly, might well be conceived undesigned and accidental; but that they should *all* be such, is morally impossible.

Testimonies Mutually Confirmatory

And here it may be observed that there may be such a concurrence of Testimonies or other Signs as shall have very considerable weight, even though they do not relate directly to *one* individual conclusion, but to *similar* ones. *E. G.* Before the reality of aërolites [meteoric stones] was established as it now is, we should have been justified in not giving at once full credit to some report, resting on ordinary evidence, of an occurrence so antecedently improbable as that of a stone's falling from the sky. But if twenty distinct accounts had reached us, from various parts of the globe, of a like phenomenon, though no two of the accounts related to the *same individual* stone, still, we should have judged this a decisive concurrence; (and this is in fact the way in which the reality of the phenomenon was actually established;) because each testimony, though given to an individual case, has a tendency towards the general conclusion in which all concur; viz. the *possibility* of such an event; and this being once admitted, the antecedent objection against each individual case is removed. The same reasoning applies to several of the New Testament Parables, as that of the Prodigal Son, the Labourers in the Vineyard, the Rich Man and Lazarus, &c., each of which contains an allusion to the future Call of the Gentiles, so little obvious however that it would have been hardly warrantable so to interpret any one of them, if it had stood alone.

Great care is requisite in setting forth clearly, especially in any popular discourse, arguments of this nature; the generality of men being better qualified for understanding (to use Lord Bacon's words) "particulars, one by one," than for taking a comprehensive view of a whole; and therefore in a *Galaxy* of evidence, as it may be called, in which the brilliancy of no single star can be pointed out, the lustre of the combination is often lost on them.

Fallacy of Composition

Hence it is, as was remarked in the Treatise on Fallacies, that the sophism of "Composition," as it is called, so frequently misleads men. It is not improbable, (in the above example,) that *each* of the stones, considered *separately,* may have been thrown at random; and therefore the same is concluded of *all,* considered in *conjunction.* Not that in such an instance as this, any one would reason so weakly; but that a still greater absurdity of the very same kind is involved in the rejection of the evidences of our religion, will be plain to any one who considers, not merely the individual force, but the *number* and *variety* of those evidences.[37]

5

What Is Meant by the Chances against any Supposition

And here it may be observed, that though the easiest *popular* way of practically refuting the Fallacy just mentioned (or indeed any Fallacy) is, by bringing forward a parallel case, where it leads to a manifest absurdity, a metaphysical objection may still be urged against many cases in which we thus reason from calculation of chances; an objection not perhaps likely practically to influence any one, but which may afford the Sophist a triumph over those who are unable to find a solution; and which may furnish an excuse for the rejection of evidence which one is previously resolved not to admit. If it were answered then, to those who maintain that the Universe, which exhibits so many marks of design, might be the work of nonintelligent causes, that no one would believe it possible for such a work as *e. g.* the Iliad, to be produced by a fortuitous shaking together of the letters of the alphabet, the Sophist might challenge us to explain why even this last supposition should be regarded as less probable than any other; since the letters of which the Iliad is composed, if shaken together at random, must fall in *some* form or other; and though the chances are millions of millions to one against that, or any other *determinate* order, *there are precisely as many chances against one as against another,* whether more or less regular. And in like manner, astonished as we should be, and convinced of the intervention of artifice, if we saw any one draw out all the cards in a pack in regular sequences, it is demonstrable that the chances are not more against that order, than against *any one determinate* order we might choose to fix upon; against that one, for instance, in which the cards are at this moment actually lying in any individual pack. The multitude of the chances, therefore, he would say, against any series of events, does not constitute it improbable; since the like happens to every one every day. *E. G.* A man walking through London streets, on his business, meets accidentally hundreds of others passing to and fro on theirs; and he would not say at the close of the day that anything *improbable* had occurred to him; yet it would almost baffle calculation to compute the chances against his meeting precisely those very persons, in the order, and at the times and places of his actually meeting each. The paradox thus seemingly established, though few might be practically misled by it, many would be at a loss to solve, and an effect may sometimes thus be produced analogous to that of what is sometimes, in war, called a "barren victory"; *i. e.* one which has no direct imme-

[37] Mr. Davison, in the introduction to his work on Prophecy, states strongly the cumulative force of a multitude of small particulars. See ch. iii. § 4. of this Treatise.

diate result, but which yet will often produce a most important moral result, by creating an impression of military superiority.

What Is Meant by an Improbability in the Sense of Its Having Many Chances against It

The truth is, that any supposition is justly called improbable, not from the number of chances against it, considered *independently,* but from the number of chances against it *compared* with those which lie against some *other* supposition. We call the drawing of a prize in the lottery improbable; though there be but five to one against it; because there are *more* chances of a blank: on the other hand, if any one were cast on a desert island under circumstances which warranted his believing that the chances were a hundred to one against any one's having been there before him, yet if he found on the sand pebbles so arranged as to form distinctly the letters of a man's name, he would not only conclude it probable, but absolutely certain, that some human Being had been there; because there would be *millions* of chances against those forms having been produced by the fortuitous action of the waves. Yet if, instead of this, I should find some tree on the island such that the chances appeared to me five to one against its having grown there spontaneously, still, if, as before, I conceive the chances a hundred to one against any man's having planted it there, I should at once reckon this last as the more unlikely supposition.

So also, in the instance above given, any *unmeaning* form into which a number of letters might fall, would not be called improbable, countless as the chances are against that particular order, because there are *just as many* against each one of all other *unmeaning* forms; so that no *one* would be *comparatively* improbable; but if the letters formed a coherent poem, it would then be called incalculably improbable that this form should have been fortuitous, though the chances against it remain the very same; because there must be much *fewer* chances against the supposition of its having been the work of *design.* The probability in short, of any supposition, is estimated from a *comparison* with each of its alternatives. The inclination of the balance cannot be ascertained from knowing the weights in one scale, unless we know what is in the opposite scale. So also the pressure of the atmosphere (equivalent to about 30,000 pounds on the body of an ordinary man) is unfelt, while it is equable on all parts, and balanced by the air within the body; but is at once perceived, when the pressure is removed from any part, by the air-pump or cupping-glass.

The foregoing observations however, as was above remarked, are not confined to Arguments from Testimony, but apply to all cases in which the degree of probability is estimated from a calculation of chances.

For some further remarks on this subject the reader is referred to § 17 of the Treatise on Fallacies,[38] where the "Fallacy of Objections" is discussed.

---

[38] *Logic,* Bk. iii.

Disbelieving Is Believing

It is most important to keep in mind the self-evident, but often-forgotten maxim that *Disbelief is Belief;* only, they have reference to *opposite conclusions. E. G.* To disbelieve the real existence of the city of Troy, is to believe that it was feigned: and *which* conclusion implies the greater credulity, is the question to be decided. To some it may appear more, to others, less, probable, that a Greek poet should have celebrated (with whatever exaggerations) some of the feats of arms in which his countrymen had actually been engaged, than that he should have passed by all these, and resorted to such as were wholly imaginary.

So also, though the terms "infidel" and *"un*believer" are commonly applied to one who rejects Christianity, it is plain that to *dis*believe its divine origin, is to believe its human origin: and *which* belief requires the more credulous mind, is the very question at issue.

Ignorance or Doubt Opposed to Belief

The proper opposite to Belief is either conscious *Ignorance,* or *Doubt.* And even Doubt may sometimes amount to a kind of Belief; since deliberate and confirmed Doubt, on a question that one has attended to, implies a "verdict of *not proven";—*a *belief that there is not sufficient evidence* to determine either one way or the other. And, in some cases this conclusion would be accounted a mark of excessive credulity. A man who should doubt whether there is such a city as Rome, would imply his belief in (what most would account a moral impossibility) the *possibility* of such multitudes of independent witnesses having concurred in a fabrication.

A State of Doubt, Difficult to Some Persons

It is worth remarking, that many persons are of such a disposition as to be nearly incapable of *remaining* in doubt on any point that is not wholly uninteresting to them. They speedily make up their minds on each question, and come to *some* conclusion, whether there are any good grounds for it or not. And judging—as men are apt to do in all matters—of others, from themselves, they usually discredit the most solemn assurances of any one who professes to be in a state of doubt on some question; taking for granted that if you do not adopt their opinion, you must be of the opposite.

Others again there are, who are capable of remaining in doubt as long as the reasons on each side seem exactly *balanced;* but not otherwise. Such a person, as soon as he perceives any—the smallest—preponderance of probability on one side of a question, can no more refrain from deciding immediately, and with full conviction, on that side, than he could continue to stand, after having lost his equilibrium, in a slanting position, like the famous tower at Pisa. And he will accordingly be disposed to consider an acknowledgment that there are somewhat the stronger reasons on one side, as equivalent to a confident decision.

The tendency to such an error is the greater, from the circumstance that there are so many cases, in practice, wherein it is essentially necessary to come to a *practical* decision, even where there are no sufficient grounds for feeling *fully convinced* that it is the right one. A traveller may be in doubt, and may have no means of deciding with just confidence, which of two roads he ought to take; while yet he must, at a venture, take one of them. And the like happens in numberless transactions of ordinary life, in which we are obliged practically to make up our minds at once to take one course or another, even where there are no sufficient grounds for a full conviction of the understanding.

Decision Difficult to Some Minds

The infirmities above-mentioned are those of *ordinary* minds. A smaller number of persons, among whom however are to be found a larger proportion of the intelligent, are prone to the opposite extreme, that of not deciding, as long as there are reasons to be found on both sides, even though there may be a clear and strong preponderance on the one, and even though the case may be such as to call for a practical decision. As the one description of men rush hastily to a conclusion, and trouble themselves little about premises, so, the other carefully examine premises, and care too little for conclusions. The one decide without inquiring, the other inquire without deciding.

6

Progressive Approach

Before I dismiss the consideration of Signs, it may be worth while to notice another case of combined Argument different from the one lately mentioned, yet in some degree resembling it. The combination just spoken of is where several Testimonies or other Signs, singly perhaps of little weight, produce jointly, and by their coincidence, a degree of probability far exceeding the *sum* of their several forces, taken separately: in the case I am now about to notice, the combined force of the series of Arguments results from the *order* in which they are considered, and from their *progressive* tendency to establish a certain conclusion. *E. G.* one part of the law of nature called the *vis inertiæ*, is established by the Argument alluded to; viz. that a body set in motion will eternally continue in motion with uniform velocity in a right line, so far as it is not acted upon by any causes which retard or stop, accelerate or divert, its course. Now, as in every case which can come under our observation, some such causes do intervene, the assumed supposition is practically impossible; and we have no opportunity of verifying the law by direct experiment: but we may *gradually approach* indefinitely near to the case supposed: and on the result of such experiments our conclusion is founded. We find that when a body is projected along a rough surface, its motion is speedily retarded, and soon stopped; if along a smoother surface, it continues longer in motion; if upon ice, longer still; and the like with regard to wheels, &c. in proportion as we gradually lessen the friction of the machinery: and if we remove the resistance of the air, by setting a wheel or pendulum in motion under an exhausted receiver, the motion is still longer continued. Finding then that the effect of the original impulse is more and more protracted, in proportion as we more and more remove the impediments to motion from friction and resistance of the air, we reasonably conclude that if this could be *completely* done (which is out of our power), the motion would never cease, since what appear to be the only causes of its cessation, would be absent.[39]

Progressive Argument for the Being and Attributes of God

Again, in arguing for the existence and moral attributes of the Deity from the authority of men's opinions, great use may be made of a like progressive course of Argument, though it has been often overlooked. Some have argued for the being of a God from the universal, or at least, general, consent of mankind; and some have appealed to the opinions of the wisest and most cultivated portion, respecting both the existence and the moral excellence of the Deity. It cannot be denied that there is a presumptive force in each of these Arguments; but it may be answered, that it is conceivable, an opinion common to almost all the species, may possibly be an error resulting from a constitutional infirmity of the human intellect; [40]—that if we are to acquiesce in the belief of the majority, we shall be led to Polytheism; such being the creed of the greater part:—and that though more weight may reasonably be attached to the opinions of the wisest and best-instructed, still, as we know that such men are not exempt from error, we cannot be perfectly safe in adopting the belief they hold, unless we are convinced that they hold it *in consequence* of their being the wisest and best-instructed;—*so far forth* as they are such. Now this is precisely the point which may be established by the above-mentioned progressive Argument. Nations of Atheists, if there are any such, are confessedly among the rudest and most ignorant savages: those who represent their God or Gods as malevolent, capricious, or subject to human passions and vices, are invariably to be found (in the present day at least) among those who are brutal and uncivilized; and among the most civilized nations of the ancients, who professed a similar creed, the more enlightened members of society seem either to have rejected altogether, or to have explained away, the popular belief. The Mahometan nations, again, of the present day, who are certainly more advanced in civilization than their

---

39 See the argument in Butler's Analogy to prove the advantage which Virtue, if perfect, might be expected to obtain.
40 One of Bacon's *"Idola Tribus"* *(Idols of the Tribe)*.

Pagan neighbours, maintain the unity and the moral excellence of the Deity; but the nations of Christendom, whose notions of the Divine goodness are more exalted, are undeniably the most civilized part of the world, and possess, generally speaking, the most cultivated and improved intellectual powers. Now if we would ascertain, and appeal to, the sentiments of Man *as* a rational Being, we must surely look to those which not only prevail most among the *most* rational and cultivated, but towards which also a *progressive* tendency is found in men in *proportion* to their degrees of rationality and cultivation. It would be most extravagant to suppose that man's advance towards a more improved and exalted state of existence should tend to obliterate true and instil false notions. On the contrary, we are authorized to conclude, that those notions would be the most correct, which men would entertain, whose knowledge, intelligence, and intellectual cultivation should have reached comparatively the highest pitch of perfection; and that those consequently will approach the nearest to the truth, which are entertained, more or less, by various nations, *in proportion as* they have advanced towards this civilized state.

Progressive Argument for Tolerance

Again, "if we inquire what is the lesson that Scripture is calculated to convey to mankind, we should look not to the conclusions adopted by the majority of mankind, but, to the conclusions towards which there has been more or less *tendency,* in proportion as men have been more or less attentive, intelligent, and candid searchers into Scripture.

"Before the Gospel appeared, we find all Legislators and Philosophers agreed in regarding '*human good* universally,' as coming under the cognizance of the Civil Magistrate; who accordingly was to have a complete control over the moral and religious conduct of the citizens.

"We find again that, when the Scriptures were wholly unread by all but one in ten thousand of professed Christians, the duty of Rulers to wage war against Infidels and to extirpate Heretics was undisputed.

"When the Scriptures began to be a popular study, but were studied crudely and rashly, and when men were dazzled by being brought suddenly from darkness into light, intolerant principles did indeed still prevail, but some notions of religious liberty began to appear. As, towards the close of a rigorous winter, the earliest trees begin to open their buds, so, a few distinguished characters begun to break the icy fetters of bigotry; and principles of tolerance were gradually developed.

"As the study,—and the intelligent study—of Scripture, extended, in the same degree, the opening buds, as it were, made continually further advances. In every Age and Country, as a general rule, tolerant principles have (however imperfectly) gained ground wherever scriptural knowledge has gained ground. And a presumption is thus afforded that a still further advance of the one would lead to a corresponding advance in the other." [41]

41 See Essays on the Kingdom of Christ, Note A. Appendix.

Many other instances might be adduced, in which truths of the highest importance may be elicited by this process of Argumentation; which will enable us to decide with sufficient probability what consequence would follow from an hypothesis which we have never experienced. It might, not improperly, be termed the *Argument from Progressive Approach.*

Analogy

The word Analogy again is generally employed in the case of Arguments in which the instance adduced is somewhat more remote from that to which it is applied; *e. g.* a physician would be said to know by *Experience* the noxious effects of a certain drug on the human constitution, if he had frequently seen men poisoned by it; but if he thence conjectured that it would be noxious to some other species of animal, he would be said to reason from *analogy;* the only difference being that the resemblance is less, between a man and a brute, than between one man and another; and accordingly it is found that many brutes are not acted upon by some drugs which are pernicious to man.

But more strictly speaking, Analogy ought to be distinguished from *direct* resemblance, with which it is often confounded, in the language, even of eminent writers (especially on Chemistry and Natural History) in the present day. Analogy being a "resemblance of ratios," that should strictly be called an Argument from Analogy, in which the two things (*viz.* the one *from* which, and the one *to* which, we argue) are not, necessarily, themselves alike, but stand in similar *relations* to some other things; or, in other words, that the common *genus* which they both fall under, consists in a *relation.* Thus an egg and a seed are not in themselves alike, but bear a like relation, to the parent bird and to her future nestling, on the one hand, and to the old and young plant on the other, respectively; this *relation* being the genus which both fall under: and many Arguments might be drawn from this Analogy. Again, the fact that from birth different persons have different bodily constitutions, in respect of complexion, stature, strength, shape, liability to particular disorders, &c. which constitutions, however, are capable of being, to a certain degree, modified by regimen, medicine, &c. affords an Analogy by which we may form a presumption, that the like takes place in respect of mental qualities also; though it is plain that there can be no direct resemblance either between body and mind, or their respective attributes.

Errors Respecting Analogy

In this kind of Argument, one error, which is very common, and which is to be sedulously avoided, is that of concluding the *things* in question to be *alike,* because they are *Analogous;*—to resemble each other in themselves, because there is a resemblance in the relation they bear to certain other things; which is manifestly a groundless inference.

Sometimes the mistake is made of supposing this direct resemblance to *exist,* when it does not; sometimes, of supposing, or sophistically repre-senting, that such resemblance is *asserted,* when no such thing was intended. One may often hear a person reproached with having *compared* such and such a person or thing to this or that, and with having in so doing intro-duced a most unjust, absurd, and indecorous comparison; when, in truth, the object in question had not been, properly speaking, compared to any of these things; an *Analogy* only having been asserted. And it is curious that many persons are guilty of this mistake or misrepresentation, who are, or ought to be, familiar with the Scripture-Parables; in which the words "com-pare" and "liken" are often introduced, where it is evident that there could have been no thought of any direct resemblance. A child of ten years old would hardly be guilty of such a blunder as to suppose that members of the church are literally "like" plants of corn,—sheep,—fish caught in a net—and fruit-trees.

Another caution is applicable to the whole class of Arguments from Ex-ample; viz. not to consider the Resemblance or Analogy to extend further (*i. e.* to more particulars) than it does. The resemblance of a picture to the object it represents, is direct; but it extends no further than the one sense, of *Seeing,* is concerned. In the Parable of the unjust Steward, an Argument is drawn from Analogy, to recommend prudence and foresight to Christians in spiritual concerns; but it would be absurd to conclude that fraud was recommended to our imitation; and yet mistakes very similar to such a perversion of that Argument are by no means rare.

"Thus, because a just Analogy has been discerned between the metropolis of a country, and the heart of the animal body, it has been sometimes con-tended that its increased size is a disease,—that it may impede some of its most important functions, or even be the cause of its dissolution." [42]

Precautions against the Above Mistakes

Against both these mistakes our Lord's Parables are guarded in two ways. 1st. He selects, in several of them, images the most *remote* possible from the thing to be illustrated, in almost every point except the one that is essential; as in the Parable referred to just above,—in that of the unjust judge and importunate widow, &c. 2ndly. He employs a great *variety* of images in illustrating each single point; *e. g.* a field of corn,—a net cast into the sea,—a grain of mustard-seed,—a lump of leaven,—a feast,—a treasure hid-den in a field, &c. For as the thing to be illustrated cannot have a *direct* resemblance, or a *complete* analogy, to *all* these different things, we are thus

---

[42] See Copleston's *Inquiry into the Doctrines of Necessity and Predestination,* note to Disc. iii. q. v. for a very able dissertation on the subject of Analogy, in the course of an analysis of Dr. King's *Discourse on Predestination.* (See Appendix [E].) In the preface to the last edition of that Discourse, I have offered some additional remarks on the subject; and I have again adverted to it (chiefly in reply to some popular objections to Dr. King) in the Dissertation on the Province of Reasoning, subjoined to the *Elements of Logic.* Ch. v. § 1.

guarded against taking for granted that this is the case with any one of them.

It may be added, that the variety, and also the extreme *commonness* of the images introduced, serve as a help to the memory, by creating a multitude of *associations*. Our Lord has inscribed, as it were, his lessons on almost every object around us.

And moreover, men are thus guarded against the mistake they are so prone to, and which, even as it is, they are continually falling into, of laying aside their common-sense altogether in judging of any matter connected with religion; as if the rules of reasoning which they employ in temporal matters, were quite unfit to be applied in spiritual.

It may be added, that illustrations drawn from things considerably remote from what is to be illustrated will often have the effect of an *"a fortiori"* argument: as in some of the Parables just alluded to, and in that where Jesus says, "If ye then, being evil, know how to give good gifts to your children, *how much more,*" &c.

So also in the Apostle Paul's illustration from the Isthmian and other Games: "Now they do it to obtain a corruptible crown; but we, an incorruptible."

Important and Unimportant Resemblances and Differences of Cases

Sound judgment and vigilant caution are nowhere more called for than in observing what differences (perhaps seemingly small) do, and what do not, nullify the analogy between two cases. And the same may be said in regard to the applicability of Precedents, or acknowledged *Decisions* of any kind, such as Scripture-precepts, &c.; all of which indeed are, in their essence, of the nature of Example; since every recorded Declaration, or Injunction, (of admitted authority) may be regarded—in connexion with the persons to whom, and the occasion on which, it was delivered—as a *known case;* from which consequently we may reason to any other *parallel* case; and the question which we must be careful in deciding will be, to whom, and to what, it is *applicable.* For, as I have said, a seemingly small circumstance will often destroy the analogy, so as to make a precedent—precept, &c.—inapplicable: and often, on the other hand, some difference, in itself important, may be pointed out between two cases, which shall not at all weaken the analogy in respect of the argument in hand. And thus there is a danger both of being misled by specious arguments of this description, which have no real force, and also of being staggered by plausible objections against such examples or appeals to authority, &c. as are perfectly valid. Hence Aristotle observes, that an opponent, if he cannot show that the majority of instances is on his side, or that those adduced by his adversary are inapplicable, contends that they, *at any rate, differ in something* from the case in question.

Analogy of the Precious Metals to Other Commodities, How Far Imperfect

Many are misled, in each way, by not estimating aright the degree, and the *kind*, of difference between two cases. *E. G.* it would be admitted that a great and permanent diminution in the quantity of some useful commodity, such as corn, or coal, or iron, throughout the world, would be a serious and lasting loss; and again, that if the fields and coal-mines yielded regularly double quantities, with the same labour, we should be so much the richer; hence it might be inferred, that if the quantity of gold and silver in the world were diminished one-half, or were doubled, like results would follow; the utility of these metals, for the purposes of coin, being very great. Now there are many points of resemblance, and many of difference, between the precious metals on the one hand, and corn, coal, &c. on the other; but the *important* circumstance to the supposed argument, is, that the *utility* of gold and silver (as coin, which is far the chief) *depends on their value*, which is regulated by their scarcity; or rather, to speak strictly, by the difficulty of obtaining them; whereas, if corn and coal were ten times more abundant, (*i. e.* more easily obtained,) a bushel of either would still be as useful as now. But if it were twice as easy to procure gold as it is, a sovereign would be twice as large; if only half as easy, it would be of the size of a half-sovereign: and this (besides the trifling circumstance of the cheapness or dearness of gold-ornaments) would be all the difference. The analogy, therefore, fails in the point essential to the argument.

Mandeville's Argument

Again, Mandeville's celebrated argument against educating the labouring classes, "if a horse knew as much as a man, I would not be his rider," holds good in reference to *Slaves,* or subjects of a tyranny; governed, as brutes, *for the benefit of a Master,* not, for their own; but it wholly fails in reference to men possessing civil rights. If a horse knew as much as a man,—*i. e.* were a rational Being,—it would be not only unsafe, but *unjust,* to treat him as a brute. But a government that is for the benefit of the *Subject,* will be the better obeyed, the better informed the people are as to their real interests.

Paul's Preference of Celibacy, How Far Applicable

Again, the Apostle Paul recommends to the Corinthians celibacy as preferable to marriage: hence some Religionists have inferred that this holds good in respect of all Christians. Now in many most important points, Christians of the present day are in the same condition as the Corinthians; but *they* were liable to plunder, exile, and many kinds of bitter persecutions from their fellow-citizens; and it appears that this was *the very ground* on which celibacy was recommended to them, as exempting them from many afflictions and temptations which in such troublous times a family would entail; since, as Bacon observes, "He that hath a wife and children hath given pledges to Fortune." Now, it is not, be it observed, on the *intrinsic importance* of this difference between them and us that the question turns; but on its importance *in reference to* the advice given.

Analogy of the French Revolution to Those of Ancient Greece

On the other hand, suppose any one had, at the opening of the French Revolution, or at any similar conjuncture, expressed apprehensions, grounded on a review of history, of the danger of anarchy, bloodshed, destruction of social order, general corruption of morals, and the long train of horrors so vividly depicted by Thucydides as resulting from civil discord, especially in his account of the sedition at Corcyra; it might have been answered, that the example does not apply, because there is a great difference between the Greeks in the time of Thucydides, and the nations of modern Europe. Many and great, no doubt, are the differences that might be enumerated: the ancient Greeks had not the use of fire-arms, nor of the mariner's compass; they were strangers to the art of printing; their arts of war and of navigation, and their literature, were materially influenced by these differences: they had domestic slaves; they were inferior to us in many manufactures; they excelled us in sculpture, &c. &c. The historian himself, while professing to leave a legacy of instruction for future ages in the examples of the past, admits that the aspect of political transactions will vary from time to time in their particular forms and external character, as well as in the *degrees* in which the operation of each principle will, on different occasions, be displayed; but he contends, that "as long *as human nature remains the same,*" like causes will come into play, and produce, substantially, like effects.

In Corcyra, and afterwards in other of the Grecian States, such enormities, he says, were perpetrated as were the *natural result*—of pitiless oppression, and inordinate thirst for revenge on the oppressors;—of a craving desire, in some, to get free from their former poverty, and still more, in others, to gratify their avarice by unjust spoliation;—and of the removal of legal restraints from "the natural character of man," which, in consequence, "eagerly displayed itself as too weak for passion, too strong for justice, and hostile to every superior." Now the question *important to the argument,* is, are the differences between the ancient Greeks, and modern nations, of such a character as to make the remarks of Thucydides, and the examples he sets before us, inapplicable? or are they (as he seems to have expected) merely such as to alter the external shape of the transactions springing from similar human passions? Surely no mere external differences in customs, or in the arts of life, between the ancient Greeks and the French (our supposed disputant might have urged) can produce an *essential* and *fundamental* difference of results from any civil commotion: for *this,* some new vital principle of Action must be introduced and established in the heart;—something capable of over-ruling man's natural character. "As long as this remains the same," (as the historian himself remarks), substantially the same results may be looked for.

Alleged Analogy between France and England

Again, when the French Revolution did break out, in all its horrors, many apprehended that the infection would spread to England. And there are not a few who are convinced at this day, that but for the interruption of intercourse between the two Countries by the war, and the adoption of certain other measures, we should have had a revolution, and one accompanied by nearly equal extravagances and atrocities. Now the justness of this inference must of course depend on the correctness of the *"Analogy,"* in respect of the points most important to the question. All History teaches that the *probability* of a revolution, and also the *violence* with which it is conducted, depend, chiefly, on the degree in which a People has been not only exasperated, but also degraded and brutalized by a long course of oppressive misgovernment, and partly on the character of the people themselves (whether arising from those or from any other causes) in respect of blind and precipitate rashness, gross ignorance, and ferocity of disposition. In proportion as these causes exist, a nation is more or less a heap of combustibles ready to catch fire from a spark, and to blaze into a fierce conflagration. A small number of persons endeavoured, with very little success, to persuade the English that they were nearly as much oppressed as the French had been: and the French were partly so far persuaded of this, that they laboured to kindle among us a conflagration, from their own. And on the other hand, there were (and still are) a much greater number who conceived the former condition of the French People to be much nearer our own than in fact it was;—who were to a great degree unaware of the full extent of misgovernment under which that Country had long suffered, and of the ignorant and degraded, as well as irritated state of the great mass of its population; and who consequently saw no reason to feel confidence that an outbreak nearly resembling that in France might not be apprehended here.

Analogy between the Jews of Old and at Present

Again, "the argument drawn from the Babylonian and other ancient States having employed Jews in civil capacities, without finding them disloyal, or experiencing any disadvantage from their national attachment, or their peculiar opinions and customs, was met by the reply, that the case of those ancient Jews is not parallel to that of Jews in the present day; the former having not been guilty of the sin of rejecting the Messiah, but being professors of the only true religion then revealed.

"My reason for saying that the above objection is irrelevant, is that the whole question turns on the *discrepancy* likely to exist between the Jews and those of another religion; and that, modern Judaism is not *more hostile* to Christianity, than ancient Judaism was to heathen idolatry. The religious opinions and observances of the Jews, in the days of Daniel for instance, do not appear (it has been urged) to have unfitted them for the civil service of Babylonian or Median princes. And as no one will contend that Daniel, and the rest, were less at variance, in point of religion, with the idolatry of Babylon, than the modern Jews are with Christianity, it is inferred (and surely with great fairness), that these last are as fit for civil employments under Christian princes, as their ancestors, under Pagan.

"If the question were, what judgment ought to be formed in a religious point of view, of the ancient and of the modern Jews, respectively, we should of course take into account the important distinction which the advent of Christ places between the two. But in a question respecting civil rights and disabilities, this distinction is nothing to the purpose. To allege that the ancient Jews at Babylon professed a true religion in the midst of falsehood, and that their descendants adhere to an erroneous religion in the midst of truth, does not impair the parallel between the two cases, in respect of the present argument, so long as it is but admitted (which no one denies) that the Jews are not now led, by their religion, to entertain a greater repugnance for Christianity, than their ancestors did, for Paganism." [43]

Analogy of States to Individuals, in Respect of Questions of Political Economy

Again, to take an instance from another class of political affairs; the manufacture of beet-sugar in France, instead of importing West Indian sugar at a fourth of the price, (and to the English corn-laws nearly similar reasons will apply,) and the prohibition, by the Americans, of British manufactures, in order to encourage home production, (*i.e.* the manufacture of inferior articles at a much higher cost,) &c. are reprobated as unwise by some politicians, from the analogy of what takes place in private life; in which every man of common prudence prefers buying, wherever he can get them cheapest and best, many commodities which he could make at home, but of inferior quality, and at a greater expense; and confines his own labour to that department in which he finds he can labour to the best advantage. To this it is replied, that there is a great difference between a Nation and an Individual. And so there is, in many circumstances: a little parcel of sugar or cloth from a shop, is considerably different from a ship-load of either; and again, a Nation is an object more important, and which fills the mind with a grander idea, than a private individual; it is also a more complex and artificial Being; and of indefinite duration of existence; and moreover, the transactions of each man, as far as he is left free, are regulated by the

---

[43] Remarks on the Jews' Relief Bill, volume of Charges, &c. pp. 454-457. It is remarkable that the very persons who spoke against me on that occasion (1833), have, since, brought forward and carried the very measure I then advocated.

very person who is to be a gainer or loser by each,—the individual himself; who, though his vigilance is sharpened by interest, and his judgment by exercise in his own department, may yet chance to be a man of confined education, possessed of no general principles, and not pretending to be versed in philosophical theories; whereas the affairs of a State are regulated by a Congress, Chamber of Deputies, &c. consisting perhaps of men of extensive reading and speculative minds. Many other striking differences might be enumerated: but the question *important to the argument,* is, does the expediency, in private life, of obtaining each commodity at the least cost, and of the best quality we can, *depend* on any of the circumstances in which an Individual differs from a Community?

These instances may suffice to illustrate the importance of considering attentively in each case, not, what differences or resemblances are intrinsically the greatest, but, what are those that do, or that do not, affect the argument. Those who do not fix their minds steadily on this question, when arguments of this class are employed, will often be misled in their own reasonings, and may easily be deceived by a skilful sophist.

In fact it may be said almost without qualification, that "Wisdom consists in the *ready* and *accurate* perception of Analogies." Without the former quality, knowledge of the past is nearly uninstructive: without the latter, it is deceptive.

Arguments from Contraries

The argument from *Contraries,* noticed by Aristotle, falls under the class I am now treating of; as it is plain that Contraries must have something in common; and it is so far forth only as they *agree,* that they are thus employed in Argument. Two things are called "Contrary," which, coming under the same class, are the *most dissimilar* in that class. Thus, virtue and vice are called Contraries, as being, *both,* "*moral habits,*" and the most *dissimilar* of moral habits. Mere dissimilarity, it is evident, would not constitute Contrariety: for no one would say that "Virtue" is contrary to a "Mathematical Problem;" the two things having nothing in common. In this then, as in other arguments of the same class, we may infer that the two Contrary terms have a similar relation to the *same* third, or, respectively, to two *corresponding* (*i. e.* in this case, Contrary) terms; we may conjecture, *e. g.* that since virtue may be acquired by education, so may vice; or again, that since virtue leads to happiness, so does vice to misery.

The phrase "Parity of Reasoning," is commonly employed to denote Analogical Reasoning.

This would be the proper place for an explanation of several points relative to "Induction," "Analogy," &c. which have been treated of in the *Elements of Logic.* I have only to refer the reader therefore to that work, Bk. iv. ch. 1 & 5; and Appendix, article "Experience."

8

Real and Invented Examples

Aristotle, in his *Rhetoric,* has divided Examples into *Real* and *Invented:* the one being drawn from actual matter of fact; the other, from a supposed case. And he remarks, that though the latter is more easily adduced, the former is more convincing. If however due care be taken, that the fictitious instance,—the supposed case, adduced, be not wanting in *probability,* it will often be no less convincing than the other. For it may so happen, that one, or even several, historical facts may be appealed to, which, being never-theless exceptions to a general rule, will not prove the probability of the conclusion. Thus, from several known instances of ferocity in black tribes, we are not authorized to conclude, that blacks are universally, or generally, ferocious; and in fact, many instances may be brought forward on the other side. Whereas in the supposed case, (instanced by Aristotle, as employed by Socrates,) of mariners choosing their steersman by lot, though we have no reason to suppose such a case ever occurred, we see so plainly the *probability* that if it did occur, the lot might fall on an unskilful person, to the loss of the ship, that the argument has considerable weight against the practice, so common in the ancient republics, of appointing magistrates by lot.

Fictitious Cases Must Be Probable

There is, however, this important difference; that a fictitious case which has *not* this intrinsic probability, has absolutely *no* weight whatever; so that of course such arguments might be multiplied to any amount, without the smallest effect: whereas any matter of fact which is well established, however *unaccountable* it may seem, has *some* degree of weight in reference to a parallel case; and a sufficient number of such arguments may fairly establish a general rule, even though we may be unable, after all, to account for the alleged fact in any of the instances. E. G. no satisfactory reason has yet been assigned for a connexion between the absence of *upper cutting teeth,* or of the presence of *horns,* and *rumination;* but the instances are so numerous and constant of this connexion, that no Naturalist would hesitate, if, on examination of a new species, he found those teeth absent, and the head horned, to promote the animal a ruminant. Whereas, on the other hand, the fable of the countryman who obtained from Jupiter the regulation of the weather, and in consequence found his crops fail, does not go one step towards proving the intended conclusion; because that consequence is a mere gratuitous assumption without any probability to support it. In fact the assumption there, is not only gratuitous, but is in direct contradiction to experience; for a gardener *has,* to a certain degree, the command of rain and sunshine, by the help of his watering-pots, glasses, hot-beds, and flues; and the result is not the destruction of his crops.

There is an instance of a like error in a tale of Cumberland's, intended to prove the advantage of a public over a private education. He represents two brothers, educated on the two plans, respectively; the former turning out very well, and the latter very ill: and had the whole been matter of fact, a sufficient number of such instances would have had weight as an Argument; but as it is a fiction, and no reason is shown why the result would be such as represented, except the supposed superiority of a public education, the Argument involves a manifest *petitio principii;* and resembles the appeal made, in the well-known fable, to the picture of a man conquering a lion; a result which might just as easily have been reversed, and which would have been so, had lions been painters. It is necessary, in short, to be able to maintain, either that such and such an event *did* actually take place, or that, under a certain hypothesis, it would be *likely* to take place.

Supposed Cases Assert Nothing

On the other hand it is important to observe, with respect to any imaginary case, whether introduced as an argument, or merely for the sake of explanation, that, as it is (according to what I have just said) requisite that the hypothesis should be *conceivable,* and that the result supposed should follow *naturally* from it, so, *nothing more* is to be required. No fact being *asserted,* it is not fair that any should be *denied.* Yet it is very common to find persons, "either out of ignorance and infirmity, or out of malice and obstinacy," joining issue on the question whether this or that ever actually took place; and representing the whole controversy as turning on the literal truth of something that had never been affirmed. [See treatise on Fallacies, ch. iii. § "Irrelevant conclusion:" of which this is a case.] To obviate this mistake more care must be taken than would at first sight seem necessary, to remind the hearers that you are merely *supposing* a case, and not *asserting* any fact: especially when (as it frequently happens) the supposed case is one which might actually occur, and perhaps does occur.

I can well sympathize with the contempt mingled with indignation expressed by Cicero against certain philosophers who found fault with Plato for having, in a case he proposes, alluded to the fabulous ring of Gyges, which had the virtue of making the wearer invisible. They had found out, it seems, that there *never was* any such ring.

It is worth observing, that Arguments from Example, whether real or invented, are the most easily comprehended by the young and the uneducated; because they facilitate the exercise of Abstraction; a power which in such hearers is usually the most imperfect. This mode of reasoning corresponds to a *geometrical* demonstration by means of a Diagram; in which the Figure placed before the learner, is an *individual,* employed, as he soon comes to perceive, as a *sign,*—though not an *arbitrary* sign,[44]—repre-

---

44 The words, written or spoken, of any language, are *arbitrary* signs; the characters of Picture-writing or Hieroglyphic, are *natural* signs.

senting the whole class. The *algebraic* signs again, are arbitrary; each character not being itself an individual of the class it represents. These last therefore correspond to the *abstract* terms of a language.

Fable and Illustration

Under the head of Invented Example, a distinction is drawn by Aristotle, between Parabole and Logos. From the instances he gives, it is plain that the former corresponds (not to Parable, in the sense in which we use the word, derived from that of Parabole in the Sacred Writers, but) to Illustration; the latter to Fable or Tale. In the former, an *allusion* only is made to a case easily supposable; in the latter, a fictitious story is *narrated*. Thus, in his instance above cited, of Illustration, if any one, instead of a mere allusion, should relate a tale, of mariners choosing a steersman by lot, and being wrecked in consequence, Aristotle would evidently have placed that under the head of Logos. The other method is of course preferable, from its brevity, whenever the allusion can be readily understood: and accordingly it is common, in the case of *well-known* fables, to allude to, instead of narrating, them. That, *e. g.* of the Horse and the Stag, which he gives, would in the present day, be rather alluded to than told, if we wished to dissuade a people from calling in a too powerful auxiliary. It is evident that a like distinction might have been made in respect of historical examples; those cases which are well known, being often merely alluded to, and not recited.

Fable and Tale

The word "Fable" is at present generally limited to those fictions in which the resemblance to the matter in question is not direct, but analogical; the other class being called Novels, Tales, &c.[45] Those resemblances are (as Dr. A. Smith has observed) the most *striking,* in which the things compared are of the most *dissimilar* nature; as is the case in what we call Fables; and such accordingly are generally preferred for argumentative purposes, both from that circumstance itself, and also on account of the greater *brevity* which is, for that reason, not only allowed but required in them. For a Fable spun out to a great length becomes an Allegory, which generally satiates and disgusts; on the other hand, a fictitious Tale, having a more direct, and therefore less striking resemblance to reality, requires that an interest in the events and persons should be created by a longer detail, without which it would be insipid. The Fable of the Old Man and the Bundle of Sticks, compared with the Iliad, may serve to exemplify what has been said: the moral conveyed by each being the same, viz. the strength acquired by union, and the weakness resulting from division; the latter fiction would be perfectly insipid if conveyed in a few lines; the former, in twenty-four books, insupportable.

[45] A Novel or Tale may be compared to a Picture; a Fable, to a Device.

Of the various uses, and of the real or apparent refutation, of Examples (as well as of other Arguments), I shall treat hereafter; but it may be worth while here to observe, that I have been speaking of Example as a kind of *Argument,* and with a view therefore to that purpose alone; though it often happens, that a resemblance, either direct or analogical, is introduced for other purposes; viz. not to prove anything, but either to illustrate and *explain* one's meaning (which is the strict etymological use of the word Illustration), or to amuse the fancy by ornament of language: in which case it is usually called a *Simile:* as, for instance, when a person whose fortitude, forbearance, and other such virtues, are called forth by persecutions and *afflictions,* is compared to those herbs which give out their fragrance on being bruised. It is of course most important to distinguish, both in our own compositions and those of others, between these different purposes. I shall accordingly advert to this subject in the course of the following chapter.

CHAP. III—OF THE VARIOUS USE AND ORDER OF THE SEVERAL KINDS OF PROPOSITIONS AND OF ARGUMENTS IN DIFFERENT CASES

1

Arguments of Confutation and of Satisfaction

The *first rule* to be observed is, that it should be considered, whether the principal object of the discourse be, to give *satisfaction to a candid mind,* and convey *instruction* to those who are ready to receive it, or to *compel* the assent, or silence the objections, of an opponent. For, cases may occur, in which the arguments to be employed with most effect will be different, according as it is the one or the other of these objects that we are aiming at. It will often happen that of the two great classes into which Arguments were divided, the *"A priori"* [or Argument from cause to effect] will be principally employed when the chief object is to instruct the Learner; and the other class, when our aim is to refute the Opponent. And to whatever class the Arguments we resort to may belong, the general tenour of the reasoning will, in many respects, be affected by the present consideration. The distinction in question is nevertheless in general little attended to. It is usual to call an Argument, simply, *strong* or *weak,* without reference to the purpose for which it is designed; whereas the Arguments which afford the most *satisfaction* to a candid mind, are often such as would have less weight in *controversy* than many others, which again would be less suitable for the former purpose. *E. G.* There are some of the internal evidences of Christianity which, in general, are the most satisfactory to a believer's mind, but are not the most striking in the refutation of unbelievers: the Arguments from Analogy, on the other hand, which are (in refuting objections) the most *unanswerable,* are not so pleasing and consolatory.

My meaning cannot be better illustrated than by an instance referred to in that incomparable specimen of reasoning, Dr. Paley's *Horæ Paulinæ*. "When we take into our hands the letters," (*viz.* Paul's Epistles,) "which the suffrage and consent of antiquity hath thus transmitted to us, the first thing that strikes our attention is the air of reality and business, as well as of seriousness and conviction, which pervades the whole. Let the sceptic read them. If he be not sensible of these qualities in them, the argument can have no weight with him. If he be; if he perceive in almost every page the language of a mind actuated by real occasions, and operating upon real circumstances; I would wish it to be observed, that the proof which arises from this perception is not to be deemed occult or imaginary, because it is incapable of being drawn out in words, or of being conveyed to the apprehension of the reader in any other way, than by sending him to the books themselves."

There is also a passage in Dr. A. Smith's *Theory of Moral Sentiments*, which illustrates very happily one of the applications of the principle in question. "Sometimes we have occasion to defend the propriety of observing the general rules of justice, by the consideration of their necessity to the support of society. We frequently hear the young and the licentious ridiculing the most sacred rules of morality, and professing, sometimes from the corruption, but more frequently from the vanity of their hearts, the most abominable maxims of conduct. Our indignation rouses, and we are eager to refute and expose such detestable principles. But though it is their intrinsic hatefulness and detestableness which originally inflames us against them, we are unwilling to assign this as the sole reason why we condemn them, or to pretend that it is merely because we ourselves hate and detest them. The reason, we think, would not appear to be conclusive. Yet, why should it not; if we hate and detest them because they are the natural and proper objects of hatred and detestation? But when we are asked why we should not act in such or such a manner, the very question seems to suppose that, to those who ask it, this manner of acting does not appear to be so for its own sake the natural and proper object of those sentiments. We must show them, therefore, that it ought to be so for the sake of something else. Upon this account we generally cast about for other arguments; and the consideration which first occurs to us, is the disorder and confusion of society which would result from the universal prevalence of such practices. We seldom fail, therefore, to insist upon this topic." [1]

Foundations of Our Judgments of Individuals

It may serve to illustrate what has been just said, to remark that our judgment of the character of any individual is often not originally derived from such circumstances as we should assign, or *could* adequately set forth in language, in justification of our opinion. When we undertake to give our reasons for thinking that some individual, with whom we are personally

[1] Part II. sec. ii. pp. 151, 152, vol. i. ed. 1812.

acquainted, is, or is not, a gentleman,—a man of taste,—humane,—public-spirited, &c. we of course appeal to his conduct, or his distinct avowal of his own sentiments; and if these furnish sufficient proof of our assertions, we are admitted to have given *good reasons* for our opinion: but it may be still doubted whether these were, in the first instance at least, *our* reasons, which led us to form that opinion. If we carefully and candidly examine our own mind, we shall generally find that our judgment was, originally (if not absolutely decided), at least strongly influenced, by the person's looks—tones of voice—gestures—choice of expressions, and the like; which, if stated as reasons for forming a conclusion, would in general appear frivolous, merely because no language is competent adequately to describe them; but which are not necessarily insufficient grounds for beginning at least to form an opinion; since it is notorious that there are many acute persons who are seldom deceived in such indications of character.

In all subjects indeed, persons unaccustomed to writing or discussion, but possessing natural sagacity, and experience in particular departments, have been observed to be generally unable to give a satisfactory reason for their judgments, even on points on which they are actually very good judges.[2] This is a defect which it is the business of education (especially the present branch of it) to surmount or diminish. After all, however, in some subjects, no language can adequately convey (to the inexperienced at least) all the indications which influence the judgment of an acute and practised observer. And hence it has been justly and happily remarked, that, "he must be an indifferent physician, who never takes any step for which he cannot assign a satisfactory reason."

2

Presumption and Burden of Proof

It is a point of great importance to decide in each case, at the outset, in your own mind, and clearly to point out to the hearer, as occasion may serve, on which side the *Presumption* lies, and to which belongs the [*onus probandi*] *Burden of Proof*. For though it may often be expedient to bring forward more proofs than can be fairly *demanded* of you, it is always desirable, when this is the case, that it should be *known*, and that the strength of the cause should be estimated accordingly.

According to the most correct use of the term, a "Presumption" in favour of any supposition, means, not (as has been sometimes erroneously imagined) a preponderance of probability in its favour, but, such a *pre-occupation* of the ground, as implies that it must stand good till some sufficient reason is adduced against it; in short, that the *Burden of proof* lies on the side of him who would dispute it.

Thus, it is a well-known principle of the Law, that every man (including

2 See Aristotle's *Ethics*, Bk. vi.

a prisoner brought up for trial) is to be *presumed* innocent till his guilt is established. This does not, of course, mean that we are to *take for granted* he is innocent; for if that were the case, he would be entitled to immediate liberation: nor does it mean that it is antecedently *more likely than not* that he is innocent; or, that the majority of these brought to trial are so. It evidently means only that the "burden of proof" lies with the accusers;— that he is not to be called on to prove his innocence, or to be dealt with as a criminal till he has done so; but that they are to bring their charges against him, which if he can repel, he stands acquitted.

Thus again, there is a "presumption" in favour of the right of any individuals or bodies-corporate to the property of which they are in *actual possession.* This does not mean that they are, or are not, *likely* to be the rightful owners: but merely, that no man is to be disturbed in his possessions till some claim against him shall be established. He is not to be called on to prove his right; but the claimant, to disprove it; on whom consequently the "burden of proof" lies.

Importance of Deciding on Which Side Lies the Onus Probandi

A moderate portion of common-sense will enable any one to perceive, and to show, on which side the Presumption lies, when once his attention is called to this question; though, for want of attention, it is often overlooked: and on the determination of this question the whole character of a discussion will often very much depend. A body of troops may be perfectly adequate to the defence of a fortress against any attack that may be made on it; and yet, if, ignorant of the advantage they possess, they sally forth into the open field to encounter the enemy, they may suffer a repulse. At any rate, even if strong enough to act on the offensive, they ought still to keep possession of their fortress. In like manner, if you have the "Presumption" on your side, and can but *refute* all the arguments brought against you, you have, for the present at least, gained a victory: but if you abandon this position, by suffering this Presumption to be forgotten, which is in fact *leaving out one of, perhaps, your strongest arguments,* you may appear to be making a feeble attack, instead of a triumphant defence.

Such an obvious case as one of those just stated, will serve to illustrate this principle. Let any one imagine a perfectly unsupported accusation of some offence to be brought against himself; and then let him imagine himself— instead of replying (as of course he would do) by a simple denial, and a defiance of his accuser to prove the charge,—setting himself to establish a negative,—taking on himself the burden of proving his own innocence, by collecting all the circumstances indicative of it that he can muster: and the result would be, in many cases, that this evidence would fall far short of establishing a certainty, and might even have the effect of raising a suspicion against him,[3] he having in fact kept out of sight the important

---

3 Hence the French proverb, "Qui s'excuse, s'accuse."

circumstance, that these probabilities in one scale, though of no great weight perhaps in themselves, are to be weighed against absolutely nothing in the other scale.

The following are a few of the cases in which it is important, though very easy, to point out where the Presumption lies.

Presumption in Favour of Existing Institutions

There is a Presumption in favour of every *existing* institution. Many of these (we will suppose, the majority) may be susceptible of alteration for the better; but still the "Burden of proof" lies with him who proposes an alteration; simply, on the ground that since a change is not a good in itself, he who demands a change should show cause for it. No one is *called on* (though he may find it advisable) to defend an existing institution, till some argument is adduced against it; and that argument ought in fairness to prove, not merely an actual inconvenience, but the possibility of a change for the better.

Presumption of Innocence

Every book again, as well as person, ought to be presumed harmless (and consequently the copy-right protected by our courts) till something is proved against it. It is a hardship to require a man to prove, either of his book, or of his private life, that there is no ground for any accusation; or else to be denied the protection of his Country. The Burden of proof, in each case, lies fairly on the accuser. I cannot but consider therefore as utterly unreasonable the decisions (which some years ago excited so much attention) to refuse the interference of the Court of Chancery in cases of piracy, whenever there was even any *doubt* whether the book pirated *might* not contain something of an immoral tendency.

Presumption against a Paradox

There is a "Presumption" against any thing *paradoxical,* i. e. contrary to the prevailing opinion: it may be true; but the Burden of proof lies with him who maintains it; since men are not to be expected to abandon the prevailing belief till some reason is shown.

Hence it is, probably, that many are accustomed to apply "Paradox" as if it were a term of reproach, and implied absurdity or falsity. But correct use is in favour of the etymological sense. If a Paradox is unsupported, it can claim no attention; but if false, it should be censured on *that* ground; but not for being *new.* If true, it is the more important, for being a truth not generally admitted. *"Interdum vulgus rectum videt; est ubi peccat."* Yet one often hears a charge of "paradox and nonsense" brought forward, as if there were some close connexion between the two. And indeed, in one sense this is the case; for to those who are too dull, or too prejudiced, to admit any notion at variance with those they have been used to entertain, *that* may appear nonsense, which to others is sound sense. Thus "Christ crucified" was "to the Jews, a stumbling-block," (paradox,) "and to the Greeks, foolishness;" because the one "required a sign" of a different kind from any that appeared; and the others "sought after wisdom" in their schools of philosophy.

Christianity, Presumptions against and for

Accordingly there was a Presumption against the Gospel in its first announcement. A Jewish peasant claimed to be the promised Deliverer, in whom all the nations of the Earth were to be blessed. The Burden of proof lay with Him. No one could be fairly called on to admit his pretensions till He showed cause for believing in Him. If He "had not done among them the *works* which none other man did, they had not had sin."

Now, the case is reversed. Christianity *exists;* and those who deny the divine origin attributed to it, are bound to show some reasons for assigning to it a human origin: not indeed to prove that it *did* originate in this or that way, without supernatural aid; but to point out some conceivable way in which it *might* have so arisen.

It is indeed highly expedient to bring forward evidences to establish the divine origin of Christianity: but it ought to be more carefully kept in mind than is done by most writers, that all this is an argument "ex abundanti," as the phrase is,—over and above what can fairly be called for, till some hypothesis should be framed, to account for the origin of Christianity by human means. The Burden of proof, *now,* lies plainly on him who rejects the Gospel: which, if it were not established by miracles, demands an explanation of the greater miracle,—its having been established, in defiance of all opposition, by human contrivance.

The Reformation

The Burden of proof, again, lay on the authors of the Reformation: they were bound to show cause for every *change* they advocated; and they admitted the fairness of this requisition, and accepted the challenge. But they were *not* bound to show cause for *retaining* what they left unaltered. The Presumption was, in those points, on their side; and they had only to reply to objections. This important distinction is often lost sight of, by those who look at the "doctrines, &c. of the Church of England as constituted at the Reformation," in the mass, without distinguishing the altered from the unaltered parts. The framers of the Articles kept this in mind in their expression respecting infant-baptism, that it "ought by all means to be *retained.*" They did not introduce the practice, but left it as they found it; considering the burden to lie on those who denied its existence in the primitive church, to show *when* it did arise.

The case of Episcopacy is exactly parallel: but Hooker seems to have overlooked this advantage: he sets himself to *prove* the apostolic origin of the institution, as if his task had been to *introduce* it.[4] Whatever force there may be in arguments so adduced, it is plain they must have far *more* force if the important Presumption be kept in view, that the institution had notoriously existed many ages, and that consequently, even if there had been no direct evidence for its being coeval with Christianity, it might fairly be at least supposed to be so, till some other period should be pointed out at which it had been introduced as an innovation.

Tradition

In the case of any *doctrines* again, professing to be essential parts of the Gospel-revelation, the fair *presumption* is, that we shall find all such distinctly declared in Scripture. And again, in respect of commands or prohibitions as to any point, which our Lord or his Apostles did deliver, there is a presumption that Christians are bound to comply. If any one maintains, on the ground of Tradition, the necessity of some additional article of faith (as for instance that of Purgatory) or the propriety of a departure from the New Testament precepts (as for instance in the denial of the cup to the Laity in the Eucharist) the burden of proof lies with him. We are not called on to prove that there is no tradition to the purpose;—much less, that no tradition can have any weight at all in *any* case. It is for *him* to prove, not merely generally, that there is such a thing as Tradition, and that it is entitled to respect, but that there is a tradition relative to each of the points which he thus maintains; and that such tradition is, in each point, sufficient to establish that point. For want of observing this rule, the most vague and interminable disputes have often been carried on respecting Tradition, generally.

It should be also remarked under this head, that in any one question the Presumption will often be found to lie on different sides, in respect of different parties. *E. G.* In the question between a member of the Church of England, and a Presbyterian, or member of any other Church, on which side does the Presumption lie? Evidently, to each, in favour of the religious community to which he at present belongs. He is not to separate from the Church of which he is a member, without having some sufficient reason to allege.

A Presumption evidently admits of various degrees of strength, from the very faintest, up to a complete and confident acquiescence.

Deference

The person, Body, or book, in favour of whose decisions there is a certain Presumption, is said to have, so far, "Authority"; in the strict sense of the

---

4 On the ambiguous employment of the phrase "divine origin"—a great source of confused reasoning among theologians—I have offered some remarks in Essay II. "On the Kingdom of Christ," § 17. 4th edit.

word.[5] And a recognition of this kind of Authority,—an *habitual* Presumption in favour of such a one's decisions or opinions—is usually called "Deference."

It will often happen that this deference is not recognized by either party. A man will perhaps disavow with scorn all deference for some person,—a son or daughter perhaps, or an humble companion,—whom he treats, in manner, with familiar superiority; and the other party will as readily and sincerely renounce all pretension to Authority; and yet there may be that "habitual Presumption" in the mind of the one, in favour of the opinions, suggestions, &c. of the other, which we have called Deference. These parties however are not using the *words* in a different sense, but are unaware of the state of the *fact*. There is a Deference; but *unconscious*.

Arrogance

Those who are habitually wanting in Deference towards such as we think entitled to it, are usually called *"arrogant"*; the word being used as distinguished from self-*conceited*, *proud*, *vain*, and other kindred words. Such persons may be described as having an habitual and exclusive "self-deference."

Of course the persons and works which are looked up to as high authorities, or the contrary, will differ in each Age, Country, and Class of men. But most people are disposed,—measuring another by their own judgment,—to reckon *him* arrogant who disregards what *they* deem the best authorities. That man however may most fairly and strictly be so called who has no deference for those whom he *himself* thinks most highly of. And instances may be found of this character; *i. e.* of a man who shall hold in high estimation the ability and knowledge of certain persons—rating them perhaps above himself—whose most deliberate judgments, even on matters they are most conversant with, he will nevertheless utterly set at nought, in *each particular case* that arises, if they happen not to coincide with the idea that first strikes his mind.

Admiration and Deference, Distinct

For it is to be observed that *admiration, esteem,* and *concurrence in opinion,* are quite distinct from "Deference," and not necessarily accompanied by it. If any one makes what appears to us to be a very just remark, or if we acquiesce in what he proposes on account of the reasons he alleges,—this is not Deference. And if this has happened many times, and we thence form a high opinion of his ability, this again neither implies, nor even necessarily produces Deference; though in reason, such *ought* to be the result. But one may often find a person conversant with two others, A, and B, and estimating A without hesitation as the superior man of the two; and yet, in any

---

[5] See article "Authority," in Appendix to *Elements of Logic*.

case whatever that may arise, where A and B differ in their judgment, taking for granted at once that B is in the right.

Grounds of Deference

Admiration, esteem, &c. are more the result of a judgment of the *understanding;* (though often of an erroneous one;) "Deference" is apt to depend on *feelings;*—often, on whimsical and unaccountable feelings. It is often yielded to a vigorous *claim,*—to an authoritative and overbearing demeanour. With others, of an opposite character, a soothing, insinuating, flattering, and seemingly submissive demeanour will often gain great influence. They will yield to those who seem to yield to them; the others, to those who seem resolved to yield to no one. Those who seek to gain adherents to their School or Party by putting forth the claim of *antiquity* in favour of their tenets, are likely to be peculiarly successful among those of an arrogant disposition. A book or a Tradition of a thousand years old, appears to be rather a *thing* than a *person;* and will thence often be regarded with blind deference by those who are prone to treat their contemporaries with insolent contempt, but who "will not go to compare with an old man." They will submit readily to the authority of men who flourished fifteen or sixteen centuries ago, and whom, if now living, they would not treat with decent respect.

With some persons, again, Authority seems to act according to the law of Gravitation; inversely as the squares of the *distances.* They are inclined to be of the opinion of the person who is *nearest.* Personal *Affection,* again, in many minds, generates Deference. They form a habit of first, *wishing,* secondly, *hoping,* and thirdly, *believing* a person to be in the right, whom they would be *sorry* to think mistaken. In a state of morbid depression of spirits, the same cause leads to the opposite effect. To a person in that state, whatever he would be "sorry to think" appears probable; and consequently there is a Presumption in his mind *against* the opinions, measures, &c. of those he is most attached to. That the degree of Deference felt for any one's Authority ought to depend not on our feelings, but on our judgment, it is almost superfluous to remark; but it is important to remember that there is a danger on *both* sides;—of an unreasonable Presumption either on the side of our wishes, or *against* them.

Deference as to Particular Points

It is obvious that Deference ought to be, and usually is, felt in reference to particular points. One has a deference for his physician, in questions of medicine; and for his bailiff, in questions of farming; but not *vice versâ.* And accordingly, Deference may be misplaced in respect of the *subject,* as well as of the person. It is conceivable that one may have a *due* degree of Deference, and an *excess* of it, and a *deficiency* of it, all towards the same person, but in respect of different points.

Men Often Self-Deceived As to Their Feelings of Deference

It is worth remarking, as a curious fact, that men are liable to deceive themselves as to the degree of Deference they feel towards various persons. But the case is the same (as I shall have occasion hereafter to point out [6]) with many other feelings also, such as pity, contempt, love, joy, &c.; in respect of which we are apt to mistake the *conviction* that such and such an object *deserves* pity, contempt, &c. for the *feeling* itself; which often does not accompany that conviction. And so also, a person will perhaps describe himself (with sincere good faith) as feeling great Deference towards some one, on the ground of his *believing* him to be *entitled* to it; and perhaps being really indignant against *any one else* who does not manifest it. Sometimes again, one will mistake for a feeling of Deference his *concurrence* with another's views, and admiration of what is said or done by him. But this, as has been observed above, does not imply Deference, if the same approbation would have been bestowed on the same views, supposing them stated and maintained in an anonymous paper. The converse mistake is equally natural. A man may fancy that, in each case, he acquiesces in such a one's views or suggestions from the dictates of judgment, and for the reasons given; ("What she does seems wisest, virtuousest, discreetest, best" [7];) when yet perhaps the very same reasons, coming from another, would have been rejected.

Statements of Facts Liable to Be Disregarded, When Coming from Those Whose Judgment Is Undervalued

It is worth observing also, that though, as has been above remarked, (ch. ii. § 4) questions of *fact,* and of *opinion,* ought to be decided on very different grounds, yet, with many persons, a statement of facts is very little attended to when coming from one for whose judgment (though they do not deliberately doubt his veracity) they have little or no Deference. For, by common minds, the above distinction, between matters of fact and of opinion, is but imperfectly apprehended.[8] It is not therefore always superfluous to endeavour to raise a Presumption in favour of the judgment of one whom you wish to obtain credit, even in respect of matters in which judgment has, properly, little or no concern.

It is usual, and not unreasonable, to pay more Deference—other points being equal—to the decisions of a *Council,* or *Assembly* of any kind, (embodied in a Manifesto, Act of Parliament, Speech from the Throne, Report, Set of Articles, &c.,) than to those of an individual, equal, or even superior

[6] Part II. ch. 1. § 2.
[7] Milton.
[8] It is a curious characteristic of some of our older writers, that they are accustomed to cite authorities,—and that most profusely,—for matters of opinion, while for facts they often omit to cite any.

to any member of such Assembly. But in one point,—and it is a very important one, though usually overlooked,—this rule is subject to something of an exception; which may be thus stated: in any composition of an individual who is deemed worthy of respect, we presume that whatever he says must have *some* meaning,—must tend towards *some* object which could not be equally accomplished by *erasing* the whole passage. He is expected never to lay down a rule, and then add exceptions, nearly, or altogether coextensive with it; nor in any way to have so modified and explained away some assertion, that each portion of a passage shall be virtually neutralized by the other. Now if we interpret in this way any *joint*-production of several persons, we shall often be led into mistakes. For, those who have had experience as members of any deliberative Assembly, know by that experience (what indeed any one might conjecture) how much *compromise* will usually take place between conflicting opinions, and what will naturally thence result. One person, *e. g.* will urge the insertion of something, which another disapproves; and the result will usually be, after much debate, something of what is popularly called "splitting the difference:" the insertion will be made, but accompanied with such limitations and modifications as nearly to nullify it. A fence will be erected in compliance with one party, and a *gap* will be left in it, to gratify another. And again, there will often be, in some document of this class, a total *silence* on some point whereon, perhaps, most of the Assembly would have preferred giving a decision, but could not agree *what* decision it should be.

A like character will often be found also in the composition of a single individual, when his object is to *conciliate several parties* whose views are conflicting. He then *represents,* as it were, in his own mind, an Assembly composed of those parties.

Any one therefore who should think himself bound in due deference for the collective wisdom of some august Assembly, to interpret any joint-composition of it, exactly as he would that of a respectable individual, and never to attribute to it anything of that partially-inconsistent and almost nugatory character which the writings of a sensible and upright man would be exempt from,—any one, I say, who should proceed (as many do) on such a principle, would be often greatly misled.[9]

It may be added, that the Deference due to the decisions of an Assembly, is sometimes, erroneously, transferred to those of some individual member of it; that is, it is sometimes taken for granted, that what they have, jointly, put forth, is to be interpreted by what he, in his own writings, may have said on the same points. And yet it may sometimes be the fact, that the strong expressions of his sentiments in his own writings, may have been omitted in the *joint*-production of the Assembly, precisely because *not* approved by the majority in that Assembly.

[9] In studying the Scriptures we must be on our guard against the converse mistake, of interpreting the Bible as if it were *one* Book, the joint-work of the Sacred Writers, instead of, what it is, several distinct books, written by individuals independently of each other.

Transferring the Burden of Proof

It is to be observed, that a Presumption may be *rebutted* by an opposite Presumption, so as to shift the Burden of proof to the other side. *E. G.* Suppose you had advised the removal of some *existing* restriction: you might be, in the first instance, called on to take the Burden of proof, and allege your reasons for the change, on the ground that there is a Presumption against every Change. But you might fairly reply, "True, but there is another Presumption which rebuts the former; every *Restriction* is in itself an evil; [10] and therefore there is a Presumption in favour of its removal, unless it can be shown necessary for prevention of some greater evil: I am not bound to allege any *specific* inconvenience; if the restriction is *unnecessary, that* is reason enough for its abolition: its defenders therefore are fairly called on to prove its necessity." [11]

Again, in reference to the prevailing opinion, that the *"Nathanael"* of John's Gospel was the same person as the Apostle *"Bartholomew"* mentioned in the others, an intelligent friend once remarked to me that *two names* afford a *prima facie* Presumption of two persons. But the name of *Bar*tholomew, being a "Patronymic," (like Simon Peter's designation *Bar*-Jona, and Joseph's surname of *Bar*sabas, mentioned in Acts;—he being probably the same with the Apostle "Joseph Barnabas," &c.,) affords a Counter-presumption that he must have had *another* name, to distinguish him from his own kindred. And thus we are left open to the arguments drawn from the omission, by the other Evangelists, of the name of Nathanael,—evidently a very eminent disciple,—the omission by John of the name of the Apostle Bartholomew,—and the recorded intimacy with the Apostle Philip.

Presumption against Logic

In one of Lord Dudley's (lately published) letters to Bishop Copleston, of the date of 1814, he adduces a presumption against the Science of Logic, that it was sedulously cultivated during the dark periods when the intellectual powers of mankind seemed nearly paralysed,—when no discoveries were made, and when various errors were wide-spread and deep- rooted: and that when the mental activity of the world revived, and philosophical inquiry flourished, and bore its fruits, Logical studies fell into decay and contempt. To many minds this would appear a decisive argument. The author himself was too acute to see more in it than—what it certainly is—a fair Presumption. And he would probably have owned that it might be met by a counter-presumption.

[10] See *Charges and Other Tracts*, p. 447.
[11] See Essay II. "On the Kingdom of Christ," § 33.

Counter-Presumption

When any science or pursuit has been unduly and unwisely followed, to the neglect of others, and has even been intruded into their province, we may presume that a *re-action* will be likely to ensue and an equally excessive contempt, or dread, or abhorrence, to succeed.[12] And the same kind of re-action occurs in every department of life. It is thus that the thraldom of gross superstition, and tyrannical priestcraft, have so often led to irreligion. It is thus that "several valuable medicines, which when first introduced, were proclaimed, each as a panacea, infallible in the most opposite disorders, fell, consequently, in many instances, for a time, into total disuse; though afterwards they were established in their just estimation, and employed conformably to their real properties." [13]

So, it might have been said, in the present case, the mistaken and absurd cultivation of Logic during ages of great intellectual darkness, might be expected to produce, in a subsequent age of comparative light, an association in men's minds, of Logic, with the idea of apathetic ignorance, prejudice, and adherence to error; so that the legitimate uses and just value of Logic, supposing it to have any, would be likely to be scornfully overlooked. Our ancestors, it might have been said, having neglected to raise fresh crops of corn, and contented themselves with vainly thrashing over and over again the same straw, and winnowing the same chaff, it might be expected that their descendants would, for a time, regard the very operations of thrashing and winnowing with contempt, and would attempt to grind corn, chaff, and straw, altogether.

Such might have been, at that time, a statement of the counter-presumptions on this point.

Presumption Overthrown

Subsequently, the presumption in question has been completely done away. And it is a curious circumstance that the very person to whom that letter was addressed should have witnessed so great a change in public opinion, brought about (in great measure through *his own* instrumentality) within a small portion of the short interval between the writing of that letter and its publication, that the whole ground of Lord Dudley's argument is cut away. During that interval the Article on Logic in the *Encyclopaedia Metropolitana* (great part of the matter of it having been furnished by Bishop Copleston) was drawn up; and attracted so much attention as to occasion its publication in a separate volume: and this has been repeatedly reprinted both at home and in the United States of America, (where it is used as a textbook in, I believe, every College throughout the Union,) with

12 I dwelt on this subject in a Charge to the Diocese of Dublin, 1843.
13 *Elements of Logic*, Pref. p. x.

a continually increasing circulation, which all the various attempts made to decry the study, seem only to augment: while sundry abridgements, and other elementary treatises on the subject, have been appearing with continually increased frequency.

Certainly, Lord Dudley, were he *now* living, would not speak of the "general neglect and contempt" of Logic at present: though so many branches of Science, Philosophy, and Literature, have greatly flourished during the interval.

The popularity indeed, or unpopularity, of any study, does not furnish, alone, a decisive proof as to its value: but it is plain that a presumption—whether strong or weak—which is based on the fact of general neglect and contempt, is destroyed, when these have ceased.

It has been alleged, however, that "the Science of Mind" has not flourished during the last twenty years; and that consequently the present is to be accounted such a dark period as Lord Dudley alludes to.

Supposing the statement to be well-founded, it is nothing to the purpose; since Lord Dudley was speaking, not, of any one science in particular, but of the absence or presence of intellectual cultivation, and of knowledge, generally;—the depressed or flourishing condition of Science, Arts, and Philosophy on the whole.

But as for the state of the "science of mind" at any given period, *that* is altogether a matter of opinion. It was probably considered by the Schoolmen to be most flourishing in the ages which we call "dark." And it is not unlikely that the increased attention bestowed, of late years, on Logic, and the diminished popularity of those Metaphysicians who have written against it, may appear to the disciples of these last a proof of the low state (as it is, to Logical students, a sign of the improving state) of "the Science of Mind." That is, regarding the prevalence at present of logical studies as a sign that ours is "a dark age," this supposed darkness, again, furnishes in turn a sign that these studies flourish only in a dark age!

Presumptions for and against the Learned

Again, there is a presumption, (and a fair one) in respect of each question, in favour of the judgment of the most eminent men in the department it pertains to;—of eminent physicians, *e. g.* in respect to medical questions,—of theologians, in theological, &c. And by this presumption many of the Jews in our Lord's time seem to have been influenced, when they said, "have any of the Rulers, or of the Pharisees believed on Him?"

But there is a counter-presumption, arising from the circumstance that men eminent in any department are likely to regard with jealousy any one who professes to bring to light something unknown to themselves; especially if it promise to *supersede,* if established, much of what they have been accustomed to learn, and teach, and practise. And moreover, in respect of the medical profession, there is an obvious danger of a man's being regarded as a dangerous experimentalist who adopts any novelty, and of his thus losing practice even among such as may regard him with admiration as a philosopher. In confirmation of this, it may be sufficient to advert to the cases of Harvey and Jenner. Harvey's discovery of the circulation of the blood is said to have lost him most of his practice, and to have been rejected by every physician in Europe above the age of forty. And Jenner's discovery of vaccination had, in a minor degree, similar results.

There is also this additional counter-presumption against the judgment of the proficients in any department; that they are prone to a bias in favour of everything that gives the most palpable *superiority* to themselves over the uninitiated, (the Idiotae) and affords the greatest scope for the employment and display of their own peculiar acquirements. Thus, *e. g.* if there be two possible interpretations of some Clause in an Act of Parliament, one of which appears obvious to every reader of plain good sense, and the other can be supported only by some ingenious and far-fetched legal subtlety, a practised lawyer will be liable to a bias in favour of the latter, as setting forth the more prominently his own peculiar qualifications. And on this principle in great measure seems founded Bacon's valuable remark; *"harum artium saepe pravus fit usus,* ne sit nullus." Rather than let their knowledge and skill lie idle, they will be tempted to misapply them; like a schoolboy, who, when possessed of a knife, is for trying its edge on everything that comes in his way. On the whole, accordingly, I think that of these two opposite presumptions, the counter-presumption has often as much weight as the other, and sometimes more.

No Necessary Advantage to the Side on Which the Presumption Lies

It might be hastily imagined that there is necessarily an *advantage* in having the presumption on one's side, and the burden of proof on the adversary's. But it is often much the reverse. *E. G.* "In no other instance perhaps" (says Dr. Hawkins, in his valuable "Essay on Tradition,") "besides that of Religion, do men commit the very illogical mistake, of first canvassing all the objections against any particular system whose pretensions to truth they would examine, before they consider the direct arguments in its favour." (p. 82.) But why, it may be asked, *do* they make such a mistake in *this* case? An answer which I think would apply to a large proportion of such persons, is this: because a man having been brought up in a Christian-Country, has lived perhaps among such as have been accustomed from their infancy to *take for granted* the truth of their religion, and even to regard an *uninquiring* assent as a mark of commendable *faith;* and hence he has probably never even thought of proposing to himself the question,—Why should I receive Christianity as a divine revelation? Christianity being nothing *new* to him, and the *presumption* being in favour of it, while the burden of proof lies on its opponents, he is not stimulated to seek reasons for believing it, till he finds it controverted. And when it *is* controverted,—when an opponent urges—How do you reconcile this, and that, and the other, with the idea of a divine revelation? these objections strike by their *novelty,*—by their being opposed to what is generally received. He is thus excited to inquiry; which he sets about,—naturally enough, but very unwisely,—by seeking for answers to all these objections: and fancies that unless they can all be satisfactorily solved, he ought not to receive the religion.[14] "As if (says the Author already cited) there could not be truth, and truth supported by irrefragable arguments, and yet at the same time obnoxious to objections, numerous, plausible, and by no means easy of solution." "There are objections (said Dr. Johnson) against a *plenum* and objections against a *vacuum;* but one of them must be true." He adds that "sensible men really desirous of discovering the truth, will perceive that reason directs them to examine first the argument in favour of that side of the question, where the first presumption of truth appears. And the presumption is manifestly in favour of that religious creed already adopted by the country. . . . Their very earliest inquiry therefore must be into the direct arguments, for the authority of that book on which their country rests its religion."

But reasonable as such a procedure is, there is, as I have said, a strong temptation, and one which should be carefully guarded against, to adopt the opposite course;—to attend first to the objections which are brought against what is established, and which, for that very reason, rouse the mind from a state of apathy. Accordingly, I have not found that this "very illogical mistake" is by any means peculiar to the case of religion.

When Christianity was first preached, the state of things was reversed. The Presumption was against it, as being a novelty. "Seeing that these things *cannot be spoken against,* ye ought to be *quiet,*" was a sentiment which favoured an indolent acquiescence in the old Pagan worship. The stimulus of novelty was all on the side of those who came to overthrow this, by a new religion. The first inquiry of any one who at all attended to the subject, must have been, not,—What are the objections to Christianity?— but on what grounds do these men call on me to receive them as divine messengers? And the same appears to be the case with those Polynesians among whom our Missionaries are labouring: they begin by inquiring— "Why should we receive this religion?" And those of them accordingly who *have* embraced it, appear to be Christians on a much more rational and deliberate conviction than many among *us,* even of those who, in general maturity of intellect and civilisation, are advanced considerably beyond those Islanders.

I am not depreciating the inestimable advantages of a religious education; but, pointing out the *peculiar* temptations which accompany it. The Jews and Pagans had, in their early prejudices, greater difficulties to surmount than ours; but they were difficulties *of a different kind.*[15]

Thus much may suffice to show the importance of taking this preliminary view of the state of each question to be discussed.

---

[14] See the Lessons on Objections, in the *Easy Lessons on Christian Evidences* (published by Parker, West Strand, and also by the Christian Knowledge Society).
[15] *Logic,* Appendix.

3

Matters of Fact and of Opinion

Matters of opinion, (as they are called; *i. e.* where we are not said properly to *know,* but to *judge,* see ch. ii. § 4,) are established chiefly by Antecedent-probability, [Arguments of the *first class,* viz. from Cause to Effect:] though the *Testimony* (*i. e.* authority) of wise men is also admissible: past Facts, chiefly by *Signs,* of various kinds; (that term, it must be remembered, including Testimony;) and future events, by Antecedent-probabilities, and *Examples.*

Example, however, is not excluded from the proof of matters of Opinion; since a man's judgment in one case, may be aided or corrected by an appeal to his judgment in another similar case. It is in this way that we are directed, by the highest authority, to guide our judgment in those questions in which we are most liable to deceive ourselves; viz. what, on each occasion, ought to be our conduct towards another; we are directed to frame for ourselves a similar supposed case, by imagining ourselves to change places with our neighbour, and then considering how, in that case, we should in fairness expect to be treated.

This however, which is the true use of the celebrated precept "to do as we would be done by," is often overlooked; and it is spoken of as if it were a rule designed to supersede all other moral maxims, and to teach us the intrinsic character of Right and Wrong. This absurd mistake may be one cause why the precept is so much more talked of than attempted to be applied. For it could not be applied with any good result by one who should have no notions already formed of what is just and unjust. To take one instance out of many; if he had to decide a dispute between two of his neighbours, he would be sure that each was wishing for a decision in his own favour; and he would be at a loss therefore how to comply with the precept in respect of either, without violating it in respect of the other. The true meaning of the precept plainly is, that you should do to another not necessarily what you would *wish,* but what you would *expect as fair and reasonable,* if you were in his place. This evidently pre-supposes that you have a knowledge of what is fair and reasonable: and the precept *then* furnishes a formula for the *application* of this knowledge in a case where you would be liable to be blinded by self-partiality.

A very good instance of an argument drawn from a "parallel case" in which most men's judgments would lead them aright, I have met with in a memoir of Roger Williams, a settler in North America in the 17th century, who was distinguished as a zealous missionary among the Indians, and also as an advocate of the then unpopular doctrine of religious liberty.

"He was at all times and under all changes, the undaunted champion of religious freedom. It was speedily professed by him on his arrival among those who sought in America a refuge from persecution; and strange as it may seem, it was probably the first thing that excited the prejudices of the

Massachusetts and Plymouth rulers against him. He was accused of carrying this favourite doctrine so far, as to exempt from punishment any criminal who pleaded conscience. But let his own words exculpate him from this charge. 'That ever I should speak or write a tittle that tends to such an infinite liberty of conscience, is a mistake, and which I have ever disclaimed and abhorred. To prevent such mistakes, I at present shall only propose this case. There goes many a ship to sea with many hundred souls in one ship, whose weal and woe is common; and is a true picture of a commonwealth, or an human combination or society. It hath fallen out, sometimes, that both Papists and Protestants, Jews and Turks, may be embarked into one ship. Upon which supposal, I affirm, that all the liberty of conscience, that ever I pleaded for, turns upon these two hinges, that none of the Papists, Protestants, Jews, or Turks, be forced to come to the ship's prayers, nor compelled from their own particular prayers, or worship, if they practise any. I further add, that I never denied, that notwithstanding this liberty, the commander of this ship ought to command the ship's course; yea, and also command that justice, peace, and sobriety be kept and practised, both among the seamen and all the passengers. If any of the seamen refuse to perform their service, or passengers to pay their freight; if any refuse to help in person or purse, toward the common charges or defense; if any refuse to obey the common laws and orders of the ship concerning their common peace or preservation; if any shall mutiny and rise up against their commanders and officers; if any should preach or write, that there ought to be no commanders nor officers, because all are equal in Christ, therefore no masters nor officers, no laws nor orders, no corrections nor punishments, I say I never denied but in such cases, whatever is pretended, the commander or commanders may judge, resist, compel, and punish such transgressors, according to their deserts and merits.' "

Explanatory Examples

It happens more frequently than not, however, that when in the discussion of matters of Opinion, an Example is introduced, it is designed, not for Argument, but, strictly speaking, for *Illustration;*—not to *prove* the proposition in question, but to make it more *clearly understood;* e. g. the Proposition maintained by Cicero (*de Off.* book iii.) is what may be accounted a matter of Opinion; viz. that "nothing is expedient which is dishonourable;" when then he adduces the Example of the supposed design of Themistocles to burn the allied fleet, which he maintains, in contradiction to Aristides, would have been inexpedient, because unjust, it is manifest, that we must understand the instance brought forward as no more than an Illustration of the general principle he intends to establish; since it would be a plain begging of the question to *argue* from a particular assertion, which could only be admitted by those who assented to the general principle.

It is important to distinguish between these two uses of Example; that, on the one hand we may not be led to mistake for an Argument such a one as the foregoing; and that on the other hand, we may not too hastily charge with sophistry him who adduces such a one simply with a view to explanation.

Our Lord's Parables are mostly of the explanatory kind. His discourses generally indeed are but little argumentative. "He taught as one having authority;" stating and explaining his doctrines, and referring for *proof* to his *actions.* "The *Works* that I do in my Father's name, they bear witness of me."

Illustration and Simile Distinguished

It is also of the greatest consequence to distinguish between Examples (of the invented kind) properly so called,—*i. e.* which have the force of Arguments,—and *Comparisons* introduced for the ornament of Style, in the form, either of Simile, as it is called, or Metaphor. Not only is an ingenious Comparison often mistaken for a proof, though it be such as, when tried by the rules laid down here and in the treatise on LOGIC, affords no proof at all; [16] but also, on the other hand, a real and valid argument is not unfrequently considered merely as an ornament of Style, if it happen to be such as to produce that effect; though there is evidently no reason why that should not be fair Analogical Reasoning, in which the new idea introduced by the Analogy chances to be a sublime or a pleasing one. E. G. "The efficacy of penitence, and piety, and prayer, in rendering the Deity propitious, is not irreconcilable with the immutability of his nature, and the steadiness of his purposes. It is not in man's power to alter the course of the sun; but it is often in his power to cause the sun to shine or not to shine upon him: if he withdraws from its beams, or spreads a curtain before him, the sun no longer shines on him; if he quits the shade, or removes the curtain, the light is restored to him; and though no change is in the mean time effected in the heavenly luminary, but only in himself, the result is the same as if it were. Nor is the immutability of God any reason why the returning sinner, who tears away the veil of prejudice or of indifference, should not again be blessed with the sunshine of divine favour." The image here introduced is ornamental, but the Argument is not the less perfect; since the case adduced fairly establishes the general principle required, that "a change effected in one of two objects having a certain relation to each other, may have the same practical result as if it had taken place in the other." [17]

The mistake in question is still more likely to occur when such an argu-

16 The pleasure derived from taking in the author's meaning, when an ingenious Comparison is employed, (referred by Aristotle to the pleasure of the act of learning,) is so great, that the reader or hearer is apt to mistake his apprehension of *this* for a perception of a just and convincing analogy. See Part III. ch. 2. § 3. See Appendix [F.] for two instances of "explanatory illustration," both of them highly ornamental also.

17 For an instance of a highly beautiful, and at the same time argumentative comparison, see Appendix, [G.] It appears to me that the passage printed in italics affords a *reason* for thinking it probable that the causes of the apostles' conduct are rightly assigned.

ment is conveyed in a single term employed metaphorically; as is generally the case where the allusion is common and obvious; *e. g.* "We do not receive as the genuine doctrines of the primitive Church what have passed down the *polluted stream* of Tradition." The Argument here is not the less valid for being conveyed in the form of a Metaphor.[18]

The employment, in questions relating to the future, both of the Argument from Example, and of that from Cause to Effect, may be explained from what has been already said concerning the connexion between them; some Cause, whether known or not, being always *supposed,* whenever an Example is adduced.

4

Arguments from Cause to Effect Have the Precedence

When Arguments of each of the two formerly-mentioned classes are employed, those from Cause to Effect (Antecedent-probability) have usually the precedence.

Men are apt to listen with prejudice to the Arguments adduced to prove anything which appears *abstractedly* improbable; *i. e.* according to what has been above laid down, *unnatural,* or (if such an expression might be allowed) *unplausible;* and this prejudice is to be removed by the Argument from Cause to Effect, which thus prepares the way for the reception of the other arguments. *E. G.* If a man who bore a good character were accused of corruption, the strongest evidence against him might avail little; but if he were proved to be of a covetous disposition, this, though it would not alone be allowed to substantiate the crime, would have great weight in inducing his judges to lend an ear to the evidence. And thus in what relates to the future also, the *a priori* Argument and Example support each other, when thus used in conjunction, and in the order prescribed. A sufficient Cause being established, leaves us still at liberty to suppose that there may be circumstances which will prevent the effect from taking place; but Examples subjoined show that these circumstances do not, at least always, prevent that effect. On the other hand, Examples introduced at the first, may be suspected (unless they are very numerous) of being exceptions to the general rule, instead of being instances of it; which an adequate Cause previously assigned will show them to be. *E. G.* If any one had argued, from the temptations and opportunities occurring to a military commander, that Buonaparte was likely to establish a despotism on the ruins of the French Republic, this argument, by itself, would have left men at liberty to suppose that such a result would be prevented by a jealous attachment to liberty in the citizens, and a fellow-feeling of the soldiery with them; then, the Examples of Caesar and of Cromwell, would have proved that such preventives are not to be trusted.

[18] See Part III. ch. 2. § 4.

Aristotle accordingly has remarked on the expediency of not placing Examples in the foremost rank of arguments; in which case, he says, a considerable number would be requisite; whereas, in *confirmation,* even one will have much weight. This observation, however, he omits to extend, as he might have done, to Testimony and every other kind of Sign, to which it is no less applicable.

Another reason for adhering to the order here prescribed is, that if the Argument from Cause to Effect were placed after the others, a doubt might often exist, whether we were engaged in *proving* the point in question, or (assuming it as already proved) in seeking only to *account* for it; that Argument being, by the very nature of it, such as *would* account for the truth contended for, supposing it were granted. Constant care, therefore, is requisite to guard against any confusion or indistinctness as to the object in each case proposed; whether that be, when a proposition is admitted, to assign a cause which *does* account for it, (which is one of the classes of *Propositions* formerly noticed,) or, when it is *not* admitted, to *prove* it by an *Argument* of that kind which *would* account for it, if it *were* granted.

With a view to the Arrangement of arguments, no rule is of more importance than the one now under consideration; and Arrangement is a more important point than is generally supposed; indeed it is not perhaps of less consequence in Composition than in the Military Art; in which it is well known, that with an equality of forces, in numbers, courage, and every other point, the manner in which they are drawn up, so as either to afford mutual support, or, on the other hand, even to impede and annoy each other, may make the difference of victory or defeat.[19]

E. G. In the statement of the Evidences of our Religion, so as to give them their just weight, much depends on the Order in which they are placed. The Antecedent-probability that a Revelation should be given to Man, and that it should be established by miracles, all would allow to be, considered by itself, in the absence of strong direct testimony, utterly insufficient to establish the Conclusion. On the other hand, miracles considered abstractedly, as represented to have occurred without any occasion or reason for them being assigned, carry with them such a strong intrinsic improbability as could not be wholly surmounted even by such evidence as would fully establish any other matters of fact. But the evidences of the former class, however inefficient alone towards the establishment of the conclusion, have very great weight in preparing the mind for receiving the other arguments; which again, though they would be listened to with prejudice if not so supported, will then be allowed their just weight. The writers in defence of Christianity have not always attended to this principle; and their opponents have often availed themselves of the knowledge of it, by combating in detail,

---

[19] A great advantage in this point is possessed by the *Speaker* over the *Writer.* The Speaker *compels* his hearers to consider the several points brought before them, in the order which he thinks best. Readers on the contrary will sometimes, by dipping into a book, or examining the Table of Contents, light on something so revolting to some prejudice, that though they might have admitted the proofs of it if they had read *in the order designed,* they may at once close the book in disgust.

arguments, the combined force of which would have been irresistible.[20] They argue respecting the credibility of the Christian miracles, abstractedly, as if they were insulated occurrences, without any known or conceivable purpose; as *E. G.* "what testimony is sufficient to establish the belief that a dead man was restored to life?" and then they proceed to show that the probability of a Revelation, abstractedly considered, is not such at least as to establish the fact that one *has* been given. Whereas, if it were *first* proved (as may easily be done) merely that there is no such abstract improbability of a Revelation as to exclude the evidence in favour of it, and that if one *were* given, it must be expected to be supported by miraculous evidence, then, just enough reason would be assigned for the occurrence of miracles, not indeed to establish them, but to allow a fair hearing for the arguments by which they are supported.[21]

Importance of Arrangement

The importance attached to the Arrangement of arguments by the two great rival orators of Athens, may serve to illustrate and enforce what has been said. Aeschines strongly urged the judges (in the celebrated contest concerning the Crown) to confine his adversary to the same order, in his reply to the charges brought, which he himself had observed in bringing them forward. Demosthenes, however, was far too skilful to be thus entrapped; and so much importance does he attach to this point, that he opens his speech with a most solemn appeal to the Judges for an impartial hearing; which implies, he says, not only a rejection of prejudice, but no less also, a permission for each speaker to adopt whatever *Arrangement* he should think fit. And accordingly he proceeds to adopt one very different from that which his antagonist had laid down; for he was no less sensible than his rival, that the same Arrangement which is the most favourable to one side, is likely to be the least favourable to the other.

It is to be remembered, however, that the rules which have been given respecting the Order in which different kinds of Argument should be arranged, relate only to the different kinds adduced in support of each separate Proposition; since of course the refutation of an opposed assertion, effected (suppose) by means of "Signs," may be followed by an *a priori* argument in favour of our own Conclusion; and the like, in many other such cases.

5

When the Premises and When the Conclusion Should Come First

A Proposition that is *well-known,* (whether easy to be established or not,) and which contains nothing particularly offensive, should in general be stated at once, and the Proofs subjoined; but one not familiar to the

---

20 See ch. 2. § 4.
21 See Paley's *Evidences,* Introd.

hearers, especially if it be likely to be unacceptable, should not be stated at the outset. It is usually better in that case to state the arguments first, or at least some of them, and then introduce the Conclusion: thus assuming in some degree the character of an *investigator*.

There is no question relating to Arrangement more important than the present; and it is therefore the more unfortunate that Cicero, who possessed so much practical skill, should have laid down no rule on this point, (though it is one which evidently had engaged his attention), but should content himself with saying that sometimes he adopted the one mode, and sometimes the other, (which doubtless he did not do at random), without distinguishing the cases in which each is to be preferred, and laying down principles to guide our decision. Aristotle also, when he lays down the two great heads into which a speech is divisible, the Proposition and the Proof, is equally silent as to the order in which they should be placed; though he leaves it to be understood, from his manner of speaking, that the Conclusion [or Question] is to be first stated, and then the Premises, as in Mathematics. This indeed is the usual and natural way of speaking or writing; viz. to begin by declaring your opinion, and then to subjoin the Reasons for it. But there are many occasions on which it will be of the highest consequence to reverse this plan. It will sometimes give an offensively dogmatical air to a composition, to begin by advancing some new and unexpected assertion; though sometimes again this may be advisable when the arguments are such as can be well relied on, and the principal object is to excite attention, and awaken curiosity. And accordingly, with this view, it is not unusual to present some doctrine, by no means really novel, in a new and paradoxical shape. But when the Conclusion to be established is one likely to hurt the feelings and offend the prejudices of the hearers, it is essential to keep out of sight, as much as possible, the point to which we are tending, till the principles from which it is to be deduced shall have been clearly established; because men listen with prejudice, if at all, to arguments that are avowedly leading to a conclusion which they are indisposed to admit; whereas if we thus, as it were, mask the battery, they will not be able to shelter themselves from the discharge. The observance accordingly, or neglect of this rule, will often make the difference of success or failure.[22]

It may be observed, that if the Proposition to be maintained be such as the hearers are likely to regard as *insignificant*, the *question* should be at first suppressed; but if there be anything *offensive* to their prejudices, the *question* may be stated, but the *decision* of it, for a time, kept back.

Gradual Statement of the Conclusion

And it will often be advisable to advance very gradually to the full statement of the Proposition required, and to prove it, if one may so speak, by

---

22 See note in § 4. It may be added, that it is not only nothing dishonest, but is a point of pacific charitableness as well as of discretion, in any discussion with any one, to *begin* with points of agreement rather than of disagreement.

instalments; establishing separately, and in order, each part of the truth in question. It is thus that Aristotle establishes many of his doctrines, and among others his definition of Happiness, in the beginning of the *Nicomachean Ethics;* he first proves in what it does *not* consist, and then establishes, one by one, the several points which together constitute his notion.

Thus again, Paley (in his *Evidences*) first proves that the apostles, &c. *suffered;* next that they encountered their sufferings *knowingly;* then, that it was *for* their testimony that they suffered; then, that the events they testified were *miraculous;* then, that those events were the *same* as are recorded in our books, &c.

Resolutions at Public Meetings

In public meetings the measure ultimately adopted will usually have been proposed in a *series* of resolutions; each of which successively will perhaps have been carried by a large majority, in cases where, if the whole had been proposed in a mass, it would have been rejected; some persons feeling objections to one portion, and others to another.

Advance from General to Particular

It will often happen again that some *general principle* of no very paradoxical character may be proposed in the outset; (just as besiegers break ground at a safe distance, and advance gradually till near enough to batter;) and when that is established, an unexpected and *unwelcome application* of it may be proved irresistibly.

And it may be worth observing, that we shall thus have to *reverse,* in many cases, the order in which, during the act of composition, the thoughts will have occurred to our minds. For in reflecting on any subject, we are usually disposed to *generalize;*—to proceed from the particular point immediately before us, successively, to more and more *comprehensive* views; the opposite order to which will usually be the better adapted to engage and keep up attention, and to effect conviction. *E. G.* Suppose I am thinking of engaging the co-operation of the laity in some measure designed for the diffusion of the Gospel; which they are perhaps disposed to regard too much as the business of the Clergy exclusively: this may lead me to reflect, generally, how prone laymen are in many points to confound Christian duties with clerical duties, and to speak and act as if they thought that a less amount of Christian virtue were amply sufficient for those who have not taken Holy Orders: and this again might carry me on to reflect yet more generally, on the prevalent error of imagining two kinds of Christianity, one, for a certain select and pre-eminent few, and the other, for the generality; and of supposing that those whom in later ages it has been customary to denominate "Saints," [23] namely the Apostles, Evangelists, and others,

[23] The term by which *all Christians* are denoted in Scripture.

who possessed inspiration, and other miraculous gifts, (such as Judas, among others, exercised,) had a degree of personal holiness, and a kind of Christian character, beyond what is at all expected of Christians generally, and which it would be even presumptuous for *us* to emulate.

Now to bring forward these topics in this order would not produce so good an effect as to reverse it; beginning with the more general remarks, and gradually narrowing, as it were, the circle, till the particular point in question was reached. The interest is the better kept up by advancing successively from the more to the less general: and moreover, as has been just remarked, the establishment of some general principle will in many cases be less unwelcome, and more fairly listened to, than the particular application of it.

Waiving a Question

It is often expedient, sometimes unavoidable, to *waive* for the present, some question or portion of a question, while our attention is occupied with another point. Now it cannot be too carefully kept in mind, that it is a common mistake with inaccurate reasoners (and a mistake which is studiously kept up by an artful sophist) to suppose that what is thus *waived* is altogether *given up.* "Such a one does not attempt to prove this or that": "he does not deny so and so:" "he tacitly admits that such and such may be the case;" &c. are expressions which one may often hear triumphantly employed, on no better grounds. And yet it is very common in Mathematics for a question to be waived in this manner. Euclid, *e. g.* first asserts and proves, that the exterior angle of a triangle is greater than either of the interior opposite angles;—without being able to determine at once, *how much* greater;—and that any two angles of a triangle are less than two right angles; *waiving* for the present, the question, *how much less.* He is enabled to prove, at a more advanced stage, that the exterior angle is equal to the two interior opposite angles together; and that all the three angles of a triangle are equal to two right angles.

The only remedy is, to state distinctly and repeatedly that you do not abandon, as untenable, such and such a position, which you are not at present occupied in maintaining;—that you are not to be understood as admitting the truth of this or that, though you do not at present undertake to disprove it.

6

When Needful to Account for Any Fact

If the Argument *à priori* has been introduced in the proof of the main Proposition in question, there will generally be no need of afterwards adducing Causes to account for the truth established; since that will have been already done in the course of the Argument: on the other hand, it will often be advisable to do this, when arguments of the other class have alone been employed.

For it is in every case agreeable and satisfactory, and may often be of great utility, to explain, where it can be done, the Causes which produce an Effect that is itself already admitted to exist. But it must be remembered that it is of great importance to make it clearly appear *which* object is, in each case, proposed; whether to *establish* the fact, or to *account* for it; since otherwise we may often be supposed to be employing a feeble argument. For that which is a satisfactory explanation of an admitted fact, will frequently be such as would be very insufficient to prove it, supposing it were doubted.

7

Refutation

Refutation of Objections should generally be placed in the midst of the Argument; but nearer the beginning than the end.

If indeed very strong objections have obtained much currency, or have been just stated by an opponent, so that what is asserted is likely to be regarded as paradoxical, it may be advisable to begin with a Refutation; but when this is not the case, the mention of Objections in the opening will be likely to give a paradoxical air to our assertion, by implying a conscious-ness that much may be said against it. If again all mention of Objections be deferred till the last, the other arguments will often be listened to with prejudice by those who may suppose us to be overlooking what may be urged on the other side.

Sometimes indeed it will be difficult to give a satisfactory Refutation of the opposed opinions, till we have gone through the arguments in support of our own: even in that case however it will be better to take some brief notice of them early in the Composition, with a promise of afterwards considering them more fully, and refuting them. This is Aristotle's usual procedure.

Sophistical Evasion

A sophistical use is often made of this last rule, when the Objections are such as cannot really be satisfactorily answered. The skilful sophist will often, by the promise of a triumphant Refutation hereafter, gain attention to his own statement; which, if it be made plausible, will so draw off the hearer's attention from the Objections, that a very inadequate fulfilment of that promise will pass unnoticed, and due weight will not be allowed to the Objections.

It may be worth remarking, that Refutation will often occasion the introduction of fresh Propositions; *i. e.* we may have to disprove Propo-sitions, which though incompatible with the principal one to be main-tained, will not be directly contradictory to it: *e. g.* Burke, in order to the establishment of his theory of beauty, refutes the other theories which have been advanced by those who place it in "fitness" for a certain end—in "proportion"—in "perfection," &c.; and Dr. A. Smith, in his *Theory of Moral Sentiments,* combats the opinion of those who make "expediency the test of virtue"—of the advocates of a "Moral sense," &c., which doctrines respectively are at variance with those of these authors, and *imply,* though they do not express, a contradiction of them.

Two Modes of Refuting

Though I am at present treating principally of the proper *collocation* of Refutation, some remarks on the conduct of it will not be unsuitable in this place. In the first place, it is to be observed that there is no distinct class of refutatory Argument; since they become such merely by the circumstances under which they are employed. There are two ways in which any Proposition may be refuted; first, by proving the contradictory of it; secondly, by overthrowing the Arguments by which it has been supported. The former of these is less strictly and properly called Refutation; being only *accidentally* such, since it might have been employed equally well had the opposite Argument never existed; and in fact it will often happen that a Proposition maintained by one author, may be in this way refuted by another, who had never heard of his Arguments. Thus Pericles is represented by Thucydides as proving, in a speech to the Athenians, the probability of their success against the Peloponnesians; and thus, virtually, refuting the speech of the Corinthian ambassador at Sparta, who had laboured to show the probability of their speedy downfall.[24] In fact, every one who argues in favour of any Conclusion is virtually refuting, in this way, the opposite Conclusion.

But the character of Refutation more strictly belongs to the other mode of proceeding; viz. in which a reference is made, and an answer given, to some specific arguments in favour of the opposite Conclusion. This Refutation may consist either in the denial of one of the *Premises,*[25] or an objection against the *conclusiveness* of the reasoning. And here it is to be observed that an objection is often supposed, from the mode in which it is expressed, to belong to this last class, when perhaps it does not, but consists in the contradiction of a Premise; for it is very common to say, "I admit your principle, but deny that it leads to such a consequence;" "the assertion is true, but it has no force as an Argument to prove that Conclusion;" this sounds like an objection to the Reasoning itself; but it will not unfre-

---

[24] The speeches indeed appear to be in great part then of the historian; but he professes to give the substance of what was either actually said, or *likely* to be said, on each occasion: and the arguments urged in the speeches now in question are undoubtedly such as the respective speakers would be likely to employ.

[25] If the Premise to be refuted be a "Universal," (See *Logic,* b. ii. ch. ii. § 3) it will be sufficient to establish its Contradictory, which will be a Particular; which will often be done by an argument that will naturally be exhibited in the third figure, whose conclusions are always Particulars. Hence, this may be called the *refutatory* Figure. (See *Logic,* b. ii. ch. iii. § 4.)

quently be found to amount only to a denial of the *suppressed* Premise of an Enthymeme; the assertion which is admitted being only the expressed Premise, whose "force as an Argument" must of course depend on the other Premise, which is understood.[26] Thus Warburton admits that in the Law of Moses the doctrine of a future state was not revealed; but contends that this, so far from disproving, as the Deists pretend, his divine mission, does, on the contrary, establish it. But the objection is not to the Deist's *Argument* properly so called, but to the other Premise, which they so hastily took for granted, and which he disproves, viz. "that a divinely-commissioned Law-giver would have been sure to reveal that doctrine." The objection is then only properly said to lie against the Reasoning itself, when it is shown that, granting all that is assumed on the other side, whether expressed or under-stood, still the Conclusion contended for would not follow from the Pre-mises; either on account of some ambiguity in the Middle Term, or some other fault of that class.

Fallacies

This is the proper place for a treatise on Fallacies; but as this has been inserted in the *Elements of Logic,* I have only to refer the reader to it (Book iii).

Direct and Indirect Refutation

It may be proper in this place to remark, that "Indirect Reasoning" is sometimes confounded with "Refutation," or supposed to be peculiarly con-nected with it; which is not the case; either Direct or Indirect Reasoning being employed indifferently for Refutation, as well as for any other pur-pose. The application of the term "elenctic," (from the Greek word mean-ing to refute or disprove,) to Indirect Arguments, has probably contributed to this confusion; which, however, principally arises from the very circum-stance that occasioned such a use of that term; viz. that in the Indirect method the absurdity or falsity of a Proposition (opposed to our own) is proved; and hence is suggested the idea of an *adversary* maintaining that Proposition, and of the Refutation of that adversary being necessarily ac-complished in this way. But it should be remembered, that Euclid and other mathematicians, though they can have no opponent to refute, often employ the Indirect Demonstration; and that, on the other hand, if the Contra-dictory of an opponent's Premise can be satisfactorily proved in the Direct method, the Refutation is sufficient.

[26] It has been remarked to me by an intelligent friend, that in common discourse the word "Principle" is usually employed to designate the *major* premise of an Argument, and "Reason," the *minor.*

The Indirect Method Sometimes Preferred

It is true, however, that while, in Science, the Direct method is considered preferable, in Controversy, the Indirect is often adopted by choice, as it affords an opportunity for holding up an opponent to scorn and ridicule, by deducing some very absurd conclusion from the principles he maintains, or according to the mode of arguing he employs. Nor indeed can a fallacy be so clearly exposed to the unlearned reader in any other way. For it is no easy matter to explain, to one ignorant of Logic, the grounds on which you object to an inconclusive argument; though he will be able to perceive its correspondence with another, brought forward to illustrate it, in which an absurd conclusion may be introduced, as drawn from true premises.

Proving Too Much

It is evident that either the *Premise* of an opponent, or his *Conclusion,* may be disproved, either in the Direct, or in the Indirect method; *i. e.* either by proving the truth of the Contradictory, or by showing that an absurd conclusion may fairly be deduced from the proposition you are combating. When this latter mode of refutation is adopted with respect to the *Premise,* the phrase by which this procedure is usually designated, is, that the "Argument proves too much;" *i. e.* that it proves, besides the conclusion drawn, another, which is manifestly inadmissible. *E. G.* The Argument by which Dr. Campbell labours to prove that every correct Syllogism must be nugatory, as involving a *"petitio principii,"* proves, if admitted at all, more than he intended; since it may easily be shown to be equally applicable to *all* Reasoning whatever.

It is worth remarking, that an Indirect argument may easily be altered in form so as to be stated in the Direct mode. For, strictly speaking, that is Indirect reasoning in which we assume as true the Proposition whose Contradictory it is our object to prove; and deducing regularly from it an absurd Conclusion, infer thence that the Premise in question is false; the alternative proposed in *all* correct reasoning being, either to admit the Conclusion, or to deny one of the Premises. But by adopting the form of a Destructive Conditional,[27] the same argument as this, in substance, may be stated *directly. E. G.* We may say, "let it be admitted, that no testimony can satisfactorily establish such a fact as is not agreeable to our experience; thence it will follow that the Eastern Prince judged wisely and rightly, in at once rejecting, as a manifest falsehood, the account given him of the phenomenon of ice; but he was evidently mistaken in so doing; therefore the Principle assumed is unsound." Now the substance of this Argument remaining the same, the form of it may be so altered as to make the Argument a direct one; viz. *"if* it be true that no testimony, &c. that Eastern Prince

---

[27] See *Logic,* b. ii. c. iv. § 6.

must have judged wisely, &c., but he did not; therefore that principle is not true."

Character of Conditional Propositions

Universally indeed a Conditional Proposition may be regarded as an assertion of the validity of a certain Argument; the Antecedent corresponding to the Premises, and the Consequent to the Conclusion; and neither of them being asserted as true, only, the *dependence* of the one on the other; the alternative then is, to acknowledge as a conclusion, either the truth of the Consequent, as in the Constructive Syllogism, or, (as in the destructive,) the falsity of the Antecedent: and the former accordingly corresponds to Direct reasoning, the latter to Indirect; being, as has been said, a mode of stating it in the Direct form; as is evident from the examples adduced.

Ironical Effect of Indirect Arguments

The difference between these two moaes of stating such an Argument is considerable, when there is a long chain of reasoning. For when we employ the Categorical form, and assume as true the Premises we design to disprove, it is evident we must be speaking *ironically,* and in the character, assumed for the moment, of an adversary; when, on the contrary, we use the hypothetical form, there is no irony. Butler's *Analogy* is an instance of the latter procedure: he contends that *if* such and such objections were admissible against Religion, they *would* be applicable equally to the constitution and course of Nature. Had he, on the other hand, assumed, for the argument's sake, that such objections against Religion *are* valid, and had thence proved the condition of the natural world to be totally different from what we see it to be, his arguments, which would have been the same in substance, would have assumed an ironical form. This form has been adopted by Burke in his celebrated "Defence of Natural Society, by a late noble Lord;" in which, assuming the person of Bolingbroke, he proves, according to the principles of that author, that the arguments he brought against ecclesiastical, would equally lie against civil, institutions. This is an Argument from *Analogy,* as well as Bishop Butler's, though not relating to the same point; Butler's being a defence of the *Doctrines* of Religion; Burke's, of its *Institutions* and practical effects. A defence of the *Evidences* of our religion, (the third point against which objections have been urged,) on a similar plan with the work of Burke just mentioned, and consequently, like that, in an ironical form, I attempted some years ago, in a pamphlet, (published anonymously, merely for the preservation of its ironical character,) whose object was to show, that objections, ("Historic Doubts,") similar to those against the Scripture-history, and much more plausible, might be urged against all the received accounts of Napoleon Buonaparte.[28]

28 To these examples may be added the "Pastoral Epistle to Some Members of the University of Oxford," (Fellowes,) first published in 1835, and now reprinted in the "Remains

It is in some respects a recommendation of this latter method, and in others an objection to it, that the sophistry of an adversary will often be exposed by it in a *ludicrous* point of view; and this even where no such effect is designed; the very essence of jest being its *mimic sophistry*.[29] This will often give additional force to the Argument, by the vivid impression which ludicrous images produce; but again it will not unfrequently have this disadvantage, that weak men, perceiving the wit, are apt to conclude that nothing *but* wit is designed; and lose sight perhaps of a solid and convincing Argument, which they regard as no more than a good joke. Having been warned that "ridicule is not the test of truth," and "that wisdom and wit" are not the same thing, they distrust every thing that can possibly be regarded as witty; not having judgment to perceive the combination, when it occurs, of Wit with sound Reasoning. The ivy-wreath completely conceals from their view the point of the Thyrsus.

Danger of Irony

And moreover if such a mode of Argument be employed on serious subjects, the "weak brethren" are sometimes scandalized by what appears to them a profanation; not having discernment to perceive when it is that the ridicule does, and when it does not, affect the solemn subject itself. But for the respect paid to Holy Writ, the taunt of Elijah against the prophets of Baal, and Isaiah's against those who "bow down to the stock of a tree," would probably appear to such persons irreverent. And the caution now implied will appear the more important, when it is considered how large a majority they are, who, in this point, come under the description of "weak brethren." He that can laugh at what is ludicrous, and at the same time preserve a clear discernment of sound and unsound Reasoning, is no ordinary man. And moreover the resentment and mortification felt by those whose unsound doctrines, or sophistry, are fully exposed and held up to contempt or ridicule,—this, they will often disguise from others, and sometimes from themselves, by representing the contempt or ridicule as directed against serious or sacred subjects, and not, against their own absurdities: just as if those idolators above alluded to had represented the Prophets as ridiculing *devotional feelings,* and not, merely the absurd misdirection of them to a log of wood. And such persons will often in this way exercise a powerful influence on those whose understanding is so cloudy that they do not clearly perceive against what the ridicule is directed, or who are too dull to understand it at all. For there are some persons so constituted as to be altogether incapable of even comprehending the plainest irony; though they have not in other points any corresponding weakness of intellect. The humorous

---

of Bishop Dickinson." It is the more valuable, now, from the *verification* of the predictions it contains, which, when it first appeared, many were disposed to regard as extravagant.

[29] See *Logic,* Chapter on "Fallacies," at the conclusion.

satirical pamphlet, (attributed to an eminent literary character,) entitled "Advice to a Reviewer," I have known persons read without perceiving that it was ironical. And the same, with the "Historic Doubts" lately referred to. Such persons, when assured that such and such a Work contains ridicule, and that it has some reference to matters of grave importance, take for granted that it must be a work of profane levity.

There is also this danger in the use of irony; that sometimes when titles, in themselves favourable, are applied (or their application retained) to any set of men, in bitter scorn, they will then sometimes be enabled to appropriate such titles in a serious sense; the ironical force gradually evaporating. I mean, such titles as "Orthodox," "Evangelical," "Saints," "Reformers," "Liberals," "Political-Economists," "Rational," &c. The advantage thus given may be illustrated by the story of the cocoa-nuts in Sinbad the Sailor's fifth voyage.

It may be observed generally, that too much stress is often laid, especially by unpractised reasoners, on Refutation; (in the strictest and narrowest sense, *i. e.* of Objections to the Premises, or to the Reasoning;) I mean, that they are apt both to expect a Refutation where none can fairly be expected, and to attribute to it, when satisfactorily made out, more than it really accomplishes.

Unanswerable Arguments May Exist on Both Sides

For first, not only specious, but real and solid arguments, such as it would be difficult, or impossible to refute, may be urged against a Proposition which is nevertheless true, and may be satisfactorily established by a *preponderance* of probability.[30] It is in strictly scientific Reasoning alone that all the arguments which lead to a false Conclusion must be fallacious. In what is called moral or probable Reasoning, there may be sound arguments, and valid objections, on both sides.[31] *E. G.* It may be shown that each of two contending parties has some reason to hope for success; and this, by irrefragable arguments on both sides; leading to conclusions which are not (strictly speaking) contradictory to each other; for though only one party can obtain the victory, it may be true that each has some reason to expect it. The real question in such cases is, which event is the *more* probable;—on which side the evidence preponderates. Now it often happens that the inexperienced reasoner, thinking it necessary that every objection should be satisfactorily answered, will have his attention drawn off from the arguments of the opposite side, and will be occupied perhaps in making a weak defence, while victory was in his hands. The objection perhaps may be unanswerable, and yet may safely be allowed, if it can be shown that more

---

[30] See above, ch. ii. § 4, and also *Logic*, Part III. § 17.
[31] Bacon, in his rhetorical common-places—heads of arguments *pro* and *contra*, on several questions—has some admirable illustrations of what has been here remarked. I have accordingly (in Appendix A.) inserted some selections from them.

and weightier objections lie against every other supposition. This is a most important caution for those who are studying the Evidences of Religion. Let the opposer of them be called on, instead of confining himself to detached cavils, and saying, "how do you answer this?" and "how do you explain that?" to frame some consistent hypothesis to account for the introduction of Christianity by human means; and then to consider whether there are more or fewer difficulties in his hypothesis than in the other.

Sophistical Refutation

On the other hand, one may often meet with a sophistical refutation of objections, consisting in counter-objections urged against something else which is taken for granted to be, though it is not, the *only alternative. E. G.* Objections against an unlimited Monarchy may be met by a glowing description of the horrors of the mob-government of the Athenian and Roman Republics. If an exclusive attention to mathematical pursuits be objected to, it may be answered by deprecating the *exclusion* of such studies. It is thus that a man commonly replies to the censure passed on any vice he is addicted to, by representing some other vice as worse; *e. g.* if he is blamed for being a sot, he dilates on the greater enormity of being a thief; as if there were any need he should be either. And it is in this way alone that the advocates of Transportation have usually defended it: describing some very ill-managed penitentiary-system, and assuming, as self-evident and admitted, that this must be the *only possible substitute* for Penal-Colonies. This fallacy may be stated logically, as a Disjunctive Hypothetical, with the Major, false.

Over-Estimate of the Force of Refutation

Secondly, the force of a Refutation is often over-rated: an argument which is satisfactorily answered ought merely to *go for nothing:* it is possible that the conclusion drawn may nevertheless be true: yet men are apt to take for granted that the Conclusion itself is disproved, when the Arguments brought forward to establish it have been satisfactorily refuted; assuming, when perhaps there is no ground for the assumption, that these are *all* the arguments that could be urged.[32] This may be considered as the fallacy of denying the Consequent of a Conditional Proposition, from the Antecedent having been denied: "if such and such an Argument be admitted, the Assertion in question is true; but that Argument is inadmissible; *therefore the Assertion is not true.*" Hence the injury done to any cause by a weak advocate; the cause itself appearing to the vulgar to be overthrown, when the Arguments brought forward are answered.

"Hence the danger of ever advancing more than can be well maintained;

32 "Another form of *ignoratio elenchi,* (irrelevant conclusion,) which is rather the more serviceable on the side of the respondent, is, to prove or disprove *some part* of that which is required, and dwell on *that,* suppressing all the rest."

since the refutation of *that* will often quash the whole. A guilty person may often escape by having too much laid to his charge; so he may also by having too much evidence against him, *i. e.* some that is not in itself satisfactory: thus a prisoner may sometimes obtain acquittal by showing that one of the witnesses against him is an infamous informer and spy; though perhaps if that part of the evidence had been omitted, the rest would have been sufficient for conviction." [33]

The maxim here laid down, however, applies only to those causes in which, (waiving the consideration of honesty,) first, it is wished to produce not merely a temporary, but a lasting impression, and that, on readers or hearers of some judgment; and secondly, where there really *are* some *weighty* arguments to be urged. When no charge *e. g.* can really be substantiated, and yet it is desired to produce some present effect on the unthinking, there may be room for the application of the proverb, "Slander stoutly, and something will stick:" the vulgar are apt to conclude, that where a great deal is said, *something* must be true; and many are fond of that lazy contrivance for saving the trouble of thinking,—"splitting the difference;" imagining that they show a laudable caution in believing *only a part* of what is said. And thus a malignant Sophist may gain such a temporary advantage by the multiplicity of his attacks, as the rabble of combatants described by Homer sometimes did by their showers of javelins, which encumbered and weighed down the shield of one of his heroes, though they could not penetrate it.

Objections Should Be Stated in Their Full Force

On the above principle,—that a weak argument is positively hurtful, is founded a most important maxim, that it is not only the fairest, but also the wisest plan, to *state Objections in their full force;* at least, wherever there does exist a satisfactory answer to them; otherwise, those who hear them stated more strongly than by the uncandid advocate who had undertaken to repel them, will naturally enough conclude that they are unanswerable. It is but a momentary and ineffective triumph that can be obtained by manœuvres like those of Turnus's charioteer, who furiously chased the feeble stragglers of the army, and evaded the main front of the battle.

And when the objections urged are not only unanswerable, but (what is more) *decisive,*—when some argument that has been adduced, or some portion of a system, &c. is perceived to be really unsound, it is the wisest way fairly and fully to confess this, and abandon it altogether. There are many who seem to make it a point of honour never to yield a single point,—never to retract: or (if this be found unavoidable) "to back out"—as the phrase is—of an untenable position, so as to display their reluctance to make any concession; as if their credit was staked on preserving unbroken the talisman of professed infallibility. But there is little wisdom (the question of

[33] See *Logic,* b. iii. § 18.

honesty is out of the province of this treatise) in such a procedure; which in fact is very liable to cast a suspicion on that which is really sound, when it appears that the advocate is ashamed to abandon what is unsound. And such an honest avowal as I have been recommending, though it may raise at first a feeble and brief shout of exultation, will soon be followed by a general and increasing murmur of approbation. Uncandid as the world often is, it seldom fails to applaud the magnanimity of confessing a defect or a mistake, and to reward it with an increase of confidence. Indeed this increased confidence is often rashly bestowed, by a kind of over-generosity in the Public; which is apt too hastily to consider the confession of an error as a proof of universal sincerity. Some of the most skilful sophists accordingly avail themselves of this; and gain credence for much that is false, by acknowledging with an air of frankness some *one* mistake; which, like a tub thrown to the whale, they sacrifice for the sake of persuading us that they have committed *only one* error. I fear it can hardly be affirmed as yet, that "this trick has been so long used in controversy, as to be almost worn out."

≈≈≈≈≈≈

Part IV Of Elocution

CHAP. I—GENERAL CONSIDERATIONS RELATIVE TO ELOCUTION

1

On the importance of this branch, it is hardly necessary to offer any remark. Few need to be told that the effect of the most perfect composition may be entirely destroyed, even by a Delivery which does not render it unintelligible;—that one, which is inferior both in matter and style, may produce, if better spoken, a more powerful effect than another which surpasses it in both those points; and that even such an Elocution as does not spoil the effect of what is said, may yet fall far short of doing full justice to it. "What would you have said,"—observed Aeschines, when his recital of his great rival's celebrated Speech on the Crown was received with a burst of admiration,—"what would you have said, had you heard *him* speak it?"

The subject is far from having failed to engage attention. Of the prevailing deficiency of this, more than of any other qualification of a perfect Orator, many have complained; and several have laboured to remove it: but it may safely be asserted, that their endeavours have been, at the very best, entirely unsuccessful. Probably not a single instance could be found of any one who has attained, by the study of any system of instruction that has hitherto appeared, a really good Delivery; but there are many,—probably nearly as many as have fully tried the experiment,—who have by this means been totally spoiled;—who have fallen irrecoverably into an affected style of *spouting*, worse, in all respects, than their original mode of Delivery. Many accordingly have, not unreasonably, conceived a disgust for the subject altogether; considering it hopeless that Elocution should be *taught* by any rules; and acquiescing in the conclusion that it is to be regarded as entirely a gift of nature, or an accidental acquirement of practice.

It is to counteract the prejudice which may result from these feelings, that I have thought it needful to profess in the outset a dissent from the principles generally adopted, and to lay claim to some degree of originality in my own. Novelty affords at least an opening for hope; and the only opening, when former attempts have met with total failure.[1]

2

Requisites of Elocution

The requisites of Elocution correspond in great measure with those of Style: *Correct Enunciation,* in opposition both to *indistinct* utterance, and to *vulgar* and *provincial* pronunciation, may be considered as answering to Purity, Grammatical Propriety, and absence of Obsolete or otherwise *Unintelligible* words. These qualities, of Style, and of Elocution, being equally required in common conversation, do not fall within the proper province of Rhetoric. The three qualities, again, which have been treated of, under the head of Style, viz. Perspicuity, Energy, and Elegance, may be regarded as equally requisites of Elocution; which, in order to be perfect, must convey the meaning *clearly, forcibly*, and *agreeably*.

3

Reading and Speaking

Before, however, I enter upon any separate examination of these requisites, it will be necessary to premise a few remarks on the distinction between the two branches of Delivery; viz. *Reading* aloud, and *Speaking*. The object of *correct* Reading is, to convey to the hearers, through the medium of the ear, what is conveyed to the reader by the eye;—to put them in the same situation with him who has the book before him;—to exhibit to them, in short, by the voice, not only each word, but also all the stops, paragraphs, italic characters, notes of interrogation, &c.[2] which his sight presents to him. His

---

1 This is, in substance, one of Bacon's Aphorisms.
2 It may be said, indeed, that even tolerable Reading aloud, supplies more than is exhibited by a book to the eye; since though italics, *e. g.* indicate which word is to receive the emphasis, they do not point out the *tone* in which it is to be pronounced; which may be essential even to the right understanding of the sentence. *E. G.* in such a sentence as in Genesis i. "God said, Let there be light; and there *was* light:" here we can indicate in-

voice seems to indicate to them, "thus and thus it is written in the book or manuscript before me."

Impressive Reading

Impressive reading superadds to this, some degree of adaptation of the tones of voice to the character of the subject, and of the style.

What is often termed *fine* Reading seems to convey, in addition to these, a kind of admonition to the hearers respecting the feelings which the composition ought to excite in them: it appears to say, "This deserves your admiration;—this is sublime;—this is pathetic, &c."

Speaking

But Speaking, i. e. *natural* speaking, when the Speaker is uttering his own sentiments, and is thinking exclusively of *them,* has something in it distinct from all this: it conveys, by the sounds which reach the ear, the idea, that what is said is the immediate effusion of the Speaker's own mind, which he is desirous of imparting to others. A decisive proof of which is, that if any one overhears the voice of another, to whom he is an utter stranger—suppose in the next room—without being able to catch the sense of what is said, he will hardly ever be for a moment at a loss to decide whether he is *Reading* or *Speaking;* and this, though the hearer may not be one who has ever paid any critical attention to the various modulations of the human voice. So wide is the difference of the tones employed on these two occasions, be the subject what it may.[3]

---

deed to the eye that the stress is to be upon *"was;"* but it may be pronounced in different tones; one of which would alter the sense, by implying that there *was* light *already.*

This is true indeed; and it is also true, that the very words themselves are not always presented to the eye with the same distinctions as are to be conveyed to the ear; as, *e. g.* "abuse," "refuse," "project," and many others, are pronounced differently, as nouns and as verbs. This ambiguity, however, in our written signs, as well as the other, relative to the emphatic words, are imperfections which will not mislead a moderately practised reader. My meaning, in saying that such Reading as I am speaking of puts the hearers in the same situation as if the book were before them, is to be understood on the supposition of their being able not only to read, but to read so as to take in the full sense of what is written.

[3] "At every sentence let them ask themselves this question; How should I utter this, were I *speaking* it as my own immediate sentiments?—I have often tried an experiment to show the great difference between these two modes of utterance, the natural and the artificial; which was, that when I found a person of vivacity delivering his sentiments with energy, and of course with all that variety of tones which nature furnishes, I have taken occasion to put something into his hand to read, as relative to the topic of conversation; and it was surprising to see what an immediate change there was in his Delivery, from the moment he began to read. A different pitch of voice took place of his natural one, and a tedious uniformity of cadence succeeded to a spirited variety; insomuch that a blind man could hardly conceive the person who read to be the same who had just been speaking."—Sheridan, *Art of Reading.*

Attention Connected with Sympathy

The difference of effect produced is proportionably great: the personal *sympathy* felt towards one who appears to be delivering his own sentiments, is such, that it usually rivets the attention, even involuntarily, though to a discourse which appears hardly worthy of it. It is not easy for an auditor to fall asleep while he is hearing even perhaps feeble reasoning clothed in indifferent language, delivered extemporaneously, and in an unaffected style; whereas it is common for men to find a difficulty in keeping themselves awake, while listening even to a good dissertation, of the same length, or even shorter, on a subject, not uninteresting to them, when *read,* though with propriety, and not in a languid manner. And the thoughts, even of those not disposed to be drowsy, are apt to wander, unless they use an effort from time to time to prevent it; while, on the other hand, it is notoriously difficult to withdraw our attention, even from a trifling talker of whom we are weary, and to occupy the mind with reflections of its own.

Both Reading and Speaking, Connected with Rhetoric

Of the two branches of Elocution which have been just mentioned, it might at first sight appear as if one only, that of the Speaker, came under the province of Rhetoric. But it will be evident, on consideration, that both must be, to a certain extent, regarded as connected with our present subject; not merely because many of the same principles are applicable to both, but because any one who delivers (as is so commonly the case) a written composition of his own, may be reckoned as belonging to either class; as a Reader who is the author of what he reads, or as a Speaker who supplies the deficiency of his memory by writing. And again, in the (less common) case where a speaker is delivering without book, and from *memory* alone, a *written* composition, either his own or another's, though this cannot in strictness be called Reading, yet the tone of it will be very likely to resemble that of Reading. In the other case,—that where the author is actually reading his own composition,—he will be still more likely, notwithstanding its being his own, to approach, in the Delivery of it, to the Elocution of a Reader; and on the other hand, it is possible for him, even without actually deceiving the hearers into the belief that he is speaking extempore, to approach indefinitely near to that style.

The difficulty however of doing this, to one who has the writing actually before him, is considerable: and it is of course far greater when the composition is *not* his own. And as it is evident from what has been said, that this (as it may be called) Extemporaneous style of Elocution, is—in any case where it is not improper—much the more impressive, it becomes an interesting inquiry, how the difficulty in question may be best surmounted.

4

Artificial Style of Elocution

Little, if any, attention has been bestowed on this point by the writers on Elocution; the distinction above pointed out between Reading and Speaking, having seldom, or never, been precisely stated, and dwelt on. Several however have written elaborately on "good Reading," or on Elocution, *generally;* and it is not to be denied, that some ingenious and (in themselves) valuable remarks have been thrown out relative to such qualities in Elocution as might be classed under the three heads I have laid down, of Perspicuity, Energy, and Elegance: but there is one principle running through all their precepts, which being, according to my views, radically erroneous, must (if those views be correct) vitiate every system founded on it. The principle I mean is, that in order to acquire the best style of Delivery, it is requisite to fix the attention on the *voice;*—to study analytically the emphases, tones, pauses, degrees of loudness, &c. which give the proper effect to each passage that is well delivered—to frame *rules* founded on the observation of these—and then, in practice, deliberately and carefully to conform the utterance to these rules, so as to form a complete artificial system of Elocution.

That such a plan not only directs us into a circuitous and difficult path, towards an object which may be reached by a shorter and straighter, but also, in most instances, completely fails of that very object, and even produces, oftener than not, effects the very reverse of what is designed, is a doctrine for which it will be necessary to offer some reasons; especially as it is undeniable that the system here reprobated, as employed in the case of *Elocution,* is precisely that recommended and taught in this very Treatise, in respect of the conduct of *Arguments.* By analyzing the best compositions, and observing what kinds of arguments, and what modes of arranging them, in each case, prove most successful, general rules have been framed, which an author is recommended studiously to observe in Composition: and this is precisely the procedure which, in Elocution, I deprecate.

Excellence in Matter and in Delivery to Be Aimed at in Opposite Ways

The reason for making such a difference in these two cases is this: whoever (as Dr. A. Smith remarks in the passage lately cited [4]) appears to be attending to his own utterance, which will almost inevitably be the case with every one who *is* doing so, is sure to give offence, and to be censured for an affected delivery; because *every one is expected to attend exclusively to the proper object of the action* he is engaged in; which, in this case, is the expression of the thoughts—not the sound of the expressions. Whoever therefore learns, and endeavours to apply in practice, any artificial rules of

[4] See "Essay on the Imitative Arts," Part III. chap. iii. §4.

Elocution, so as deliberately to modulate his voice conformably to the principles he has adopted, (however just they may be in themselves,) will hardly ever fail to betray his intention; which always gives offence when perceived. Arguments, on the contrary, *must* be deliberately framed. Whether any one's course of reasoning be sound and judicious, or not, it is necessary, and it is expected, that it should be the result of thought. No one, as Dr. Smith observes, is charged with affectation for giving his attention to the proper object of the action he is engaged in. As therefore the proper object of the Orator is to adduce convincing Arguments, and topics of Persuasion, there is nothing offensive in his appearing deliberately to aim at this object. He may indeed weaken the force of what is urged by *too great* an appearance of elaborate composition, or by exciting suspicion of rhetorical *trick;* but he is so far from being expected to pay no attention to the sense of what he says, that the most powerful argument would lose much of its force, if it were supposed to have been thrown out casually, and at random. *Here* therefore the employment of a regular system (if founded on just principles) can produce no such ill effect as in the case of Elocution: since the habitual attention which that implies, to the choice and arrangement of arguments, is such as *must* take place, at any rate; whether it be conducted on any settled principles or not. The only difference is, that he who proceeds on a correct system, will think and deliberate concerning the course of his Reasoning, to *better purpose,* than he who does not: he will do *well* and *easily,* what the other does ill, and with more labour. Both alike must bestow their attention on the *Matter* of what they say, if they would produce any effect; both are not only allowed, but expected to do so.

The two opposite modes of proceeding therefore, which are recommended in respect of these two points, (the Argument and the Delivery,) are, in fact, both the result of the same circumstance; viz. that the speaker is expected to bestow his whole attention on the proper business of his speech; which is, not the Elocution, but the matter.[5]

5

Natural Style of Elocution

When however I protest against all artificial systems of Elocution, and all *direct* attention to Delivery, *at the time,* it must not be supposed that a *general* inattention to that point is recommended; or that the most perfect Elocution is to be attained by never thinking at all on the subject; though it may safely be affirmed that even this negative plan would succeed far better than a studied modulation. But it is evident that if any one wishes to *assume the Speaker* as far as possible, *i. e.* to deliver a written composition

[5] Style occupies in some respects an intermediate place between these two; in what degree each quality of it should or should not be made an object of attention *at the time of composing,* and how far the appearance of such attention is tolerated, has been already treated of in the preceding Part.

with some degree of the manner and effect of one that is extemporaneous, he will have a considerable difficulty to surmount: since though this may be called, in a certain sense, the Natural Manner, it is far from being what he will naturally, i. e. *spontaneously*, fall into. It is by no means natural for any one to *read* as if he were *not* reading, but speaking. And again, even when any one is reading what he does not wish to deliver as his own composition, as, for instance, a portion of the Scriptures, or the Liturgy, it is evident that this may be done better or worse, in infinite degrees; and that though (according to the views here taken) a studied attention to the sounds uttered, at the time of uttering them, leads to an affected and offensive delivery, yet, on the other hand, an utterly careless reader cannot be a good one.

CHAP. II—ARTIFICIAL AND NATURAL METHODS COMPARED

1

Reading

With a view to Perspicuity then,—the first requisite in all Delivery, viz. that quality which makes the meaning fully understood by the hearers,—the great point is, that the Reader (to confine our attention for the present to that branch) should appear to *understand* what he reads. If the Composition be, in itself, intelligible to the persons addressed, he will make them fully understand it, by so delivering it. But to this end, it is not enough that he should himself *actually* understand it: it is possible, notwithstanding, to read it as if he did not. And in like manner with a view to the quality, which has been here called Energy, it is not sufficient that he should himself feel, and be impressed with the force of what he utters; he may, notwithstanding, deliver it as if he were unimpressed.

2

Sheridan

The remedy that has been commonly proposed for these defects, is to point out in such a work, for instance, as the Liturgy, *which* words ought to be marked as emphatic,—in what places the voice is to be suspended, raised, lowered, &c. One of the best writers on the subject, Sheridan, in his "Lectures on the Art of Reading," [1] (whose remarks on many points coincide with the principles here laid down, though he differs from me on the main

---

[1] See note, ch. i. § 3. It is to be observed, however, that most of the objections I have adduced do not apply to this or that system in particular; to Sheridan's, for instance, as distinguished from Walker's; but, to *all* such systems generally; as may be seen from what is said in the present section.

question—as to the System to be practically followed with a view to the proposed object,) adopted a peculiar set of marks for denoting the different pauses, emphases, &c., and applied these, with accompanying explanatory observations, to the greater part of the Liturgy, and to an Essay subjoined; [2] recommending that the habit should be formed of regulating the voice by his marks; and that afterwards readers should "write out such parts as they want to deliver properly, without any of the usual stops; and, after having considered them well, mark the pauses and emphases by the new signs which have been annexed to them, according to the best of their judgment," &c.

To the adoption of any such artificial scheme there are three weighty objections; first, that the proposed system must necessarily be *imperfect;* secondly, that if it were perfect, it would be a *circuitous* path to the object in view; and thirdly, that even if both those objections were removed, the object would *not* be effectually obtained.

Imperfection of the Artificial System

First, such a system must necessarily be imperfect; because though the *emphatic* word in each sentence may easily be pointed out in writing, no variety of marks that could be invented,—not even musical Notation,[3]— would suffice to indicate the different *tones* [4] in which the different emphatic words should be pronounced; though on this depends frequently the whole force, and even sense of the expression. Take, as an instance, the words of Macbeth in the witches' cave, when he is addressed by one of the Spirits which they raise, "Macbeth! Macbeth! Macbeth!" on which he exclaims, "Had I three ears I'd hear thee;" no one would dispute that the stress is to be laid on the word "three;" and thus much might be indicated to the reader's eye; but if he had nothing else to trust to, he might chance to deliver the passage in such a manner as to be utterly absurd; for it is possible to pronounce the emphatic word "three," in such a tone as to indicate that "since he has but *two* ears he cannot hear." Again, the following passage, (Mark iv. 21,) "Is a candle brought to be put under a bushel, or under a bed," I have heard so pronounced as to imply that there is *no other alternative:* and yet the emphasis was laid on the right words. It would be moreover a task almost equally hopeless to attempt adequately to convey, by any written marks, precise directions as to the *rate,*—the degree of rapidity or slowness,—with which each sentence and clause should be delivered. Longer and shorter pauses may indeed be easily denoted; and marks may be used, similar to those in music, to indicate, generally, quick, slow, or moderate time; but it is evident that the variations which actually

2 See Appendix [N].
3 And even in Music, the Notation, though so much more complete than any that could be adapted to Speaking, yet leaves much to be supplied by the intelligence, taste, and feeling, of the performer.
4 See first note, ch. i. § 3.

take place are infinite—far beyond what any marks could suggest; and that much of the force of what is said depends on the degree of rapidity with which it is uttered; chiefly on the *relative* rapidity of one part in comparison of another. For instance, in such a sentence as the following, in one of the Psalms, which one may usually hear read at one uniform rate; "all men that see it shall say, This hath God done; for they shall perceive that it is his work;" the four words "this hath God done," though monosyllables, ought to occupy very little less time in utterance than all the rest of the verse together.

Circuitousness of the Artificial System

Secondly, but were it even possible to bring to the highest perfection the proposed system of marks, it would still be a circuitous road to the desired end. Suppose it could be completely indicated to the eye, in what tone each word and sentence should be pronounced according to the several occasions, the learner might ask, "But *why* should this tone suit the awful,—this, the pathetic,—this, the narrative style? *why* is this mode of delivery adopted for a command,—this, for an exhortation,—this, for a supplication?" &c. The only answer that could be given, is, that these tones, emphases, &c. are a part of the language;—that nature, or custom, which is a second nature, suggests spontaneously these different modes of giving expression to the different thoughts, feelings, and designs, which are present to the mind of any one who, without study, is speaking in earnest his own sentiments. Then, if this be the case, why not leave nature to do her own work? Impress but the mind fully with the sentiments, &c. to be uttered; withdraw the attention from the sound, and fix it on the sense; and nature, or habit, will spontaneously suggest the proper delivery. That this will be the case, is not only true, but is the very supposition on which the artificial system proceeds; for it professes to teach the mode of delivery *naturally* adapted to each occasion. It is surely, therefore, a circuitous path that is proposed, when the learner is directed, first to consider how each passage ought to be read;—*i. e.* what mode of delivering each part of it would *spontaneously* occur to him, if he were attending exclusively to the *matter* of it (and *this* is what, it appears to me, should *alone* be studied, and most attentively studied) ;—then, to observe all the modulations, &c. of voice, which take place in such a delivery; then, to note these down, by established marks, in writing; and, lastly, to pronounce according to these marks. This seems like recommending, for the purpose of raising the hand to the mouth, that he should first observe, when performing that action without thought of any thing else, what muscles are contracted,—in what degrees,—and in what order; then, that he should note down these observations; and lastly, that he should, in conformity with these notes, contract each muscle in due degree and in proper order; to the end that he may be enabled, after all, to—lift his hand to his mouth; which by supposition he had already done. Such instruction is like that bestowed by Molière's pedantic tutor upon his *Bourgeois Gentilhomme,* who was taught, to his infinite surprise and delight, what configurations of the mouth he employed in pronouncing the several letters of the alphabet, which he had been accustomed to utter all his life, without knowing how.

Appearance of Affectation Resulting from the Artificial System

Lastly, waiving both the above objections, if a person could learn thus to read and speak, as it were, *by note,* with the same fluency and accuracy as are attainable in the case of singing, still the desired object of a perfectly *natural* as well as correct Elocution, would never be in this way attained. The reader's attention being fixed on his own voice, (which in singing, and there only, is allowed and expected,) the inevitable consequence would be that he would betray more or less his studied and artificial Delivery; and would, in the same degree, manifest an offensive affectation.

It should be observed, however, that, in the reading of the Liturgy especially, so many gross faults are become quite familiar to many, from what they are accustomed to hear, if not from their own practice, as to render it peculiarly difficult to unlearn, or even detect them; and as an aid towards the exposure of such faults, there may be great advantage in studying Sheridan's observations and directions respecting the delivery of it; provided care be taken, *in practice,* to keep clear of his faulty principle, by *withdrawing* the attention from the sound of the voice, as carefully as he recommends it to be *directed* to that point.

3

Natural Manner—How to Be Secured

The practical rule then to be adopted, in conformity with the principles here maintained, is, not only to pay no studied attention to the Voice, but studiously to *withdraw* the thoughts from it, and to dwell as intently as possible on the Sense; trusting to nature to suggest spontaneously the proper emphases and tones.

Many persons are so far impressed with the truth of the doctrine here inculcated, as to acknowledge that "it is a great fault for a reader to be *too much* occupied with thoughts respecting his own voice;" and thus they think to steer a middle course between opposite extremes. But it should be remembered that this middle course entirely nullifies the whole advantage proposed by the plan recommended. A reader is sure to pay *too much* attention to his voice, not only if he pays *any at all,* but if he does not strenuously *labour to withdraw* his attention from it altogether.

He who not only understands fully what he is reading, but is earnestly occupying his mind with the matter of it, will be likely to read as if he understood it, and thus to make others understand it; [5] and in like manner,

---

[5] Who, for instance, that was really *thinking* of a resurrection from the dead, would ever tell any one that our Lord "rose *again* from the dead;" (which is so common a mode of reading the Creed,) as if He had done so more than once?

with a view to the *impressiveness* of the delivery, he who not only feels it, but is exclusively absorbed with that feeling, will be likely to read as if he felt it, and to communicate the impression to his hearers. But this cannot be the case if he is occupied with the thought of what their opinion will be of his reading, and, how his voice ought to be regulated;—if, in short, he is thinking of *himself,* and, of course, in the same degree, abstracting his attention from that which ought to occupy it exclusively.

It is not, indeed, desirable, that in reading the Bible, for example, or any thing which is not intended to appear as his own composition, he should deliver what are, avowedly, another's sentiments, in the same style, as if they were such as arose in his own mind; but it is desirable that he should deliver them as if he were *reporting* another's sentiments, which were both fully understood, and felt in all their force by the reporter: and the only way to do this effectually,—with such modulations of voice, &c. as are suitable to each word and passage,—is to fix his mind earnestly on the *meaning,* and leave nature and habit to suggest the utterance.

4

Difficulties in the Natural Manner

Some may, perhaps, suppose that this amounts to the same thing as *taking no pains at all;* and if, with this impression, they attempt to try the experiment of a natural Delivery, their ill-success will probably lead them to censure the proposed method, for the failure resulting from their own mistake. In truth, it is by no means a very easy task, to fix the attention on the meaning, in the manner and to the degree now proposed. The thoughts of one who is reading any thing very familiar to him, are apt to wander to *other* subjects, though perhaps such as are connected with that which is before him. If, again, it be something new to him, he is apt (not indeed to wander to *another* subject, but) to get the start, as it were, of his readers, and to be thinking, while uttering each sentence, not of that, but of the sentence which comes next. And in both cases, if he is careful to avoid those faults, and is desirous of reading well, it is a matter of no small difficulty, and calls for a constant effort, to prevent the mind from wandering in another direction; viz. into thoughts respecting his own voice,—respecting the effect produced by each sound,—the approbation he hopes for from the hearers, &c. And this is the prevailing fault of those who are commonly said to take *great pains* in their reading; pains which will always be taken in vain with a view to the true object to be aimed at, as long as the effort is

---

It is to be observed, however, that it is not enough for a reader to have his mind fixed on the *subject;* without regard to the *occasion,* &c. It is possible to *read* a prayer well, with the tone and manner of a man who is not *praying,* i. e. addressing the Deity, but addressing the *audience,* and *reciting* a form of words for their instruction: and such is generally the case with those who are commended as "fine readers" of the Liturgy. Extemporaneous prayers again are generally delivered, with spirit indeed, but (after the first few sentences) not *as* prayers, but as *exhortations* to the *congregation.*

thus applied in a wrong direction. With a view, indeed, to a very different object, the approbation bestowed on the reading, this artificial delivery will often be more successful than the natural. Pompous spouting, and many other descriptions of unnatural tone and measured cadence, are frequently admired by many as excellent reading; which admiration is itself a proof that it is not deserved; for when the delivery is *really* good, the hearers (except any one who may deliberately set himself to observe and criticise) *never think about it,* but are exclusively occupied with the sense it conveys, and the feelings it excites.

Advantages of Imitation Precluded by the Adoption of the Natural Manner

Still more to increase the difficulty of the method here recommended, (for it is no less wise than honest to take a fair view of difficulties,) this circumstance is to be noticed, that he who is endeavouring to bring it into practice, is in a great degree precluded from the advantage of *imitation.* A person who hears and approves a good *reader in the Natural manner,* may, indeed, so far imitate him with advantage, as to *adopt his plan,* of fixing his attention on the matter, and not thinking about his voice; but this very plan, evidently, by its nature, precludes any further imitation; for if, while reading, he is thinking of copying the manner of his model, he will, for that very reason, be unlike that model; the main principle of the proposed method being, carefully to exclude every such thought. Whereas any artificial system may as easily be learned by imitation as the notes of a song.

Advantages of Practice Less Easily Obtained by the Adoption of the Natural Manner

Practice also (*i. e.* private practice for the sake of learning) is much more difficult in the proposed method; because, the rule being, to use such a delivery as is suited, not only to the *matter* of what is said, but also, of course, to the *place* and *occasion,* and this, not by any studied modulations, but according to the spontaneous suggestions of the matter, place, and occasion, to one whose mind is fully and exclusively occupied with these, it follows, that he who would practise this method in *private,* must, by a strong effort of a vivid imagination, figure to himself a place and an occasion which are *not* present; otherwise, he will either be *thinking of his delivery,* (which is fatal to his proposed object,) or else will use a delivery suited to the situation in which he actually *is,* and not, to that for which he would prepare himself. Any system, on the contrary, of studied emphasis and regulation of the voice, may be learned in private practice, as easily as singing.

5

Importance of Practice in Elocution

It has been thought best, as has been above said, to state fairly the difficulties of a regular training in really good elocution; not, of course, with a view to discourage exertion for an object so important, but as a reason for labouring the more sedulously to overcome those difficulties.

In fact, nothing tends more to discourage assiduous study in this department, than the ill effect produced by the faulty methods commonly in use. For when it is found—as it too often will be—that those who have taken most pains in the study, acquit themselves even worse than those who have wholly neglected it, the natural result will be, that, instead of inquiring whether a better plan might not be adopted, men will be apt to sit down contented with the ordinary slovenly style of delivery, supposing that whatever superiority any one may manifest is altogether a gift of nature.

Accordingly, little or no care is usually taken, either in schools or in private families, to teach young persons to read well. What is called the "English-master" in most seminaries, is usually a person of very humble qualifications; and for the most part, either contents himself with making his pupils "mind their stops," or else teaches them an affected spout. And the consequence is, that, of men otherwise well-educated, a considerable number are found to have acquired an offensively artificial delivery, and a far greater number, a habit of reading as if they neither felt nor even understood what they read.

Unconscious Imitation of What Is Faulty

And even men of good sense and good taste, often acquire, through undesigned and unconscious *imitation,* an absurd style of reading those passages which they have been from infancy accustomed to hear ill-read by others. To the members of our Church accordingly, the difficulty of reading the *Liturgy* with spirit, or even with propriety, is greatly enhanced by the long established and inveterate faults to which almost every one's ears are become familiar; so that such a delivery as would shock any one of even moderate taste, in any other composition, he will, in this, be likely to tolerate, and to practise. Some, *e. g.* in the Litany, read, "have mercy *upon* us, miserable sinners;" and others, "have mercy upon *us,* miserable sinners;" both, laying the stress on a wrong word, and making the pause in the wrong place, so as to disconnect "us" and "miserable sinners;" which the context requires us to combine. Every one, in expressing his own natural sentiments, would say, "have *mercy* upon us-miserable-sinners."

Many are apt even to commit so gross an error, as to lay the chief stress on the words which denote the *most important things;* without any consideration of the emphatic *word* of each sentence: *e. g.* in the Absolution, many read, "let us beseech Him to grant us *true repentance;*" because, forsooth, "true repentance" is an important thing; not considering that, as it has been just mentioned, it is not the *new idea,* and that to which the attention should be directed by the emphasis; the sense being, that since God pardoneth *all* that *have* true repentance, therefore, we should "beseech Him to *grant* it to *us."*

In addition to the other difficulties of reading the Liturgy well, it should be mentioned, that prayer, thanksgiving, and the like, even when avowedly not of our own composition, should be delivered as (what in truth they ought to *be*) the genuine sentiments of our own minds at the moment of utterance; which is not the case with the Scriptures, or with any thing else that is read, not professing to be the speaker's own composition.

Different Modes of Teaching the Different Points of Good Elocution

But the department of education I am speaking of, instead of being entrusted to such persons as usually conduct it, is one which calls for the assiduous attention of some one well-qualified in point of good taste and sound judgment. Let young persons be accustomed much to reading aloud to a parent or other teacher thus qualified, and who shall be ready to point out and correct any faults they may commit; and let this be done in strict conformity with the principles above laid down. Let the instructor, accordingly, remember that the pupils' attention is then, and then only, to be called to the *sounds* uttered, when the fault is one which he would wish corrected (and which indeed he should be ready to correct) in the utterance of *ordinary conversation. E. G.* many young persons have habits,—and such as, not seldom, grow up with them,—either of an indistinct pronunciation, which makes the vowels audible, while the *consonants* are slurred,[6] or of dropping the voice toward the close of each sentence so as to be nearly inaudible, or of rising into a scream, or of too rapid and hurried an utterance, or of some provincial vulgarity, &c. All such faults should,—as has been said,—be corrected not in reading only, but in ordinary speaking.

But on the other hand, all those faults of delivery, which, though common in reading, do not occur in ordinary speaking, constitute a distinct class, and must be carefully indeed corrected, but in a totally different manner. For hardly any one in ordinary conversation speaks as if he did not understand, or did not really mean, what he is saying. In reference therefore to *correct* reading, (in respect of the sense,) and *impressive* reading,—such as shall convey the true import, and full force, of what is said,—the appeal must be made to the learner's own mind; and his attention should be drawn *from* the sound, to the *sense* of what he is reading. And the instructor should give admonitions, when needed, not, as in the other case, by saying "You have pronounced that word wrong; pronounce it so and so:" or "You read too quick," &c.; but "Read that passage as if you understood it: read

---

[6] A useful maxim as to this point, is, to "take care of the consonants, and the vowels will take care of themselves."

this suitably to a *command,* that, to an *interrogation,* &c.: express the scorn—the exultation—the earnestness, &c. of that passage, as if you were expressing such a feeling of your own in your own words," &c.

That such an exercise as this, under a judicious guide, will have most beneficial result, I am convinced from experience. And if the study of Elocution, thus conducted, were made, as it manifestly ought to be, an indispensable part of a liberal education, I have no doubt that good reading would be no longer the exception, but the rule. For though the method I have been recommending, will not, as I have said, so readily and so easily accomplish its object, as the opposite method does *its own* object, on the other hand this latter is in reality no benefit at all, but a great evil; while, on the other plan, the student is at least put on the right course, and will be in the way of indefinitely improving himself in after-life.

Learning by Rote

It is almost superfluous to remark, how utterly at variance with all that I have been here recommending, is the practice of setting children to learn by heart and recite, before they are able to understand, poems, chapters of the Bible, collects, &c., to which they attach little or no meaning, while they repeat the words by rote. A habit of reading in an artificial tone, offensive to those of good taste, and tending to impair the force of what is so read, is one natural result—though far from the worst [7]—of such a practice. If any who have been thus brought up are found, in after-life, to have a good elocution,—and, I may add, to have their intellectual and moral powers unimpaired,—this must be, not in consequence of such a training, but in spite of it.

CHAP. III—CONSIDERATIONS ARISING FROM THE DIFFERENCES BETWEEN READING AND SPEAKING

1

Some additional objections to the method I have recommended, and some further remarks on the counterbalancing advantages of it, will be introduced presently, when I shall have first offered some observations on *Speaking,* and on that branch of Reading which the most nearly approaches to it.

When any one delivers a written composition, of which he is, or is supposed to profess himself, the author, he has peculiar difficulties to encounter, if his object be to approach as nearly as possible to the extemporaneous style. It is indeed impossible to produce the *full* effect of that style, while the audience are aware that the words he utters are before him: but he may approach indefinitely near to such an effect; and in proportion as he succeeds in this object, the impression produced will be the greater.

[7] See Appendix [O].

Comparative Advantages of Written and Extemporary Addresses

It has been already remarked, how easy it is for the hearers to keep up their attention,—indeed, how difficult for them to withdraw it,—when they are addressed by one who is *really speaking* to them in a natural and earnest manner; though perhaps the discourse may be encumbered with a good deal of the repetition, awkwardness of expression, and other faults, incident to extemporaneous language; and though it be prolonged for an hour or two, and yet contain no more matter than a good *writer* could have clearly expressed in a discourse of half an hour; which last, if read to them, would not, without some effort on their part, have so fully detained their attention. The advantage in point of style, arrangement, &c. of written, over extemporaneous discourses, (such at least as any but the most accomplished orators can produce,) is sufficiently evident: [1] and it is evident also that *other* advantages, such as have been just alluded to, belong to the latter. Which is to be preferred on each occasion, and by each orator, it does not belong to the present discussion to inquire; but it is evidently of the highest importance, to *combine*, as far as possible, in each case, the advantages of both.

A perfect familiarity with the rules laid down in the First Part of this Treatise, would be likely, it is hoped, to give the extemporaneous orator that habit of *quickly* methodizing his thoughts on a given subject, which is essential (at least where no very long premeditation is allowed) to give to a *speech* something of the weight of argument, and clearness of arrangement, which characterize good Writing.[2] In order to attain the corresponding advantage,—to impart to the delivery of a written discourse, something of the vivacity and interesting effect of real, earnest, *speaking*, the plan to be pursued, conformably with the principles I have been maintaining, is, for the reader to draw off his mind as much as possible from the thought that he *is* reading, as well as from all thought respecting his own utterance;—to fix his mind as earnestly as possible on the *matter*, and to strive to adopt as his *own*, and as his *own at the moment* of utterance, every sentiment he delivers;—and to *say* it to the audience, in the manner which the occasion and subject spontaneously suggest to him who has abstracted his mind both from all consideration of *himself*, and from the consideration that he is reading.

[1] Practice in public speaking generally,—practice in speaking on the particular subject in hand,—and (on each occasion) premeditation of the matter and arrangment, are all circumstances of great consequence to a speaker.

Nothing but a *miraculous gift* can supersede these advantages. The Apostles accordingly were forbidden *to use any premeditation*, being assured that it "should be *given* them, in that same hour, what they should say;" and, when they found, in effect, this promise fulfilled to them, they had experience, within themselves, of a sensible miracle.

[2] Accordingly, it may be remarked, that, (contrary to what might at first sight be supposed,) though the preceding parts, as well as the present, are intended for general application, yet it is to the *extemporary speaker* that the rules laid down in the former Part (supposing them correct) will be the most peculiarly useful: while the suggestions offered in this last, respecting Elocution, are more especially designed for the use of the *reader*.

2

Most Men Speak Well in Common Discourse

The advantage of this NATURAL MANNER—*i. e.* the manner which one naturally falls into who is *really speaking*, in earnest, and with a mind *exclusively* intent on what he has to say—may be estimated from this consideration; that there are few (as was remarked in the preceding chapter) who do not *speak* so as to give effect to what they are saying. Some, indeed, do this much better than others. Some have, as I observed above, in ordinary conversation, an indistinct or incorrect pronunciation,—an embarrassed and hesitating utterance, or a bad choice of words: but hardly any one fails to deliver (when speaking earnestly) what he does say, so as to convey the sense and the force of it, much more completely than even a good reader would, if those same words were written down and read. The latter might, indeed, be more *approved;* but that is not the present question; which is, concerning the *impression* made on the hearers' minds. It is not the polish of the blade that is to be considered, or the grace with which it is brandished, but the keenness of the edge, and the weight of the stroke.

There is, indeed, as I have said, a wide difference between different men, in respect of the degrees of impressiveness with which, in earnest conversation, they deliver their sentiments; but it may safely be laid down, that he who delivers a written composition with the same degree of spirit and energy with which he would naturally speak on the same subject, has attained, not indeed, necessarily, *absolute* perfection, but the utmost excellence attainable by *him.* Any attempt to outdo his own Natural manner, will inevitably lead to something worse than failure.

On the contrary, it can hardly be denied that the elocution of most readers, even when delivering their own compositions, (suppose, in the Pulpit,) is such as to convey the notion, at the very best, not that the preacher is expressing his own real sentiments, but that he is making known to his audience what is written in the book before him: and, whether the composition is professedly the reader's own, or not, the usual mode of delivery, though grave and decent, is so remote from the energetic style of real Natural Speech, as to furnish, if one may so speak, a kind of running comment on all that is uttered, which says, "I do not mean, think, or feel, all this; I only mean to recite it with propriety and decorum:" and what is usually called *fine* Reading, only superadds to this, (as has been above remarked,) a kind of admonition to the hearers, that *they* ought to believe, to feel, and to admire, what is read.

3

Natural Manner Not to Be Confounded with the Familiar

It is easy to anticipate an objection which many will urge against, what they will call, a *colloquial* style of delivery; viz. that it is undignified, and unsuitable to the solemnity of a serious, and especially, of a religious discourse. The objection is founded on a mistake. Those who urge it, derive all their notions of a Natural Delivery from two, irrelevant, instances; that of ordinary *conversation*, the usual objects of which, and consequently its usual tone, are comparatively light;—and, that of the coarse and extravagant *rant* of vulgar fanatical preachers. But to conclude that the objections against either of these styles, would apply to the Natural delivery of a man of sense and taste, speaking earnestly, on a serious subject, and on a solemn occasion,—or that he would *naturally* adopt, and is here advised to adopt, such a style as those objected to, is no less absurd than, if any one, being recommended to walk in a natural and unstudied manner, rather than in a dancing step, (to employ Dr. A. Smith's illustration,) or a formal march, should infer that the natural gait of a clown following the plough, or of a child in its gambols, were proposed as models to be imitated in walking across a room. Should any one, on being told that both tragic-acting and comic-acting ought to be a *natural representation* of man, interpret this to mean, that Tragedy ought to be performed *exactly like* Comedy, he would be thought very absurd, if he were supposed to be speaking seriously. It is evident, that what is *natural* in one case, or for one person, may be, in a different one, very unnatural. It would not be by any means natural to an educated and sober-minded man, to speak like an illiterate enthusiast; or to discourse on the most important matters in the tone of familiar conversation respecting the trifling occurrences of the day. Any one who does but notice the style in which a man of ability, and of good choice of words, and utterance, delivers his sentiments in *private*, when he is, for instance, earnestly and seriously admonishing a friend,—defending the truths of religion,—or speaking on any other grave subject on which he is intent,—may easily observe how different his tone is from that of *light* and familiar conversation,—how far from deficient in the dignified seriousness which befits the case. Even a stranger to the language might guess that he was not engaged on any frivolous topic. And yet, when an opportunity occurs of observing how he delivers a written discourse, of his own composition, on perhaps the very same, or a similar subject, will it not often be perceived how comparatively stiff, languid, and unimpressive is the effect?

Natural Manner Is Accommodated to the Place, Subject, and Occasion

It may be said indeed, that a sermon should not be delivered before a congregation assembled in a place of worship, in the same style as one would employ in conversing across a table, with equal seriousness on the same subject. This is undoubtedly true: and it is evident that it *has been implied* in what has here been said; the Natural manner having been described as accommodated, not only to the *subject*, but to the *place, occasion*, and all other circumstances; so that he who should preach exactly as if he were speaking in private, though with the utmost earnestness, on the same subject, would, so far, be *departing* from the genuine Natural manner. But it may be safely asserted, that even *this* would be far the less fault of the two. He who appears, unmindful, indeed, of the place and occasion, but deeply impressed with the *subject,* and utterly forgetful of *himself,* would produce a much stronger effect than one, who, going into the opposite extreme, is, indeed, mindful of the place and the occasion, but not fully occupied with the subject, (though he may strive to *appear* so;) being partly engaged in thoughts respecting his own voice. The latter would, indeed, be the less likely to incur censure; but the other would produce the deeper impression.

The object, however, to be aimed at, (and it is not unattainable,) is to avoid *both* faults;—to keep the mind impressed both with the matter spoken, and with all the circumstances also of each case; so that the voice may spontaneously accommodate itself to *all;* carefully avoiding all studied modulations, and, in short, all thoughts of *self;* which, in proportion as they intrude, will not fail to diminish the effect.

4

A Familiar Delivery One Species of the Natural

It must be admitted, indeed, that the different kinds of Natural delivery of any one individual on different subjects and occasions, various as they are, do yet bear a much greater resemblance to each other, than any of them does to the Artificial style usually employed in reading; a proof of which is, that a person familiarly acquainted with the speaker, will seldom fail to *recognise his voice,* amidst all the variations of it, when he is *speaking* naturally and earnestly; though it will often happen that, if he have never before heard him *read,* he will be at a loss, when he happens accidentally to hear without seeing him, to know who it is that is reading; so widely does the artificial cadence and intonation differ in many points from the natural. And a consequence of this is, that the Natural manner, however perfect,— however exactly accommodated to the subject, place, and occasion,—will, even when these are the most solemn, in some degree *remind* the hearers of the tone of conversation. Amidst all the differences that will exist, this one point of resemblance,—that of the delivery being unforced and unstudied, —will be likely, in some degree, to strike them. Those who are good judges will perceive at once, and the rest, after being a little accustomed to the Natural manner, that there is not necessarily any thing irreverent or indecorous in it; but that, on the contrary, it conveys the idea of the speaker's being deeply impressed with that which is his proper business. But, for a time, many will be disposed to find fault with such a kind of elocution; and, in particular, to complain of its indicating a want of respect for the audience. Yet even while this disadvantage continues, a preacher of this kind may be assured that the *doctrine* he delivers is much more forcibly impressed, even on those who censure his style of delivering it, than it could be in the other way.

A discourse delivered in this style has been known to elicit the remark, from one of the lower orders, who had never been accustomed to any thing of the kind, that "it was an excellent sermon, and it was great pity it had not been *preached:*" a censure which ought to have been very satisfactory to the preacher. Had he employed a pompous spout, or modulated whine, it is probable such an auditor would have admired his *preaching,* but would have known and thought little or nothing about the *matter* of what was taught.

Which of the two objects ought to be preferred by a Christian Minister on Christian principles, is a question, not indeed hard to decide, but foreign to the present discussion. It is important, however, to remark, that an Orator is bound, as such, not merely on moral, but (if such an expression may be used) on *rhetorical* principles, to be mainly, and indeed exclusively, intent on *carrying his point;* not, on gaining approbation, or even avoiding censure, except with a view to that point. He should, as it were, adopt as a motto, the reply of Themistocles to the Spartan commander, Eurybiades, who lifted his staff to chastise the earnestness with which his own opinion was controverted; "Strike, but hear me."

I would not, indeed, undertake to maintain (like Quintilian) that no one can be an Orator who is not a virtuous man; but there certainly is a kind of moral excellence implied in that renunciation of all effort after display,—in that forgetfulness of self,—which is absolutely necessary, both in the manner of writing, and in the delivery, to give the full force to what is said.

5

Natural Manner not Praised

Besides the inconvenience just mentioned,—the censure, which the proposed style of elocution will be liable to, from perhaps the majority of hearers, till they shall have become somewhat accustomed to it,—this circumstance also ought to be mentioned, as what many, perhaps, would reckon (or at least feel) to be one of the disadvantages of it; that, after all, even when no disapprobation is incurred, no *praise* will be bestowed, (except by observant critics,) on a truly Natural delivery; on the contrary, the more perfect it is, the more will it withdraw, from itself, to the arguments and sentiments delivered, the attention of all but those who are studiously directing their view to the mode of utterance, with a design to criticise or to learn. The credit, on the contrary, of having a very fine elocution, is to be obtained at the expense of a very moderate share of pains; though at the expense also, inevitably, of much of the force of what is said.

6

Bashfulness Felt on First Adopting the Natural Manner

One inconvenience, which will at first be experienced by a person who, after having been long accustomed to the Artificial delivery, begins to adopt the Natural, is, that he will be likely suddenly to feel an embarrassed, bashful, and, as it is frequently called, *nervous* sensation, to which he had before been comparatively a stranger. He will find himself in a new situation,—standing before his audience in a different character,—stripped, as it were, of the sheltering veil of a conventional and artificial delivery;—in short, delivering to them his thoughts, as one man *speaking to* other men; not, as before, merely *reading in public*. And he will feel that he attracts a much greater share of their attention, not only by the novelty of a manner to which most congregations are little accustomed, but also, (even supposing them to have been accustomed to extemporary discourses,) from their perceiving themselves to be personally *addressed,* and feeling that he is not merely reciting something *before* them, but saying it *to* them. The speaker and the hearers will thus be brought into a new and closer relation to each other: and the increased interest thus excited in the audience, will cause the Speaker to feel himself in a different situation,—in one which is a greater trial of his confidence, and which renders it more difficult than before to withdraw his attention from himself. It is hardly necessary to observe that this very change of feelings experienced by the speaker, ought to convince him the more, if the causes of it (to which I have just alluded) be attentively considered, how much greater impression this manner is likely to produce. As he will be likely to feel much of the bashfulness which a really extemporary speaker has to struggle against, so, he may produce much of a similar effect.[3]

After all, however, the effect will never be completely the same. A composition delivered from writing, and one actually extemporaneous, will always produce feelings, both in the hearer and the speaker, considerably different; even on the supposition of their being word for word the same, and delivered so exactly in the same tone, that by the ear alone no difference could be detected: still the audience will be differently affected, according to their knowledge that the words uttered, are, or are not, written down and before the speaker's eyes. And the consciousness of this will produce a corresponding effect on the mind of the speaker. For were this not so, any one who, on any subject, can speak (as many can) fluently and correctly in private conversation, would find no greater difficulty in saying the same things before a large congregation, than in reading to them a written discourse.

[3] The question between preaching extempore and from a written discourse, it does not properly fall within the province of this treatise to discuss on any but what may be called rhetorical principles. It may be worth while however to remark, incidentally, that one who possesses the power of preparing and arranging his matter, and retaining it in his memory, and expressing it fluently in well-chosen language, extempore,—in short, who is qualified to produce the best effects of this kind of preaching,—should remember, as a set-off against its advantages, that he may be holding out an *example* and encouragement to others who are *not* thus qualified. He may perhaps find himself cited as *approving* of extemporary preaching, and appealed to as an authority, and imitated by those who perhaps resemble him *only* in fluency, and who, by not merely speaking extempore, but also *thinking* extempore, leave some of their hearers disgusted, and the rest, unedified.

7

Inquiry Respecting the Bashfulness Felt in Addressing a Large Audience

And here it may be worthwhile briefly to inquire into the causes of that remarkable phenomenon, as it may justly be accounted, that a person who is able with facility to express his sentiments in private to a friend, in such language, and in such a manner, as would be perfectly suitable to a certain audience, yet finds it extremely difficult to address to that audience the very same words, in the same manner; and is, in many instances, either completely struck dumb, or greatly embarrassed, when he attempts it. Most persons are so *familiar* with the fact, as hardly to have ever considered that it requires explanation: but attentive consideration shows it to be a very curious, as well as important one; and of which no explanation, as far as I know, has been attempted. It cannot be from any superior deference which the speaker thinks it right to feel for the judgment of the hearers; for it will often happen that the single friend, to whom he is able to speak fluently, shall be one whose good opinion he more values, and whose wisdom he is more disposed to look up to, than that of all the others together. The speaker may even feel that he himself has a decided and acknowledged superiority over every one of the audience; and that he should not be the least abashed in addressing any two or three of them, separately; yet still all of them, collectively, will often inspire him with a kind of dread.

Powerful Excitement Produced in a Large Audience

Closely allied in its causes with the phenomenon I am considering, is that other curious fact, that the very same sentiments expressed in the same manner, will often have a far more powerful effect on a large audience, than they would have on any one or two of these very persons, separately. That is in a great degree true of all men, which was said of the Athenians, that they were like sheep, of which a flock is more easily driven than a single one.

Different Language Employed According to the Number Addressed

Another remarkable circumstance, connected with the foregoing, is the difference in respect of the style which is suitable, respectively, in addressing a multitude, and two or three even of the same persons. A much *bolder,* as well as less accurate, kind of language is both allowable and advisable, in speaking to a considerable number; as Aristotle has remarked, in speaking of the *Graphic* and *Agonistic* styles,—the former, suited to the closet, the latter, to public speaking before a large assembly. And he ingeniously compares them to the different styles of painting; the greater the crowd, he says, the more distant is the view; so that in scene-painting, for instance, coarser and bolder touches are required, and the nice finish, which would delight a close spectator, would be lost. He does not, however, account for the phenomena in question.

from CHAP. IV—PRACTICAL DEDUCTIONS FROM THE FOREGOING VIEWS

3

Natural Delivery More Easily Heard

The last circumstance to be noticed among the results of the mode of delivery recommended, is, that the speaker will find it much easier, in this Natural manner, to *make himself heard:* he will be heard, that is, much more distinctly—at a greater distance,—and with far less exertion and fatigue to himself. This is the more necessary to be mentioned, because it is a common, if not prevailing opinion, that the reverse of this is the fact. There are not a few who assign as a reason for their adoption of a certain unnatural tone and measured cadence, that it is necessary, in order to be heard by a large congregation. But though such an artificial voice and utterance will often appear to produce a *louder sound,* (which is the circumstance that probably deceives such persons,) yet a natural voice and delivery, provided it be clear, though it be less laboured, and may even seem low to those who are near at hand, will be distinctly heard at a much greater distance. The only decisive proof of this must be sought in experience; which will not fail to convince of the truth of it any one who will fairly make the trial.

The requisite degree of loudness will be best obtained, conformably with the principles here inculcated, not by thinking about the voice, but by *looking* at the most *distant* of the hearers, and addressing one's self especially to him. The voice rises *spontaneously,* when we are speaking to a person who is not very near.

It should be added, that a speaker's being well heard does not depend near so much on the *loudness* of the sounds, as on their *distinctness;* and especially on the clear pronunciation of the *consonants.*

That the organs of voice are much less strained and fatigued by the natural action which takes place in real speaking, than by any other, (besides that it is what might be expected *à priori,*) is evident from daily experience. An extemporary Speaker will usually be much less exhausted in two hours, than an elaborate reciter (though less distinctly heard) will be in one. Even the ordinary tone of *reading* aloud is so much more fatiguing than that of conversation, that feeble patients are frequently unable to continue it for a quarter of an hour without great exhaustion; even though they may feel no inconvenience from *talking,* with few or no pauses, and in no lower voice, for more than double that time.

4

Recapitulation of Advantages and Disadvantages

He then who shall determine to aim at the Natural manner, though he will have to contend with considerable difficulties and discouragements, will not be without corresponding advantages, in the course he is pursuing.

He will be at first, indeed, repressed to a greater degree than another, by emotions of bashfulness; but it will be more speedily and more completely subdued; the very system pursued, since it forbids all thoughts of *self*, striking at the root of the evil.

He will, indeed, on the outset, incur censure, not only critical but moral;—he will be blamed for using a *colloquial* delivery; and the censure will very likely be, as far as relates to his earliest efforts, not wholly undeserved; for his manner *will* probably at first too much resemble that of conversation, though of serious and earnest conversation: but by perseverance he may be sure of avoiding deserved, and of mitigating, and ultimately overcoming, undeserved, censure.

He will, indeed, never be praised for a "very fine delivery;" but his *matter* will not lose the approbation it may deserve, as he will be the more sure of being heard and attended to. He will not, indeed, meet with many who can be regarded as models of the Natural manner; and those he does meet with, he will be precluded, by the nature of the system, from minutely imitating; but he will have the advantage of carrying with him an *Infallible Guide,* as long as he is careful to follow the suggestions of Nature; abstaining from all thoughts respecting his own utterance, and fixing his mind intently on the business he is engaged in.

And though he must not expect to attain perfection at once, he may be assured that, while he steadily adheres to this plan, he is in the right road to it; instead of becoming,—as on the other plan,—more and more artificial, the longer he studies. And every advance he makes will produce a proportional effect: it will give him more and more of that hold on the attention, the understanding, and the feelings of the audience, which no studied modulation can ever attain. Others indeed may be more successful in escaping censure, and ensuring admiration; but he will far more surpass them, in respect of the proper object of the Orator, which is, *to carry his point.*

5

Action

Much need not be said on the subject of *Action,* which is at present so little approved, or, designedly, employed, in this country, that it is hardly to be reckoned as any part of the Orator's art.

Why Action Is Generally Disused

Action, however, seems to be natural to man, when speaking earnestly: but the state of the case at present seems to be, that the disgust excited, on the one hand, by awkward and ungraceful motions, and, on the other, by studied gesticulations, has led to the general disuse of action altogether; and has induced men to form the habit (for it certainly *is* a *formed* habit) of keeping themselves quite still, or nearly so, when speaking. This is supposed to be, and perhaps is, the more rational and dignified way of speaking: but so strong is the tendency to indicate vehement internal emotion by some kind of outward gesture, that those who do not encourage or allow themselves in any, frequently fall unconsciously into some awkward trick of swinging the body, folding a paper, twisting a string, or the like. But when any one is reading, or even speaking, in the Artificial manner, there is little or nothing of this tendency; precisely, because the mind is *not* occupied by that strong internal emotion which occasions it. And the prevalence of this (the artificial) manner may reasonably be conjectured to have led to the disuse of all gesticulation, even in extemporary speakers; because if any one, whose delivery is artificial, does use action, it will of course be, like his voice, studied and artificial; and savouring still more of disgusting affectation; from the circumstance that it evidently might be entirely omitted. And hence, the practice came to be generally disapproved and exploded.

It need only be observed, that, in conformity with the principles maintained throughout this Book, no *care* should, in any case, be taken to use graceful or appropriate action; which, if not perfectly unstudied, will always be (as has been just remarked) intolerable. But if any one spontaneously falls into any gestures that are unbecoming, care should *then* be taken to break the habit; and that, not only in public speaking, but on all occasions. The case, indeed, is the same with utterance: if any one has, in common discourse, an indistinct, hesitating, provincial, or otherwise faulty delivery, *his* Natural manner certainly is not what he should adopt in public speaking; but he should endeavour, by care, to remedy the defect, not in public speaking only, but in ordinary conversation also. And so also, with respect to attitudes and gestures. It is in these points, principally, if not exclusively, that the remarks of an intelligent friend will be beneficial.

If, again, any one finds himself naturally and spontaneously led to use, in speaking, a moderate degree of action, which he finds from the observation of others not to be ungraceful or inappropriate, there is no reason that he should study to repress this tendency.

6

Action Naturally Precedes the Words

It would be inconsistent with the principle just laid down, to deliver any *precepts* for gesture: because the *observance* of even the best conceivable precepts, would, by destroying the natural appearance, be fatal to their object: but there is a *remark,* which is worthy of attention, from the illustration it affords of the erroneousness, in detail, as well as in principle, of the ordinary systems of instruction in this point. Boys are generally taught to employ the prescribed action either *after,* or *during* the utterance of the words it is to enforce. The best and most appropriate action must, from this circumstance alone, necessarily appear a feeble affectation. It suggests the idea of a person speaking to those who do not fully understand the language, and striving by signs to explain the meaning of what he has been saying. The very same gesture, had it come at the proper, that is, the *natural,* point of time, might, perhaps, have added greatly to the effect; viz. had it *preceded* somewhat the utterance of the words. *That* is always the natural order of action. An emotion, struggling for utterance, produces a tendency to a bodily gesture, to express that emotion more *quickly* than *words* can be framed; the words follow, as soon as they *can* be spoken. And this being always the case with a real, earnest, unstudied speaker, this mode of placing the action foremost, gives (if it be otherwise appropriate) the appearance of earnest emotion actually present in the mind. And the reverse of this natural order would alone be sufficient to convert the action of Demosthenes himself into unsuccessful and ridiculous pantomime.